Keith Hancock

A graduate of the University of Melbourne, Keith Hancock took his doctorate at the London School of Economics in 1959. He was then a Lecturer in Economics at the University of Adelaide before becoming the Foundation Professor of Economics at Flinders University in 1964. In 1980, he became Vice-Chancellor of Flinders University. He left Flinders University in 1987 to become a Presidential Member of the Australian Conciliation and Arbitration Commission (later the Australian Industrial Relations Commission). Since his retirement in 1997, Hancock has held honorary appointments at Adelaide and Flinders Universities.

He was one of the founders of the Industrial Relations Society of South Australia. He also founded the Flinders University (later the National) Institute of Labour Studies.

Hancock is a Fellow and former President of the Academy of the Social Sciences in Australia. He has served as President of the Industrial Relations Society of Australia and the Economic Society of Australia (South Australian Branch).

This book is available as a free fully-searchable pdf from
www.adelaide.edu.au/press

Australian Wage Policy

INFANCY AND ADOLESCENCE

by

Keith Hancock

School of Economics
The University of Adelaide

UNIVERSITY OF
ADELAIDE PRESS

Published in Adelaide by

University of Adelaide Press
The University of Adelaide
Level 1, 230 North Terrace
South Australia 5005
press@adelaide.edu.au
www.adelaide.edu.au/press

The University of Adelaide Press publishes externally refereed scholarly books by staff of the University of Adelaide. It aims to maximise the accessibility to its best research by publishing works through the internet as free downloads and as high quality printed volumes on demand.

Electronic Index: This book is available from the website as a downloadable PDF with fully searchable text.

© 2013 Keith Hancock

This book is copyright. Apart from any fair dealing for the purposes of private study, research, criticism or review as permitted under the *Copyright Act 1968* (Cth), no part may be reproduced, stored in a retrieval system, or transmitted, in any form or by any means, electronic, mechanical, photocopying, recording or otherwise without prior written permission. Address all inquiries to the Director at the above address.

For the full Cataloguing-in-Publication data please contact the National Library of Australia: cip@nla.gov.au

ISBN (paperback) 978-1-922064-47-9
ISBN (ebook) 978-1-922064-46-2

Cover design: Emma Spoehr
Book design: Zoë Stokes

To Joe Isaac—Teacher, scholar, critic, and lifelong friend

Contents

Foreword — vii

1   Inception and setting — 1

The Higgins era 1907–1921

2   The setting — 43

3   The basic wage 1907–1921 — 55

4   Broadening the scope of wage policy — 151

Caution and restraint 1921–1929

5   The setting — 187

6   The Powers era — 217

7   The new regime — 279

Wage policy in Depression and recovery 1929–1939

8   The setting — 331

9   Wage policy and the onset of Depression — 359

10   The depths of the Depression — 465

11   The basic wage in the recovery — 543

12   Other aspects of wage policy 1935–1939 — 595

The economic critique

13   The economics of wage regulation — 653

References — 711

Index — 723

Foreword

The system of industrial conciliation and arbitration was, for most of the 20th century, a distinctive feature of the Australian economy and society. It was hailed by some as a source of equity and a mechanism of economic management; by others, it was condemned as a market friction and a brake on economic progress. In the 1990s, the system was relegated to a diminished role, partly because of a shift of opinion toward the latter perception and partly because the trade union movement, frustrated by restraints on the exercise of its power, withdrew its support for the traditional system. Though no one can foresee with certainty future industrial relations arrangements, the revival of a system of centralised regulation seems improbable.

Australian society is, nevertheless, a product of its history, and is better understood if we do not lose sight of that history. This study describes a small part of it. It is confined to the period between the inception of conciliation and arbitration and World War II. If, as I believe, the history of the system is worth telling, the study needs to be carried forward for the remainder of the 20th century. I hope that there are scholars who will take on that task.

In addition to the time limitation, there is one of scope. My focus is the regulation of the terms of employment, the attitudes and goals underlying it, the economic settings in which it occurred and the economic consequences. Except when they bear directly on my central inquiry, I do not deal with industrial disputes, or with constitutional and other legal issues that surrounded the operation of the arbitration system, or with the politics of arbitration. There is some literature in these areas, but the book is not closed.

In this book, there are many citations of cases published in the *Commonwealth Arbitration Reports* (CAR). I have elected not to refer to these cases in the conventional legal manner (*Amalgamated Engineering Union v Alderdice*) but to use titles which give some indication of the contents of the decision (*Main Hours* case). It was the practice of the Judges, in their decisions, to refer to previous cases in this way. In some cases, the reports themselves use descriptive titles (*Basic Wage and Wage Reduction Inquiry*) and I have adopted these. I have also used short titles which appeared in later numbers of the CAR (*Judgment—Saddlery Industry (Tanning Section)*).

I am grateful, for the photographs, to the Australian Bureau of Statistics, Fairfax Media Limited, Fair Work Australia (now the Fair Work Commission), the National Library of Australia, the State Library of South Australia and the State Library of Victoria.

I should like to thank Rachel Franklin, at the relevant time Librarian of the Australian Industrial Relations Commission and Fair Work Australia, for helping to assemble primary materials for my study; Tom Sheridan for making available his copy of the *Harvester* case transcript; the University of Adelaide and Flinders University for conferring honorary appointments on me and providing access to facilities for my work; the Directors of the National Institute of Labour Studies for their encouragement and support; the South Australian Industrial Court and Commission for accommodating me in their library while I worked on limited-circulation documents; Joe Isaac and Stuart Macintyre for reading my manuscript and making many helpful suggestions; Sheila Cameron, my proficient and helpful copyeditor; and the University of Adelaide Press—especially John Emerson and Zoë Stokes—for publishing this book.

My wife, Sue Richardson, and my four children—Jim, Kate, Bill and Ben—have given me every encouragement and shown much forbearance as I have worked on the project.

Keith Hancock

March 2013

1

Inception and setting

The advent of industrial regulation by tribunal came close to the turn of the century. Wages boards began in Victoria in 1896 and courts of arbitration in 1900. The first day of the new century was also the first day of the Commonwealth of Australia, endowed with a parliament that was empowered to institute its chosen models of conciliation and arbitration for the prevention and settlement of interstate industrial disputes. This book is a study of the operation of conciliation and arbitration, especially by the Commonwealth Court of Conciliation and Arbitration, from the inception of the system until World War II. It is not, however, a general history of conciliation and arbitration. It does not, for example, deal with the successes and failures of the tribunals in preventing strikes and lockouts; or with the manifold legal issues to which the system gave rise, unless they affected significantly the tribunals' exercise of their power to fix wages and conditions.[1] Rather, it is about fixing the terms of employment; and it attempts to set the tribunals' performance in an economic context. It is about 'wage policy', if the term is interpreted broadly enough to include both prescribed wages and other factors that affect the cost of labour, including working hours and leave.

---

[1] For an historical account of arbitration and industrial disputation, see Harley (2004). For an account of the legal issues, see Kirby and Creighton (2004).

1.1 The origins of wage fixation[2]

In the late 19th century, in Australia as in some other countries, the presumption that wages (like other prices) were best left to the interplay of market forces was confronted by a growing body of opinion that market outcomes were intolerable.[3] If Australia, with New Zealand, moved ahead of other countries in responding to this perception, a reason may be that policy-making was more pragmatic and less cognisant of the prescriptions of orthodox economics. As we shall see in Chapter 13, formal economics was virtually non-existent. An educated reformer was likely to be either a lawyer or a clergyman, little affected by economic doctrine.[4] Within the colonial parliaments, there were politicians prepared to judge proposals for state intervention with fewer and less strongly held preconceptions against them. Australia did not have a strong *laissez-faire* tradition. Governments had 'intervened' in various ways, including the establishment of state-owned enterprises and encouragement of immigration. Because this is a study of wage fixation, the issues of strike prevention and dispute resolution receive less attention than would be appropriate in a general history of arbitration. But it is certainly not my intention to underplay the impact of either the strikes of the 1890s or the desire of the labour movement to redress by legislation the industrial impotence of unions.[5] Both were of great importance in creating a climate for state intervention, partially displacing 'the market', to find a place on the political agenda.

---

[2] This topic is more extensively discussed in Macintyre and Mitchell (1989).
[3] A useful summary of the kinds of labour market regulation practised before the advent of arbitration is provided by Shanahan (1999, especially pp. 221–226).
[4] Jenny Lee writes of the Victorian legislation of 1896—establishing wages boards—that 'the measure was less the brainchild of the labour movement than of the liberal Christian small-bourgeois and professionals of the Anti-Sweating League. The liberal anti-sweaters ... sought particularist, moralistic explanations for the misery engulfing the working class in the 1890s, and fashioned their legislation accordingly' (Lee 1987, p. 352).
[5] Macintyre and Mitchell (1989, pp. 15–17) argue that a major reason for the adoption of compulsory arbitration was the opportunity for unions to gain assured recognition. Without disputing this, I would contend that the necessary support for arbitration of people not aligned with the unions was largely a result of their concerns about inadequate wages and unacceptable conditions of work.

Tolerance of active government was a permissive factor for interference with the labour market. The first actual intervention was the result of a specific concern—'sweating'—soon to be overtaken by the drive for the living wage (discussed in Chapter 3). The notion of sweating was fluid. Evelyn M Burns, writing in 1926, noted the vagueness of the idea:

> The exact meaning of the term 'sweating' is difficult to determine, partly because it has changed considerably since its first use, and partly because it is now a complex of vague ideas very generally held. As used today, it is roughly synonymous with the payment of 'very' or 'unduly' low wages, while some couple with it the idea of employment under unhealthy conditions, and often for very long hours. The crucial terms, 'unduly' or 'very low', are most generally taken to mean less than a very low living wage, in itself a none too precise concept, which … expands and contracts with changing economic circumstances, but they are sometimes used to imply wages 'very much lower than the normal rates prevailing throughout the country.' [*Fifth Report of the Select Committee of the House of Lords on the Sweating System* (1890)] (Burns 1926, p. 9)

A Committee of Inquiry in South Australia in 1904 identified sweating with the payment of an 'unduly low wage'. This meaning, said Burns, 'was becoming increasingly popular, possibly because it is the definition of one unknown in terms of another'.

Sweating is by no means the only concept that lacks precision but may yet be an ingredient of intelligent conversation and even policy. 'Poverty', 'fairness', 'reasonableness', 'equality' and 'equity' are but a few others. In the late 19th and early 20th centuries there were people working under conditions so offensive to many observers as to leave no room for semantic nicety. The concern was widespread. Differences of opinion emerged when the discussion focused on the extent of the problem. Was it narrowly confined to pockets of industry where, for one reason or another, employers were unable or unwilling to comply with bare minimum standards of adequacy; or did it embrace much larger proportions of the working class?

The Age, in 1890, returned to the attack on sweating; and the Chief Inspector of Factories issued a report confirming stories coming from unofficial investigators of low wages and long hours. A Factories Act Inquiry Board of 1893–94 offered suggestions about ways of dealing with the sweating problem (Hammond 1914–15, p. 107).

Victorian legislation to counter sweating provided for the creation of wages boards. A board would comprise equal numbers of employer and employee representatives presided over by a neutral chairman. The responsible Minister was Alexander Peacock. M B Hammond, an American economist who visited Australia to investigate the operation of wages boards, provides an account of his interview with Peacock:

> The author of the wages boards plan which was incorporated in the Factories Act of 1896 was Mr (now Sir) Alexander Peacock, who had recently become Chief Secretary in the Turner ministry. The agitation against sweating was at its height, and Mr Peacock interested himself in the matter and personally visited the homes of many of the out-workers. 'I found', he says, 'that these people were working excessive hours at grossly sweated rates of pay in poor and cheerless homes and generally under wretched conditions'. Sir Alexander has told me that he and the Chief Inspector of Factories, Mr Harrison Ord, held many conferences in which they endeavoured to find a practicable solution for the sweating evil. … The plan which was adopted was suggested to Mr Peacock by his own experience when, as a youth, he had been a clerk in a mining company's office near Ballarat. The owner of the mining property, a rough man who had himself been a miner, had announced a reduction of 3s a week in the wages of his men, who offered bitter opposition and asked for a conference with their employer. At this conference young Peacock acted as secretary. The employer argued that as there had been a decline in the prosperity of the business, the men ought to be willing to share in the reduction of profits. The men replied to this by pointing out the way in which they were obliged to live and successfully appealed to the employer's knowledge, as an old time comrade, of what effect a reduction of 3s a week would have on their standard of living. The

recollection of this crude experiment in collective bargaining led Mr Peacock to think that what had been done in mining might be done in other industries by compelling employers to meet with their employees to arrange wage scales. (Hammond 1914–15, pp. 108–109)

The Bill that Peacock introduced, however, would have limited the scope of wage board regulation to women and young people, 'except so far as the Chinese are concerned, in order to limit their power to contract for what wages and hours they please' (Second Reading Speech, quoted by Davey 1975, p. 44). A combination of Labor and Liberal protectionist members (the latter including Alfred Deakin and H B Higgins) secured amendments that extended the boards' coverage to adult males. Initially, five boards were set up, for the baking, boot and shoe, clothing, shirts, and underclothing trades; and a sixth board, for furniture, was appointed soon afterwards (Davey 1975, p. 58). By uneven steps, the coverage of board regulation expanded. This process was accompanied by an expansion of the accepted meaning of sweating. Davey, the author of the largest study of Victorian wages boards, says:

> Over time the meaning [of sweating] changed considerably, such changes generally reflecting alterations in the public's attitude towards state wage regulation. Thus as the public's attitude towards state regulation of wages became more favourable, so the term 'sweating' was given wider meaning. In the late nineteenth century the term was applied to a system of outwork and subcontract in certain industries in which the employer paid excessively low wages. In 1904 a wider meaning was given to the term as a result of a Committee of Inquiry Report made in South Australia, which identified sweating with the payment of an unduly low wage. From that time, opponents of sweating maintained that the term applied to almost any method of work under which workers were extremely ill-paid or overworked. (Davey 1975, p. 1)

By 1920, three-quarters of the workers in Victorian manufacturing were covered by wages boards. Coverage would have been still wider had some boards not been displaced by awards of the Commonwealth Court (Davey 1975, p. xviii). In 1910, the Victorian Parliament legislated to permit the Governor-in-Council 'to … appoint wages boards for any process, trade, business or occupation, define the area or locality within which the determination of each board should be operative, and adjust the powers which such boards or any [sic] may lawfully exercise.' This enabled the government, for the first time, to create boards for agricultural industries. The Legislative Council's objections to wages boards for agricultural callings were increasingly overshadowed by its fear of Commonwealth Arbitration Court interference in state industrial matters (Davey 1975, pp. 87–88). Within the first decade of the 20th century, the idea that the boards' role was to eliminate sweating gave way to an acceptance of their having a more general function of regulation.

South Australia was the other colony wherein sweating emerged as a significant, albeit less effective, pressure in the drive toward wage prescription. A Shops and Factories Commission was appointed in 1892 to inquire into sweating in certain trades; the first *Factories Act* was passed in 1894 (coming into effect in 1895), requiring the appointment of two Inspectors—one male and one female; and from 1896 onward the Reports of Chief Inspector of Factories located sweating in various trades, especially clothing. Not until 1900, however, did South Australia follow Victoria in making legislative provision for wages boards, and boards were not actually appointed until 1905, because of the refusal of the Legislative Council to allow the necessary regulations (Burns 1926, p. 11; Dabscheck 1983, p. 79; Finnimore 1995, p. 27). By 1905, sweating was probably a less important 'driver' than it had been in Victoria in the 1890s. Ernest Aves, an observer sent to Australia by the British Government to report on wages boards, reported of his visit to Adelaide:

> There were no signs of 'sweating' as a basis upon which industry could be said to rest, but many to show that there was a good deal of pressure in the factories. This, indeed, appears to be the form that 'sweating' assumed, and I was myself more impressed by a certain intensity of application here in the few factories I visited than elsewhere. Perhaps the impression was strengthened by the contrast presented by this 'Garden

City of the South', with its parklands and beautiful hills, its exquisite climate, its fruit and its flowers—and inside the factories some touch in the middle of all this beauty of what is regarded as old world pressure. (Aves 1908, p. 80)

Elsewhere, anti-sweating movements were less prominent. Coghlan, who surveyed all colonies, mentions them only for Victoria, South Australia, and (very briefly) New South Wales. Victoria was the colony where the need to combat sweating had the most concrete effect in the establishment of wage-fixing machinery. The gradual corruption of the term, moving it from specific evils such as uncontrolled outworking, with a concomitant exploitation of female and juvenile labour, to low pay, long hours, and tough working conditions in general, entailed its absorption into a broader assault on the operation of the market. Of this, the movement for a living wage was a major component.

The Victorian wages boards inaugurated wage regulation in Australia. Subsequently, boards were introduced in every State except Western Australia. But wages boards did not lend themselves to the application of wide-ranging concepts. Their composition emphasised the working-out of solutions acceptable within specific and narrowly defined trades. The neutral chairman (typically a magistrate), who might exercise a casting vote, could be expected to operate within bounds set by employer and employee members. This limitation of focus was, at times, strengthened by statutory requirements that boards apply the standards set by 'reputable employers'. Davey sees the continuing importance of boards in Victoria as symptomatic of the political weakness of labour. As Labor Parties in New South Wales, South Australia, and Queensland became more powerful, industrial labour gained the political capacity to implement its policy of compulsory arbitration (Davey 1975, p. 336).

Two models of conciliation and arbitration—the court and the wages board—jostled with each other for acceptance in the formative years of the Australian system. The Commonwealth's choice of the former was a decisive step.⁷ A court or like tribunal afforded greater scope than did boards for the development and application of concepts such as the living wage. This was probably a reason why labour and interventionist legislators preferred the adjudicatory tribunal; and why employers' associations and political conservatives might, if driven, accept boards as the lesser evil.⁸ It was, of course, possible for systems of regulation to be so constituted that boards operated within policy frameworks defined by overarching authorities. Courts of Industrial Appeals did, to some degree, provide such frameworks, as did the Board of Trade established in New South Wales in 1918. The court model was, however, to be the instrument of more adventurous and comprehensive policies.⁹

1.2 THE AUSTRALIAN ECONOMY

1.2.1 The population

Within three months of federation, the State Statisticians conducted a census. They had previously met to agree on uniform methods of collection and compilation. In the words of the yet-to-be-appointed Commonwealth Statistician, the 1901 census was carried out 'on a fairly uniform plan'.¹⁰ It indicated a population of 3.774 million (excluding Aborigines). Thirty-five per cent of these people lived in the six capital cities. Melbourne was the largest, with 494,000 inhabitants. Sydney had 488,000; Adelaide 162,000; Brisbane 119,000; Perth 36,000; and Hobart 32,000. Sixty-one per cent of the people were aged 15 to 64, with 35 per cent being younger than 15 and only 4 per cent 65 or older. Those born in Australia constituted 77 per cent of the total;

---

[7] The historical literature throws little light on the reasons for the choice or the reasons for constituting the Court with a judge of the High Court. There is, however, some related discussion in Macintyre (2004, pp. 57–61).
[8] The attitudes of employers to the emerging methods of regulation are thoroughly explored by Plowman (1989).
[9] H B Higgins (1922, pp. 32–33) argued that employee representatives on wages boards were exposed to intimidation by employers.
[10] Data provided by the 1901 census are from Commonwealth Bureau of Census and Statistics (1908), *Official Year Book of the Commonwealth of Australia*, No. I.

Occupational Category	Males (%)	Females (%)	Total (%)
Professional	5.5	11.9	6.9
Domestic	3.9	43.8	12.4
Commercial	14.5	10.1	13.8
Transport & communication	9.4	0.9	7.5
Industrial (excluding construction)	20.3	22.0	20.6
Construction	7.3	0.0	5.8
Primary (excluding mining)			
Agriculture	19.8	7.2	17.1
Pastoral	7.7	4.1	6.9
Other	2.1	0.0	1.7
Total primary (excluding mining)	29.6	11.3	25.7
Mining & quarrying	9.3	0.0	7.3
Total occupied	100	100	100

Table 1.1: 1901 Census: the occupied population
Note: Numbers may not sum to 100 because of rounding.

10 per cent had been born in England or Wales, 5 per cent in Ireland, and 3 per cent in Scotland. Asia accounted for less than 1 per cent.[11] The number of people described as 'occupied' was 1.617 million. Seventy-eight per cent of these were males; and the number of occupied males (including aged and juvenile workers) exceeded the male population aged 15–65. The composition of the occupied population is shown in Table 1.1.

These bare statistics attest to a small, young, and racially homogeneous population, somewhat urbanised, but with a substantial rural base, and geographically dispersed. Apart from the heavy concentration of females in domestic service, those who worked for their living were spread over a range of occupations and industries. The working population was moderately industrialised, but only moderately. The census showed that 3.5 per cent of males worked in the industrial category 'metals and minerals'; 5.4 per cent were in 'art and mechanic'; 2.6 per cent in food, drink, etc; and 2.2 per cent in textiles and related trades. For females, the only significant secondary industry

---

[11] The great majority of Asians were Chinese males.

was textiles and related trades, which accounted for 19.4 per cent of occupied women and girls.

Censuses were conducted in 1911, 1921, 1933, and 1947. The intercensal rates of population growth (percentages per annum) were:

1901–11	1.67
1911–21	2.01
1921–33	1.63
1933–47	0.96

There was no census close in time to the beginning of World War II. By the time of the 1947 census, the population was 7.579 million—double the 1901 level.[12] The proportion living in the six State capitals had risen to 50.7 per cent. Sydney now had 1.484 million people; Melbourne 1.226 million, Brisbane 402,000, Adelaide 382,000, Perth 272,000, and Hobart 77,000. Eighteen per cent of the population was categorised as 'provincial' (a designation that took in the 10,000 inhabitants of Canberra), and 31 per cent as 'rural'. The 15 to 64 age group now accounted for 67 per cent of the population. There had been a marked reduction in the relative size of the under-15 cohort—down to 25.1 per cent; the people aged 65 or more now constituted 8.1 per cent of the total. The proportion born in Australia was 90.2 per cent, with 7.9 per cent born in the British Isles. There were only 24,000 'Asiatics'—about 0.3 per cent of the population.

Table 1.2 shows the changes in the occupational composition of the labour force which were revealed by the censuses conducted between 1911 and 1947. (The classifications used in the 1911 and later censuses differed from those of 1901.) Although the 1933 figures indicate seemingly temporary changes that may have been due to the Depression, some long-term trends are reasonably clear—notably the relative decline in farming and the growth of clerical work. In short, proportionally fewer people worked 'on the land' and proportionally more 'in the office'. The proportion in mining declined.

---

[12] The 1947 census data are from the *Year Book of the Commonwealth of Australia*, No. 38 (1951) and No. 39 (1953).

	1911	1921	1933	1947
Upper professional	1.8	1.7	1.8	1.4
Lower professional	3.2	3.5	3.9	4.5
Managerial	5.0	3.7	4.5	5.9
Farmers and farm workers*	23.9	21.7	20.4	15.7
Shop workers**	7.6	7.6	7.5	7.0
Clerical workers	4.1	6.6	9.9	13.9
Craftsmen	17.3	17.0	12.2	15.9
Operatives	7.5	8.8	8.4	10.0
Drivers	5.2	5.4	5.1	5.5
Service workers	11.4	11.1	11.3	7.6
Miners	4.8	2.5	2.2	1.2
Labourers	7.7	9.7	12.3	9.9
Armed services, police	0.6	0.6	0.5	1.6
Total	100	100	100	100

Table 1.2: Occupations of the labour force 1911–1947 (%)
*Includes graziers
**Includes proprietors
Note: Numbers may not sum to 100 because of rounding.
Data derived from a table in Withers (1987), p. 261.

1.2.2 Productive performance

Maddock and McLean (1987) have summarised the processes of development that produced the economic and population structures observable early in the 20th century:

> It may be helpful to characterise Australian economic development in the nineteenth century as having been shaped essentially by the interaction of two very broad sets of forces. From the supply side, the influences were the progressive expansion of the natural resource base as a result of the discovery of land suitable for farming and of mineral deposits; the expansion of the workforce as a result not only of the natural rate of increase in the initially small resident population but also by immigration; and the augmentation of domestic savings and investment through foreign borrowing. Other things being equal, the growth of the economy was closely and positively related

to the rate at which these factors of production were accumulated. From the demand side, a high rate of population growth stimulated certain types of production, especially the provision of foodstuffs, building and construction activity, and the supply of other non-tradable goods and services. In addition, Australia exported large (in per capita terms) quantities of natural resource-intensive commodities in strong international demand, exploiting a comparative advantage, and importing those commodities that either could not be produced domestically or could be produced only at very great cost. The level of aggregate demand in the economy was therefore subject to both domestic and foreign influences. (Maddock and McLean 1987, p. 9)

Meredith and Dyster (1999, p. 5) refer to the 'dual economy' that existed at the turn of the century: one part rural and export-oriented and the other urban. The counterpart of the large export sector was a high dependence on imported consumer goods—a dependence accentuated by the funds emanating from capital inflow. Reliance on imports was both a cause and an effect of the limited development of manufactures.

Australians, on average, had enjoyed a standard of living that was high by international standards. It had come back to the field somewhat in the 1890s, but at the beginning of the new century, Australia remained one of the more affluent countries of the world. Critics of Australia's economic performance in the 20th century often assert that there was a relative decline, and some attribute this to the country's industrial relations arrangements. In assessing that contention, we must remember that the principal sources of high per capita incomes in the late 19th and early 20th centuries were productive primary industries (including mining) favoured by natural endowments, favourable terms of trade, and a low population. There was no good reason to expect that if the population grew and the country became more self-reliant, Australia's relative advantage would necessarily endure. Whether or not the industrial relations system added to or subtracted from the relative decline is another question.

The last decade of the 19th century had, in fact, been a bad period for many Australians. Beginning with a depression that was imported, but was exacerbated by domestic speculation, financial immaturity, and industrial disputation, the deterioration in economic outcomes was prolonged by drought. Recovery was slow. N G Butlin (1962) estimated that the Gross Domestic Product (GDP) per head fell, in real terms (1910–11 prices), from £66 in 1889 to £48 in 1897 and that the earlier peak was not regained until 1907 (Meredith and Dyster 1999, p. 60). Bryan Haig has criticised Butlin's estimates and provided his own. Haig's numbers suggest a shallower depression in the 1890s (Haig 2001). Whatever the truth of the disagreement, Australia, at the advent of the new century, was far from being a place of confidence and optimism. The environment was conducive to social conflict and to an increased concern about the role of the state in furthering or protecting the interests of embattled groups. This was the economic context wherein regulation of the terms of employment came onto the agenda.

There is a widely held view that the half-century before World War II was a period of little growth in productivity and *per capita* income. This view owes much to the work of Butlin, who wrote that between 1891 and 1939

> a drastic retardation occurred. It is important to note that this was much less marked in terms of population, work force and labour inputs. Indeed, these grew much faster in Australia than elsewhere in the West; it is of some significance that, in these terms, Australian *expansion* was relatively better sustained, and this raises the question whether Australian policy, pursuing expansion and increased scale of the economy, should not properly be judged on its own terms of aggregate rather than *per capita* real product (over the whole period 1890–1939, the compound growth rate was perhaps between 0.3 and 0.6 per cent per annum). If the figures are to be treated literally, output per worker and per unit of labour input may even have fallen in the interwar period but, at best, appears to have risen very slowly. The figures should not, of course, be taken too literally. Nevertheless, it would appear probable that adjustments for very large errors indeed would still allow only a very slow rise in these measures during the whole fifty years. This is in

marked contrast with, at all events, several significant Western countries, including Britain and the United States, where *per capita* and per worker growth rates tend to follow reasonably closely along the long-term trend (subject only to major fluctuations). In the Australian case this simple tabulation conceals some brief spurts of relatively rapid growth. These were not sustained, and in considerable measure, represented recovery from preceding down-swings of activity. (Butlin 1970, pp. 284–285)

As noted above, Butlin's estimates of the real GDP have been criticised by Haig (2001), who has calculated an alternative set. To adjudicate between the rival estimates, even if I could do so, would take me too far from focus of this book.[13] Figure 1.1 reproduces both Butlin's and Haig's estimates of the real GDP in the first four decades of the 20th century. Perhaps the main differences between the Butlin and Haig series are that:

- Butlin shows a stronger growth in the pre-World War I period than does Haig;
- Haig indicates a lesser slackening of growth in the later 1920s than Butlin's numbers imply; and
- Haig's estimates suggest a stronger recovery from depression in the 1930s.

Over the long term, the difference between the rival estimates is not large. The trend rate of growth of the GDP was around 2 per cent per annum (1.98 per cent on the Butlin estimates and 2.09 per cent on Haig's).[14] We also see in Figure 1.1 the growth of the population aged from 15 to 64. The trend rate of growth of the 'working-age' population was 2.00 per cent—similar to that of the GDP. This lends support to the view that the performance of the economy was poor. A more refined analysis would take into account changes

---

[13] Haig criticises both Butlin's estimates of the nominal GDP and his conversion of those estimates into real values. Whereas Butlin deflated nominal values of value added in sectors of the economy by selected price indices, Haig's basic technique was to ascertain the real quantities of various products and attach (constant) prices to them. Neither technique is inherently superior to the other. Both Butlin and Haig had to resort to simplifications and assumptions to allow for missing data. Haig argues that the economic history of Australia cannot be interpreted on the basis of Butlin's estimates.

[14] The trends are calculated by fitting lines of best fit to the logarithms of the actual values.

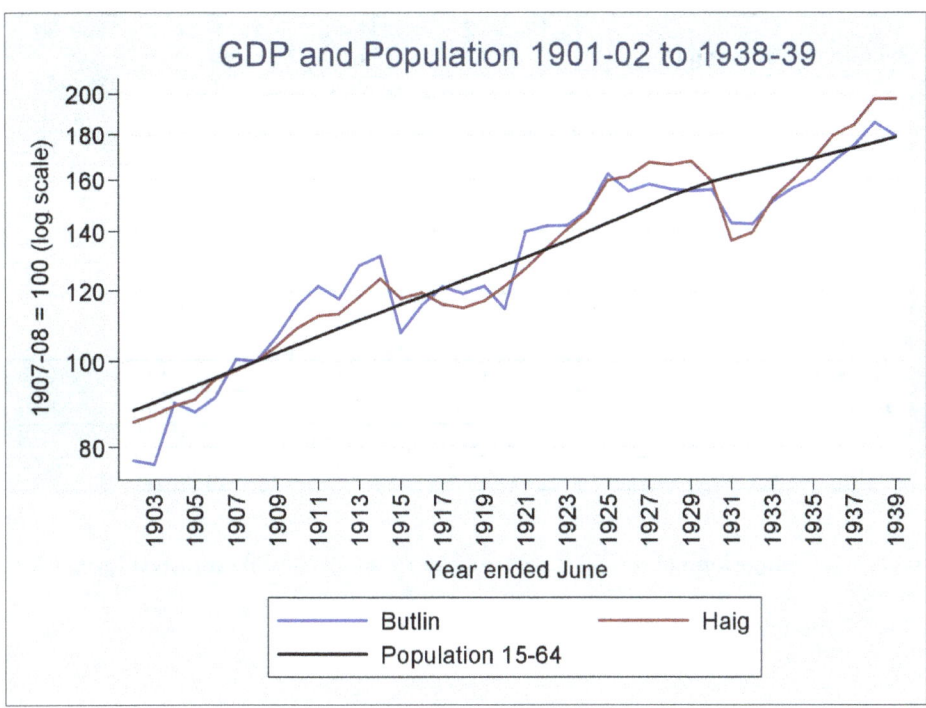

Figure 1.1
Sources: For GDP, Butlin (1962), p. 461 and Haig (2001), pp. 28–30; for population, ABS, *Historical Population Statistics, 2008*, cat. 3105.0.65.001.

in the proportion of the population in the work force and in working time. Certainly, as we see below, working hours fell; and there were increases in paid leave. Hence, there is likely to have been some improvement in the real product generated by an hour's labour; but if the GDP figures (either set) are correct, the increase was modest.

Butlin also argued that the period was one of slight change in the *structure* of economic activity. Table 1.2 above lends some support to this in respect of a broad occupational dissection of the workforce. Table 1.3 relies on Butlin's computations of the real GDP, in which production is valued at 1910–11 prices. What is striking about this table is the stability of the shares of most of the sectors. The only dramatic change in the sectoral structure of the economy was a decline in the relative importance of mining. The relative

Sectors Contributing to Real GDP	1901–02 to 1910–11	1911–12 to 1920–21	1921–22 to 1930–31	1930–31 to 1938–39
Pastoral	13.8	12.9	11.2	12.2
Other rural	10.1	10.6	11.4	13.5
Mining	8.3	6.5	5.1	2.0
Manufacturing	12.4	13.6	13.5	14.7
Construction	6.8	7.6	7.5	5.5
Distribution	14.2	15.4	16.6	18.6
Public undertakings and services	8.1	9.0	9.9	10.0
Other services	14.1	12.9	12.9	10.6
Rents	9.0	8.5	8.9	10.5
Other	3.0	3.0	3.1	2.5
Total	100.0	100.0	100.0	100.0

Table 1.3: Composition of real GDP 1901–02 to 1938–39 (Butlin estimates) (percentage shares)
Note: Numbers may not sum to 100 because of rounding.
Source: Butlin (1964), p. 461.

Sectors Contributing to Real GDP	1901	1911–12	1921–22	1931–32
Pastoral	12.4	9.3	8.4	9.0
Other rural	16.5	11.5		
Mining	11.8	5.4	2.9	2.9
Manufacturing	16.1	22.4	23.3	23.0
Building	4.5	7.1	9.1	7.8
Services	29.5	36.5	36.9	35.3
Rent	9.2	7.8	7.5	7.7
Total	100.0	100.0	100.0	100.0

Table 1.3A: Composition of real GDP 1901–02 to 1938–39 (Haig estimates) (percentage shares)
Note: Numbers may not sum to 100 because of rounding.

contribution of rural production was no smaller in the 1930s than it had been 30 years earlier. There was modest growth in the relative role of manufacturing. In Butlin's view, manufacturing contributed little to productivity growth and may actually have impeded it. Butlin adds, however, that in this respect manufacturing was not exceptional: there was 'a remarkable lack of leadership in productivity in every area of the economy ...' (Butlin 1970, p. 304). Distribution increased somewhat in importance. Services became slightly less important. Overall, however, the table suggests that the economy underwent no pronounced structural change.

Table 1.3A presents a compositional analysis of the GDP based on Haig's estimates.[15] The major differences between the two sets of estimates are the higher share for manufacturing and the greater increase in the manufacturing share between the first two periods suggested by Haig.

Colin Forster, relying on Butlin's research, wrote in 1987:

> In the period from the end of the 1880s to the end of the 1930s, Australian real Gross Domestic Product grew at roughly the same rate as population and work force. It would be an overstatement to say that output per head was stationary, and indeed the quantitative estimates of national income must be treated cautiously, but any growth in output per head was small. The Australian experience contrasted with many Western countries, and also contrasted with the preceding and following periods in Australia. (Forster 1987, p. 4)

Forster also comments on the limited structural change in the economy, though pointing out that *within* the manufacturing sector there was significant compositional change.

The view of the economy's performance suggested in the preceding discussion is puzzling in two respects. One is that it seems at odds with what we know about changes occurring in these decades that could be expected to have caused substantial increases in productivity—for example, the increasing mechanisation of production and transport, the advent of electric power, and

---

[15] We should note that there is a discontinuity in Haig's statistics because of a change in the prices applied to his real estimates. For years before 1911, Haig used the prices of 1910–11; but for later years he used the prices of 1938–39. This change affects the relative values of commodities. Hence the differences between the numbers in the first column of Table 1.3A and those in the subsequent columns may be due in part to alterations in relative prices. Similarly, differences between the percentage shares based on Haig's numbers and those based on Butlin's for the last three periods may be due in part to different relative prices.

the growing adoption of techniques of mass production. The other is that it also seems inconsistent with the growth in real wages (accompanied by reductions in working time) discussed in the next section, modest though it was. One does not need to have a mechanistic view of the link between productivity and real wages to find surprising an increase in real wages in excess of 20 per cent (more for females) in the period 1914–1939, when production—if Butlin and Haig are approximately correct—grew no faster than the working-age population.

In 1946, the Commonwealth Statistician, Roland Wilson, presented to ANZAAS a paper on *Facts and Fancies of Productivity* (Wilson 1947).[16] He discussed various methods of productivity measurement from both a conceptual and a practical standpoint. One possibility was to measure the estimated value of production in terms of some selected constant—'to postulate some article or group of articles whose absolute utility we are prepared to accept as constant'. Wilson explained:

> Given such a (necessarily hypothetical) standard we can, by pricing the standard from time to time, secure comparative measurements of any other aggregation of commodities and services by reference only to their total values at the corresponding times. The very considerable advantage of this method is that it enables us to dispense with the rarely procurable data as to the quantities of all the commodities in the aggregation with which we are concerned. If such a method is to be used I can think of no more suitable a standard than the basic necessities of life, whose total utility to the consumer is probably as constant as anything else. Professor L F Giblin may then be commended for the perspicacity which led him to introduce for the first time into an official statistical publication a general measure of productivity calculated by dividing an index of all material production by an index of retail prices and rents. (p. 17)

Wilson alludes here to a decision that Giblin had taken as Acting Commonwealth Statistician. The *Labour Report* for 1930 (No. 21, p. 67) records it:

---

[16] Wilson had previously discussed this and related issues in 1937 (Wilson 1937).

Roland Wilson

In previous issues an attempt has been made to measure the quantity of material production by means of production price index-numbers. These index numbers have never been regarded as satisfactory over a long period, and there is danger in continuing them further in respect to manufacturing production. In the absence of a satisfactory measure of the quantity of production, all that is offered here is a measure of 'real' production, i.e., the value of production measured in the same retail purchasing power, which was used to find 'real' wages.

From a modern viewpoint, deflating the nominal GDP by the consumer price index seems a crude method of computing the real GDP. Wilson noted the argument of convenience arising from data limitations, but also suggested a more respectable rationale for the technique. What it provides is a measure of the purchasing power of the income generated by production. It is, of course, a problem that not all of that income is expended on consumption. The seriousness of that problem is reduced if prices of non-consumption goods and services vary in a manner similar to that of consumer items; or if the share of consumption in total expenditure is roughly constant. We do not know whether either possibility holds good. The real-purchasing-power approach must be treated with great caution. It is, nevertheless, of interest to notice the perspective that Wilson's analysis provided. His data of per capita output underlie Figure 1.2. The 'all industries' series indicates an increase of 42.3 per cent, or almost 2 per cent per year. This implies a degree of success in generating 'real purchasing power' that contrasts with the more dismal assessments of economic performance of Butlin and Haig.

The sombre view suggested by Butlin's estimates was also challenged by McLean and Pincus (1983), who believed that the standard of living had increased between 1890 and 1939 to a significantly greater extent than Butlin's numbers had suggested. They argued for an alternative method of price adjustment that raised the trend rate of growth of real income per person from 0.61 per cent per year to 0.82 per cent. Further, they argued that the standard of living had benefited from an accumulation of capital, particularly government-owned infrastructure, which enhanced the consumption opportunities of Australians over and above the increase made possible by the growth of current income. McLean and Pincus invoked, too, a range of partial indicators of living standards—quality of housing, education, access to cars, telephones, radios and household appliances, life expectancy, age of retirement, and working hours—which suggest that well-being was considerably higher on the eve of World War II than it had been a half-century earlier. They proposed valuations of the increased life expectancy, earlier retirement, and shorter working hours, the cumulative effect being to raise the per capita growth rate from 0.8 per cent to 1.5 or 1.7 per cent. They did not attach values to the increased enjoyment of the capital stock and specific consumer goods. Presumably, these *ought* to have been included in the underlying growth rate of 0.8 per cent, but they may be a reason for suspecting that the underlying rate is too low.

McLean and Pincus's analysis relates to the average standard of living of the population and not specifically to real wages. Obviously, the two are

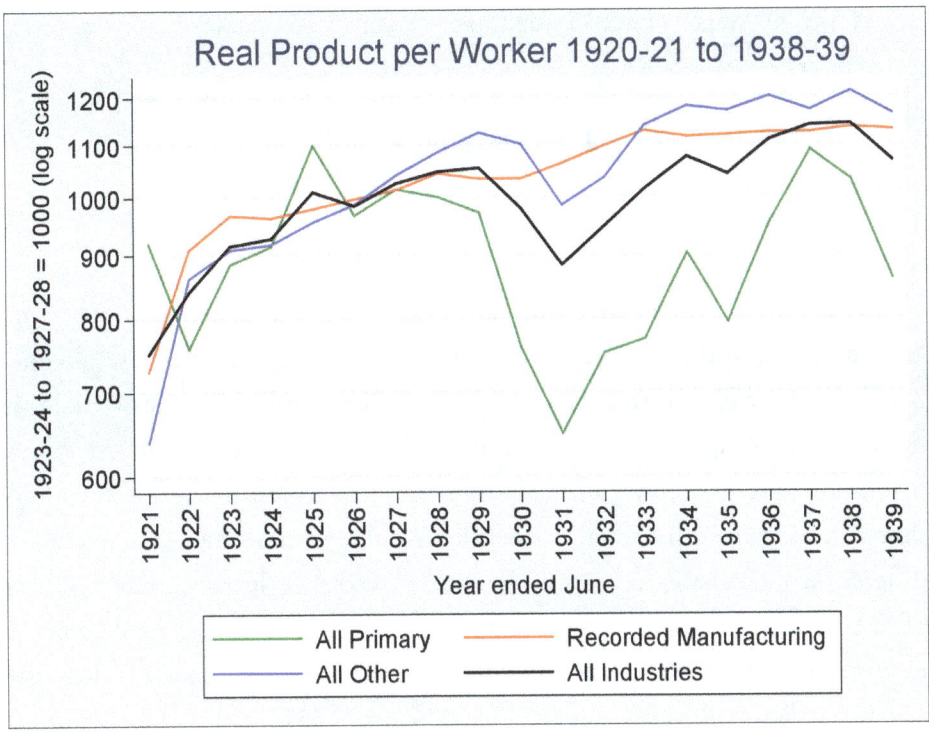

Figure 1.2
Notes: The data used for this figure are net of depreciation. The estimated numbers of workers are male equivalents.
Source: Wilson (1947), p. 45.

related but different. We may assume that a given growth rate of real wages would have been consistent with a faster rise in living standards of employees and their households because of a long-term fall in family size. Real weekly wage estimates would not take in the rise in life expectancy or the reduction of working hours. Hence McLean and Pincus's calculations are consistent with a low growth rate of real weekly wages. Wilson's much earlier estimates seem to suggest a significantly better performance.[17]

We can only conclude that there is much uncertainty about Australia's long-term economic performance in the period of this study. Contemporary

---

[17] The time periods of the two sets of calculations differ. It is unclear how far this difference influences the results.

discussion of wage policy tended, as we shall see, toward a pessimistic assessment.

1.2.3 Unemployment

The only continuous statistics of unemployment before World War II were derived from trade union returns. Union secretaries supplied to the Commonwealth Statistician information about the numbers of members of their unions and the numbers known to be unemployed. There are obvious possibilities for bias in such statistics, even if the union secretaries were both honest and competent.[18] For example, the experiences of non-members of unions may well have differed from those of unionists; and the unions that recorded their members' unemployment may have had characteristics different from those of unions without such records. Moreover, the numbers of members of reporting unions were initially quite small. In 1908, for example, 68 reporting unions had 18,685 members, of whom 1,117 (6.0 per cent) were unemployed (*Labour Report*, No. 8, 1917, p. 18). The coverage increased significantly in 1912, and in 1913, 464 unions with 251,716 members reported that 13,430 (5.3 per cent) were unemployed. (Figure 1.4 below begins with the year 1913.) In the *Labour Report* for 1923 (No. 14, pp. 21–22), the Commonwealth Statistician wrote:

> The particulars in the following tables are based upon information furnished by the secretaries of trade unions in the several States, and the membership of unions regularly reporting has now reached nearly 400,000. Unemployment returns are not collected from unions whose

---

[18] J L K Gifford (1928), drawing on the Minutes of Evidence of the Royal Commission on National Insurance of 1926, gave two reasons for regarding the unemployment statistics as unreliable: 'First, because the secretaries of many of the unions have no unemployment registers and are obliged to guess the number unemployed, and second, that it is against the interest of the unions to make correct returns, it being sometimes in the interest of some members to conceal unemployment if they are anxious to obtain an increase in wages from an arbitration court, and sometimes in their interest to exaggerate the amount of unemployment if they wish to close their books to new members or restrict the number of apprentices. It seems clear that if a secretary wished to supply wrong information the Census and Statistics Bureau in present circumstances would not be able to check it. Mr Sutcliffe admitted as much in his evidence' (p. 5).

Figure 1.3
Source: *Labour Report*, various numbers.

members are in permanent employment, such as railway and tramway employees or from unions whose members are casually employed (wharf labourers, etc). Very few unions pay unemployment benefit, but the majority of the larger organisations have permanent secretaries and organisers who are in close touch with the members and with the state of trade within their particular industries. In many cases unemployment registers are kept, and provision is made in the rules for members out of work to pay reduced subscriptions. It may, therefore, be affirmed that percentage results based on trade union information fairly show the general trend of unemployment.[19]

During the period covered by Figure 1.3, there were two censuses which afford some check on the reliability of the union data. On April 4, 1921, 9.6 per cent of wage and salary earners were unemployed (*Year Book Australia* 1923, p. 952). The *Year Book* commented: 'The number returned as unemployed in

---

[19] Similar statements appeared in other numbers of the *Labour Report*.

1921 was nearly three times as great as in 1911, and it is of interest to note that these results are substantially confirmed by the Labour and Industrial Branch of this Bureau' (p. 951). In fact, the union-based percentages for the first and second quarters of 1921 were 11.4 and 12.5, respectively (*Labour Report*, No. 12, 1921, p. 18)—rather higher than the census suggested. At the census of 30 June 1933, the unemployment percentage was 22.4 (*Year Book Australia* 1935, p. 552). The union percentages for the second and third quarters of 1933 were 25.7 and 25.1 (*Labour Report*, No. 25, 1935, p. 103). Thus the relativity of the union-based unemployment percentages to the census result was the reverse of that of 1921. But the comparisons with the census data do not suggest that the union-based series is seriously misleading as an indicator of changes in the state of the labour market.

The impact of the Depression on unemployment is sufficiently evident in Figure 1.3 and requires no further comment at this stage. In earlier years, except for 1921, unemployment varied between 5 and 10 per cent. After the recession of 1921, it failed to return to the levels that had been reached between 1916 and 1920. This accords with contemporary dissatisfaction about economic performance in the 1920s to which later chapters further refer.

1.3 Wages, prices, and hours of work to World War II: a conspectus

1.3.1 Nominal wages

For the period before 1914, there are no comprehensive wage data. From that year, however, there are estimates of nominal weekly wage rates. These data were compiled by the Commonwealth Statistician, who provided the following explanation:

> The collection of data respecting the nominal rates of wages payable in different callings and in occupations in various industries was first undertaken by this Bureau in the early part of the year 1913. Owing to the difficulty of obtaining reliable particulars of the numbers of apprentices, improvers and other juvenile workers to whom progressive

rates of wages fixed according to increasing age or experience were payable from year to year, the inquiry was confined to the rates of wages payable to adult workers only, and was further limited generally to those industries in operation within the metropolitan area of each State. In order to make the inquiry comprehensive, however, certain industries were included which were not carried on in the capital cities, e.g. mining, shipping, agriculture, and pastoral. The particulars acquired were obtained primarily from awards, determinations and industrial agreements under Commonwealth and State Acts, and related to the minimum wage prescribed. In cases where no award, determination or agreement was in force, the ruling union or predominant rate of wage was ascertained from employers and secretaries of trade unions. For convenience of comparison weekly rates of wages were adopted. In many instances, however, the wages were based on daily or hourly rates, since in many industries and occupations in which employment is casual or intermittent wages are so fixed ... The information thus obtained referred to the weekly rate of wage in upwards of 400 specific occupations. Rates of wage were not of course available for each of these occupations in every State but the aggregate collection for the six States amounted to 1,569 male occupations or callings. (*Labour Report*, No. 28, 1937, p. 55)

The occupations were assigned to industry groups. For each industry group within a State, an unweighted average of the occupational rates was calculated. In aggregating these separate averages, weighting formulae were applied to reflect the numbers of workers in the industries and the States. Thus the overall averages are a hybrid of weighted an unweighted data.

As the Statistician made clear, nominal wages were, for the most part, wages prescribed in industrial instruments. (No data of actual earnings for a full-time week, exclusive of overtime, are available.) This means that comparisons of nominal wages over time do not register the effects on actual wages of changes in the composition of the work force. (In this respect, the nominal wage series is akin to the modern Labour Price Index rather than the series for Average Weekly Earnings.) The nominal wages data do not reflect either over-award or below-award payments.

1.3.2 Retail prices

The Commonwealth Statistician began publication of quarterly retail price index numbers in 1912.[20] The construction of these numbers is described in detail in the *Labour Report* for 1912 (No. 3). The initial index, which became known as the 'A series', measured the weighted average prices of 46 items of food and groceries plus house rents. The items included were dictated to some extent by the problems of assembling reliable data and to some extent by a 'cost of living' survey, covering 999 people, which had been conducted in 1910–11. The data were obtained from retailers—not by direct purchase of commodities, but by asking the retailers to supply the information. They were collected from 30 towns—five in each State (including the capital cities). At the inception of the A series index, the Statistician asked retailers to provide data for the years 1901–1911. This retrospective information was collected on an annual basis only and its reliability obviously depended on the accuracy of the retailers' records and recollections.[21]

In 1925, following the advice of a conference of statisticians, the Commonwealth Bureau published an alternative version—the B series index—which differed from the A series by confining rent to four and five-roomed houses.[22] The B series index incorporated the rent component of the A series up to the time of the change.

---

[20] During the hearing on the 1933 application for restoration of the 10 per cent wage reduction, the union advocate H C Gibson said: 'Mr King O'Malley claims to have been the originator of the Commonwealth Bank and also the originator of these index figures. I have had several chats with that gentleman as to what was behind his mind, and what was his intention in requesting the Commonwealth Statistician to undertake this investigation, but he is the haziest individual I have ever met' (transcript, p. 142).

[21] In the 1930–31 basic wage case, Gibson disputed the index number for 1907—a matter of some consequence because it affected the wage level necessary to maintain the *Harvester* standard (see Chapter 9, Subsection 9.2.8).

[22] Because the Commonwealth Arbitration Court preferred the old index for wage adjustment, the Statistician continued to provide the A series data (commonly described as the 'All Houses' index). Movements of the two indices differed very little.

An obvious limitation of the A and B series indices was their failure to cover clothing and many items of miscellaneous expenditure. The Statistician repeatedly said that food, groceries, and house rents represented about 60 per cent of household expenditure. He also asserted, until the 1930s, that the index numbers for food, groceries, and housing gave an accurate picture of the overall behaviour of retail prices. The Royal Commission on the Basic Wage, which reported in 1920, constructed a regimen of commodities which included clothing and miscellaneous items.[23] Subsequently, the Statistician began publication of the C series (or 'All Items') index. This added clothing and miscellaneous items to the items in the A series (later the B series) index. The C series index is available on a quarterly basis from the second quarter of 1922. Annual values were provided for November of each year from 1914 to 1921.

Because of their relevance to wage setting, the price indices were the subject of controversy. I discuss some of the criticisms in later chapters. For a broad perspective, however, I rely on the C series index because of its greater comprehensiveness.[24]

1.3.3 Wages, prices, and real wages

Figure 1.4 describes (subject to data limitations) the behaviour of adult male wages, consumer prices, and real wages over the period 1907–1939. The most notable features of this story are:

- a high rate of inflation, reflected in both the price and the wage data, between 1914 and 1920: over the six-year period, prices rose by 68 per cent and wages by 51 per cent;
- severe deflation between 1929 and 1933, with prices and wages falling by 20 per cent and 18 per cent, respectively;

---

[23] The Royal Commission and its report are discussed in Chapter 3.
[24] Because the C series index begins in November 1914, I use the A series index to measure the price level in the previous three quarters. For the years 1915–21, quarterly values of the C series index are estimated by interpolation between the November numbers.

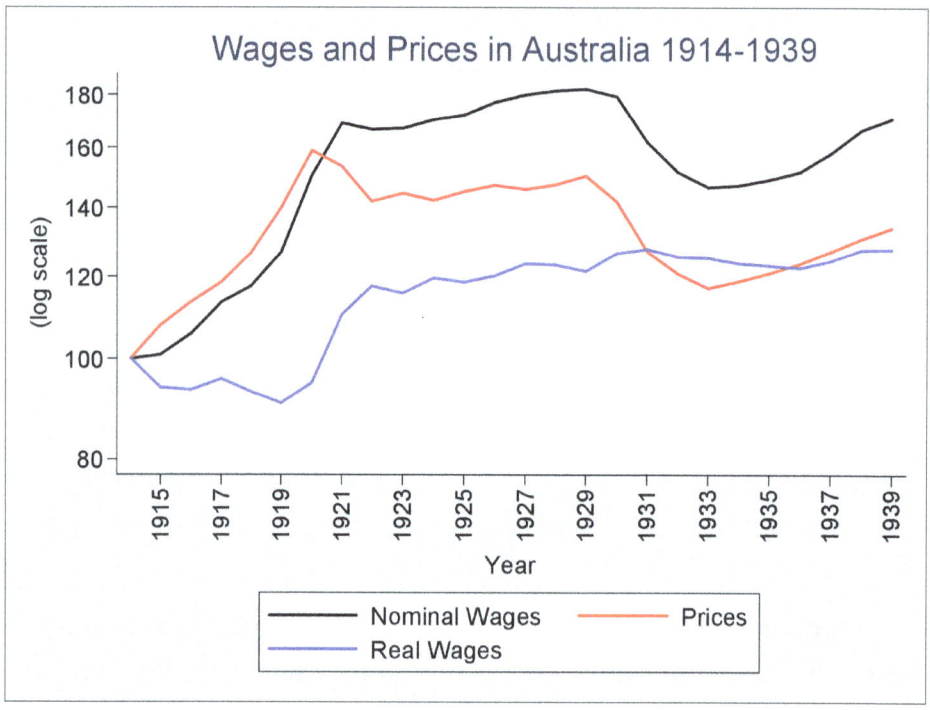

Figure 1.4
Source: *Labour Report*, various numbers.

- subsequent increases in both prices and wages, but leaving 1939 prices still 5 per cent below and wages 6 per cent below their 1929 levels;
- a fall of 14 per cent in real wages between 1914 and 1919, as the rise in nominal wages lagged behind that of prices;
- a 30 per cent rise in real wages between 1919 and 1922, taking real wages in that year to a level 11 per cent higher than in 1914, the increase being linked to a continuing rise in money wages after prices had begun to fall;
- a modest further increase (3 per cent) in real wages between 1922 and 1929;
- virtual constancy of real wages during the 1930s, with a 1939 level 21 per cent above that of 1914; and

- over the whole period, a rise in real wages of just under 1 per cent per year. For the years 1922–39, the average increase was 0.5 per cent per year.

All of these aspects of the period will, of course, be more fully discussed in later chapters.

1.3.4 Real wages and well-being

The sluggish growth in real wages, as in productivity, is—if the statistics are reliable—a significant characteristic of the period. Wilson in his 1946 lecture commented on this perplexing fact:

> We have no doubt all been struck … by a feeling of slight wonder that real wages in Australia, as measured by the nominal wage index divided by the index of retail prices, should have risen so little in the last thirty or forty years. The annual rate of increase between 1907 and the three years ending in June 1940 was only 0.61 per cent. As there is not much evidence to suggest that the distribution of incomes over that period has changed greatly to the detriment of the wage-earner, real wages must be accepted as a not altogether unreasonable indication of the long-term trend of productivity, at any rate as measured in the composite units of the retail price index. On the other hand, the impressions of many of those who have lived through this period record an improvement in the well-being of the average worker out of all proportion to the measured rise in real wages. (Wilson 1947, p. 17)

'The real question to be answered', said Wilson, 'is whether well-being can change without a corresponding change in productivity as measured by currently accepted methods.' He suggested several reasons why well-being might have grown faster than the data of real wages and productivity suggested.

First, there was a growing *supply* of 'free goods'. An important example was 'the gradual increase in the community's stock of owner-occupied houses, the imputed rentals of which sometimes find a place in estimated money-values of the national income, but never to my knowledge in a directly costed index of productivity. Owner-enjoyed property of other kinds, such as books, pictures, furniture and so on may also be mentioned as items which may appear in a productivity index as new products but which do not affect it in their capacity of continuous producers of current satisfactions.' The market, and measures of production, failed to capture 'satisfactions arising from the enjoyment of property such as museums, public gardens, schools and universities, bequeathed to the people by governments and public benefactors of earlier days' (p. 18).

Second, there was greater *access* to free goods, 'partly as the result of increasing economies in the cost and time of travel, partly because of the general trend to greater leisure'. The Lancashire millhand of a century earlier had little or no opportunity to enjoy the Scottish Highlands, or even Blackpool. Now a visit to Palm Beach or the Blue Mountains was 'only an incident to the industrial worker of Sydney' (p. 19).

Third, there was a 'growing tendency for work to become play, and thus to fall outside the Statistician's measurement of productivity'. Greater leisure afforded to people the opportunity to 'produce' for their own benefit by such means as 'household repairs, gardening, and simple manufacture'.

Finally, estimates of productivity growth were biased downward because of the statisticians' inability to allow adequately for the emergence of new products and the disappearance of old ones. The standard technique to adjust indices of real output for changes in the composition of production was chain-indexing. But this was an imperfect technique. Wilson illustrated the problem:

> Suppose, for instance, that buggies disappeared entirely at the end of 1910 and were replaced by cars as from the beginning of 1911. We should then compare the whole product of 1910 with the whole product of 1909, the product of 1911 (excluding cars) with the product of 1910 (excluding buggies), the whole product of 1912 with the whole product of 1911, and chain the results together to form an index.
>
> The important omission, for the present purpose, is that at no time have we compared buggies directly with cars. We have allowed for any

> increase or decrease in the 'productivity' of car manufacturers after car manufacture started, and any decrease or increase in the productivity of buggy manufacturers before buggy manufacture ceased. But this does not get us out of the basic difficulty that, in effect, we have assumed that the contribution to well-being of the man making the last buggy is exactly equal to the contribution of the man making the first car. This leaves out of account the improvement in well-being made possible by the substitution of car-travel for buggy-travel. (p. 19–20)

The buggy-car substitution does not, of course, have to be instantaneous for the point to hold: if, year by year, there are more cars and fewer buggies produced, the measure of total production may be flawed. An objection to the argument is that the relative prices of cars and buggies may reflect the benefit that users derive from them. If the price of a car is twice that of a buggy, the nominal GDP will register this. The problem then shifts to the deflator for the GDP: we wish to adjust the nominal GDP for pure price increases but not for enhanced quality. It may, however, be difficult or impossible to disentangle them. A chained price index entails the same difficulty as Wilson noted for chained quantity measures. It is a familiar difficulty of price indices that they may not capture fully increases in quality and may therefore treat as price increases what are in truth improvements of quality.

That problem is very likely to have applied to the retail price indices of our period. There was little or no allowance for the changing content of consumption or for changes in quality. Hence the indices are likely to have overestimated the rise in prices (or underestimated the falls). There is no way of quantifying the error. But we may reasonably suppose that the employed wage-earner did fare somewhat better than Figure 1.4 implies.

1.3.5 The basic wage

Much will be said in this study about the basic wage. Although the federal basic wage had its origin in the *Harvester* case of 1907, no meaningful statistics of the basic wage can be provided for years before 1922. The reason is that in those early years the basic wage was set award-by-award, usually when the award fell due for renewal but sometimes upon application for variation. Moreover, the practices of the judges in fixing the basic wage varied. As a result, there was not one basic wage, but a range of them.[25] In 1922, however, the Commonwealth Court adopted the practice of prescribing a general basic wage (subject to geographical differences and some departures from general practice in particular awards). From this time, it is meaningful to speak of *the* basic wage.

From 1922 onwards, the federal basic wage was subject to automatic quarterly adjustment with reference to a price index. In addition, discretionary changes were imposed by the Arbitration Court in 1931, 1933, 1934, and 1937. Figure 1.5 shows the levels of the (federal) basic wage over the period 1922–39.[26] These are weighted averages for the six capital cities. The figure also shows the real basic wage and the relativity of the basic wage to nominal adult male wages. (All three curves are constructed from index numbers, with the values for the second quarter of 1922 set at 100.) The federal basic wage increased during the 1920s, and in 1929 was 15 per cent higher than in mid-1922. Between 1929 and 1933, it fell by 29 per cent. Although it increased thereafter, in 1939 it was still barely at the 1922 level. In real terms, it was above the 1922 level, but below that of the later 1920s. The relativity of the basic wage to total nominal wages was lower in 1939 than at any time in the 1920s. One reason for the differences between the movements of the basic wage and of nominal rates is the fact that the latter encompass components of wages additional to the basic wage, mainly margins for skill. Another is the adoption by State tribunals of policies different from those of the Commonwealth Court. An important example of divergent policy was the failure of some State tribunals to follow the federal 'lead' when the Court cut wages by 10 per cent in 1931.

---

[25] The setting of the basic wage in this earlier period will be discussed in chapters 3 and 6.
[26] I thank Rachel Franklin, formerly Librarian of Fair Work Australia, for providing data showing the basic wage obtaining in each of the six capital cities and the weighted average for all six cities. During the 1920s, the wage adjustment times were the beginning of February, May, August, and November. I have constructed data for quarters ended in March, June, September, and December by calculating averages. The March quarter number, for example, comprises one-third of the November number and two-thirds of the February number.

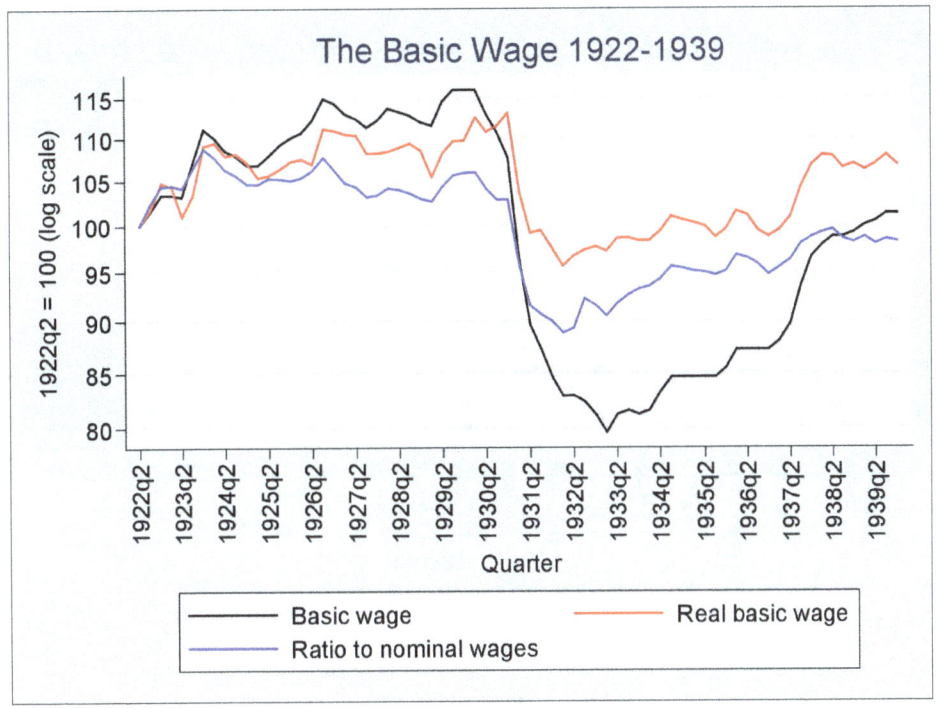

Figure 1.5
Source note: Basic wage levels calculated from data supplied by the Librarian of Fair Work Australia; other data are from various numbers of the *Labour Report*.

Basic or living wages were also set by State tribunals in four of the States: New South Wales, Queensland (from 1921), South Australia, and Western Australia (from 1926). Figure 1.6 shows the relativities of the basic or living wage to the corresponding federal wage in each of four capital cities in the years 1923–1939.[27] It is plain that there were significant differences between the State and the federal wage policies. This was particularly evident in Depression years, when the States (whether by legislation or tribunal decision) acted independently of the Commonwealth Court and resisted the Court's policy of wage reduction.[28]

---

[27] I should acknowledge that the data on which Figure 1.6 is based have been in my possession for many years and are of uncertain provenance.
[28] The prescription of a living wage in New South Wales was complicated by the adoption of child endowment, which at various times was associated with a reduced living wage and

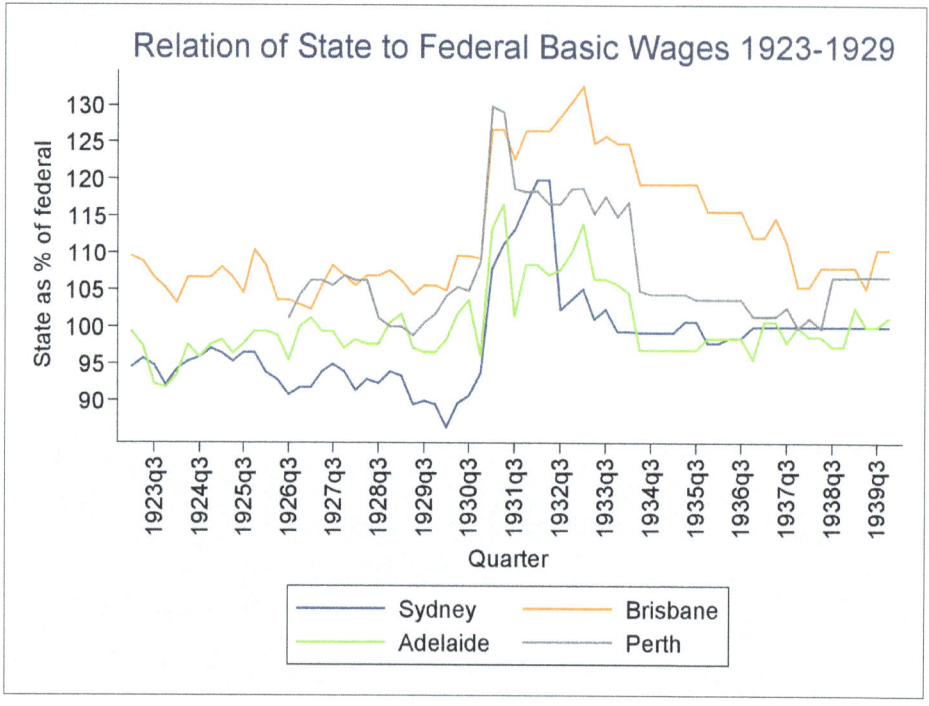

Figure 1.6

1.3.6 Female wages

Nominal wage data were compiled for adult females in a similar manner to those for males, though the female series covered a narrower range of occupations. Figure 1.7 shows real female wages and the ratio of female rates to those for males. Although the time-pattern of changes in female real wages was much the same as for male wages, women's relative position improved somewhat. In 1914, the average female wage was 49 per cent of the male wage; by 1939 it reached 55 per cent.

---

employer contributions to an endowment fund. Further references to State policies are made in later chapters.

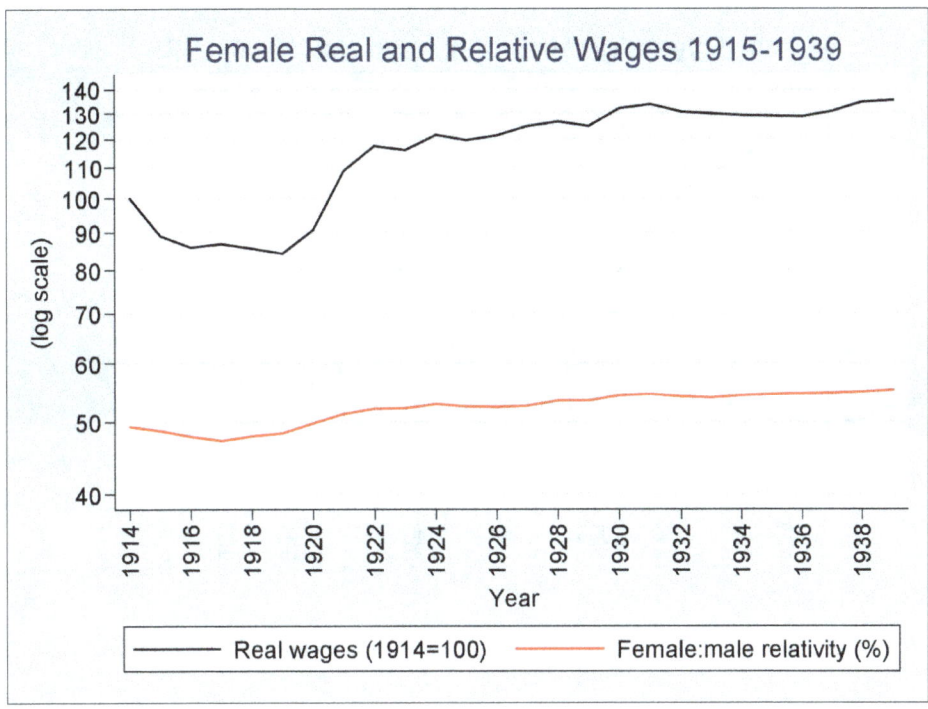

Figure 1.7
Source: *Labour Report*, various numbers.

1.3.7 Working hours

Like the wage data, those of working hours are derived from legal instruments such as awards.[29] There are no statistics of actual working time. The best interpretation of the published statistics is that they represent the maximum hours that employers could legally demand of their workers without paying overtime. Of course, the maxima varied from instrument to instrument and the numbers published are averages.[30] The hours prescribed for adult males and females are shown in Figure 1.8.

---

[29] In the case of some State awards, hours were at times controlled by statute.
[30] As averages, they are subject to similar limitations as those of the nominal wage data. In some industries, there were no prescribed maximum hours. These industries were excluded from the Statistician's calculations.

38 *Australian Wage Policy*

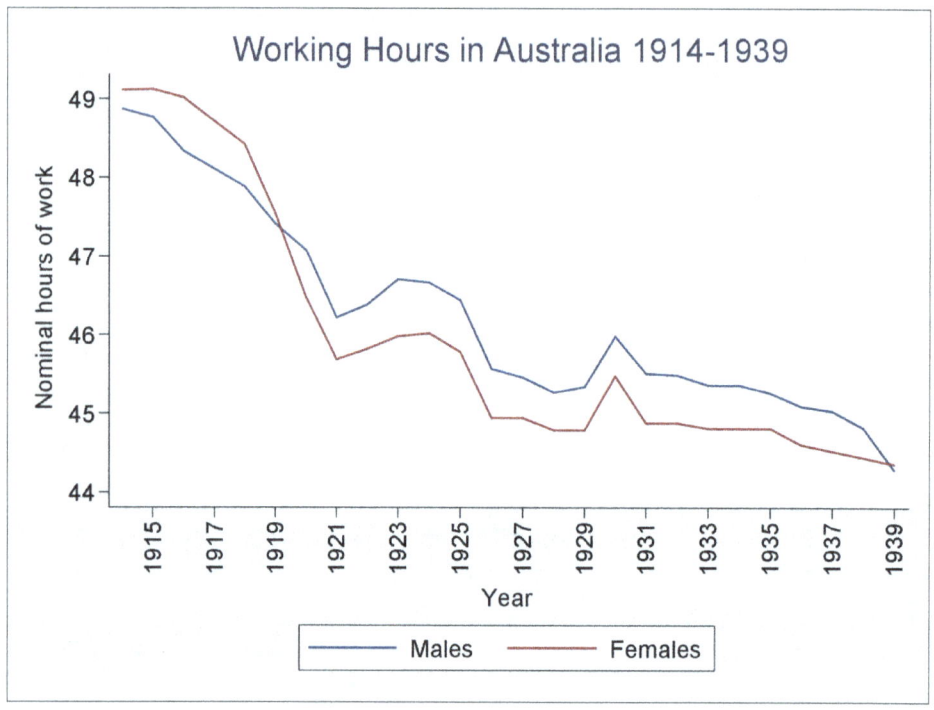

Figure 1.8
Note: The observations plotted in the chart pertain to the end of the year.
Source: *Labour Report*, various numbers.

Over the quarter-century covered by Figure 1.8, average weekly hours fell from 48.9 to 44.3 for adult males and from 49.1 to 44.4 for adult females. More than half of the reduction occurred between 1914 and 1921. As the figure shows, females initially worked slightly longer hours than did males. This was reversed between 1918 and 1921. It appears that the reduction of hours that gathered strength after 1937 affected men more than women; and by the end of 1939 the average hours of males and females were virtually equal. The reduction of 9.4 per cent in male working time, combined with an increase of about 27.6 per cent in real weekly wage rates, implies a rise of about 41 per cent in hourly real wages. A similar calculation for females indicates an increase of about 50 per cent.

Ideally, statistics of weekly working hours would be supplemented by data of paid leave, giving a comprehensive picture of the division between working and other time. There are no such data. In the course of this study, references will be made to tribunal decisions about leave; but this is qualitative evidence, which falls far short of the requirements of a data series. In brief, the qualitative evidence is of an early movement toward the awarding of paid public holidays (8 to 10 per year) and sick leave. Annual leave came later. By World War II, one week's leave was common for manual workers and in white-collar work longer periods were general.

THE HIGGINS ERA 1907–1921

2

The setting

2.1 THE COURT

The original *Commonwealth Conciliation and Arbitration Act 1904* provided for a specialist Court—the Commonwealth Court of Conciliation and Arbitration—comprising a single Judge (designated as President), who would be one of the Judges of the High Court, appointed for a term of seven years. One of the initial three appointees to the High Court, R E O'Connor, was appointed to the Arbitration Court in 1905 and served until 1907, when he resigned. O'Connor's contributions were limited, his main decision being the making of an award for merchant seamen (Macintyre 2004, pp. 55, 59). He was succeeded by Henry Bournes Higgins, who served almost two terms (resigning in June 1921, shortly before the end of his second term).[1] Higgins was the sole member of the Court for six years. An amendment of the Act then allowed for the appointment (also from the High Court) of Deputy Presidents, and Charles Powers was so appointed in 1913. From then until 1921 Higgins and Powers shared the great bulk of the Court's workload, with some help from Isaac Isaacs and Hayden Starke in 1917 and 1920–21 respectively.

Initially, the workload of the Court was modest. In its first five years, it made only five awards: three related to merchant shipping, one for employees of the BHP Company at Broken Hill and Port Pirie, and one for the boot

---

[1] The best biography of Higgins is Rickard (1984).

trades. The pace began to quicken about 1912, probably because unions judged that they could get better results from the Commonwealth Court than from some of the State tribunals.[2] At the end of 1913, there were 17 Commonwealth awards in force; at the end of 1921, there were 99 (*Labour Report*, No. 13, 1922). In 1920, Powers observed that 'so many Federal unions are knocking at the door for awards that the two Judges of the Court cannot possibly get within reasonable distance of dealing with the many applications filed in the Court' (14 CAR vii). Apart from the *Harvester* case, which did not involve an award, it was in the making and occasional variation of the awards that the Court's policies were fashioned.

Higgins's departure from the Court was the culmination of an intense dispute between him and Prime Minister Hughes about the correct response to industrial disputation. Higgins adhered staunchly to the policy of refusing to arbitrate while unions were on strike, contending that any concessions made would only cause more future resort to direct action. Hughes, on the other hand, was more concerned to settle particular disputes with a view to resumption of work. His strategies included personal intervention to meet the demands of strikers and the creation of special tribunals which would displace the Court (Hancock 1979a, pp. 17–18; Rimmer 2004, pp. 283–284).

2.2 The economic setting

At the time of inception of federal arbitration, Australia was reasonably prosperous, having recovered from the depression of the 1890s and a severe drought. Butlin's estimates indicate that between 1900–01 and 1910–11, the real GDP increased by 62 per cent or 4.9 per cent per year (Butlin 1962, p. 461). Haig's estimates suggest a less exuberant growth, with the real GDP rising by 30 per cent (2.6 per cent per year) between 1901 and 1911 (Haig 2001, p. 30). In the intercensal period from 1901 to 1911, the growth of the workforce was about 19 per cent (1.8 per cent per year) (*Year Book Australia*, No. 1, 1908; No. 7, 1914). The improvement in productivity—substantial

---

[2] The coverage of unions also increased. According to the *Labour Report* (No. 8, 1917, p. 10; No. 13, 1922, p. 11), there were 433,000 union members in 1912 and 703,000 in 1921.

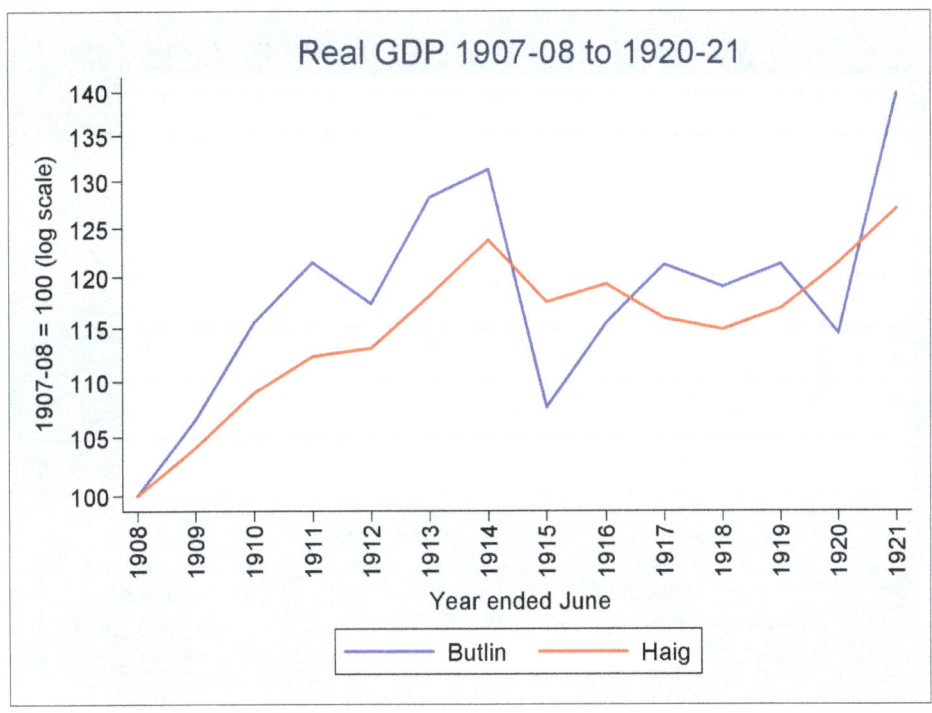

Figure 2.1
Note: As indicated in Subsection 1.2.2 of Chapter 1, the Haig series combines two separate sets of estimates: one (to 1911) based on 1891 prices and computed for calendar years; the other (from 1911–12) based on 1938–39 prices and computed for July to June. The adjustments necessary to combine the two series are likely to have imported minor errors into the composite series.
Sources: Butlin (1962, p. 461), Haig (2001, pp. 28–30).

on Butlin's GDP estimates, more modest on Haig's—may have been due in considerable degree to improved seasonal conditions. Whether the process of recovery from the depression or the end of drought was the more potent driver of growth in this period is a debatable issue.

Figure 2.1 shows the movement of the real GDP from 1907–08 to 1920–21 according to the Butlin and Haig estimates. Butlin's estimates are more volatile than Haig's, but both indicate a peak in 1913–14 and a downturn thereafter. Through the war years, production was below the pre-war peak. Both sets of estimates show strong growth in 1920–21.

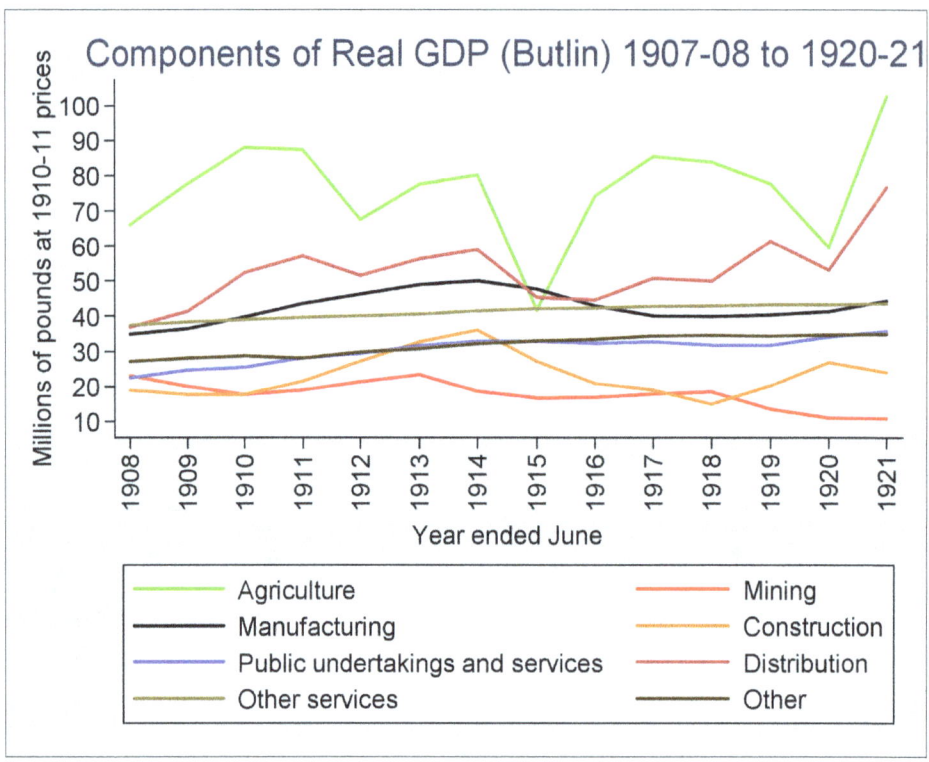

Figure 2.2
Note: 'Agriculture' includes pastoral and dairying. Water transport (1.6% of the GDP in 1907–08) and finance (2.0%) are included in 'other services'.

Figure 2.2, based on Butlin's estimates, shows the movements of the components of the real GDP over the period. It suggests that the GDP fluctuations of the period were dominated by the experience of the rural sector. A second feature of the figure is the relative growth in the size of 'distribution'. In this sector, fluctuations mirrored to some extent those of agriculture, but were more muted. Third, manufacturing and construction both peaked in 1913–14, and neither sector had regained its 1913–14 product by the end of the period. There is little sign of a manufacturing 'take-off' in these years. Fourth, there was a falling trend in the gross product of mining.

Figure 2.2A shows Haig's estimates. Because of the changes in the price deflator used by Haig—separating the period to 1911 and the period from

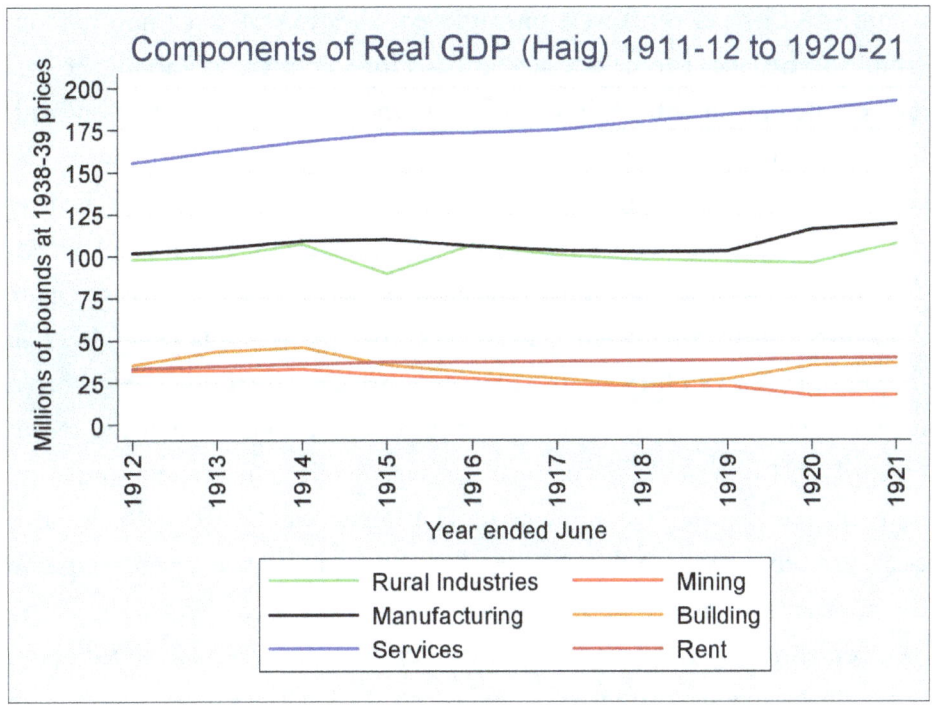

Figure 2.2A

1911–12 onward—we cannot use his figures to analyse the composition of the GDP over the entire period from 1907–08 to 1920–21. Hence Figure 2.2A is confined to the period from 1911–12 to 1920–21. It suggests much less volatility in the component segments of the GDP than is indicated by Butlin's figures. Both sets of estimates show a declining trend in mining; and both show falls in several components of the real GDP in 1914–15. Haig's figures confirm that there was no overall growth in manufacturing. The differences between the estimates reduce the confidence that we can have in the GDP data to indicate the compositional changes in the GDP in this period.

Data specific to the labour market are scarce. The only continuing measures of unemployment at this time were the returns, provided by trade union secretaries, of unemployment among union members (see Chapter 1, Subsection 1.2.3). The *Labour Report* (No. 13, 1922, p. 23) shows that at the end of 1907 there were returns from 51 unions with 13,179 members, of whom 757 (5.7 per cent) were unemployed. Clearly, this small non-random sample of the labour force is a slender basis for any inferences about the true level of unemployment. At the end of 1910, the returns from 109 unions with 67, 961 members showed that 1,857 (5.6 per cent) were unemployed. The coverage of the returns increased markedly in 1912 and continued to rise over the next decade, reaching 361,744 in 1921. From 1913, the unemployment data derived from these returns are available on a quarterly basis. Figure 2.3 shows the unemployment percentages from the first quarter of 1913 to the second quarter of 1921. In Chapter 1, we noted that the union-based unemployment percentages in 1921 were somewhat higher than the census of April 1921 indicated. The comparison suggests that the union returns may have overstated 'true' unemployment. The impact of the 1914–15 slump is clear, but otherwise it is difficult to relate the unemployment percentages to the variations in the real GDP. The poor 'fit' is particularly evident in 1920–21. Contemporary reports and commentary, including that of the tribunals, point unambiguously to an economic crisis at that time; they accord with the unemployment percentages, but not with the real GDP estimates. Notwithstanding the possible conflict between the measures of performance, there is little doubt that the period from 1914 to 1921 was (with a possible respite in 1920) less 'comfortable' than the early Higgins years.

So far as I can discover, there is no published analysis of the short-term economic effects of World War I. To investigate those effects thoroughly would be a separate research project. According to Butlin, between 1913–14 and 1914–15 gross private capital formation (in 1910–11 prices) fell from £35 million to £19 million, and in 1917–18 was only £13 million. Thereafter there was some recovery, with the level of private investment rising to £20 million in 1918–19 and £24 million in both 1919–20 and 1920–21 (Butlin 1962, p. 463). These estimates point to a wartime slump in business confidence, accentuated perhaps by the difficulty of obtaining imported supplies. Whether the slump was caused by the war is a question that I cannot answer. It may be that the relatively low levels of unemployment between 1916 and 1920 were

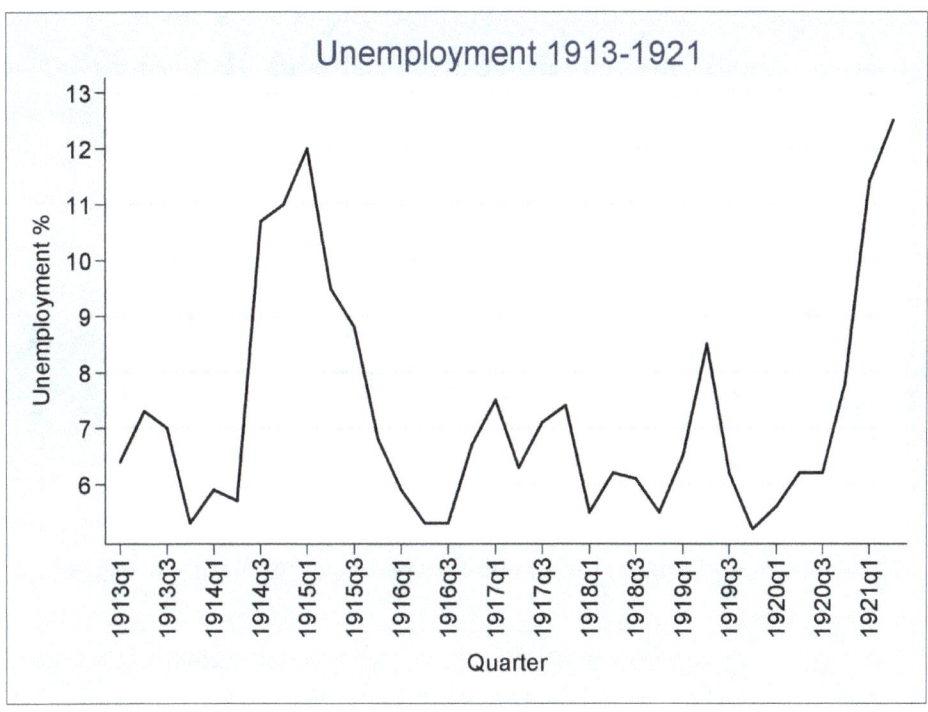

Figure 2.3
Source: *Labour Report*, various numbers.

due in some measure to the absorption of men into the forces and that the increase thereafter owed something to their discharge.

2.3 WAGES AND PRICES

Statistics of wages and prices, compiled by the office of the Commonwealth Statistician, began to emerge in the second decade of the 20th century. By today's standards, these data were rudimentary. They do, nevertheless, throw some light on the realities of a troubled period. Quarterly data of nominal wages are available from 1914.[3] (The manner of construction of these data is described in Chapter 1, Subsection 1.3.1.) The Commonwealth Statistician also estimated nominal wages for the year 1911. It is possible, therefore, to

---

[3] There are data for 30 April 1914. Thereafter, the data are for the end of June, September, December and March.

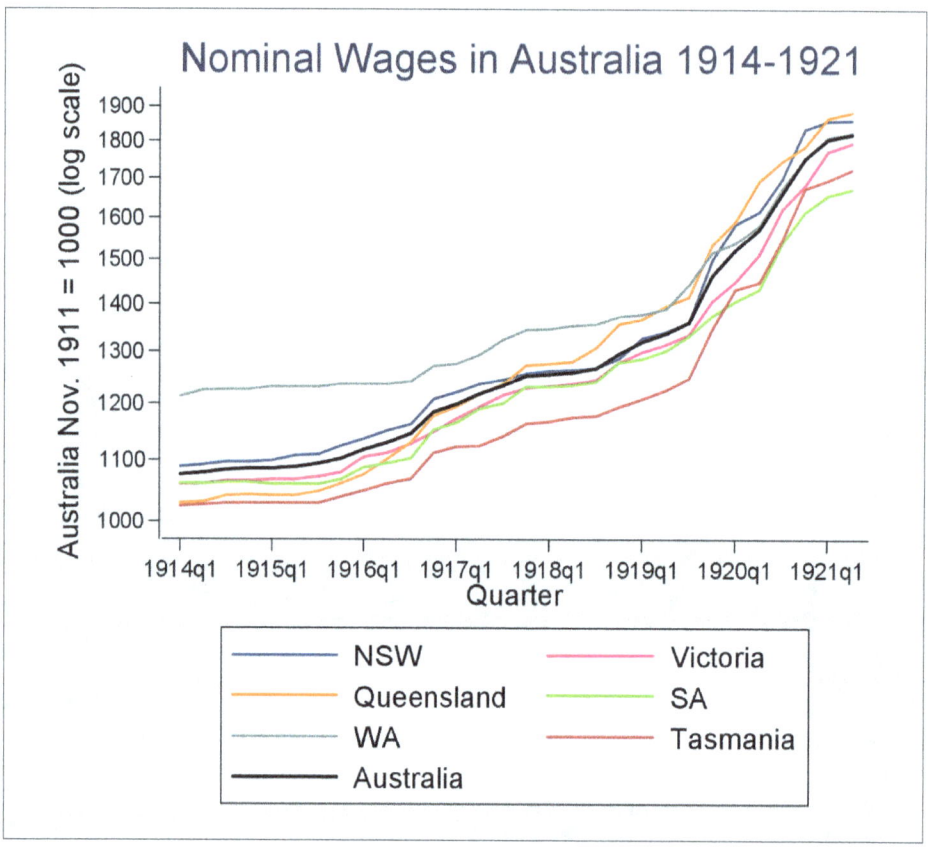

Figure 2.4
Note: The wage data are for adult males.
Source: *Labour Report*, various numbers.

calculate the changes that occurred between that year and the various dates in the quarterly series. The extent of deviations of actual wages from those that underlie the nominal wage data is unknown. Figure 2.4 shows, for the States and the whole of Australia, the movements of adult male wages over the period from April 1914 to May 1921.[4]

At the beginning of 1914, average nominal wages (for the whole of Australia) were 7.5 per cent higher than in 1911; in mid-1921, they were 81.9 per cent higher. It is evident that the increase was concentrated in the latter

---

[4] The observation for quarter 1 of 1914 relates to 30 April.

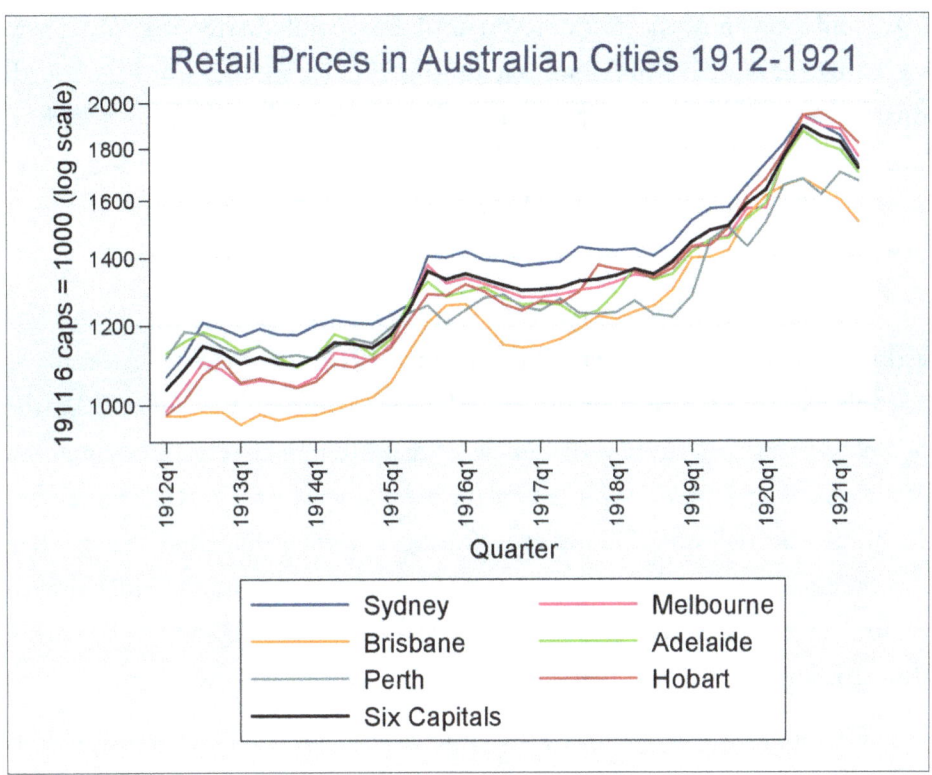

Figure 2.5
Source: *Labour Report*, various numbers.

part of the period. The figure permits comparisons across the States: Western Australia was for some time a high-wage State, but by the end of the period was no longer so. South Australia and Tasmania were low-wage States.

In Subsection 1.3.2 of Chapter 1, I explained that the A series index was confined to food, groceries, and rent. The more comprehensive C series index is not available in quarterly form until 1922. Annual data show that between the end of 1914 and the end of 1921 the C series index increased by 47 per cent, while the A series grew by 44 per cent.[5] The A series shows a reduction of 3 per cent between 1901 and 1907 and an increase of 13 per cent between 1907 and 1911. Figure 2.5 makes use of the quarterly numbers which begin in

---

[5] There were, however, wider divergences during the 1914–21 period.

1912 and shows how the index moved until the second quarter of 1921.[6] There were three episodes of inflation: one during 1912; a second, from the fourth quarter of 1914 to the fourth quarter of 1915; and the third, from the third quarter of 1918 to the third quarter of 1920. By the end of the period, prices were falling. Sydney was generally the most expensive capital and Brisbane usually the cheapest (though prices were sometimes lower in Perth).

Combining the wage and price data to compute real wages, we get the estimates represented in Figure 2.6.[7] In April 1914 real wages for Australia as a whole were 3.8 per cent below their 1911 level; and only in June 1921 (the last observation in Figure 2.6) did they regain the 1911 level. In September 1915, real wages were 19.7 per cent below the level of 1911; in September 1920, the shortfall was 12.2 per cent. It is little wonder that complaints of low wages (noted more fully in later chapters) were rife. Queensland and Western Australia were generally States with high real wages, with Queensland moving dramatically ahead in 1920–21.

Nominal wage data are also available for 14 industrial groups. It is not practical to depict in one graph the movements over time of wages in so many groups. Table 2.1, however, shows the relative wages prevailing in 1914 and 1921. As we see later, the tribunals in this period tended to raise the basic wage in response to increased prices, but to leave margins for skill constant in money terms. This policy might be expected to have caused some compression of inter-industry differentials. A casual inspection of the table seems to bear out that expectation. A more formal analysis, involving the fitting of an equation to the logarithms of average wages, confirms it.[8] The equation indicates, for example, that if industry A in 1914 had wages that

---

[6] The base of the index numbers, both for the separate capital cities and for the average of them, is the six-capitals index number for 1911. For example, the Melbourne index number for the third quarter of 1917 is 1300. This shows that the items in the index cost 30 per cent more in Melbourne in that quarter than the average cost of the same items in the six capitals in 1911.

[7] Having regard to the range of occupations covered by the nominal wage data, I think it more appropriate to deflate them by the capital cities price indices than to use the five-towns numbers.

[8] The equation is: $\ln w_{21} = 0.565 \ln w_{14} + 2.014$; $r^2 = 0.80$.

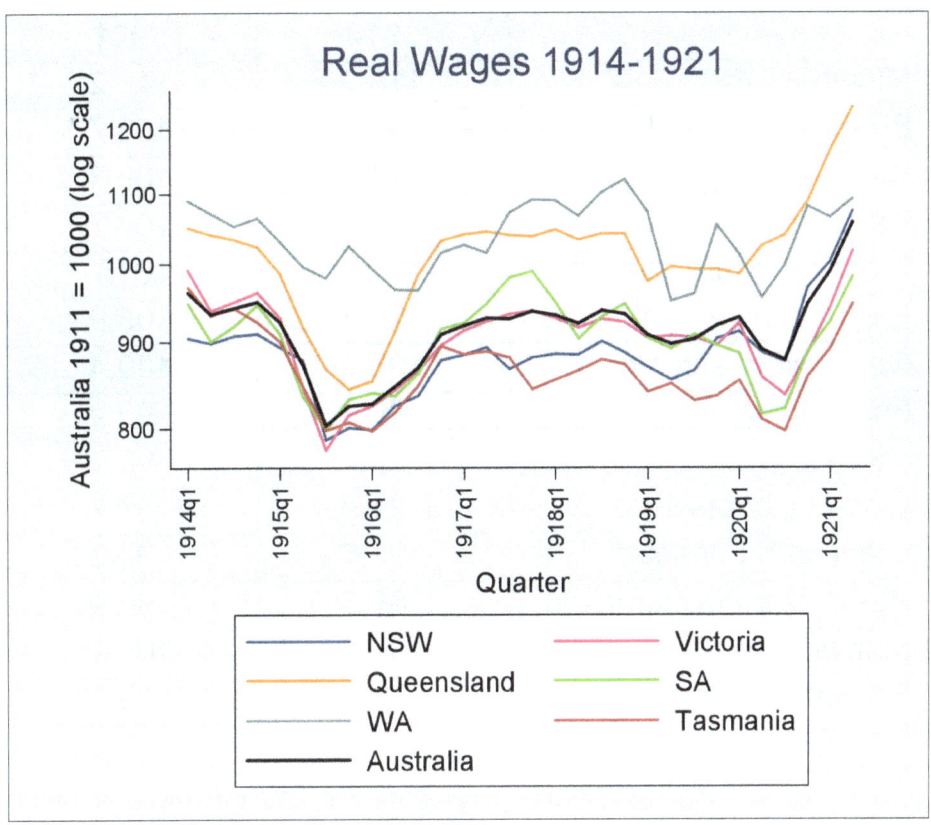

Figure 2.6
Source: *Labour Report*, various numbers.

exceeded the wages of industry *B* by 10 per cent, the difference would have been reduced by 1921 to 5.5 per cent. (This is, of course, an average tendency and does not necessarily apply to any two specific industries.) The 'squeeze' on inter-industry relativities was much severer in this period than in any other period before World War II. We later provide similar data for other periods and find that in those periods the relationships between the end-of-period and beginning-of-period industry relativities were tighter than in 1914–21. It would seem that the economic turbulence of the war and post-war periods had the effect of disturbing relativities. The largest change was in shipping, where wages rose from 89 per cent of the average in 1914 to 102 per cent in 1921.

	1914	**1921**
Mining	118.2	113.2
Building	118.1	108.7
Books, printing, etc.	114.9	109.3
Rail and tram services	108.4	104.7
Wood, furniture, etc.	106.2	104.7
Engineering, metal works	103.5	105.0
Other manufacturing	100.0	100.4
Food, drink, etc.	99.9	99.2
Miscellaneous	97.3	95.7
Clothing, boots, etc.	94.9	97.7
Other land transport	92.6	97.3
Pastoral, agricultural, etc.	89.8	94.4
Shipping, etc.	88.7	102.1
Domestic, hotels etc.	85.4	88.0

Table 2.1: Relative wages in industry groups, 1914 and 1921 (percentage of average wage)
Note: The 1914 numbers are for the first quarter of that year; the 1921 numbers are for the second quarter. In some cases the industry titles shown are abbreviations of fuller titles.
Source: *Labour Report*, various numbers.

2.4 Conclusion

Making due allowance for the imperfections of the data, we can see that the Higgins era—at any rate, after 1911—was a difficult one for a tribunal that was in its infancy and had both a limited comprehension of what was happening and only rudimentary techniques for responding to a changing environment. In the next two chapters, we see how it responded to the challenges.

3

The basic wage 1907–1921

The idea of a minimum wage, payable to unskilled adult male workers but also serving as the foundation element of the total wage structure, emerged, but was not completely articulated, during the Higgins era. The process is described in this chapter.

3.1 The living wage

The doctrine of the living wage had a central position in discussions of wage policy for the first quarter of the 20th century and, to a lesser extent, beyond. The underlying idea was that the employer had a responsibility to provide for the worker some minimum standard of living—one that permitted the worker to maintain himself and his family at a level consistent with prevailing concepts of adequacy. In this definition, there are obvious areas of vagueness. Imprecision of meaning gave rise to differences of opinion about policies.

The concept of a living wage was not invented in Australia, even if the Australian wage-fixers were to contribute significantly to its development as a policy goal and to give it a local flavour. Classical economics—from Adam Smith onward—contained a notion of a natural wage that would suffice to ensure the maintenance and reproduction of the working population. Smith himself regarded a rate 'sufficient to maintain the labourer and to enable him to bring up a family' as the 'lowest rate which is consistent with common humanity' (quoted by Sawkins 1933, p. 11). In classical economics, the natural wage was not biologically determined, but would adjust to moveable standards of subsistence. David Ricardo wrote:

> Labour, like all other things which are bought and sold, and which may be increased or diminished in quantity, has its natural and its market price. The natural price of labour is that which is necessary to enable the labourers, one with another, to subsist and perpetuate their race, without either increase or diminution … The market price is the price which is really paid for it, from the natural operation of the proportion of the supply to the demand. However much the market price of labour may deviate from its natural price, it has, like commodities, a tendency to conform to it. … It is not to be understood that the natural price of labour, estimated even in food and necessaries, is absolutely fixed and constant. It varies at different times in the same country, and very materially differs in different countries. It essentially depends on the habits and customs of the people … Many of the conveniences now employed in an English cottage would have been thought luxuries at an earlier period of our history. The friends of humanity cannot but wish that in all countries the labouring classes should have a taste for comforts and enjoyments, and they should be stimulated by all legal means in their exertions to procure them. There cannot be a better security against a superabundant population. (Ricardo 1962, pp. 93–100)

Ricardo certainly did not advocate wage regulation: 'Like all other contracts, wages should be left to the fair and free competition of the market, and should never be controlled by the interference of the legislature' (p. 105). Yet if 'the natural price of labour' were conventionally determined, adjusting to 'the habits and customs of the people', might there not be scope for regulatory intervention directed at raising, over time, the people's expectations?

That question was rarely, if ever, asked and certainly not answered affirmatively during the greater part of the 19th century. By its end, however, the doctrine that payment of a sufficient wage was an obligation upon employers, and that 'market forces' should not necessarily prevail, was making some, albeit slow, headway. Its most celebrated statement was in the pontifical encyclical *Rerum Novarum* of 1891. This was the Catholic Church's attempt to provide a definitive response to the 'social problem'—the conflicts between the haves and the have-nots that had emerged in 19th century Europe (Coleman and Baum 1991). It affirmed the right of private property, but also rights of workers. Leo XIII declared that the worker who accepted less than a just wage because the employer would pay no more was 'the victim of force and injustice'; and a just wage was one that would support the worker in conditions of 'reasonable and frugal comfort'. The encyclical provided no guidance as to the family for which the wage should provide, as Burns noted:

> If the wage earner was entitled to receive enough to support him 'in reasonable and frugal comfort', did this include the comfort of a wife, and of possible children? The question was a delicate one. It was referred by the Pope to Cardinal Zigliaria, who unhelpfully replied that though an employer who paid less than a 'family' wage would not violate justice, yet such action might sometimes be contrary to charity or to natural righteousness. No further solution came from the Church. (Burns 1926, p. 326)

'Once again', said Burns, 'it was in Australia that the work was done.'

In 1906, John A Ryan, a Catholic priest who was Professor of Ethics and Economics in the St Paul Seminary, Minnesota, published *A Living Wage* (Ryan 1906). He observed that 'the doctrine that every labourer has the right to a Living Wage is obviously in direct conflict with existing business practice and theory' (p. 3). The wage paid was the outcome of relative bargaining power, which did not ensure a living wage.[1] The claim to a living wage was grounded in the natural rights of the human being. Ryan discussed at length the issue referred to Cardinal Zigliaria and his response, which had apparently engendered much controversy. The Cardinal's answer turned on the consideration that the worker's family were not contributors to production and were, therefore, beyond the employer's direct responsibility. Ryan and

---

[1] Ryan's discussion of bargaining over wages is reminiscent of Higgins' comments on the 'higgling of the market'.

others found this reasoning to be at odds with the principle that receipt of a living wage was a right that flowed from the worker's claim to human dignity.[2]

In the United Kingdom, the germ of the idea of a living wage can be found in the 'Fair Wages Resolution'. This was pioneered in 1889 by the London School Board. Fair Wages Resolutions were passed by the House of Commons in 1891 and 1893. The 1893 Resolution was:

> That in the opinion of this House, no person should, in Her Majesty's Naval Establishments, be engaged at wages insufficient to maintain a proper maintenance, and that the conditions of labour as regards hours, wages, insurance against accidents, provision for old age, etc, should be such as to afford an example to employers throughout the country.

This was passed without dissent and was regarded as applicable to all public departments (Snowden 1913, p. 18). It was renewed from time to time, in different forms, and was extended to government contractors. It remained operative policy until the time of the Thatcher Government.

In late 19th century Britain, the agitations and inquiries of social reformers, such as Booth and Rowntree, awakened attention to the plight of much of the working population. The demands that were generated could be assigned to the 'anti-sweating' category as much as to the living wage, but the latter had certainly become part of the lexicon. The economist Alfred Marshall, writing in 1890, discussed the adequacy of wages from the viewpoint of industrial efficiency:

> But it will serve to give some definiteness to our ideas, if we consider here what are the necessaries for the efficiency of an ordinary agricultural or an unskilled town labourer and his family, in England, in this generation. They may be said to consist of a well-drained dwelling with

---

[2] Ryan devoted a chapter of his book to estimates of the dollar amount of a living wage in the United States. Some of these estimates were made by the Department of Labor. The Church's ambivalence about the claim of the wage-earner to an amount sufficient for a family, as well as himself, seems to have been resolved later. For example, in the encyclical *Divini Redemptoris* of 1937, Pius XI said: 'But social justice cannot be said to have been satisfied so long as working men are denied a wage that will enable them to secure proper sustenance for themselves and their families …' (cited in Fogarty 1961, p. 272).

several rooms, warm clothing, with some changes of underclothing, pure water, a plentiful supply of cereal food, with a moderate amount of meat and milk, and a little tea, etc, some education and some recreation, and lastly, sufficient freedom for his wife from other work to enable her to perform properly her maternal and her household duties. If in any district unskilled labour is deprived of any of these things, its efficiency will suffer in the same way as that of a horse that is not properly tended, or a steam-engine that has an inadequate supply of coals. All consumption up to this limit is strictly productive consumption; any stinting of this consumption is not economical, but wasteful. (Marshall 1961, pp. 69–70)[3]

The edition of *Palgrave's Dictionary of Political Economy* published in 1906 contains an entry on the 'Living Wage', written by William Smart, Professor of Economics in the University of Glasgow. The term, said Smart,

came to the front during the great coal strike of 1893. But it is impossible to limit the claim of a living wage to any section of workers—by whom, indeed, it might be attainable given strict combination, limitation of numbers, and maintenance of price—and the expression seems likely to take root as the claim of labour generally to a preference share in the total product of industry. (p. 617)

Philip Snowden's *The Living Wage* was written in 1913. Snowden was a Labour MP (and a future Chancellor of the Exchequer). He had strong religious convictions and propounded a highly idealised view:

It may be impossible to give a precise or satisfactory definition of a Living Wage. But it expresses an idea, a belief, a conviction, a demand. A thousand questions may be asked of those who advocate the Living Wage which it may be difficult to answer, but the faith of its advocates

---

[3] In a footnote, Marshall estimated the cost of 'the strict necessaries for an average agricultural family' at 15 to 18 shillings per week. 'Conventional necessaries' required an extra 5s. Different estimates were given for other classes of labour: 'For a man whose brain has to undergo great continuous strain the strict necessaries are perhaps two hundred or two hundred and fifty pounds a year if he is a bachelor; but more than twice as much if he has an expensive family to educate. His conventional necessaries depend on the nature of his calling' (p. 70).

in its justice and possibility is not shaken by these objections. The idea of a Living Wage seems to have come from the fount of justice, which no man has ever seen, which no man has ever explained, but which we all know is an instinct divinely implanted in the human heart. (Snowden 1913, p. 3)

Not only was the living wage a *right* of the worker as a human being; it also accorded with the dictates of efficiency, for there was 'an incalculable loss of national wealth by the underpayment of large bodies of workers, who in consequence of low wages are underfed, insufficiently clothed, badly housed, poorly educated, industrially inefficient and politically incompetent' (p. 7). Many employers had discovered the benefit of treating workers well, but often were defeated by what we now call the 'race to the bottom', wherein competition enforced a neglect of external costs and benefits. In the unorganised and unskilled industries, conditions were set by 'the least scrupulous employer, who finds it more profitable to draw upon (at the expense of the community) the unlimited supply of half-starved and helpless labour, which he quickly uses up'.

In terms strongly reminiscent of H B Higgins and his counterparts in State tribunals, Snowden expressed strong antipathy to the strike as a method of achieving a just wage. Invoking the examples of Australia and New Zealand, he favoured compulsory arbitration.

Also occurring in 1913 was a church-based conference on *The Industrial Unrest and the Living Wage*. 'The industrial unrest' alluded especially to the coal strike of 1911, which had led the Asquith Government to enact, reluctantly, a *Coal Mines (Minimum Wage) Act 1912*. A number of speakers, mainly churchmen, strongly advocated the living wage. The Reverend A J Carlyle, for example, said that 'the living wage is not a matter of philanthropic consideration but of justice—that is to say, it is something that is, or ought to be, regarded as an inherent feature of the social system just as a man's right to his life or his person is a necessary feature of a social order. ... it is not something which individual employers should grant out of consideration, generosity or mercy, it is something which morality and law should guarantee as a right which work can claim' (*The Industrial Unrest and the Living Wage* 1913, p. 67). Contrary views were put by the Reverend Philip H Wicksteed, a well-known economist, and Miss Mary Theresa Rankin, also an economist, who later published a book about the Australian and New Zealand wage-fixing systems (Rankin 1916).[4]

Miss Constance Smith presented a paper about the International Association for Labour Legislation. Clearly a forerunner of the International Labour Organisation (ILO), this had two sections: the International Labour Bureau (located in Switzerland), which collected, classified, and published countries' labour laws; and the Federation of Labour Sections. The Federation had the objective of *improving* labour laws. It met every two years and comprised (said Miss Smith) 'Parliamentary representatives of all parties, ministers of different Churches, men of science and social reformers, University professors and Trade Union Secretaries'. Miss Smith described the movement of the Federation's thinking from a concentration on sweating towards the enforcement of minimum wages through wages boards, observing that 'the little fire kindled in Australia in the nineties is already beginning to light country after country of the Old World'. 'And so', she said, 'the general movement in favour of a living wage, towards which the establishment of a minimum wage must be considered the first necessary step, tends to proceed on Christian lines, dealing first with the poorest, the humblest, the most helpless' (*The Industrial Unrest and the Living Wage* 1913, pp. 158–168).

It was indicative of the extent to which the idea of the living wage had taken hold that the Peace Treaty of 1919 called upon the High Contracting Parties to promote 'the payment to the employed of a wage adequate to maintain a reasonable standard of life as this is understood in their time and country' (quoted by Anderson 1929, p. 188). Achieving compliance with Article 427 of the Treaty became a concern of the ILO. In 1928 the Chief of the Statistical Section wrote that 'it would be a great success for international policy if every

---

[4] Whether she visited Australia and New Zealand is unclear. She was a Carnegie Research Scholar in 1911–12 and 1912–13. J Shield Nicholson, in an introduction to her book, writes that 'in all cases the sources used were official reports and publications'.

State were to accept a binding obligation to provide suitable machinery for the payment of a minimum wage wherever the individual worker, owing to his economic helplessness, fails to earn enough by a full day's work to cover his recognised minimum needs—an obligation which at bottom is almost self-evident' (Pribram 1928, p. 331).

Thus, in the early decades of the 20th century, the living wage was very much 'in the air'. It was a revolt against perceived evils of 19th century capitalism and industrialism. At the same time, the support that it captured owed much to the economic advances, and the rising average income levels, which these had caused. Evelyn Burns, in 1926, described the living wage as the most widely accepted principle of wage prescription, having by then been adopted in a number of American States and some of the Canadian Provinces (Burns 1926, p. 260). It would be a major research endeavour, beyond the scope of this study, to analyse and to explain fully the emergence, in a number of advanced countries, of a sentiment favouring the implementation of a living wage. Adoption of the idea in Australia owed something to the influence of overseas opinion, but Australia's experiments were, in turn, an inspiration to proponents of the living wage elsewhere. The Australian wage-fixers were involved at the level of application, and had to face practical issues—prescription of a specific amount, determining the family unit for which the wage was to provide, and adjusting the wage to the changing value of money—that might be glossed over if the living wage were merely an aspiration.

I cannot say when the idea first entered Australian discourse. A well-known affirmation of it, however, was made in 1890 by Samuel Griffith, who brought into the Queensland Parliament a strange Bill 'to declare the natural law relating to the acquisition and ownership of property'. It resembled the yet-to-be-published *Rerum Novarum* inasmuch as it affirmed both the right of private property and the claim of labour to a sufficient wage. The Bill (which did not pass) referred thus to wages: 'The natural and proper measure of wages is such a sum as is a fair immediate recompense for the labour for which they are paid, having regard to its character and duration; but it can never be taken at a less sum than such as is sufficient to maintain the labourer and his family in a state of health and reasonable comfort' (Sawkins 1933, p. 9).

The development of thought about a living wage was stultified in the 1890s by economic depression, the industrial defeats of labour, and the priorities of establishing wage-setting mechanisms and of countering sweating. None of the studies of early wage fixation of which I am aware refers to the enunciation of a living-wage principle before the first decade of the 20th century. The index to Coghlan's monumental study (which extends to 1901) has no entry for 'living wage', the closest approximation being one for minimum rates prescribed in New South Wales (1894) and Victoria (1896) for contractors on public works (Coghlan 1969, vol. IV, pp. 2027–2028; 2051–2052; 2214). More intensive research might uncover opinions about the living wage that have escaped my notice; but they would not be abundant. The idea did not feature in the Convention debates on the proposal that led to section 51(xxxv) of the Constitution or in the parliamentary debates on the Commonwealth Conciliation and Arbitration Bill.

That it first makes its appearance *within* the wage-fixing system probably reflects the practicality that tribunals had to find bases for their decisions. There were several possibilities: a living wage, what the trade could bear, what 'reputable employers' were paying, and compromise between the positions of the disputants. The statutory requirement for wages to be 'fair and reasonable' (embodied, for example, in the *Excise Tariff Act 1906*) might seem, at first sight, to be another criterion, but was so wide as to leave the arbitrator virtually undirected.

All of the above options found places in early decisions of the tribunals. Indeed, none—except perhaps 'reputable employers'—was discarded. The living wage, however, was the most likely to appeal to an adjudicator wishing to invoke a principle applicable to different cases—a typical aspiration of courts of law. Hence, the establishment of arbitration courts enhanced the likelihood of the tribunals adopting the living wage. If the *Harvester* case (discussed below) is any indication, the living wage was an idea that judges, rather than the parties, brought into the practice of wage fixation. As educated men, they had some awareness of the discussions in other countries. Higgins, for example, corresponded with Seebohm Rowntree and Sidney Webb, and it can be taken for granted that social considerations relevant to wage adequacy would have been discussed (Macarthy 1969, pp. 19–38).

Sawkins states (and I have no contrary evidence) that the first clear mention of a living wage in an arbitral decision was that of Justice Heydon in 1905 in the New South Wales Court of Arbitration (Sawkins 1933, p. 12). Heydon referred to 'the duty of assisting to, if possible, so arrange the business of the country that every worker, however humble, shall receive enough to enable him to lead a human life, to marry and bring up a family and maintain them and himself with, at any rate, some small degree of comfort; this … may be shortly defined as the duty to prevent sweating …'. But it was necessary to 'keep the law of supply and demand carefully in view' and 'I can discover nothing in or out of the Act to prevent full effect being given to this in the case of all labour above the lowest or living wage limit …'. Heydon did not, on this occasion, attempt any quantification of needs. That was a task to which Higgins purportedly addressed himself in *Harvester*.[5]

3.2 THE *HARVESTER* CASE[6]

3.2.1 The legislation

The agricultural implements industry, one of the few branches of engineering involved in manufacture, as opposed to jobbing, was exposed to growing competition from North America, from which it sought relief. After an inquiry, this relief was afforded by import duties imposed under the *Custom Tariff Act 1906*.

---

[5] Macarthy (1968, pp. 127–128) argues that before 1907 Victorian wages boards and the Industrial Appeals Court virtually ignored the living wage principle. In those determinations which included a minimum wage for unskilled labour, the predominant rate was 36s. The *Harvester* standard was not generally adopted until the 1917–21 period.

[6] For other perspectives on the case, see Macarthy (1969), and Fahey and Lack (2007).

The proposal to impose duties on imported agricultural machinery was before the Parliament in August 1906 upon a motion of Sir William Lyne (Minister of Customs and Excise) in the Committee of Ways and Means. During his speech, interjectors asserted the need for complementary action to benefit workers. Mr Hume Cook asked: 'Will the Massey Harris Company pay fair wages?'; and Mr Page said: 'If we are going to have protection for the manufacturer, we must have protection for the worker.' Lyne said: 'I think—and I believe it is the desire of the Committee—that some conditions will have to be imposed in the Bill, or a Wages Board will have to be appointed, to prevent the payment of unduly low wages to those engaged in the industry'. (Mr Tudor interjected—'And to prevent the employment of too many boys'.) Lyne explained that the motion 'is intended really for the information of the Committee, and is not part and parcel of the Bill to be hereafter submitted' (*Commonwealth Parliamentary Debates*, vol. 33 [33 CPD], pp. 3443–3445).

The policy of New Protection sought to ensure that employees benefited from the protection provided to employers. New Protection, Alfred Deakin explained,

> aims at according to the manufacturer that degree of exemption from unfair outside competition which will enable him to pay fair and reasonable wages ... It does not stop there. Having put the manufacturer in a position to pay good wages, it goes on to assure the public that he does pay them. (*New Protection* ... 1907, p. 1)

When Deakin spoke (in the week after that of the debate reported above) about the proposed legislative package, an interjector asked how he would define reasonable wages. He replied: 'So far as Victoria is concerned, that point would be decided according to the decisions of the Wages Boards. In other cases, they would be decided according to the current rates in the locality, under a power similar to that vested in the Minister of Trade and Customs with regard to the sugar industry in Queensland' (34 CPD, p. 3969). Sixteen days later, Deakin said that 'to my mind protective duties which benefit only the manufacturer fall far short of conferring any real advantage upon the community. It is desirable that some portion of the direct benefit derived

Alfred Deakin

from the imposition of duties should, if possible, go to the employees'. By then, however, the proposal to exempt from duty employers who complied with decisions of Victorian wages boards had been abandoned. The reason, said Deakin, was the view of the Attorney-General that exemptions from duty upon compliance with decisions of State tribunals would infringe the constitutional prohibition of taxation that discriminated between the States (34 CPD, pp. 5137–5138).

The *Custom Tariff Act 1906* imposed the import duties. For example, the price of a stripper-harvester was around £70, and the duty payable from 7 September 1906 was £12. Consistent with Deakin's expressed concern for consumers, there were specified maximum prices for Australian stripper-harvesters and drills. If these were not observed, the Governor-General could reduce the import duties by 50 per cent. Complementary to this measure was the *Excise Tariff Act 1906*. This imposed excise duties equal to half of the import duties, but with the proviso that

> this Act shall not apply to goods manufactured by any person in any part of the Commonwealth under conditions as to the remuneration of labour which—
>
> (a) are declared by resolution of both Houses of Parliament to be fair and reasonable; or
>
> (b) are in accordance with an industrial award under the *Commonwealth Conciliation and Arbitration Act 1904*; or
>
> (c) are in accordance with the terms of an industrial agreement filed under the *Commonwealth Conciliation and Arbitration Act 1904*; or
>
> (d) are, on application made for the purpose to the President of the Commonwealth Court of Conciliation and Arbitration, declared to be fair and reasonable by him or by a Judge of the Supreme Court of a State or any person or persons who compose a State Industrial Authority to whom he may refer the matter.

As the agriculture implement industry was not subject to either a Commonwealth award or a filed agreement, it may be that the exemption routes were intended for wider application, to be embodied in other legislation. Deakin said that he expected route (a) to be used rarely. The terms of (d) deserve brief notice. An application for exemption would be made to the President of the Arbitration Court and an exemption would be granted if *he* deemed the wages to be fair and reasonable. That is, the application, was made, not to *the Court*, but to *the President* and adjudged by him. Alternatively, the President could refer the matter to a Judge of a State Court—not to the State Court—or to a person or persons composing a State authority—not to the authority. The procedure of imposing responsibility on the officer, but not the tribunal itself, may have reflected a constitutional concern. During the hearing of *Harvester*, Higgins said that the matter was not before the Court, but before him. An implication was that he could choose his method of inquiry, and that an arbitration-like procedure was not a requirement. This view, which appears to be correct, did not emerge in the judgment (2 CAR 1, 1).

It is a matter for speculation whether the legislative technique of affording conditional protection would have been deployed more widely if the High Court had not disallowed the *Excise Tariff Act 1906*.

3.2.2 The case

Neither Higgins' short-serving predecessor O'Connor nor Higgins himself delegated any of the manufacturers' applications. Each took the responsibility of certifying, or not certifying, that the wages paid by an applicant were fair and reasonable. O'Connor, earlier in 1907, had dealt with the question in a manner summarised by Anderson:

> In Bagshaw's case certain interested unions were allowed representation, and at a conference arranged by Mr Justice O'Connor between representatives of employers and of employees at Adelaide in June, 1907, an agreement as to rates of wages was reached. This agreement was important, because it enabled the President to adopt it as a standard by which to judge 'fair and reasonable' rates, and it enabled manufacturers to know the wage rates which would pass the test of 'fair and reasonable'. Mr Justice O'Connor granted the applications of 108 manufacturers whose wage rates were not less than those provided in the agreement. The rate fixed by the agreement for an unskilled worker was 39s per week of forty-eight hours. The margin for skill for blacksmiths, fitters, turners, woodworkers, and wheelwrights was 15s per week; semi-skilled workers and tradesmen of less than average capacity, from 6s to 9s per week. (1939, pp. 66–67)

There is no indication, in either the hearing of *Harvester* or the decision, that Higgins ascribed any persuasive authority to the Bagshaw precedent.

Confronted by a long queue of applications, he adopted, in effect, a test-case strategy. 'I selected Mr McKay's application out of some 112 applications made by Victorian manufacturers', he said, 'because I found that the factory

H B Higgins

was one of the largest, and had the greatest number and variety of employees; and because his application was to be keenly fought' (2 CAR 1, 2). Other applicants would not be allowed to traverse the same issues, but would be afforded opportunities to show that their situations differed materially from McKay's.

The hearing began on 7 October 1907 and concluded on 1 November. The decision was given on 8 November. McKay was represented by counsel, William Schutt, who was later a judge in the Victorian Supreme Court. Very few of McKay's workers were union members. Nevertheless, there was union representation. 'Certain unions of ironworkers' were represented by Frank Gavan Duffy, later Chief Justice of Australia. Duffy became ill during the case and his place was taken by his junior, J A Arthur, who became a Minister in the Fisher Labor Government (but died soon after taking office). Some other unions were jointly represented by one of their secretaries. None of the unions comprised unskilled labourers.

Higgins made it clear that *he* would determine the structure of the case and define the questions to be considered. He did not hesitate to tell the representatives to desist from particular lines of argument or to insist on the importance of others. Except when witnesses were in the box, the proceedings were essentially dialogues between Higgins and those at the bar table.

It is well known that, in his decision, Higgins attended first to the wage for adult unskilled labourers. Having done that, he moved on to the rates appropriate for skilled and semi-skilled workers.

3.2.3 The cost of living

Nothing in Duffy's opening address suggests any prior intention of treating as an issue the adequacy of the living standards of the employees and their families. Duffy strove unsuccessfully to persuade Higgins to take into account the profitability of McKay's business and the claim of employees to share in the benefit that the firm enjoyed from tariff protection. Higgins' insistence on the priority of 'the cost of living' seems to have forced the parties to review their positions. In advance of the unions' evidence being called, Higgins inquired of Duffy whether there would be 'any direct evidence of a workman's wife or housekeeper'. Duffy replied that there would, and Higgins observed that 'there is no one can give better evidence as to the way the shoe pinches, if it does pinch, than the workman's wife' (transcript, p. 333).[7] The manner in which the evidence of living costs was given—mostly by men whose primary task was to describe the work performed at McKay's and elsewhere—suggests that calling this evidence was something of an afterthought. McKay's counsel was certainly caught off guard, as the following exchange shows:

---

[7] Duffy then said: 'These women do not wish, naturally, to have their names published in the newspapers and I will ask Your Honour, when the time comes, to make an order that they shall not be published.' Higgins asked Schutt whether he would have any objection to this. When he replied that he would not, Higgins said 'I should certainly do it'.

Mr Schutt: Before we proceed with the examination of the witness, I might say the remarks of Your Honour came somewhat as a surprise to me and the gentlemen instructing me, viz: … that Your Honour expected us in our case to go into questions of the cost of living.

His Honour: You need not unless you like. I only thought it fair you should have an opportunity, if you thought fit, as well as the other side to do so.

Mr Schutt: What I mean is this, that although the matter had naturally entered into our calculation we were not shaping our case from that point of view. What we thought was this. Supposing we put a case before Your Honour showing the conditions under which these wages were earned, that is to say, conditions of work, that then would be sufficient for our case, and if the other side disputed the fact that people should be comfortable under those conditions that then we might be allowed by Your Honour to have a rebutting case to rebut anything put in evidence by them.

His Honour: I could not allow a rebutting case. The burden lies on you to show that the conditions of remuneration are fair and reasonable. Then if you go and work that out you will see it is impossible to find that the conditions are fair and reasonable without going into the question of the cost of living. The way it strikes my mind is this. The legislature says that I am to declare whether the conditions as to remuneration are fair and reasonable. It gives me no guide as to what it means to be fair and reasonable. When you say fair and reasonable it must mean fair and reasonable according to some standard. Then what is the standard? On looking for the standard it cannot be fair and reasonable on the standard of competition, individual employer against individual employee. It must be having regard to the needs of the employee as a human being in the first instance. As you interfere with the principle of competition between the individual employer and the individual employee, that is the only thing we can fall back on. What I propose to do is this. I think the basic matter is—what is necessary for the ordinary unskilled labourer?

Mr Schutt: From the point of view of living?

His Honour: Yes … what is fair and reasonable in order that he may live as a human being first of all. (p. 255)

Schutt sought an adjournment for McKay's representatives to get evidence about living costs. Higgins refused, saying that they had had months to think about the matter (p. 261). On Friday 25 October, he warned Schutt that if he was to call such evidence, he must do so on the following Monday (p. 490). On the Monday, Schutt said that all that he could have done was to call upon some of McKay's workmen to give evidence, and he had no wish to do that. 'We did make some enquiries as to rents', he said, 'and we do not think the estate agents can be contradicted' (p. 517). In the decision, Higgins said: 'I allowed Mr Schutt … an opportunity to call evidence upon this subject even after his case had been closed; but notwithstanding the fortnight or more allowed him for investigation, he admitted that he could produce no specific evidence in contradiction [of the union evidence]' (2 CAR 1, 6).

Eleven witnesses called by the unions gave evidence about the expenditures of their households. Higgins said in his decision that 'some very interesting evidence has been given by working men's wives and others' (p. 5). In fact, three wives gave evidence. Eight men provided statements of household expenditure, but most said that these either had been prepared by their wives or were constructed in consultation with them.[8]

A simple average of the budgets would be misleading, because it is clear that some witnesses omitted items. For example, two excluded rent, three excluded clothing, one excluded fruit and vegetables, and one omitted tea and flour. (Higgins in his decision itemised some of the omissions.) Some witnesses probably excluded items because they were treated as 'husband's' rather than household expenditure. Tobacco, personal insurance, and contributions to accident funds are in this category. It is possible, however, to construct

---

[8] Duffy also led evidence from an estate agent (discussed below) and a wood and coal merchant. The burden of the latter's evidence was that the prices of wood and coal had risen over the previous two years. It throws no light on the actual prices of these items or the quantities consumed.

	Shillings	%
Food	27	50
Rent	10	19
Clothing	8	15
Wood, gas and light	2.5	5
Fares	1.5	3
Lodge, insurance and accident fund	2	4
School requisites	0.5	1
Newspapers	0.5	1
Tobacco	1	2
Union	0.5	1
Total	53.5	100

Table 3.1: *Harvester* **evidence—constructed budget**
Note: Numbers in the last column do not sum to 100 because of rounding.

a synthetic budget which takes such items into account and is unlikely to be seriously inaccurate *for the class of worker to whose households the evidence related*. Table 3.1 is such a budget.

This budget does not include some miscellaneous items. Insofar as the witnesses referred to such items, the burden of their evidence was that they could not afford them. But it is unlikely that they entirely forwent them. One witness said that he frequently attended football matches. Some professed to be teetotallers, but it is probable that the expenses of an average household included some alcohol.

Clearly, a labourer on 6s per day (McKay's standard) or even the 7s that Higgins adopted could not afford weekly expenditure of £2 13s 6d (nearly 9s a day) or thereabouts. The discrepancy is largely explained by the fact that none of the workmen concerned was a labourer. Some were journeymen; and several were union officials, paid at journeymen rates or better. Of the five whose wages were disclosed, one received £3 per week and three—probably four—received £2 14s. All had children, the number ranging from one to seven. In three instances, there was evidence that working children contributed to the household funds.

Several of the witnesses spoke of the difficulty of making ends meet. There is little evidence, however, about the quantity or quality of the purchases made within the budget. There is little, either, about the adjustments made to confine the expenditures of labourers' households within the lesser amounts available to them.

An exception is housing. Smith Aumont, called by Duffy, was an auctioneer and estate agent. Although he carried on business in Collingwood, he claimed to have contact with agents in other districts and to be familiar with current rents. He said:

> I have got 36s a week men amongst my tenants. They live in places that have no conveniences, such as baths and coppers. I have several houses that have not got baths and coppers with tenants in but I could not tell you what their wages are—I should gather from their occupation that 36s was their wage. They may get less. If there is a bath and a copper I can claim at least another shilling a week. The owner would require a shilling a week extra if he had to go to the expense of connecting a bathroom with the sewer. ... At present a labourer as a rule does not care to go beyond seven shillings a week. It would be a very inferior place at that. He could not possibly go lower than that, and if he did it would be a very inferior house. He could not possibly get a place for human habitation for less than six shillings and that would only be for three rooms. The artisan class go from 8s 6d up to 12s 6d. (transcript, pp. 502–503)

A three-room house comprised two bedrooms and a kitchen. A fourth room, if there was one, was usually a dining room. Aumont's evidence accords with that of the workers or the wives who commented on housing costs. Mrs Bayliss said that her family occupied a four-room house in North Brunswick. It cost eight shillings and was unsewered. The sewer would be there soon and its advent would raise the rent (p. 505). C J Bennett lived in a four-room house in Spencer Street, North Melbourne, for 12s 6d per week (pp. 487–488); presumably his house was sewered. Ernest Wilkinson paid 8s 6d per week for a four-room house, with a bath and copper in a detached room outside (pp. 473–474). Mrs Russell's family of eight lived in a five-room double-storey brick house, comprising three bedrooms, a living room and a kitchen—'not a good house at that' (p. 441). There was no bathroom, but there were a bath and a copper in a shed. This house cost 12s 6d a week. Mrs Smith, living at Port Melbourne with her husband and seven children, also paid 12s 6d rent:

> The kitchen is counted in the five rooms. We use one room for the boys, one for myself and girls, and one for a dining room—we have no bathroom. We have a copper and troughs. It is a portable copper outside. (p. 440)

Mrs Smith added:

> I cannot say how our neighbours live who only earn 38s a week. I can only say the houses they live in are not fit for habitation and it would be better to live in the fresh air. They are wooden houses, tumbling down. (p. 441)

David Skidmore said that the average rent for a mechanic's house would be 10s 6d. Labourers had 'to go less': 'Labourers live in very poor houses, from 5s and 5s 6d up to 7s 6d. But they are not fit to live in' (p. 429).

A rough assessment, based on the evidence, is that labourers paid between 2s 6d and 6s a week less in rent than the witnesses. Higgins' estimate of seven shillings as the labourer's weekly rent (*Harvester* decision 2 CAR 1, 6) was probably based on Aumont's evidence. The 'saving' goes a small way to reconciling the synthetic budget, derived from the evidence, with the actual wages of labourers. The 'cost' of this economy was the occupation of distinctly inferior housing (and the artisan's house was far from luxurious). On the evidence, a 7s house was typically cramped, dilapidated and unsewered. Higgins simply took the seven shillings estimate at face value, without reflecting on the efficacy of such housing in meeting 'the normal needs of the average employee, regarded as a human being living in a civilised community' (p. 3).

At the time of putting Schutt on notice that he must provide any evidence about living costs on the following Monday, Higgins said that in any event 'I think I have enough'. It is hard to take this seriously. Higgins at one point said that 'in order to know what is fair and reasonable remuneration I should like to know in the present state of the markets what food, clothing and shelter can be got for a certain wage' (p. 253), but neither he nor the parties pursued that question. The evidence (with the limited exception of that about housing) dealt with the *actual* expenses of families receiving *artisans'* wages.[9] The sum required to sustain *labourers'* families in conditions of 'frugal comfort' was a separate topic. That there was no evidence about it is explicable by the employee representation—the unions were those of skilled and semi-skilled workers. Apart from the estate agent and the wood and coal merchant, the unions' witnesses were drawn from their ranks and their members' wives.

One route that Higgins followed for a certain distance was to derive a partial 'budget' from the evidence of actual expenses, incorporating the seven shillings per week standard for rent. The amount of £1 12s 5d represented 'the necessary average weekly expenditure for a labourer's home of about five persons' in respect of rent, groceries, bread, meat, milk, vegetables, and fuel. It was 'the average of the list of nine housekeeping women' (p. 6). As we have seen, there were 11 household 'budgets'—eight presented by husbands and three by wives. The numbers of people in the 11 households ranged from three to nine, with an average of just over five. For this group, then, Higgins'

---

[9] A failure to notice this is a fault in Macarthy's article. Macarthy provides a table of 'Unskilled Workingman's [sic] Budgets (Lists offered in evidence at the *Harvester* hearing)', but there was no such evidence (Macarthy 1969, p. 32).

calculation of an average family of 'about five' was correct. Such slender evidence, it would seem, was the basis of what was to become a vexed issue in basic wage fixation—the size of the family unit.

Higgins then noted numerous items not comprehended in the £1 12s 5d: 'light …, clothes, boots, furniture, utensils … rates, life insurance, savings, accident or benefit societies, loss of employment, union pay, books and newspapers, tram and train fares, sewing machine, mangle, school requisites, amusements and holidays, intoxicating liquors, tobacco, sickness and death, domestic help, or any expenditure for unusual contingencies, religion, or charity'. These items would clearly amount to more than 3s 7d—the gap between £1 16s and £1 12s 5d. Hence he could be confident that £1 16s was an insufficient wage. The difficulty with this reasoning is inherent in the derivation of the £1 12s 5d. It comprises seven shillings—the estimated rent of a labourer's house—and £1 5s 5d allowed for food on the basis of the evidence of actual expenditure. By parity of reasoning, the amount required for the labourer's household might have been set at £2 13s 6d (as in the synthetic budget) less a 'saving' of 3s on rent (achieved by adopting a lower standard of housing)—a total of £2 10s 6d (say £2 10s). Such an amount was not founded on any identification of need—it was the amount (subject to the rent adjustment) spent by households where the breadwinners earned more than £2 10s; and they spent it because they could.

Schutt commented on the lack of evidence about the living conditions of labourers and their families:

> I expected to be more enlightened by the other side on this point. It is perfectly true they called a lot of witnesses, but they did not call witnesses who were in receipt of the lowest rates of pay. … The witnesses they called were people who spent what they got or very near it, and their rate of living depended upon the amount they received. But the difficulty is that there was nobody called who got 36s a week. There was a reference made by one witness, Mrs Russell, to a time when her husband got 30s some time before. (transcript, p. 624)

Higgins responded:

> I also remarked that there was no evidence called of the labourer himself. But at the same time, it is almost *a fortiori* the case, that when these people who are receiving £2 5s, £2 10s or £3 a week find themselves unable even with that to get anything in the way of luxuries or anything more than bare necessaries, that the others would be in a worse position. Then Mrs Russell said something that ought to impress one, that her husband, who was working at a candle factory, a man doing physical work, sometimes was not able to get any meat. Of course, there are some people who have theories that meat does not do them any good, but if you have not meat you must have something else. For a grown man working hard with his back, arms and legs all day and not be able to get strong food impresses me as a strong case. (p. 625)

Mrs Russell referred to a time when her husband's wage was £1 16s per week. (He was now, as a union secretary, receiving enough to 'give' his wife £2 10s.) Mr Russell's restricted consumption of meat was mentioned in the decision. 'This inability to procure sustaining food', said Higgins, 'is certainly not conducive to the maintenance of the worker in industrial efficiency'. He did not mention that Mr and Mrs Russell had six children.[10]

In truth, the gap in living standards between the synthetic budget and the consumption possibilities of the labourer's family was greater than is suggested if we assume a daily wage for the labourer of six or seven shillings. The labourer might earn such an amount in a week of 48 hours *if he were fully employed*. But the evidence showed that there were various impediments to his securing that amount. Most important—at least at McKay's factory—was the seasonality of demand for the product. Higgins referred to this in his decision:

> There is no constancy of employment, as the employer has to put a considerable number of men off in the intervals between the seasons. The seed-drill and plough season, I am told, is in the earlier part of the year, about April; but the busiest time is the harvester season, about

---

[10] The eldest child—a daughter aged 15—earned five shillings a week at bookbinding and probably contributed most of her wage to the household budget (p. 441).

August to November. But even if the employment were constant and interrupted, is a wage of 36s fair and reasonable, in view of the cost of living in Victoria? (p. 5)

Seasonality was not the only cause of discontinuous employment. George Bult, a foreman in the harvester department at Sunshine, referred to the holidays observed at the factory—a fortnight at Christmas, Foundation Day in January, a stock-taking day in February, four days at Easter, Eight Hours Day, King's Birthday, and Show Day. These were all *unpaid*, though a bonus was given at Christmas (p. 244). If there were an interruption of work through mechanical failure, the idle employees were not paid for the period of the interruption, although the employer might extend the working day to make up the lost time. There is no indication in the decision that Higgins made any attempt to factor loss of working time into his assessment of fair and reasonable wages.

In summary, the seven shilling standard lacked any real basis in measured or estimated needs. For what it was worth—but it was worth very little—the evidence suggested that a 'needed' wage was significantly above seven shillings. To be taken seriously, a 'needs' criterion required the identification of necessary items of consumption and their prices. It required, too, a more deliberate consideration of family size than reliance on the average of the 11 households.

3.2.4 The seven shillings standard

What, then, was the basis for the seven shillings? A key consideration in Higgins' mind was the desirability of *improving* the workers' lot. He virtually argued in his decision that this was a statutory duty:

> The provision of fair and reasonable wages is obviously designed for the benefit of the employees in the industry; and it must be meant to secure to them something which they cannot get by the ordinary system of individual bargaining with employers. If Parliament meant that the conditions shall be such as they can get by individual bargaining—if it meant that those conditions are to be fair and reasonable, which employees will accept and employers will give, in contracts of service—

> there would have been no need for this provision. The remuneration could safely have been left to the 'higgling of the market' for labour, with the pressure for bread on one side, and the pressure for profits on the other. (p. 3)

This was a position that Higgins had clearly signalled during the hearing. For example, when Schutt suggested that the best approach was 'to see whether the rate paid [by McKay] to the unskilled labourer is in accord with rates usually paid and accepted', Higgins responded: 'That would never do. … You must have regard to current rates for ratios and the rest, but the whole idea of the Act is interference with what is called free contract between an individual employer and employee' (p. 258). Higgins *could* have taken the view that his task was to inquire whether a *particular* applicant, such as McKay, observed generally prevailing standards—an approach suggested by Deakin in the Parliamentary debate noted in Subsection 2.2.1.

That said, it is fair to add that the evidence lent substance to Higgins' concern about the 'higgling of the market'.

The principal witness called by Schutt was H V McKay's brother, George, who was factory manager. His frank evidence was that he set all of the wages, taking some account of the advice of foremen. 'In fixing the wages', he said, 'I have endeavoured to get labour at the cheapest price that I honestly could' (p. 133). The wages book was tendered, showing the amounts paid to 495 men. The classifications of labour shown in the book had been entered only after the application was made. Previously, there was simply a rate for each man, determined by George McKay. Men performing what seemed to be tradesmen's work, but receiving less than might have been expected for such jobs, were designated by George McKay as 'improvers'. J B Garde, manager of the plough department, said that the men 'get small rises from time to time as they are deemed worthy. As Mr George McKay thinks fit he gives them small rises …' (p. 535). In effect, Higgins was being asked to bless the wages that George McKay chose to offer. It is no surprise that he bridled at that idea.

It was in his interpretation of 'improvement' that Higgins, in his decision, invoked the standard of a wage appropriate to 'the normal needs of the average employee, regarded as a human being living in a civilised society'. Elaborating on this standard, he said:

> If A lets B have the use of his horses, on the terms that he give them fair and reasonable treatment, I have no doubt that it is B's duty to give them proper food and water, and such shelter and rest as they need; and, as wages are the means of obtaining commodities, surely the state, in stipulating for fair and reasonable remuneration for the employees, means that the wages shall be sufficient to provide these things, and clothing, and a condition of frugal comfort estimated by current human standards. (p. 4)

The analogy of the horses seems to imply a concept of subsistence wages. It is unlikely that Higgins intended that.

What other standard was there? The rates paid by other employers and those set by wages boards were possibilities. And Higgins moved from needs to accepted standards:

> Then, on looking at the rates ruling elsewhere, I find that the public bodies which do not aim at profit, but which are responsible to electors or others for economy, very generally pay 7s. The metropolitan Board has 7s for a minimum; the Melbourne City Council also. Of seventeen municipal councils in Victoria, thirteen pay 7s as a minimum; and only two pay a man so low as 6s 6d. The Woodworkers' Wages Board, 24th July, 1907, fixed 7s. In the agreement made in Adelaide between employers and employees, in this very industry, the minimum is 7s 6d.[11] On the other hand, the rate in the Victorian railways workshops is 6s 6d. But the Victorian Railway Commissioners do, I presume, aim at a profit; and as we were told in the evidence, the officials keep their fingers on the pulse of external labour conditions, and endeavour to pay not more than the external trade minimum. My hesitation has been

---

[11] This was incorrect. The 'Adelaide agreement', in Bagshaw's case, included a rate of 6s 6d for unskilled labour (Anderson 1939, p. 67).

> chiefly between 7s and 7s 6d; but I put the minimum at 7s, as I do not think that I could refuse to declare an employer's remuneration to be fair and reasonable, if I find him paying 7s. (pp. 6–7)

The implication that pursuit of profit—a dubious enough assumption for the railways—reduced the relevance of an employer's wages did not emerge in the hearing itself. It was Higgins' strongly asserted position that the fairness and reasonableness of wages was *independent* of the employer's profitability. At the outset, Duffy sought an order requiring McKay to produce his 'books'. McKay made it easier for Higgins to refuse by conceding capacity to pay, and Higgins expressed unwillingness 'to make a man's financial position known to his competitors' (transcript, p. 5). But Higgins' objection was more fundamental. When Duffy sought to cross-examine George McKay about profits, Higgins again rebuffed him. 'The idea of the Act', he said, 'is to treat reasonable and fair wages as a first charge on the receipts whether there are profits or not' (p. 187). He might, perhaps, have argued that the profit motive would cause an employer to exploit unduly his bargaining strength in the 'higgling of the market'. This was not a view that he put to the parties.

The decisions of wages boards, on the other hand, were a subject of repeated comment. The boards were established under Victorian law and comprised equal numbers of employers and employees with independent chairmen. If, after negotiation, there was an equality of employer and employee votes, the chairman exercised a casting vote. Higgins acknowledged, in principle, the potential persuasive power of a wages board decision, but only inasmuch as an agreed outcome was the result of a bargaining process: '… it would be a tremendous advantage to me if I could have a wages board determination provided it was a joint determination of both employers and employees' (transcript, p. 256). But there was a difficulty. Wages boards established since October 1903 were subject to a statutory limitation that precluded them from imposing wages above those paid by 'reputable employers'.[12] Moreover, an

---

[12] Davey (1975, p. 73) writes that the 'reputable employer' clause was inserted 'at labour's request, and the intention was to prevent the boards from fixing a minimum wage which was too low'. But 'it failed to help those it was supposed to protect'.

appeal lay from a Board decision to a Court of Industrial Appeals comprising a Supreme Court judge plus an employer and an employee representative. These constraints, in Higgins' view, reduced the relevance of Board decisions:

> I should attach ten times as much importance to a wages board determination if it were the concurrent opinion of both sides than I would do to the determination of a wages board which is limited by what the employers think. Then there is again the other consideration—there is the Appeal Court. Under these present circumstances I understand the wages board comes to its decision oppressed with the fact that there may be an Appeal Court over them which will decide on the evidence which is submitted. Now the wages board's merit, if it has any, is that it is composed of men who know the conditions, without evidence, and there is an appeal from the men who know to the court that must inform itself by evidence, and I, of course, should not be so much helped by the wages board decision as I should like. (transcript, p. 256)

The boards were required to enforce at least a living wage, but Higgins perceived this as something less than fair and reasonable. 'Wages boards', he said, 'were not told to find fair and reasonable conditions of remuneration, and I am' (p. 625). The following exchange occurred between Schutt and Higgins:

> Mr Schutt: I think six shillings would give [a labourer] the necessaries of life.
>
> His Honour: How can you say that when you say you cannot contradict the evidence which has been given and the prices as to rent and butchers' meat?
>
> Mr Schutt: All the same, we say a man earning 36s a week can live comfortably. On the other hand, I find on the wages board determinations over and over again adults over 21 years were given various sums ranging from 30 shillings to 36 shillings.
>
> His Honour: Were those boards influenced by the reputable employers' clause mostly?
>
> Mr Schutt: Well, I can find out for Your Honour.

> His Honour: Well, the only thing I can say is that on the evidence I have here I should not follow those standards. (pp. 626–627)

The Woodworkers' Wages Board, to which Higgins referred with approval, had been established before October 1903 and was not subject to the 'reputable employers' clause. Neither was the Furniture Board, which had fixed a labourer's rate of eight shillings. Although Sutch, for some of the unions, urged this rate on Higgins (p. 546), it was obviously outside his contemplation.

The answer to the question why Higgins chose seven shillings as the labourer's wage thus combines two elements. One was a determination that the *Excise Tariff Act 1906* should be the means of enhancing the worker's position—for providing to him a benefit that he was unlikely to achieve by the operation of the market. (Whether at that time Higgins envisaged using the Court's award-making role to generalise the *Harvester* standard is unknown.) The other element was a sense that seven shillings was a rate that could not be represented as excessive, because a number of employers were already paying that amount. Did the 'cost of living'—the needs of the wage-earner and his family—play *any* role? Perhaps it strengthened Higgins' resolve to enforce an increase. But the link between the seven shillings and living costs was so tenuous that nothing more is arguable.

3.2.5 *Harvester* and the living wage principle

As we saw earlier in this chapter, the goal of a living wage was widely advocated in the early decades of the 20th century, and *Harvester* occurred in that context. During the *Harvester* hearing, Higgins suggested that a mere 'living wage' fell below the standard at which he should aim:

> 'Fair and reasonable' means something between a good wage and a living wage. I think Mr Duffy is right in saying it is not merely on what a labourer can live. At the same time I do not think I am entitled to refuse a man excise remission if he does not give a good wage. It is something between a mere living wage in that sense and a good wage. (p. 253)

In the event, the distinction came to nothing, and in arbitral discourse terms such as the basic wage and the living wage were interchangeable. 'Basic wage' seems to have been coined by Higgins in 1911, with the purely functional purpose of identifying the labourer's wage as a foundation upon which secondary wages were superimposed.[13] Although 'basic wage' became common usage in the Court, Powers, as Deputy President, often used 'living wage'.

In the aftermath of *Harvester*, as we shall see, Higgins endowed the basic wage with a 'sacrosanct' quality that was quite at odds with the process by which he had arrived at the seven shillings standard. There were three fundamental problems with the process:

- the subjectivity of the very concept of wage adequacy;
- the tenuous connection between the seven shillings and identified consumption possibilities; and
- the superficiality of Higgins' attention to family size.

The conceptual inadequacies of the *Harvester* standard as a measure of household needs, combined with the inadequacy of the methods of adjusting it to a rising price level, were to lead ultimately to the Piddington Commission (see Section 3.6). In fairness, it should be admitted that the circumstances of the *Harvester* case—the limited information, the parties' narrow agendas, and the pressure for an early decision—did not lend themselves to sophistication in Higgins' judgment. If he is to be criticised, it is not so much for the intellectual shortcomings of the decision as for his subsequent endeavours to endow it with a mystique that its origins and its contents belied.

3.3 THE COMMONWEALTH BASIC WAGE

3.3.1 The foundation element of award rates

Higgins' first award, a year after *Harvester*, was for marine cooks, bakers and butchers (2 CAR 65). He adopted the *Harvester* standard for the lowest grade (the sculleryman), making adjustments for the fact that the workers' 'keep'

---

[13] He used the term in the *Engine-Drivers' and Firemen's* case (5 CAR 9).

was partially provided by the employer. In the *Broken Hill* case of 1909, he was confronted by evidence that the BHP Company's mine was becoming uneconomic. Higgins deemed the *Harvester* wage to be inviolable, declaring that 'unless great multitudes of people are to be irretrievably injured in themselves and in their families, it is necessary to keep this living wage as a thing sacrosanct, beyond the reach of bargaining' (3 CAR 1, 32). Reinforcing his concern about 'injury' to the workers and their families was a contention that maintaining the living wage was necessary for industrial peace:

> I cannot conceive of any such industrial dispute as this being settled effectively which fails to secure to the labourer enough wherewith to renew his strength and to maintain his home from day to day. He will dispute, he must dispute, until he gets this minimum; even as a man immersed can never rest until he gets his head above the water. (p. 20)[14]

The linkage between the wage and the level of unrest was taken for granted. It was a further—and unargued—step to suppose that the specific rate for unskilled workers set in *Harvester* was the amount that separated peace from turmoil.

It was the repeated stance of Higgins and Powers that the basic wage-earner should not be called upon to share any burdens of economic adversity, although workers receiving additional amounts might be expected to do so. This principle accorded with Higgins' decision of 1909 in the *BHP* case. But it had wider import as prices rose during the war, and the Court held margins constant in money terms while increasing the basic wage. Powers, in 1915, expounded the principle in patriotic terms:

> The war necessarily causes loss and self-sacrifice, and although a worker is entitled to claim a living wage in times of war as well as in times of peace, and to get it if he can do so by the methods provided by Parliament—it is to be hoped that those who are employed in industries which cannot afford to pay higher wages for skilled workmen than are at

---

[14] In *A New Province for Law and Order* (1922, p. 6), Higgins wrote (in 1915): 'One cannot conceive of industrial peace unless the employee has secured to him wages sufficient for the essentials of human existence'.

present paid—for their own sakes and for the Empire's sake—will follow the example of their fellow-workers in Great Britain and Ireland who, although receiving lower wages have, apparently—when convinced that the industry cannot pay all they demand—accepted, during the war, what can in fairness be paid. By doing so they will help, by their work, to keep our industries going—prevent further depression—and bring the war to a successful issue at as early a date as possible. ... A country that pays 8s 6d a day to labourers in time of war—and considers claims for increases of such wages in war time—is surely worth fighting for and worth some self-sacrifice in time of need. (*Tanners and Leather-Dressers'* case 9 CAR 209, 211–212)

In 1916, Powers referred to a decision of President Jethro Brown in the South Australian Industrial Court, wherein Brown had said that he felt justified 'in expecting even the unskilled worker in time of war to exercise an abnormal economy'. 'In this Court', said Powers, 'we do not feel justified in forcing abnormal economy on the unskilled worker ...' (*Storemen and Packers'* case 10 CAR 629, 643). 'The war', said Higgins in 1918, 'causes suffering everywhere, deprivation nearly everywhere; and the extra commodities purchasable by the secondary wage are not so vital to healthy, fully nourished life as the commodities to which the basic wage is to be appropriated. The basic wage, which is meant to secure the proper sustenance of the children, the future citizens, must be provided at all costs; anything, everything must be cut down before the basic wage' (*Coopers'* case 12 CAR 427, 428).

3.3.2 Adjustment for rising prices

Until 1912, Higgins made no attempt to review the adequacy of the *Harvester* 7s in relation to changing prices. In the *Engine-Drivers' and Firemen's* case of 1911, the union claimed a higher wage because of an alleged increase in the cost of living. Higgins said that the cost of living was rising, but that the evidence did not justify his setting a higher rate in that case; in future he might need to take the higher cost of living into account (5 CAR 9, 14; Anderson

1929, p. 230). In the *Rural Workers'* case of 1912,[15] however, he set a minimum rate of 8s (6 CAR 61). Late in 1912, the Commonwealth Statistician began publication of his first price index, covering food and grocery prices and house rentals—the A series index (see Chapter 1, Subsection 1.3.2). In the *Gas Employees'* case, heard between March and September of 1913, Higgins referred to these statistics:

> I have found many indications that the minimum of 7s has become too low, owing to the increased cost of living; and I have allowed the fact to influence my awards; but I have never yet had presented to me, before this case, evidence sufficiently specific to show me what the advance in the basic wage should be ... According to the Commonwealth Statistician, the sum of 17s 4d would purchase in Melbourne in 1907 as much of the necessaries of life as 20s 11d would purchase in 1912. From another statement, it appears that, if the year 1911 be taken as the normal year, the cost of living in Melbourne has increased from 1907 to 1913 in the proportion of 922 to 1,111. In other words, 7s in 1907 were worth as much in Melbourne, in real wages, as 8s 5¼d today. This, if taken by itself, would suggest an increase to nearly 8s 6d. (7 CAR 58, 69)

Higgins set 8s 6d as the daily basic wage for Melbourne. The Statistician's figures also allowed comparisons of the cost of the regimen in different places, and Higgins accordingly set specific rates for different capital cities. In the *Engine-Drivers' and Firemen's* case, decided in October 1913, he set out the comparative costs in the June quarter. The basis of comparison was the purchases that could have been made in 1907 with £1, on average of the six capital cities. The same items would by June of 1913 have cost 23s 10d in Sydney, 22s 11d in Adelaide and Perth, 21s 3d in Hobart, 21s 2d in Melbourne, and 19s 7d in Brisbane (7 CAR 132, 141). In some cases thereafter, the Court set differential rates reflective of the estimated costs of living, but quite often the relevant parties requested uniform rates, and the Court usually complied.

---

[15] Also known as the *Fruitpickers'* case.

Once the publication of the price index had begun, it was the subject of frequent reference and discussion. In many cases, evidence was given by staff of the Labour and Industry Branch of the Commonwealth Statistician's office, principally J T Sutcliffe, the officer in charge of the Branch. It appears from the decisions, moreover, that unions, employers' representatives and the members of the Court freely contacted the office to get its advice about the construction and interpretation of the index. The tenor of references to the Statistician and his staff was invariably one of respect.

Initially, Higgins took note of the Statistician's figures, but both he and Powers (from 1914) treated them simply as one factor—an important one—in the set of considerations upon which the decisions were to be based. In the *Waterside Workers'* case, decided in April 1914, Higgins said that wharf labourers 'clearly belong to the category of unskilled labourers'. Continuing, he said:

> The cost of living in Melbourne was in 1907, and is still, somewhat lower than the Australian average; on the Australian average, the basic wage would have been 43s. Taking 43s as the proper basic wage for the Australian in the capital cities in 1907, the basic wage should now be 53s per week.

But the actual conclusion was a little different:

> On the whole, and after weighing all the circumstances, I think that with the evidence available, and on a comparison with other industries, and on a moderate and conservative estimate, the minimum rate per hour should be fixed at such a sum as should generally insure for the worker a sum of 51s per week, or 8s 6d per day. This is the wage which has been found by Heydon, J, in his recent elaborate and valuable inquiry as to the cost of living (for the purpose of NSW) to be the proper minimum wage for ordinary work ... It is also the minimum wage prescribed by myself for yardmen in cokeyards in Melbourne in the *Gas Employees'* case, August 1913, and by the Victorian Coal and Coke Board in the determination gazetted 4th December 1913. (8 CAR 53, 64–65)

Anderson (1929, p. 232) accurately summarises the position: 'In May, 1914, Mr Justice Powers awarded 8s 6d per day to labourers engaged in tanneries. At that time the Court was awarding a basic rate of about 8s 6d to labourers in Melbourne, Sydney, and Brisbane; and that was about the rate when the Great War commenced in August, 1914.' What had happened, in effect, is that '*Harvester*' had become 8s 6d in lieu of 7s. The increase of 21 per cent over the original 7s compares with the 20 per cent rise in the cost of living (measured by the A series index) between 1907 and 1914.

Continuing increases in prices, especially in the early years of the war, led to a greater reliance on the index. Two important qualifications must be borne in mind, however, because they affected significantly the reality of the *Harvester* standard. One is that the basic wage was set when an award was made. Awards typically ran for periods of three to five years. The basic wage *might* be increased on application for variation of the award, but not before the union could point to a substantial increase in living costs. The other qualification is that Higgins and Powers, in responding to price increases, exercised discretion in their choice of index numbers. Generally, the choice was between the average prices of the previous calendar year and the average for the immediately preceding four quarters, with Higgins leaning to the former and Powers to the latter. For both reasons, the basic wage in any award might be well out of date in respect of living costs. At a time of rising prices, this meant a reduction relative to the *Harvester* equivalent. An example of the two effects is provided by Higgins' decision of July 1915 in the *Artificial Manure* case:

> It appears from the most recent publication of the Commonwealth Statistician ... that in 1907 a sum of 17s 6d in Melbourne would go as far in securing groceries, food, and rent, as 22s 1d would go in 1914, taking the year as a whole. It also appears that the corresponding figure for 1914 in Adelaide is 22s 10d. The basic wage as ascertained and found in 1907 for Melbourne was 7s per day; and if that finding was correct—there has been no evidence produced to impugn it—the basic

wage should not be less than 8s 10d for Melbourne, or less than 9s 1d or 9s 2d for Adelaide. Of course, we are now at the end of July, 1915; and according to a return furnished by the Commonwealth Statistician, the cost of living has, since 1914, been increasing in a startling degree. For Melbourne, the Statistician's figure for the first quarter of 1915 is 22s 11d; for the second quarter 25s 3d. For Adelaide, the figure for the first quarter of 1915 is 23s 2d; for the second quarter 25s 4d. But I have to make an award for some years to come (both sides are willing that the term should be three years); and as the recent exceptional rapidity of the rise in prices seems to be due chiefly to the war and to the drought, I think it better to award according to figures for the last full year available, 1914. … But, although I do not propose to fix the wage on the basis of the cost of living figures for the first half of 1915, I have to take these figures as a warning, and therefore I think it right to give full effect to the figures for 1914. The strain of present conditions must at present be very great for the wage-earners. The Court has always power to vary the award; and if prices persistently increase, the union may apply for an increase on the basic wage awarded; while if prices go down, the employers may apply for a decrease. (9 CAR 181, 189–190)

Higgins fixed the basic wage for Victoria in this award as 53s a week (8s 10d a day).

In October 1915, Powers dealt with the first application for an award *variation* based on the increase in the cost of living. This was in the *Tanners and Leather-Dressers'* case. The award still had 18 months to run. Powers said that it was 'out of the question' to fix a basic wage by reference to prices in the August quarter (the most recent for which figures were to hand). There was a likelihood that at least some of the items in the index would return to 'normal prices' by the end of the year because of the breaking of the drought. 'This Court', he said, 'cannot, in fairness to employers, employees or the public, make awards on the figures available for a month or for a few months preceding the day the different awards are made—nor can it vary awards from time to time because of a temporary change in the cost of food and groceries, or in the cost of living generally. ...' (9 CAR 209, 215). Powers decided, 'under all the circumstances mentioned', to raise the basic wage in the award from 8s 6d to 9s.

The continued rise in prices led Higgins in September 1916, in the *Meat Industry Employees'* case, to fix a Melbourne basic wage of 10s per day. This was based on a comparison of the Statistician's index numbers for 1907 and 1915. 'It is true', said Higgins, 'that the figures are still higher for the present year 1916, so far as it has gone; but I do not think it expedient to act on the figures of the latest fraction of a year' (10 CAR 465, 484). This entailed a lag of about 15 months between prices and the wage level. As the award ran its course, the interval grew correspondingly. In the early part of 1917, Higgins moved to a 10s 6d standard. 'The cost of living is higher for 1916 than for 1915', he said; 'but even in 1915 the figures would point to about 10s 5d as the minimum daily wage. I do not see how I could be justified in prescribing less than 10s 6d per day, 63s per week' (*Glass Manufacturers'* case 11 CAR 31, 33). In the following June, Powers refused to adopt the 10s 6d standard. In the *Engine-Drivers'* case, the union drew his attention to the two cases in which Higgins had fixed that rate. There had in recent months been some fall in prices. Higgins had acted on the basis of prices for the whole of 1916. 'It has been my practice', said Powers,

> to make awards based on the Statistician's figures available for twelve months prior to the award, and not to be guided in making an award on any monthly or quarterly figures, and I understood that to be the practice of the President, but I see he based his last award on the fact that 1916 as a whole was higher than 1915 as a whole. The tables supplied to me by Mr Sutcliffe satisfy me that awards made on the Statistician's tables for twelve months prior to April 1917 should not (except in the case of Perth) be made (if the figures of the Statistician are solely relied upon) for more than awards made on the same tables for twelve months prior to January 1917, or prior to October 1916, or to July 1916. (11 CAR 197, 212)

A reading of decisions between late 1917 and mid-1919 indicates that in fixing the basic wage the Court hovered between 10s and 10s 6d. This was for Melbourne. For other places, the wage might be higher or lower according to the Statistician's estimates of prices of food and groceries and of house rents.

The adjustment—however crude—of the basic wage to a price index raised issues about the reliability of the index. Little was said about the collection of the data, perhaps because of the Statistician's insistence that his 'tables' measured accurately what they purported to measure. Criticisms centred, rather, on two aspects of the index:

- it encompassed only prices of food and groceries and house rents; and
- the regimen of items included in the index was fixed.

The categories excluded from the index were clothing and miscellaneous items.[16] It was commonly supposed that these represented about 40 per cent of the household expenditure of basic wage-earners. The Court's attitude generally was that, in the absence of evidence to the contrary, it would suppose that the index accurately measured the decline in the purchasing power of the sovereign; that is, that the prices of items in the excluded categories moved in much the same proportions as food and grocery prices and house rents. There was 'a general fall in the value of money in relation to all commodities, in all parts of the civilised world, and whether there are wages boards or arbitration Courts or not; and the burden lies on the employers to show that the price of clothes, furniture, fuel, etc, does not increase in substantially as high a ratio as the price of groceries, food, and rent' (*Artificial Manure* case 9 CAR 181, 190). Unless the employers showed otherwise, said Higgins in 1916, 'I must assume that the value of the pound sterling has fallen generally as to the commodities of a worker's family, in the same ratio as it has fallen in relation to the Statistician's selected commodities' (*Merchant Service Guild* case 10 CAR

---

[16] Of course, the regimen did not include all items of expenditure within the categories of food and groceries and rent.

214, 225). He did not discuss the possibility that the prices of the excluded items might have risen *more* than those covered by the index.

Going into more detail, Higgins said in a later case:

> Mr Knibbs [the Commonwealth Statistician] has taken food, groceries and house rent, and has treated the variations in their prices as best showing the variations in the value of money against commodities generally; and he has shown good reasons for the course which he has taken. These commodities are in steady uninterrupted demand. It is said that since the war began the price of clothes has increased in a somewhat greater ratio. But the need to purchase clothes is intermittent, irregular, casual, controllable. ... Several of the 'miscellaneous' items have not increased at all: for instance, tram fares, union subscriptions, insurance premiums, newspapers etc. To my mind, it is better not to disturb the Statistician's careful estimate as to the increase in the cost of living by inserting in it incomplete estimates of one's own as to the increase for a portion of the period of some one or more of the miscellaneous commodities, not being all of them. (*Gas Employees'* case 1919 13 CAR 437, 457)

There may here have been an implied response to Powers' decision in the 1918 *Public Service* case (discussed below).

The possibility of variations in the *composition* of household consumption was raised by employers as a reason why the basic wage need not be increased to the full extent of the increase in prices. In some cases, there was the added suggestion that an adjustment of the menu would be a reasonable contribution by the wage-earner to the war effort. As we shall see, this contention was discussed in some detail in the New South Wales tribunal. The Commonwealth Court lent support to it in relation to secondary wages, but it had limited impact on the Court's decisions about the basic wage. In the 1916 *Clerks'* case (10 CAR 16) the employers tendered a letter from the Commonwealth Statistician, who said:

> The price-index given in the Labour Bulletin accurately and unequivocally expresses the changing value of the sovereign for this

particular regimen, and for any regimen sensibly the same. ... But I may point out that when prices are abnormally high for a particular commodity, people diminish the use thereof. ... *As prices become abnormal so will any given regimen cease* to represent actual usage; and to the extent to which it differs from actual usage, so will it fail to be a true indication of the *actual cost of living*.

Powers, in his decision, noted that pork had gone up 100 per cent since the beginning of the war, and that people could fare quite well on other meats and foods. He declined to give full effect to the index (Anderson 1929, pp. 236–237). Discounting of the index was rare, however. In the *Meat Workers'* case (below), Higgins made plain his rejection of the focus on specific items, such as pork, and little more was heard of this. Normally, the index was accepted as an accurate measure of the change in the cost of living.

3.3.3 Basic wage principles

In two cases, the principles of basic wage fixation were discussed in more than usual depth.

The earlier of the two was the *Meat Workers'* case (10 CAR 465). Higgins in September 1916 made the first federal award for the meat industry. 'In this case', he said,

> I have welcomed—at last—a rational discussion of the principles on which the Court has hitherto ascertained the 'basic' wage—(I think the name was first given by me)—both as to its elemental factors and as to the mode of ascertaining the appropriate variations from time to time. On both subjects, Mr Parsons [the KC representing South Australian respondents] has very properly referred me to the elaborate and interesting pronouncements of Mr Justice Heydon, as reported in the New South Wales *Industrial Gazette* for March 1914, and of the same learned Judge, with Mr Justice Edmunds, in their recent consideration of the matter on August 18th last. I have also had the advantage of reading, since I reserved my judgment, a similar pronouncement made by Professor Jethro Brown, as President of the Industrial Court

of South Australia, in connexion with the Tinsmiths' case. Criticism is desirable—is essential—on a subject so novel and difficult; and I have not seen any other Australian criticism which approaches these utterances in value. I am far more surprised at the number of points of agreement found in the three several and independent Courts than at the points of difference. No Court in Australia … rejects the principle of a living wage as an essential first condition in any bargain between employer and employee. It is also reassuring to see a consensus of opinion as to the need for finding a basic wage, based on the cost of living, as distinguished from the secondary wage, based on skill or other exceptional qualifications; to find also agreement as to the fundamental principles and methods for ascertaining the basic wage; and to find even approximately similar results. … I had feared that the difference would be greater; for the State tribunals are naturally and—if I may presume to say so—properly, influenced by considerations of inter-State competition—considerations which do not embarrass this Court. (p. 475)

The 1907 basic wage had been fixed without the assistance of any 'statistician's tables'. It was, rather, 'the result of the selected and sifted evidence of thrifty and careful housekeeping women whose husbands were wage-earners'. 'I recollect', said Higgins,

> that counsel for the union did not propose to call any such evidence till I suggested it; and when these witnesses came, without notes or preparation, they showed, each in her artless fashion, how every shilling, almost every penny, was earmarked for some necessary family commodity. … This was my starting point—7s per day in Melbourne; though I had doubt whether it should not be 7s 6d. (p. 479)[17]

---

[17] In *A New Province for Law and Order* (1922, p. 4), reproducing an essay written in 1915, Higgins said: 'At my suggestion many household budgets were stated in evidence, principally by housekeeping women of the labouring class; and, after selecting such of the budgets as were suitable, I found that in Melbourne … the average necessary expenditure on rent, food, and fuel, in a labourer's household of about five persons, was £1 12s 5d …; but that, as these figures did not cover light, clothes, boots, furniture, utensils, rates, life insurance, savings, accident or benefit societies, loss of employment, union pay, books and newspapers, tram or train fares, sewing machine, school requisites, amusements and holidays, liquors, tobacco,

If my earlier account of *Harvester* is a fair one, Higgins' recollection could most kindly be characterised as romantic. It *is* true that Higgins 'suggested' ('demanded' might be the better word) the calling of evidence about the cost of living. *Three* housewives and eight men gave evidence about weekly expenses. But, as we have seen, the link between their evidence and the 7s standard was tenuous.

Since 1907, prices had risen; and since the outbreak of war, the increase had been 'violent'. But by *how much* had prices increased? 'It is at this point', Higgins said, 'that I make use of the Statistician's tables; but I make use of them as *prima facie* evidence only':

> The tables purport to show the variations in the purchasing power of money, so far as the variations in the prices of his selected regimen, with its 47 items, show it. The Statistician does not affect to believe that these same staple commodities in the same quantities are purchased always by all classes in all localities, or by all families in a class; but he says that 'in normal circumstances properly computed index numbers of food and groceries and house rent combined form one of the best possible measures of those variations in the purchasing power of money which affect the cost of living'. ... These index numbers do not deal with all the commodities purchased by the wage-earning classes, and some of the selected commodities may not be purchased by these classes at all; but—until the contrary be shown—I infer that the depreciation in the value of money which is found in relation to the selected commodities is to be found also in relation to the other commodities; that the same causes produce the same effects; and the contrary has not been shown. (pp. 479–480)

Higgins turned to the possibility of the wage-earners offsetting higher living costs by changing the consumption mix. For the basic wage-earner,

> a compulsory change of regimen ... must mean generally an inferior regimen, less sustenance, a failure to satisfy the normal needs of civilised

---

sickness or death, religion or charity, I could not certify that any wage less than 42s per week for an unskilled labourer would be fair and reasonable.'

men, a diminution of physical power, a decrease in efficiency; whereas a change of regimen on the part of people with larger incomes is not likely to have any such result. When it appears, as in this case, that one respondent has opened since the war a shop or stall for the sale of ox cheek and cuttings off the head, for which he had no market before, but which people buy now as meat is so dear, such a fact makes one think. … I notice that Mr Justice Powers, in his judgment delivered in the Federated Clerks' case, March, 1916, has spoken as to the necessity of changing one's regimen from things which are dear to things which are cheap. He has spoken of the duty of all under present circumstances, to make some sacrifices; but he has carefully guarded his words by making them apply only to the secondary wage—'once the living wage is secured.' …Yet even as to the living wage it is always open to employers, to prove, if they can, that there is a complete regimen which is physiologically as good as the kind contemplated in the calculations of the living wage, and which is at the same time cheaper. It is of no use, however, to point out merely that there is this or that possible substitute for this or that favourite article, and to show that it would be cheaper. It is of no use merely to show, for example, that ox cheek is cheaper than rump steak or than ribs of beef. I am told that ox cheek is actually richer in grammes of protein, but that it has only half as many calories as steak—half the fuel value, half the value for energy. If 3,500 calories and 125 grammes of protein be required for the worker per day, the deficiency must be made up somehow; so that it is idle to compare the different regimens except in their totality. But although the Court may fairly be asked to revise its conclusions as to the living wage on being shown that there is as good a regimen which is cheaper, it must avoid the morass of faddism. It must decline to be led into the absurd position of deciding between rival theories as to diet—for example, between a vegetarian diet and a diet in which animal food is allowed. It must take the habits of the people as they are, must refuse to dictate what to eat and what not to eat; must accept the practice of thrifty wage-earners' homes—which make economies under pressure of stern necessity, but whose bread-winner's strength has to be renewed from day to day—as affording usually the best practical test as to the suitable regimen. (pp. 480–481)

Notwithstanding his earlier deference to the evidence of the artless housewives, Higgins now postulated that the *Harvester* standard might be 'quite wrong'. It was always open to the parties to show this, and his acceptance of the 1907 standard was 'tentative only'. The subject was 'too novel, too difficult, too formidable in all its consequences, to make that finding of 1907 a fundamental dogma' (pp. 481–482). In this case, the 1907 decision had been criticised for the assumption made about the size of the labourer's family—'about five'. The assumption had also been criticised by Mr Justice Heydon in the New South Wales tribunal, citing statistics suggesting that the actual number of children aged below 14 was fewer than two. 'But', said Higgins,

> if my judgment in the *Harvester* case be examined, it will be seen that I did not attempt to lay down the average of three as being the actual average. … I took the family of 'about five' persons as a fair type; just as Professor Bowley … takes a family of six (four children) as a fair type … As for Australia, the most satisfactory indication of the average that I can find is contained in tables furnished by the Commonwealth Statistician—furnished since Mr Justice Heydon's inquiry. In these tables, the dependent children in families with incomes under £3 per week—and this is the class of families to be observed—the children under fourteen years are stated at 2.24 per family. … If we are to be so meticulous as is urged, we must take into the estimate of a living wage 2.24 children; and if we are to provide for the feeding of .24, or one-quarter of a child, may we not as well provide for the child's other three-quarters? … I feel strongly that our problem does not turn on the actual average number of dependent children per family—even if the average is confined to wage-earners' families, and at the best wage-earning period. The problem is not to find any existing needle in any existing haystack, but to find what sum can be most reasonably laid down, in the circumstances of the time, as the foundation or basic wage—a wage below which employers ought to be forbidden by the state to employ its citizens who are labourers. I can only say that I can see no sufficient

reason for departing from the hypothetical case of a family of 'about five' for the purpose of fixing the basic wage. (pp. 482–484)

Anderson (1929, p. 195) drily observed: 'As most people find it difficult to understand what is meant by a family of "about five", the statement is usually made that the *Harvester* wage was fixed for a family of five, and that the Court's present basic wage is fixed for a family of five.' As we shall see, the issue of family size, as well as being a point of divergence between federal and State tribunals, was to be a major topic of consideration in the aftermath of the Piddington inquiry. Despite the criticisms, Higgins was given to remarking that—whatever might have been said of the price index—the *Harvester* 7s had not been impugned.[18]

The other decision that stands out for the depth in which the issue of basic wage prescription was debated was the *Public Service Clerical* case, decided by Powers in October 1918 (12 CAR 531). The applicant associations sought an increase in the basic wage of Commonwealth public servants, then £150 per year (9s 7d per day for 313 days). If granted, the increase would be by way of a war bonus for a limited term. The Public Service Commissioner and other respondents argued that there should be no increase. They contended, said Powers,

> that public servants were not entitled to any increased basic wage, and that we must all recognise the times as abnormal, and submit to them in the best way we possibly can. That course is possible to those who receive from £300 to £3,000 a year, and the higher the income the easier it is to say it, and to do it; but it appears to me unreasonable to expect those on the basic wage in the Public Service to quietly submit to the greatly increased cost of living without at least applying to get the basic wage allowed outside the Public Service. ... It is difficult to see how a man, his wife and family, can be expected to live on the wage fixed before the war. (pp. 535–536)

---

[18] See, for example, the *Artificial Manure* case (1915) (9 CAR 181, 189), the *Glassmakers'* case (1917) (11 CAR 31, 34) and the *Coopers'* case (1918) (12 CAR 427, 426).

Powers permitted employers' federations to participate in the case. They argued that no increase in the basic wage beyond 63s per week (10s 6d per day) should be granted. This, they said, was the amount to which the pre-war wage should be raised to match the increase in the price index.

Powers' very detailed decision included a long discussion of the level and composition of expenditure consistent with living on the basic wage. At the risk of oversimplifying this discussion, we can summarise it in the following terms. The assumption that food and rent represented about 60 per cent of the household's expenditure was false: on pre-war evidence compiled by the Commonwealth Statistician, these items absorbed considerably more. This meant that the sum available for other items, including clothing, was intolerably low; and this inadequacy had been exacerbated by wartime increases in the cost of clothing that exceeded the growth in the price index. Powers also listed the items which, in the unions' contention, the basic wage should cover. They included rent, food and groceries, clothing, fuel and light, and fares; and also a number of other items such as children's school requisites, lodge and friendly society fees, union dues, a newspaper, maintenance and replacement of furniture, crockery and linen, occasional medical attendance and children's dentistry, stamps and stationery, toys, tobacco and drink, and some provision for old age. In Powers' view, the public would not see these aspirations as unreasonable.

The great amount of evidence tendered to Powers and his analysis of it might perhaps have been the basis of a 'new start'. Had he moved in that direction, his relations with Higgins could well have been strained. In the event, he drew back: 'I do not feel justified as a Deputy President of the Court in adopting an entirely new basis for the living wage in making this award at the present time' (p. 546). He would adhere to existing practice and merely adjust the wage to the increase in the cost of living, granting a war bonus so as to raise the basic rate for married officers to £162 per year (about 10s 4d per day).

At the end of the war, then, the practice of the Court, when making a decision about the basic wage, was simply to award an approximation of the *Harvester* standard, with imperfect allowance for the increase in prices.

3.3.4 The call for review

Both Higgins and Powers, however, had for some time been advocating a separate inquiry into the living wage. Powers appears to have taken the lead. He said in November 1916:

> I certainly think that an inquiry should be made as soon as we get back to normal times, to ascertain as nearly as possible what a fair living wage for a Commonwealth award should be, based on the ordinary regimen of a working man and his family and the cost of all of the items taken into consideration ... The Statistician informs me that it would be possible in normal times to ascertain what it does in fact cost an average working man and his family of two or three to live in reasonable comfort in the Commonwealth ... (*Storemen and Packers'* case 10 CAR 629, 644)

'It is remarkable', said Higgins in March 1917,

> that though an attempt has been made to impugn the soundness of the Statistician's estimate of the change in the cost of living, no attempt has yet been made in this or any other case to impugn the soundness of my finding in 1907 as to 7s as the proper basic wage in Melbourne in that year. ... An inquiry on this subject is eminently desirable, now that the finding of 1907 has stood for nearly ten years but I cannot force parties to an arbitration to undertake the labour of such an inquiry. I hope however that some party will exercise his undoubted right to challenge the figures as to the existing cost of living. The matter is one of extreme importance to the industries of the Commonwealth. (*Glass Founders'* case 11 CAR 31, 34)

Soon afterwards, Higgins said that an inquiry would resolve issues surrounding both the 1907 decision and the measurement of price movements (*Gas Employees'* case 11 CAR 267, 277). In the *Engine-Drivers' and Firemen's* case, decided in June 1917, Powers gave as an additional reason for holding an inquiry the differences in the living wages fixed by the Commonwealth and State tribunals: the inquiry 'should enable all the Courts to have a common basis on which uniform awards would be possible' (11 CAR 197, 219). In the *Public Service* case of 1918, discussed above, he referred to the necessity for the Court 'to reconsider the assumptions as to the percentages of expenditure, on which awards have, up to the present, been made; unless that is avoided by a full inquiry by a Commission, or by the Statistical department, on the questions: What sum should be fixed as a Federal living wage? Including (1) What average family should be allowed for; (2) What items of expenditure should be allowed in fixing a basic wage; (3) What proportion each item of expenditure approved of bears to the total sum suggested as a living wage' (12 CAR 531, 538). Powers said in the same case:

> At the conclusion of the evidence the representative of the Acting Public Service Commissioner, the representative of the Employers Federation of Victoria and NSW, and the representative of the seven unions now before the Court, joined in urging that the Federal Government should appoint a Commission or some body to take evidence with a view to fixing a Federal living wage for a man, his wife, and family of three, on a scientific and humane basis, or to authorise the Commonwealth Statistician to do so. The President of this Court and I have, on more than one occasion, recommended that course to the Federal Government because we know that men, although they obey awards, feel that they are not getting more than a wage on which they can exist ... (pp. 542–543)

Higgins and Powers, in 1919, made further calls for an inquiry. In July, for example, Powers said:

> I again make the suggestion [for a Royal Commission] because I feel sure the discontent that is existent here, and in other countries, can only be removed by removing the cause. Prosecutions and imprisonment of employers or employees are necessary if they by illegal actions starve the community and violate the laws of the country, but the only real remedy is to remove the cause of the discontent wherever possible.

> I also do so because I am not satisfied that the basic wage is a living wage within the meaning placed on it by this Court before the war. ... No one who has any knowledge of the subject could make himself believe that £3 a week would allow a man and his wife and family of three to live up to the standards mentioned at the present prices of food, clothing and rent. (*Carters and Drivers'* case 13 CAR 214, 239)

In September, Powers said that 'the President of the Court has, and so have I, on several occasions publicly protested against having to continue to go on with the work of the Court without information obtained by an Inquiry Board or Commission (sometimes called a living wage inquiry) as to the reasonable needs of a man and his wife and family in these times ...' (*AWU* case 13 CAR 563, 582–583).

3.4 THE LIVING WAGE IN STATE TRIBUNALS

In the formative years of arbitration, the State tribunals played some part in the development of wage-fixing principles, including those pertaining to the basic or living wage. Some of the State Acts, in fact, enshrined the concept in one way or another, whereas no such recognition was to be found in the *Commonwealth Conciliation and Arbitration Act 1904* (Burns 1926, p. 300). New South Wales and South Australia were the States where the tribunals gave fullest consideration to the principle. There was, of course, no formal mechanism for consultation between tribunals—that did not come until the 1970s. But tribunal members read the decisions that emerged in other jurisdictions and, from time to time, commented on them.

The New South Wales counterpart of Higgins was Mr Justice Heydon. I have previously referred to Heydon's observations of 1905 about the desirability of equating the minimum wage with a living wage. Heydon did not then attempt to measure the living wage. In 1908, the structure of the New South Wales system was altered. Under the new structure, the primary power of wage-setting rested with Boards. Their decisions, however, were subject to appeal. (A further, less fundamental, restructure occurred in 1912.) F A A Russell, the Chairman of 11 Industrial Boards, said in 1914:

> It must be a function of the Court of Appeal to co-ordinate the work of the Boards and to regulate them; if the Boards make mistakes and fix minimum wages too high the appeal is to the Court—in the New South Wales system this heavy responsibility has been placed almost altogether upon the patient shoulders of a single indefatigable judge— and the Court has power to reduce any minimum wages that may have been unduly increased as well as to level up any that have been kept too low. (Russell 1915, pp. 344–345)

The 'indefatigable judge' was Heydon. In 1914, he reviewed 60 awards made by Industrial Boards between 1912 and 1914, finding that the minimum rate set by them was typically 8s per day (Sawkins 1933, p. 15). 'This', he said, 'is the first inquiry of any extent carried out by any arbitral tribunal in order to fix a living wage of general application in the State' (Board of Trade (NSW) 1918, p. 4). The Boards had spent much time in trying to apply the *Harvester* standard to the circumstances of the cases before them. 'Accordingly, the opportunity afforded by an appeal from an award was taken, and this inquiry was begun' (p. 16). What was required was 'an authoritative declaration as to the basic or living wage in New South Wales, together with the ascertainment of some method (if such can be found) of raising or lowering it with the rise or fall in the cost of living' (p. 5).

Heydon reviewed the *Harvester* decision and rejected it. His feeling was 'that I cannot safely take the *Harvester* wage as a starting point, and that the living wage must be sought by an independent inquiry' (p. 24). One ground for rejection was Higgins' assumption of a family containing three children. The Commonwealth Statistician had supplied information, based on the 1911 census, showing that the average number of children was less than two. Knibbs had also in 1911 made a survey of household food expenditures, which indicated that Higgins' allowance for food was excessive (pp. 18–19). Heydon's commentary on the evidence given in *Harvester* shows that he had not read the transcript and was too charitable to Higgins:

> The means thus provided, after three years, by the Commonwealth Statistician, of testing the figures for food expenditure of the *Harvester*

witnesses, to my mind throws serious doubt upon them. Certainly … the nine group have the advantage of having been called, and subjected to cross-examination, and seen by the Court, and it seems evident that they were (as, in my experience, such witnesses nearly always are) worthy wives and mothers, whose recital in Court of their household cares and troubles moves both sympathy and respect. On the other hand they are but nine, and living in one spot. The strongest and best feelings of their natures, their love for their husbands and children, their regard for the opinion of their neighbours, their loyalty to their class, appeal to them to make their evidence as strong as possible—for I can feel no doubt that they knew the object of the hearing, and it had probably been frequently discussed. Then they were open to selection. When the managers of the case knew that heavy budgets would help them while light budgets would injure them, can it be doubted which they would choose? (pp. 20–21)

The evidentiary basis of *Harvester* was weaker than this passage implies, but Heydon's criticisms were justified.

Heydon himself received much evidence about household budgets. The unions had put a great deal of effort into collecting it. 'This', said Heydon, 'was really valuable material'. Having said that, he went on to make a fundamental criticism of the reliance on actual expenditures to identify needs:

The weakness of the evidence, so far as it was weak, lay in the nature of the method of investigation by ascertaining actual expenditure. It is quite evident that when a living wage is sought, the mere fact that a witness spends, say, £3 a week, proves nothing. If such a fact proved that £3 a week was a living wage, the same method might equally prove that £2, or £4, or £10 a week was a living wage. Nothing was brought out more clearly in this inquiry than the fact that nearly all the witnesses simply lived according to their income, whatever it might be. Of several of them the wage had gone up or down, or the rent had been raised, or a child had begun to earn money, quite recently. The expenditure immediately expanded or contracted as the case might be. … The real question is one of standard. One has to ask one's self whether the family life as disclosed exhibits hardship which should not be tolerated, or falls below what should be guaranteed to the humblest class, and in fixing the standard one has to bear in mind that it is not a thing which is stationary, and if it has risen the wage should rise too. (pp. 41–42)

The point seems self-evident. And yet it seems commonly to have eluded tribunals, advocates and researchers; the equation of needs with actual expenditure recurs across the 20th century.

Notwithstanding the breadth and depth of his inquiry, however, Heydon arrived at a superficial endorsement of the existing standard, which was below the *Harvester* equivalent. 'I know of no case', he said, 'in which the [Commonwealth] Court has made an inquiry as full as the present, and I think that I should not hesitate to express what seems to me to be its true lesson. That is, that the living wage in Sydney, for the average family of two parents and two dependent children, is not more than £2 8s per week' (p. 60). The Commonwealth Court's basic wage was then typically £2 11s—itself below the true *Harvester* equivalent.

Heydon did not leave the matter there. His task was to recommend a minimum wage to the boards. The times, he said (without citing any evidence), were prosperous, and the wage-earner 'should have his share in prosperous times'. That would happen in a labour market unregulated by Courts, and regulation should not deprive the worker of a benefit that he might otherwise have enjoyed. An adjustment might be made on either of two bases: (1) an upward revision of the notions of adequacy underlying the determination of the living wage; or (2) simply paying more than the living wage. Heydon chose the latter:

> it might be said that as prosperity increases the standard of living rises and carries the living wage with it. This would be true, but I do not think it is well to call what may be a mere temporary change, which may last for only a few years, a change of standard. To my mind, that expression should be limited to change of a more fixed and permanent character, such as become generally accepted as necessary conditions; such, for instance, as the adoption of footwear, both boots and stockings,

> a change not yet, I think, quite universal in the case of children. This is very different from the changes wrought by a wave of prosperity, and to my mind (though I can understand others taking a different view) it is better to keep the two things separate, and to have the true living wage in sight, even when one departs from it … (p. 61)

Heydon's recognition of the relativity of 'needs' was, for the time, an interesting but isolated one. He suggested to the boards that unskilled workers in Sydney should receive for light work 8s 6d per day, for ordinary work 8s 9d and for heavy work 9s (p. 62). The prosperity component raised the living wage to, or above, the Commonwealth standard. He offered no solution to the need for 'some method (if such can be found) of raising or lowering it with the rise or fall in the cost of living'.

By the time of the next determination of a minimum wage—December 1915—the country was at war and there was serious inflation. Heydon said that he and Mr Justice Edmonds had decided, for no explicitly stated reason, that the minimum wage should be £2 12s 6d. They were unwilling simply to raise the wage to match the increased prices:

> As to the great variations shown by Mr Knibbs' tables, in the purchasing power of the sovereign, they are in themselves too violent, and their causes too obscure, and their future course too uncertain to enable us to rely upon them at this time, even if the war and the course of events should not make it necessary in some cases to abandon their use. However, beyond what we have said we cannot go; the prospect is too dark and difficult to permit us to attempt any conclusive determination. (p. 66)

In August 1916, the Court—Heydon sitting with Edmonds—issued a new judgment, far more expansive than that of the previous December. Referring to the 1914 decision, Heydon said that the prosperity component had fallen into abeyance. Much of the 1916 decision was a discussion of the weight to be accorded to the increase in prices, as reported by the Commonwealth Statistician. There were three subjects of discussion: (1) the meaningfulness of the statistics as a measure of the increase in the cost of living; (2) the causes of the rise in prices; and (3) the appropriateness of maintaining real wages during the war.

The point at issue in relation to (1) was the household's ability to counter the effects of higher prices by altering the composition of its consumption toward goods and services that had become relatively cheaper. Of course, there was no measurement of this effect, but Heydon put it forward as a reason for not automatically adjusting the wage to the value of the sovereign.

As to (2), he considered three causes of the inflation. One was the expansion of the Commonwealth note issue. This was 'a war tax; and should not every man pay his own taxes? Is taxation which is deliberately imposed upon the whole community to be converted by the Court into double taxation upon a part of the community?' (p. 73). The other two causes were 'slow working' and strikes. Heydon seized the opportunity to condemn these nefarious labour practices—the work of 'saboteurs':

> Conscience, country, and God appear to be all alike repugnant to them. The real parents of such doctrines, as stupid as they are abominable, seem to be hatred, envy, fraud, and laziness; feelings directly opposite to the manly and upright instincts which mankind has in all ages admired. (p. 75)[19]

But in the final analysis, Heydon ascribed to the war itself his refusal to compensate for higher prices:

> The main circumstance, however, which we have to consider is that we are at war, and we have determined to admit that fact alone as a modifying circumstance, and setting aside the questions hereinbefore discussed, of paper money, slow work, and strikes. We have repeatedly said that the war, in all its portentous magnitude, cannot be disregarded by us in considering at what the living wage should be fixed. It is impossible to define the living wage in terms which make it inelastic. All such seducing words, as 'fair' and 'reasonable', are essentially relative, and introduce existing circumstances into the problem. (p. 78)

---

[19] Graham (1995, p. 77) describes the criticism that Heydon, a Catholic, made of Archbishop Mannix's opposition to conscription.

The decision was to fix the sum of £2 15s 6d as the living wage to be incorporated in new awards. Existing awards would be reopened, and the living wage in those awards be raised to £2 14s. No explanation of either amount was given, other than the fact that 'an application of the method adopted by Mr Justice Higgins in the *Artificial Manures* case on the 20th July last year … would show a smaller wage than [£2 15s. 6d] by 1s 8d per week' (p. 82). (Higgins' 'method' was to set a basic wage equivalent to the *Harvester* 7s, adjusted for the increase in prices up to the average of the previous calendar year.)

No new declaration of the living wage was made until September 1918. By then, the *Industrial Arbitration Act* had committed this function to the newly established Board of Trade. The Board was required from year to year to make 'public inquiry into the increase or decrease in the average cost of living' with a view to then declaring living wages (p. 113). Heydon, as President, sat with four Commissioners representing employers and employees. The Board began its reasoning with the 1914 declaration, 'taking the last two quarters of 1913 as the period covered by the living wage inquiry, and following the practice of the Court of Industrial Arbitration of taking the present figure at the average of the last four quarters, in this case up to 30th June, 1918 …' (p. 114). J T Sutcliffe, who gave evidence, had applied the formula to calculate a living wage of £2 18s 5d, which would normally be rounded to £2 18s 6d. The employers argued that the proper basis for the calculation was not the wage set in 1914, which included the prosperity supplement, but the lesser amount identified as the cost of living. The Board disagreed:

> It is true that the investigation of the material then before the Court brought out a cost of living of about £2 6s 6d, but the Court did not accept that result; for various reasons which may be gathered from the judgment, it added 1s 6d to that figure, and treated the resulting £2 8s as showing the cost of living, and as pointing to a living wage of the same amount.

In fact, the Board decided to grant *more* than £2 18s 6d because of the abnormality of 'the times':

> In a general way everyone complains of the increase in the cost of living, though even more money seems to be spent than ever before. Whether this is permanent, or whether the close of the war or anything else will end it, we cannot possibly say. It is true that everyone ought to economise and avoid waste as much as possible; but still we think, under the very special circumstances of the present time, and for the present time only, that something might be done for the lowest class of workers. We deal only with the living wage and nothing else, and as we have to consider it every year we are able to take short views … We find that the living wage proper is £2 18s. 6d. per week, but we add to it (for the living-wage workers only, and until our next inquiry only) another 3d per day, making the minimum wage … £3 0s 0d per week. (pp. 120–121)

Thus the Board added a 'loading' to a standard that was itself above the 'cost of living' identified in 1914, the combined addition being of the order of 5 per cent.

In October 1919, the Board (presided over by Edmunds as Acting President) discussed a union claim for the living wage to be related to the needs of a family comprising a man, a wife, and three children, as in the Federal Court's decisions. The Board refused:

> If the number of dependent children, three, adopted by Mr Justice Higgins in the *Harvester* case of 1907, was not taken by him because it was presumed to be an average, it is impossible for the Board to say upon what grounds it was taken. The statistical inquiry into the subject shows that, as an average for this State, that number is wrong. The Board finds that during the past year this average number of dependent children is under two. (*Compendium* … 1921, p. 11)

This finding was based on analysis (by the Commonwealth Statistician) of the 1911 census. Although there was no evidence about subsequent demographic change, the long-term trend in dependency was one of decline: in 1881, there were 2.41 children under 15 years of age per married, widowed, or divorced male; by 1911, the number was 1.75 (p. 16).

The Board fixed a living wage of £3 17s. The increase of 17s exceeded the rise in the index and was explained by the Board's taking into account evidence about the actual costs of fuel and light, clothing and boots, and other miscellaneous items. Alarmed by the amount of the increase, the New South Wales Government announced a scheme whereby the living wage would be set for a man and wife only. Payments related to the number of children would be made from a fund into which employers would pay amounts determined by the numbers of employees. The scheme was not approved by Parliament (Burns 1926, pp. 328–329). A similar measure would be proposed by Piddington in 1920 (see Subsection 3.6.7).

The following is a comparison of the declared living wages in New South Wales and the amounts generally being prescribed by the Commonwealth Court for Sydney (the latter being, for various reasons, approximate):

End of	NSW Living Wage	Commonwealth Basic Wage
1914	48s-54s	51s
1915	52s 6d	54s
1916	55s 6d	60s
1917	55s 6d	60s
1918	60s	63s
1919	77s	69s

Thus in the years 1915–18 the Commonwealth basic wage exceeded its New South Wales counterpart. Although an even larger difference might be 'explained' by different assumptions about family size, it is questionable whether this was the essence of the matter. Rather, the New South Wales Court seemed to regard the *Harvester* standard as an excessive impost on employers, and found an easy justification for rejecting it in Higgins' ostensible assumption of three children. The 1919 New South Wales decision was a rather radical departure from previous practice.

In South Australia, under the terms of the *Factories Act 1907*, a Court of Industrial Appeals was appointed to hear appeals from the wages boards. Mr Justice Gordon, hearing an appeal from the Brushmakers Board in 1908, said that the Court had no power to vary a Board decision without securing a living wage to the workers affected (Anderson 1929, p. 213). Unlike the *Commonwealth Conciliation and Arbitration Act 1904*, the South Australian *Industrial Arbitration Act 1912* formally defined the 'Living Wage': it would be a sum 'sufficient for the normal and reasonable needs of an average employee living in the locality where the work under consideration is done ...' (Burns 1926, p. 301). Regular reports of Court decisions date from 1916, when the Court was constituted by Mr President Jethro Brown (formerly Professor of Law at Adelaide University). As in the Commonwealth jurisdiction, decisions about the living wage in South Australia were made in the context of specific cases.

Brown, like Higgins, Powers, and Heydon, was given to articulating his views about the principles underlying the prescription of a living wage. In the *Salt* case of 1916 (1 SAIR 1, 6, cited by Anderson 1929, p. 214), he declared that the living wage must be based on the normal and reasonable needs of a married man with a wife and children to support, and that the higher comfort of living and the higher standard of social conditions which the general community in Australia allowed to those who lived by labour had also to be taken into consideration. In the *Tinsmiths'* case of 1916, he said that it was 'natural that I should pay considerable deference to awards of the Commonwealth Court of Conciliation and Arbitration', but proceeded to criticise the Commonwealth Statistician's price index, which should be used with caution (1 SAIR 55, 57, 63, cited by Anderson 1929, pp. 207 and 234). Brown also felt justified 'in expecting even the unskilled worker in time of war to exercise an abnormal economy' (cited by Powers, with disapproval, in the *Storemen and Packers'* case 10 CAR 629, 643; see below). In 1918, Brown said that while it had been held by the Court that a living wage must be paid even if it involved the closing down of particular industries, 'when we come to interpret "living wage" in precise figures, we must remember that it must be a wage which is reasonable under all the conditions of the community or locality where it is prescribed' (*Storemen and Packers'* case, 2 SAIR 111, 116–117, cited by Anderson 1929, p. 193).

Brown also advocated the creation of machinery for fixing an Australian living wage. Dealing in 1919 with the assumptions underlying the male (as opposed to the female) living wage, he said:

> The family living wage is assessed on the assumption that the husband requires no 'skill', and that the general conditions in the industry in which he works are such that no conclusive ground can be alleged for fixing a primary minimum which is higher than the bed-rock wage. But the Court has to assume, for practical and quite irresistible reasons, that the man may have children. He may have none. He may have six under 14 years of age. The Industrial Court cannot base its calculations on the abnormal. As a matter of fact, this Court proceeds on the assumption that the wage-earner will, or may have, three children under 14 years of age. (*Women's Living Wage (Cardboard Box Makers')* case, 3 SAIR 11 at 26–27, cited by Anderson 1929, p. 214)

Higgins and Powers from time to time referred to State decisions. I referred in the previous section to Higgins' reliance in the *Waterside Workers'* case of 1914 (8 CAR 53, 65) on a recent decision of Heydon to justify a daily basic wage of 8s 6d. There was a hint of self-congratulation in a comment by Higgins, referring to Victoria, in the *Artificial Manure* case of 1915:

> The Court of Industrial Appeals, on an appeal from the Wages Board … reduced the 51s to 48s … but it is now made clear and well recognised that the cost of living, with the resulting pressure on the poor, had already risen to an unexpected height. The decision on appeal very nearly produced a strike; but such an extreme measure was averted because this federation of Victorian and South Australian chemical workers had been formed, and the men hoped for relief from this Court. The federation, though formed as early as December 1912, was registered on the 19th September 1913, just ten days after the decision of Hodges J. (9 CAR 181, 185)

In the 1916 *Meat Workers'* case, Higgins both reflected upon the gratifyingly small differences between federal and State wages and defended his three-child household against the criticisms of Heydon and Edmunds.

Powers, in the *Storemen and Packers'* case of 1916 (10 CAR 629), rejected an employer proposal that he adopt the various State living wages rather than impose a higher basic wage commensurate with the movement of prices. The issue, he said, had been discussed so thoroughly by Higgins in the *Meat Workers'* case that he did not need to deal with it in detail. He noted that the New South Wales Court provided for only two children (p. 642). Moreover, he referred to Jethro Brown's suggestion that even the living wage-earner should exercise 'abnormal economy' in time of war. 'In this Court', he said, 'we do not feel justified in forcing abnormal economy on the unskilled worker' (p. 642). Powers continued:

> It is my duty as deputy president of this Court ... to adopt so far as I can the principles laid down from time to time by this Court, instead of causing unrest and confusion by following judgments of other Courts based on different principles. It is easy for me to do so because, if equally free to adopt any one of the three principles on which the living wage was fixed (a) by this Court, (b) by the New South Wales Court, or (c) by the South Australian Court, I would adopt the one laid down by this Court in 1907 and since followed. (p. 644)

Powers, in 1917, referred to differences in minimum wages as an additional ground for the appointment of an inquiry into the basis wage:

> The Industrial Courts in Victoria, New South Wales, South Australia, and Western Australia award less for a labourer's wage than this Court does, while the Industrial Court in Queensland—where the Statistician shows the cost of living is less than in New South Wales or Victoria in the latter part of 1916—awarded, in some cases, higher rates to labourers than this Court awarded in 1916 to employees in New South Wales and Victoria as a labourer's wage. The Queensland Court by a late Act cannot fix less than a reasonable wage for a man, his wife, and three children. ... [The] result of an inquiry such as is suggested should enable all the Courts to have a common basis on which uniform awards would be possible. The position caused by the divergent views expressed by the Commonwealth and State Courts as to a basic wage ... is not in the public interest, nor in the interests of industrial peace. ... The

> difficulty might, I think, be met to some extent by a conference of the presidents of the Commonwealth and the State Industrial Courts to see if some common basis could be found upon which awards could be made pending the inquiry mentioned. (*Engine-Drivers' and Firemen's* case 11 CAR 197, 218–219)

Powers wrote to like effect in the *Public Service* case of 1918 (12 CAR 531, 543–544).

Higgins, in the *Gas Employees'* case of 1919, returned to the question of family size and his disagreement with Heydon:

> It is enough for my present purpose to say that I still follow the general practice of sociological inquirers of looking for the expenditure of a labourer's home of 'about five persons'; whereas Mr Justice Heydon looks for the expenditure of a house of four persons two children. The statistical returns which the learned Judge used were not limited to the wage-earning classes or to definite ages; and yet it is well known that the proportion of dependent children in the wage-earning classes is greater than in the middle classes. Since my decision in the Butchers' case there has appeared a book written by Mr Seebohm Rowntree, 'The Human Needs of Labour'; and his investigation has confirmed me in my view. The families were all the families *of all classes*, in the city of York, where the mother was between 40 and 45. All children over fourteen were ignored. Mr Rowntree finds finally 'that if we were to base minimum wages on the human needs of families with less than three children, 80 per cent of the children of fathers receiving the bare minimum wage would for a shorter or longer period be inadequately provided for, and 72 per cent of them would be in this condition for five years or more.' He even recommends a scheme whereby the State should supplement the minimum in the case of larger families. But, as between employer and employee, I do not put on the employer any obligation to pay a basic wage calculated on more than three dependent children. (13 CAR 437, 458)

In December 1919, in the *AWU* case (13 CAR 823), Higgins attempted a more detailed critique of the Board of Trade's decision. It went essentially to two issues—the implicit allowance for clothing and miscellaneous items, and family size. We need not follow Higgins in revisiting the latter. As to the former, the Board's discussion had some resonance with that of Powers in the 1918 *Public Service* case. Using the Statistician's index as a measure of the rate of increase of all prices entailed the assumption that, taken together, the excluded components of expenditure—clothing and miscellaneous—moved at the same proportional rate as the included items. The Board thought that it had evidence that the excluded items had in fact risen substantially more. Hence, a wage that reflected only the rate of increase of food, groceries, and rent would provide for a diminished level of overall consumption. It increased the living wage by 3s in recognition of the increased cost of fuel and light and 14s for clothing 'The Commonwealth Statistician', said Higgins

> for various sound reasons which he has repeatedly stated, has treated food groceries and house rent as giving the best practical test of the variations in the purchasing power of money generally. The demand for food and shelter is universally continuous, always urgent; the demand for clothing is of a very different character. There is a marked difference between casual expenditure and constant. Taking food groceries and house rent as constituting about 60 per cent of the worker's expenditure, it may fairly be assumed, until the contrary be shown, that for the remaining 40 per cent the value of the shilling has fallen to an equivalent degree; but if we lift clothing out of the 'miscellaneous', we should make sure that the other 'miscellaneous' expenses, of the same casual, unstable character—such as on furniture and pots and cups, medical attendance, etc—have been similarly examined, and for the same period, on the same basis. (p. 840)

A reading of Higgins' decision leaves an impression of resentment of any other wage-setter who seemed to be 'taking the lead' in the development of principles and policy. That impression is not allayed by his assurance that, notwithstanding his criticisms, he held 'in genuine respect the great efforts which the Board has made, and the light which it has focused on one of the most difficult problems presented to our industrial tribunals' (p. 843).

3.5 Summary: the basic wage from 1907 to 1919

The idea of a living wage, appropriate for the unskilled male labourer, was a key component of wage prescription in these formative years of arbitration. In one way or another, the tribunals came to treat the living wage as the foundation amount of award wages. But there were various unresolved issues. These were the product of a range of factors: reliance on lawyers who lacked experience and training in broader social science; the rudimentary state of statistics; techniques of wage-setting that were ill-adapted to rapid change in the economic and social environment; lack of coordination between the various tribunals; war; and inflation. Foremost among the issues were:

- the definition of the standard of adequacy;
- the elasticity of that standard in times of economic change;
- the nature of the family unit for which the living wage was intended to provide;
- the measurement of price changes; and
- the method of adjustment for changing prices.

These were the essential questions confronted by the Piddington Commission.

3.6 The Piddington challenge

3.6.1 Background to the inquiry[20]

Powers and Higgins, as we have seen, had since 1916 been advocating an inquiry into the basic wage. Their statements were generally vague about its subject matter. It would, in fact, be a mistake to see them as the major reason for the appointment of a Royal Commission, for there is no evidence that the federal government took notice of them. Much greater importance attaches to the industrial and political circumstances of the later war years, and the first year of peace, and the Arbitration Court's failure *in practice* to maintain the basic wage at even the *Harvester* standard. Worker discontent with the reduced

---

[20] In writing this subsection, I have drawn freely on Graham (1995) and Whillier (1977).

purchasing power of the wage was certainly a factor in the thinking of Prime Minister Hughes.

The years 1917–19 were turbulent. Early consensus about the war had eroded and the issue of conscription was especially divisive. An important by-product was the splitting of the Labor Party, with one segment, led by W M Hughes, entering into a National Government and the remainder going into Opposition. Great bitterness surrounded the shattering of political Labor. Industrial discontent was evident in a higher incidence of time lost through strikes, relative to the size of the labour force, than at any other stage of the 20th century. There was a decline in support for arbitration, and left-wing union leaders denounced Higgins (Whillier 1977, p. 10). Undoubtedly, ideology played an important part, with the Industrial Workers of the World (IWW) encouraging union militancy. If the IWW's influence was diminishing by the end of the war, the events of 1917 in Russia maintained a fear of industrial disorder in other countries, including Australia. Although these extraneous forces were widely seen as causes of the strikes, there was also a measure of acceptance of the 'fertile ground' thesis: that the readiness of workers to be led into militant action was due significantly to real grievances, especially inadequacy of wages.[21]

Hughes, with his union and Labor background, sympathised with this interpretation of events. And he was anxious to do what he might to reduce strikes. (This brought him into headlong conflict with Higgins, who saw Hughes' methods, including the making of concessions to strikers and the establishment of special tribunals, as disruptive of the Arbitration Court's orderly approach.) He lent a sympathetic ear to a union delegation that waited on him shortly before the 1919 election—the first since the Labor 'split'. The delegation sought an inquiry into the basic wage. Hughes told them that the Government had already considered the question and was prepared to appoint

---

[21] A view endorsed by the New South Wales Board of Trade in its Living Wage Declaration of 8 October 1919: '… interesting details were furnished of devices resorted to by housewives to readjust their method of living to higher costs, and anyone engaged in investigations of this kind is forced to the conclusion that the constant increase in the cost of commodities has become the most prolific source of industrial ferment' (Board of Trade (NSW) 1921, p. 33).

W M Hughes

an inquiry. It would be constituted of employer and employee representatives, who would choose their own chairman (Whillier 1977, pp. 26–27). It is possible that Hughes, recently returned from the Peace Conference, was influenced by the support for joint consultation prevalent in the United Kingdom under the banner of Whitleyism. Not only did he promise an inquiry; he also told the delegation: 'I am asking for power to deal with all industrial matters and this minimum wage, once we get it, will apply to all wage-board people and to everybody else. They will all have to come under it' (Whillier 1977, p. 28). Here he foreshadowed the 'Powers Referendum' that was held concurrently with the election of 13 December 1919. This, if it had succeeded, would have given the Commonwealth a general power to regulate the terms of employment.[22]

In his policy speech of 30 October 1919, Hughes said that 'the cause of much of the industrial unrest, which is like fuel to the fires of Bolshevism and

---

[22] The referendum was neither supported nor opposed by the Labor Opposition. It failed narrowly.

direct action, arises with the real wages of the worker'. The Government was appointing a Royal Commission:

> The Commission will be fully clothed with power to ascertain what is a fair basic wage and how much the purchasing power of the sovereign has been depreciated during the war; also how the basic wage may be adjusted to the present purchasing power of the sovereign, and the best means when once so adjusted of automatically adjusting itself to the rise and fall of the sovereign. The Government will at the earliest date create effective machinery to give effect to these principles. ... The fundamental question of the basic wage having been thus satisfactorily—because permanently—settled, there remain other causes of industrial unrest which must be dealt with ... (Royal Commission 1920, pp. 7–8)

If there was no explicit promise to adopt the Royal Commission's findings and recommendations, such a commitment was surely implied.

Hughes had, no doubt, a political purpose. But his view about the need for action to alleviate the grievances that contributed to industrial discontent was strongly held. In January 1920 he received an employer delegation which sought (unsuccessfully) changes in the letters patent of the Royal Commission. According to the record of that meeting, which Whillier has extracted from the archives, Hughes said:

> Class hatred is not a complaint without a root, nor did it spring up in a night. It is a deep-seated disease, and it had its roots in the injustices suffered by the workers in the days that are gone, and we are now reaping where those who went before us have sown. ... My experience of unions is this, that the great bulk of the men, if you take them by and large, are free from this bitter class consciousness. Unfortunately men have been from the beginning of time led by the few who have got their minds made up. The great bulk of our fellow-citizens are law-abiding, peaceful and genial people, and of course the great mass of our fellow-citizens [are also], like all of us, credulous, and likely to be beguiled by alluring statements, lying statements, propaganda which has for its objective overturning the state and the existing condition of things. If we are

to combat their propaganda, and prevent the great mass of the people acknowledging these men as their leaders, we must find something to put in its place. It was for that reason I put the basic wage proposition forward … [It] was an attempt to remove one of the most prolific causes of industrial unrest …The standard by which this effort to get industrial peace is tried is not what it will cost, but what it will do. If it won't do anything, it is dear at any price. If it will do what we want it to do, it won't matter what it costs. (Whillier 1977, pp. 40–41)

3.6.2 The Royal Commission

The letters patent of the Royal Commission on the Basic Wage were proclaimed in December 1919, soon after the election. The Commission was to report on:

1. The actual cost of living at the present time, according to reasonable standards of comfort, including all matters comprised in the ordinary expenditure of a household, for a man with a wife, and three children under fourteen years of age, and the several items and amounts which make up that cost.
2. The actual corresponding cost of living during each of the last five years.
3. How the basic wage may be automatically adjusted to the rise and fall from time to time of the purchasing power of the sovereign. (Royal Commission 1920, p. 1)

The Government appointed equal numbers of employer and employee representatives, who in turn agreed on the Chairman. The employer members were E E Keep of Melbourne, appointed on the nomination of the Central Council of Employers of Australia; J A Harper from Adelaide, President of the Associated Chambers of Manufactures of Australia; and G M Allard from Sydney, nominated by the Associated Chamber of Commerce of Australia. Harper resigned in February 1920 and was replaced by G D Gilfillan. The three employee members, elected by the Conference of Federated Unions, were: H C Gibson (Federated Engine-Drivers and Firemens' Association); R

Cheney (Federated Carters and Drivers' Industrial Union); and T C Maher (Commonwealth Public Service Clerical Association). The agreed Chairman was A B Piddington KC (then Chairman of the Interstate Commission).[23] J T Sutcliffe, officer in charge of the Labour and Industrial Branch of the Commonwealth Statistician's Office, was appointed Statistician and Secretary (Whillier 1977, p. 49). He probably deserved much of the credit for the thoroughness and sophistication of the Royal Commission's work.

The Commission held 184 meetings, including 115 public hearings. There were nearly 800 witnesses; and the Commission received 580 statistical reports and other exhibits. Having completed its public inquiry in September 1920, it submitted its report to the Governor-General on Saturday 20 November 1920 (Whillier 1977, pp. 36 and 56).[24]

3.6.3 Constructing a standard

The Commission began by rejecting the *Harvester* standard; for although *Harvester* had laid down a requirement that the minimum wage be sufficient to meet the cost of living, 'the decision in the case was given without the cost of living having been ascertained by evidence except to a partial extent'. The context suggests that the Commission's review of *Harvester* was confined to a reading of the decision, from which inferences were drawn—and guesses made—about the evidence provided to Higgins. That some of these were wrong was probably due in part to statements made over the years by Higgins—statements that gave a misleading impression of the depth of his inquiry. 'With regard to food and groceries', it said, 'there was presumably evidence from the nine housewives examined that the amount of £1 5s 5d

---

[23] Piddington had in 1913 been appointed to the High Court, but before he sat he resigned in response to criticism of the appointment from the Bar. Later in 1913, he was appointed Chairman of the newly formed Inter-State Commission. The appointment was for seven years. During Piddington's term, the Commission was much exercised in determining criteria for protection, and Piddington was seen to give much weight to labour standards. The Commission itself was emasculated by a High Court decision that denied it the authority to exercise judicial power (Graham 1995, pp. 52–53 and Chapter 5).

[24] A supplementary report (Royal Commission 1921) was tendered on 2 April 1921.

… did afford a sufficient supply of food.'[25] (Royal Commission 1920, p. 10). There was no such evidence from either the three housewives or the eight husbands. The Royal Commission contrasted Higgins' allowance of 7s for rent with a later finding of the Commonwealth Statistician that the rental of a four-room house in Melbourne in 1907 was 8s 11d. It explained the difference by supposing that Higgins' four-room house was in Sunshine, rather than Melbourne (p. 11). Nothing in the *Harvester* case evidence supports this explanation. The key factor in the cost of housing was the inferior quality of houses occupied by labourers and their families.

The Royal Commission was confronted with the issue of whether it should identify a standard of comfort specific to low-paid wage-earners and their families. The employer deputation to the Prime Minister, mentioned above, sought an amendment of the letters patent to limit the inquiry to 'the humblest worker'. In the hearing, as the Commission records, A W Foster (for the unions) suggested 'that the Commission should not select any special occupation, whether skilled or unskilled, and ascertain the cost of living of the family of an employee in the occupation so selected, but should endeavour to picture the "typical Australian man" and determine what is his "reasonable standard of comfort"'. On the other hand, Russell Martin, for the Employers' Federation, contended 'that the Commission should (as he put it) "first catch its man" or in other words select a man in some definite calling, which, he maintained, should be that of "an unskilled labourer" or "the humblest worker" or the "lowest-paid employee" or "basic wage earner", and ascertain for that family the reasonable standard of comfort' (Royal Commission 1920, p. 14). Later in the inquiry, an employer representative said: 'If we start with a man on the lowest level, whoever he may be, it will be very easy for the Arbitration Court, if our determination comes before it, to use that as a starting point and decide how much to give above that amount, but if we are to take the average Australian and start on an indefinite basis, then the Court would be in a difficulty as to where to start and how much to work upwards or downwards.'

---

[25] Higgins had specified £1 12s 5d as the amount required for food, groceries, and rent. Seven shillings was the amount ascribed to rent.

Piddington replied that this was a curious line of reasoning, for at no time had the Court awarded a margin above the basic wage on the ground that one worker required a higher standard of living than another (Whillier 1977, pp. 67–68).

The Commission's stance was that the appropriate standard of comfort was one appropriate to wage-earners, but not specifically low-paid ones. It referred to 'the pitfall of supposing that, because the humblest worker ought to be paid the "actual cost of living according to reasonable standards of comfort", therefore that "actual cost of living according to reasonable standards of comfort" must be ascertained by finding out what the humblest worker does actually spend'.[26] In the main, the Commission found, there was no difference between skilled and unskilled workers in what was required for 'reasonable standards of comfort':

> It was not contended at any time during the inquiry that it makes a difference to the amount necessary for a reasonable standard of comfort under the section of rent or of Food or of Miscellaneous requirements whether the employee is a skilled or an unskilled worker. Nor was an attempt made to establish any distinction in the section of Clothing, as far as the employee's wife or his children are concerned. The only point, therefore, in which a difference is arguable is as to the regimen of clothing for the man. There is no decision to suggest to the Commission the conclusion that the skilled labourer ought to have a different 'reasonable standard of comfort' in respect of clothing than the unskilled. What is more important than the absence of decisions is that there was no

---

[26] In the light of the Commission's rejection of the notion that needs could be inferred from actual expenditures, it is unclear why it sought evidence of actual household budgets. It did so by distributing some 9000 forms on which respondents were to record expenditures over a four-week period. This proved to be an unfruitful line of inquiry. Only 400 forms were returned—'a result due, no doubt, to the exacting labour necessary to fill in a multitude of details, every one of which is essential if safe inferences are to be drawn'. 'An examination of the returns', said the Commission, 'leaves no doubt that this method, though frequently adopted, is not effective even to discover what is the general level of expenditure. And, of course, the level of expenditure is not *per se* a criterion of the level of comfort' (Royal Commission 1920, p. 18).

> evidence before the Commission establishing such a difference as being found to exist in actual fact. On the contrary, all the evidence showed that, except for special occupational clothing, sensible wage-earners of all occupations dress very much alike. (p. 17)

Thus the Commission saw its task as one of identifying consumption standards 'not by reference to any one type or group of employees, but by reference to the needs which are common to all employees, following the accepted principle that there is a standard of living below which no employee should be asked to live'. The needs of employees and their families had to be ascertained by specific inquiry, uncontaminated by awareness of the wages actually being paid.

How, then, did the Commission establish these needs? A family unit of five was specified in the letters patent, and the Commissioners agreed that it would contain a boy of 10½, a girl of 7, and a boy of 3½ (Royal Commission 1920, pp. 25–26).[27] The Commissioners were able to refer to a Tentative Budget Inquiry conducted in Washington DC in 1919 by Royal Meeker, Commissioner of the Bureau of Labor Statistics, United States Department of Labor. Meeker distinguished three standards of living: (1) the pauper or poverty level; (2) the minimum of subsistence level; and (3) the minimum of health and comfort level. He had adopted the last of these. 'Your Excellency's Commissioners', said the Royal Commission, 'have pursued a similar aim and sought to find the amount which will provide real but moderate comfort in each section of this Inquiry', adding that nothing less would meet the expectations implicit in the letters patent.[28]

---

[27] Corresponding to the agreed position of the unions and the employers, except for the substitution of the younger boy for an infant.

[28] Meeker's description of this standard was as follows: 'This represents a slightly higher level than that of subsistence, providing not only for the material needs of food, shelter, and body covering, but also for certain comforts, such as clothing sufficient for bodily comfort and to maintain the wearer's instinct of self-respect and decency, some insurance against the more important misfortunes—death, disability, and fire—good education for the children, some amusement, and some expenditures for self development' (Royal Commission 1920, p. 17).

3.6.4 Measuring needs

The Commission structured its analysis of necessary expenditures under the obvious headings of housing, clothing, food, and miscellaneous.

In respect of rent, the Commission noted that at the time of the 1911 census the capital cities and suburbs contained 116,308 owner-occupied houses and 202,135 rented houses. The former, it said, would include the houses of the well-to-do and those in the course of rent purchase. The Commission would not modify its treatment of rent to take into account owner occupation (Royal Commission 1920, pp. 21–22). A critical issue was the assumption to be made about the number of rooms—four or five. In *Harvester*, the Commission said, Higgins had adopted a standard of four rooms. (The *Harvester* decision, in fact, is silent on the issue; but the evidence was that houses were generally of three or four rooms.) The requirement of at least five

> appeared so clear to the Commission that, at a certain stage, the Commission having got the impression that the point would not be disputed, announced its intention of confining the evidence for the future to houses of that size. In deference, however, to the protest of Mr Ferguson [for the Victorian Employers' Federation], the matter was reopened. The only consequence was a loss of time in collecting evidence as to smaller houses, while not one witness—either house agent or medical authority or architect—was found to maintain that a four-roomed house was a proper standard for the typical family. The Commission had learnt from an officer of the Commonwealth Statistician's Department that in 75% of the cases, of a family of three children under fourteen, two would be of one sex, and the third of the opposite sex. This necessitates two bedrooms at least, apart from that of the husband and wife, and, as the kitchen is always counted as a room, the four-roomed house leaves the worker without any other sitting room or social room than the kitchen. (p. 20)

Ferguson argued that many families did live in four-roomed houses because of the shortage of houses; and employers should not have to provide money for housing that was not obtainable. The Commission's answer was that 'the amount over and above their actual rent while living in four-roomed houses may fairly be regarded as enabling [families] to obtain other comforts as a balance or compensation for the deficiency in their housing accommodation forced upon them by existing circumstances' (p. 22).

A secondary issue to that of room numbers was amenities. 'Accepting current standards', the Commission said, 'no house for the typical family can be considered to comply with that family's requirements unless it has the three elementary household conveniences of bath, fixed copper, and fixed tubs' (p. 20).[29]

The standard of adequacy for clothing was elusive, but the Commission relied heavily on the evidence of consumers:

> In no branch of the inquiry was more ample evidence adduced by both parties, and in no branch was the value of popular participation in the investigation more clearly shown, than with regard to Clothing. Only by such means was it possible to arrive at clear determinations of a matter involving so many complicated considerations, as does the question of the amount necessary to provide a reasonable standard of comfort in dress. ... A number of housewives and some working men gave evidence as to the amount spent in the home upon Clothing and the requirements of the various members of the family. The general trend of such evidence was that at present prices and with present wages, families of the typical size or larger, have gone short of necessary clothing or lived to some extent upon what they already had, without being able to make necessary replacements. There can be no doubt, either, that since 1914, the standard of clothing enjoyed by families has been lowered, or that the evidence visible every day in the streets of a higher standard of dress than that obtaining before the war is confined

---

[29] The Commission said: 'In some of the capitals the copper and the tubs frequently belong to the tenants, and are movable; the houses being, in this respect, below the standard which should be observed in Australia.'

to employees of either sex who have benefited by the increase of wages, based on a typical family's requirements, without having the liabilities of such a family. ... The findings of the Commission as to Clothing will remedy whatever is well-grounded in such complaints coming from the typical family. (pp. 26–27)

The Commission reduced its allowance for clothing, having regard to the opportunities for economy that existed by taking advantage of sales (3 per cent) and by making down clothes at home (5 per cent) (p. 32). In relation to the latter, it said:

the Commission declined to adopt the argument that all clothing should be obtained upon a ready-made footing ... It was thought by the Commission that savings by cutting-down, etc, are an admirable form of thrift, and that the work involved is not in itself the most laborious of a housewife's duties. Indeed, it is far from distasteful, as appealing to the exercise of skill and an age-long feminine art. (p. 47)

Food lent itself to a more sophisticated treatment:

The prime conditions in the provision of a family's food are—

> First—that it shall be sufficient in food values, expressed in Calories, to provide warmth and energy, to renew tissue so as to maintain the weight of the body, and to satisfy the requirements of growing and developing children.
>
> Second—that it shall contain a proper proportion of the three main constituents of food, viz., Proteins, which produce new growth or replace tissue lost, Fats and Carbohydrates to supply energy.
>
> Third—the supply must permit of a sufficient variety of food for the preparation of palatable and digestible meals.
>
> Fourth—the varieties of food must conform generally to the habits of the community. (p. 34)

The first two of these criteria were the subject of scientific evidence, both oral and written. The Commission adopted 3500 calories as the standard for a working man (and was scathing in its criticism of Professor Osborne of Melbourne University, a union witness, who advocated a much higher intake). Recognising that calorific requirements varied with the work performed, the Commission opted for a man doing moderate muscular work. The assumed family of five was equated, for its food needs, with 3.3 man-units (pp. 36–41; 85–87).

In relation to the composition of the food budget, the Commission noted a substantial fall since 1914 in the consumption of meat (probably due to an increase in its relative price). The Commission would have allowed for the 1914 standard of meat consumption 'if it had considered that this consumption was necessary for the health or comfort of the community, since it could not be reasonably contended that the standard of comfort in Australia ought to be lower in the present year than it was in 1914'. It rejected the 1914 standard, however, because

> the authorities seem to be overwhelming in support of the position that the altered habit of our people, in consuming less meat, is far from inflicting any injury to health or any hardship, provided that the total amount of food which is necessary is obtained. The Commission has, therefore, accepted what appear to be the present habits of the people in respect to the eating of meat. (p. 44)

Miscellaneous items required case-by-case treatment. Only a selection of the items is discussed here. Many of the union claims were rejected.

Claims for household equipment were weighed against the considerations that such items could be bought before the worker had a full household of dependents and that many could be kept in service until the number of dependants diminished (p. 45). Life insurance of the breadwinner was an aspect of 'reasonable comfort', but could not be included because the Commission could not determine the actuarial probability of the worker's demise while the family was of the prescribed size and structure. Unemployment insurance was excluded for similar reasons and also because arbitration tribunals, in fixing occupational rates, took into account the relative probabilities of unemployment (p. 46). Nothing was included for 'Church and Charity', because the basic wage-earner was unlikely to spend much on them. This was partly because help was given in kind: 'People of limited means help one another wonderfully here, as in all countries, but this help is not so much in money-donations as in the kindly personal offices and sacrifices that make such mutual help far more acceptable and helpful.' Nor was any allowance made for alcoholic and soft drinks. 'There seems no reason', the Commission said, 'for regarding the regular consumption of alcoholic or soft drinks as essential to a reasonable standard of comfort'. The unions had claimed allowance for domestic help in four weeks of the year to afford the housewife some relief from her toils. The Commission rejected this claim, but allowed £4 a year for a holiday to achieve a similar benefit (p. 47). For dentistry, the Commission included a sum 'thought to be sufficient as a general amount to be expended in the year' (p. 50). In relation to 'amusement recreation and library', it said:

> The claim of the federated Unions ... was supported by the argument that families should have a due share of the intellectual and social enjoyments of life. The argument may be conceded to be just, but it is not to be forgotten that the best part of such enjoyments is often to be found in a family's own resources when this family is not oppressed by poverty or the fear of poverty. The mistake is in supposing that life has no pleasures other than bought excitements. It is probable that few communities possess easier access, or access to a greater variety, of pleasure than the Australian community possesses, and can exploit at little, if any, cost in money. Nor could anything be done to earmark any sum for recreations of an intellectual character. The Commission has, therefore, included a sum under the one heading of Recreation, Amusement, and Library, leaving the use of the sum thus included to the choice of the wage-earner. (p. 50)

The report lists in full the items deemed to be necessary for life at the required standard, and shows their respective prices.[30] For Melbourne, the total costs were:

---

[30] For food, the list covers each of the six capital cities. The lists for clothing and miscellaneous items are for Melbourne only.

Rent	19s 6d
Clothing	£1 9s 0d
Food	£2 6s 1½d
Miscellaneous	£1 0s 10½d
Total	**£5 15 s 6d**

The totals for other capital cities ranged from £5 6s 2½d in Brisbane to £5 17s ¾d in Sydney.

These amounts greatly exceeded the current basic wage. The excess cannot be precisely stated, because there was not then a uniform basic wage, even for a single city. According to the Royal Commission, the most recent Commonwealth award contained a basic wage of £4 2s. This had been set on the basis of prices in the 12 months to September 1920. If it had been related to the September quarter price level, the amount would have been £4 13s (Royal Commission 1920, p. 93). That amount, perhaps, is the best approximation to the *Harvester* standard—the September quarter 1920 equivalent of £2 2s in 1907. This was 80 per cent of the Royal Commission standard. But the failure of the basic wage to keep pace with price changes meant that the average increase in the basic wage needed to give effect to it would be greater. According to the Royal Commission (p. 93), the basic wage in some Commonwealth awards was £3 8s—73 per cent of the *Harvester* standard and 59 per cent of the Royal Commission's. Subsequently, Piddington (still advised by Sutcliffe) said that the prevalent basic wage under Commonwealth awards at the date of the report was £3 17s (Piddington 1921, p. 6). Piddington also wrote that the 1907 equivalent of the Royal Commission's standard, in Melbourne, was £2 13s 8d (p. 13). As we saw earlier, the evidence of household budgets in *Harvester* pointed to an amount of this order, but Higgins unsurprisingly sidestepped the evidence to 'award' £2 2s. On the basis of rates then in force, both within and outside the agricultural implement industry, the higher amount would have been an unrealistic wage for the unskilled labourer. But the truth of the matter is that Higgins did not conduct a serious inquiry into 'the normal needs of the average employee'. The Royal Commission did just that.

In *The Next Step*, Piddington remarked: 'If it be objected that the standard of comfort determined by the Commission to be reasonable may be higher than that determined by the *Harvester* case, the answer is that no standard was determined in that case' (Piddington 1921, p. 14). This was a fair comment.

3.6.5 Wage adjustment

As the Royal Commission was directed to report on 'how the basic wage may be automatically adjusted to the rise and fall from time to time of the purchasing power of the sovereign', it was insufficient for it simply to determine an amount appropriate to the time of its report. A way must be found of altering the basic wage automatically to offset variations in the cost of living. This required, in practice, (1) a price index that measured the changes in the cost of the regimen of goods and services that constituted the Royal Commission's basic wage, and (2) a method of using that index to adjust the wage automatically.

The A series index, on which the Court had relied since 1913, comprised 47 items, limited to food, groceries and rent. Although the Commonwealth Statistician had not developed the index for use in wage adjustment, he and his officers (especially Sutcliffe) gave much help to both the Court and State tribunals in their efforts to interpret and to apply it. As Higgins and Powers recognised, decisions about the basic wage that were based on the index might over-compensate or under-compensate for price changes if the prices of items within the index had risen at greater or lesser rates than those excluded. The unrepresented items were categorised as 'clothing' and 'miscellaneous'. As we have seen, the Royal Commission's regimen not only extended the food and groceries list and specified a standard for housing; it also contained clothing and miscellaneous items. The Commission collected information about the prices of items in its regimen between 1914 and 1920. These were annual data, but a beginning-and-end comparison (for Melbourne) shows that over the six years, when the average increase in prices was 72 per cent, the component increases were: rent, 26 per cent; food, 103 per cent; clothing, 82 per cent; and miscellaneous, 62 per cent. Rent and food together rose by 71 per cent (Royal Commission 1921, p. 102). By chance, therefore, there was little difference between the broad index and one confined to rent and food. But within the six years, there were periods when they diverged significantly. If the goal were to measure as accurately as possible the changes in *the* cost of living, the more comprehensive index was to be preferred.

For the ongoing collection of the necessary data, the Commission proposed that a Bureau be created within the Commonwealth Statistician's Office. It would be organised from existing members of the Public Service and 'should ascertain from time to time the rise or fall in the purchasing power of the sovereign in relation to the reasonable standards of comfort' of the family defined in the letters patent (Royal Commission 1920, p. 55). The hand of Sutcliffe may be discerned in this suggestion. The Commission pointed to the role of the United States Bureau of Labor Statistics within the Department of Labor and emphasised that it was not recommending for Australia the creation of a separate department. Despite Hughes' refusal to adopt the Commission's main recommendation, the Secretary of his department advised Piddington that 'on the subject of the organisation from existing Public Service of a Bureau of Labour Statistics to undertake the work of adjustment of the basic wage to the cost of living, I am directed to inform you that arrangements are being made to give effect to the recommendations of the Commission, and that the Commonwealth Statistician is being consulted as to the methods to be followed in this connection' (Royal Commission 1921, p. 97).

I have referred in Section 3.3 to the delays in the adjustment of the basic wage inherent in the procedures adopted by Higgins and Powers. Because there was no single basic wage, we cannot specify the effects of these delays on *the* basic wage. To illustrate their significance, however, let us assume that at any point of time the wage was, on average, two years out of date. This assumption seems conservative. If we suppose that the basic wage for the last quarter of 1916 corresponded to the *Harvester* standard adjusted to the price level of the last quarter of 1914, the shortfall (in Melbourne) was 14 per cent. Moving forward by years, we have a 'surplus' in 1917 of 1 per cent (prices being slightly less than at the end of 1915); a deficiency in 1918 of 7 per cent; in 1919, 16 per cent; and in 1920, 27 per cent.[31] Discrepancies such as these lend a degree of unreality to the prevailing debates about the adequacy of the *Harvester* 'standard': had that standard actually been achieved, the living standards of the basic wage-earner and his family would have been materially higher. D T Sawkins later wrote:

> The deputy Industrial Registrar of the Commonwealth Court has courteously provided a tabulation of the basic rates of Commonwealth awards current at 1st November, 1920, as an example. It appears that the basic rates in force at that date (all being 'equivalents' of the '*Harvester*' finding) ranged from £2 11s to £4 2s, and averaged £3 7s 3d, or nearly 15s less per week than the latest awarded '*Harvester*' equivalent. (Sawkins 1933, p. 19)

The Commission recommended quarterly adjustments. A quarter, it said, was 'an interval which will reduce to a not substantial figure the risk of the wage-earner being paid too little'. It was necessary, however, 'that the adjustment should take place upon a system which recognises the seasonal character of the fluctuations in price of staple commodities'. Hence the wage adjustment should be based on the cost of living data for the previous year: 'thus the declaration to be made in November 1921 would be based on the average of the cost of living determinations at November 1920, February 1921, May 1921, August 1921' (Royal Commission 1920, p. 56). This would remove the seasonal effects thought to be present in quarter-by-quarter changes in prices. But the basic wage would still lag prices (on average) by more than half a year—a point of arithmetic on which the Commission did not comment.

3.6.6 The Piddington standard

Piddington, noting that the 'prevalent' basic wage was two-thirds of the recommended amount, wrote:

---

[31] Divergences computed from a table in Royal Commission (1921, p. 104).

> In other words, all families with three children are receiving only two-thirds of what is necessary according to current human standards. Let the reader turn to the summary of the Commission's Indicator lists as to Food and Clothing, and take two-thirds of the stated quantities and then, using his own knowledge of family needs, say whether a reasonable standard of comfort can possibly be enjoyed on such quantities. Could a family of five even satisfy hunger with two-thirds of the dietary set out? (Piddington 1921, p. 6)

That the Royal Commission's basic wage differed so far from current reality was open to several responses (or a combination of them):

- Its standards were excessive.
- The family unit prescribed in the letters patent was unrealistic.
- Whatever the merits of the Commission's finding, the Australian economy simply could not meet it.

I refer here to the first of these points, the others being discussed later.

The notion of a benchmark living standard is disputable because of the arbitrary and subjective judgments involved in it. All such benchmarks, including modern poverty lines, are open to this objection. That said, it is of interest to consider the kind of living standard that Piddington implied. Would most regard it as reasonable or as luxurious? That question is obviously time-dependent: the perspective of 2013 is not that of 1921. Yet the following comments are to the point.

First, the report was unanimous as to the requirements of reasonable comfort. This meant that the finding (though not the policy consequence) carried the support of three employer and three employee representatives, as well as that of the Chairman. Those familiar with the workings of such committees will know that 'unanimous' recommendations commonly entail compromises. Nevertheless, we may infer that Commission members with divergent backgrounds were broadly persuaded that the standard was indeed one of reasonable comfort by contemporary standards.[32]

---

[32] Two of the employer members, Keep and Gilfillan, though signatories to the main report,

Second, the regimen adopted by the Commission was detailed and evinced a great deal of consideration.

Third, it was similar to that used in the Washington survey of Dr Meeker (Piddington 1921, p. 9).

Fourth, a reading of the report does not suggest that the Commission was 'soft' in its attitude to union claims.[33]

Fifth, one can scrutinise the items approved and those rejected so as to judge whether 'needs' were defined at luxury levels. This is a difficult area of judgment. Some of the quantities may, indeed, seem excessive. Did the family really need each week 5½ pounds of sugar, 2 pounds of jam, 2 pounds of butter, and 8 pounds of beef? (But it must be remembered that these food items were within an overall calorie limit, so that less of one item would have entailed more of others.) Some critics (including, as we shall see, Powers) criticised the clothing 'requirements' specified in the Report; and the all-male Commission's assessments of women's clothing needs did not escape ridicule. On the other hand, the absence of any provision for church and charity or for alcohol and soft drink seems to border on the frugal.

Finally, the Commission (in its supplementary report) noted that 'Mr H [sic] F Giblin, the Government Statist of Tasmania, in his Budget Inquiry in 1920 also selected families who were known to be workers living in reasonable comfort with thrifty management, and that his finding for Hobart in August, 1920, was £6 per week.'

These considerations suggest that the Piddington standard was *not* extravagant for the family unit to which it related.

---

tendered a memorandum of dissent going to two issues: (1) an implication which they discerned in the majority report, that the amount determined should be enforced as the basic wage; and (2) the finding that the basic wage awarded by the Court from time to time, and especially in 1914, did not provide a reasonable standard of comfort (Royal Commission 1920, pp. 61–62). It is difficult to reconcile the latter point of dissent with Keep and Gilfillan's endorsement of the main finding.

[33] The unions had claimed sums ranging from £10 16s in Brisbane to £11 13s 6d in Hobart.

3.6.7 Implementation?

As the Royal Commission's deliberations drew to a close, there was, apparently, some expectation of a recommendation that might embarrass Hughes. On 16 November, the Leader of the Opposition sought an assurance that the recommendation, once received, would be promptly put into effect.[34] Hughes was equivocal:

> May I remind honourable members opposite that when I put forward this proposal for a Commission at the election, they sneered at it? They had a quite different way of getting into the Kingdom of Heaven. But they have lost the keys to their paradise; they now say that this Commission is the thing to save Sodom and Gomorrah. When I receive the report, and it has been considered by my colleagues, I shall state the intention of the Government; more than that I cannot say. (Whillier 1977, p. 56)

Hughes, in all likelihood, foresaw the problem that lay ahead. Having received the report from the Governor-General on Sunday 21 November, he immediately summoned Knibbs, the Commonwealth Statistician. On the next day, Knibbs supplied a Confidential Memorandum asserting that the implementation of the Royal Commission's basic wage was impossible, for wages would then exceed the total value added by industries. Hughes thereupon asked Piddington to submit a memorandum on a range of matters, including 'the effect upon industry, domestic and for foreign countries, of making a basic wage for all employees of £5 16s 0d' (Royal Commission 1920, p. 89).

Piddington answered that night: 'Having received your request at 5 pm to-day, there has been no opportunity to summon my colleagues to ascertain whether they desire to take part in the matter, therefore I do not sign this Memorandum as Chairman' (Royal Commission 1920, p. 93). Piddington

---

[34] Whether Hughes could have implemented the recommendations within the Commonwealth's constitutional powers (as then understood) is doubtful. Piddington's personal opinion was that he could. Any legal difficulty would, of course, have been obviated by the carriage of the 'Powers' referendum.

George Knibbs

provided arithmetic (possibly the work of Sutcliffe) showing the effect of attempting to enforce the Royal Commission's basic wage (p. 91). Assuming the present wage to be £4, allowing for an increase to £5 16s, and treating the increase as payable to 1,000,000 workers, he calculated the total cost as £93,000,000 per year. That amount, he said, represented 31 per cent of production in 1918, but the present percentage would be a little less because of the subsequent rise in prices. The effect on local prices would diminish the value of the wage increase; industries manufacturing for export would be ruined; and 'the increase in the price even of the products of our primary industries would before long be a formidable drawback to their development, and possibly to their continuance.' Hence Piddington endorsed the thrust of Knibbs' advice, if not its details (which were apparently not provided to him).

But the 1911 census showed that the dependants of the average male wage-earner were far fewer than the letters patent had postulated. Adjusting the 1911 numbers slightly, Piddington said that there were about one million male wage-earners in 1920. If each of these were paid at a level to maintain a wife and three children, then industries would be supporting 450,000 non-existent wives and 2,100,000 non-existent children. The true cost of living, therefore, was much less than the amount computed on the basis of a family of five.

He proposed a scheme that took this into account. The basic wage should be set for a man with a wife but *no* children. Piddington rejected any discounting of the wage for the non-existent wives. Every employee should receive enough to keep a man and wife '(1) because during bachelorhood, which ends, on the average for the whole Commonwealth, at the age of 20, ample opportunity should be provided to save up for equipping the home; (2) because a man should be able to marry and support a wife at an early age'. Children were different. Employers should pay a tax to the Commonwealth from which it would fund payments of child endowment. The specific amounts proposed were:

Basic wage	£4 00s
Endowment tax per worker	10s
Endowment per child aged 14 or under	12s

Thus a worker with three children would receive £5 16s, but the total payment that an employer would make in respect of a basic wage-earner would be only £4 10s (Royal Commission 1920, p. 90).

The idea of child endowment as a solution to the problems of varying family size was not novel. It was seen by some as a measure, not only of equity, but also of race survival—a response to prevalent concerns about the declining birth rate. A Member of the New South Wales Parliament had unsuccessfully proposed a scheme of endowment in 1916. After the 17s increase in the State living wage of 1919 (discussed above), the New South Wales Government proposed legislation to reduce the amount of increase and to institute endowment funded by employer contributions. The Bill (opposed by both employers and unions) was rejected by the Legislative Council (Graham 1995,

p. 87). Thus Piddington was suggesting a measure that already had both supporters and opponents.

When Hughes tabled the report on Tuesday 23 November, he said that the Government could not possibly advocate payment of the Commission's wage. This was, by the Chairman's own admission, impossible (Whillier 1977, pp. 57–58). But Piddington's endowment proposal had 'much to recommend it'. Three weeks later, Hughes introduced for the Public Service a scheme that provided a £4 basic wage plus 5s per child (funded by a 'tax' on Public Service salaries). Otherwise, nothing came of the proposal. Whillier reports that it was not generally supported. *The Bulletin* declared:

> If you are going to pay men according to their success as breeders and not according to their merits as workers there will be no inducement for a man to excel in his vocation … Australia has no time to waste on fancy schemes of this description. (Whillier 1977, pp. 61–62)

The endowment 'solution' was not supported by the unions, which focused their efforts on securing the implementation of the Royal Commission wage. They did not have access to Knibbs' memorandum, but focused their criticisms on Piddington's arithmetic. Knibbs, responding to a further inquiry by Hughes, lent some support to their criticisms, but again insisted on the impossibility of paying the Commission's wage (Whillier, p. 69). Piddington *had* erred. His error was to treat the £298 million as the value of *all* production in 1918. This sum did not include the value of services produced, although many of the workers were employed in service industries. Piddington should have used *either* a smaller amount than £93 million for the cost of the wage increase *or* a larger sum than $298 million for the value of production. (An intriguing question is whether Sutcliffe was implicated in the mistake.) Knibbs confined his calculations to manufacturing and coal. If the whole of the interest and profit of manufacturing industry had been diverted to paying the basic wage, the maximum amount payable would have been £5 13s 10d; and similar reasoning for coal yielded a sum of £5 5s 7d. Thus the payment of £5 16s to every adult male wage-earner was impossible. 'The only way by which such a standard of comfort can be attained by the wage-earning class,' said Knibbs, 'is

142 *Australian Wage Policy*

by increase in the production per worker, either (a) by improved organisation, (b) by increased effort on the part of the wage-earners, or (c) by both improved organisation and increased effort.'[35]

Child endowment was a recurrent issue in federal and State politics at the federal and State levels in the 1920s.[36] In the years 1925–29, it was at the heart of political disputation in New South Wales, with Piddington himself—a judge in the State system—a major actor (Graham 1995, chapters 8 and 9). Commonwealth child endowment was eventually introduced—with a view to averting a basic wage increase—in 1941.

3.7 The Court's response to the Royal Commission

The first reference in a Court decision to the Royal Commission was made by Powers, who said in November 1919: 'I have already stated that I propose—until my finding in the Public Service (living wage) case is proved by evidence or by the findings of the proposed "Living Wage Commission" to be incorrect—to be guided by the decision I arrived at in that case' (*Tanners and Leather-Dressers*' case 13 CAR 803, 805)[37] Higgins' first comment was made in December 1919 in the *AWU* case (13 CAR 823). He referred to the uncertainties of the miscellaneous items (including clothing) in household needs:

> There is, certainly, an urgent need for a scientific study of the miscellaneous items; but a Royal Commission composed of representatives of employers and employees is not a suitable body for such a study. Such a Commission is to be appointed for Australia, as I understand from the newspapers. The intention is good, and

---

[35] Knibbs' reasoning and comments are contained in documents in the Commonwealth Archives Office, CRS.A40, Item E5/2/–.

[36] Graham (1995, p. 88) writes that Hughes attributed his non-adoption of Piddington's scheme to the failure of the Powers Referendum. His election promise had, he claimed, been premised upon its passage. Piddington twice (in 1921 and 1922) ran unsuccessfully for election to the federal parliament to press the case for child endowment. In 1922, his sole opponent was Hughes (Graham 1995, pp. 94–99).

[37] This was one of the numerous cases in which the Court relied on Sutcliffe's evidence in allowing for price levels and changes.

the Commission may achieve indirectly some useful results; but one might as reasonably throw the question of the influence of gravity on light as a bone to be fought for in a Commission of employers and employees as leave to such a Commission the scientific question as to the miscellaneous expenditure. It would be even safer; for on such a subject as the cost of living members would be only too liable to be swayed by affiliations and sympathies; and the result—perhaps by majority vote or by compromise—will be, at the best, only another big guess. A cold and neutral inquiry made by competent statisticians on various defined bases of living and of regimen is the thing needed; and to the industrial tribunals should be left the responsibility of fixing the wages on the result of the inquiry. (pp. 841–842)

Viewed against his pronouncements in favour of an inquiry to fix a living wage, this commentary tends to confirm that Higgins really wanted to remain 'in charge' of the principles of wage-setting and was jealous of other contenders for the role. He had made a like comment in an article written for the *Harvard Law Review*, published in December 1920 and reprinted in *A New Province for Law and Order* (Higgins 1922, pp. 94–95).

During the currency of the Royal Commission, the Court adhered to its existing practices in setting the basic wage. Higgins continued to rely upon the 1907 decision and to 'update' it by means of the Statistician's price index averaged for the previous calendar year. The reference wage used by Powers was the amount set in his *Public Service* decision of 1918, discussed in Subsection 3.3.3.[38] A problem noted by both Higgins and Powers was that in some instances the rise in prices implied a basic wage that the Court could not grant, because it would exceed the ambit of the unions' plaints. This, of course, was a further reason why the Court's basic wage might fall below the *Harvester* standard. In the *Chemical and Fertiliser* case, Powers reported that many of the employers had agreed to comply with the amount that he set as an 'ordinary arbitrator', but that some employers would exercise their legal right

---

[38] Powers left the Court in April and was replaced in May by Mr Justice Starke. Although Starke made important decisions, he attempted no innovation affecting the basic wage.

to pay 6s per week less (14 CAR 161, 164). When the AWU sought variations of the Pastoral Award, Higgins said that he could not fully match the rise in the cost of living because 'according to the decisions of the Full High Court, the award must not exceed the original claim, under any circumstances' (14 CAR 386, 389).

Not surprisingly, unions asked the Court to adopt the Piddington wage. The principal discussion of the issue was in a case decided by Powers after his return to the Court and discussed in Chapter 6. Higgins considered the issue in the *ASE* case, decided in May 1921—the month before his departure from the Court (15 CAR 297, 302–306). Because of his role in the history of the basic wage, and especially in embedding the criterion of family need, his response to Piddington is of interest and importance. His principal objection to the Commission's finding was its failure to propose an amount specific to the basic wage-earner. For this, he blamed the letters patent, relishing, perhaps, the opportunity for an implied 'dig' at Hughes. 'I had hoped', he said,

> that I should get further illumination as to the absolute existing cost of living from what is called the Basic Wage Commission, created by the Federal Government; but my hope has not been fulfilled. What the Commissioners have reported is not a 'basic wage' at all. This is the result of the faulty drafting of the commission under which they acted ... There is no mention in clause 1 of a basic wage, or of the wage relation at all; no mention of employees, and no distinction between skilled employees and unskilled. Yet there is no 'wage' without employment, and no 'basic wage' unless a higher class of employees, entitled to higher pay, a higher standard of life, be assumed. There is no meaning in 'basic' except in relation to something higher. (pp. 302–303)

He went on to say that, not liking to quote himself (a reticence not hitherto obvious), he endorsed a dictum of Heydon that 'the living wage must relate to the humblest class of worker'. Referring to the Royal Commission's intimation that, in relation to items other than clothing, no one had contended that the requirements of reasonable comfort were affected by the worker's level of skill, Higgins said:

> Probably such a contention was not raised because the words of the Commission preclude it; and as a result the finding is a finding of what the Commissioners think to be a proper standard of living for a man with a wife and three children, whether the man is a messenger or a roll-turner, a millionaire or a street sweeper. Such a finding is of no use to this Court for immediate purposes. (p. 303)

He desired it to be understood that he did not dissent from the Commissioners' finding 'under the terms of their commission'.

What was necessary, said Higgins, was a properly directed inquiry; for 'the evidence on which the [*Harvester*] judgment was given was very meagre, and should be supplemented by an up-to-date inquiry—preferably of statisticians, on cool scientific lines—as to the present appropriate basic wage'. The terms of the letters patent should have been more carefully weighed.

> On a matter so vitally affecting the working of this Court, the psychology of industrial employees, industrial peace, and society as a whole, it is not, I hope, too much to say that my brother Powers or myself should have been consulted before the language of the letters patent was adopted. (p. 304)

It would be better 'for all parties—union and employers—to begin again and to press for an inquiry which will replace the *Harvester* finding on scientific lines, rather than to press for payment of this so-called "basic wage" of the Commission, which is not a true basic wage, but a will o' the wisp that will lead them into the ditch'.

Higgins observed, 'in justice to the Commissioners', that they had not recommended payment of £5 16s. The Commonwealth Statistician had reported that to pay such a wage would more than exhaust the whole produced wealth of the country, including profits. 'There seems', said Higgins, 'to be a storm coming up, with widespread scarcity of employment, and it is wise to keep the moorings which we have until we make certain of better.'

Notwithstanding the protestations of the unions, it was unrealistic to suppose that the Court would simply substitute the Piddington basic wage for the *Harvester* equivalent. What is indefensible, however, is Higgins' casuistry about the Royal Commission's letters patent. The members of the Royal Commission were well aware that their appointment stemmed from dissatisfaction with the basic wage; theirs was no mere abstract inquiry. As we have seen, the Commission explicitly discussed the question whether the amount needed to afford reasonable comfort was affected by the employee's level of skill, the issue having also been highlighted by the employers' abortive deputation to Hughes. 'Reasonable standards of comfort' is obviously a nebulous concept, but it was not nonsensical to identify needs that were common to workers of diverse skills. Meeting them was another matter: perhaps they were unachievable for the unskilled workers, who therefore could not live in reasonable comfort; perhaps they were achievable and the skilled worker could have something more. The Royal Commission said, and meant to say, that *any* worker with a wife and three children needed £5 16s (in Melbourne) to have a reasonable standard of comfort. In its supplementary report of April 1921, the Commission said:

> It remains only to add that between the theoretical basis of the standard which this Commission has determined and the standard as defined in the *Harvester* Case there is no difference. The term used in the letters patent was 'reasonable standards of comfort, including all matters comprised in the ordinary expenditure of the household for a man with a wife and three children under 14 years of age.' The standard as defined in the *Harvester* Case is 'the normal needs of the average employee regarded as a human being living in a civilised community.' … [T]his Commission has throughout its task considered that 'the normal needs of the average employee regarded as a human being living in a civilised community' are exactly paraphrased in the letters patent by the term 'reasonable standards of comfort,' the word 'man' being used as

the equivalent of the words average employee …' (Royal Commission 1921, p. 106)

Here, surely, was an unambiguous finding that the *Harvester* standard was insufficient *for its avowed purpose*. Though it was published about a month before Higgins delivered his decision in the *ASE* case, he did not refer to it.

For the Court, there were several responses that would have been logically defensible. One was to quarrel with the finding itself. The subjectivity of 'reasonable comfort' and 'need' left room for a regimen different from that selected by the Commission. For this, however, the crudeness of *Harvester* was a problem. There is no comparison between the levels of sophistication of Higgins' and the Royal Commission's estimates. Another was to abandon the needs criterion and simply to portray the basic wage as an amount that could realistically be provided for the unskilled worker—an assessment that would have regard to the income of the society and other claims upon it. A combination of these responses would have been to accept the Commission's standard as an aspiration, to find that it was not achievable, but to consider what movement (if any) might be made toward it. Finally, the Court might, in the spirit if not the letter of Piddington's personal response, have revised the family size to which the basic wage was ostensibly related without altering its amount. That Higgins chose none of these responses, but focused on the letters patent, was not to his credit.

He was, however, correct in observing that the appointment, deliberations, and report of the Royal Commission had given rise to expectations that were likely to be disappointed. From that perspective, the creation of the Commission was a mistake. But although the unions condemned the Court's rejection of the Piddington wage (Whillier 1977, pp. 69–70), little or nothing came of their discontent. The economic conditions of 1921 are a likely cause. Rising unemployment and a stiffening of employer resistance as prices fell were not conducive to either an increase in industrial action or abandonment of arbitration.

3.8 HARVESTER AND FAMILY NEEDS

The Royal Commission had shown that *Harvester* did not meet the needs of a family of five. Its analysis, though inevitably subjective, was far more sophisticated than any that had been attempted (or would in the future be attempted) by the Court. Higgins and Powers insisted, nevertheless, on the relevance of the *Harvester* basic wage to the needs of the family of five. Certainly, there were compelling reasons for not adopting the Commission's standard. But these were reasons of economic possibility and expedience. In addition to the issue raised by Knibbs and Piddington himself, namely whether the productive capacity of the economy would support the higher standard—and the depressed state of the economy in 1921—there was then under way the remarkable increase in real wages generated by an unintended change in the relation between nominal wages and prices. An attempt by the Court to impose a further increase of, say, 40 per cent, would have had dire economic consequences, or broken the federal arbitration system, or both.

Yet the notion that the *Harvester* wage was grounded in family needs stood exposed as a fiction. But it was an influential fiction. As late as 1970, the researchers into Melbourne poverty set a poverty line (for 1966) of $33 for a man, non-working wife, and two children. This amount was the basic wage plus child endowment. Their book explains:

> This is a definition of poverty so austere as, we believe, to make it unchallengeable. ... We chose this basic-wage content of the poverty line because of its relevance to Australian concepts of living standards—the basic wage being the lowest wage which can be paid to an unskilled labourer on the basis of, in the famous words of Mr Justice Higgins, 'the normal needs of an average employee regarded as a human being living in a civilised community'.[39] (Henderson, Harcourt, and Harper 1970, p. 1)

The 'Henderson' poverty line was adopted by the Australian Government Commission of Inquiry into Poverty (1975) and, with subsequent

---
[39] A footnote records that the quoted passage was written by R I Downing.

adjustments for prices and earnings, remains the official poverty line today. But its original justification was neither more nor less than that set out in the above quotation.[40] The Royal Commission, on the other hand, made a serious attempt to measure needs. Adjusting its finding to a smaller family unit, which the letters patent precluded, would have brought its conclusion much more into line with economic reality. If Australia were to have a poverty line, an inquiry replicating its techniques (but taking account of changed consumption patterns) was surely appropriate.

---

[40] 'We should like to emphasise the importance of giving assistance first to those at the bottom of the ranking. To try to ensure that our recommendations have this effect we have drawn our "poverty line" at an austere low level—the same level as that in the Melbourne 1966 survey, updated by average earnings since then. It cannot seriously be argued that those below this austere line, whom we describe as "very poor", are not so' (Australian Government Commission of Inquiry into Poverty 1975, p. 13).

4

Broadening the scope of wage policy

•———•

The issues demanding the arbitrators' consideration were not, of course, confined to the basic wage (however termed). This chapter surveys the policies that emerged in other areas.

4.1 Wage differentials

The setting of rates above the basic wage was dominated by four practices. First, the Federal Court's usual approach, in its initial setting of rates, was to add to the basic wage amounts equal to the differences—proportional or absolute—previously established in the market or by wages boards.[1] Second, these amounts were not adjusted thereafter for movements in prices. Third, although there was little attempt to determine independently the 'value' of jobs, the Court did, on various grounds, fix amounts modestly above the basic wage for some that had hitherto been regarded as unskilled. This meant that the relevant classification would be awarded a wage that was slotted in between the basic wage and the tradesman's rate. Fourth, whereas the living wage was 'sacrosanct', additional payments might be set at lower levels than otherwise if the Court were persuaded that industries needed relief from the burden of labour costs. The cases discussed in this section illustrate these practices.

---

[1] Higgins (writing in 1915) said in *A New Province for Law and Order* (1922, p. 7): 'The secondary wage, as far as possible, preserves the old margin between the unskilled labourer and the employee of the skilled or exceptional class.'

In the *Harvester* hearing, Higgins made it clear that he intended not merely to answer 'yes' or 'no' to the question whether McKay's were paying fair and reasonable wages, but to lay down a scale of rates for the guidance of both McKay's and other applicant employers. The other employers would bear the onus of showing that the scale should not apply to them. During Duffy's submissions, the following exchange occurred:

> His Honour: I think I can speak freely to you with regard to the skill. It is very much a matter of opinion and it is also a matter of custom and the employers. If you once fix your datum point, the unskilled labourer, then may I not lean with confidence upon the ratios fixed by the wages board decisions in the other industries which have these trades?
>
> Mr Duffy: I should think you could.
>
> His Honour: I think it will save a great deal of trouble. (transcript, p. 333)

The guidance that Higgins had from the evidence is illustrated by the statement of Henry William Goodall:

> I am a correspondence clerk in the Metropolitan Board of Works. I am acquainted with the wages paid by the Board to its employees. I produce a list showing the particular classes of labour I understood I should be asked about. Labourers unskilled receive 7s a day. That is the minimum. Blacksmiths 10s, engine fitters 10s, carpenters 10s, sewerage plumbers 10s, water supply plumbers 9s, and painters 8s per day … (pp. 402–403)

Towards the end of the hearing, Higgins said:

> I can assure you that if I make any standard I shall not follow my own judgment—imperfect as it is. I shall follow more the opinions of those who have worked in the trade, who have discussed the necessary wages, and who know the ratios on which the men should be paid. I have got far more trust in that than I have in my own judgment. … Take the unskilled labourer, and the cost of living—that is one thing. Take the other men who are paid by recognised standards fixed by the wages

boards and unions—that is another thing.[2] That will guide me in my judgment. I have no means in the time given me to go into the interests of those twenty trades in order to find out what degree of skill is required for each. (p. 622)

There was, in fact, little discussion of skill differentials, but a great deal about McKay's practice of paying below the recognised tradesmen's rates by classifying men as 'improvers'.

The idea that existing differentials should generally be accepted flowed through into early awards. In his first award, for marine cooks, bakers and butchers (2 CAR 55), Higgins adopted the *Harvester* standard for the base grade—sculleryman—and for most other grades continued existing absolute differences.

In the 1911 *BHP* case, however, this practice was challenged. Higgins was called upon to deal with an employer that had not subscribed to an agreement between the union and other mining companies (3 CAR 32). The BHP Company's Broken Hill mine was fast becoming uneconomic. Higgins laid down three rules that had an enduring effect. First, the wages fixed must include the *Harvester* wage as the least permissible rate. Second, the condition of an *industry* might be taken into account in fixing the rates for higher grades of labour; for example, skilled workers might get less than their proper wages so as to safeguard employment. Finally, payment of less than the proper wages should not be sanctioned on account of the difficulties of a particular employer.

In the *Telegraphic Linesmen's* case of 1914 (8 CAR 119), Higgins said that the linesmen were 'not to be treated either as skilled artisans or as unskilled labourers'. Accordingly, they should receive more than the basic wage and less than the artisan's wage. In this case, Higgins also stipulated that the rate to be paid should reflect the highest functions that the employee was required to perform. 'Otherwise', he said, 'every wages board determination may be evaded.' He explained:

---

[2] Unions were sometimes able to enforce 'union rates'. They did so by binding their members not to accept less than these rates. Obviously, the practice was confined to unions of skilled workers.

> For instance, a skilled plumber may be out of work and in sore need; he may be offered a job by the employer as a labourer for several weeks, at a labourer's wage, with the stipulation that he is to do plumbing work if and when required. It would be extraordinary if the employer could get his plumbing work done by this man at a labourer's rate, and defeat a prosecution on the ground that the man was hired as a labourer. If the employer choose to use a skilled plumber to do labouring work as well, he must pay for the luxury. (p. 129)

The 'highest function' rule became standard arbitral practice.

Powers, in the *Tanners and Leather Dressers'* case of 1914 (8 CAR 145), acquiesced in the wage differences fixed in determinations of wages boards. 'The amounts to be fixed for skill over and above the living wage is not so difficult to decide', he said, 'because the respondents, in all the States except South Australia, admitted that the amounts allowed in the Boards' Awards over and above the living wage, in their opinion, represented the differences in the work done by the different employees' (p. 166). Included in the rates so set was one of 52s per week for limejobbers, compared with 51s for labourers. The differential of 1s was supported by a Queensland wages board decision, evidence tendered about the United States and the fact that limejobbers were generally selected as the class from which men moved to higher rates (p. 162).

In the *Mining Employees'* case of 1915 (9 CAR 330), Powers said that in determining classification rates for skill he proposed to follow 'the rule laid down by the learned President' in the *BHP* case, when Higgins said that 'the relative values of the different classes of workers may generally be safely left to the practice of the employers and the employed' (p. 358). Higgins himself invoked the 'rule' in the *BHP* case of 1916 (10 CAR 155): 'The minimum wage for those who now get more than the basic wage—artisans, furnacemen, and others—I fix … by adding to the new basic wage the old margin for skill or other necessary exceptional qualities' (p. 193).

The pre-war and wartime inflation obviously affected both the real value of the skill differential and its proportional relation with the basic wage. Surprisingly, this did not become a significant issue in the Court before 1916: unions, apparently, acquiesced in the mere continuance of the previous absolute differentials. Higgins dealt with the question, however, in his decision of June 1916 in the *Merchant Service* case (10 CAR 214). 'It may fairly be urged', he said,

> that, in the absence of evidence to the contrary, the decrease in the value of the sovereign must be treated as applying to all the commodities required by a man in the position of an officer as well as to the commodities required for a family's support on a labourer's standard of living; and it is quite true that the pressure of social forces makes the extra expenditure for the officer almost as essential for him as the labourer's expenditure for the labourer. But the fact remains that it is not so absolutely essential; and in a time of violent disturbance of prices such as the present, in a time when war has combined with the drought of 1914–1915 to produce the rather alarming figures for 1915 on which I have to act, I do not think it advisable, in framing an Award for three or five years to come, to push principles to an extreme. (p. 226)

Higgins increased the monthly salary of each grade by £3. 'Probably some of the more highly paid masters', he said, 'will think the increase too small in their cases; but I have explained my reasons, and if we should hereafter reach the haven of settled times, their claims will have to be further considered' (p. 227). The implication that the 'freeze' on differentials was temporary, to be reconsidered in 'settled times', was to create problems for the Court after the war.

In the *Meat Industry* decision of September 1916 (10 CAR 465), Higgins retained the existing margin for slaughtermen. This was 'not ideally just', because the increase in the cost of living affected 'the additional commodities which convention and social habits dictate for the skilled worker'. But these were abnormal times; and whereas it was necessary 'to secure to the labourer sufficient wages to keep himself and his family in healthy sufficiency', it was 'by no means so imperatively necessary to secure to the skilled worker to the full extent all the other commodities to which he has been accustomed'.

Nevertheless, the absolute margin had to be preserved. 'I must do nothing', said Higgins,

> to diminish the recognised margin between the man of skill and the man without skill. It would be a fatuous step, on the part of this Court, to lessen the inducement to learn a trade, to attain superior skill and efficiency. Not only would it invite industrial discontent and unrest—and industrial peace is the objective of this Court; but it would encourage the employment of men in work for which they are not fully qualified, and foster the too prevalent tendency to be content with what is 'good enough'—to be content with imperfect workmanship. (p. 485)

It does not seem to have occurred to Higgins that the diminishing *real* value of the margin for skill did indeed 'lessen the inducement to learn a trade, to attain superior skill and efficiency'.

Higgins took a similar stance in the *Postal Electricians'* case, decided in September 1916 (10 CAR 578). And in the *Pastoral* case of 1917 (11 CAR 389) the increases that he granted in shearing rates represented a notional adjustment of the basic wage component only. In April 1918, he gave a decision affecting 343 senior employees in the public service (12 CAR 114). 'The Australian communities', he said,

> have earned for themselves a good name in the world by insisting that every labourer shall have enough wages wherewith to provide for himself and a family the essentials for a healthful existence; but the fact that a man has secured himself enough for these essentials is not an adequate reason for refusing to him the extra reward which induces men to face the drudgery of study and close application. In an ideal world it may be otherwise; but in the world as it is we cannot hope for a perpetual flow of highly trained men for the King's services which involve laborious training without reasonable reward for that training. (p. 125)

'In the stress of the present war', however, he had generally refused to increase the skill margin 'on the ground of the increase in prices, the depreciation in the value of money'; and he would do the same in this case (p. 126).

In the *Coopers'* case (12 CAR 427), decided in September 1918, Higgins again acknowledged that holding margins constant was 'not strictly logical'. But it was a moderate course to take, and it had the assent of the unions. 'The war', said Higgins,

> causes suffering everywhere, deprivation nearly everywhere; and the extra commodities purchasable by the secondary wage are not so vital to healthy, fully nourished life as the commodities to which the basic wage is to be appropriated. The basic wage, which is meant to secure the proper sustenance of the children, the future citizens, must be provided at all costs; anything, everything must be cut down before the basic wage. (p. 428)

Higgins foreshadowed a change of course in an *Engineers'* case of 1920 related to Broken Hill and Port Pirie (14 CAR 22). If the 10s fitter's rate was appropriate when the basic wage was 7s per day, then 'if the 7s man has to be raised to 12s, the 10s man ought, *prima facie*, to be raised to about 17s'. This implied a fitter's margin of 5s. In fact, the margin remained at 3s. The reason for the discrepancy', Higgins said,

> is that, during the war, I thought it proper, under the very special circumstances, not to apply the increase in the cost of living to the secondary wage, but only to the basic wage; at the same time preserving the secondary wage which I found to have prevailed in practice, 3s. ... It is only fair to say that the skilled unions which appeared before me accepted the position, as it seemed to me, patriotically, under the pressure of the great national emergency. These skilled men, and their families, certainly suffered ... The question is now, should this sacrifice be continued indefinitely? It is very important for our industries that the lads (and their parents) should feel it to be worth the trouble to learn crafts and to learn them thoroughly. ... During the course of the discussion in this case I stated, and I now repeat, that my mind is strongly inclined in favour of now granting the relief which these highly skilled artisans seek—at least to the extent of making the secondary wage 4s instead of 3s per day. (pp. 25–26)

Because the case was limited to the two towns, Higgins deferred any increase until other employers had the opportunity to put arguments to the Court. On the same day that Higgins gave this decision, Powers gave one for *Letter Carriers* continuing the existing policy (14 CAR 40).

> In the *Harvard Law Review* for December 1920, Higgins wrote:
>
> During the violent financial upheaval caused by the Great War, and because of the widespread uncertainty as to what would follow, the Court has not increased the secondary wage in proportion to the increased cost of living; it has merely maintained the same absolute margin ... Now that the war has ended, the question arises whether this cautious and conservative course should still be followed; but as the subject is to be discussed at an early date I refrain from further comment. (Higgins 1922, p. 98)

The first actual change came in the *Merchant Services* case, decided by Higgins in September 1920 (14 CAR 459). Referring back to his 1916 promise of a review when 'settled times' returned, Higgins said: 'Well, the war is over; and, although we cannot be said to have reached the desired haven in all respects, it would not be fair to withhold from these trained men their proper secondary wage for ever' (p. 465). Calculation of the increase was complicated by the need to allow for on-board keep; but the amount granted represented the increase necessary to restore the proportional relativity of 1907. For 'the proper wage must be restored if we are to keep up a succession of trained men for the merchant service—and if we are even to keep our men in Australia' (pp. 465–466).

In May 1921—only weeks before his already-announced resignation took effect—Higgins gave a decision that signified 'restoration' of margins to proper levels. This was a decision for *Engineers* (15 CAR 297). Higgins set out the background:

> During the war, as the cost of living was rising to a remarkable degree, I found it necessary to raise the basic wage in proportion to the decrease in the purchasing power of money; but, in the great uncertainty as to

the future, I thought it well not to raise the secondary wage. I left the secondary wage at 3s per day as in 1907. Yet this course was not strictly fair to the skilled workers ... The skilled men were really entitled to more than the 3s, but under the abnormal circumstances they accepted uncomplainingly the old margin of 3s. I promised, however, that when the war ended they should have restored to them the proper margin as represented in true wages, not nominal (Merchant Service Guild) [10 CAR 214, 226]; and in a case of the same guild, decided last year but not yet reported, I applied the Statistician's figures ... to the secondary wage as well as the basic ... If I adhere to the old margin of 3s per day, then the rate of unskilled to skilled, which was 7:10 in 1907, will be 14:17 in 1921. This is not fair play to the skilled worker, or likely to induce lads to undertake the burden of learning a craft. (pp. 306–307)

Higgins increased the tradesman's margin to 6s a day. He also expressed distaste for fine distinctions and for 'specialist' classifications below the tradesman's rate. He rejected a claim for an extra 6d per day for blacksmiths, which the union justified by their scarcity. Scarcity was no ground for prescribing a higher *minimum* wage, and the work of the blacksmith was not of itself worth more than that of the general tradesman (p 310). It was useless to resist the spread of specialisation under the pressure of competition, 'however injurious such specialisation may be to the employee as a man, however much it tends to monotony, to a sense of servitude to the machine, to industrial discontent' (p. 314). But this was no reason to pay the specialist less than the full tradesman: 'The best way to discourage the manufacture of imperfect tradesmen, and to prevent slavery to the machine, is to prescribe for them [machinists] the same minimum rate as for the full tradesman' (p. 315). But he was not free to act fully on this view, for the union in its claim had accepted lower rates for 'drillers, screwers, etc'; and the three grades of machinists in the award were there by union consent (p. 316). Thus Higgins' concept of a simple scale, containing few semi-skilled rates, was already eroded.

The first explicit challenge to the idea of restoring differentials in the post-war environment appears to be a decision of Starke in September 1920, in the *Commonwealth Railways'* case (14 CAR 496), given four days before Higgins decision in *Merchant Services'*. The unions argued for increases in margins commensurate with the increased cost of living. 'I see neither justice nor expediency in this contention', said Starke:

> It is asserted that the comparative standard of living will otherwise be affected, and to some extent the assertion is true. I say 'to some extent' advisedly, because the exercise of economy, so necessary in these times, will still enable the skilled workman to maintain the same standard of living without making the proportionate increase sought by their representatives. However, the proposition appears to me to overlook a vital point. The base wage, according to the settled doctrine of this Court, is fixed, in industrial concerns, to enable the unskilled workman to keep himself, a wife and three children in reasonable comfort without feeling the pinch of poverty. It has little or no relation to the value of his work. The cost of living determines this wage; but it does not or ought not determine the wage of the skilled workman. He is not on the poverty line. The value of the work of the skilled tradesman ought, in my opinion, to be the guiding principle in fixing his wage, though an increase in the cost of commodities must not be ignored as a factor in arriving at a just result. Furthermore, the wage of the skilled workman must be sufficiently high to induce men to acquire the necessary skill. I admit the difficulty of forming any accurate opinion of the value of work apart from the economic causes which, uncontrolled, regulate the rate of wages, but the Court is given that control and must do what it considers fair and just. (p. 569)

The implication was that the value of the skilled worker should not be assessed by harking back to the past.

The major repudiation of Higgins' post-war policy, however, came in Powers' decision of October 1921 in the *Engine Drivers'* case (15 CAR 883), which Chapter 6 discusses.

	Males	Females	Total	Female Proportion
I. Professional	6.6	17.2	8.7	39.7
II. Domestic	2.7	34.5	9.1	76.2
III. Commercial	14.9	17.2	15.3	22.4
IV. Transport & Communication	10.8	1.6	9.0	3.5
V. Industrial	32.6	25.6	31.2	16.4
VI. Primary Producers	31.7	2.2	25.8	1.7
VII. Independent	0.7	1.7	0.9	38.0
Total Breadwinners	100.0	100.0	100.0	20.0

Table 4.1: Gender composition of employment 1921 (per cent)
Source: *Commonwealth Yearbook*, vol. 16, 1923, pp. 950–951.

4.2 WAGE POLICY FOR FEMALE WORK

At the 1921 census, females were 20 per cent of all breadwinners. Table 4.1 shows the population of breadwinners as recorded by the census. Admittedly, the crude set of occupational classes allows only broad judgments to be made about the nature of women's work. The most instructive column is probably the last, except that the percentages shown there need to be read in the context of the earlier columns; for example, the high female component in the 'independent' class is unimportant when the overall size of this class is taken into account. The 'domestic' class, where females predominated, was unlikely (with few exceptions) to attract the jurisdiction of the Federal Court. The most promising areas were the 'professional', 'commercial', and 'industrial' classes. Obviously, these classes would need to be unpackaged to determine more reliably their potential for arbitral regulation. State tribunals had greater relevance to women employed in many areas, including teaching and the health services.

In the Commonwealth Court, issues of female employment arose in cases affecting fruitpicking, felthatting, journalists, clerical grades in the federal public service, telephonists, the clothing trades, marine stewards, and (to a small extent) hotels. The Court's decisions were sporadic; its principles and their application confused. They were given at a time when gender segregation of the workforce and marked differentiation in pay were widely accepted norms (Lee 1987).

The most famous of these cases was the *Fruitpickers'* case of 1912 (6 CAR 61), when Higgins first discussed the principles to be followed in setting female rates. It concerned fruit pickers and packers in the Mildura area. Higgins fixed hourly rates. Males received 1s per hour. In dealing with women, Higgins sought to distinguish between the circumstances in which women should receive the same amount and those in which they should get less. This led him to discuss two criteria—the requirements of a living wage and the protection of males against female competition. In fruitpicking itself, employers were likely to be indifferent at equal rates, and lower pay for females would jeopardise men's employment. Higgins set equal rates. Packing was different:

> I have had the advantage of seeing the women performing packing at a factory; and I have no doubt that the work is essentially adapted for women with their superior deftness and suppleness of fingers. The best test is, I suppose, if the employers had to pay the same wage to women as to men, they would always, or nearly always, employ the women (p. 72).

Packing, then, was women's work and competition with men was not an issue. A female rate was appropriate. In Higgins' view, his task was 'to find a fair minimum wage for these women, assuming that they have to find their own food, shelter, and clothing'. With little consideration as to what these needs actually were, he came to the conclusion that 'as the minimum for men and women pickers is to be fixed at 1s per hour, the minimum for women workers in these processes, in which men are hardly ever employed, should be fixed at 9d per hour' (p. 73). The implication was that women should be paid *less* than men if their skills were inherently *superior* for the task in question. I am not aware, however, that the Court again used this test to identify 'women's work'. That aspect of the decision may therefore be regarded as a curiosity. The more important implications were that a living wage for women should apply where women were doing women's work; that the women's living wage was less than men's; and that women should receive equal pay where they were in competition with men. The living wage differential was due to the presumption that women did not have the family responsibilities attributed to men. Higgins made no effort, in this case, to quantify the difference, and arbitrarily fixed a rate equal to three-quarters of the male rate.

In the *Felthatting* case (8 CAR 346), decided in September 1914, the union claimed a minimum wage for women of 30s. At the time, the basic wage for men in new awards was generally 54s. The employers argued for a female rate of 22s. Powers said that 'women as well as men are entitled to a "living wage" as defined by this Court, namely, "sufficient to provide proper food, shelter, rest, clothing, and a condition of frugal comfort estimated by current human standards"' (p. 376). He granted the 30s (56 per cent of the basic wage), saying that, in his view, the work done by women was worth this amount, whether or not it was a living wage. He does not seem to have considered the possibility that the living wage for a woman might be *more* than 30s—a defensible omission when he was granting the full amount of the union's claim.

Powers referred briefly to female pay in the *Public Service Clerks'* case (10 CAR 58), decided in April 1916. The respondents admitted the equal value of male and female work, and Powers awarded equal pay in the classifications without discussing the possibility of a lower living wage component in the women's rates.

Isaacs, serving temporarily as a Deputy President, made an award for journalists in April 1917 (11 CAR 67). With little comment, he noted that all provisions of the award applied to both sexes (p. 111). This, presumably, accorded with the practice of the trade. It could have been said, no doubt, that women were in competition with men.

Powers discussed the female living wage at greater length in May 1917, in the *Theatrical and Amusement Employees'* case (11 CAR 133):

> Before proceeding, I think it only right to mention that this Court has, since 1912, laid it down that women and men should be paid equal

> wages if women are employed to do a man's work—or where the work done by a woman is of as great a value as the man's work.
>
> It is only where the work in question is woman's work—suitable work for women—that the Court awards what it considers the value of the work as woman's work; or if the value is less than a living wage for a woman then it allows a living wage for a woman for a week's work. (pp. 145–146)

The 'principles' implied by this decision were, first, that the Court would identify the value of work. If this were work performed equally by men and women, its value would be assessed without regard to gender. If, however, it was 'woman's work', it would be assessed as such. Powers did not discuss why the value of the work might be affected by gender. Second, any assessment of value might be overridden by the primary requirement of the living wage. Third, the living wage for women differed from that for men. The problem with this formula—apart from the large issue of assessing 'value'—is that it did not describe the Court's practice. For the Court did *not* determine first the value of work—male or female—and then superimpose a living wage, but rather it *began* with the basic wage and added to it 'margins' related to skill and the circumstances of the work. Even if equal margins were awarded, the difference in the base rate would apply at all levels in the pay structure.

Powers did give thought to the amount that a woman needed to support herself. Under an agreement of 1913 that was still in effect, the women's wage was £1 5s. But, said Powers, the cost of living had increased,

> and board and lodging in reasonable comfort cannot now be obtained in Melbourne or Sydney at less than 17s a week. Tram fares to and from the city where most of the work is done, it is said, average 3s a week. These two items on an average cost about £1 a week without allowance for even a light lunch. At the present wage [of] £1 5s that would only leave 5s a week for clothes, laundry expenses, and the many other expenses that a woman must incur to live in reasonable comfort honestly. … On the evidence before me as to the increased cost of living and the greatly increased cost of clothes, I propose to fix £1 15s as

the minimum Federal wage for women working in the industry under existing circumstances for 48 hours. I know that is higher than has been allowed as a woman's minimum wage, but the war prices do not justify me in allowing less. (p. 146)

The basic wage being set for males at this time was around £3 3s. Once again, the minimum female rate was 56 per cent of the basic wage.

In October 1918, Powers awarded bonuses related to the cost of living to lower-paid male public servants. He did not grant them to females, because no argument had been advanced for doing so (12 CAR 531, 609). In another public service case, about female note sorters and others doing similar work in government departments, Powers observed that the work was 'admittedly work suitable for women'. The minimum rate—£110 per annum—was well below the minimum for males in the public service, but the employees' association 'did not contend that the wage paid to adult females employed as sorters and checkers was less than a living wage, or call any evidence to show that it was not [adequate for their living costs]' (13 CAR 69, 73).

Higgins in May 1919 returned to the question of the female living wage. This was in a *Clothing Trades* case (13 CAR 647). He awarded 65s—the amount claimed—as the basic wage for men. Referring back to *Fruitpickers*, he said that 'Mr B Seebohm Rowntree … takes practically the same view, that a woman's minimum rate in women's appropriate employments should not be a family rate'. After investigating the conditions of 516 women workers in York, and taking account of their responsibilities for dependants, Rowntree had estimated the appropriate post-war minimum rates as 44s for men and 25s for women. Applying the same ratio in the case before Higgins would give a female minimum rate of nearly 37s. The union had claimed £2. It produced some 'schedules of a few [seven] girls selected by the union officials', but this was unsatisfactory evidence. (Its similarity to the kind of evidence provided, at Higgins' urging, in *Harvester* is striking.) 'There is', said Higgins, 'no subject as to which more care is necessary in the collection of evidence than the subject of the cost of living, and there is no subject on which less care is used. … But I must do my best on the materials available' (p. 693). There was some guidance from decisions of President Jethro Brown in South Australia and the New South Wales Board of Trade; and the Superintendent of a Domestic Arts Hostel had given evidence about clothing costs. Higgins allowed 22s for lodging and 12s 6d for clothing. Without commenting on other needs, he fixed a minimum wage for women of 35s.

Thirty-five shillings was the amount awarded by Powers two years earlier in the *Theatrical and Amusement Employees'* case. In the interval, prices had risen about 12 per cent (March quarter numbers). The female minimum rate of 35s set by Higgins in *Clothing Trades* was 54 per cent of the male basic wage of 65s. Higgins noted that in *Fruitpickers'* the relativity was 75 per cent, but did not comment on his choice of a lower fraction in *Clothing Trades*. The 54 per cent relativity, which was to become the *de facto* standard until World War II, seems to have originated in the *Clothing Trades* case.

Higgins, in a further decision in the same case, given in October 1919, returned to the issue of gender-related pay differences. In the previous April, there was published in the United Kingdom a Cabinet Committee report on 'the relation which should be maintained between the wages of women and men'. The majority of the Committee held that 'women doing similar or the same work should receive equal pay for equal work in the sense that pay should be in proportion to efficient output'. Higgins commented:

> I confess that for the practical purpose of making an award in this case the attractive theory of paying according to 'efficient output' on time-work rates seems to be unworkable. It is surely much better to leave it to the employer to select the person, man or woman, who seems to him most suitable for the job, but at the same time-work rate. ... But it is important to notice that even this majority report does not favour a discrimination in wages on the mere ground of sex. The minority report of Mrs Sidney Webb is even more drastic. Mrs Webb ... asserts—'That for the production of commodities and services women no more constitute a class than do persons of a particular creed or race.' ... To my mind, Mrs Webb's conclusion is sounder for all practical purposes. The only difference between this lady's position and the position which

> I took up in the Fruit case is that I prescribed a lower minimum rate for women where they are engaged in what is distinctively women's work, such as millinery. This difference seems to be due to the fact that I approached the subject from a somewhat different point of view, and that I gave more effect to the fact that, normally, women have not such responsibilities for supporting a family as a man has. This is also the position taken up by Mr Seebohm Rowntree … But on the question of wages in this tailoring industry, where men and women are fairly in competition, where employers would even (as I am told) prefer men but for women having lower wages, there seems to be no difference between Mrs Webb's doctrine and the principle of the Fruit case. (pp. 703–704)

Higgins' portrayal of his own position as somehow akin to Beatrice Webb's is laughable. The very basis of the Court's practice was that women *were* a separate class—separate both with respect to needs and with respect to their capacities to perform various kinds of work.

In June 1920, in the *Marine Stewards'* case (14 CAR 392), Higgins said that the Court was called upon for the first time to fix the terms for stewardesses:

> Equal rates are not claimed; and even if they were, I should be inclined to follow the system which I adopted in the Fruit case. As these stewardesses attend mainly to the needs of women and children passengers, as they do not compete with men, do not displace men by accepting a lower wage, as they do not normally have the responsibility, legal or actual, for a family, I do not think that a family wage is appropriate. In the Fruit case, I find that, for the reasons there stated, I prescribed for the women three-fourths of the minimum wage prescribed for men. In this case the Commonwealth Government has agreed to £9 per month; but for the 1st saloon, or 2nd class saloon, or 3rd class stewardesses, £10. This seems to be a very fair arrangement, where the steward's minimum is £13. (pp. 399–400)

Because stewards and stewardesses received free on-board accommodation the relativities of female to male wages cannot be simply calculated, but it was clearly more than 54 per cent. As Higgins indicated, he acquiesced in the view of one employer—the Commonwealth Government.

The 1920 *Public Service* case (14 CAR 639)—conducted shortly before the jurisdiction passed to the Public Service Arbitrator—was heard by Starke, serving as Deputy President of the Arbitration Court. He offered a rather different explanation of the gender difference in rates awarded by the Court: 'Experience shows', he said,

> that women have always been remunerated on a lower scale than men. … Typists, telephonists, sorters, and checkers illustrate this fact in the present case, and if their work were appraised on the same scale as that of men the tendency would be to close to them a most suitable avenue of employment. Again in positions such as assistants, in which both men and women are employed, the work is also very suitable for women, and a similar tendency must, in my opinion, develop if the Court makes no distinction on the ground of sex. 'Equal pay for equal work' is an attractive phrase, but it is ambiguous, and if equal pay would close or tend to close the door to women's employment in suitable occupations then it can hardly be denied that the work is not equal. It is therefore expedient, in my opinion, that some distinction should be made on the ground of sex in the interests of women themselves, and also just from the point of view of the community which must find the money to remunerate its officers. (pp. 686–687)

Starke was the first member of the Court to include in his reasons the fact that women *normally* were paid less than men. If the Court were to impose equal rates, it would be departing from its own principles *and* reversing a pattern that prevailed independently of Court decisions. Starke was also the first to argue that unequal pay served the function of protecting women's employment. Whereas Higgins, and to a lesser extent Powers, had emphasised the necessity of preserving *male* employment by granting equal pay where the sexes were in competition, Starke saw lower pay for women as an offset to their allegedly lesser value.

In summary, the Court's treatment of the minimum wage for women was confused. There was general agreement that, on average, women *needed* less than men, because of the difference in family responsibilities. There was no systematic attempt to quantify the difference, though in some cases attention *was* given to the actual needs of a single female worker. There was also agreement that there were some jobs that were men's work and others that were women's, though the criteria for distinguishing them were ill-defined. It is not so clear that there was recognition of gender-free work, but the judges, if asked, would probably have said that there was. In 'women's work', females would be paid less. The main reason for this was the difference in needs, but in Starke's *Public Service* decision there was also a suggestion that lower rates would preserve the employment opportunities for women that these tasks provided.[3]

In the period under review, there were decisions of State tribunals that contributed to the climate in which the Federal Court dealt with the gender issue.[4]

Mr Justice Cussen, in the Victorian State Court of Industrial Appeals, heard in 1913 an appeal from a decision of the Victorian Commercial Clerks' Wages Board, which had prescribed equal rates for male and female clerks. The relevant State Act required the sex of the workers to be taken into account. Cussen expressed general agreement with Higgins' approach in *Fruitpickers'*. The evidence indicated that if female clerks were paid as much as males, fewer would be employed. The principle of 'equal pay for equal work' had a clear meaning when people worked on piece rates, but otherwise the problem of identifying equal and unequal work deprived it of practical value. If, in reality,

---

[3] Higgins also discussed gender pay differences in *A New Province for Law and Order* (1922, pp. 11–12): 'The principle of the living wage has been applied to women, but with a difference, as women are not usually legally responsible for the maintenance of a family. A woman's minimum is based on the average cost of her own living to one who supports herself by her own exertions. A woman or girl with a comfortable home cannot be left to underbid in wages other women or girls who are less fortunate.' Higgins went on to describe the circumstances where women were paid the male rates and those where they were not, setting out the principles followed in *Fruitpickers'*.

[4] I rely for these on Anderson (1929, Chapter XIX).

'equal pay for equal work' meant that men and women should be paid the same amount, it failed to recognise that women were inferior to men in physical strength and endurance and the capacity for sustained work. If the principle meant that equal pay should be given for work of equal return to the employer, this implied that for unequal work there should be unequal pay; but this was opposed to the principle of the minimum wage, which was independent of result or value (Anderson 1929, pp. 406–408).

In 1917, the full Court of Industrial Arbitration in Queensland was asked to construe a requirement of the *Industrial Arbitration Act 1916* that 'the same wage be paid to persons of either sex performing the same work or producing the same return of profit to the employer'. The Federated Clerks' Union asked the Court to say that female clerks were doing the same work as males and should therefore be paid the same wages. The Court held that it was necessary to look behind the classifications and to inquire whether the work done was the same, not only in kind, but also in quantity and quality. This was a matter of evidence. If the Court or Board were satisfied that in this sense males and females were doing the same work, then it should fix the same wage; if not, different rates could be set (Anderson 1929, pp. 409–410). Clearly, however, the Queensland Act did not envisage differences based on need and was at odds with the practice of the Federal Court.

In two South Australian cases, in 1918 and 1919, President Jethro Brown in the Industrial Court considered the living wage for women. There was a statutory requirement that no worker be paid less than a living wage. In the *Printing Trades* case of 1918, Brown said that some women asked for wages to be assessed on the basis of equal pay for work of equal value; but a Court that tried to fix the minimum wage for unskilled labour on this basis would be lost in a sea of fallacy and contradiction. A judge was naturally driven to the standard of needs, which led to different results for men and women. In an industry where men might be threatened by female competition, evidence would need to be introduced to establish that they should be retained in the industry or the grade (Anderson 1929, pp. 397–399). In 1919, in the *Women's Living Wage (Cardboard Box Makers')* case, Brown sat with two women assessors. The approach adopted was to start with the family living wage and work backwards to the living wage for single women. If this were assessed too liberally, the result would be unfair to women deprived of employment. The Court arrived at 30s per week (pp. 412–413). This was around half the amount then being set for males.

Clearly, unequal pay was the norm, reflecting several factors: custom and practice, a perception that women needed less than men because of their different family obligations, and resistance to any notion that women and men ordinarily performed work of equal value.

4.3 Working hours

The Court, until 1921, was given to pronouncing a general rule of 48 hours per week. The 48 hours were usually worked over 5½ days—8¾ hours Monday to Friday and 4¼ hours on Saturday, or some variant thereof. There were exceptions to the 48-hour standard, based on existing practice in the industry concerned, the characteristics of particular jobs, and gender. The Commonwealth Statistician's series for average hours, registering the requirements of statutes, awards, and registered agreements, begins in 1914 (see Chapter 1, Subsection 1.3.5). It shows a gradual decline, in the case of males, from 48.9 hours in 1914 to 46.2 in 1921. For women, the reduction was from 49.1 hours in 1914 to 45.7 in 1921. The Court's contribution to these reductions cannot be disentangled from that of agreements, State Acts, and State tribunals.

The *Harvester* wage of 7s per day was equated by Higgins and others to a weekly wage of 42s. But the 7s was simply a benchmark against which the rates being paid by employers could be judged. There was no requirement that the employer actually employ the worker for a whole day, let alone a week; and we saw in Chapter 3 that H V McKay's practice was to suspend payment when work was interrupted by a breakdown in the machinery. The *Excise Tariff Act 1906* did not require the employer to get a certificate that the working hours, as well as the wages, were 'fair and reasonable'. It *might* have allowed Higgins to specify that the fair and reasonable wage was for 48 hours per week, but the unions did not claim this and it was not argued. This, no doubt, reflected a shared assumption that the wage was intended for 48 hours.

In his early awards, Higgins adhered to the 48-hour standard. There was a minor departure in the *Builders' Labourers'* case of 1913 (8 CAR 15), when he granted a 44-hour week, but on the condition of a reduction in wages commensurate with the hourly rate for 48 hours. In the *Waterside Workers'* case of 1914 (8 CAR 53), he dealt with the issue of irregular hours in casual employment. Treating the waterside worker as an unskilled labourer, he sought to fix an hourly rate that would, over the week, provide 8s 6d per day. Adopting an estimate of 30 hours per week, he set an hourly rate of 1s 9d. 'If a man keeps a horse', said Higgins,

> he has to feed the horse on days when he does not use him, as well as on the days when he does. If he keep two or more horses, and use them in rotation, they must be fed all the time. If people expect cabmen to be ready for a call at the stand, they must pay an extra rate to cover the time lost in waiting. It would be absurd to say, as has been urged here, that the obligation of the master ceases with the actual physical exertion. (p. 73)

This decision did not entail any softening of the 48-hour rule but affected its application to irregular employment.

By 1914, however, there were some departures from the rule, based on the characteristics of the work. In the *Telegraphic Linesmen's* case (8 CAR 119), Higgins dealt with a group of workers who were already on a 46-hour week, but whose union sought a reduction to 44. Higgins said that there would need to be some special ground for moving even further from 'the Australian standard' of 48 hours:

> I never depart from that standard except for some special reason; and the burden lies on the Union to show me a sufficient special reason. In the case of the builders' labourers, I prescribed forty-four hours, because the men have to 'follow the jobs' from place to place, and lose much

time in coming from and going to their homes. In the case of the postal electricians, I prescribed forty-four hours, because there is much indoor work, and much racking of the nerves. But, except in such work as tunnel work, these linesmen carry on their operations, almost wholly, in the open air; and there is little or no irritation to the nerves. I confess that I should like to see the hours of actual work reduced to eight on five days in the week, with a half-holiday on Saturday; but I do not feel justified in making the reduction. Except in an extreme case, it is for Parliament, not for this Court, to interfere with the existing standard of hours. (p. 135)

The principle that it was for Parliament rather than the Court to change the standard week was repeated several times by both Higgins and Powers. Neither ever explained why this potential cause of industrial disputation differed from others; or how the prescription of standard hours by the federal legislature could be supported by the Constitution.

In 1915, Higgins granted a 44-hour week (instead of the existing 46½ hours) for letter carriers, because of the broken day that they worked and the consequent length of time (5:30am to 5:45pm) from beginning to end (9 CAR 52, 81).

In the *BHP* case of 1916 (10 CAR 155), conducted in the aftermath of a strike about working hours, he said that it was his duty 'to accept recognised standards, not to create them' and that 'if a further general limitation of hours has to be made, it ought to be made deliberately by the Legislatures' (pp. 185–186). But the adverse health effects of mining were a special factor. While it was his practice not to increase wages because of risk to body or health, the risk could well be taken into account on a question of hours (p. 187). He was, apparently, leaning to a reduced working week for the miners; but before he gave his decision, the New South Wales Parliament prescribed a maximum of 88 hours per fortnight for underground work. This Act, said Higgins, 'will have to be obeyed whatever I award' (p. 190). He granted a 44-hour week for underground men, but refused it for others.

Making the first award for the meat industry in 1916 (10 CAR 465), he refused the 44-hour week for abattoir workers: there were no unhealthy or dangerous conditions such as those of miners (p. 491). For shop butchers, existing hours ranged between 50 and 52. Higgins prescribed 48 hours, to be worked between 6am and 6pm Monday to Friday and between 6am and 1pm on Saturdays. For carters and drivers, all of the wages board determinations that he had seen prescribed more than 48 hours. Given the variety and open-air character of the work, he did not feel justified in enforcing the 48-hour standard, and awarded 52 (pp. 491–496).

In the *Storemen and Packers'* case of 1916 (10 CAR 629), the union sought a 44-hour week on the ground of the strenuous character of the work. Powers was unconvinced. But since the case had begun, the union had reached agreement with New South Wales employers for 48 hours for 6 months of the year and 44 for the other 6, and with Queensland employers for 46. In the wool stores at Port Adelaide 45½ to 46 hours 'have for some time been recognised as the hours of duty … In Adelaide, again, the recognised hours have always been 48'. Powers set a maximum of 46 hours in Melbourne wool stores from 1 April to 30 September and at Port Adelaide 46 hours throughout the year. He fixed Saturday finishing times at 12.00 or 12.30 (pp. 635–637). Clearly, the negotiators were leading the arbitrator. Likewise in the *Miners'* case (10 CAR 681; 11 CAR 17), Powers observed that 44 hours prevailed in New South Wales, Victoria, and Queensland. He did not feel justified in retaining 48 hours for Mount Lyall and two other mines when the 44-hour week was general for underground work in the eastern States.

Powers was asked in 1917 to set a maximum of 48 hours in the *Theatrical and Amusement Employees'* award (11 CAR 133). The employers said that a 60-hour week was absolutely essential and that they paid extra for it (apparently at standard rates). Powers provided for a 48-hour week, with the effect that work in excess of 48 hours was at higher rates. 'In that way', he said, 'the wage for 48 hours for a resident carpenter will be £4 12s, and if I had fixed 60 hours it would have been £5 15s for 48 hours and overtime, and if 60 hours are worked it will amount to £6 5s 6d.' That is, fixing the standard week at 48 hours had the effect of raising the pay of the 60-hour worker by 10s 6d.

In the 1917 *Pastoral* case (11 CAR 389), Higgins refused the union's plea for a limit of 44 hours, rather than 48, for shearers' work: 'I cannot find any sufficient ground for departing from the Australian standard of 48 hours. One does not find here any conditions analogous to the conditions of builders' labourers, or of miners' (p. 408).

The *Gas Employees'* case of 1917 (11 CAR 267) is of interest because Higgins commented on inequitable differences in working hours. Some gas companies had conceded working weeks of fewer than 48 hours. 'But the question remains' said Higgins, 'should I force it on [other] employers?':

> It is evident that … the men of the union contrast their treatment with the treatment of the office staff. In the South Australian company, for instance, it appears that the employees of the staff, clerks and others, have 38½ hours of work, get all holidays on full pay, and also get fourteen days per annum leave of absence on full pay. How is this difference between the office staff and the employees at the works to be justified? … If I granted the claim, I should be altering recognised standards; and as in the case of the 48 hour week, the Australian standard of hours, I do not like to take on myself the responsibility of altering recognised standards except on very definite exceptional grounds. … I confess that I should like to see leave of absence conceded, as the metropolitan Gas Company concedes it, voluntarily. The concession may have a good basis even in business expediency, as tending to keep tried men attached to the works. It is not well that all the relations between employer and employed should rest on compulsion. I refuse the claim. (pp. 284–285)

The seeming inequity was again illustrated in the *Commonwealth Public Service Professional Officers'* case of 1917 (12 CAR 114), a case that concerned 343 officers in the Professional Division. Higgins noted that the working week was 36¾ hours, with the officers also enjoying 18 days of recreation leave.

Disparities were also evident in the terms of a consent award for hotels made by Higgins in April 1919 (13 CAR 84). There were differences between

States, but the provisions for Victoria can be taken as an example (pp. 106–111). Adults who handled or distributed liquor, other than barmaids, had a working week of 54 hours, for which the pay was 61s. (At the time, the basic wage in new awards was around 65s.) Barmaids had a 50-hour week for 44s. For other kinds of labour specified in the award, the hours were 58 (males) and 56 (females). The male rates of pay, without board and lodging, ranged from 44s (day porter, pantryman, kitchenman) to 79s (first cook where kitchen staff exceeded eight); for females, the range was 32s (pantrymaid, kitchenmaid) to 53s (first cook, more than eight employees). I cite the rates of pay lest it be thought that the long hours were compensated by higher wages. Clearly, the 'Australian standard' of 48 hours was not universal.

In May 1919, Higgins made a new award for the meat industry (13 CAR 153). The only change to working hours was for carters and drivers (previously 52 hours). The employers wanted 50 hours. Higgins prescribed an option of 48 or 50 hours, with the extra two hours to be paid at ordinary rates.

Powers in July made a new general award for carters and drivers (13 CAR 214). The existing working week was 50 hours (48 for motor drivers). 'The war is now over', he said,

> and many old conditions are passing away and will pass away in all countries by granting fair conditions to workers or by revolutions which can only make things worse for every one. In Old England industries which were working 56 to 60 hours are working and have to prepare to work 48 hours a week. The Sunlight Company recently reduced its hours of duty to 36 hours instead of 48 hours without any reduction of wages. The League of Nations has declared for 48 hours a week and Australians are not likely to rest content with longer hours now the war is over. … I do not see why carters and drivers should continue to be forced to remain on duty longer than 48 hours a week for wages based on the recognised basic wage for 48 hours. (p. 230)

Powers granted the 48-hour week.

Higgins, in 1919, made a new award for the clothing trades (13 CAR 647). The workers were predominantly female, and at Higgins' request the Attorney-General 'appointed a lady, highly qualified for the purpose, to make a report to me as to the appropriate hours for females, having regard to health, efficiency, and output' (p. 689). In due course, Mrs Osborne, from 'the University', tendered her report, favouring 44 hours. Drawing upon it, Higgins made much of the draining conditions, especially noise, in the factories. He was concerned, too, that some factories, at the girls' urging, worked the 48 hours over five days, which was bad for them (p. 706). He proposed to grant the claim for 44 hours,

> and inasmuch as this is mainly a women's industry, the women in the union outnumbering the men by nearly five to one, the hours fixed must be the hours appropriate for the women. In the factories it would, indeed, rarely pay the employer to spend electric power and light for the few men who would be left; and, as I have pointed out, the whole team system would be deranged, and discontent would be aroused. (p. 711)

The clothing trades decision could be seen as part of a slow erosion of the 48-hour standard. From another perspective, it met the requirement that some special factor or factors should be present to justify a deviation from the 'Australian standard'. The same ambivalence is evident in the decision of Powers, in March 1920, in the *Flour Mills* case (14 CAR 114). The employers had not raised their customary dire predictions about the effects of shorter hours. Powers presented a broad view of the issue:

> The recognised working hours in industries have been reduced by the Court where it is considered necessary to do so in the interests of the health of the employees, and in some other cases where the recognised hours have been more than 48 hours. ... I reduced the recognised hours for horse-drivers in the carriers' industry from 56 hours to 48 hours per week; in the theatrical business from 60 hours to 48 hours; and in the mining industry for *underground* workers from 48 hours to 44 in the States in which 48 hours were previously worked.

> In all civilised countries in the world it appears the workers have, at the present time, decided that the hours of duty they were required to work before the war were not fair and were not necessary; and very many large employers of labour in England and America have found that they were not necessary, from any point of view, and have granted much shorter hours than were recognised as necessary before the war. The workers generally have decided to work shorter hours than they did before 1914; and if they cannot get shorter hours from Parliament; and if this Court will not even consider claims for shortening the hours … the workers will secure them in their own way by not working more than the hours they fix, whether reasonable or unreasonable. … In the light of the fact that it has been proved that shorter hours, with rest periods, enable workers to produce as much as they produced working longer hours, this Court must, I think, reconsider the position as to claims for shorter hours, especially as the federal Parliament cannot properly legislate on matters left to the States and the different States from time to time fix different hours in the same industries. (pp. 123–128)

It would have been reasonable to infer, in 1920, that Higgins and Powers were feeling their way toward a more general reduction of hours.

At this time, the Government brought in legislation to amend the *Commonwealth Conciliation and Arbitration Act 1904*, requiring that reductions in hours below 48 per week, along with all increases in hours, be approved by a Full Court.[5] This was the first legislative endorsement of the practice of important issues being dealt with by multiple judges. Consistency, to the extent that it had previously been achieved, turned on the respect that the judges (Higgins and Powers particularly) accorded to each other's decisions. Starke alluded to the impending change, with evident approval (which Higgins and

---

[5] The change was contained in an amendment moved by the Government in the committee stage of a Bill that was said to be chiefly a machinery matter (92 CPD, pp. 3593; 4076; 4077). The amendment allowed the appointment of more than one Deputy President and authorised multiple-judge benches, but the *requirement* of a Full Court was limited to hours. No explanation was given for this, other than the fact that the basic wage was then under review by a Royal Commission. Suspicions were expressed by the Labor Opposition that it was directed against Higgins.

Powers might or might not have endorsed), in the *Commonwealth Railways* case (14 CAR 496):

> The Court is not dealing with principles or rules of law in which the settled practice is for one Judge to accept and loyally carry out the decisions of another Judge of equal authority until reversed by higher authority. It is dealing with matters of fact; with what is just and proper in the circumstances of a given case, and its award, on matters within the Court's jurisdiction, is not open to challenge or appeal in any other Court on any account whatever. On such a vital point as the reduction of hours, each member of the Court must therefore give the matter separate and independent consideration and cannot shelter himself from responsibility under cover of an award in another case. It is to be regretted, in my opinion, that the members of the Court do not, and perhaps cannot, in the present state of the law, sit and hear together matters such as this. A most difficult and an intolerable position may easily arise. (p. 567)

The new requirement did not apply to matters already begun—an exclusion that allowed Higgins to make two important decisions, for timber workers and engineers.[6]

In May 1920, he had given a preliminary indication of his thinking in the *Timber Workers'* case (14 CAR 811). He then decided to substitute weekly for hourly hiring, noting that hitherto the men had gone without pay when the work was interrupted, even if the causes were outside their control. He rejected the union contention that the dusty and unhealthy conditions in sawmills justified a shorter working week. But that was not the end of the matter:

> The question still remains, are 48 hours necessary, are 48 hours appropriate, for industries generally, under present conditions. May 44 hours be prescribed unless special reasons be shown to the contrary …
> At present we have established in Australia a standard of 48 hours per

---

[6] This exclusion was introduced near the end of the debate on the clause, possibly to counter the anti-Higgins interpretation.

> week—a standard long envied by workers in other countries, a standard which is now being generally adopted. But we have not in Australia established the 8 hours day. In order to get the boon of a Saturday half-holiday, the workers here have to add three-quarters of an hour, generally, to the 8 hours ... Is this sacrifice to continue for ever? The unions do not now, so far as my experience goes, keep up the hopeless fight against new machinery; but are they to get no direct advantage from the introduction of labour-saving devices? (pp. 841–842)

This was not an issue for one industry. In the course of the hearing, the representative of an employer body contended that changing standard hours was a matter for the legislature—a position that Higgins and Powers had previously adopted. 'I shall be very glad', said Higgins, 'if the Legislature would take it in hand, but as it has not done so, I must act. The difficulty is that this question is continually coming up before me' (p. 845).

He adjourned the matter to allow the Council of Employers and the Trades Hall Councils to put evidence and arguments and delivered a further judgment in November 1920. The federal government had declined an invitation to appear; and the Federal Council of Employers, having said that it intended to appear, failed to do so. The decision sets out at great length instances of the introduction of 44 hours in Australia and overseas. Higgins saw as one of the main issues the likely effect of shorter hours on production. His conclusion was equivocal. The unions had not satisfied him that the reduction of hours would have no adverse effect; nor had the employers satisfied him that any effect would be proportional to the reduction in hours. Another issue was the claim of workers on the benefits of increased use of machinery. The employers agreed that machinery did raise output, but denied that the workers had any claim upon the increase: they were neither the inventors nor the patentees. Inventions, said Higgins, were a social product, to which the workers often made unrecognised contributions. Consumers benefited from the greater cheapness that machinery caused; and the employer who was not the inventor got the benefit of higher profit. Why should the employee not share in the benefit by a reduction of working hours? (p. 862)

Higgins reduced the weekly hours for timber workers to 44, with the clear indication that he saw this as a new standard.[7] There was, however, only one other case not covered by the amendment to the Act. This was the *ASE* case, decided by Higgins in May 1921 (15 CAR 297). In respect of hours, his decision was brief. 'In accordance with my decision in the timber workers' case', he said, 'I propose to make 44 hours per week the limit for ordinary hours of work—the limit unless payment be made for the overtime' (p. 320).

Thus Higgins, at the end of his tenure, was clearly of a mind to substitute a 44-hour standard week for the earlier 48 hours. As we see in Section 6.3 of Chapter 6, the continuing members of the Court, influenced by deteriorating economic conditions, were not persuaded.

4.4 Other awarded benefits

In the Higgins years, there were few other alterations in working conditions which could be attributed to the Court's intervention. Provisions of awards going to leave and penalty rates were commonly among the terms settled by the parties on which the Court was not required to arbitrate.

In our discussion of the *Harvester* case, we noted that employees of H V McKay had no paid leave. Various holidays were taken, but no payment was made. Higgins was not invited to interfere with this arrangement. He might have taken the unpaid leave into account in assessing the fairness of McKay's wages, but there is no evidence in the transcript or the decision that he did so. I do not know how typical McKay's practice was in 1907. Some later decisions of the Court suggest that it had become usual for employers to allow paid leave on a number of special days. In 1915, Powers fixed the holidays to be observed in the mining industry, the employers having resisted the *extent* of the union claim:

---

[7] Higgins described this case in *A New Province for Law and Order* (Higgins 1922, pp. 124–125). He said: 'But the Court refused to accept the argument for the union to the effect that hours should be lowered because thereby more men would have to be employed; it treated relief from the bane of unemployment on such a ground as illusory'.

> The majority of respondents allow their employees the number of days asked for, but do not grant a holiday for State and federal elections. Some employers allow holidays at Christmas from Christmas Eve to the 3rd January and other days in the year. It was not shown that any employee was ever prevented from voting at elections. I propose to allow as a minimum New Year's Day, Good Friday or Easter Monday, Eight Hours Day, Christmas Day, Boxing Day, and Union Picnic Day, or ANA, or such other day or days in lieu of any of the days named as the local officers of the Organisation and the respective respondents agree to recognise as a holiday. (*Mining Employees'* case 9 CAR 330, 369)

The number of holidays in awards was commonly eight or nine. In 1918, in the *Coopers'* case, Higgins observed: 'As the respondents consent to a picnic day, I prescribe 9 holidays' (12 CAR 427, 444).

Annual leave was common in the public sector, but not in private employment. The Court was reluctant to grant it, except where the employees worked seven-day weeks. In November 1916 Powers had contemplated making a leave provision in a storemen and packers' award, but after the speaking to the minutes said that annual holidays were not as general as he had thought:

> I asked Mr Pemberton [for the union] to point out any agreement or award under which storemen and packers outside the Government service are allowed an annual holiday but he could not do so; and I find on inquiry that no such award has been made by this Court except to persons on ships who do not get the ordinary holidays, Saturday afternoons, and Sundays off, and to public servants. ... In the circumstances, as it is objected to, I do not propose to cause unrest and dissatisfaction in other industries by granting an annual holiday to the members of this organization who are being granted increased pay, increased overtime, more public holidays, and shorter hours in the wool and grain business. (*Storemen and Packers'* case 10 CAR 629, 659–660)

I do not recount in detail the Court's other interventions in prescribing the terms of employment. There had been a variety of decisions made in specific cases and commonly based on special factors, all of which amounted to a not inconsiderable overall improvement. Chapter 5 will note the attempts of Powers and Webb to demonstrate the substantial gains made by labour under the aegis of the Court.

CAUTION AND RESTRAINT: 1921–1929

5

The setting

5.1 THE COURT

Powers became President of the Commonwealth Court of Conciliation and Arbitration on 1 July 1921. (He left the Court in April 1920, but returned as Deputy President in February 1921.) Two other judges of the High Court—Duffy and Rich—were appointed Deputy Presidents in August 1921. They resigned in June 1922 and two lawyers who were not High Court Judges—Quick and Webb—were appointed as Deputy Presidents.[1] From then until 1926, the members of the Court were Powers, Quick, and Webb. In June 1926, Powers relinquished his position, and the Court was reconstituted in response to a High Court requirement that judicial functions be exercised only by judges with life tenure. A chief justice (Dethridge) and two judges (Lukin and Beeby) were appointed.[2] Another judge (Drake-Brockman) was appointed in April 1927.[3] Neither Quick nor Webb was given judicial status

---

[1] An amendment to the Act had removed the requirement for Deputy Presidents to be drawn from the High Court. Sir John Quick was a distinguished jurist, active in the federation movement, and a former politician. N A Webb was a former Adelaide solicitor and Deputy President of the South Australian Industrial Court.

[2] George Dethridge was a judge of the Victorian County Court; in 1919 he had been a Royal Commissioner inquiring into conditions of wharf labourers at Port Melbourne. Lionel Lukin had recently resigned from the Queensland Supreme Court. George Beeby had been a controversial politician in New South Wales. Since 1920, he had been a Judge of the Industrial Court of Arbitration and President of the Board of Trade. Biographies of these judges and Drake-Brockman (see the next footnote) appear in the *Dictionary of Australian Biography*.

[3] Edmund Alfred Drake-Brockman was a former President of the Central Council of

in the reconstituted Court. Webb resigned as Deputy President in February 1927. Quick remained until 1930 so as to complete the making of awards for the railway industry.[4]

A reading of the *Commonwealth Arbitration Reports* gives the impression of a rising work load for the Court. Various industries came under its awards for the first time, partly as a consequence of High Court decisions about the Arbitration Court's jurisdiction (Kirby and Creighton 2004). Railways and printing were perhaps the most important. Speaking at the welcome to Drake-Brockman in April 1927, Attorney-General Latham referred to the rise in the number of matters pending as the reason for the additional appointment. There is no entirely satisfactory statistical evidence of the extent of the Court's influence. The *Labour Reports* for these years provide data of *changes* in wages. They show that in the five years 1919–23, the number of workpeople who experienced wage changes averaged 796,000 per year; by 1924–29 the number had increased to 1,170,000. Between the two periods, the proportion of these workpeople whose wage changes flowed from Commonwealth awards and registered agreements increased from 23 to 63 per cent. Measuring the changes by amount, rather than numbers of workpeople, gives a rather different impression. The amount of the changes, in weekly terms, fell from £194,000 to £84,000. In 1919–23, Commonwealth awards and agreements accounted for 17 per cent of the monetary changes; in 1924–29, the percentage was 28. The difference between the two measures may be due substantially to the automatic adjustment system, whereby there were frequent small changes in Commonwealth awards, whereas under the State arbitration systems there were occasional larger increases. These data suggest a rise in Commonwealth coverage, but the statistical evidence is tenuous.

Foenander (1937, pp. 26–27) offered a less equivocal account of the Court's *de facto* authority:

Employers of Australia and his appointment generated strong union condemnation. He was a Senator from Western Australia from 1924 to 1926 (Hagan 1981, pp. 87–88; Plowman 1989, p. 18).

[4] A M Stewart, who had been Registrar since the inception of the Court, was appointed in 1926 as a Conciliation Commissioner and combined the two functions.

> It will be understood that, by the close of the year 1926, the Commonwealth Court had, in point of prestige and authority, far outstripped its sister tribunals in the States. The balance in the arrangement of a dual concurrent industrial control between the Commonwealth and the States had tilted strongly in favour of the Commonwealth. Of approximately 2,000,000 wage-earners in Australia, about 711,000 were members of Federal trade unions and 139,000 were registered with industrial associations not affiliated with the Commonwealth Court. In round figures, therefore, 84 per cent of Australian trade unionists were subject directly to the Federal jurisdiction. But the State industrial authorities as a whole have always, in their decisions, been strongly influenced by Federal award rates. This is particularly so in Victoria and Tasmania, and even in the non-industrial States (Queensland and Western Australia) the bearing is fairly well marked. On an estimate it can be calculated that the awards of the Federal Court directly extended to somewhat more than one-third of the workers of Australia. Indirectly, however—by reason of the tendency of State authorities and employers of non-union labour to be guided by the Federal decisions—Commonwealth awards could be said to be decisive in determining the general level of wages and conditions in Australian industries.

I have no difficulty with Foenander's estimate of a one-third direct coverage of federal awards. The indirect effects are more conjectural, and Foenander may have exaggerated the readiness of State authorities to fall in line with the Court's decisions. The Depression would underscore their exercise of an independent role.

A significant development affecting the Court's ability to conduct a wage policy and to displace State regulation was the 1926 decision of the High Court in *Clyde Engineering Company v Cowburn* (37 CLR 466; Foenander 1937, p. 26). New South Wales legislation in 1925 provided for a general 44-hour week. Earlier decisions of the High Court suggested that the State law providing for the 44-hour week would be binding in New South Wales on employers operating under federal awards. This was because 48 hours in federal awards represented a maximum, and it was possible for an employer to comply with the State Act without violating the federal award. *Cowburn's* case, however, established that where a federal award prescribed working hours, the State law as to hours was of no effect as between the parties to the federal award. If the Federal Court intended to 'cover the field'—in this instance the 'field' of working hours—the award displaced the State law.

The *Commonwealth Conciliation and Arbitration Act 1904* was extensively amended in 1928 (Anderson 1928). The changes were due in large measure to criticisms of the operation of the system, some of which are described in Chapter 13 (see also Foenander 1937, chapters II, III, and IV). For this study, a relevant amendment was the insertion of section 28D, which required the Court, except when dealing with the basic wage, to take into account the economic effects of its decisions. In the event, this section was repealed in 1930. It does not seem to have affected the Court's decision-making in the interval between enactment and repeal.

Continuing dissatisfaction with the conciliation and arbitration system, intensified by the British Economic Mission (see Chapter 13), together with a recommendation from the Royal Commission on the Constitution, crystallised in the Bruce Government's decision to abandon federal conciliation and arbitration and to the ensuing fall of the Government in October 1929.

5.2 The Economic Climate

There are considerable uncertainties and differences of opinion about the performance of the economy in the 1920s. Not the least of the sources of uncertainty are the differences between the GDP estimates of Butlin and Haig, discussed in Chapter 1. Figure 5.1 shows the alternative estimates. It draws upon the same data as those represented in Figure 1.1, but converts the estimates to a base of 1920–21 = 100. We saw in Chapter 2 that there was a sizeable increase in the real GDP between 1919–20 and 1920–21—larger on Butlin's estimates than on Haig's. Butlin's figures suggest that the real GDP then increased slowly until 1922–23, with a more rapid increase occurring

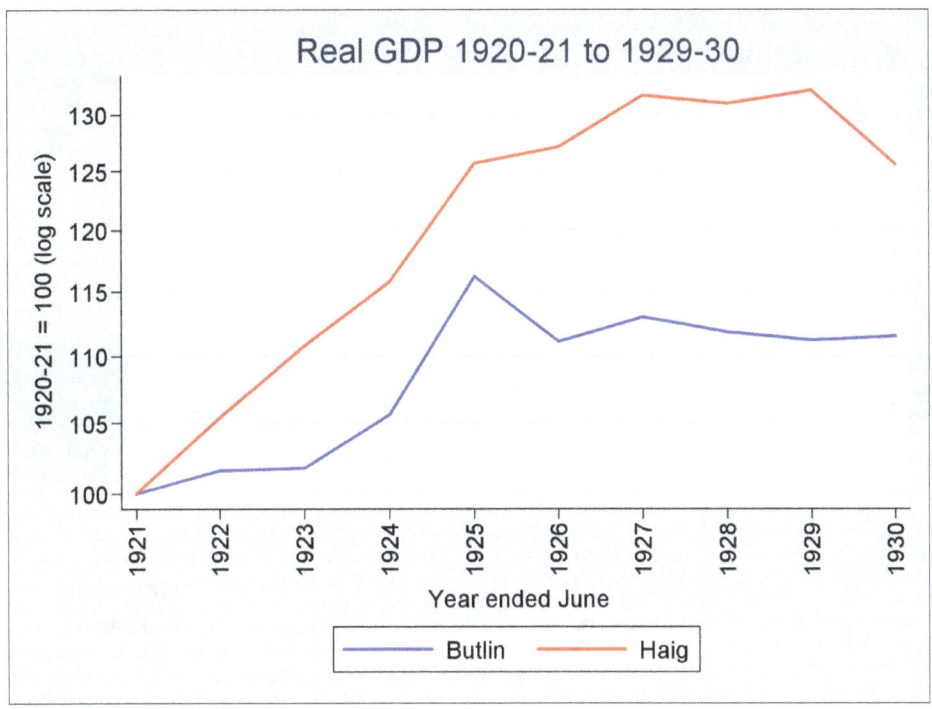

Figure 5.1
Source: See Figure 1.1.

between the latter year and 1924–25, when the GDP peaked at 16 per cent above its level of four years earlier. For the remainder of the decade, on Butlin's estimates, the real GDP stagnated. Haig depicts a much stronger growth, with the peak occurring in 1928–29 at 32 per cent above the 1920–21 level. There is a modicum of agreement that the growth rate of the earlier 1920s tailed off in the latter part of the decade. If the alternative estimates are related to other evidence of the economic history of the period, it may be conjectured that:

- Haig's more exuberant picture conforms better to the known technological and structural changes of the 1920s, including the spread of electrical energy, the increasing use of cars and trucks, and the emergence of various new industries (Merrett and Ville 2011).

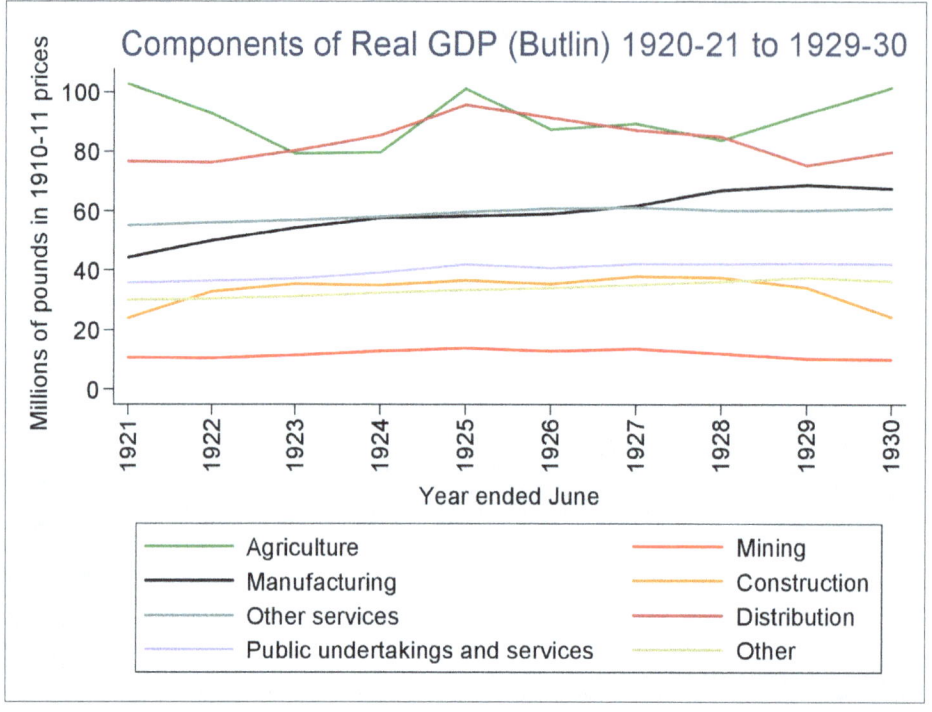

Figure 5.2

- Butlin's estimates are the more plausible for the period from 1920–21 to 1922–23. Contemporary evidence is that this was a period of some economic difficulty, unlikely to have witnessed the kind of growth suggested by Haig.
- The downturn after 1924–25, suggested by Butlin's estimates, may be too early. Haig's estimates, suggesting that the period of growth came to an end in about 1926–27, seem more probable as to timing (though not necessarily as to the level of the index).
- There is abundant evidence that the later 1920s were a difficult period, and Butlin's estimates, which suggest that the loss of momentum was more severe than do Haig's numbers, capture this more convincingly.

It is, of course, an unsatisfactory situation that the accuracy of the GDP estimates has to be guessed on the basis of more general information, rather than the GDP estimates being taken as a firm measure of economic performance. But that is the fact of the matter.

Figure 5.2, based on Butlin's estimates, shows the movements of the main components of the GDP. As in the earlier period, the contributions of the rural sector to the GDP were volatile, but there is no clear sign of a trend. The principal source of growth was manufacturing, which contributed 12 per cent of the GDP in 1920–21 and 16 per cent in 1929–30. Distributive industries constituted a growing sector of the economy until 1924–25, but thereafter declined. Construction, for most of the period, contributed 8 to 9 per cent of the GDP, but was a smaller contributor in 1920–21 and at the end of the period.

Haig's estimates of the components of the GDP are shown in Figure 5.2A. Once again, Haig's estimates for the rural sector suggest less volatility than do Butlin's estimates for agriculture (which includes the pastoral industry). Haig's rural estimates also indicate a rising trend. There is rough agreement about a rising trend in manufacturing, though Haig suggests an earlier levelling-off of growth than does Butlin. Butlin's estimates suggest a rise until 1924–25 and then a decline in the contribution of distribution, while Haig's estimates for services in general show growth until 1926–27 and then a levelling-off. Taking the two sets of estimates into account, we can reasonably say that during the decade there was a modest growth in the share of manufacturing and services in the economy. Little more can be said with confidence.

Forster (1987), relying on Butlin's estimates, saw the period from the end of the 1880s to the end of the 1930s as a time when the growth in population and the workforce roughly matched the growth in output. 'It would be an overstatement', he said, 'to say that output per head was stationary, and indeed the quantitative estimates of national income must be treated cautiously, but any growth in output per head was small' (p. 4). In this, Australia's experience

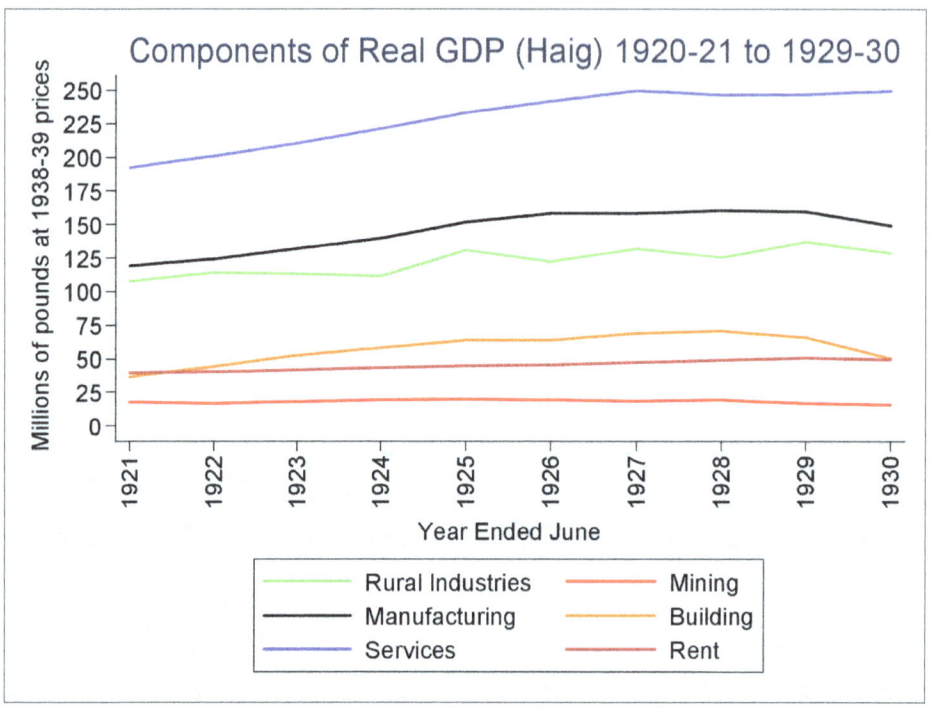

Figure 5.2A

contrasted with those of many other Western countries and its own experience in earlier and later periods.

It is always difficult to identify the contribution of policy to economic change. The growth in population—in which immigration played a significant part—and the growth of manufacturing both accorded with the objectives of government. But governments also wanted continued growth in agriculture and invested heavily in infrastructure to encourage it. Much of the farm sector, however, had a difficult time. This was due partly to climate; and the government-sponsored schemes of agricultural settlement placed many of new farmers on land that was marginal. The tariff raised the cost of some of the items that farmers bought, and the sale of much of the rural product in external markets meant that there was little opportunity to recoup higher costs through adjustment of prices. Policy pursued objectives that were not entirely consonant—an expanded total population, a bigger agricultural sector, a

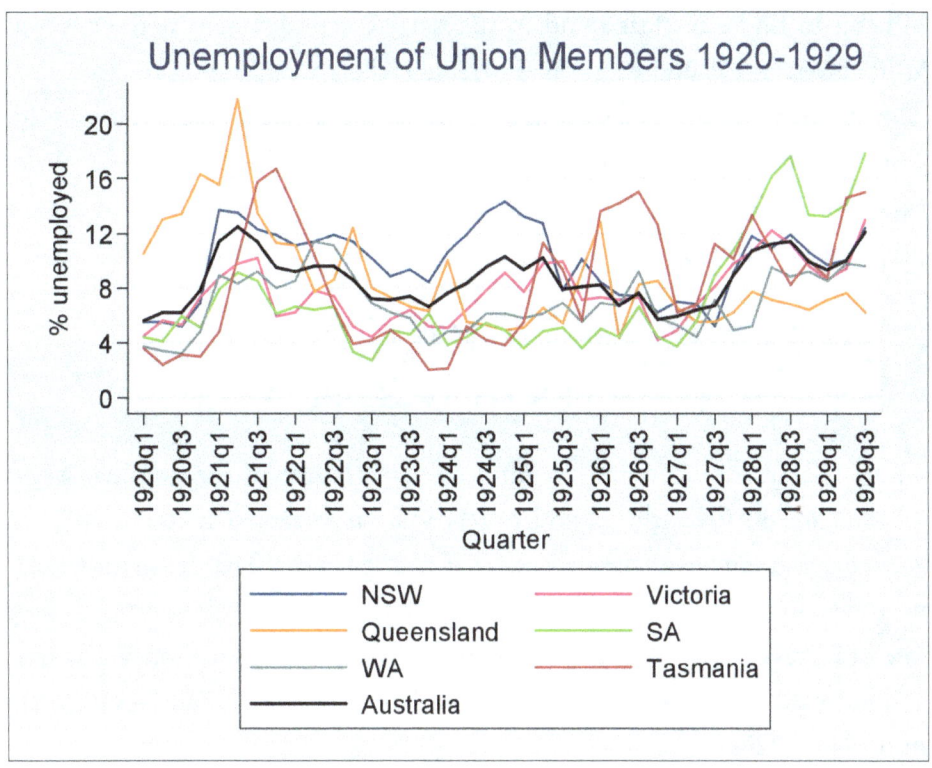

Figure 5.3
Source: *Labour Report*, various numbers.

growing manufacturing sector shielded against foreign competition, and high labour standards.

If the 1920s could be considered a period of restored normality, they could hardly be seen as times of prosperity. Unemployment in 1921 was 11.2 per cent, and in 1922 it was 9.3 per cent. Thereafter, the annual rates ranged between 7.0 and 11.1 per cent, the average for the years 1923–29 being 8.7 per cent. These rates were well above the pre-war level. The Australia-wide and State percentages are shown in Figure 5.3. These percentages, as we have previously noted, are computed from returns submitted by trade unions. (I have referred in Subsection 1.2.3 of Chapter 1 to the limited checks on the reliability of the data afforded by the censuses.) The slump of 1921, persisting until early 1923, is evident in the national average. If we put that aside, it is difficult to find any clear trend in the data. Unemployment nationally was at its lowest at the end of 1926. Thereafter, there was a substantial increase. The different States varied strikingly. Queensland's relative position improved, while South Australia's deteriorated. In the early 1920s New South Wales experienced more severe unemployment than Victoria, but, as the decade progressed, unemployment in these two large States converged.

5.3 Wages and prices

5.3.1 Nominal wage rates

Figure 5.4 describes the movement across the decade of the nominal wages of adult males. Over the period of 9¾ years represented in this chart, the Australia-wide increase averaged 1.4 per cent per year. The fluctuations that were evident in the early years gave way, from the end of 1923, to a more stable rate of increase. Queensland was generally a high-wage State; South Australia and Tasmania, low-wage States. New South Wales became a high-wage State in the late 1920s.

5.3.2 Retail prices

The movement of retail prices is shown in Figure 5.5. This is based on the C series ('All Items') price index rather than the A series or B series indices. The A and B series indices were confined to food, groceries, and rent. The All Items Index includes those items but also clothing and miscellaneous items, the additional components being modelled on the Piddington Commission's regimen of households' requirements. Chapter 2 used the A series numbers because they were available for a greater proportion of the relevant period. We now refer to the C series Index because of its greater comprehensiveness, despite the Court's continued reliance on the food, groceries, and rent index numbers for basic wage adjustment. (In Subsection 5.3.5, I return to the divergence of the indices because of its relevance to the basic wage.) Figure 5.5 demonstrates the dramatic fall in prices which occurred in 1921 and 1922. Over the two years from the last quarter of 1920 to the last quarter of 1922, the reduction

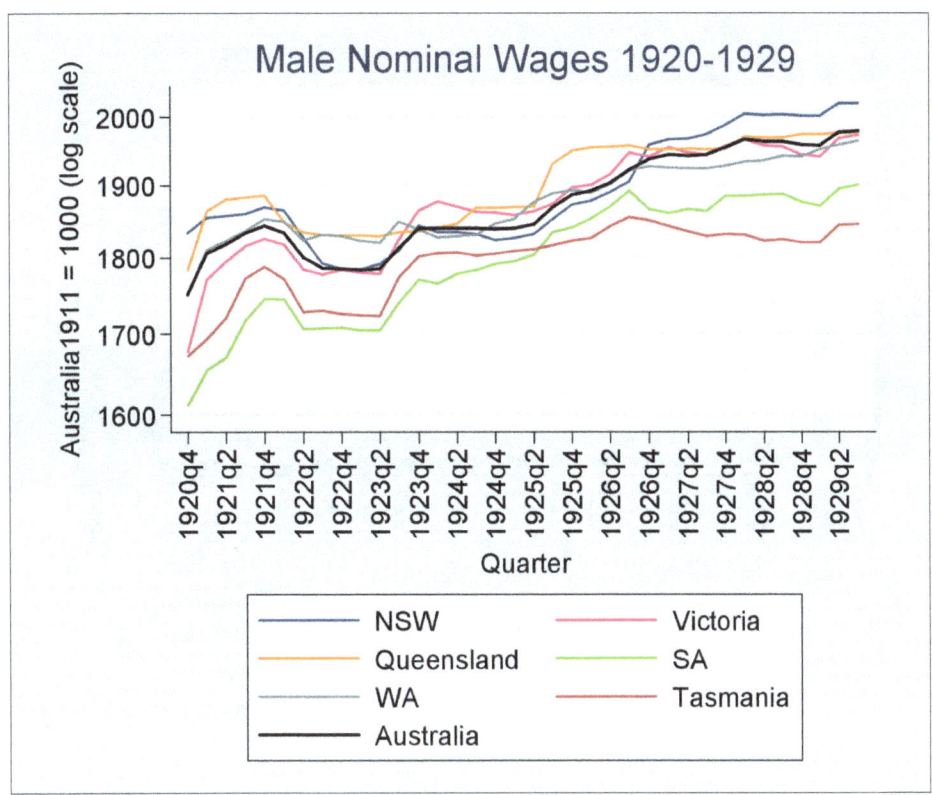

Figure 5.4
Source: *Labour Report*, various numbers.

in the six-capitals number was 16.5 per cent. Thereafter, the index fluctuated around a slowly rising trend. In the third quarter of 1929, it was 7.6 per cent higher than in the last quarter of 1922. Prices were conspicuously lower in Brisbane than in the other capitals. In the latter part of the decade, Sydney prices rose significantly above those of the other capital cities.

5.3.3 Real wages

Deflating the nominal wages represented in Figure 5.4 by the retail prices described in Figure 5.5, we get the real wage levels shown in Figure 5.6. A combination of rising nominal wages and falling prices had the effect that over one year—from the last quarter of 1920 to the last quarter of 1921—real

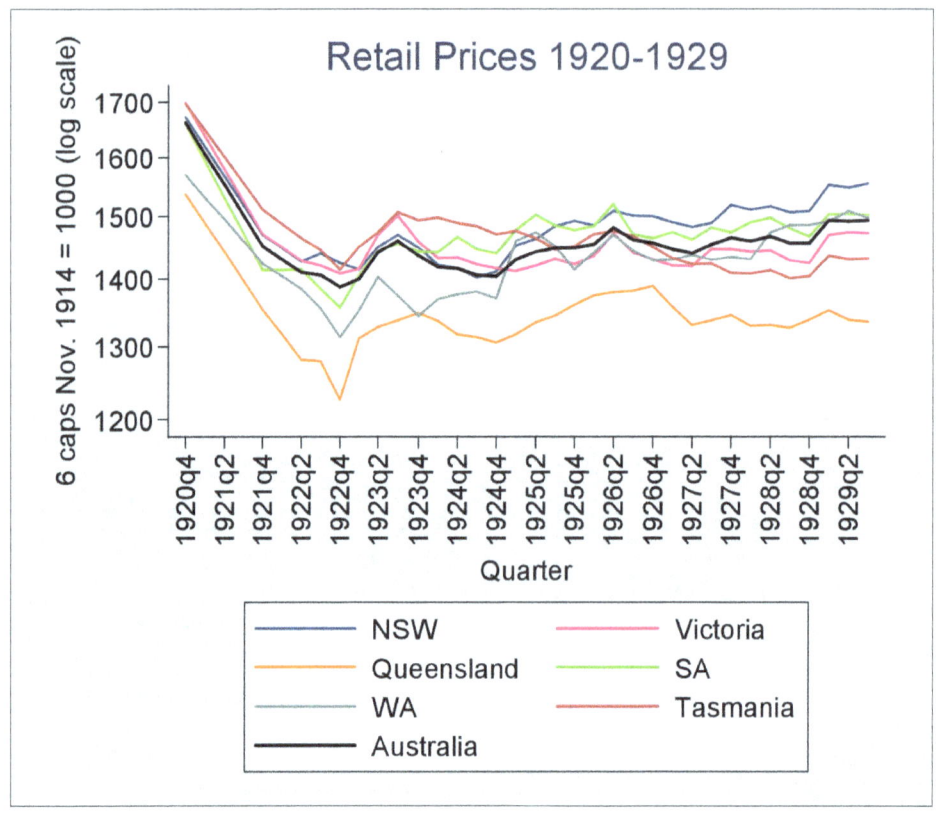

Figure 5.5
Note: The vertical scale shows index numbers, where the average for the six capital cities in 1914 is 1000. The numbers for the first three quarters of 1921 and the first quarter of 1922 are estimated by interpolation.
Source: *Labour Report*, various numbers.

wages rose by 21 per cent. Thereafter, however, changes were slight. Between the fourth quarter of 1921 and the third quarter of 1929, the average increase in real wages was 0.5 per cent per year. Fixing wages and conditions in the 1920s was a difficult task, because further advances in employment standards were hard to achieve. At the State level, Queensland workers enjoyed real wages about 10 per cent above the national average; South Australian and Tasmanian real wages were, on average, about 5 per cent below the all-Australian level; and Western Australia, where real wages were relatively high at the beginning of the decade, returned to the national average by its end.

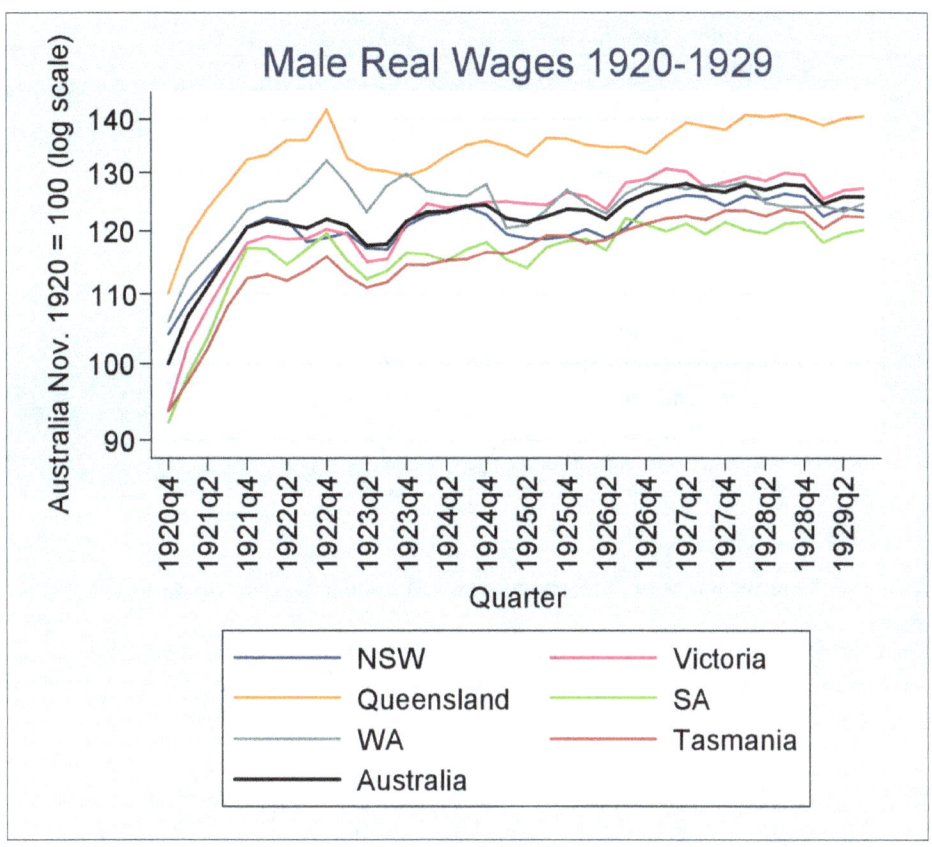

Figure 5.6

5.3.4 Industry wages

As noted in Section 2.3 of Chapter 2, nominal wage data were computed for 14 industrial groups. Such data continued to be available for later periods. Table 5.1 shows the relative wages in the various groups in 1921 and 1929. There were three conspicuous high-paid industries—books, printing, etc.; mining; and building—and two low-paid—agriculture and domestic. There was some reshuffling of the pack. The industry with the highest average wages in 1921—mining—had fallen to third place in 1929, behind books, printing, etc. (second in 1920), and building (third in 1920); and shipping, which was in ninth place in 1921, rose to fourth in 1929; but otherwise there were

Industry Group	1921	1929
Mining	113.2	109.0
Books, printing, etc.	109.3	117.6
Building	108.7	111.9
Engineering, etc.	105.0	102.5
Railways, etc.	104.7	103.7
Wood, furniture, etc.	104.7	103.2
Shipping, etc.	102.1	105.1
Other manufacturing	100.4	101.1
Food, drink, etc.	99.2	99.7
Clothing, boots, etc.	97.7	98.5
Other land transport	97.4	96.3
Miscellaneous	95.7	95.7
Agricultural, etc.	94.3	94.5
Domestic, etc.	88.0	92.1

Table 5.1: Relative wages in industry groups, 1914 and 1921 (percentage of the average wage)
Note: The 1921 data are for the second quarter, and the 1929 data are for the third quarter. In some cases the industry titles shown are abbreviations of fuller titles.
Source: *Labour Report*, various numbers.

only minor changes in the rankings. We saw in Chapter 2 that during the years 1914–21 the inter-industry pay structure became more equal. A similar calculation shows that between 1921 and 1929 there was little change.[5]

5.3.5 The federal basic wage

As we shall see in Chapter 6, in 1921 and 1922 the Arbitration Court adopted practices that made it meaningful to speak of *the* basic wage. This does not mean that there was a single rate, for there were geographical differences. But the new approach entailed simultaneous adjustment of the basic wage in most awards, whereas previously the amounts prescribed depended largely on the times at which the awards were made or (occasionally) varied.

---

[5] The regression line fitted to the logarithms of the relativities in Table 5.1 implies that if industry *A* in 1921 had an average wage 10 per cent greater than that of industry *B*, the difference in 1929 would have been 10.05 per cent.

The price index used in adjusting the basic wage combined the prices of 46 items of food and groceries and house rent. According to the Commonwealth Statistician, it represented about 60 per cent of the living costs of basic-wage earners. In respect of housing, rents of all houses were taken into account until 1925. The *Labour Report* for that year reported a change of practice: in future only houses of four or five rooms would be included.[6] The Court, however, apparently did not approve any change in the index used for wage adjustment.[7] The *Labour Report* stated that 'the preparation of index-numbers for food, groceries and rent of all houses in the 30 towns of the Commonwealth will be continued for the use of the Commonwealth Court of Conciliation and Arbitration ... and the results will be published in the Quarterly Summary of Statistics' (*Labour Report*, No. 16, 1925, p. 20). The Statistician's revised index for food, groceries, and rent became known as the 'B series' Index, and the alternative as the 'All Houses' or 'Court' Index.

The Piddington Commission had provided—no doubt with Sutcliffe's help—measurements of price movements taking into account clothing and miscellaneous items, as well as food, groceries, and rent. Moreover, it recommended that the Commonwealth Statistician maintain and publish an index based on the more comprehensive regimen. The Government accepted this recommendation. The *Labour Report* for 1920 (p. 25) said that the Bureau had been authorised 'to extend its investigations to cover the whole of the ordinary expenditure of a household' and that this was being done. It added, however, that 'the index-numbers computed for food, groceries and rent in the past can be accepted in general as a near approximation of the variation in the whole ordinary household expenditure'; and that it was 'only in abnormal

---

[6] This accorded with a resolution of the 1924 Conference of Statisticians of Australia and New Zealand. The *Labour Report* commented: 'Up to the present time the practice followed in computing the retail price index-number has been to take into account the rentals of all houses ranging from those of three rooms and under to those of seven rooms and upwards. In respect to rent this practice is, to some extent, a departure from the principle adopted with regard to food and groceries, i.e., that of taking the price of the predominant type of commodity, inasmuch as the rent of houses other than the predominant type has been included'.

[7] I have not discovered any reference to the matter in reported decisions.

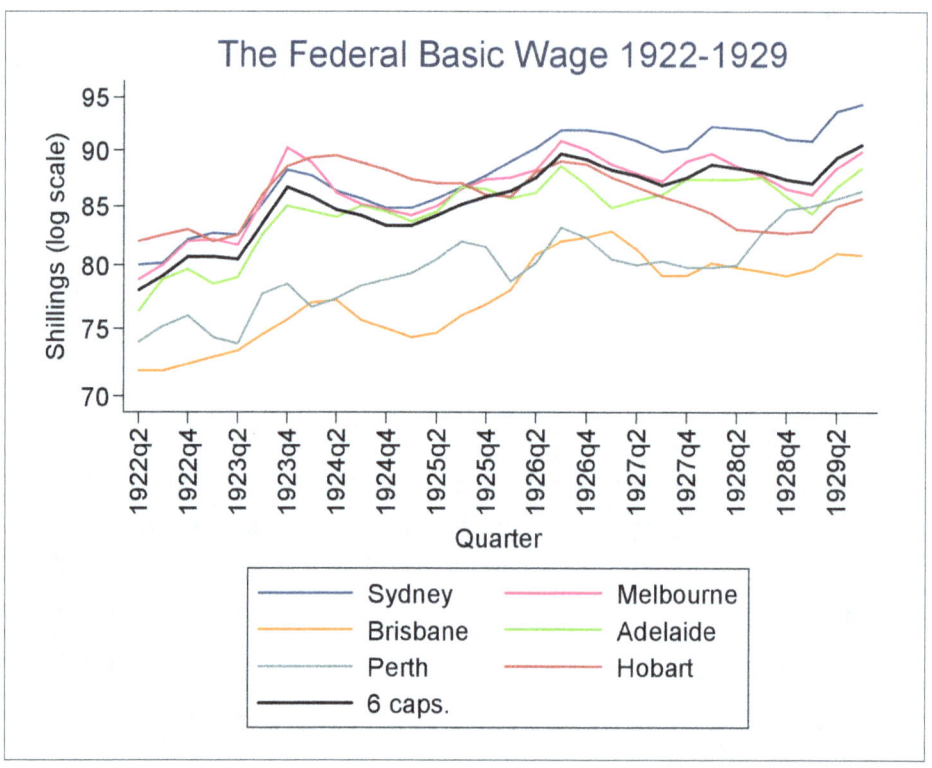

Figure 5.7
Source: Data supplied by the Librarian of Fair Work Australia.

times that the results based upon the cost of food, groceries and rent can be vitiated to any great extent'. In the *Labour Report* for 1921 (p. 52), the Statistician said that the existing index numbers were satisfactory measures of the movements of food and grocery prices and house rents.[8] The Bureau used the Royal Commission's 'indicator lists' for clothing and miscellaneous items.

The new price index—the future C series Index—had a base number of 1000 for November 1914, whereas the index for food, groceries, and housing had its base in 1911. The difference was due to the lack of data for the added items before 1914. For the 1920s, the two indices may readily be compared.

---

[8] The Royal Commission had stipulated a standard of five-roomed houses. The Statistician did not apply this requirement, but said that the movements in rents reflected in the Bureau's existing index numbers provided a reliable guide to movements in rents of five-roomed houses.

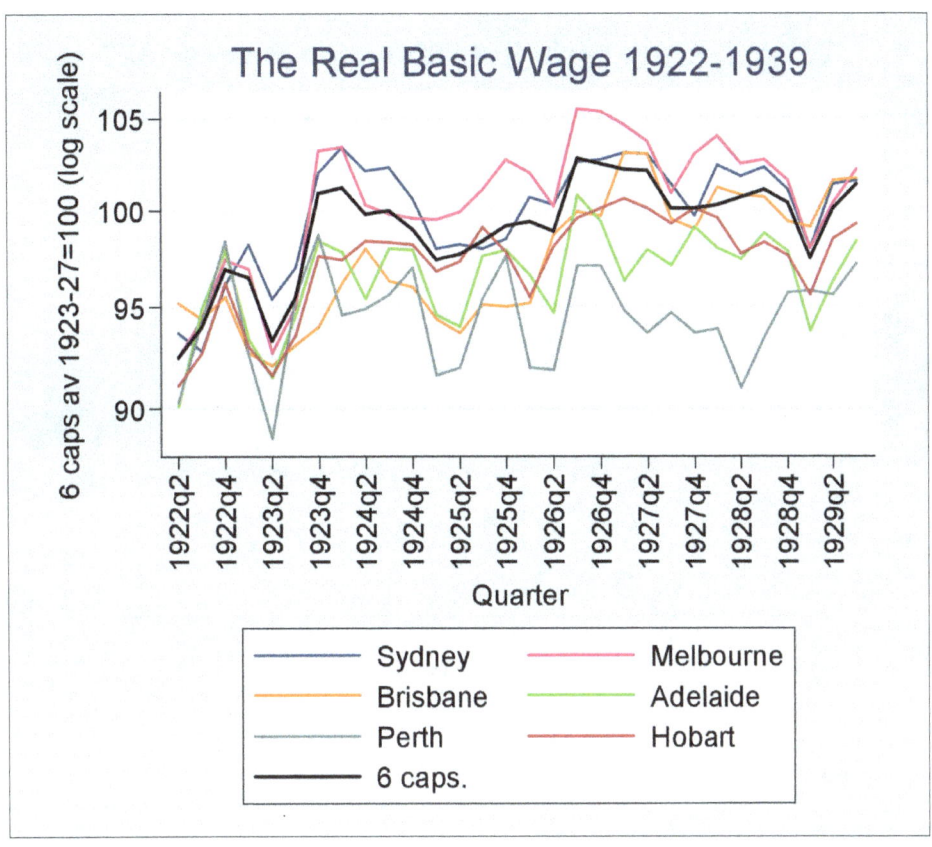

Figure 5.8
Source: Basic wage—see Figure 5.7; prices—*Labour Report*, various numbers.

Quarterly data are available of the basic wage for each capital city and the six capitals combined from the second quarter of 1922 onward.[9] Figure 5.7 shows the amounts of the basic wage up to the third quarter of 1929. For the six capital cities, the wage increased from 78s to 90s 6d—an increase of 16 per cent. Most of this increase occurred by the end of 1923: over the remainder of the period, the increase was just 4 per cent. For most of the period, the basic wage was above the average level in Sydney and below it in Brisbane and Perth.

Converting the quarterly wage levels to real equivalents, we get the results shown in Figure 5.8. The price index used for this purpose is the C

---

[9] See Chapter 1, Subsection 1.3.3 for explanation of these data.

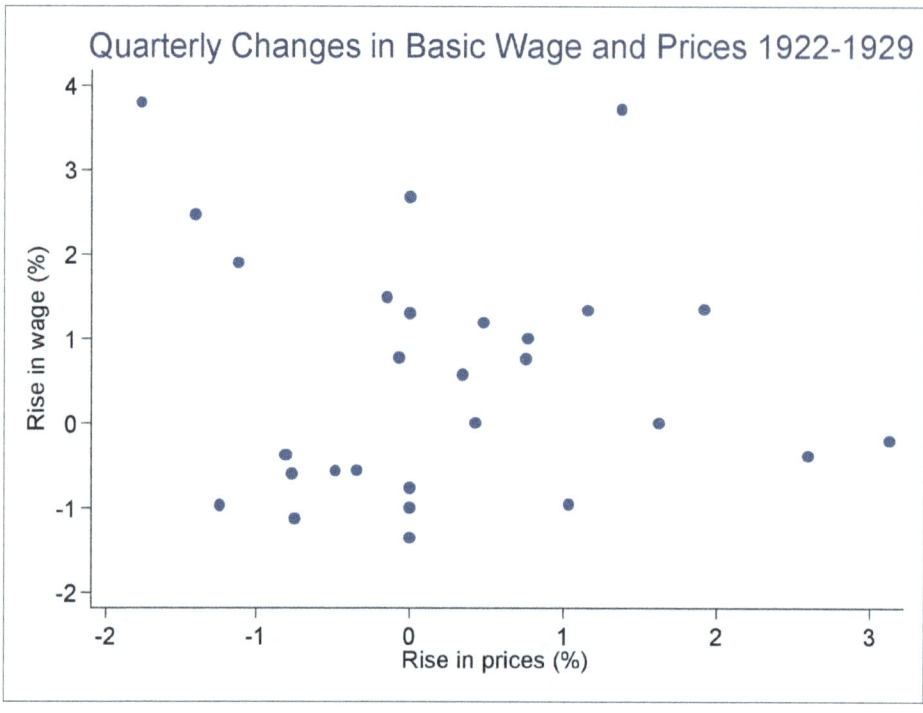

Figure 5.9

series Index. For the six-capitals average, the increase over the period was 11 per cent. This was concentrated in 1922 and 1923; thereafter, the increase was just above zero. The figure indicates both surprising volatility in the real basic wage and surprising differences between the capital cities.

Some temporal variation could be expected, because of the lags inherent in wage adjustment and because of the nominal wage being adjusted by minima of a shilling. But the changes shown in the figure seem greater than such factors would entail. The fact is that the quarterly movements of the basic wage were not well correlated with movements in the price index. This is apparent from Figure 5.9. To allow for the possibility that the quarterly data assume too close an alignment in time between wage and price movements, Figure 5.10 shows four-quarter moving averages, which should absorb most of any accidents of timing. The correlation is little improved.

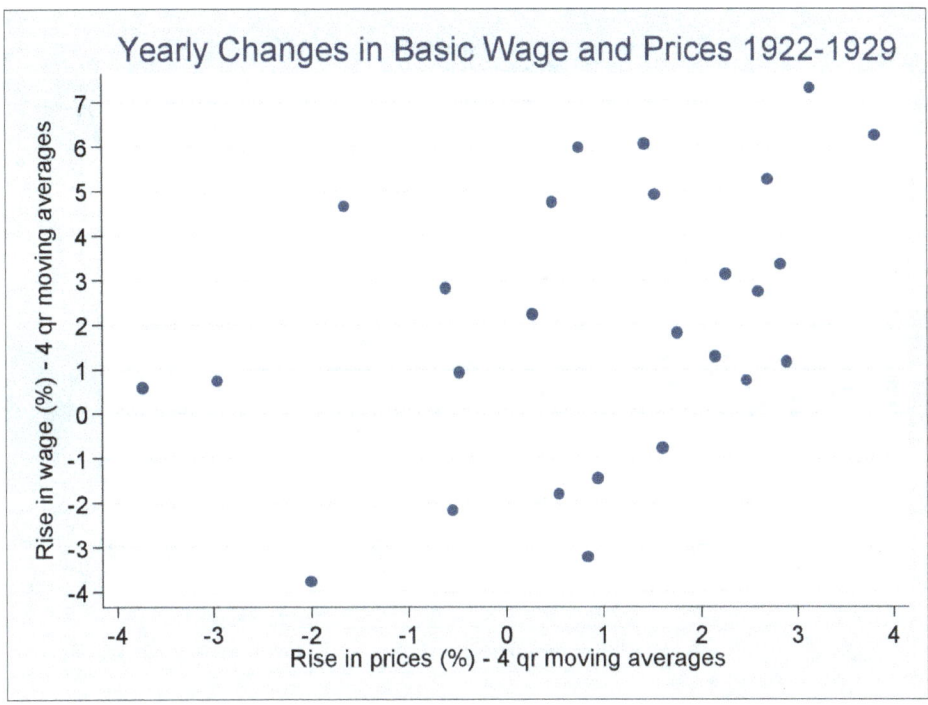

Figure 5.10

The All Items (C series) Index was not, however, the index used by the Court for adjusting the basic wage. The Court (supported by the Commonwealth Statistician) preferred the less-comprehensive index covering food, groceries, and house rent and until 1933 used this index for basic wage adjustment. In Figure 5.11, we compare the six-capitals B series and C series indices. For this purpose, the data, taken from the *Labour Report*, are shown with a base of 100 in November 1914—the commencing date for the C series Index.[10] Annual data for the years 1914–21 show that the C series Index rose considerably more than the B series—a divergence highlighted by the Piddington Commission. By early 1922, however, the two indices were close together. Thereafter the B series Index was above the C series. In the second quarter of 1926, the B series exceeded the C series by 9.1 per cent. The average excess over the period 1922–29 was 6.3 per cent. If a basic wage

---

[10] C series index data are annual until 1921; quarterly data begin with May 1922.

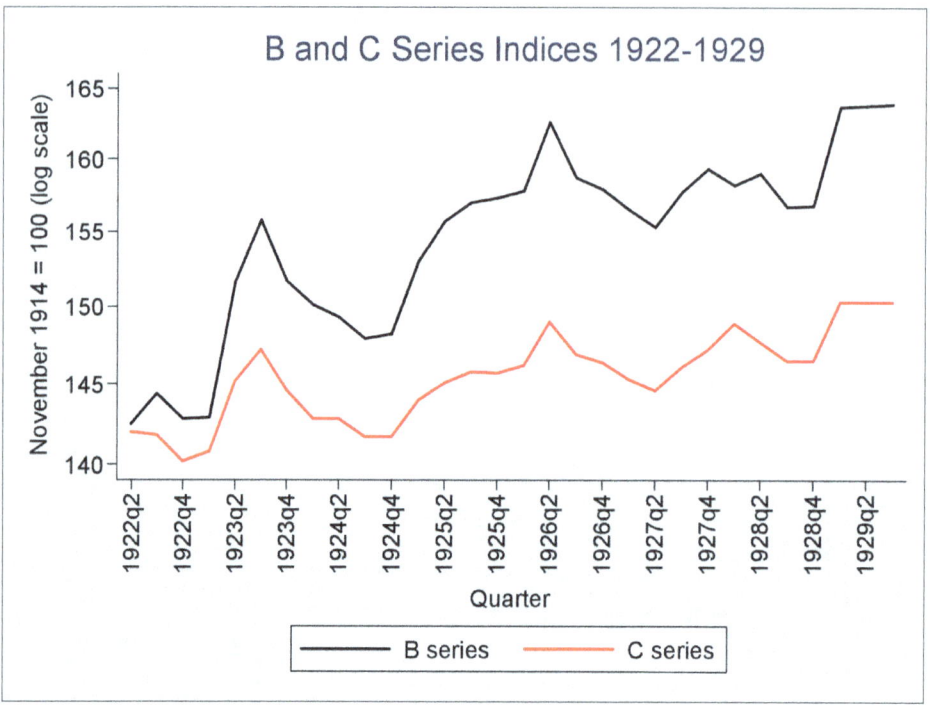

Figure 5.11
Source: *Labour Report*, various numbers.

adjusted to the C series Index was 'correct'—in the sense of compensating for price movements since 1914—a wage adjusted to the B series Index entailed an unintended bonus for the basic wage earner. The two indices shared two components: food and groceries, and housing (rents); but the C series Index had two extra components: clothing and miscellaneous.[11] Between the years 1921 and 1929, the percentage changes in the four components were:

Food and groceries	9.7
Housing	24.1
Clothing	-10.4
Miscellaneous	-0.5

---

[11] Gifford (1928) argued that because of deficiencies in the collection of data, the clothing and miscellaneous components of the C series index seriously understated the rise in prices (p. 36). Further criticisms of the index were made by union advocates in the 1930–31 basic wage case, discussed in Chapter 9.

The increase in the B series Index over this period was 15 per cent; of the C series Index, 5.8 per cent. The prices of clothing and miscellaneous items prices were not accurately proxied by the prices of food and groceries, and house rents. The average benefit to the basic wage earner (in the period represented in Figure 5.11) of linking the wage to the more limited index was 6.3 per cent, or over 5s per week—considerably more than the gain that he realised from Powers' 3s.

Does the use of the B series Index remove some or all of the volatility and inter-city disparities indicated in Figure 5.8? A comparison between Figure 5.8 and Figure 5.12 suggests that the answer is 'only a little'.

Figure 5.8 also showed differences between the capital cities in the levels of the real basic wage. These are contrary to expectation, because the application of the price index was intended to equalise the real wage.[12] Table 5.2 shows the average real basic wage in each of the six capital cities as a percentage of the 6-capitals real wage, distinguishing between the two index numbers. The choice of index clearly affects the comparison, and the differences were less with the B series Index as the deflator.

Overall, however, the volatility of the real basic wage and the inter-city differences remain mysterious.

It might have been expected that employers would make something of the difference between the alternative price indices, since deflation by the C series suggests that there was an unintended rise in the real wage. They did, but only toward the end of the period. The issue assumed importance in employer arguments in the 1930–31 basic wage case, discussed in a later chapter. In that case, the union advocates criticised the C series Index. One of their advocates was H C Gibson, who had been a member of the Royal Commission on the Basic Wage. Gibson elicited from C H Wickens, the Commonwealth Statistician, acknowledgement that some of the items in the miscellaneous category were priced at constant amounts. The amounts had

---

[12] This is not quite accurate, because Powers' 3s (see Chapter 6) was not adjusted for prices.

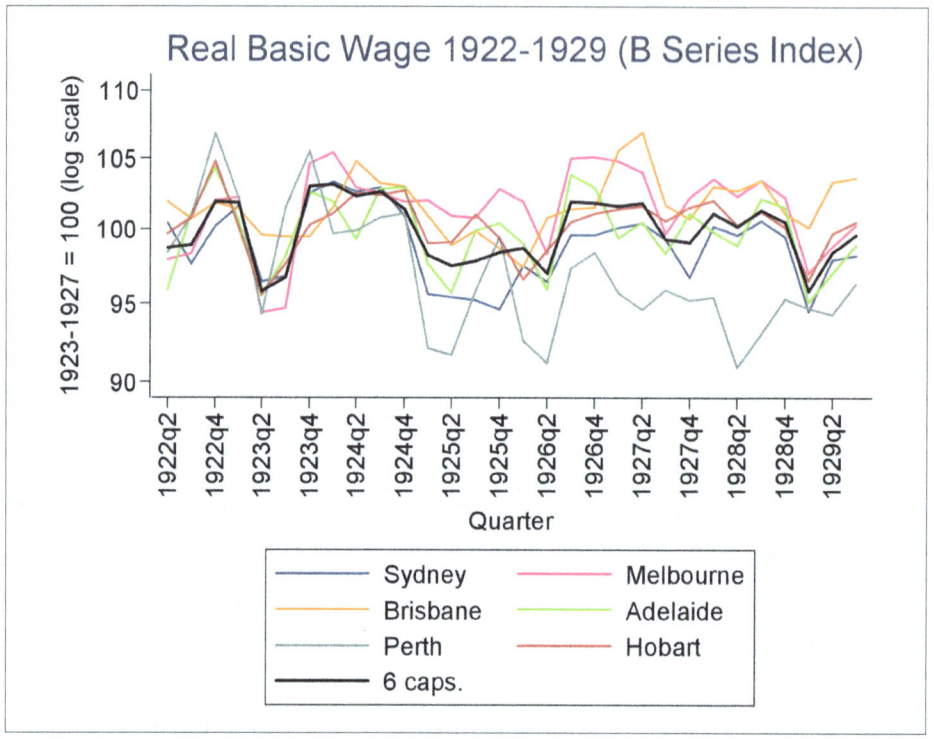

Figure 5.12

been identified by the Royal Commission in 1920. Hence for the whole of the 1920s the prices entered the index at the 1920 values. Among the items so recorded were fares, cinema tickets, smoking requisites, and school requisites. Gibson contended that the items whose prices were assumed to be constant had in fact become dearer, with the result that the index had a downward bias. Wickens claimed that the prices in question were difficult to ascertain. Gibson replied that the Royal Commission had been able to get them (transcript, pp. 199–209). Whether or not there was a systematic bias, as Gibson alleged, the substitution of assumed prices for prices obtained by inquiry obviously reduced the reliability of the miscellaneous component of the index.[13]

---

[13] The unions advanced other criticisms of the indices. Mention is made of these in Chapter 9.

	B series	C series
Sydney	-1.0	0.9
Melbourne	1.5	1.5
Brisbane	1.7	-1.6
Adelaide	-0.1	-2.5
Perth	-2.9	-4.6
Hobart	0.4	-1.8

Table 5.2: **The real basic wage in capital cities (percentage differences from 6-capitals average)**

5.4 WORKING HOURS

For Australia as a whole, the average working week of adult males—as measured by the hours prescribed in awards, statutes, and formal agreements—was 47.07 hours on 31 December 1920. By the end of 1929, it had fallen to 45.34 hours. Figure 5.13 shows the movements of hours in the several States and Australia between 1919 and 1930.[14]

In three States—Victoria, South Australia, and Tasmania—nominal hours were similar and above those in the rest of the country. They also varied little across the decade. In Western Australia, there was a more gradual (though not uninterrupted) fall in working hours due mainly to decisions of the State tribunal.

It would appear that the Australia-wide pattern was significantly affected by State regulation in New South Wales and Queensland.[15] In 1920 the New South Wales Parliament passed the *Eight Hours (Amendment) Act*

---

[14] I can throw little light on the reliability of the data, but note that there are several instances in which the averages within States do not change from one year to the next. As they are given to two decimal points, this is somewhat surprising.

[15] The ensuing outline of State provisions is based on Anderson (1929, p. 527), various numbers of the *Labour Report*, and Nyland (1987, pp. 42–44).

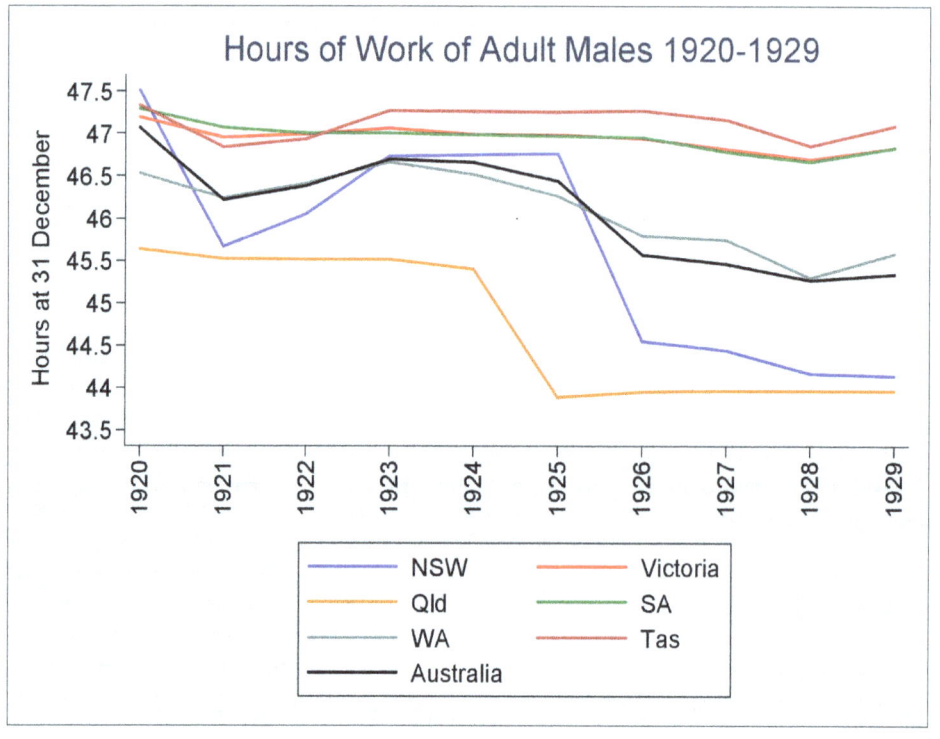

Figure 5.13

1920. This created a special mechanism for dealing with applications for a 44-hour week and created a presumption that such applications would normally be granted. Under this legislation, the 44-hour week was applied in many industries. In 1922, after a change of government, the Act was repealed and the discretion with respect to working hours was restored to the Court of Industrial Arbitration. Existing provisions for 44 hours remained in force until altered by the Court. Late in 1925, the New South Wales Parliament passed the *Forty-four Hours Week Act 1925*, which made the 44-hour week a general standard (with limited exceptions). The statutory provision for a 44-hour week was repealed in June 1930 and restored in the following December. The Queensland Parliament in 1924 passed an Act that provided for a maximum working week of 44 hours, with few exceptions.

5.5 Labour standards and economic constraints

Forster (1987) observed that a long-run situation in which *per capita* output rises little is likely to be a difficult one for labour relations, because it limits the scope for raising real wages and is likely to engender disputes over income shares. This observation has particular relevance to the 1920s, when labour clearly aspired to significant advances in wages and conditions. There was, in fact, a large increase in real wages in the years 1921 and 1922. The limitations of the data preclude precise statements of the orders of change, but the statistics suggest that the net effect of the wartime deterioration and the post-war resurgence was a rise in average real wages of 10 to 20 per cent. Superimposed on an apparently sluggish growth in productivity, this could only lead to a circumstance in which further improvements were difficult to achieve. It was not, however, an intended effect of wage-setting and went largely unnoticed. In demanding advances in wages and conditions, labour focused on the intention rather than the reality.

There is little sign, indeed, that the 'jump' in real wages in 1921 and 1922 played much part in the thinking of the Court or the parties that appeared before it. Certainly, the trade unions appeared to believe that little or no progress had been made. Their attitudes were affected, no doubt, by the continued role of the 14-year-old *Harvester* standard as a benchmark for the basic wage and the refusal of the Court to adjust skill margins for inflation. This study is not about industrial disputation, but it is well known that much of the period was turbulent. One of the causes of the turbulence was the difficulty of satisfying labour's aspirations. For its part, the Court was inclined to argue that the unions understated the improvements that had been achieved, but it evinced no strong presumption that rising standards were the norm. There was no expectation of continuous improvement supported by rising productivity. Indeed, the possibility of standards having to be wound back was taken seriously, both in 1921–22 and in the later 1920s.

In 1922, Powers reflected on a union contention that workers had benefited little from the Court's policies and practices:

Mr Gibson[16] ... asks—Is the *Harvester* standard fixed in 1907 to stand as it was in 1907? The answer to that is certainly not. As soon as some better standard is shown to be necessary based on what people really need to live in reasonable comfort, it will be altered ... But as a matter of fact it has already been altered for the benefit of the workers generally and especially for those on the basic wage.

Since 1907, men have secured payment for holidays never granted in 1907 or for many years after.

Since then the weekly wage has been granted to secure the standard wage for the week.

Since then the wage has been based on the cost of living on the quarter preceding the award which prevents losses complained of by the workers.

Quarterly adjustments have been introduced to secure the living wage during the award.

3s a week has been added to the *Harvester* standard to prevent the possibility of loss during any quarter.

The actual wage received by the worker has been greatly increased since 1907 apart from the increased cost of living, and the standard of living has necessarily been raised because it has been proved that it was fair to do so.

For instance, very many classes of skilled work have been reclassified at higher rates since 1907 and some work for which the basic rate only was allowed in 1907 is now paid for as slightly skilled work at rates above the basic wage. Rates for work done on Sundays and holidays have been raised. Public holidays have been increased. Annual holidays are given in proper cases.

In addition hours of work generally have been reduced to the Australian standard of 48 hours, in some cases from 60 hours a week and in others from 56, 54, 52, and 50 a week to 48. Where the health of the worker is endangered and in the industries where the work is intermittent the

---

[16] Gibson had been a member of the Piddington Commission.

> hours have been reduced to 44 hours or even less to secure to the worker the basic wage for the week.
>
> Workers in continuous processes who were required to work seven days in the week for 8 hours for 365 days in the year, now only work six days in the week, working on one Sunday in seven.
>
> The conditions of work generally have been greatly improved for the worker by State and Federal Arbitration Awards. (*Engine-Drivers'* case, 16 CAR 1107, 1120–1121)

Powers might have added to this list the spread of the Court's wages and conditions and those set by State tribunals across the labour force. Of its nature, this is a process whose effects cannot be measured. But they may well have been large.

Soon afterwards, the union representative in a *Carpenters and Joiners'* case (16 CAR 1136) told Webb that 'what we want is some tangible benefit, something that will improve our actual social and economic position, something that will enable us to get comforts that we are not now able to purchase, and to keep them all the year round'. Webb responded by quoting remarks of Higgins in *A New Province for Law and Order*:

> I am not unaware of the far-reaching schemes, much discussed elsewhere, which contemplate conditions of society in which adjustment of labour conditions between profit-makers and wage-earners may become necessary. Our Australian Court has nothing to do with these schemes. It has to shape its conclusions on the solid anvil of facts, in the fulfilment of definite official responsibilities. It has the advantage, as well as the disadvantage, of being limited in its powers and objects. Its objective is industrial peace, as between those who do the work, and those who direct it. It has no duty, it has no right, to favour or condemn any theories of social reconstruction. It neither hinders nor helps them. (pp. 1139–1140)

Webb said that although it was no function of the Court 'to alter our social laws', there was a 'striking contrast between the social and industrial conditions of Australia and those in any other part of the world'; and it was 'not unfair to say that the Industrial Courts of Australia have been the main factor in bringing about the conditions ... which stand in such marked contrast to the wretched conditions which exist in so many other lands'. These results had been achieved 'by following the simple duty of awarding fair wages and conditions according to definite and carefully considered principles' (p. 1140).

In 1925, Powers again reflected on the advances in working standards that had been achieved under arbitration, emphasising the breadth of the changes:

> Since [1907] the standard then fixed has been altered by increasing the basic wage, by increasing overtime rates, by fixing weekly instead of hourly rates—or allowances if the rate is daily or hourly—by allowances for pay during sickness, by fixing shorter hours and better conditions, by preventing employees being required to work seven days a week for 365 days a year in continuous processes, by increasing the standard wage for women workers, and greatly improving their conditions, by basing the rate on the cost of living at the time the award is made instead of on the preceding calendar year, by ordering quarterly adjustments of wages to secure to the workers the living wage during the term of the award, by discouraging the employment of men for long periods in high temperatures, in mines and other places, by special conditions, rest periods, reduced hours or extra rates, and in many other ways to which it is not necessary to refer. (Resignation statement, 18 December 1925, 22 CAR xxxi, xxxvi)

Powers might have added to his list the gradual award of margins to many classes of labour that hitherto had been paid only the basic wage. On the other hand, he could also have noted the failure of the system to preserve the real value of the margins paid to skilled workers.

In the *Main Hours* case of 1926–27 (24 CAR 755),[17] Charlie Crofts (one of the principal union advocates) spoke of the stagnation of real wages since 1907:

---

[17] Discussed, at length, in Chapter 7.

> The basic wage man has remained stationary since 1907, so far as his economic position is concerned. But the artisan has gone back. He has not maintained his position. In 1907, in the *Harvester* judgment, he received 3s per day above the basic wage. Today the Court allows 4s. The cost of living has gone up from 7s to 15s 1d, which is over 100 per cent, but the artisan's margin has only increased from 3s to 4s. Therefore, he has receded in his economic position since 1907. (transcript, p. 215)

The advance of labour standards was restricted by perceptions of poor economic performance. In the course of this case, there was much debate as to whether the economy was more or less productive than it had been before World War I. No one claimed more than a modest gain. In his closing address for the unions, Crofts complained of his adversaries' standpoint that 'everything has to be judged from the period 1910–14'. Was everything, he asked, 'to be judged by the highest peak of prosperity'? It had been shown 'that even as compared with the peak years chosen by the employers, we are within about 3 per cent of the production of that period' (transcript, p. 5616–A). From today's perspective, celebration of a GDP within 3 per cent of the level reached 15 years earlier seems extraordinary.

A discussion of the determinants of long-term change in labour standards occurred in the *Merchant Service Guild* case decided by Dethridge in 1928 (27 CAR 482). The Guild was concerned about a decline in the living standards of ships' officers, but painted on a wider canvas. Dethridge's decision discusses the movements of both 'productivity' and labour's share in the 'national dividend'. Of the former, he said:

> As to Captain Lawrence's contention that Australia has now reached the same extent of productivity per head of population as in or about 1910, it is not at all certain that this is correct. Probably, as I said in the hours' case, we are now not far short of that achievement, but one cannot feel a comfortable certainty on the point. ... The production statistics on the whole rather suggest that in the years 1910–12 there was an abnormal increase in productivity generally, which of course

> facilitated the granting of higher marginal wages at that time, and that that increase would not have been maintained even if the war had not intervened. (p. 499)

Dethridge's perception, right or wrong, that there had been little or no productivity growth over nearly two decades is striking. It implies a limited scope for improvement of conditions of the employment, and it accords with the tenor of many of the Court's decisions. As to income shares, Captain Lawrence had evidently argued that there had been a long-term shift to profits which the Court should try to correct. Dethridge could find little support for this thesis in J T Sutcliffe's recently published book, *The National Dividend*. But he also sought the advice of C H Wickens, the Commonwealth Statistician, who told Dethridge that the only available data about the share of interest and profits in output were for manufacturing.

> Mr Wickens has been good enough to furnish me with a table extracted from the manufacturing statistics, which shows that after deducting from the total factory output the cost of 'materials' used, fuel and light' and 'salaries and wages', the percentage of the margin available for 'profit and miscellaneous expenses', which in 1913 was 17.52 per cent, and in 1914 was 17.57 per cent, was practically the same in 1924 to 1927, viz., 17.27 per cent in 1924–5, 17.16 per cent in 1925–6, and 17.56 per cent in 1926–27. (p. 498)

Overall, the decisions of the Court in the 1920s—especially the later years—convey an assumption that the opportunities for advancing wages and conditions were severely limited. As we shall see in Chapter 7, the Court became convinced that the adoption of piecework would solve the problem of low productivity and deplored union opposition to it. It both held out the prospect of better terms if piece work were accepted and threatened to remove existing benefits if the unions continued to reject it. Its exhortations had little effect.

6

The Powers era

———•———

In the light of the discussion in Chapter 5, it is not surprising that wages policy during the 1920s was conducted in an atmosphere of stringency. In this chapter, we see the effects of the perceived stringency on the kinds of decisions made in the period of Powers' Presidency, before the Court's reconstruction in 1926.

6.1 THE BASIC WAGE

6.1.1 Powers and the Royal Commission

Having succeeded Higgins as President, Powers held his own inquiry into the application of the Piddington standard. The *Gas Employees'* case, decided in September 1921, was a 'test case'. Powers allowed unions and employers generally to be represented. He described the dimensions of the case:

> During the hearing of this inquiry the parties have submitted numerous text-books, judgments, awards, statistical records, and other documentary evidence, and some oral evidence. The whole of the evidence taken before the Royal Commission, covering 2,879 pages of printed foolscap, has also been submitted; and the report of the Commission itself; the subsequent memorandum of the Chairman; the Supplementary Report of the Royal Commission; a pamphlet entitled *The Next Step* (by the Chairman, Mr A B Piddington); and one entitled *The Basic Wage Betrayal,* published by the Committee of the Conference

of Federated Unions. In addition I have before me the shorthand report of the addresses of the representatives of the parties, which occupied over four days. It is impossible in a judgment on the question before this Court, under the circumstances, to deal in detail with the evidence, or the reasons urged by the parties, or to do much more than state the decisions arrived at on the principal questions raised. (15 CAR 838, 841–842)

It was necessary, said Powers, to consider 'fully' the Royal Commission's report. He recalled that 'the Court itself, to make sure that it was going on safe lines, strongly recommended the appointment of a Royal Commission to report on the basic wage question on a scientific and humane basis. Although the Commission suggested by this Court was not appointed, it makes it none the less necessary to seriously consider the report and finding of the Commission …' (p. 842). Like Higgins in the *ASE* case (discussed in Chapter 3), Powers made much of the Royal Commission's letters patent. The issue now was

> whether the Royal Commission was asked to find, or did find, a basic, or living wage, as recognised by the Courts in Australia, viz., one in which the interests of employees, employers and the public should be considered—or to find any basic wage at all;—or, whether the members were only asked to consider what the actual cost of living at a certain date was, according to what the members of the Commission considered were reasonable standards of comfort, for a man (not an unskilled worker only), his wife and three children under fourteen years of age, without having to consider the question of whether the amount they found could, or should, be paid by the employers, or by the public of Australia. (p. 843)

The answer was that the members of the Commission 'were not bound to consider the basic-wage earner only, or the effect of their recommendations on industry generally, or the interests of employers, or of the community, and it is clear they did not consider the matters mentioned' (p. 844). Moreover, two of the employer representatives had stated in a minority report that they

Charles Powers

did not concur in the main report 'if it could be construed as a report on what the basic wage should be'.

The Royal Commission, in its supplementary report, denied that it had made any recommendation as to what the basic wage should be or how the cost of living should be taken into count. Powers commented that 'if that statement had been made with the original report, it would not have raised false hopes and it would have saved an immense amount of misunderstanding, and unrest, and dissatisfaction among workers with the wages that are being paid under the different Courts' awards, and Wages Boards determinations, throughout the Commonwealth'.

Notwithstanding his emphasis on the letters patent, Powers was otherwise critical of aspects of the Report. The Royal Commission had allowed for 'a quantity and quality of clothes which, I know from my experience in this Court, are not necessary for men, women and children to live in reasonable comfort, even when in receipt of £400 a year' (p. 852). He cited newspaper advertisements offering suits for less than the prices allowed by the Commission (p. 854). As to food, much evidence had been taken about the calorie requirements of the family; but 'whatever mistakes Mr Justice Higgins is supposed to have made, it was not contended that he did not allow sufficient for food and groceries' (p. 855). Powers did not think it necessary 'to trouble about the necessary number of calories that scientific men consider necessary'.[1]

'The Commission', Powers concluded, 'approached the question of a standard of living from an entirely different point of view to that from which this Court has to approach the question of a basic wage, and it may account for the Commission itself—and the Chairman in particular—not recommending its finding to be adopted as a basic wage' (p. 855). But were there other grounds for increasing the basic wage? Here Powers resorted to the 'onus' principle that has so often been used by arbitrators to answer difficult questions. It would have to be proved that *Harvester* 'did not in 1907 give to the unskilled worker a fair wage based on current human standards'; that his own decision of October 1918, given 'after full inquiry into the cost of living including food, groceries, rent and clothing, and all items of miscellaneous expenditure' was wrong; and that various decisions of State tribunals were also wrong (p. 856). Moreover, it was now established that the typical family contained fewer than three children under fourteen. But he did not propose to reduce the basic wage, because 'the community has accepted the wage for a family of five as a fair thing' (p. 860). Further indicators of the sufficiency of current wage levels were the growth of savings and the amounts spent on alcohol, gambling, and smoking:

> No one objects to the working man having a smoke, or begrudges him his picture-shows, sports, or recreation; and this Court has to recognise

---

[1] It is true that the amount allowed by Higgins in 1907 *for food alone*, adjusted for price changes, met or exceeded the Royal Commission's standard. The Royal Commission did not say otherwise; but it could hardly have taken the food component of the wage as a given without taking evidence on the point. Higgins' 'measurement' of the food requirements of the family of five could not have been treated as conclusive by a serious commission of inquiry: if Higgins got it right, that was fortuitous.

'current human standards', and that many people will smoke, drink, and gamble, and live in houses of less than five rooms to enable them to do so. It is not within the Court's function to preach to the community, but I think it right to point out that the benefits the worker enjoys, some of which I have referred to, could not be enjoyed ... if the Court's awards, which are attacked by the unions as insufficient, did not at least secure a fair and reasonable wage to the workers generally, as long as they only have families of three children. (pp. 862–863)

Finally, Powers discussed the question whether the country could pay the Royal Commission rates. Authorities for thinking that it could not were the Commonwealth Statistician, the Prime Minister, and the Chairman of the Royal Commission. Respondent employers had submitted statistical returns supporting this position. The unions' attempts to refute these contentions were not convincing. Knibbs' report to the Prime Minister had not been produced and Knibbs was not called as a witness; but Powers assumed 'that he could have satisfactorily defended his report if he had been called' (p. 864).

The 'fallacy' had been pressed in this and other cases that higher wages were made possible by better machinery and labour-saving devices. This, said Powers, was wrong because these developments 'cannot enable the employer to grant to workers better conditions if competitors in other countries, with equally good machinery and labour-saving appliances, sell their goods in Australia at a price which will not let the producer get a larger profit than he did with the inferior machinery, and that is the case at present' (pp. 864–865). The technical improvements were necessary 'to allow industry to be carried on at all'. Powers did not explore the question: if the improved productivity made possible by machinery and labour-saving devices did not flow to higher real wages or higher real profits, who were the beneficiaries?

Employers, it was true, always said that the time was inopportune for wage increases; but 'there is no doubt about the truth of the objection this time'. Powers continued:

> We are living in a time of world-wide depression, causing unemployment everywhere, a reduction of wages in all countries, and in many countries longer working hours. As the world is now one market, Australia must be affected by what is going on elsewhere, and has already been affected by it ... The common enemy of employers and employees at the present time is the economic position, and both labour and capital should work together instead of fighting each other, and help to secure *greater production*, so as to allow industries to be carried on and a decent standard of living to be maintained in Australia ... I am satisfied that this Court, if it granted the [union application for £5 16s], would do so much harm to the workers of Australia that they would have to abandon their unions to get employment clear of award rates, or parliament would have to brush aside the Court and its awards to let industries be carried on. (pp. 865–866)

The decision was 'to continue the fair and practicable minimum wage the Court has adopted for so many years, instead of adopting the higher standard fixed by the Royal Commission, which is not practicable at the present time as a flat rate' (p. 873).

Piddington's child-endowment proposal was 'worthy of the most serious consideration by the Parliaments of the Commonwealth, for, at present, a very great injustice is done to families of over three dependent children', but its implementation was beyond the present power of the Court.

6.1.2 Applying *Harvester*

It is plain from earlier discussion that between 1907 and 1920 the Court's methods of adjusting the basic wage so as to align it with the *Harvester* standard were crude. The long intervals between wage changes (made award by award) and the use of price index numbers that were outdated had the effect that, for much of the period, the real basic wage was significantly below *Harvester*. As we saw above, the Royal Commission proposed a method of automatic adjustment that would have reduced the lags; but the use of annual price data would still have left room for discrepancies between the assumed and the actual cost of living.

In 1921, however, the economic context was significantly different from that of earlier years. Business was depressed, prices were falling and real wages were rising. The stickiness of money wages, relative to prices, turned in the wage-earners' favour (if they retained their jobs). Frequent and up-to-date adjustments became less favourable to employees than the previous slow processes. A continuation of the assumption described in Subsection 3.6.5 (involving a two-year delay) implies a Melbourne basic wage for the last quarter of 1922 exceeding the *Harvester* standard by 9 per cent. By contrast, a delay of only one quarter entailed a rise of less than 1 per cent.

In this environment, some employers and unions began to agree on automatic adjustment arrangements. I cannot say whether the predominant motivation was that of employers wishing to avoid paying excessive wages or of unions thinking that rising prices might soon return. In the *ASE* case, Higgins said:

> It is very gratifying to find that a practice has grown up and is increasing, now that employers and employees have come to understand the ways of this Court, of agreeing to vary the basic wage periodically according to the fluctuations of the tables of the Commonwealth Statistician. The tables are applied to my rough and tentative finding of 7s per day, 42s per week, in the *Harvester* case of 1907. (15 CAR 297, 302)

In August, Powers said in the *Wallaroo and Moonta* case:

> It is clear that some alterations in the war methods should now be made to prevent employees receiving less than the living wage fixed by the Court in future awards during the term of the award ... I think the method lately introduced into consent awards and agreements between registered unions and employers during the last twelve months will be found to be fair, namely, to fix a rate for the time of the award subject to adjustment each quarter on the Statistician's figures. This would save expense, delay, and uncertainty to the parties and the time of the

employers, employees, and of the Court taken up at present in variations of awards to meet the cost of living. (15 CAR 704, 716)

Also in August, Powers in the *Clothing Trades* case made a consent award that provided for half-yearly adjustments of the basic wage: an adjustment would be made on 1 February for the prices of the year ended on the previous 31 December, and another on 1 August for prices of the year ended 30 June. Powers added, however, that 'the wages adjustment clauses are only made by consent and special request of the parties and cannot be used as a precedent in other cases as I have already announced that the Court is now considering the claim for a different basic wage and the Court intends to reconsider the method of fixing the basic wage in view of the continued and rapid decrease of the cost of living since October last' (15 CAR 746, 747).

While both Higgins and Powers resisted the unions' attempt to substitute the Royal Commission's standard for *Harvester*, Powers in particular was exercised by the possibility that the *Harvester* standard, now closer to being achieved, might be too high for some employers. In the *Wallaroo and Moonta* case, decided in August 1921 (15 CAR 704), both the level of prices and the economic crisis were factors in his decision. The Wallaroo and Moonta Mining and Smelting Company had closed its mines because of the depressed price of copper, but later told employees that it would reopen them if it were assured that no award would be made for 6 months on plaints lodged earlier in the year. It would guarantee a minimum wage of 11s per shift, although the basic wage would ordinarily be over 12s. Most ex-employees (1354 out of 1400) had signified their willingness to accept this, but the unions did not. The Company asked the Court to exercise its discretion not to make an award. Powers granted the application.[2]

This decision differed from one that Powers had given in June in the *Mt Lyall* case (15 CAR 604). Mt Lyall was the only copper producer that remained in operation, and the company had stated that it would close unless

---

[2] He added the proviso: 'I do not definitely decide that no award shall be made for six months, but so long as the price of copper remains at its present price (or less than £77 a ton) I do not propose, on the facts at present before me, to make any award' (p. 711).

it were given relief from increases granted earlier in the year by Higgins. Some unions had agreed to a six-month deferral of the increases. Powers granted the deferral *except* for the basic wage; that is, the higher basic wage would be 'absorbed' into the margins of the skilled workers.[3]

In the *Wallaroo and Moonta* case he argued both that it was proper to adapt the basic wage to maintain employment and that his decision did not entail a violation of established principles. As to the former, he did not feel justified 'by any order of this Court in preventing 1,400 men from obtaining employment in these times at rates they think fair and reasonable' (p. 711). 'The Court's living wage', he said, 'was not made to prevent men working for nine-tenths of what the Court thinks a living wage, if they wish to do so without the intervention of the Court—when, if they do not, they will not get any wage at all—or because they know they can live in any particular locality for less than the Court on the evidence before it believes to be a living wage' (p. 714). Even if the Court had treated the basic wage as 'sacrosanct', it had not so treated any particular method of varying it. For a time, Higgins and Powers had followed different practices in that Higgins related the basic wage to prices in the previous calendar year, whereas Powers had referred to prices in the immediately previous four quarters (though Higgins had adopted the latter method in the 1919 *Gas* case). Powers mentioned this

> to show that the Court has not laid down any method of fixing the basic wage as 'sacrosanct'; on the contrary it has always fixed it on the basis that seemed to it fairest at the time of the award to secure to employees a living wage during the term of the award. ... The Court has always heretofore, by adopting different methods for fixing the basic wage, adjusted itself to existing conditions as changes take place, and it must continue to do so in the interests of employees, employers, and the community. (pp. 715–716)

It was true, Powers acknowledged, that if the *Harvester* 7s in Melbourne were adjusted to prices for the 12 months to the previous June, the amount in Wallaroo and Moonta would be 12s 11d. But this was an inappropriate

---

[3] The issue of increases in margins had a wider context, discussed in Section 6.2 below.

benchmark. 'I would not be justified', said Powers, 'in ordering the closing of an industry causing further unemployment, because in September and October of 1920 the cost of living was abnormal and not likely to recur again in Australia for some time to come.' He reproduced a 'rough graph' prepared at the Statistician's Office demonstrating, for Sydney and Wallaroo, the 1920 peak. 'The figures quoted and a reference to the graph', he said, 'confirm what I have already stated and show the necessity of adopting some method of fixing the basic wage different from that adopted during the years 1914 to 1920 inclusive' (pp. 719–720).

Moreover, Powers continued, Higgins and he had always taken special factors into account in setting a basic wage in a locality rather than 'slavishly' following the Statistician's figures. The company provided sanitation and street lighting without cost to the resident. It had agreed to supply at cost, for the life of the agreement, working boots, work clothing, and other items. And the threepence per day for train and tram fares 'usually allowed for in a basic wage' was not necessary in Wallaroo.

Thus Powers found, at least to his own satisfaction, that the lesser wage was consistent with *Harvester*. Whether he would in any event have acquiesced in the 11s wage so as to ensure the miners' employment is a question that he left unanswered. Certainly, there are passages in the judgment that could be taken to imply that he would. For example:

> One of the matters which I feel bound to consider in the case is that 1,354 out of 1,400 have registered for work on the terms offered by the company. Some have lived there for over 40 years. A great many have worked there for ten years or more and have worked with this company. They apparently are satisfied they can live in fair and reasonable comfort under the special conditions under which they are living at Wallaroo and Moonta on a basic wage of 11s. (p. 722)

In the *Engine Drivers'* case (15 CAR 883) Powers dealt with pleas from the mining industry at large for relief from the rigorous enforcement of the

Harvester standard. In speaking to the minutes, on 20 December 1921, he said that 'the Court cannot fairly consent to make employees work for less than a fair living wage in dividend-paying mines or in non-dividend paying mines against their wish', though it could 'deal with exceptional cases when exceptional circumstances are shown to warrant it, such as were shown in the Wallaroo and Mount Lyell cases' (p. 907). He drew a distinction between mines making profits or paying dividends, on the one hand, and the others. The former would be subject to the normal terms of the award. For the latter, there were two concessions. One was to allow the basic wage to be set on the basis of the Statistician's figures for the particular districts. 'This,' said Powers, 'is in itself a concession to a very depressed industry because, except in special cases, the total difference between city and country rates are not allowed in awards of the Court.' The other was to allow the union and the respondent employer to agree to set the basic wage by reference to the Statistician's figures for the September quarter, rather than the four quarters to September. Because of the reduction of prices, this would produce a lesser amount. If the parties could not agree, application could be made to the Court 'on special grounds, as in the case of the Mount Lyell and Wallaroo Mining Companies'.[4]

For industries other than mining that were subject to the *Engine-drivers'* award, Powers rejected a union request that he use the price numbers for the year to the June quarter rather than the lower numbers for the year to September. 'I was again pressed [by the union]', he said in October 1921,

> to take the figures for the 30th June instead of the 30th September; but I do not see my way to altering the practice of the Court by adopting any other figures than those available for the last twelve months prior to the making of the award. As the practice of making a fixed rate for a long term has proved unfair to employees in 1920 and to employers in 1921, I have decided to act on the lines employers and employees have lately adopted in many cases, and to order wages to be adjusted quarterly after six months from the date of the awards, on the basis of

---

[4] In March 1922, Powers bound the Wallaroo and Moonta Mining Company to the award, but subject to the concessional terms for loss-making mining companies (16 CAR 69).

> the Statistician's figures for the preceding twelve months prior to the quarterly adjustments. (*Engine-drivers' and Firemen's* case 15 CAR 883, 913)

This decision serves to emphasise that automatic adjustments of the basic wage were brought into effect at a time when they operated to the benefit of employers.

Later in the same month, Powers commented at greater length on the timing issue. In the past, he said, the Court had assumed that the experience of the preceding twelve months would be a fair indicator of the year following the award, 'and in normal times it would be'. The Court had refused to use quarterly figures because 'it is well known that awards based for a time on the cost of living on winter or summer quarters particularly would be unfair to either employer or employee'. While the cost of living was rising, the Court's practice 'has not been proved to be quite fair to the employee, for they have received less than the figures for the different quarters alone showed was the actual cost of living'. But during the past twelve months the cost of living had been falling. As a result, 'the employees have been benefited, and under existing awards, are being paid, at present, more than the figures for the quarter ending 30th September, 1921, only would warrant' (*Gas Employees'* case 16 CAR 4, 15). Powers had 'obtained from Mr Sutcliffe' comparative figures of annual and quarterly prices. Assuming that 7s a day was a fair rate for Melbourne in 1907, Sutcliffe had told him that the six-capital basic wage for the twelve months to the September quarter would be £4 4s 6d per week; for the September quarter alone, it was £3 19s 6d. The union, using figures for the year to the June quarter, was seeking £4 10s 6d. Powers proposed to use the year to September, noting that this afforded workers '5s a week more than is necessary to secure to them the full benefits of the *Harvester* judgment at the present time and prevents the possibility of them getting less than the *Harvester* judgment standard even if the cost of living increases again before April, 1922'. From April 1922, the basic wage would be adjusted automatically each quarter with reference to the A series numbers for the previous twelve months (pp. 28–32).

By December, after the speaking to the minutes, Powers had changed his mind. He abandoned the previously announced basis of adjustment and decided on quarterly adjustments based simply on the previous quarters' figures. 'A wrong method', he said, 'should be altered when it has been clearly proved that it must act unfairly to any party or to both parties'. The union, apparently, preferred the method proposed in October, but Powers assured them that that the alternative now adopted would be to their members' advantage. His reasoning is unclear, but 'an interview with Mr Sutcliffe would, I think, convince the union representatives that that will be the case'. It appears that Powers intended to apply the automatic adjustments to the wage proposed in October, thereby continuing the above-*Harvester* standard. He intended,

> when two new judges had been appointed, to suggest a meeting of the Full Court to discuss and decide what method should be adopted to secure to the workers the benefit of the *Harvester* judgment recognising the fact that the workers did not during the abnormal increases receive the full benefit of the living wage, when the Court anticipating a decrease in the cost of living during the term of the award fixed rates either on the figures for the preceding calendar year or on the figures for the twelve months immediately preceding the award. (p. 33)

During the 1930–31 basic wage case, the union advocate H C Gibson gave an account of the transition to automatic adjustments based on the price index for the previous quarter plus an addition (later to be known as Powers' Three Shillings):

> It was expected by all parties that the Court would continue the practice which had been set by the late President, Mr Justice Higgins, and that practice was to make the awards on the average of the four previous quarters, on the last known figure. ... The average for the four quarters ending September 30th gave the wage for Melbourne of £4 7s per week; the actual equated *Harvester* wage, as equated by the tables the Court now uses, was £4 1s 6d for Melbourne. The wage fixed for Melbourne was £4 5s. The announcement dropped like a bombshell in our camp, at any rate. We interviewed his Honour—when I say 'we' I mean Mr

> Crofts and myself—to see if a mistake had not been made. His Honour declined to discuss it with us, stating that he intended to take his vacation as during the previous year through stress of work he had been deprived of his vacation, and he would go into the matter immediately on resuming early in the New Year. In the New Year it was the first we heard of this proposal that 3s had been added to the last quarter's figures for the purpose of meeting the lag. As a matter of fact, it was 3s 6d on to the last quarter's figures. Under the system that had then been in vogue … the workers working under awards of this Court had, to use a book-keeping phrase, piled up a debit balance of at least £50 per worker. … By the new method, it must necessarily have taken some time to wipe out that debit balance and to have created a credit balance. (transcript, pp. 297–298)

A Full Court hearing did not occur until October 1922. In the meantime, a variety of adjustment methods operated. In a *Clothing Trades* decision of February 1922, Powers referred to an arrangement, proposed by an employer representative, which had been agreed to in July 1920. The matter was before Powers in 1922 because the union maintained—contrary to the employers' contention—that the agreement provided only for increases: once the basic wage was increased, it would not be reduced, even if prices fell. The union, represented by R G Menzies, unsuccessfully sought an award variation to give effect to its understanding of the agreement (16 CAR 50). In April 1922, Powers noted 'the practice lately established so as to preserve to the workers the *Harvester* standard of living in the event of any increase in the cost of living … namely [allowing] 3s a week above the [previous] quarter's figures' (*Boilermakers'* case 16 CAR 172, 177). During 1922, until August, he generally added three or four shillings to the *Harvester* equivalent as of the previous quarter.[5]

In August 1922, Powers dealt with an application by steamship owners to vary the seamen's award by imposing quarterly adjustments plus the 3s, but

---

[5] In an *ASE* case, he granted 4s, reducing to 3s at the end of October (16 CAR 311, 325).

with the cost of living determined on the average of the previous year, rather than the numbers for the previous quarter. Powers responded:

> What the workers are entitled to is the *Harvester* standard for the time they are working and it is useless to continue to tell them they ought to be content with what it was twelve months ago or twelve years ago. What the workers are entitled to is the full rate at the time they are working under the Court's awards.
>
> It is truly said that under the present practice the workers may during a quarter receive 3s more than the *Harvester* standard, if the cost of living falls again, but under the old system it appears that they had to accept 10s or even 12s less than the cost of living at times because of the unexpected increase in the cost of living during the award and for more than a quarter, and at other times where adjustments were agreed to during the awards the employer had for a time to pay higher rates than the *Harvester* standard for the quarter.

'The old method', he said, 'did not secure the *Harvester* standard' (16 CAR 517, 519).

The recently appointed Deputy President, Sir John Quick, in September 1922 adjourned an application to vary an agreement so that the matter of basic wage adjustment could be considered by the Full Court. The Court (Powers, Quick, and Webb) invited representatives of unions and employers to appear, and gave its decision on 20 October in a case reported as *The Fairest Method of Securing the 'Harvester Judgment Standard' to the Workers* (16 CAR 822). It soon emerged that quarterly adjustment, based on the previous quarter's figures, was not an issue in dispute. The matter that was contested was the extra 3s. The employers apparently advanced a 'swings and roundabout' argument, contending that the small delay between the change in prices and the consequent wage adjustment might sometimes benefit workers, just as they lost something at a time of rising prices. Powers would have none of this: his priority was to ensure that *at all times* the basic wage delivered the *Harvester* standard: 'The fact that [workers] were sometimes paid more than

John Quick **Noel Webb**

the standard rate did not meet the objection that what the worker is entitled to is the wage necessary to live on when the prices are high, and the cost of living is increasing' (p. 830). The shortfall at some times while prices are high prevented the basic-wage earner 'getting what is reasonably necessary for himself and his family to live in reasonable comfort—and if he gets into debt the possible increase may not be realised' (p. 832). Quick and Webb wrote concurring decisions.

Automatic adjustments based on the previous quarters' data responded to the perceived unfairness of reliance on a year's index numbers, which were lagged an average of 2½ quarters behind the quarter in which the adjusted wage was paid. There remained the lag of about 2½ months that was inescapable with the current quarter's value of the index necessarily being an unknown.[6] Powers' Three Shillings, as it became known, was meant to cure this problem.

---

[6] For example, the price index for the three months to the end of June (centred in mid-May) would be reflected in a wage adjustment at the beginning of August. A delay was necessary, of course, to await the publication of the index.

It constituted an addition to the basic wage equal, at the time, to about 3¾ per cent.

Some sense of the dimensions of the problems caused by the lags can be gained from analysing the quarterly index numbers from their inception in 1912 to the end of 1922. Across that period, the average excess of the quarterly index numbers over the index for the four quarters ended in the same quarter was 1.4 per cent. Adjustments based on quarterly, rather than annual, numbers took care of this problem. There remained the lag inherent in the collection and publication of the quarterly price data and the delay in altering the wage. The average excess of a given quarter's index number over that of the previous quarter was 1.1 per cent. From the beginning of 1919 to the end of 1922, the initial inflation and subsequent deflation lent great significance to the lags. In the third quarter of 1920, a basic-wage earner receiving a wage related to the previous four quarters' prices would be getting only 86 per cent of the full *Harvester* standard; and had he received a wage related to the immediately previous quarter's index, he would have received 93 per cent. In the fourth quarter of 1921, on the other hand, the worker getting a basic wage based on the preceding four-quarter average would be getting 11 per cent 'too much'.[7] It is not surprising that, in a period of falling prices, unions would favour the lengthening of lags and employers their shortening.

The automatic adjustment system plus Powers' 3s, approved by the Full Court in 1922, was the platform of basic-wage fixation for the remainder of the decade. In April 1923, the Full Court (Powers, Quick, and Webb) promulgated 'rules of practice'. The rules for the basic wage were:

1. The basic wage adopted by the Full Court is the one based on the Statistician's figures for food, groceries and rent for the preceding quarter plus 3s a week assuming 7s a day was a fair basic wage for a labourer in Melbourne in 1907, and the method decided upon will not be departed from by a single Judge until it is decided by the Full Court to vary that method.

---

[7] The calculations referred to in this paragraph are based on the A series price index for six capitals.

2. The Court will continue its practice of fixing one rate only when the parties desire it, or when the Court thinks it just to do so, and it will continue its practice of fixing uniform rates for groups of capital cities—or of country towns—or of districts as heretofore—where the parties desire it or when the Court thinks it just to do so. Where one rate only is fixed or one rate for each group it will be fixed on the Statistician's figures showing the average of the capitals or places (as the case may be) in which the respondents employ members of the union.

3. The Full Court has already decided that in new awards the adjustment of rates shall be quarterly based on the increased or decreased purchasing power of a sovereign shown by the Statistician's figures.

4. The basic rates are to be fixed on the Statistician's figures showing the cost of food, groceries and rent for the preceding quarter and not on any new basis until approved by the Full Court, but such allowances as may be deemed fair in country districts will be allowed on any ground the presiding Judge thinks just.

Rule 1 affirmed the Court's continued reliance on the *Harvester* standard. Rule 2 allowed some room for manoeuvre in choosing between geographical variants of the price index. Rules 3 and 4 dealt with the adjustment system. Rule 4 specified that the price index to be used was that for food, groceries, and rent—not the broader index that the Statistician had recently begun to publish. Formally, these rules were no more than advisory to the individual arbitrators. The Act did not then reserve the basic wage to the Full Court; nor did it provide for appeals. By the late 1920s there were signs of discomfort (noted more fully in Chapter 7) within the reconstituted Court with existing practices in setting the basic wage; but they remained in effect until the Depression.

Automatic adjustments were implemented by means of tables included in the awards.[8] These tables specified ranges of the price index; for each range,

---

[8] There were some exceptions, normally by consent, to the automatic adjustment system. For

there was a monetary amount. Lukin, in 1928, described the origin of this practice:

> In June, 1922, Mr Justice Powers held a consultation with Mr Sutcliffe, and some of the representatives of employers and employees, at which, apparently, a desire held in common by employers and employees was expressed, so I am informed, that the principle of no fraction of a shilling should be applied in making the quarterly adjustments from time to time. Mr Sutcliffe proposed a formula which was revised and amended in detail, and inserted in subsequent awards of the Court. (*Timber Workers'* case 27 CAR 577, 608)

Although automatic adjustments were not seriously criticised, Powers' 3s was a subject of contention, both before and within the Court and especially after the reconstitution of 1926. In October 1924, Powers commented that employers had sought the omission of the 3s on the ground that, with the cost of living no longer rising, it was unnecessary; but 'as I pointed out to the respondents, until the Full Court alters the rule, I feel bound to add the 3s to the basic wage in ordinary cases' (*Engineers'* case 20 CAR 1135, 1152–1153). Quick, in 1924, began the task of making awards for the railways (following the High Court decision in the *Engineers'* case). In 1925, he acceded to an application that he make an interim award for the Victorian Railways (22 CAR 886). This occurred because the relevant State tribunal, the Railways Classification Board, had not adopted the automatic adjustment system or added the 3s to its basic wage. Quick set a basic wage that was 4s 6d a week above the Board's basic wage and added the Board's margins to that higher amount.

In his resignation statement of December 1925,[9] Powers referred to the 3s:

---

example, in the *Liquor Trades'* case (for maltsters) of 1925, Webb said that he had included the standard adjustment clause in the award, but the parties had jointly requested its omission, and he agreed to their request. The purpose was to allow certainty in contracting for the supply of malt (22 CAR 675, 685).
[9] This did not become effective until mid-1926.

> The Court, as at present constituted, has continued to carry out the work of the Court on the principles and practices laid down by Mr Justice Higgins, and we have, where practicable, granted new and better conditions and permanently increased the basic wage by 3s a week, which 3s I first allowed as a temporary measure to secure the basic wage during the term of the award. (22 CAR, xxxi)

The implication that the 3s had mutated from a device for *preserving* the *Harvester* standard into a permanent *addition* to it troubled some members of the reconstituted Court. After 1926, they were prepared, in some special instances, to dispense with it (see Chapter 7).

6.1.3 Raising the standard

Some unions, in their formal plaints, avowedly sought basic wages that exceeded the *Harvester* standard. These claims were invariably rejected. For example, in a *Carters and Drivers'* case of 1923, Quick said that the union had asked him to state a case for the opinion of the Full Arbitration Court on the question of the basis and fairness of the *Harvester* judgment. He refused to do so: 'In view of the decision of the Full Court to continue to make awards on the *Harvester* judgment basis and that the method of fixing the basic wage would not be altered by any one judge for any one union or one set of employers, the only way in my opinion to have the basis and fairness of the *Harvester* judgment again considered is by some of the important unions to join in an application to the Full Court to reconsider it' (17 CAR 194, 199). Webb, in another *Carters and Drivers'* case (21 CAR 232), said in 1924 that the union had demanded a higher basic wage because employees were 'entitled to share in the increased productivity of the nation'. The Court, said Webb,

> has no mandate from the Legislature to take the profits of an industry into consideration when fixing wages in an industry. Some Industrial Courts are expressly directed to consider such matters, but this Court is not, and it has always acted on the principle that such considerations are not within the scope of its work, nor could any one Judge take into consideration such a factor as a general increase in productivity. The

Judges of this Court have laid down certain principles to guide them in fixing the basic wage. It is essential that the Judges should act in harmony on this matter, and until all the Judges agree to an alteration, no single Judge could depart from the principles which have been adopted.

6.1.4 Variations around the standard

There were two 'fringe' issues in basic-wage fixation which we should notice. These were geographical differences in the wage and the concessions made to employers seen to be in financial difficulty. In some instances the two issues overlapped.

The Statistician produced price index numbers for 30 towns (which included the capital cities). These, he stated, could be used to link the prices prevailing in any of the towns to those of Melbourne in 1907, so that *Harvester* equivalents could be computed. If the basic wage were regarded strictly as the means of securing the *Harvester* standard, it would vary from place to place according to the levels of the price index. Exact equivalences would be unachievable, because a mere 30 numbers could not reflect the full diversity of local conditions. But the Court had the opportunity to select the 'town' most relevant to the workers covered. In reality, there was a range of practices, varying from a moderately close observance of local differences to a high level of averaging. The justifications for the former were twofold: that it was desirable for the basic wage to conform to the *Harvester* standard; and that the lower nominal wages that this permitted in some instances were beneficial to the employers concerned and might even contribute to their survival. Averaging, on the other hand, avoided or lessened issues in the identification of the right price indices; and it was sometimes portrayed as allowing employers to compete on equal terms. (The question whether 'equal terms' entailed the same money wages or the same real wages was overlooked.)

Webb, in 1924, made the first federal award for general printing, covering the metropolitan areas in Sydney, Melbourne, Adelaide, and Hobart. He fixed a uniform basic wage on 'the weighted average of the figures of the Commonwealth Statistician for the four cities concerned', explaining that 'in an industry which lends itself to Inter-State competition I think it is beneficial to fix a flat rate if such a course can be followed without injustice' (22 CAR 247, 249).

In 1925, Powers rejected a union claim for a uniform basic wage for locomotive enginemen, but set a single wage for each State (using the 'five towns' index number) (*Locomotive Enginemen's* case 21 CAR 442, 448). Later in 1925, he said that 'where work is done in the country … it is usual for this Court to fix the basic wage on the weighted average of what is known as the four towns of each State, omitting the capital cities, because the four towns, except in Tasmania, give a fair idea of the cost of living in the country' (*AWU* case 22 CAR 973, 975). In a 1926 decision about shearers, Powers granted a uniform basic wage based on the weighted average index number for all 30 towns (including the six capitals): 'I do not see how that can be fairly avoided where employment for twelve months in country districts cannot be guaranteed' (*Pastoral* case 23 CAR 458, 478).

Powers, in 1925, discussed the complexities of setting country basic wages:

> The question of fixing [basic] rates for country towns has always been a very difficult one to decide. If the rates are fixed much lower than the capital city rates then the employees on the first opportunity leave for the city to get higher rates and the advantages obtainable in the cities. On the other hand, if the rates are not less than the city rates, large industries cannot be carried on in the country districts (not seaport towns) and employees are forced into the city. It is recognised that it is not in the interests of the country to get all industrial or other workers in the cities. … I propose to ask my colleagues to join me in considering the whole question of country rates and allowances for disadvantages recognised by all parties—to see if we can agree upon some uniform basis for country districts and special country towns instead of (1) on the capital cities rate in some cases, (2) on the five towns' basis in others, (3) on the four towns' basis in others, and (4) on the special town figures (as at Ballarat) in others. (*Ironworkers'* case 22 CAR 707, 708)

Unless it was done informally, the joint consideration of local rates did not happen.

We have noted above the convoluted endeavours of Powers to set a basic wage that reflected economic crises in the mining industry. The problems of mining confronted Webb in 1924 in respect of operations at Bendigo (*Mining* case 20 CAR 669). The attitude of the union, he said, had been very definitely stated by its representative:

> He says that the union requests the Court to accede to its claim and substantially increase wages in the industry whatever the consequences may be. If the result is that the industry is destroyed, the men must find work in other avenues of life. The union contends that men ought not to be required to work in the industry at the rates which at present prevail, and if the increasing of the wages destroys the industry, the industry must be destroyed. The union takes the full responsibility of pressing its demand. (pp. 671–672)

Webb decided, however, that

> in the interests of the industry, in the interests of the men employed in it, and in the interests of the public it is my duty to follow as nearly as possible what was done by Mr Justice Starke in 1920 and Mr Justice Powers in 1921, in the hope that the industry may continue to be carried on. It is not in the interests of any one that this Court should be the instrument of bringing about the calamity which I feel certain would be precipitated if the claims of the union were granted. (p. 673)

In several awards, said Webb, the basic wage for Bendigo had been set on the basis of the local *Harvester* equivalent (then £3 10s) plus 3s plus half the difference (6s) between that amount and the Melbourne rate—a total of £3 19s. If he increased the rate in mining (currently £3 10s) by 9s, 'I have little doubt that the industry would be at an end'. Webb's solution was to differentiate between non-profitable and profitable mines. For the former, he fixed the basic wage at £3 13s (the local *Harvester* rate plus 3s). In profitable mines, an extra 6s would apply.

Webb, in 1925, also dealt with the basic wage in the dried-fruit industry (*Dried Fruit* case 21 CAR 334). When the industry was in its infancy before the war, practically all of the product was marketed in Australia and was heavily protected. The producers did well, and people were attracted to the industry. After the war, many returned soldiers entered the industry and an extensive settlement was established at Red Cliffs. Now, much of the greatly expanded output had to be marketed overseas at prices well below the Australian. Past practice had been to set a basic wage on the Melbourne price index, because the Mildura rate would have been higher. Sutcliffe's evidence was that a Mildura-based rate would be £4 15s. Webb now fixed a rate of £4 2s, or 2s 6d less than the Melbourne rate. Despite the wage being 14 per cent below *Harvester*, the growers protested that the concession took insufficient account of their predicament. Webb said that, if he were looking at this case from the point of view of the growers only, 'I think I should almost be justified in saying that [the industry] cannot afford to pay any wages at all, and the workers must work for very little or nothing'; but 'I must prescribe for these workers a wage which in some measure conforms to the principles which the Court has laid down' (p. 349). Webb also set rates for Renmark and Leeton that were well below the local *Harvester* equivalents. The conformity of this decision to 'the principles which the Court has laid down' was slight indeed.[10]

The interaction of the geographical and the economic aspects of basic-wage prescription was illustrated in a *Printing* case, also decided (in March 1926) by Webb (23 CAR 124). This was about newspaper printing in Adelaide and Hobart. The Hobart employers tendered the report (submitted in September 1925) of a Committee appointed by the Premier of Tasmania to inquire into the State's disabilities under federation.[11] The Committee said:

> Generally, it may be said that on account of her isolated position, her different characteristics of climate, her small population and low state

---

[10] Webb's acceptance of the growers' account of their predicament was criticised in 1939 by O'Mara (*Judgment—Fruit Growing, etc.* 41 CAR 285, 302–303).
[11] Committee members were Sir N E Lewis, a former Premier (Chairman), Sir A H Ashbolt, a former Agent-General for Tasmania, J B Brigden, Professor of Economics, L F Giblin, State Statistician, and W A Woods, a former Labor MP.

of development of secondary industries, all the defects of the Federal Arbitration Court methods, which in the larger States are in many cases of no great practical importance, have an exaggerated effect in Tasmania and constitute an appreciable handicap. An inquiry has shown that the overwhelming majority of employees in Tasmanian secondary industries come under Federal awards, and for the remainder the local Wages Board cannot, in practice, make a determination sensibly below the Federal standard. In the depressed state of Tasmanian secondary industry any consideration given to the wage-paying capacity would lead to Tasmanian rates rather under the general Australian level; but the crude principle of the cost of living criterion combines with the imperfections of its application to impose rates considerably higher than the Australian average. This puts an additional burden on Tasmanian enterprise and competitive production, which are already suffering from high coastal freights, with consequent aggravation of unemployment and loss of production. (quoted by Webb, p. 126)

Webb commented that there were two outstanding reasons for federation: defence and inter-State free trade. It was difficult for fair inter-State competition to exist unless industrial conditions were reasonably similar. The use of the Statistician's price numbers in setting the basic wage had operated to Tasmania's advantage:

> The Commonwealth Statistician publishes with every Labour Report a return which shows the weighted hourly rate of wage for each State. The last of such returns … shows that for each year between 1914 and 1924 the wages paid in Tasmania have almost invariably been the lowest in the Commonwealth. If low wages are an advantage to the industries of a State, then Tasmania has, for many years, in common with South Australia, had an enormous industrial advantage over the rest of the Australian States. (p. 127)

The Committee's report and Webb's response seem to conflict on the facts—either the Court's policies raised Tasmanian wages above those of the mainland (the Committee) or they did not (Webb). The evidence is ambiguous.[12] The clear implication of Webb's comment, however, was that wages should not be an instrument of inter-State economic adjustment. Other members of the Court would generally have agreed.

6.1.5 State basic wages

Four of the six States—New South Wales, Queensland, South Australia, and Western Australia—had explicit basic or living wages. The wages boards in Victoria and Tasmania did not declare basic wages, but seem to have taken account of notional basic wages in fixing their rates for various tasks. None of the States followed the Commonwealth Court into an automatic adjustment system. In the four States where a basic or a living wage was declared, there were tribunals responsible for the task, though subject in some instances to statutory direction. In New South Wales, the Board of Trade declared living wages until 1926, when the responsibility was transferred to the newly constituted Industrial Commission. The Commission was subject to changing statutory directions about the nature of the family unit for which the wage should provide. In Queensland, the Court of Industrial Arbitration made its first formal declaration of a basic wage in February 1921, setting an amount of 85s when the *Harvester* equivalent was 78s 6d. It reserved the right to set higher or lower amounts according to the level of prosperity of the industry concerned. In March 1922, the wage was reduced to 80s, at which it remained until September 1925. The State Parliament enacted a law fixing the rate at 85s until September 1926, when discretion reverted to the Court. In South Australia, the *Industrial Code 1920* committed the task of declaring a basic wage to the Board of Industry, which could alter the amount at minimum intervals of six months. In Western Australia, there was no mechanism for declaring a basic wage until 1925, when the Court of Arbitration was required to make an annual declaration.[13] Figure 1.6 in Chapter 1 compares the State and federal basic wages.

---

[12] Between 1923 and 1925, the price index was higher for Tasmania (5 towns) than for Australia (30 towns); thereafter the relation was reversed.

[13] The foregoing summary of State arrangements is based on Anderson (1929, pp. 119–121) and the *Labour Reports*.

6.2 THE WAGE STRUCTURE

The two-tier wage structure was often, and increasingly, explicit, with awards containing separate clauses for the basic wage and margins. In other cases, it was implicit: wages were prescribed as total amounts, but with the arbitrators (and presumably the parties) having clear understandings about their composition. Additions to the basic wage were generally characterised as 'margins'. (There were also a few 'industry allowances'.) Setting wages for specific grades of labour was perhaps the major task of the arbitrators of the 1920s. There was no formal mechanism of coordination, such as appeals or references to Full Benches. Consistency depended on agreement or collegiality. (Members of the Court sometimes said that they had consulted with their colleagues, who agreed with the pronouncements that they were making.)

6.2.1 The appeal to the past

We saw in Chapter 4 that Higgins, in the year before his departure from the Court, embarked on a policy of increasing margins so as to restore something like the proportional relativities that had existed before the war. This policy had been rejected by Starke. The major repudiation, however, came in Powers' decision of October 1921 in the *Engine Drivers'* case (15 CAR 883). 'A new claim' said Powers, 'has been pressed in this and in every case lately ... for what is called the full or effective margin for skill, over and above the basic wage, based on what was allowed in 1907 for skill; and in some cases later than 1907' (pp. 896–897). This claim was based principally on two grounds: (1) that during the war margins for skill were not increased at all or not in proportion to the cost of living; and (2) 'that the claim was recognised by the late President for the first time in the last award made before he resigned'.

Powers said with respect to (1) that even before the war margins had been awarded, not on the basis of what they might have been in 1907, but on 'what the skill was worth at the time'. The basic wage, in contrast, had not been related to the value of work but was set 'to carry out the principles adopted by the Court in fixing a minimum wage, namely that each adult worker should be paid enough to keep himself, his wife and three children under fourteen years in reasonable comfort'. During the war, some margins had actually been reduced (as in the public service), and in these cases the Court had promised to review them when times became normal. But honouring this promise was 'an entirely different proposition to the one now pressed for, namely, to grant increased margins allowed by this Court based on the value of the margins granted by some Board or Court or otherwise in 1907 or later under entirely different conditions and different hours of duty' (pp. 897–898).

As to (2), Powers could only assume that Higgins was satisfied on the evidence presented to him 'that the employees in question were entitled at the date he made the award to the full amount he allowed as margins for skill at that date'. The work of fitters and turners might well be worth what Higgins had awarded, 'but that cannot, in my opinion, be determined by what they received in 1907'. He did not think that Higgins had based his decision 'on anything but the value of the skill at the date of the award under 1921 conditions'; but if he did, as was alleged, base it solely on the ground that 1907 margins ought to be doubled, then 'I cannot see my way to admit that decision as a guide to this Court'. Powers concluded:

> The principal reason why this Court does not feel justified in fixing margins in 1921 on the ground that certain margins were paid in 1907, and then double them automatically, is because the whole industrial position has been changed since 1907 principally—through direct legislation affecting labour conditions—through the constant activities of the unions in insisting on and obtaining better conditions for their members, shorter hours, standards [of] work, etc—through the awards of the Court since 1907 improving conditions and shortening hours for the workers and through the improved machinery and appliances of to-day greatly lightening the labour of employees. Again in some cases new duties have been added. In some, duties have been reduced. In numerous other ways skill and duties required in 1921 are not the same as in 1907, and the marginal rates are not necessarily the same. (p. 900)

At first sight, the idea that the wages of the skilled and semi-skilled should reflect the value of the work at the time when they were set, rather than movements in prices or the basic wage since some earlier time, such as 1907, seems compelling. On closer inspection, however, it entailed significant complexities.

First, it implied that, when setting margins, the Court would actually undertake the task of evaluating the jobs. How would this be done? Higgins' approach in *Harvester* was based on the judgment that people in the trade understood better than he the relative worth of the different jobs. This was at least arguable; and an independent assessment of 'worth' would hardly have been consistent with the time constraints of dealing with the many applications for relief from the excise. Starke and Powers turned their back on the simple formula. They might, for example, have noted the 'custom and practice' element of pre-war relativities and asked whether there were reasons for increasing or narrowing the spread. But having rejected the unions' attempts to invoke the pre-war relativities, they offered no alternative method of evaluation.

Second, in the absence of a serious re-evaluation whenever margins were set or reviewed, what was the 'default option'? The three conceivable choices were constant money amount, constant real amount, and constant relativities. Starke and Powers chose the first of these without seriously weighing the respective merits of all three options.

Third, there were unstated and perhaps unrecognised issues as to the interrelation of the basic wage and margins. The basic-wage component of the total wage was understood to be equal to the unskilled labourer's rate, and changes in that rate were translated into equivalent alterations in all award rates. But if wage differences were to reflect the relative values of jobs, the total wages were surely the relevant comparators. And if the general principle was subject to an overriding and socially based requirement of ensuring at least a living wage, one method of achieving this would have been to fix all rates on the basis of 'worth' (if that could be done) but to add the proviso that not less than the living wage must be paid to every worker. (This principle was adopted in the 1970s with the 'minimum wage'.) The technique of allowing margins to *ride on top* of the basic wage, but only as money amounts, is almost impossible to reconcile with setting wages by absolute or relative worth.

This is not to deny a pragmatic justification for such a practice—that it might be expedient to limit the movements of wages by adjusting only a portion of them, the basic wage, for the cost of living. That is what the Court did between 1907 and 1921. But it is idle to suggest that such a policy is consistent with fixing wages by worth, unless 'worth' is so defined that the argument is tautologous.

Powers further considered the level of margins in the *Engineers'* case, decided in June 1922 (16 CAR 231). In this case, the decisions of Higgins made a year earlier about margins and hours were under review (though the matter of hours had to be reserved for a Full Court and is discussed in the next section). 'I am asked', he said,

> to reconsider an important award made after a very lengthy hearing by the late President of this Court just before his resignation as President, by which the learned Judge … increased margins for skill beyond any margins recognised by employers, employees and Wages Boards in the engineering industry, and contrary to the practice of this Court previous to the award in question, except in one award—the Merchant Service Guild. (p. 232)

He did not think for a moment that the rates set by Higgins were not fair on the evidence before him and at the time of his decision. But he was 'also satisfied that on the evidence before me at the present time that the late President would not today make the award he did in June, 1921'.

Powers now said—contrary to what he had said in the *Engine Drivers'* case—'that the late President did allow the extra 2s a day [for fitters and turners] on the ground of the increased cost of living since 1907, not the increased value of skill in 1921, and to carry out his promise to give increased margins according to the cost of living when he thought it could fairly be done' (p. 262). But he was 'quite satisfied that the late President would not in June, 1922, consider it opportune or fair to add new burdens never imposed' on industries (p. 265).

There is no evidence in Powers' decision that the margins awarded in any way reflected an evaluation of the work. He gave as his principal reason for reducing margins the 'mass of evidence' which showed 'that the rates awarded in June last year cannot now be paid by any of the manufacturing industries at the present time, because the rates for all engineering and other classes of work in America, England, France, and Belgium have been reduced to a very great extent since June last year, and rates for margins are now much below what was proved to be the margins in June, 1921, in those countries' (p. 262). He thought that it would be in the public interest to increase the pre-1921 margin by 1s per day (to 4s for tradesmen), recognising that 'employers will even then have a hard task to face the competition while they have to pay wages so much higher than in England and in other continental countries, including Germany, with which country it is said trade relations are to be resumed in August' (p. 271).

Thus the metal tradesman's margin, which had been 18s a week between *Harvester* and 1921, and was raised to 36s by Higgins, became 24s. There it stayed until after the Depression.

During the 1920s, the Court consistently resisted attempts by unions to raise margins where the ground for the increases sought was either the erosion of proportional relativities or the rise in prices since pre-war years. The near-consistent position of the Court was that margins should correspond to the value of the work entailed in the given classification, and that this did not move in proportion to the basic wage or retail prices.

In the *Engineers'* case of 1924 (20 CAR 1135), the unions claimed a fitter's margin of 31s per week (in place of the existing 24s). This amount was derived by assuming a 1907 margin of 18s and adjusting it for the rise in the cost of living. Rejecting this appeal to the past, Powers said that 'to fix margins for skill on any other basis than its value in the market at the time the awards are made would be contrary to the practice of every other Arbitration Court in Australia, contrary to the practice of every tribunal appointed to fix wages, and contrary to every State Wages Board decision in all the States of the Commonwealth' (p. 1149). There were several answers to the unions' argument about the declining rewards for skill:

- 'That the industrial world has not stood still since 1907. That machinery has been invented to make the work of tradesmen much easier, and in many cases to do the work the fitters and turners did in 1907 by hand. In some cases it has simplified the work. In other cases, many classes of work then paid for at basic rates only have since been classified as skilled or slightly skilled, and if I allowed only the rates for skill of the 91 classes of work I have now to deal with on the basis of rates allowed in 1907 only, the rates would be much lower than they will be under the award.'
- 'The market value of the margin for skill has not increased in any country at the same rate as the basic wage has increased.'
- '[T]he unions have argued strongly that I should allow fitters and turners' rates to workers whose work I have the greatest difficulty in fixing as high as a margin as 24s a week, and some for which I cannot see any way to fix 24s a week margin, leave alone 31s a week. If I gave these men margins based on what they were getting as labourers in 1907, the union would strongly object.'
- If the argument from the cost of living had been available to fitters and turners, it should, in fairness, have been extended to other groups: 'Every man who received any sum above the basic wage would then automatically be entitled to nearly double the amount whatever it was—all tradesmen of any sort, all clerks, foremen, accountants, and Government officials—including the Commissioner for Railways—and if it is fair for one it is fair for all. Why not a Justice of the High

Court, who has not even had an increase in keeping with the cost of living, and whose salary has, in addition, been further reduced by some hundreds a year through taxation? If the union's contention is correct, the salaries should be raised by £2,500' (p. 1150–1151).

Rejection of the historical link (whether direct or via the cost of living) would seem to raise two significant questions. If the margin for any grade of labour was to be determined on the basis of its contemporary 'value', how was that measured? And why was it that the value of the work of the more skilled grades had risen less (in proportional terms) than that of the unskilled labourer? In the passages quoted above, Powers did not confront the former question. As to the latter, he offered two answers. One was that mechanisation has reduced the demands made of the skilled worker. The other was that wage gains conferred on lower-paid workers (chiefly by awarding margins where none previously existed) had absorbed benefits that might otherwise have been available for the more highly skilled and qualified.

6.2.2 Fixing specific margins and industry allowances

A study of the many decisions wherein specific rates were awarded reveals a bewildering variety of practices and principles. Generalisation is difficult. I refer to a selection of decisions which will serve to demonstrate this.

The role of agreement: Agreement between the parties played a large role. Many awards were made by consent, giving rise to little or no commentary by the Court. Commonly, there would be agreement about the ranking of classifications; and very often there was agreement about the margins themselves. In these cases, no doubt, the terms of the agreements were influenced by the parties' awareness of the likely attitude of the Court. In some decisions, however, the members of the Court emphasised their dependence on the parties to resolve issues that might otherwise have taxed their capacities. For example, Quick, in a case about electrical workers in South Australia, said in 1923: 'It has been most satisfactory to notice the business-like and friendly spirit shown by the representatives of all the parties concerned, without which it would have been impossible to have arrived at settlements solving difficult and complicated questions relating to the rates of pay to be made applicable to numerous sections of a trade so technical and having so many ramifications as that of electrical work' (*Electrical Trades* case 18 CAR 685, 691).

The tradesman's rate: The notion of a tradesman's rate had some influence; and the most representative tradesman was commonly seen as the engineering fitter. It is convenient, therefore, to refer to the structure of wages set by Powers in 1924 for the engineering trades (20 CAR 982, 1135). This is shown in Table 6.1. About 30 classifications were distributed between 14 levels of pay. Between the basic wage and the tradesman's rate were six levels of margins for semi-skilled workers.

The margin of 24s for tradesmen was adopted in the first federal award for printing, made by Webb in 1924 (*Printing Industry* case 22 CAR 247). 'In most industries,' said Webb, 'there is one tradesman whose work is representative of the standard of skill usually achieved by the skilled worker in the industry. In this industry, the hand compositor is generally taken as being the tradesman who fixes such standard' (p. 249). It was impossible, Webb said, 'to compare things which are so widely different as the skill of men in different skilled trades, and I cannot properly and fairly compare one trade with another, although it is very natural that one should try to do so. … Each industry must stand on its own merits'. Nevertheless, without explicit reason, he fixed the hand compositor's margin at 24s (p. 253).

In 1925, Powers made the first federal award for locomotive enginemen, adopting the rates currently paid in New South Wales. These included a margin for skill of 24s in the first year, rising by 6s in successive years to 42s in the fourth year, with an additional 6s for drivers of express and passenger trains *Locomotive Enginemens'* case (21 CAR 442, 453).

Where the adoption of the 'tradesman's rate' involved a large wage increase, however, the Court might hold its hand. In the *Clothing Trades* case of 1923 (18 CAR 1033), Webb observed:

Margin (shillings)	Wage as a % of basic wage	Classification
0	100	General labourers
6	107	Tradesmen's helpers
9	111	Casting attendants; motor attendants
12	114	Third class machinists; furnacemen (brass); switchboard attendants; wetstone grinders (ordinary)
16	119	Second class machinists; furnacemen (iron); electroplater while doing second class work
18	121	Electrical wiremen or linemen
21	125	Annealers; case hardeners
24	128	Tradesmen; first class machinists; fitters
26	131	Electrical fitters
27	132	Toolmakers of machine tools; toolsmiths making machine tools; die-makers; gauge-makers; fitters—special no. 1; angle-iron smiths
28	133	Oxy-acetylene operators; electric welders; electrical fitters on signal maintenance work other than in workshops
30	136	Fitters—special no. 2
33	139	Patternmakers
36	143	Forgers

Table 6.1 Margins in the engineering trades, 1924

> In this industry margins for skill are very low; indeed, I know of no other trade in respect of which it is necessary to serve as long periods of apprenticeship [5 years] as are required in this trade, where the margins for skill are so low. The employees contend that the reason of this is that in no instance has any margin for skill in this industry been fixed by the Court, the margins have been fixed in conferences and under circumstances where employees have accepted less than they thought they were entitled to. (p. 1046)

In a 1919 (consent) award, the margin for tailors had been set at 10s (compared with the fitter's margin of 18s). This was obviously too low, and in 1921 the employers had agreed to a margin of 15s. The union now sought 25s, and Webb noted that in many trades the tradesman received a margin of 24s. The employers, however, said that they were faced with severe overseas competition and brought evidence to that effect. 'On the other hand', said Webb, 'the employees press that their claims should be dealt with on their intrinsic merits, and contend that any simple measure of justice must greatly increase the wages which they are receiving' (p. 1048). It was impossible to make an award that would meet these contrary positions, but 'I must do the best I can'. His decision was to raise the tailor's margin to 18s. The clothing trades remained a low-pay industry.

In 1925, the agricultural implement and machinery industry came before the Court (in the person of Quick) for the first time since Higgins had dealt with it (outside the arbitration jurisdiction) in 1907 (*Ironworkers'* case 22 CAR 479). Higgins had set the basic wage at 7s and the rate for fitters and turners at 10s—an implied margin of 3s per day or 18s per week. (Quick noted that in 1909 the agricultural implements wages board in Victoria had set a basic wage of 6s 6d and a margin for fitters and turners of 2s 6d.) When Higgins set an engineering tradesman's margin of 36s in 1921, his intention was to restore the 10:7 ratio of 1907. Since the 36s margin had subsequently been replaced by one of 24s, there might have been an expectation that the latter would now be the amount awarded in the agricultural implement industry. The employers, however, strenuously resisted this:

> Mr Myhill, on behalf of the employers, said that in his opinion if Mr Justice Higgins, who in 1907 had found that a man doing fitting and blacksmithing work in connection with a plough was then worth an 18s margin, were to assess the work which is done today, he would probably fix a margin of something like 9s per week owing to the altered conditions of the industry. The skill which was then required had almost all gone and no notice should therefore be taken of what was done in 1907. The employers have, by the introduction of modern methods and up to date machinery, eliminated a large amount of the skill which was required in this particular industry, and they contended that they are morally entitled to a reduction of the margins. In spite of this the employers, said Mr Myhill, had been fair. In 1909 the margin of the implement fitter and the implement smith was determined by the Wages Board at

> 15s per week. Although the employers had spent thousand of pounds in introducing modern methods and modern machinery, they had not asked for a reduction of the 15s margin, so they considered the union had been very well treated. (p. 485)

Quick was persuaded. 'I am convinced', he said, 'that agricultural fitting is of a very crude nature as compared with engineering fitting' (p. 493). He retained the margin of 15s set by the wages board in 1909.

Margins for other grades: In two cases of 1922, the Court articulated a view that mechanisation had reduced the call for higher levels of manual skill but had created semi-skilled jobs that justified modest margins. Webb distinguished between the levels of skill required of different kinds of 'carpenters'. 'A carpenter,' he said,

> is a highly skilled tradesman. A carpenter on a building is, in my opinion, the most skilled tradesman on a building. A carpenter is entitled to a high margin for skill. The margin should be at least 4s per day … But there is a class of employee who is termed a carpenter who is employed on work known as stock work. This is putting together stock doors, stock sashes and work of a similar nature. The bulk of the work is done by machinery … I have inspected the work done by these employees—it does not require the degree of skill as is required by a general carpenter. His margin should not be more than 3s per day. (*Carpenters and Joiners'* case 16 CAR 1136, 1142)

In a *Glassworkers'* case, also in 1922 (16 CAR 1276), Quick described the changing skill requirements of the industry:

> Glass bottle making was at one time exclusively a hand and mouth worked process, but in recent years this process has been largely superseded by bottle-blowing machines which are fed with liquid glass by skilled glass workers. More recently machines … which automatically feed the blowing machines have been installed. These feeders take the place of the skilled glass worker. (p. 1278)

But he awarded a margin of 3s 6d a week to lehrmen, who looked after ovens to ensure that a stable temperature was preserved. Their work was hot and required a certain amount of skill plus continuous and undivided attention (p. 1293). He also awarded 2s 6d per week to sorters, who have 'to swiftly exercise sound judgment and discretion in determining whether bottles are fit to go into use or whether they should be rejected' (p. 1294). Higgins had refused any margin to sorters because they were not skilled.

Webb, in 1923, dealt with an application for an increased margin for wool sorters (*Wool and Basil Workers'* case 17 CAR 598). Under a 1920 award, sorters received a margin of 1s 2d per day. This, apparently, accorded with then-existing standards and the union claim. The Court, said Webb,

> necessarily places great reliance on previous customs in an industry, and especially voluntary agreements between the parties when fixing a secondary wage. Almost universally these have been of the utmost value in guiding the Court. … Indeed, it would be an almost impossible task on the Court if the Judges had to perform the work of fixing a secondary wage without a knowledge of previous customs in the industry to guide them. It is true that at times some margins are seriously challenged and new margins are fixed. But even in fixing new margins one of the important factors that a Judge takes into consideration is the relative margins fixed by long usage and custom in the industry. (p. 599)

Initially, Webb raised the margin to 1s 4d per day. The union, however, asked for a variation of this decision. It was now obvious, said Webb, that a 'claim was being made to fix a new and special secondary wage for the skilled work of a body of men whose interests had always been completely overlooked'. He asked the union representative how this had happened and was told that the sorters had been unorganised and had never had their case pressed. Webb appointed two assessors to advise him, and raised the daily margin to 3s.

Webb described his approach to setting margins for the timber industry. This passage shows the miscellany of considerations guiding the outcomes:

I have seen most of the work done. I know that a No. 1 benchman is a highly skilled man, and is entitled to the full margin for a skilled worker. I know that a shaper machinist, boults carver machinist, general joiner machinist, moulding machinist, variety turning lathe machinist are very skilled machinists, and should receive an adequate margin for the work they do. Buzzer machinists, tenoning machinists, door planing machinists, timber bending machinists are doing work which is familiar to me, and I have classified them according to my knowledge of the work. I know nothing about coopers' machinists, but I have followed rates previously agreed in respect of these machinists. I know the work of carpenters and joiners and stock carpenters, for I awarded for them in another case. Mantelpiece makers should, I think, be on the same margin as stock carpenters. I have seen the work of making plywood, and have awarded for the various classes of work done. … My object as far as possible has been to give a fair margin for the individual skill of each worker, and in every case, if possible, to fix the same margin for the whole of the Commonwealth. … My great desire is to reduce this complicated matter to some degree of co-ordination, and to establish as far as possible uniform rates and conditions throughout the Commonwealth. (*Timber Workers'* case 18 CAR 325, 349–350)

In the 1923 *Tanners and Leather Dressers'* case (18 CAR 790), most of the rates had been agreed, but the parties differed over the margin for the machine shaver. It had been increased in 1920, under a consent award, from 7s to 11s. The employers were resisting a further increase. They contended that the 1920 award had placed the shaver 'in the wrong place', because it raised his relative position above that fixed by Powers in 1914. 'But, if they got into the "wrong place"', said Quick, 'then it was with the consent of 128 employers … and with the sanction of the Court' (p. 793). One of the employers had voluntarily offered an increase of 4s because of the scarcity of workers with the required skill, but had retracted the offer under pressure from other employers. 'It may well be argued', said Quick, 'that if it would be just, reasonable and profitable for Russell Brothers to increase the rates payable to their shavers it should be equally just, reasonable and profitable for other employers to do the same'; but the Court 'would not necessarily be bound by the rate paid by any employer or any limited number of employers under such circumstances' (p. 795). Quick raised the shaver's margin by 1s 6d to 12s 6d.

The *Meat Industry* case of 1924 required Quick to consider both an industry allowance and margins (20 CAR 182). An existing agreement and prevailing practice justified him 'in arriving at the conclusion that there has been an implied recognition of an industry allowance above the basic wage in the shops and factories section'. The industry was characterised by 'special industrial conditions additional to and independent of margins for skill'. Quick decided, therefore,

> to make what is commonly called an 'industry allowance' superadded to the basic wage, in consideration of the following factors, viz., distasteful and disagreeable and in some cases repulsive and repellent nature of the work, especially in the hot summer months; conditions injurious to health such as working in cellars and cold storage chambers; necessity for providing and wearing special clothing in the discharge of duties; wear and tear, renewal and laundry of clothing, and providing tools of trade.

He awarded an allowance of 4s 6d per week, 'which is the amount allowed under the New South Wales and South Australian awards …' (p. 189).

Turning to margins, Quick noted that in 1916 Higgins had allowed a margin of 10s for shopmen and general butchers. This was retained in a 1921 agreement and remained in force, but the union now sought an increase, which the employers opposed. 'It is only under very special circumstances', said Quick,

> that the Court would be disposed to interfere with existing margins, but in this case I believe that butchering has of late years been a progressive industry, showing a great increase in methods of preparing and handling meat and presenting it in a form attractive to customers. The magnificent shop-window displays of to-day to be seen in the metropolitan and country shops show a great advance in the taste and refinement of the butchering trade, compared with the rough, ready and

rude methods of earlier years. Complaint has been made that the trade has not been attracting the services of apprentices and that the standard of workmanship has been endangered. The best way in my opinion of securing apprentices and improvers to supply the shopmen and general butchers of the future is to make the trade attractive and give it a better footing and standard, instead of allowing it to be regarded as a repulsive and unprogressive occupation … Under the circumstances, I propose to make a small marginal increase of 1s 6d per week, which is of course independent of the industry allowance provided for at the bottom of the scale. (pp. 191–192)

Quick returned to the butcher's margin in December 1925, and in this case compared the butcher's work to that of the engineering tradesman:

The margin allowed to a fitter in the engineering industry is 4s per day, or 24s per week. To qualify himself to earn that he has to serve an apprenticeship of five years. The margin allowed to shopmen and general butchers by the award as it now stands is 11s 6d per week, which is not quite half that allowed to the fitter. Now, in my opinion, the general butcher is a tradesman equally as useful, necessary and indispensable in his sphere of industrial operations as a fitter in the iron industry. It is true that the butcher in cutting meat has not to work to the same exactitude and precision as the fitter, but he has to understand the anatomy of oxen, hogs, and sheep, and be able to cut to the requirements of the retail trade with a certain amount of care and skill so as to avoid waste to the employer and do justice to the employer's customer. (*Meat Industry* case 22 CAR 794, 803–804)

Quick increased the margin to 14s. There is no indication why the remaining 'gap' between the fitter and the butcher (10s) was more correct than the previous gap of 12s 6d. (With the industry allowance of 4s 6d, the gap was reduced to 5s 6d.) The structure of the butcher's wage thus became:

Basic wage	£4 8s
Industry allowance	4s 6d
Margin	14s
Total	£5 6s 6d

Another decision that appeared to turn on the arbitrator's assessment of the work was that of Webb, given in 1925, about the margin for maltsters (*Liquor Trades* case 22 CAR 675):

> When a man seeks work in a malthouse he begins his work without any special training. But he is selected for the work by the employer or his foreman. Where the employer wants a man and a man offers for the work he is given a trial if he is a 'likely-looking man'. The man may at the time know nothing about the work but there is a consensus of testimony that he has a lot to learn and that it takes him some time before he becomes proficient at the work. A maltster must be a man who can be relied on to do his work carefully and properly. There is skill in his work. It is not a high degree of skill but I am satisfied that the work requires some skill. … It is true that untrained men are put on to do the work at the full wage, but the untrained man must learn the work and unless he shows that he is capable of learning and that he is a trustworthy, reliable man he is not permitted to continue in the employment. (p. 681)

The reader may well ponder what margin would accord with this description of the maltster's work. Webb's answer was 12s.

In the *Printing Industry* case (relating to newspapers in Adelaide and Hobart), decided in March 1926, Webb was asked to include an industry allowance in the award. Having reviewed previous decisions about industry allowances, he said:

> The cases which I have quoted establish that it is the practice of the Court to reflect in its awards an industry allowance where such allowance has been previously observed in an industry, and especially when such allowance has been voluntarily conceded by agreement. Now, in this industry, such industry allowance undoubtedly exists, and the reasons why an industry allowance should be granted are to be founded in the exacting nature of the work done, but the matter is very troublesome. In no two States is the same amount fixed, and the sums granted in each State show wide divergences. (23 CAR 124, 134)

Webb granted an industry allowance of 6s in Adelaide and 3s in Hobart. He then went through the various classifications of work and, after summary descriptions, awarded margins. The following is an example:

> Rotary Machinist—The rotary printing machine in a printing office is a very wonderful piece of machinery. The man who is in charge of the machine is the machine minder or rotary machinist. His work is very responsible work, and the margin for this employee will be £1 10s per week.

In 1921, responsibility for fixing salaries in the Commonwealth Public Service was transferred to the Commonwealth Public Service Arbitrator. This removed from the Court what had hitherto been its main responsibilities for white-collar and professional work. Nevertheless, in the course of the 1920s the Court made decisions affecting other such areas, including banking, insurance, local government, and clerical and higher classifications in the railways.

In the *Insurance Clerks'* case of 1923, Quick was confronted with a claim for a long incremental scale (19 CAR 208). During the hearing, he had contrasted this claim with the normal treatment of manual workers. The fitter, for example, might receive £284 per year at age 21, but 'he then becomes a fixture unless he gains promotion to a superior position such as that of overseer or manager' (p. 223). From that point in the proceedings, 'the argument in support of the ascending scale was directed to show that the insurance clerk, unlike the stationery fitter, is constantly increasing his knowledge and usefulness and is shouldering more and more responsibility'. Further, 'the argument was advanced that the basic wage applicable to mechanical tradesmen and suitable to the age of 21 years was not sufficient for the progressive insurance clerk whose costs of living are necessarily greater than those of a mechanic'. Quick was persuaded:

> At about the age of 26 or 27 years a young man naturally approaches the age at which he may reasonably consider and prepare for marriage, and if his income at that time is not sufficient to enable him to support a

> wife and possible family his outlook is very cheerless and unsatisfactory. Unless he has some motive for looking forward to an improving career justifying the responsibilities of marriage he is in danger of losing interest in his work and is liable to drift into habits of carelessness and lack of ambition. (p. 224)

He prescribed a scale in which the rate at age 21—£220—was equated to the basic wage and a maximum of £390 was reached at age 32 (p. 226). In the *Bank Officers'* case of 1924, Quick retained a similar scale, which had been included in a consent award of 1922 (19 CAR 272). He refused, however, to prescribe rates for branch managers: 'Their appearance in such a Court as this alongside their bank officers, most of them subordinate to themselves, being members of a common labour organisation formed for the very purpose of prosecuting demands and obtaining awards against their employers, appears to me to place them as well as their employers in a false position' (p. 284).

Much of the work of *musicians and actors* was casual; individual skills varied markedly; and assessing the level of work was seen to be a difficult exercise. In 1923, Powers took refuge in the fact that he was setting only minimum rates: 'I am not asked to fix rates for the Mozarts, Mendelssohns, Kubeliks or O'Briens of the orchestra, or even the man who is worth £10 a week to managers, who can command their own rates, but the Court has to fix rates for the John Brown, Tom Jones, and Andrew Robinsons of the orchestra who would not get a fair rate for playing in the orchestra from some employers, if the Court did not fix a minimum rate for the ordinary work of an ordinary musician in the orchestra' (*Musicians'* case 17 CAR 900, 907).

Webb, in 1924, said that 'to attempt to assess the value of an actor's skill would be to embark on a hopeless task' (*Actors'* case 19 CAR 788, 795).

> One difficulty is that there is no standard by which I can measure or value such skill, and another insuperable difficulty is that there is no standard of skill or responsibility. … I am dealing with men in respect of whom there is no standard at all. Their skill may be great, or it may be negligible. I cannot assess its value. The utmost the Court can do in

an industry such as this is to fix a minimum which will provide for the normal and reasonable needs of those workers considered as human beings, and further than that the Court cannot go. It must, however, I think, be conceded that any actor is entitled to something more than an unskilled labourer's wage. He is expected to dress better than a labourer; he is expected to be a man of some education; his occupation requires that he should live under certain conditions; he is required to work at times when most people prefer to enjoy their leisure, and the needs of such a man are greater than those of an unskilled labourer. (pp. 795–796)

Webb awarded £6 for an actor and £5 5s for an actress. These amounts included allowances for travelling.

In relation to musicians, Webb said that a difficulty confronting a judge was that there was no other industry that could be used for comparison.

> The employment is more in the nature of a professional engagement than of an industrial occupation. In all cases the Court would experience great difficulties when it endeavoured to find standards by which to measure the value of professional services. Yet in some cases it must be done, and the conditions of the musicians' employment are such that it is necessary that the Court extend its protection to them. Other professions can protect themselves. The musician is a wage-earner who would be hopelessly at the mercy of exploitation if he were not protected by the Court. (*Musicians'* case 22 CAR 29, 30)

It was commonplace, said Webb,

> that the skill of musicians is a very variable matter and ranges from the artistry of a great artist to the poor skill of a moderate player … We cannot compute the true worth of genius, and there are some who claim to be musicians the value of whose work it would be just as difficult to estimate from another point of view. It is between these two extremes that this Court has to find a wage for the body of professional musicians who earn their living by playing an instrument in an orchestra at a public performance, and it is, of course, obvious that this body of

musicians will, as a rule, include neither the great artist not the very poor performer. (p. 34)

6.2.3 Conclusion

It will be plain that when the Court moved from general principles, such as refusal to match movements in the basic wage, there were, on the one hand, few consistently applied principles for the setting of margins and, on the other, a plethora of criteria applied in specific cases. Obviously, there was no systematic job evaluation. The 24s 'tradesman's' margin did provide a benchmark that encouraged consideration of inter-award relativities. A tendency to maintain existing margins was countered to a degree by the process of assigning small margins to work that hitherto would have been treated as unskilled: unfortunately, no data exist that would show the effects of this process on the degree of inequality in the wage structure. Hancock and Moore (1972) found that the degree of inequality between award wages did not change much during the 1920s. That finding, however, was derived from an analysis of the behaviour of 28 award rates across the period 1914–66. It could not allow for the effect of the insertion in the structure of new classifications that carried small margins.

6.3 Hours of work

With Higgins' resignation on 29 June 1921, Powers was for a time the sole member of the Court. Hence there was no 'quorum' to deal with possible hours reductions (below 48 hours) or increases. With unions making claims that flowed from Higgins' decisions, a queue developed. Duffy and Rich, appointed Deputy Presidents on 6 August, stayed only long enough to join Powers in deciding upon these claims. The *Standard Hours* case—the first full bench case in the Court's history—was heard in September and October and decided in December (15 CAR 1044).

Powers began his decision by listing reasons why it was necessary to deal with the issue at length:

- 'The unions concerned, and their members, and the public, are entitled to know why this Court, in November, 1921, refuses to lower standard hours when the late president of the Court ... in November, 1920, and in June, 1921, decided to lower standard hours in two important industries.'
- 'The unions concerned, and their members, should know the refusal of this Court to reduce standard hours generally is in accordance with the principles and practices laid down by this Court since its establishment up to the date of the Timber Workers' award, namely, for 13 years' (p. 1146).

Higgins had always, since inception of the Court, refused to reduce hours below 48 unless this was necessary 'on the ground that the conditions under which the employees had to work seriously affected their health, and shorter hours would tend to prevent injury to their health, or for other special reasons as in the Builders Labourers' and the Waterside Workers' cases' (p. 1048). In all other cases the Court had held that any reduction of standard hours was a matter for State Legislatures. 'That practice', said Powers, 'was followed from the establishment of the Court until the award of the late president in the Timber Workers' case, made in November last; after he had publicly announced his intention of not continuing the responsibility of conducting the work of this Court, as President, after the cases in hand had been dealt with' (p. 1049).

Powers acknowledged, nevertheless, that in the *Timber Workers'* case 'the late president dealt very fully with the question of reducing standard hours in Australia generally, and he gave reasons why he should alter the practice of this Court, and reduce the standard hours of work in Australia except where special reasons to the contrary were shown in any case' (p. 1051). He had carefully read Higgins' decision. 'Whether the learned Judge was right, or not, on the evidence submitted in that case', conditions had since changed. 'I doubt', said Powers, 'whether the learned Judge would under present conditions, and on the evidence at present before the Court, make a similar award' (p. 1052). Higgins' inquiry had been held at a time (August, September, and October

1920) 'when wages were at their highest, and when employers could and did receive the highest prices for their products' (p. 1054). Since then, 'the rates of wages in all countries have dropped considerably and the hours of labour increased except in Australia' (p. 1059). Unemployment among unionists had risen from 6.2 to 11.4 per cent, and the Court would not be justified 'in adding to the abnormal unemployment by reducing standard hours' (pp. 1060–1061).

The evidence in the present case showed that in all industries where hours had been reduced from 48 to 44, there had been reductions of output 'about equal to the proportion of the reduction of hours' (p. 1062). That increases in production due to new and better machinery should allow workers to enjoy shorter hours was, in theory, quite right; but it could not do so in practice 'unless the workers of the world act together and enforce that claim':

> I personally do not see how any employer in Australia can give his workers shorter hours because his machinery produces twice as much, or five times or twenty times as much, as the machinery of 1910 did if he has to compete with competitors in the United States and England who have as good or even better machinery and who have employees who work longer instead of shorter hours at lower wages.
>
> ... The Court will find it difficult in the light of present happenings throughout the civilised world to maintain the Australian standard of living based on the *Harvester* judgment, the living wage, the standard of 48 hours as a maximum in industries generally, and shorter hours in force in special industries and for special reasons, while the world as a whole has reduced and is reducing standards of living, reducing wages, and increasing hours of work. As at present constituted the Court will maintain those standards ... (pp. 1063; 1071)

The joint decision of Duffy and Rich reads in full:

> We have carefully considered the evidence in these cases and we are not satisfied that any of the reductions in standard hours of work asked for should be imposed on employers at the present time. We have been

pressed to make such a reduction in certain exceptional cases where the work is stated to be either distasteful or prejudicial to health or both. In our opinion such cases can be dealt with most effectually by payment of additional wages for distasteful work, and by the enforcement of more satisfactory industrial hygienic conditions by the Parliaments of the States, or, in default of parliamentary action, by award of this Court. (p. 1071)

Thus the majority decision of the Court, for all its brevity, was even stronger than that of Powers. Not only did Duffy[14] and Rich oppose the general reduction of hours envisaged by Higgins; they also rejected the 'special factors' approach that had led the Court for some time to reduce hours in specific industries and occupations.[15]

Following this decision, employers affected by Higgins' decisions in the *Timber Workers*' and the *ASE* cases sought to have the 48-hour week restored. With Duffy and Rich having left the Court, their claims could not be dealt with until new Deputy Presidents were appointed. Quick and Webb were appointed in June 1922.[16] A new Full Bench gave its decision in September (16 CAR 649). Not surprisingly, the employers' claims succeeded, and concurrent union claims for a wider application of Higgins' two decisions failed.[17]

Powers was satisfied by the evidence that 'the industries in Australia generally are in a much more depressed state than they were in September,

---

[14] Interestingly, Duffy had been the principal union counsel in *Harvester*. The *Standard Hours* case was his (and Rich's) sole involvement in the Arbitration Court.

[15] In December 1921, Powers gave a decision in a case related to gold mining at Bendigo (15 CAR 1166). Having inspected the work, he thought that the claim for a reduction of hours was reasonable. 'But as the hours cannot be reduced, and the Full Court expressed their opinion that special cases ought to be dealt with by increased rates (if at all), I propose to grant increased rates for persons working in hot places where the temperature in rises or stopes in a mine exceeds 76 degrees (wet bulb) Fahrenheit' (p. 1171).

[16] A note at the beginning of volume 16 of the CAR states that Duffy and Rich resigned on 26 June and that Quick and Webb were appointed on the same date. No doubt this is correct, but the fact is that Duffy and Rich had done no work in the Arbitration Court since *Standard Hours* and that Powers had earlier referred to them as having resigned.

[17] The issue of working hours was a cause of significant industrial disruption (Hagan 1981, p. 34).

1921, and that it would not be in the interests of employees, the employers or the public generally, to reduce the recognised standard of 48 hours in industries generally in Australia at the present time or to fix 44 hours as a week's work except in special cases or on special grounds'. Departing, however, from his earlier stance that 48 hours was a norm that only the legislatures should alter, he added:

> Finally if the Court bases its decision not to reduce standard hours because it is satisfied the industries and the country cannot at present afford to pay the extra cost of production which would necessarily follow by reduction of hours of duty, it will, I think, compel this Court to view favourably any application to grant 44 hours a week when the industries can bear the extra burden … without adding too greatly to the burdens on the general public. (p. 671)

The *Main Hours* case of 1926 (discussed in Chapter 7) could be seen as an attempt by the unions to redeem this 'promise'.[18]

Quick observed that Higgins' decisions in the *Timber Workers'* and *ASE* cases were departures not only from his earlier criteria but also from a term of the Treaty of Versailles, calling for 'the adoption of an eight hours day or a forty-eight hours week as the standard to be aimed at where it has not already been attained'. (Whether the drafters of the Treaty intended to say that employees should not work *less* than 48 hours is questionable.) He felt that the 1921 Full Court decision had 'reversed any new ideal standard of 44 hours which the late president may have had in his mind and which he may have desired to establish in Australia' (p. 708); and that 'if industries which supply the wants of the public are prejudiced, harassed and discouraged, the public whose interests are supreme will suffer' (p. 710). Webb found no evidence that 48 hours caused undue fatigue for workers in the industries concerned in the applications and was persuaded that the reduction of hours had caused proportional reductions of output (p. 728). An important factor

---

[18] It is arguable that the 1920 amendment of the Act, specifying that reductions of standard hours below 48 had to be dealt with by the Full Court, had the implication that such reductions were at least on the Court's agenda and were not reserved to the legislatures.

in his judgment was the import competition being experienced by the timber industry.

The decision left the 44-hour week intact in some sections of the timber industry, notably metropolitan timber yards. Some employers thereafter made efforts to revert to 48 hours in these areas. The Court in April 1923, however, refused to countenance further changes in hours:

> This Full Court has already decided that it will not approve of any increase of recognised standard hours unless with the consent of the parties, or unless it is quite satisfied that it should do so in the interests of employers, employees and the public. It will not approve of any increase of standard hours in industries which can be carried on at a profit simply to allow employers to increase their profits. It will not approve of any reduction of standard hours in any industry or branch of an industry except with the consent of the parties—or unless it is satisfied it should do so on the ground that the health of the employees is affected by the hours worked or that the work is so strenuous that men cannot be fairly asked to work standard hours or for any other special reasons. (*Timber Industry* case 17 CAR 244, 250)

A few weeks later, Powers refused to refer to the Full Court an application by flourmillers for an increase in hours from 44 to 48. Even if the employers could persuade the Court that there were no longer health grounds for the shorter hours, it would not increase hours, because the industry was well able to sustain the 44-hour week (*Flourmillers'* case 17 CAR 323, 324).

The Rules of Practice issued by the Full Court on 30 April 1923 (previously mentioned in discussing the basic wage) included the following statements about standard hours:

- The 'standard hours' for Federal awards generally have been fixed by the Full Court as 48 hours a week except in cases where the recognised standard hours in the industry at the time the award is to be made are less than 48 hours a week, as they are in the building industry as such (apart from mixed industries)—in mining

- (underground)—in the flour milling industry—in the shearing branch of the pastoral industry—and in other industries for special reasons.

- In all other cases the Act prevents a single Judge reducing the 'standard hours' below 48 hours a week, or increasing them—where 48 hours are the standard hours—or if the standard hours are less than 48 hours a week from increasing or reducing them, but it does not prevent a single Judge from refusing to increase or reduce hours.

- This Court has also decided that where the standard hours—in an industry as a whole—are at the present time 44 hours a week or less than 48 hours they will not be increased to 48 hours if the industry or industries are not mixed industries and can be profitably carried on working 44 hours a week or any number less than 48 hours. (17 CAR 376–377)

The Court, as it had done previously, endeavoured to combat 'long' working hours, that is, hours in excess of 48 per week. For example, in July 1923, Quick dealt with a request by owners of ships in the River Murray trade to be free of the 48-hour limitation, claiming that it was 'unworkable and impractical' in the circumstances of the trade. 'If I granted this request', said Quick,

> the result would be to return to pre-award practices in connexion with privately-owned boats in which there appears to have been no limitation or definition of hours, there being a fixed sum paid in wages irrespective of time worked. Of course there could be no overtime for there was no daily or weekly time limit beyond which overtime could be charged. Men might be required to remain on duty 12 hours per day or 84 hours per week without any extra pay. To sanction either directly or indirectly such a system would be in my judgment a reactionary step from which I would shrink to be responsible. (*Merchant Service Guild* case 17 CAR 657, 661)

In October 1924, Powers granted a union claim to reduce standard hours for ships' cooks from 63 to 56 per week (from 9 hours per day to 8 hours in a seven-day week) (*Marine Cooks'* case 20 CAR 556). He commented:

> Every attempt since the Court was established to reduce standard hours is always met by objections. In some cases it was and is said they are impracticable. In others it only means an addition to the wages in the shape of overtime. In others that the hours are reasonable and fair and ought not to be reduced. In others the parties have agreed to longer hours. In others the industries cannot pay higher rates. (p. 560)

Powers cited various examples to show that the Court had been able to counter long hours without causing the dire effects predicted by the employers. Where workers were engaged on continuous processes, such as smelting, employers had insisted that a seven-day week was essential; but the Court had provided for a six-day week without detriment to the industries. In the case of theatrical employees, hours had been reduced from 60 to 48; and carters' and drivers' hours were being reduced progressively from 56 to 48.[19]

I referred in Section 5.1 of Chapter 5 to the decision of the High Court in *Cowburn's* case, which rendered inoperative a New South Wales law prescribing a 44-hour week where the employees were subject to federal awards prescribing hours. In May 1926, Powers commented on the changed legal context:

> I think it very necessary to point out the position in which this Court, the employers, and the employees—the employees especially—are placed by the New South Wales State Act fixing 44 hours per week, coupled with the recent declaration of the law by the High Court in the 44-hour case ... The effect of the position is that Federal awards are now to be sanctuaries under which respondents to Federal awards can flee to escape all State laws, Commissions, Arbitration Courts and Wages Board decisions, which are imposed upon all other citizens in a State—that is as to rules and conditions fixed by Federal awards. If that

---

[19] In 1926, Powers wrote in similar terms in the context of a reduction of hours for marine stewards (*Marine Stewards'* case 23 CAR 284).

is the effect, and I think it is, then the unions will not assist to build the sanctuaries into which the respondents can flee, and will apply to determine the awards as soon as the period for which they were made expires. ... If nothing is done, it is clear that very few awards will in future be made for employees in New South Wales. Queensland awards are very rare at present, and so are Western Australian awards. The work of this Court will therefore be greatly reduced if the law is not amended in some way ... Personally, I deplore any political interference with the hours of duty or basic wage, but both the Federal Parliament and the State Parliaments have legislated in respect of hours. If the Court is to continue to make Federal awards, something must be done. (*A Statement of the Position of the Court, the Employers, and the Employees* 23 CAR 386, 386–387)

Powers' deprecation of 'political' interference with hours contrasts with the earlier insistence of Higgins and himself that the reduction of hours below 48 was properly a matter for the legislatures. His fears of a switch of jurisdictions proved to be exaggerated.[20]

6.4 FEMALE EMPLOYMENT

Although in 1921–22 the Federal Court moved toward recognition of *the* male basic wage (which might vary geographically), linking to it the automatic adjustment system, there was no declaration of a general basic wage for women.[21] In some, but not all, awards which provided for female employees, however, there was acceptance of the concept of a basic rate for women.

The basic wage created by Higgins was conceived as an amount appropriate to an unskilled male labourer responsible for the maintenance of

---

[20] Quick, in May 1926, granted an application by the Storemen and Packers' Union to terminate their award in respect of New South Wales. The employers consented to the application in return for the union's agreeing to a wage reduction of 5s per week (*Storemen and Packers'* case 23 CAR 402). In June 1926, Quick refused an application by the Electrical Trades' Union for a 44-hour week in the tobacco industry (without loss of pay). The union relied on the fact that a number of New South Wales employers had agreed to such an arrangement (*Tobacco* case 23 CAR 412).
[21] This remained the position until World War II.

a family of 'about five'. The Court, perceiving that the typical female worker had no similar obligations, concluded that the minimum wage appropriate to a woman was one that would provide for her support only. Though there was some variance, the wage set for unskilled female workers was commonly equal to about 54 per cent of the relevant male basic wage. There was no consistently applied principle for rewarding female skill and little discussion of the question.

Issues of women's employment were, in fact, a minor part of the Court's agenda in the 1920s. In most awards, no terms of employment of women were prescribed. Indeed, the underlying disputes and plaints mostly did not refer to females. The reason is clear—female employment was confined to a narrow range of industries and occupations. Cases in which references to women's employment can be found related to: manufacturing grocers; the clothing trades; hotels; banking; insurance; fruit picking; food preserving; actors; the entertainment industry (for, example, usherettes in cinemas); marine stewardesses, laundresses, etc.; railway cleaners; printing; and journalists.

6.4.1 Manufacturing grocers

In 1923, Powers made a new award for manufacturing grocers (*Manufacturing Grocers'* case 17 CAR 625). The parties in Melbourne had agreed to a slight reduction in the proportional minimum rate for women. Powers refused to accept this, saying that it would take the women's wage below £2 2s, which he judged to be 'the minimum to allow any adult woman to live in any sort of reasonable comfort in the capital cities in these days'. He determined that the female minimum would rise or fall proportionally with the male basic wage, but subject to the minimum of 42s. So far as I am aware, there is no explanation for the specific amount of 42s.

6.4.2 Clothing

Webb, in 1923, made a new award for the clothing trades (*Clothing and Allied Trades* case 18 CAR 1033). Under the previous award, the basic wage for males was £4 5s, and for females £2 5s 6d (a ratio of 53.5 per cent). The union sought basic wages of £4 15s for men and £2 15s for women, raising the female basic wage to 58 per cent of the male rate. 'On behalf of the employees', said Webb, 'several budgets of expenditure have been put in evidence, and these budgets have been criticised by the employers, who have submitted arguments and estimates from which they ask me to come to the conclusion that a fair basic rate for a woman would be about £1 18s 3d' (p. 1039). The Court in the past had treated women in industry 'from a liberal point of view' in relation to its assessment of their needs:

> There is a large number of women in this industry who live at home. In my recent inspections of the factories I questioned many girls, and in many cases, the girl told me that she was living at home with her father and mother, paying her mother often 15s, sometimes 17s 6d, and sometimes £1 a week for her board, and often contriving to save money out of her wage. Mr Justice Higgins, however, decided to adopt a single woman living away from her home as the type upon which to fix the wage according to the needs of such an individual. 'A woman or girl in a comfortable home cannot be left to underbid in wages other women or girls who are less fortunate,' and I think most reasonable men will agree with this view. (p. 1041)

Both sides had urged him to make an independent inquiry into women's needs, but he had come to the conclusion that he 'would not be justified in departing from the established practice in the industry with regard to the woman's basic wage'. The parties had agreed on an addition of 2s as compensation for lost time. Accordingly, Webb raised the female minimum wage to 47s 6d.

I have previously referred to Webb's comments about margins in the clothing trades. Having said that these were very low, he set a tailor's margin of 18s rather than the usual tradesman's margin of 24s. For female coat hands, he awarded 10s, but did not explain how far this was based on gender and how far on his assessment of skill.

This *Clothing Trades* case illustrates some of the reasons for the low pay of women in a predominantly female industry. One, of course, was Webb's acceptance of the needs differential in respect of the basic wage. A second was the apparent weakness of the union, which had previously agreed to margins well below those achieved by more male-dominated unions for work in other industries requiring comparable training and skill. A third was the arbitrator's acceptance of a lesser margin for the work of skilled women. A fourth was a willingness of women to accept low-paid work. The last reason raises the issue of cause and effect. The clothing trades were a low-pay industry, for both women and those men who worked in it. Had the wage levels been similar to those of the more male-dominated industries, the clothing trades would have been a smaller industry.[22] Webb (and his predecessors who made earlier awards) could have fixed rates on a par with those existing elsewhere, at the cost of reducing one of the few industries where women predominated. Hence, the low wages in clothing could be construed as the *result* of women crowding into it; or as the *cause* of job opportunities for women that would not otherwise have existed. In either case, the low pay of the female worker was due in part to the limited range of 'female' employment.

6.4.3 Insurance and banking

In the *Insurance Clerks'* case of 1923 (see Subsection 6.2.2), Quick fixed separate scales for males and females. Whereas the male scale rose by annual increments between ages 15 and 32, the female scale stopped at age 23. At age 21, the female rate was a high fraction—66 per cent—of the male rate, and at age 23 the relativity was 72 per cent. But by age 32, the female received only 46 per cent of the male wage. In the *Bank Officials'* case of 1924, Quick again awarded a long scale for males and a truncated one for females (19 CAR 272). In neither case did he comment on the differences between the scales, but it is obvious that he (and the parties) had not absorbed any notion of career scales for women. This now seems incongruous for a point in history when the casualties of World War I implied an increase in the population of single women.

---

[22] This effect might have been countered by imposing higher tariffs on imported clothing.

While the insurance and banking awards did not specify different tasks for the men and women employed under the respective scales, it may well be that differentiation existed 'on the ground'. Otherwise, we might suppose that females would have driven men from these industries. The likelihood is that the employers—perhaps responding to customers' expectations—tended to commit the more responsible work to men. For example, while bank managers were not covered by the banking award, the expectation that managers and accountants would be males is likely to have affected the assignment of work to employees on the basic scale. Thus, not only were females paid less, but they were allotted correspondingly inferior work.

6.4.4 Actors and actresses

In the 1923 *Actors'* case (see Subsection 6.2.2), Webb set minimum rates of £6 for actors and £5 5s for actresses, including allowances for travelling. He did not comment on the size of the difference, though it was less than what was usual for basic-wage and minimum-wage workers. Later in 1924, in the *Theatrical and Amusement Employees'* case (20 CAR 16), he said of the 'female basic wage':

> In the Clothing Trades case I decided that the female base wage for females working a 44 hour week should be 54 per cent of the male base wage. On a base of £4 4s 6d that would be a sum of £2 5s 7d. In this industry the base fixed for unskilled female workers in the previous award was £2 9s 1d, and this was 60 per cent of the male base of £4 2s 2d. But this base applied to a woman working 48 hours per week under the condition of hours fixed by that award. I can have no reason to alter the increased percentage fixed in the previous award … and the wages for women in this industry will be fixed on a base wage of £2 10s 6d per week, which is 60 per cent of £4 4s 6d per week, calculated to the nearest sixpence. (p. 18)

Since the 44-hour week applied to both males and females in the clothing trades, and the basic wage was supposed to be related to needs, it is not obvious why the ratio of the basic wages should be different when both sexes worked

48 hours. But in fixing travelling allowances, Webb took into account the fact that the man still had to maintain his family at home, while the woman was to some extent relieved of her normal 'home' expenses. Accordingly, he fixed the male travelling allowance at 12s 6d per day or 45s per week and the female allowance at 7s 6d per day or £1 per week.

6.4.5 Food preservers

In the *Food Preservers'* case decided in August 1924 (20 CAR 60), Quick set a female basic wage at 54 per cent of the male rate and awarded a margin of 6s per week for females engaged in cutting or pulping lemons or pineapples—work which was 'most distasteful and irritating, and frequently causes poisoning of hands, fingers and face, which is not covered by the Workers' Compensation Act' (p. 81). He and the applicant union apparently assumed that only women would be doing this work.

6.4.6 Dried fruit

Dealing with the dried-fruit industry in February 1925 (see Subsection 6.2.2), Webb decided 'to provide that the female rates and juvenile rates are to be fractional rates of the rates for adults [sic]. The sums are very simple, and the parties will have no difficulty in ascertaining the rates'. But there was a special provision:

> In recent years, a method of selling dried fruits has come into extensive use. It is that of selling the fruit in cartons or cardboard boxes. Owing to the high rate of wage which is paid to women under the award in this industry, the dried fruit are not packed at the growing centres. The fruit is sent down in bulk to the capital cities, and there packed into cartons for sale. The girls at Mildura would have this work to do if it were not for the high rate of wage which is paid there. I propose to fix a special rate of wage for packing fruit in cartons in the hope that, if the girls at Mildura desire to take on this work, they may have the opportunity to do so, and that the work may be kept in the fruit-growing centres. (*Dried Fruit* case 21 CAR 334, 345–346)

Thus the low range of job opportunities for women in the country town became a reason for holding down their award rate of pay.

6.4.7 Marine laundresses

In 1925, Powers set rates for marine stewards, laundresses and others (*Marine Stewards'* case 22 CAR 193). The union claimed for the laundress the same rate as for the assistant laundry steward—a man. The claim was made 'on the ground that it is a man's work, but as a laundress's work is generally recognised as a woman's work I propose to allow the same rate as to the assistant stewardess' (p. 195). This reflected the principle, enunciated by Higgins in the 1912 *Fruitpickers'* case, that a differentiating criterion was whether the task was men's or women's work. If the work were 'men's work', women performing it might be awarded equal pay. Unequal pay prevailed where the work was 'women's work' or, as in the insurance and banking industries, both sexes were employed.

6.4.8 Printing

Webb in April 1925, in a *Printing Industry* case (22 CAR 247), set the female basic rate at 54 per cent of the male wage, observing that this was the percentage that he had fixed in the *Clothing Trades* case. In that case, he had maintained the percentage relation set by Higgins in a previous case for the clothing trades, although Higgins did not arrive at the rate set 'by calculating a proportion of the basic wage'. He had adopted the percentage in other cases, and he proposed to adhere to it.

6.4.9 The work

The members of the Court from time to time showed a sensitivity—sometimes patronising—to a presumed need for women to be accorded special consideration as to their working conditions, especially hours. In the 1923 *Clothing Trades* case (18 CAR 1033), Webb said:

> The history of the clothing trade has, no doubt, many sad pages within its covers. I doubt if any class of worker in unregulated industry was in a more defenceless position than the needlewoman. I think it was her plight which made factory legislation possible in its beginnings. … The thought that kept constantly recurring to my mind when I was inspecting a large number of factories in Victoria, was that females engaged in this industry comprised a body of superior women and intelligent and happy-looking girls, apparently working under healthy and happy conditions. They were a fine class of workers, and appeared to me to reflect credit on Australian conditions. (pp. 1034–1035)

And he said in the *Theatrical and Amusement Employees'* case of 1924 (20 CAR 16):

> But I wholly disapprove of girls being compelled to appear as ushers and ticket takers in male costume and other costumes which are unbecoming to an Australian girl working under the conditions under which these girls work. It is quite unnecessary; it is not fair to the girls; and it is not fair to the community. The award will make a provision against this in the manner claimed by the union. (p. 20)

It was Webb, too, who said in 1925:

> I do not wish to be misunderstood about pianola playing. I am quite prepared to concede that the pianola gives great pleasure to many who hear it and many who play it. But we all know that it is possible to have too much of a good thing, and most people will agree that it is not fair to require a girl to play a pianola for eight hours a day for six days a week. When I made the award I reduced the hours for pianola players to 36 hours a week. It seemed to me that if a girl worked a pianola for six hours a day she had done a fair day's work. (*Theatrical and Amusement Employees'* case 21 CAR 769, 770)

6.5 Conclusion

The early part of Powers' presidency, from mid-1921 to late 1922, was dominated by the Court's rejection of Piddington, its response to economic contraction and falling prices, and its endeavours to reverse Higgins' policies of raising margins and reducing hours. Although Powers' commentary on Piddington in the *Gas Workers'* case stressed deficiencies in the Royal Commission's terms of reference and included specific criticisms of the Commission's assessment of needs, it also dealt with the inability of industry to pay a basic wage set at the Piddington level. In this last sense, it was an affirmation of the controlling role of 'capacity to pay'. Not until the Depression would the Court affirm that capacity to pay was pre-eminent and family needs secondary, but the truth of the matter is that after Piddington the needs criterion had little purchase.

Having negotiated the Court past Piddington, Powers (with Quick and Webb) succeeded in establishing an innovative method of basic-wage adjustment. Indeed, the federal basic wage ceased for a time to be a subject of serious contention. From 1923 until mid-1926, the balance of the Court's award-making work shifted toward micro wage-fixing, with emphasis on the establishment of margins within a framework set by two principles: rejection of any notion of adjusting margins to restore earlier proportional relativities, and acceptance of the tradesman's rate as a key element in the pay structure.

From an economic perspective, the most interesting aspect of the period is the slight attention paid by the Court to the large increase in real wages that occurred, seemingly fortuitously, in 1921 and 1922. Members of the Court did have a sense that there had been a post-war boom, followed by contraction. This contributed to the reversal of Higgins' 'generosity' with respect to margins and working hours. But the reality of the real wage increase seems to have passed unnoticed, seemingly obscured by the Court's adherence to the *Harvester* standard.

7

The new regime

The presumption which had marked the era of Powers' Presidency—that economic conditions were not conducive to any substantial advance in labour standards—continued after the reconstruction of the Court, though the newly appointed judges[1] had different views of the *degree* of restraint that the situation required. The available data analysed in Chapter 5, especially those about unemployment, indicate deterioration in the economy in the later years of the decade. Moreover, contemporary comparisons between the productivity of industry in the 1920s and in the pre-war years produced results ranging from actual decline to, at best, a small improvement. As the decade wore on and no decisive improvement emerged, there was little scope for any assumption of continuous improvement of wages and conditions. By the end of 1929, the tepid performance of earlier years was giving way to a foretaste of the crisis to come.

7.1 THE BASIC WAGE

Although there was no major innovation in the Court's approach to setting the basic wage, there was some important working-out of existing principles.

---

[1] See Chapter 5, Section 5.1.

7.1.1 The standard

Dethridge, in the *Glass Workers'* case of 1927, dealt with a union attempt to revive the Piddington wage:

> The union claims that the minimum wage in the industry shall be £5 15s 6d per week. This amount is that which was determined by the Basic Wage Commission of 1920, under the chairmanship of Mr Piddington, as to the actual cost of living at that time according to reasonable standards of comfort ... for a man with a wife and three children under fourteen years of age. Since that finding the unions have made a practice of claiming that amount as the minimum wage in industries in substitution for the *Harvester* basic wage which this Court has adopted. This claim has been disallowed, reasons for its disallowance having been given by Mr Justice Higgins on one occasion at least, and at considerable length by Mr Justice Powers in the gas employees' case. Notwithstanding the expression of those reasons, the claim is still made without regard to the fact, which is obvious to those who make any investigation into the statistics of the country, that the payment of a minimum wage of £5 15s 6d to all adult workers is quite impossible. ... The insertion of a claim for a flat minimum wage of such an amount as £5 15s 6d is harmful, inasmuch as it may mislead many of the workers into supposing that this Court, by some miraculous power, may be able to force employers to grant it. (25 CAR 289, 290)

It was not surprising that unions continued to invoke the Piddington finding, or that the Court continued to spurn it. Piddington, as we saw in Chapter 3, had acknowledged that the Royal Commission standard was unattainable, except by means of a system of child endowment which would relate income levels to family size. Dethridge, in the *Glass Workers'* case, said that

> the payment of a wage of anything like that amount to workers with a wife and three children depending upon them ... is only possible if unmarried male workers and married childless workers receive considerably less than the *Harvester* wage. Such a revolutionary change

could not be made effectively without legislative action comprising the whole of Australia. (p. 290)

Linking of the basic wage to child endowment was, at the time, a live issue in New South Wales, where Piddington had been appointed head of the State tribunal. Child endowment had also been referred, by agreement of the Commonwealth and the States, to a Royal Commission. The Commission, by a 3:2 majority, recommended against it. No action was taken.

In his 1929 *Timber Workers'* decision, Lukin took the argument as to family size a stage further. Not merely was the unreality of the wife and three-child family an objection to adopting the Piddington wage; it called into question the *Harvester* standard itself. The union had claimed an allowance in recognition of the fact that men working in the bush might have families living elsewhere. 'It may be said', Lukin commented, 'that the Court has gone beyond reason in making provision for all employees as if they were maintaining a wife and three children, when a man in fact on the average only maintains a fraction of a wife and a fraction of a child, and that it should go no further' (27 CAR 577, 628).

7.1.2 Powers' three shillings

Some of the Judges of the reconstituted Court indicated misgivings about Powers' 3s and about Powers' suggestion in his resignation statement that it was now a settled addition to the basic wage, rather than an expedient to cope with possible increases in the price level. They were prepared, in some special instances, to dispense with it.

In his 1927 decision in the *Shearers'* case, Dethridge granted a 'marginal wage' which (contrary to normal practice) took account of the increase in the cost of living since 1911, and noted:

> It will be observed that I have not added on to the basic wage for 1927 ... the 3s usually added since 1922 by the practice of this Court. I think that where the wage contains an adjustment clause, and where

> the marginal wage is increased proportionally with the increased cost of living—in this case from 9s to 15s 3d—it is equitable to leave out the customary 3s. (25 CAR 626, 632)

Drake-Brockman, in 1928, dealt with a claim for an adjustment of the basic wage in the clothing trades to recognise the unpaid loss of time in the industry. The workers were, he said, 'the equivalent of about two weeks' pay short of what the *Harvester* judgment fixed as their minimum annual requirements'. This, however, was partially 'made good' by Powers' 3s. Drake-Brockman adjusted the wage by 4s for the loss of time, but absorbed the 3s into the increase (leaving a net gain of 1s) (*Clothing Trades* case 26 CAR 76, 78). Beeby, in the same year, referred to a shipowners' endeavour to eliminate Powers' 3s from the rate for waterside workers:

> The [union] did not ask for any alteration in wage rates, but the employers contended that the 3s addition to the bare living wage should now be disallowed. I stated, during the proceedings, that this claim would not be granted, but that the application could be renewed after the Full Court had completed its proposed re-investigation of the whole problem of the living wage. (*Waterside Workers'* case 26 CAR 867, 884)

This is the first reference that I have encountered to a review of the basic wage. No such review occurred before the Depression.[2]

Later in 1928, Lukin referred to 'the Powers' 3s addition over and above [the] basic wage', commenting that 'although … the reason for its present existence is not anywhere explained its allowance has been, by an order of the Full Court, firmly established as the practice, and ought therefore, in my opinion, to be continued until the Full Court otherwise orders' (*Saddlery Workers'* case 27 CAR 156, 158). In the *Timber Workers'* case, he left no doubt about his own opinion:

---

[2] Lukin said in January 1929: 'In September, 1923, five years ago, it was evidently contemplated that the basic wage should be reconsidered at an early date. So far it has not been reconsidered, but I understand that the matter is to be reviewed by the Court, as the Court is now constituted, as soon as the other business of the Court will permit. This should really mean at an early date' (*Timber Workers'* case 27 CAR 577, 597).

George Dethridge

Lionel Lukin

George Beeby

Edmund Drake-Brockman

> I now refer to the unsatisfactory position in which the Court stands in regard to this adjunct to the basic wage. ... On 18th December, 1925, Powers J, in speaking of 'the work and history of the Court ... and the value of the work of the Court to the community', said, 'We have where practicable granted new and better conditions, and permanently increased the basic wage by 3s a week, which 3s I first allowed as a temporary measure to secure the basic wage during the term of the award.' I cannot find where the Full Court did by any direction or order *permanently* increase the basic wage, or where, even if it had purported to do so, the Court obtained power to make any such permanent order. ... If it be justifiable because the basic wage is insufficient in amount on the standard of 1907, or insufficient on an improved or a newly approved standard of to-day, or is deficient in any other respect, the sooner the Court says so the better; but I have an objection to allowing such an addition, even if it has been the practice in the past, where at present no assignable reason or justification other than the evidence of such practice can be given for so doing. ... [Mr Benham] points out that the rising prices caused the basic wage prevailing to be below the *Harvester* equivalent at most periods between 1914 and 1921, and that the 3s addition, unaccompanied by rising prices, has caused the *Harvester* equivalent to be exceeded since 1921. ... [H]as not the compensation paid since 1921 up to the present time been more than ample compensation for past losses previous to that year, and has not the time arrived when the two reasons that existed in the past having ceased, partly or wholly, to operate, the imposition as a consequence should also, partly or wholly, cease to operate? (27 CAR 577, 598–599)

In January 1930, Dethridge published a decision about wages and conditions in the dried fruits and canned fruits industries (*Dried Fruit* case 28 CAR 597). Convinced that these industries were in dire economic condition, he discussed their continuing obligation to pay the Court's basic wage. By this time, the issue was complicated by section 25D of the Act (see Chapter 5, Section 5.1). This directed the Court to take into account the probable economic effects of its awards. That consideration, however, must not 'affect the practice of the Court in fixing the basic wage'. Members of the Court found some ambiguity in the word 'practice'—specifically, whether Powers' 3s was part of it. Lukin, in the *Timber Workers'* case, held that it was. Dethridge disagreed:

> But with all respect to him, I think that this view does not give sufficient attention to the real purpose of section 25D, which is that the Court should consider the economic effect of an award. Mere details of the Court's practice used in fixing the basic wage, some of which details vary or are not used according to the circumstances of a particular case, have little bearing upon the consideration of the economic effect of an award. What does have a weighty influence is the principle upon which the basic wage is fixed. And I think therefore the word 'practice' in the proviso must be read as meaning the *guiding* principle always adopted by the Court in fixing that wage. That principle is that for an ordinary adult male, the basic wage should never be less than the true equivalent for the time being of the *Harvester* basic wage. … The section does not in my opinion prevent me from omitting the Powers' 3s, but it *does* require me to award a basic wage not less in *real* value than the *Harvester* wage *whether the industry be depressed or not.* (p. 604)

Dethridge did not explicitly refer to the 1923 Rules of Practice, but said: 'Only in a very exceptional case would a single Judge be justified in departing from the Court's ordinary practice without the Full Court's approval, but in my opinion this is an instance.' He decided that 6d, rather than 3s, was sufficient to protect the basic-wage earner against any lag in the adjustment of the wage for higher prices.

In 1925, Powers saw the 3s as an increase in the basic wage, taking it above *Harvester*. Lukin, and probably Dethridge and Drake-Brockman, saw it as an anomaly. What is conspicuously lacking from the discussion is any reflection upon the fact that, without it, the basic wage would still have been set at a standard judged appropriate as long ago as 1907.

7.1.3 The price index

Chapter 5 (Subsection 6.1.4) noted the differences in the basic wage that would have flowed from the use of the 'All Items' price index rather than the index for food, groceries and rent. Employers were slow to raise this issue. It was raised, however, in a *Municipal Officers'* case decided by Quick in October 1926 (24 CAR 409). Existing rates had been set in an agreement that had operated since 1921. The basic wage corresponded to the cost of living in September 1921: there had been no adjustments and no Powers' 3s. Sutcliffe gave evidence that the *Harvester* equivalent plus 3s was £4 12s, compared with the amount of £4 1s 6d set in the 1921 agreement. Quick commented:

> Mr Derham, one of the representatives of the municipalities, availed himself of the opportunity of putting some questions to Mr Sutcliffe as to the method adopted by the statistical office in determining these cost of living figures. In reply, Mr Sutcliffe said that the practice had been to take certain commodities, such as food, groceries, and house rent, which are the component parts or necessary elements or factors in the cost of living. These amounted only to 60 per cent of the total necessaries of life. Yet they are taken as the guiding factors in determining the cost of all, including the remaining 40 per cent. Mr Derham suggested the view that it was not correct that any statistical authority should take certain items equalling 60 per cent of the total and adjust the whole of the wage on those items. From admissions made by Mr Sutcliffe, in reply to Mr Derham, I gather—(1) that by comparing the year 1920 with 1925 on the basis of taking into consideration only 60 per cent of commodities, the cost of living has decreased by 5 per cent; and (2) that by comparing the same years and taking as a test the Basic Wage Commission's findings, which cover all commodities, the reduction in the cost of living would be about 16 per cent. (pp. 411–412)

From further comments by Quick, Sutcliffe seems to have argued that the index numbers based on the Royal Commission's regimen were more suited to higher-paid workers than to basic-wage earners. This led, with union agreement, to a tapering of wage increases for workers receiving more than £500 per year.

The issue of measurement was also noticed by Lukin in his 1929 decision in the *Timber Workers'* case (27 CAR 577). Referring to the *Labour Report*, he drew attention to the differences between the two indices, and added:

> I do not suggest, and I am not here expressing any opinion, that the standard prescribed in the *Harvester* equivalent as originally determined, or as ascertained from time to time by the Court's index figures, is excessive, sufficient, or insufficient, but I am calling attention to the peculiar results that follow from the application of these two different methods of adjustment. These marked differences, however, accentuate the necessity for a speedy and thorough inquiry into and a fresh determination of a suitable standard, of its corresponding monetary figures, and of a more accurate system of adjusting such figures in accord with the varying change in the purchasing power of the sovereign. (p. 597)

7.1.4 Local rates

The conflicting goals in the selection of a local rate, discussed at some length in Chapter 6, were illustrated in a 1928 decision of Lukin for the gelatine industry (*Gelatine Industry* case 27 CAR 156). Under the existing award, there was a uniform basic wage corresponding to the six-capitals price index. The union complained that its members working at Botany received '4s less than is sufficient, according to the *Harvester* standard, to keep an employee his wife and the three children with which he is credited properly alive'. Their employer, the Davis Gelatine Company, 'pointed out that it has only one competitor in Australia, that is in Victoria, and that if the flat rate is departed from it would be on the then existing figures 4s 6d worse off per employee in competition with its rival'. Lukin found 'some justice in the union's claim that the Sydney employees should be paid not less than the basic wage' (p. 157). He continued:

> I do not need to repeat the principle of the Court as to that wage. I would be setting aside that principle if I should award a flat rate, and although the Court has apparently frequently done so, I do not believe that I would be justified in doing so consistently with the underlying principle of the basic wage. … It is unfortunate that the Sydney employer will in this respect be at a disadvantage when compared with the Melbourne employer. It is perhaps a disadvantage of his particular State citizenship, but it is shared by all employers in that State. I have, therefore, fixed the basic wage for Sydney and Melbourne on the Commonwealth Statistician's figures for those cities. (p. 158)

7.1.5 Summary of federal policy and practice

Reviewing the Court's record in basic-wage setting between 1922 and the onset of the Depression leads to the following conclusions:

- The two-tier system of award wages (with the basic wage as the foundation wage) was treated as a given, and not discussed.
- There was no reconsideration of the *Harvester* standard, despite the long period that had elapsed since it was fixed.
- In practice, the real federal basic wage was around 10 per cent above *Harvester*, because of Powers' 3s (hardly required to avert any erosion of the real wage by inflation) and the use of a price index that exaggerated the rise in the prices paid by households.
- An economic constraint on basic-wage setting, evident in the Court's rejection of the Piddington basic wage, was also apparent in the special treatment accorded to some industries and localities, such as Bendigo mining and dried-fruit production.
- Inconsistencies in the treatment of geographically specific living costs made for significant differences in the living standard that basic wages would support.

7.1.6 State basic wages

Chapter 6 summarised the development of State basic wages in the period 1920–26.

In New South Wales, the three years from 1926 to 1929 saw much turmoil in the setting of the living wage (and in the State arbitration system more generally), associated with the personnel of the tribunal, changes of government, and the introduction of child endowment. A new Industrial Commission supplanted the former Board of Trade in 1926. It comprised representatives of employees and unions presided over by an Industrial Commissioner. The Commissioner appointed by the State Labor Government was A B Piddington. The Act directed the Commission, when setting the living wage, to proceed by two stages: first to determine a standard of living and second to declare the living wages based upon that standard for adult male and adult female employees in the State. In its decision of December 1926, the Commission adopted the Royal Commission's finding as the basis for fixing a standard for a family of five. The required amount, set by Piddington in the absence of agreement between the parties, was £5 6s. Rather than prescribe this amount, however, Piddington set a living wage of £4 4s, treating this as appropriate to a family of three—man, wife, and one child—and coupling with it a recommendation to the Parliament that child endowment be paid for children in excess of one.

The Government responded to Piddington's recommendation by securing legislation which directed the Commission to fix a living wage for a man, a wife and no children and provided for payment of child endowment at the rate of 5s per child.[3] Employers had to pay a tax of 5s per employee. The Commission then had to consider a reduction of the living wage, because the assumption of one child no longer applied. Piddington identified the reduction as 11s, but held that 'the term "living wage" implies current human standards' and that the existing wage was at a level such as a man and a wife

---

[3] Subject to a condition which meant, in effect, that endowment was reduced by any excess of the wage received over the living wage.

could expect to enjoy. Hence, in June 1927, he refused to reduce the wage and raised it to £4 5s because of a small increase in the cost of living.

A Royal Commission appointed by the New South Wales Government found that the Industrial Commission, in making this decision, had exceeded its powers. After a change of government, the Commission was reconstituted in 1928 so as to comprise three judges, including Piddington. The majority, in October 1929, overruled Piddington. Concurring in the Royal Commission's finding, it determined that the living wage should be £3 12s 6d; but it deferred action so that the Parliament could consider the position. The Act was amended to require that the wage be set for a family of man, wife, and one child, with child endowment being payable only for the second and subsequent children. The Commission then fixed a living wage of £4 2s 6d.[4]

In Queensland and South Australia, the basic or living wage was unaltered during this period. There were small variations in the annual reviews in Western Australia. The relation of State to Commonwealth basic wages is shown in Figure 1.6 of Chapter 1.

7.2 THE WAGE STRUCTURE

7.2.1 The skill differential

We have seen that the Court's failure to adjust margins so as to preserve either their real value or their relativity to the basic wage, and Higgins' abortive attempts to restore the relative position of skilled workers, caused some turmoil in the early 1920s. Unions continued to make demands on the skilled workers' behalf.

The principal discussion of the issue in the later 1920s is to be found in two decisions of Dethridge, given in December 1928. These were linked decisions for marine engineers and deck officers (27 CAR 446 and 482). Dethridge reported that his colleagues concurred in his view that 'the Court

---

[4] The above summary of living-wage setting in New South Wales is based largely on Sawkins (1933), pp. 40–42. A much more detailed account is provided by Graham (1995), chapters 8 and 9.

when assessing marginal wages must pay regard to the then existing conditions and not accept previously awarded margins as in any way binding precedents' (p. 448). Higgins had been dealing with marine officers in 1916, when he promised a restoration of pre-war relativities after normal times had returned. Dethridge said that 'an expectation was expressed by Mr Justice Higgins that at some indefinite time in the future the real pre-war ratio of the marginal wage to the basic wage would be restored by the Court, on the assumption apparently that the ratio should be invariable in normal times'. 'Mr Justice Higgins', he added, 'occasionally seemed to act on this assumption, but he by no means applied it to its full extent' (p. 486). He continued:

> In my opinion Powers, J, enunciated the correct principle, that is to say, that the Court when making an award as to marginal wages should assess the amounts thereof only according to the conditions existing at the time of the award. ... The value at the time of the special skill or qualifications for which the marginal wage is to be paid must be ascertained, although to do so may, in some cases, involve the consideration of very difficult problems. In most cases probably the recent practice in the industry will afford a sufficient guide even though the amounts paid in accordance with that practice were originally fixed by awards of this Court when the purchasing power of money was greater. The margins so fixed were only minimum amounts, and if the industrial value of the special skill or qualification had become greater than the award amounts the demand for that skill and qualification would have tended to increase its market value, and that increase would have tended to show itself in practice notwithstanding the influence of any contrary tendency to make the minimum rate the maximum. The mere fact, therefore, that in many cases the present margin is no greater in money than the pre-war margin does not necessarily show that that present margin does not represent the present full industrial value of skill or other qualification for which it is paid. Since these margins were first prescribed the conditions of industry have materially changed and the position of the skilled worker has improved in other directions, although the relative advantage in wages that he formerly enjoyed over the unskilled worker may have

> diminished; it is not improbable that those other changes have tended to lessen that advantage. (pp. 493–494)

This reasoning implied that *prima facie* the margins currently being received by skilled workers fully reflected the value of their work. If not, the market would 'take over' and provide a signal that the award margin was too low. This invites the question why the Court should be involved in fixing skilled rates at all, rather than leaving them to the market. (Of course, it had no choice, given that union claims included wages for the various grades of labour.)

Dethridge did not leave the matter where it stood in the above passage. The Court, he said, should only set minimum rates, leaving scope for bargaining about additional payments. 'How then', he asked, 'is the present minimum marginal value of skilled employees to be discovered?' He dealt with this question at some length. The market offered a partial answer:

> In a freely competitive industrial world the relative values of the various services required in industry—unskilled labour, skilled labour, management, invention, enterprise, and capital—would evidence themselves in the actual price or reward given for them as the result of the interplay of supply and demand. The relative industrial and comparative market values of the different classes of services would fluctuate with changing social or mental or material habits of life, and therefore the wages or other pay for various kinds of skill or qualification would not retain a constant proportion either to each other or to the wages or pay of unskilled labour. Unforeseeable variation would occur in the intra-varying complex of human wants and responses which actuate industry as a whole, and the highly valued skill of one period might not be sought at all in the next period. To a large extent these competitive forces do operate in real life, and their effect cannot be ignored by this Court. (p. 495)

But, said Dethridge, a completely free competitive system had never existed, and probably never would, however desirable or undesirable that ideal might be. Moreover, public opinion did not support some of the outcomes of a free market, and limitations were imposed to prevent sweating and like evils. This was done either by tribunals or by the use of collective instead of individual bargaining. Under collective bargaining,

> each group seeks to gain for its members as much as it can get from the total product of industry, employees at times doing so, unknowingly, at the expense of employees in other groups. Sometimes, indeed, groups, believing that the product of industry is greater than it is, struggle for that which is not—like blind children scrambling for imaginary pennies. In this *melee* of conflicting aims particular classes of workers may fail to gain an equitable return for their services, but it is more likely than in the case of individual competition that the wages they actually receive are just, and therefore such wages paid in countries not widely dissimilar from Australia do furnish finger posts of a sort for guidance; as will be seen, however, such of these finger posts as are available point in rather different directions. (pp. 495–496)

The outcomes of collective bargaining were not decisive, for

> the Court may be driven to the conclusion that the rates of pay thereby shown do not sufficiently reward the special skill concerned, having regard to the amount of training, education and mental or physical capacity required, the discomfort or deprivation attendant upon the work to be done, and the proportion such rates bear to those of other workmen employed in Australia, particularly in or about the same industry as that in which the special skill or qualification is required. ... It is clearly in the interests of the community that men exercising skill and responsibility in an industry such as the shipping industry should receive pay so far above that of the unskilled worker as to provide a sufficient incentive to men to qualify themselves for the work, to enable them to maintain themselves and their families in a manner consonant with their standing, and to preserve such a distinction and separation from subordinates as experience seems to show to be still necessary for the purpose of maintaining requisite authority and discipline. In other countries a much more marked difference appears between the remuneration of those in authority and that of subordinates than seems

> to be practicable, or probably desirable, in Australia, but a substantial difference is undoubtedly necessary. (pp. 496–497)

But qualifying the Court's discretion was the need to have regard to the financial state of the industry concerned:

> If the industry is waning its skilled employees may be forced to choose between a low wage and unemployment, and this Court cannot remedy that position. In a prosperous industry, however, although, of course, the Court cannot go beyond the limit imposed by economic conditions, it may, in cases where it has come to the conclusion that the minimum rates being given for skill or responsibility are inadequate, and that it can safely increase those rates without causing unemployment, reasonably make an increase. Industry and the community in general benefit by the development and exercise of superior skill and capacity, and the Court may therefore properly encourage that superior skill and capacity by providing the necessary incentive in wages corresponding to the superiority where it seems fairly clear that the increase will not ultimately cause unemployment—a much greater evil than the continuance of a rather lower rate of pay. (p. 496)

What Dethridge articulated was a confused set of principles, with elements of self-contradiction. The freely competitive market would have yielded a set of relativities, which should be taken into account. The operation of the free market, however, had some unacceptable outcomes. These had led to the intrusion of collective bargaining and tribunals. For reasons not explained, the existing (money) valuations of work, which reflected the effects of these processes, should command respect. But the Court might overrule them because of the desirability of preserving and increasing the supply of skill and maintaining the status of the skilled worker. All of these considerations, however, must yield to the state of the industry and the risk that higher pay might cause unemployment. Clear signals as to the Court's likely approach to setting margins are difficult to derive from such guideposts. Nevertheless, there is sufficient in them to rationalise the Court's reluctance to raise the money value of skilled margins.

Dethridge, like Powers in 1924, suggested a further reason for the relative decline of rewards for skill: that increases in the wages of the unskilled and semi-skilled had eroded the capacity of industry to reward the skilled worker:

> It may be that since 1910 some of that part of the national income which was formerly received by the more highly skilled and responsible wage or salary earners, as a reward for their special qualifications, has been transferred to the unskilled or low skilled wage-earners by reason of industrial awards or determinations or other pressures. Both in Great Britain and Australia the higher-paid officials certainly, and the other middle classes almost certainly, do not enjoy incomes of nearly pre-war purchasing values, and have thus suffered a change which may be regrettable for national reasons. But I am more concerned at present with the possibility that in Australia there has been since 1910, partly by reason of direct or indirect state regulation of industrial conditions, such a redistribution of the national income as will tend to make it difficult for this Court to award what it may consider an adequate wage for higher classes of capacity. (pp. 499–500)

We have here an implicit criticism of the tribunals, and perhaps the unions, for having raised unduly the pay of the low-skilled.

What *was* the explanation of the compression of the skill relativity? Approached from a purely arithmetic perspective, the answer to this question is straightforward. The tribunals raised the money value of the basic wage, but refused to raise the margins of the skilled commensurately. This policy originated during World War I, when it could be seen as a response to abnormal conditions. Failure to restore relativities after the war was the result of (1) the downward rigidity of the real basic wage and (2) reluctance to increase the nominal values of skill margins. It was because the basic wage and margins had separate lives that they could follow different paths. The stickiness of nominal margins seems to be the result of two things: the perception—clearly articulated during the war—that the special needs of the skilled were less fundamental than the basic needs of the unskilled; and the Court's reluctance to impose added burdens on employers in the economic conditions of the 1920s.

Though this is a broadly accurate account of wage-setting policy, the question remains whether there were underlying industrial, economic, or social forces which supported the directions of policy. Both Powers and Dethridge referred to the decline in the relative reward for skill in other countries. This suggests that there may be a risk of focusing unduly on the *mechanisms* whereby the process occurred. From an institutional perspective, trade unionism was becoming less of a craft phenomenon and more embracing of unskilled and semi-skilled workers. From a social viewpoint, the prevailing concerns about the conditions of life of the low-paid and their families entailed some priority for the amelioration of their condition. For economists, there were both demand and supply factors that could have tended towards narrower differentials. From the demand side, the spread of machinery could well have caused a reduction in the demand for higher-level manual skills. On the supply side, the extension of basic education is likely to have expanded the proportion of the workforce able to undertake more demanding work. Exploring these historical developments and their interactions is beyond the scope of this study; but it is necessary to remind ourselves of the context in which wage policies were formed and continued.

7.2.2 Fixing specific margins

The Court continued to face the challenge of identifying principles applicable to margins in specific industries and occupations. Possibly because many awards were now reasonably settled, the demands of this work seem to have been less than in earlier years. Examples of some of the issues that arose, and the Court's responses, are provided below.

Tramways

Beeby, in 1927, fixed margins for traffic workers on tramways (*Tramways* case 25 CAR 597). This decision is an example of the Court's moving from a description of the work, and the attributes required of the workers, to a prescription of money amounts, without an explained link between the two.

Past State prescriptions had been influenced by local practice and agreements. Beeby had 'therefore re-investigated the whole question of what should be the minimum wage of tramway employees, except craft workmen and labourers incidentally attached to the services whose wages must necessarily conform to those fixed for similar work in awards of general application' (p. 603). He turned to the work itself:

> The men engaged in traffic operations are a selected body. They must be of average intelligence, able to pass rudimentary education tests. They must be physically sound and able to pass medical and eye-sight tests. They must also be men of the right temperament, of courteous demeanour, and patient in learning. Their occupation, whilst not arduous in the ordinary physical sense, is harassing during portions of each day. … Their hours of work are necessarily irregular. … A considerable portion of their day's work is done in crowded city streets in which care, alertness, and promptness of action are always necessary. They must adapt themselves to the vagaries of the public and are responsible for large sums of money passing through their hands. … The main difficulty in fixing a wage scale arose from the employees asking for a high rate of wage because of the comparative disadvantage of their employment, and at the same time seeking for the removal of those disadvantages. The scale of wages now awarded was arrived at after careful consideration of the disabilities of the service and would have been lower if those disabilities had not been unavoidable. (pp. 604–605)

Railway conductors

In a decision about train conductors, given in 1927, Quick confronted the fact that conductors in New South Wales received smaller margins than their Victorian counterparts (*Railways'* case 25 CAR 152). The decision is of interest principally for the argument advanced by the representative of the New South Wales employer, and Quick's response:

> The question, he said, as to whether a wage is sufficient for a particular occupation should, as a general rule, be regulated in a natural way by the law of supply and demand. If a wage attached to any particular position is not regarded as sufficient, men will naturally seek other avenues of employment.
>
> The reply to that is that the Commonwealth Arbitration Court does not determine rates of pay according to any law of supply and demand. The only test is what is a fair and reasonable rate of pay for the value of services rendered. It has already been determined by this Court in connexion with the Victorian branch of this railway dispute that first class train conductors are entitled to margins of 1s 6d and 2s per day. … The duties of these men being identical in the two States, I am of opinion that, as a matter of justice and equity, the rates of pay should be the same in the two services. (p. 163)

This is one of very few instances of the Court's explicitly asserting that criteria *other than* supply and demand should determine wage relativities. The importance of supply and demand was, of course, implicit in numerous other decisions, notably those that stressed the necessity of restraining wages in the interest of preserving or increasing employment.

The Sydney Harbour Bridge

The New South Wales Government's contract with Dorman Long and Coy Limited allowed the constructor to 'pass on' to the Government extra costs caused by award wage increases. Dethridge, in 1928, dealt with a case wherein the union sought various increases to which Dorman Long consented. There had recently been a change of government, however, and the new government was represented to object to the increases. 'Under the circumstances', said Dethridge,

> I thought it desirable to hear evidence for myself as to whether the increases asked for are justified by the special nature of the work, and Dr Bradfield accordingly gave evidence upon that matter. He supports the unions' claims, saying, in effect, that the work in question is so extraordinary as to justify the increased wages asked for. No evidence to the contrary was tendered by the Government or the contractor, and I have come to the conclusion that the applications should be granted. (*AEU* case 26 CAR 353, 355)

The increases granted ranged up to 11½d per hour for work on the main arch of the bridge. They were insufficient, however, to avoid disputation and strikes, notwithstanding that they gave effect to the understanding between the union and the contractor.

The matter was again before Beeby early in 1929, when the union claimed that the men had not been in a position earlier to appreciate the difficulties and hazards of the task. Beeby chose to disregard the agreement and to determine the application for variation. By what standards should he evaluate the work? 'It is difficult', he said, 'to find any principle on which the Court can act in assessing the value of labour in circumstances such as those surrounding these applications. It is admitted that the workmen are engaged in one of the world's most difficult and hazardous engineering undertakings, and should receive wages substantially above those relating to normal work' (27 CAR 1065, 1067). Workers on similar projects in the United States and Canada received more than the Sydney workers, but those workers were in a very strong economic position:

> They can often drive a bargain in which the value of the labour to the community plays a much smaller part than the scarcity of competent workmen. In such circumstances wages are regulated solely by supply and demand. But in Australia, with its machinery for the compulsory fixing of minima, there is no way of testing what wages a particular group can command in the open market. If the work in question were left to the traditional play of economic forces, the unions might be able

to enforce their demands. But this is only conjectural, and in any event cannot be accepted as a method of assessing the fair value of labour. The Court's function is to check unfair claims by economic strength of both employers and employees. (p. 1068)

This passage is of interest for (1) the implication that the value of labour to the community is something other than its market price, (2) equation of 'supply and demand' with collective bargaining, and (3) the assertion of the Court's role in countering unfair claims reflective of the economic strength of the parties. Despite his comments on the causes of the high wages paid to comparable workers in the United States and Canada, Beeby concluded that 'the only principle on which the Court can act in all the circumstances of this case is to approximate the wages of the Sydney workmen to those paid in other countries for similar work'; and since the only information about rates elsewhere was for the United States and Canada, he 'as closely as possible awarded to the Sydney men the same effective wages which they could earn in those countries for similar work' (p. 1069). Beeby increased by 6 per cent the rates (set by Dethridge) for the first seven panels on either side of the arch and by 75 per cent the rates for the centre.

This did not end the matter. Work stopped again, because the main decision was said to maintain too wide a margin between the skilled and the less-skilled workers. The stoppage was unwarranted, said Beeby, because the Court would always correct 'proven errors'. But further adjustment was necessary:

> The extra rates having been fixed as compensation for the unusual difficulties and dangers of the work, the unskilled man should here, as in Canada and the US, more nearly approach in earnings the skilled tradesman. The percentage margins between skilled and unskilled men should, I think, be generally maintained, and their disturbance to meet the special circumstances under review must not be accepted as a precedent. (p. 1071)

Beeby increased the rates for riggers and helpers by about 4d per hour. Perhaps the chief interest of the Harbour Bridge decisions was the difficulty of maintaining a set wages policy when labour held the 'whip hand'—a rare situation in the 1920s.

Timber

The reverse situation existed, by the late 1920s, in the timber industry. This, too, experienced great industrial unrest, as a result of labour's attempts to resist the reduction of wages and the erosion of conditions.

Lukin—conspicuously the Judge least sympathetic to labour—conducted between February 1927 and August 1928 the proceedings leading to a new award, and gave his decision in January 1929 (*Timber Workers'* case 27 CAR 577). (I have discussed above his comments on the basic wage, especially his evident hostility to Powers' 3s. I also discuss below the Full Court's restoration of the 48-hour week in the timber industry.) Dealing specifically with margins, Lukin observed that previous awards, by Higgins (largely as a result of agreement) and Webb, had been made at times of greater prosperity in the industry than those now existing. He also noted, on the basis of evidence from the *Monthly Labor Review*, that while in the United States and Canada the proportion of men on the labourer's wage varied between 50 to 60 per cent of the total employed, in the Australian States subject to the Webb award (which excluded Queensland) the proportion varied between 10 and 15 per cent. 'Now', he asked, 'on what basis should I proceed?'

> Am I to assume, contrary to the fact, that the state of the timber industry is what the employers, the employees, the community, and myself would wish it to be? Am I to treat it, contrary to the fact, as if it were in the abnormally prosperous condition in which Higgins J found it, or as in the normal condition it was in when Webb DP made his award, or am I to treat it in accordance with the facts of to-day? The answer, on what it is to-day, is obvious, at the same time paying due regard to the history and lessons of the past, and to a reasonable hope and expectation of a brighter future. That, of course, means that I cannot, except in some particular case for some special circumstances,

increase the margins given by the last award and that, in some cases, I must reduce them. (p. 616)

Lukin's inspections led him to the conclusion 'that much of the work which is classed as skilled in this industry is labourer's work, or little better' (p. 618). Timber workers had been 'exceptionally well treated in the past' (p. 619). He asserted:

> A consideration of the wages paid and of the financial documents of the companies in past years leads me to the conclusion that the community has had to pay for the products of this industry a price which, while making allowances for other variations, is greater than it ought to have paid. In other words, it has been paying for the skill of a worker when that worker has not got such skill, or who, if he has, does not have to use it, that is for skill which is non-existent in the product, and for the antiquated methods and lack of organisation of a great number of employers. (p. 621)

It was possible, especially in larger establishments, said Lukin, for a few men to ensure the efficient functioning of the machines, 'while the duty of the men on the machines is merely to feed or operate them'. This was the trend of modern production, and 'unless such methods are adopted in this country its industries will not be able to compete with those overseas, and must lean all the more heavily on a constantly and ever-increasing tariff' (p. 621). He therefore provided in the award for 'machinists who are merely operators or feeders', with a margin of 3s per week, 'not for skill, but because it appears to me that, as things are at present and will be under this award, the industry can pay such margins'. This would entail a reduction in pay for many, but if piecework were adopted, there would be the opportunity to offset the loss (p. 623). Whereas the union had proposed a two-level scheme of classification, with some workers receiving a 30s margin and others 24s, and employers were generally content with the margins previously set by Webb, Lukin awarded margins for machinists ranging in seven steps from 3s to 21s. The evidence on which he acted included the confidential report of an independent expert whom he had appointed (p. 625).

White-collar work in railways

In 1928, Quick retained, with modifications, incremental scales for Victorian railway clerks previously set by the Railways' Classification Board (26 CAR 639). In this decision, he also dealt with the salaries of train-control officers, who (aided by developments in communication) played an increasingly important role in the efficient running of the system. The chief train dispatcher received a salary of £636 (a margin of £410). The Railways Commissioners had recently proposed to increase this officer's rate, but this required the approval of the State Government, which had rejected a part of the increase. The Court in 1927 had made an award giving effect to the full increase (p. 688). Quick, in 1929, dealt with the salaries of railway professional officers (*Railway Professional Officers'* case 28 CAR 173). 'In my opinion', he said, 'the most important and far-reaching question in this industrial dispute is what shall be the commencing salary of the lowest engineering grade in each State, because that will necessarily determine the relative margins in the higher grades' (p. 220). Having regard to the evidence of financial problems in the railways, Quick refused the Association's claim for increases. In this case, as in others, the Court accepted career structures previously negotiated or determined by other authorities.

Actors

Dethridge, in 1929, made a new award for actors (*Actors'* case 27 CAR 1008). The Federation had called on him to set rates that reflected the artistic content of acting. This he rejected, saying that the Court 'would be fatuous if it attempted to determine the minimum rate to be paid for artistic merit' (p. 1009). The Court had to deal with the minimum requirements of the job:

> Many of the employees now in question have little or no artistic merit, but they all require [sic] to possess some qualifications, either of education, training, or bodily capacity or appearance, not necessary for an unskilled labourer. For those engaged in ballet, for instance, just as for most artisans, some natural capacity and training of the body

is indispensable; in neither case is any higher natural qualification requisite for the ordinary performance of their work by the rank and file. Those who possess such higher qualifications must be left to bargain for themselves with the employers, if any, requiring them. The Court can only deal with employees in classes capable of being defined by ordinary qualities or attainments, and further, when dealing with a marginal wage for any such class, can only attempt to determine the *minimum* wage proper for *every* employee qualified to be in that class, although that wage may be inadequate for the more efficient employees in that class. (pp. 1009–1010)

It was of the nature of award rates of pay that they did not differentiate between the levels of skill of individual employees within the designated classifications. Employers might, if they chose, pay extra to employees whom they perceived as having higher value to them; and a worker with special skill could seek to bargain in his or her own right. The cases of the actors and the musicians may have exposed these realities more conspicuously than the occupations more commonly before the Court. The Court's reluctance to enter into issues of artistic merit is understandable and defensible. The problem that remained, however, was to identify the characteristics of the 'ordinary' actor or musician for which the award should allow. Although the Court was obliged to set minimum pay rates for actors and musicians, the processes by which it arrived at the prescribed amounts are not at all obvious.

7.3 Working hours[5]

The major area of conflict within the framework of federal arbitration in the 1920s was standard hours. As we saw in Chapter 6, Higgins after World War I took initial steps toward the granting of a 44-hour week. This had led to federal legislation removing the capacity of a single member of the Court to reduce hours below 48. The Full Court's decision of February 1927 (24 CAR 755), in the *Main Hours* case, concluded the first of the general economic inquiries that were to become a feature of the proceedings of the Court and

---

[5] See also Nyland (1987).

its successor Commissions. Over the next three years, the contest between the 48-hour and 44-hour weeks occupied much of the Court's time.

7.3.1 The jurisdiction issue

We saw in Chapter 6 (Section 6.3) that New South Wales legislation providing for a 44-hour week in the State and the High Court decision in *Cowburn's* case—to the effect that federal award provisions for 48 hours prevailed over the State law—caused Powers to fear a shift between jurisdictions. This did not happen to any marked degree. The New South Wales legislation was important, however, in generating tension within the federal jurisdiction. Unions and their members, understandably, saw the 48-hour standard as ungenerous. A number of unions did apply to terminate their federal awards in relation to New South Wales, and in October 1926 Dethridge referred one of these applications to the Full Court. In a decision with which Lukin and Beeby agreed, Dethridge said:

> In essence, the position is that unions claim that if at any time they think that better conditions of labour can be secured from a State tribunal in respect of one State they can, by application to this Court, obtain a variation exempting that State from the award of this Court. Under varying circumstances the President and Deputy Presidents of this Court have in the past granted similar applications, while others have been refused. One such application was granted by Judge Beeby since the constitution of this Court. It is now thought necessary that a general rule should be enunciated as to such applications. We do not decide how far this Court has power ... to determine an award in whole or in part. Whatever the extent of that power, it is clearly discretionary, and we are of opinion that no such application should be granted merely because an applicant, whether an employer or employee, anticipates being able to obtain more favourable conditions from a State tribunal. (*Locomotive Enginemens'* case 24 CAR 371, 373)

In August 1927, Dethridge made an award for the glass industry. The union had excluded Queensland from its log of claims, hoping to get a higher wage and a 44-hour week through the State tribunal. The employer, however, had served a log on the union, and this enabled Dethridge to extend the award to Queensland. As to working hours, he said, 'whatever the Full Court decides I shall take as being proper and as requiring me to disregard what the State tribunal may do in the matter' (*Glass Workers'* case 25 CAR 289, 294).

7.3.2 The *Main Hours* case[6]

The New South Wales, Queensland, and Western Australian adoption of the 44-hour standard was important background to the renewed efforts of unions to get the 44-hour week in federal awards.[7] The principal case was the *Main Hours* case, beginning immediately after inception of the reconstituted Court and heard, as the Act required, by the Full Court (Dethridge, Lukin and Beeby). The hearing lasted from August to December of 1926 and the decision was given in February 1927 (24 CAR 755). In the depth of the inquiry and the range of the evidence and the argument, it exceeded any previous case before the Court.[8] It was conducted on the basis that while the industry of immediate concern was engineering, the Court might make declarations that could subsequently be applied to other industries. The main union case was presented, not by representatives of the metal unions, but by those of the Trades and Labour Councils of Australia and the Commonwealth Council of Federated Unions.[9] Much of the burden of

---

[6] The Librarian of the Australian Industrial Relations Commission has made available to me parts of the transcript of this case. Unfortunately, the remainder of the transcript and the exhibits have not been found.

[7] In Western Australia, a Labor government had attempted to legislate for a 44-hour week, but was rebuffed by the Legislative Council. A compromise was eventually reached whereby a Court of Arbitration was brought into being. The 44-hour week was then imposed by arbitration.

[8] A 1926 amendment of the Act permitted the Attorney-General to intervene in the public interest 'in any proceeding before the Court in which the question of the standard hours of work in any industry or the basic wage is in dispute'. Upon any such intervention, the Court might permit anybody 'interested in the determination of the question ... to be heard and to examine and cross-examine witnesses' (Cameron 1953–55, p. 206). The Attorney-General intervened. In doing so, he made it clear that his intention was not to put a substantive position to the Court, but to activate the procedure for allowing other interventions.

[9] In the course of his submission for the unions, Charlie Crofts said that before the reconstitution of the Court, unions had been making desperate attempts to get the hours

making the case for the hours reduction was borne, however, by A W Foster, counsel for the New South Wales Government.

Though there was some variation, the usual practice under the 48-hour week was for a half-holiday to be taken on Saturday. Hence, the working days between Monday and Friday exceeded eight hours. One of the pleas of the unions was for workers to enjoy a 'clean' eight-hour day without forgoing the half-holiday on Saturdays (though in his closing address Crofts said that the unions would accommodate any employer preference for working the 44 hours over five days).

Of the many issues traversed in the hearing, some of the more interesting entailed rudimentary national income analysis. J T Sutcliffe, who had recently written *The National Dividend* (1926), gave evidence about his methods and findings (and about various other matters).[10] Among the vigorously debated questions arising from his evidence were:

- whether (as Sutcliffe contended) services, or only tangible items, should be counted in the national income. The employers' counsel produced a memorandum from the former Commonwealth Statistician, Sir George Knibbs, opposing the counting of services, while Foster cited a document written by the current Statistician, C H Wickens, which supported Sutcliffe's position;
- what was the appropriate price index for deflating the nominal values?

---

question settled. They deferred their applications on the assurance of the Government that the standard-hours matter would be the first business of the reconstituted Court (transcript, p. 242).

[10] Sutcliffe was employed from 1911 to 1924 in the Commonwealth Statistician's Office and was Head of the Labour and Industry Branch; Secretary to the Royal Commission on the Basic Wage 1919–20; from 1924 to 1927 Head of the Labour and Industrial Department in Queensland; and Chairman of the Economic Commission on the Queensland Basic Wage 1924–25. Sutcliffe moved to the private sector in 1927 as General Manager of Amalgamated Textile Pty Ltd.

The outcome of the case was a 'split' decision. Beeby favoured a wide application of the 44-hour week. Lukin would have refused any reduction below 48 hours. Dethridge's position became the decision of the Court, because each of the other Judges would support him against the third. Dethridge explained that

> what I have said in my judgment indicates the probable course of the Court in future applications; that is to say, that in industries which are similar in their conditions as to leisure, or want of leisure, to the engineering industry the Court will probably apply a similar reduction as in the case of the engineering industry, but not in other industries, or not to the extent that my brother Beeby has indicated. … The majority of the members of the Court approve of the reduction of the standard hours of work in the engineering industry to 44 per week as from the coming into operation of the award to be made herein. (p. 904)

To Dethridge, the issue was in part one of equity. Workers on a 48-hour week might not be at a disadvantage relative to the many who worked fewer hours. The relevant comparison was not simply one of hours:

> The railway porter, for instance, at the end of eight and three-quarter hours work, is in a position to obtain just as much real enjoyment or leisure as the machine worker in an engineering shop would get after finishing an eight-hour day of strain and toil. … Machine and factory workers, who have to work within four walls, frequently in the midst of nerve-racking noise, with a monotonous continuation of the same motion, and an unbroken concentration of attention upon uninteresting toil, have a higher claim to consideration than most others, and may have some reason to feel that they are not enjoying equality of treatment, seeing that workers in other occupations have already obtained the 44-hour week, although there was nothing in the work done to justify that priority. (p. 768)

There had been much argument and evidence about the impact of reduced hours on output. The unions contended that there would be no adverse effect, or that any such effect would be minimal, because the improvement in the workers' productivity would more than offset the reduction of working time. The employers disputed this. Dethridge was persuaded that there would be some reduction, which told against 'an all-round easeup', but weighed against this the likely adverse effect, in the long term, of resentments on the part of workers who were disadvantaged by the 48-hour week:

> But factory, workshop, and machine employees, like the members of the claimant union [the Amalgamated Engineering Union], working the 48-hour week are on the whole at a real disadvantage as compared with most other workers, and this contrast of condition, cumulative upon any contrast created by State laws or awards or administration, will certainly diminish zeal, efficiency, and productivity. A just standard of hours of labour in industry is that which places the workers in all industries on what is really, and not merely superficially, the same footing in point of leisure … Only a rough approximation to this general fair treatment can in practice be obtained. (pp. 790–791)

The criterion advocated by Dethridge became known as 'the equation of leisure'. It was not finally rejected until 1939 (see Chapter 12, Section 12.2).

To Lukin, the crucial concerns were the prospective loss of output, the absence of evidence (or even claims) of adverse health effects from working 48 hours, and his perception of the 44-hour week as a luxury that Australia could ill afford. He referred to the endorsement of the 48-hour week in the Treaty of Versailles, by the first International Labour Conference and by Seebohm Rowntree in *The Human Factor in Business*.

Lukin regarded as irrelevant, arguments about the capacity of industry to offset the reduction of output by mechanisation and improved methods unless these were directly attributable to the fewer working hours:

> To say that the improvements in the future under forty-four hours will make up for the deficiency now between forty-eight and forty-four is to assume covertly that the improvement will arise only under the forty-four [hour] week and to ignore the fact that improvements have always been going on, and would continue to go on under a forty-eight hour week. … If one could definitely attribute an improvement

> as being consequent only on the reduction, and not on what would in the ordinary course of events have happened, then such improvement, if it be identifiable, and if its added value be ascertainable, could be used in conjunction with the production at the lesser hours for comparison with that of the greater. I think it almost impossible, in a very great majority of cases, to identify such an improvement or to ascertain its value. (pp. 805–806)

Moreover, said Lukin, 'it must be borne in mind that the improvement of machinery, method and organisation is not peculiar to Australia but takes place on the whole contemporaneously in most of the other parts of the world, so that any resultant increase in productivity per hour will not *ipso facto* necessarily increase Australia's ability to meet the foreign competition which it is now encountering, and from which it is now suffering' (p. 806). The notion that mechanisation and better organisation were merely a means of 'standing still' if they were matched in competitor countries—an idea previously asserted by Powers—was hostile to any concept of 'distributing' to labour a share of the benefits of rising productivity.

Lukin made much of pronouncements by the Tariff Board. The Board (chiefly in its annual reports) protested strongly and repeatedly against the endeavours of unions to extract higher wages and better conditions after the Board had conferred extra protection on industries. (These pronouncements of the Tariff Board are discussed in Chapter 13, Subsection 13.1.4.) 'So far as the unions' demands are necessary to secure the normal standard of living and necessary conditions of labour', said Lukin, 'I think, with all due deference to the Tariff Board, that the unions are within their natural rights, but where, as here, the claim is not to secure the normal standard of living or necessary conditions of labour, but to provide unnecessary extra leisure, then the unions, as applicants with the employers for the tariff assistance, are in duty bound to the community … to refrain from such further claims'.

Lukin saw the suggestion of reduced working time as out of keeping with national goals:

> If we are to retain exclusive possession of this vast continent for ourselves and our posterity, is it not essential that we should develop and progress as expeditiously as possible? In order to do this is it not necessary that every Australian citizen should continuously contribute toward this end? Must not Australia develop its industries, primary and secondary, as quickly as possible to make this great country as attractive and prosperous as possible, so as to induce our fellow-members of the British Empire and other desirable members of the white races of the world to come to our shores and settle amongst us, so that when the critical time of foreign aggression arrives we will have sufficiently developed and have attained sufficient strength to resist such aggression and be enabled to retain Australia for our race? (p. 820)

The evidence left uncertainties about the economy's productive performance, but the indications were that little or no progress had been made since before World War I. The level of the national debt was a further reason for resisting the reduction of working time. Sutcliffe's evidence showed that the debt stood at £966 million, £400 million of which was war debt. The non-war debt had been used to fund assets, some of which must now be 'discounted'.

The reduction of hours, Lukin concluded,

> means an undoubted decrease in output when a substantial increase is so absolutely necessary to this young country; a seriously increased cost directly or indirectly of such reduced output ... the weakening of our power to develop our own resources and consequent delay in doing so; the weakening of our power to resist foreign competition and its inroads and the subsequent weakening of our financial stability; the weakening of our power to recapture the balance of trade by making our exports exceed our imports and provide us with the wherewithal to meet our heavy overseas debts; the discouragement of our manufacturers to continue in some cases a hopeless struggle or to invest further capital; the discouragement of prospective manufacturers to invest and commence business in Australia under such adverse conditions when better conditions, more conducive to business success, prevail elsewhere in the world; the delay in commencing and carrying into effect further public

utilities so necessary to our advancement; the still further weakening of our primary industries, which have already been over-strained by existing conditions and which are competing and must continue to compete on prices determined by competition in world markets; the creation of further dissatisfaction in the rural worker whose hours and conditions of labour appear to be out of fair proportion with that of the city worker and whose drift, already very serious, to the city, its attractions and its better living and wage conditions will be accentuated. And all for what purpose? (pp. 864–865)

Beeby had 'form' as to working hours, having presided over the New South Wales Royal Commission which in 1920 recommended the creation of a special court of inquiry to receive applications for a 44-hour week and to make recommendations (*Labour Report* 1920, pp. 109–110). Not surprisingly, one of the union advocates made considerable use of Beeby's report. 'This Court', Beeby now said, 'is not asked to introduce some novel change in industrial relationship, but rather to finalise a resistless trend and remove from the path of industry one of the most prolific causes of unrest' (p. 873). With even more emphasis than Dethridge, he wrote of the need to reduce hours so as to counter the growing 'monotony' of mechanised production:

> The expulsion of skilled artisans from industry to make way for machine operatives increases from year to year. It can be said with certainty that the proportion of trained mechanics with manipulative skill becomes relatively less each year, and that the increasing use of machinery does tend to make work more monotonous. More time for fostering other interests and for recreation is necessary to those whose natural creative instinct is suppressed by economic necessity. (p. 875)

Beeby argued that the States in which the 44-hour week had most extensively been adopted—New South Wales, Queensland and Western Australia—had fared at least as well, in economic terms, as those where the 48-hour week more fully prevailed.

Entering into the debate about the extent of economic progress, if any, since before the war, Beeby said:

A better way of judging the increase or decline of production and of the comparative prosperity or otherwise of the Commonwealth is, in my opinion, the analysis of statistics of the five years prior to the war, and of the last five years. I do not propose to follow in detail the argument between Mr Sutcliffe and Mr Benham on this point. Mr Benham had not given consideration to the practical matters before this Court; he had not made any inquiry as to the actual effect of the shorter week on production costs in industries which had changed over from 48 to 44 hours; he had not applied his mind to historical facts, or the ethical issues involved. Taking available statistical figures, and applying index numbers, he ventured the conclusion that, although in the year 1926 Australia recovered her pre-war productivity per head of population, for some years previously production had been lower than during years immediately before the war. I am not prepared to dispute or accept this conclusion. (p. 881)

At Beeby's instigation, a table had been prepared in which the pre-war and the post-war production were expressed 'per head of persons engaged in industry, instead of per head of population'. 'Mr Benham', he said,

> attached no significance to this second table, probably because of failure to understand the purpose for which it was called. If either table is sufficiently accurate to form a reliable guide, then the second one supports the contention that our material wealth has increased sufficiently to increase the number of the leisured class who have retired from active production. It also meets the oft-repeated statement that loss in average production (if any) arises from the laxity of those actually engaged in production. (p. 883)

A further table, showing manufacturing output per hour of labour, indicated a 10 per cent increase between 1914 and 1924–25. If Benham were right in asserting that there had been a decline in productivity, the fall away could only have been due to the primary sector. Prices of primary products had been high in recent years. The decline, if any, in primary output was 'clearly attributable to causes other than increased labour cost'. Partly for these reasons, and partly because of a growth in 'the annual value of all wealth produced in the Commonwealth' during the 1920s, Beeby refused to accept 'Mr Benham's forebodings'.

He also rejected Benham's forebodings about the size of the national debt. More than half of the total public debt had been subscribed in Australia, and more than half of the interest payments related to Australian-held debt. 'This', he said,

> is mainly a recent development, and is one of the substantial signs of the accumulation in Australia of surplus wealth derived from primary and manufacturing industries. Even now, after much reflection on Mr Benham's evidence, I cannot understand his persistency when considering the comparative position of countries in refusing to see any difference between a debt which is represented by great public utilities and assets, and one against which no credit entries appear. (p. 885)

The evidence of metal trades employers did not, in Beeby's opinion, outweigh the need to remove a cause of ongoing discontent. For other industries, 'little evidence was furnished in support of prophecies of disaster if the shorter week is conceded' (p. 896). The timber industry was in difficulty, due to the growing use of steel and concrete in construction, but the greater part of that industry was already working a 44-hour week. As to primary industry, Beeby was sceptical about arguments asserting that it would be damaged by the increased costs of a 44-hour week.

> Some day, I hope, this Court will have before it reliable figures disclosing dissected wage, machinery, transport, and other costs of primary production. Until that evidence is available, and for other reasons, I am prepared to agree to exemption for the present of direct primary production from a 44-hour week declaration. But I am not prepared to admit that the indirect increase in costs is sufficient to exclude favourable consideration of the claim of wage earners in secondary and distributive occupations for a review of their hours of employment. (p. 901)

One point on which the three Judges agreed was the potential economic benefit of a more widespread application of piecework. I discuss this issue in Section 7.4.

7.3.3 The aftermath

There followed a series of cases in which the Full Court dealt with the application of the *Main Hours* decision in other areas. In May 1927, the Court (by majority) approved the 44-hour week for various metal-related industries (*Standard Hours: Boilermakers, etc.* 25 CAR 64). In June, it refused (by majority) applications by the Commissioners of Railways of the Commonwealth and of the States of Victoria, South Australia, New South Wales, and Tasmania for exemption from the 44-hour week awarded in the metal trades industries (*Standard Hours: Metal Workers (Railways)* 25 CAR 216). The State Electricity Commission of Victoria was granted an exemption, and, in August, Dethridge granted an injunction against the union and members who were refusing to work more than 44 hours for the SECV (*Standard Hours: Electrical Workers* 25 CAR 283). In October, there was another three-way division in respect of the gas industry. With Beeby wishing to grant 44 hours to more grades than did Dethridge, and Dethridge favouring 44 hours for more grades than Lukin, Dethridge's decision prevailed (*Standard Hours: Gas Employees* 25 CAR 996).[11] In November, the Full Court (Dethridge and Lukin, Beeby dissenting) refused the 44-hour week in the agricultural implement and machinery industry (*Standard Hours: Agricultural Machinery* 25 CAR 1148).[12] In December, the Court (Beeby dissenting) refused the 44-hour week in the glass industry, save for certain grades deemed to be engaged in arduous work (*Standard Hours: Glass Workers* 25 CAR 1300).

The Full Court, in December 1927, published its decision on the application for a 44-hour week for locomotive enginemen, firemen and cleaners, and drivers of electric trains (*Standard Hours: Locomotive Enginemen* 25 CAR 1252). In this case, the Court was unanimous in rejecting the claim. Part of the union's case was that the 44-hour week had already been granted to locomotive men in New South Wales, Queensland and Western Australia, and in New Zealand. Dethridge commented:

---

[11] Lukin would have reduced hours for some grades because of the arduousness of the work.
[12] In two later decisions, the Court (by majority) determined that engineers working in this industry should have a 48-hour week (26 CAR 36 and 27 CAR 367).

> The Union contends that these reductions go to show that their present claim is just, but the respondents allege that in every case they were made as the result of political action without any inquiry into the merits of the reduction. This contention of the respondents is supported by the fact that, at any rate in New South Wales, Queensland and Western Australia, the reduction was part of a general reduction extended to employees regardless of the arduousness of their work. It would not be safe to take these reductions as a guide to our action in this proceeding. (p. 1253)

Dethridge was unmoved by arguments going to the enginemen's absences from home and related disadvantages: these were aspects of the work that the employees had knowingly accepted and which had influenced their wages and other conditions. The union had 'failed to show that the conditions of work of its members are such as to justify an alteration of the standard hours of work prescribed by the current award in any of the States covered by that award' (p. 1260). Lukin agreed with Dethridge. Beeby thought that introduction of the 44-hour week 'in some directions' should be gradual and that 'to impose suddenly on the railways of Australia a universal 44-hour week would seriously hamper operations and lead to additions to running cost which, on consideration of the financial condition of the different railway systems, cannot be justified'. Introduction of the 44-hour week in railways should begin with mechanics and their assistants in workshops (p. 1260). Moreover, the locomotive men were already allowed to take their lunch in working hours, which reduced their effective working hours to about 45 (p. 1262).

In the *Printing Industry* case, decided in December 1927 (25 CAR 1265), the Full Court granted the 44-hour week in the commercial and newspaper printing awards. This was a majority decision of Dethridge and Beeby, with Lukin dissenting. Dethridge again referred to the widespread operation of 44 hours under the State systems, but in this case seems to have drawn an opposite conclusion from that of the enginemen's case:

> The Court cannot disregard the fact that the 44-hour week already largely prevails in this industry. Even where this is due to State legislation or

> awards, which this Court might override in cases within its jurisdiction, the fact is of some importance where the nature of the work is not plainly of a kind to make the 44-hour week improper, having regard to the principles this Court has enunciated. Still more attention must be given to any extensive adoption of the shorter week by agreement between employers and employees. (p. 1269)

An added factor was the presence of numerous females in the industry. There was medical evidence that 48 hours caused fatigue among these women. Dethridge thought it impractical to grant a 44-hour week for females only. Lukin, though dissenting in respect of males, supported the 44-hour week for females. Beeby favoured a 42 hours for females, 42 for linotype operators on day work, and 40 for night work, 42 for night work generally, and otherwise 44 hours.

The Court's decisions about standard hours in 1928 indicate a growing resistance to the extension of the 44-hour week.[13] What this meant, in practice, was a hardening of Dethridge's attitude. This trend was evident in the *Timber Workers'* case, decided in December 1928 (27 CAR 396), when the Court restored the 48-hour week in those sections of the industry where the 44-hour week had survived the Full Court decision of 1922. The decision caused great industrial turmoil. A year later, in the *Coach-making and Motor Body Building* case (28 CAR 411), the Full Court (Dethridge and Lukin, Beeby dissenting) affirmed the 48-hour week, except for females.[14] Dethridge said that

> existing circumstances call for the gravest consideration of the likely effects of any proposed change in the conditions of an industry which may lessen its vitality. Where the demand for its products is brisk and expanding, a reduction in working hours—a desirable thing in itself— may not unreasonably be regarded by employees as worth the forgoing of some possible expansion of the field of employment in that industry.

---

[13] Nyland (1987) argues that this was due, in part, to the unions' refusal to entertain piecework. My reading of the decisions suggests a different emphasis—on deteriorating economic conditions. The Court's concerns about the economic environment might have been alleviated somewhat by union acceptance of piecework.

[14] This decision entailed an increase in hours for painters in New South Wales.

> But where the demand is likely to remain stationary for a considerable time in the future, and may possibly even shrink, that reduction, attended with a serious risk of consequent contraction in the existing amount of employment, should be shunned rather than welcomed by the employees. (p. 414)

'General unemployment', said Dethridge, was 'great', and 'so long as the other causes of that general unemployment are likely to continue with consequential unemployment in this industry … nothing should be done to increase the evil' (pp. 419–420). He recognised that some employees in the industry worked under State awards and enjoyed the 44-hour week, so that 'a disadvantageous disparity as to working hours is now suffered by most of the members of the federation' (p. 415). He also accepted that there was 'no substantial relevant difference' between the work performed in some of the trades and those metal trades for which 44 hours had already been granted: 'if conditions in respect of unemployment were the same now as when the 44 hour week was approved by this Court for the metal trades industries, I should approve it for employees in this industry' (p. 424).

By the end of the 1920s, the 44-hour week had made limited progress in the Court's awards.

7.4 Payment by results

Union resistance to piecework had been noted with disapproval by the Court during the Higgins era. After the reconstitution of the Court in 1926, the judges became more forthright in their endeavours to promote it. This was, of course, the era when Taylorist principles of management, which included piecework, were in vogue. Piecework was strenuously opposed by the unions, which saw it as a device for speeding the work with no likelihood of long-term benefit to the workers, and as a likely cause of unemployment.

The issue was canvassed during the hearing in the *Main Hours* case. For example, E J Holloway, one of the union advocates, cited an employers' official who had allegedly admitted 'that ever since the tribunals have been in existence in Australia—1901 to 1924—the workers have been losing. They have not been getting what is now given in America, namely, an incentive to do their best, and to co-operate with the management, by having a share in the industry' (transcript, p. 620). Dethridge commented:

> It may very likely be that a part explanation is what my brother Beeby referred to the other day, namely, the prevalence of payment by results in America as compared with this country. If the good worker is encouraged to work and earn more than the average worker, it follows that the share going to the workers as a class is increased. (transcript, p. 620)

Beeby said that in America not all work was piecework 'and that those on day work participate in the higher advantages also; but they probably give better results because of the standard set by the pieceworkers'. Holloway questioned the practicality of piecework at a time when new machines were continually changing the nature of the tasks, and said that 'one of the principal things which have made our people oppose piece-work in the past has been the fact that the moment men become more efficient, the rates are cut back'. Dethridge replied: 'Of course, the worker has to be protected against imposition of that kind. In many cases, apparently, the protection has been ensured by placing the control of piece-work rates in the hands of a combined body of employers and employees' (transcript, pp. 620–622).

In his judgment, Dethridge said:

> Some form of payment by result properly safeguarded in the interest of the workers seems to be a necessary incentive, but most of the unions are officially at any rate still strongly opposed to this principle of remuneration. I have had the advantage of reading my brother Beeby's judgment so far as it deals with methods of remuneration and agree with what he says as to the injury to workers themselves arising from the unions' attitude upon this matter. I hope that a practical scheme of unemployment insurance can be devised which will help to remove

> the fear of unemployment, which is the chief obstacle to payment by results as well as other instruments and methods of efficiency in output. (p. 773)

Beeby said:

> If we could have so organised industrial life as to guarantee to every worthy citizen constant employment, or insurance during periods of unavoidable unemployment, the main objection to payment by results would not exist. That organised unionism is adopting a wrong remedy is beyond argument. All unnecessary restrictions upon production reduce the possibility of continuing to improve standards of living and to provide for the needs of increasing population. (p. 874)

Beeby criticised employers for thinking 'that the introduction of new methods of payment and the fixing of piece-work and contract rates are matters of management only, and not subjects of consultation with their workmen'. The absence of joint shop committees in Australia was 'lamentable' (p. 875).

Lukin spoke of 'abundant evidence in these proceedings that the worker in the majority of cases can reasonably do more, reasonably put more effort into the work than he does, reasonably give greater output than he does'. This was shown 'by the rules of the unions which impose fines for exceeding certain limits of work, by the pronounced opposition to piece-work, by the greater production given, and the less time consumed where payment is made according to results, by frank statements made by some of the witnesses that the workers always have "a little up their sleeve"' (p. 807). If the shorter week were granted, 'it would not be unreasonable to make it a condition … that the unions should withdraw all opposition to, and give support to, payment by results under schemes that will prevent exploitation, and secure advantages both to the employers and the employees, thereby benefiting the community and making up, to some degree at any rate, for the loss that will be occasioned by the … reduction of hours' (p. 864).

The members of the Full Court returned to the subject in June 1927, in giving their decisions about the (unsuccessful) applications of the railways for exemption from the 44-hour week in respect of grades that fell within the scope of the *Main Hours* decision (25 CAR 216). Dethridge wrote:

> In my opinion the future development of industry in Australia depends upon the abolition of all influences restricting production consistently with the fair treatment of employees. One of these influences is the method of payment according to time worked, and not according to results. A system of payment by results is not possible in some branches of the metal industry, but it is applicable in very many cases. In those cases, however, where it is so applicable, the nature of modern industry is such that the system requires an exhaustive and complicated series of investigations and adjustments to be made by experts in order to ensure success in practice. … Its initiation and development must come, for the most part, from employers, and demands from them a very considerable amount of difficult work and close attention. Sporadic efforts have been made in this direction by employers in the metal trades in Australia, but with no great energy or persistence in face of the opposition of the unions. (p. 222)

Dethridge added that if he had thought that the employers were 'ready and eager' to adopt a system of payment by results, he might have made the reduction of the working week conditional on the employees' concurrence in its implementation; 'but there was no sign of this, and after much deliberation I decided to grant my approval without requiring such concurrence as a condition precedent' (p. 223). Since the *Main Hours* decision, an interstate conference of the Amalgamated Engineering Union had resolved that the union 'cannot accept piece-work, bonus, contract, or task work, or any system of payment other than an hourly, daily, or weekly rate, as is generally known and observed in the trade'. 'If this resolution … reflects the real intention of the employees', said Dethridge, 'it bodes ill for the retention of the 44-hour week'; and 'a suggestion worthy of serious consideration has been made that in view of this resolution, the Court should suspend its approval of the reduction of hours in the metal trades, but I have come to the conclusion that the employees should not be deprived of their opportunity' (pp. 223–224).

Given the unions' attitude, Lukin asked rhetorically: 'should the Court proceed further with this proposed experiment?'

> I am strongly of the opinion that this Court should take no further step in applications for reductions in standard hours, and that the present orders, though actually made, should be suspended until the unfair and unreasonable restriction and limitation of 'setting the pace' in the workshop ceases, and until this determined hostility and opposition of the unions to payment by results is withdrawn and abandoned, and a more conciliatory and favourable attitude adopted. (p. 231)

Beeby said that 'if the unions or their members place obstacles in the way of securing increased production without reduction of status or earnings, then the standard hours of work, at some future date, will have to be reconsidered' (p. 234).

In the following month, Beeby published his decision about a new award for the metal trades (the hours aspect having been determined by the Full Court in the *Main Hours* case) (*Metal Trades* case 25 CAR 364). He spoke of 'the prejudice against piece-work and other systems of payment by results, formed as the result of abuses of such systems before the days of statutory regulation of industrial conditions'. Employees were not alone to blame for the prevailing lack of cooperation.

> Every benefit which they have secured during recent years has been the result of hard fighting, either in this Court or before State tribunals. No carefully thought out proposals for a better organisation of the industry has ever been put before them. Employers and their managers voluntarily offered testimony to the capacity of their workmen, but admitted that they had made no serious effort by means of shop committees or industrial councils to get into closer contact with them ... I have therefore included in the award every possible provision for the formation of Joint Committees. (pp. 373–374)

Beeby announced the insertion in the award of a clause empowering employers and employees to make contracts for other than ordinary wages, and another providing that organised prohibition of payment by results would be a breach of the award (pp. 376–377). He cancelled the latter provision in response to union protests.[15]

In August 1928, Drake-Brockman made the first federal award for the furnishing trades (the union's 44-hour week claim having previously been rejected by the Full Court) (*Furnishing Trades* case 26 CAR 808). Margins for skill had been fixed, giving increases for some grades but causing reductions for others. Drake-Brockman added that

> broadly speaking, all the sections which have been subjected to decreases are suitable for piece-work operations, and consequently a provision for piece-work is included in the award. If this provision is used the loss to the individuals concerned can easily be made up. (p. 809)

Under the award, pieceworkers would have to receive at least 10 per cent more than the time rate.

To the best of my knowledge, there is no statistical evidence as to the effects of the Court's endeavours to promote payment by results. Hagan argues that union resistance was blunted by inter-union differences of view and by the willingness of workers to work at piece rates in spite of the hostility of their unions. He cites an estimate by Foenander that by 1937 as many as 20 per cent of all jobs were on piece rates (Hagan 1981, p. 85).

7.5 Female employment

I have commented in Chapter 6 on the limited extent of award coverage of female workers and the confined range of cases in which the terms of women's employment were an issue. In the later 1920s, too, there were few cases in which the Court specifically considered award terms for females.

In 1926, Webb gave a decision about hotels, in the course of which he set rates for barmen and barmaids (*Liquor Trades* case 24 CAR 309). The

---

[15] See Hagan (1981), p. 84. Hagan attributes the early survival of the Australian Council of Trade Unions (ACTU), founded in 1927, to its role in organising resistance to piecework.

comments below are based on the section of his decision that deals with Victoria. The union had quoted a passage from Higgins' *A New Province for Law and Order*:

> But in an occupation in which men as well as women are employed, the minimum is based on a man's cost of living. If the occupation is that of a blacksmith, the minimum is a man's minimum; if the occupation is that of a milliner, the minimum is that of a woman's minimum; if the occupation is that of fruitpicking, as both men and women are employed, the minimum must be a man's minimum. (decision, p. 313)

Webb refused to apply this reasoning to the case before him:

> No one could have a higher respect for the work done by Mr Justice Higgins than I have, but I am unable to accept the principle as applicable to this industry … The fact is that this is an industry where, from time immemorial, men have been employed on a man's wage and women have been employed on a woman's wage, and it is one of several in which a similar state of affairs exist, and must exist. I call to mind all kinds of domestic service, clerical work, work in shops, and so on where men are employed on a man's wage and women are employed on a woman's wage, and where, in my opinion, they must continue to be so employed. (p. 313)

He could understand the award of an equal basic wage for an industry 'where it is desired to push women out of employment'—an objective disclaimed in this case.

Webb was correct in identifying the failure of the *Fruitpickers'* principle to recognise the realities of mixed industries. Unequal basic wages did not necessarily cause industries or occupations to become all-female (though this may have been close to the truth in the clothing trades). The inputs of men and women may not have been fully substitutable. Just as custom and expectations may have reserved some work in banking and insurance for men, likewise in hotels there were (and probably still are) subtly different roles for barmen and barmaids.

Differential basic wages would continue. In fixing margins, Webb said:

> There has been considerable evidence called to show the nature of the work done by barmen. The existing margin is 2s 6d per week, and an increase is sought. I cannot see that there is any skill in a barman's work. There is some responsibility, but I do not think I should increase the present margin. (p. 312)

Turning to barmaids, he said:

> It must at once be conceded that a barmaid should not be on the base. A barmaid is a capable business woman who attracts custom by her personality and ability. It is essential for her work that she should spend money on clothes. She must be well dressed. In the previous case, I fixed the rate at £3 3s, when the woman's base was £2 4s 6d; but I did not have all the conditions of the industry under review then, as I now have. I have decided to fix the wage at £1 above the basic wage. (pp. 313–314)

We might have expected some explanation as to why the barmaid deserved a margin of £1—a high margin when compared with the prevalent tradesman's margin of 24s—while the barman got only 2s 6d. There is none, unless it is implied in the remarks about the barmaid's personality, ability, and clothing.

In the *Printing Industry* case of 1927 (25 CAR 1265), the Full Court gave specific attention to the working hours of women. Dethridge explained that outside printing proper—in cardboard boxes, paper bags, bookbinding and stationery—most of the employees were female, some as young as 15. Dr Ethel Osborne gave evidence of an investigation of the health of the female workers in the industry in Victoria, and suggested that there were serious problems of fatigue. 'I am disposed', said Dethridge,

> to rely on Dr Osborne's conclusions as substantially correct. Moreover, it has to be remembered that women operatives have usually to bear the burden, not only of their factory work, but also of some home duties which the mode of living of our community imposes on them. I have little doubt that in the case of women employed in this industry the introduction of a shorter working week will tend to improve their health

and increase their vigour, so that ultimately there will be no appreciable falling off in their output as the result of the reduction of hours. (p. 1274)

Even Lukin, who dissented from the award of 44 hours for males in the printing case, joined with Dethridge in favour of the 44-hour week for females. Beeby would have set the female working week at 42 hours. In the *Coach-makers' and Motor Body Builders'* case (28 CAR 411), decided in December 1929, the Full Court approved a 44-hour week for females, though refusing it for males.

In the 1928 *Clothing Trades* case (26 CAR 76), the union claimed a minimum wage for females of £5 and tendered budgets in support of the claim. Drake-Brockman said that he had carefully analysed the budgets. The claim included 19s 6d for dependants. 'I see no reason', said Drake-Brockman, 'to depart from the accepted principle of this Court that a basic wage for women should be fixed for a single woman without dependants' (p. 89). He set a female basic wage of £2 9s 6d, to be adjusted proportionally with the male rate.

Dethridge, in January 1930, reviewed the female rates in the dried and canned fruits industries (*Dried Fruit* case 28 CAR 597, 609–610).[16] Referring to Higgins' *Fruitpickers'* decision, he said:

> Mr Justice Higgins, assuming that fruit harvesting was essentially a man's occupation and that women who entered it would compete unfairly with men unless they were paid men's rates, prescribed men's rates for them. So far as the picking of grapes is concerned, I find it hard to agree with him; women have always been engaged in this part of the work to a very large extent, and it may be said that that it is as much women's work as men's work … the picking of stone fruit is almost all done by men. I do not think I should continue the male rate for female workers, but should to some extent observe the distinction between male and female rates according to the general practice of this Court and of the community. (p. 609)

---

[16] This case is discussed in Subsection 7.1.2 in connection with the setting of the basic wage.

Observing that the minimum rate for women was ordinarily about 54 per cent of the male rate, but was in some awards 60 per cent, Dethridge said that in fruit picking (though not in canneries) the difficulty of getting accommodation and maintenance warranted a higher rate, and he set a ratio of two-thirds. Dethridge accepted that in grape-picking, though not in other branches of the work, women did work of equal value to that of males. The same might be said of juniors.

> But it would not be for the benefit of the industry or of the community to give the adult basic wage to either females or juniors. The adult basic wage is given not because it is a wage which the market value of the product of an industry justifies, but because for several reasons an adult male's wage should not fall below that amount—he is assumed to have certain responsibilities which make that wage necessary. The same reasoning does not apply to females or juveniles—the wage for them has to be fixed, having regard to their individual requirements and also to economic results. (p. 610)

7.6 Conclusion

In these pre-Depression years, the principal matter of contention was working hours, reflecting the adoption of the 44-hour week in some States and the Court's limited and tentative approval of 44 hours in 1927. The momentum for reduction of hours that might have been generated by the 1927 decision was countered, however, by the Court's growing concern about deterioration in the condition of industries. In other areas, there was little or no advance in standards and numerous expressions of concern about the capacity of employers to maintain existing award conditions. The *Timber Workers'* cases signified the preparedness of the Court to retreat to lower standards than had previously been accepted. From labour's perspective, the decade ended dismally.

In the United States and the United Kingdom, the late 1920s were the period when the doctrine of 'high wages' commanded some support (for example, Rowe 1928 and Cole 1928). The idea was that high wages would yield economic benefits in three ways:

- Workers would be motivated to greater effort.
- Employers would be induced to implement measures to raise productivity.
- The high wages would constitute the purchasing power needed to absorb increased production.

Thus Cole (1928) wrote:

> The American employer pays more because he cannot get men to work at the pace he wants except by doing so. But, when he has paid his high wage in return for high output, he comes to realise that the high wage is itself the means through which the high output finds a market. This is concealed from the British employer, both because he is not subject to conditions which compel him to pay a high wage, and because his eyes are on the foreign more than on the home market. The 'economy' of high wages, therefore, has not hitherto appealed to his imagination. He still tries to cut his costs of production mainly, not by increasing output, but by reducing wage-rates and piece-work prices. He has still to realise that high output will not help him unless the workers' wages are high enough to enable them to buy it. (p. xii)

Although union advocates and some of the judges were aware of the work of Cole and others, the high-wages doctrine had little purchase in Australia. The emphasis in contemporary debate was very much on wages as a cost. As the economic situation deteriorated, the predominant issue was whether industries could 'afford' existing wages and conditions. Any suggestion that higher labour standards could be of benefit to them would have received short shrift.

WAGE POLICY IN DEPRESSION AND RECOVERY 1929–1939

8

The setting

———•———

The Depression of the 1930s was, for many reasons, a decisive episode in Australian history. Not the least of those reasons was the Commonwealth Arbitration Court's adoption of a wage policy directed toward a macroeconomic outcome. Ironically, the Court was in a position to attempt this role only because the election in 1929 of a Labor Government, which opposed the Court's strategy of wage reduction, had averted its extinction. Its efforts to counter the economic effects of the Depression are the major focus of chapters 9 and 10, without neglecting such other developments as there were in the evolution of wage policy. Chapters 11 and 12 then move to the period of recovery, in which there was an understandably more relaxed approach to wages and conditions. In one important case—the basic wage inquiry of 1937—the Court's decision was again shaped, in part at least, by a macroeconomic strategy, the converse of that of the Depression years.

8.1 The Court

The four judges appointed to the Court in 1926 and 1927 remained in office throughout most of the 1930s. In Lukin's case, this was a formality. He was appointed to the Bankruptcy Court and ceased his active membership of the Arbitration Court in May 1930. This left Dethridge, Beeby, and Drake-Brockman to hear the major cases of the Depression years. A new judge, H B

Piper, was appointed in February 1938.[1] Dethridge died in December 1938. Beeby was appointed Chief Justice in March 1939. At the same time, Thomas O'Mara became a judge of the Court.[2]

The Labor Government, elected in 1929, introduced new industrial legislation in 1930 (Foenander 1937, Chapter IV). This legislation was amended somewhat to secure its passage through the Senate, where the Opposition had a majority. The 1928 provision about the Court's taking account of economic factors, which had been strenuously opposed by Labor, was repealed. Existing provisions for conciliation were strengthened. The Act provided for the appointment of Conciliation Committees, to be presided over by a Conciliation Commissioner. Beeby and Drake-Brockman explained the effect:

> Once a Committee has been so appointed, the Court's jurisdiction as to 'all matters in dispute' is suspended until, on failure of a Committee to come to an agreement, a Conciliation Commissioner makes an award or order. If an agreement is arrived at, even on the basic wage and standard hours of employment, the dispute or application to vary is finally determined. If an award or order is made by a Commissioner, it cannot vary standard hours or the basic wage, and is subject to review by the Court on appeal. (29 CAR 436, 443)

The Government appointed E H Coneybeer to be a Conciliation Commissioner, able to preside over Conciliation Committees.[3] In December 1930 the High Court declared invalid the provisions relating to Conciliation Committees.[4] Coneybeer thereafter played a minor role in the proceedings of the Court.

---

[1] Piper was an Adelaide solicitor.
[2] O'Mara was an industrial lawyer from New South Wales, working mainly for employers.
[3] Coneybeer had been Deputy Industrial Registrar in Adelaide. He resigned as Conciliation Commissioner in May 1935.
[4] *Australian Railways' Union v Victorian Railways Commissioners* (1930) 44 CLR 319. One ground of the decision was that determination of matters by committee did not constitute arbitration and was not authorised by section 51(xxxv) of the Constitution.

A decision of the High Court in 1935 allowed the logs of claims served by unions to include demands affecting employees who were not union members.[5] Hitherto, non-members either were covered by State awards and determinations or were award-free. Though it would take time for the consequences of this decision to work through the awards, it permitted an important expansion of the Arbitration Court's coverage of the workforce.[6]

In the later 1930s, on the other hand, the Court of its own volition showed some reluctance to regulate areas of employment which could be regulated by State authorities. Beeby, dealing with the Metal Trades award in August 1937, said that the Federated Ironworkers' Association had sought the inclusion in the award of classifications and margins for employees working in steel tube and pipe making. He had come to the conclusion, however, that the Broken Hill Proprietary Co Ltd and its subsidiaries should be dealt with by the one tribunal: 'It would be better, I think, in the interests of all parties, that I should clear the deck so that the State tribunal, which is dealing with all the other branches of the metal trades in Newcastle, should also deal with this' (*Variation—Metal Trades' Awards* 38 CAR 328, 331).

The Court also reflected on its jurisdiction in 1938, when meat-industry unions sought the cancellation of awards for butchers' shops. The Full Court stated its opinion that 'the relations of employers and employees in retail butchers shops are not suitable for regulation by this Court and should have been left to State industrial tribunals'. But the Court had, since 1916, regulated the shops in Victoria and South Australia and, since 1932, those in New South Wales and Queensland and this history would be difficult to reverse. Cancellation of the awards was opposed by the employers. Their objection was no doubt due to a fear that they would fare worse under State awards; and the

---

[5] *Long v Chubbs Australian Co Ltd* (1935) 53 CLR 143.
[6] Beeby, referring to the High Court decision, said: 'Freedom to employ non-unionists on conditions different from those prescribed for unionists leads to discrimination against unionists and is frequently a source of bitter dispute. Wherever the ambit of a dispute is wide enough both unionists and non-unionists should be bound' (*Variation—Metal Trades' Award* 35 CAR 756, 758).

union admitted that its main motive for seeking the termination of the awards was the likelihood of getting better outcomes, especially in respect of hours, from the State tribunals. When the Court made the awards, it had, 'in effect, promised those concerned in the industry that it would continue to officiate as code maker unless substantially all of them desired it to discontinue'. To cancel the awards 'would savour of repudiation by the Court'. The application was refused (*Determination—Meat Industry Awards* 39 CAR 270, 271–272).

The Court's authority was challenged, to a degree which cannot accurately be measured, by the bypassing of its awards. In the Depression period, this took the form of underpayments. I refer in Subsection 10.6.1 of Chapter 10 to a statement made to the Court by an employer representative about award evasion and avoidance in the building industry. W R McLaurin visited Australia in 1934–35 from Harvard University. (He subsequently worked at the Massachusetts Institute of Technology.) Presumably, he was influenced by comments that he had heard in Australia or in subsequent correspondence when he wrote in 1938:

> The evasion of wage awards also tended to bring down the general level slightly more than the declared figure. One method was for the employee to supply a few materials with his work and make a contract for a fixed sum for a particular job; this procedure took him out of the jurisdiction of the arbitration court. Some employers violated award rates by making secret arrangements with their employees for a lower wage; but this practice was stamped out wherever possible. Employers' associations not infrequently made private investigations of companies suspected of undercutting awards, and if undercutting was proved, steps were taken to stop it. Trade unions, too, made it a practice to prosecute all such cases that came to their attention … If violation was proved, the employer was liable for the full payment of back wages and a fine as well. There were cases in which workmen appealed to employers to give them odd jobs for a few shillings a week, and, after they had worked at these odd jobs for some time, applied to the arbitration court for back wages at the full rate. … As a result of all these measures, while there was some violation, it was not very extensive and was confined for

the most part to small companies and individual employers. (McLaurin 1938, p. 74)

In the later 1930s, by contrast, the challenge to awards came from payment of wages above the ordinary award standards. Some unions could extract wage increases and other benefits by action 'on the ground'—an indication of the improved economic climate. In 1937, over-award payments of 3s to metal tradesmen were widespread.[7] Beeby, in October 1937, referred to an industry allowance of 3s in the gas industry conceded in response to a strike organised by the Boilermakers' Society (*Variation—Metal Trades' Awards* 38 CAR 440).[8] In January 1938, he decided to deregister the Amalgamated Engineering Union and the Australasian Society of Engineers for striking to gain over-award payments. 'Mr Mundy', he said

> urged that many employers are paying above award wage rates and that the union was justified in its efforts to compel others whose conditions were equally prosperous to do the same. He disregards the fact that while some groups can always command higher rates the rank and file—by far the greater proportion of members—have the advantage of standardised rates which many of them could not command in an unregulated market. All the Court can do is to fix minimum standards to apply to employers prosperous or struggling and to employees of differing efficiency leaving the securing of higher standards to individual bargaining. Unions not accepting this interpretation of the Court's powers cannot expect to maintain the corporate rights conferred by registration. (*Cancellation of Registration—Amalgamated Engineering Union, Australian Section, and Australasian Society of Engineers* 39 CAR 7, 9)

In addition to responding to union pressure, some employers no doubt paid above the awards simply to 'meet the market'.

---

[7] In 1941 O'Mara said that he had been 'under the impression that all members of the Metal Trades Employers Association were parties to an agreement made in 1937 to pay 3s per week above the award rates. On speaking to the minutes … [the representative of the Association] demurred to this … and it now appears that not all his members were parties to the 1937 agreement' (*Judgment—Foundry Employees, NSW (War-Time)* 44 CAR 215, 216).

[8] Because it became part of a formal agreement, this would have entered into the nominal wage data. Increases granted informally by employers did not enter the data.

336 *Australian Wage Policy*

The area of work with the most egregious variance from normal standards was probably local government, where the Municipal Officers Association was the relevant 'white-collar' union and registered agreements prevailed. In some—but by no means all—instances, local government employers extended their generosity to the manual grades (represented by the Municipal Employees Federation). An example is the consent variation of the *Municipal Employees' Agreement (Collingwood City Council)*, made by Beeby in September 1939 (40 CAR 604). This provided a labourer's wage of £5 when the Court's basic wage was below £4; tar gang labourers received £5 12s and a classification called 'maintenance' £6 18s. These rates were for a 40-hour week.

8.2 Economic activity

Figure 8.1 shows the alternative measures of the real GDP computed by Butlin and Haig.[9] It should be remembered that the real GDP measures the level of economic activity within the country, but not the real income of the community. An important reason for divergence between the GDP and the Gross National Income (GNI) is the terms of trade, which reflect the quantity of imports that can be bought from the proceeds of a given quantity of exports. The GDP, if accurately measured, is the appropriate measure of internal productive activity. Both the Butlin and the Haig series show a substantial reduction—more pronounced if Haig's measure is preferred—between 1929–30 and 1930–31. By comparison with 1929–30, the fall amounted to 8.4 per cent (Butlin) or 14.3 per cent (Haig). These estimates of the reduction of activity, especially Butlin's, are surprisingly low if we have regard to the rise in unemployment (discussed below) and the general contemporary perception of the severity of the Depression. Recovery began in 1931–32 (Haig) or 1932–33 (Butlin) and continued until 1937–38. Haig's estimates point to a stronger recovery than do Butlin's. In the last pre-World War II year, there was either a levelling-off (Haig) or a fall (Butlin) in the real GDP. Figure 1.1 in Chapter 1 shows that, on either set of estimates, the growth of the real GDP between the

---

[9] To facilitate comparison, each set of measures is converted to a base of 100 in 1928–29.

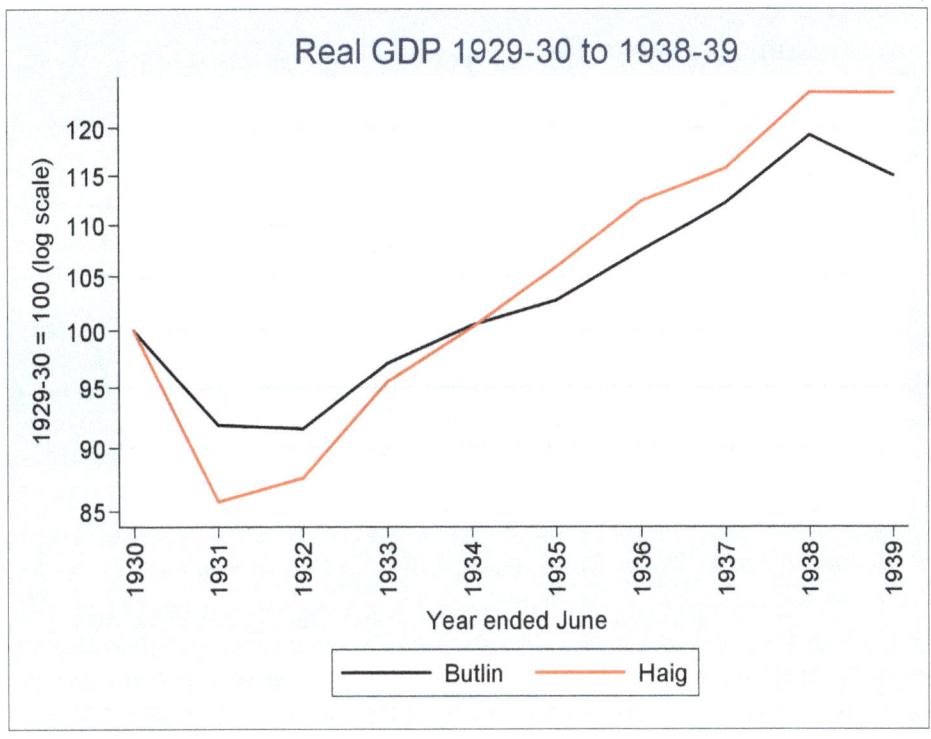

Figure 8.1

trough and the peak of the 1930s far exceeded the growth of the working-age population.

The production levels of the major components of the GDP, calculated from Butlin's and Haig's estimates, are shown in figures 8.2 and 8.2A, respectively. Neither set of estimates points to any fall in the real output of the rural sector. It seems likely that graziers and farmers attempted (unsuccessfully) to sustain their incomes by increased production. Reductions in production were pronounced in the service industries (including distribution), manufacturing, and construction. These reductions can safely be ascribed to the fall in aggregate demand caused by the collapse of export prices and the cessation of foreign borrowing.

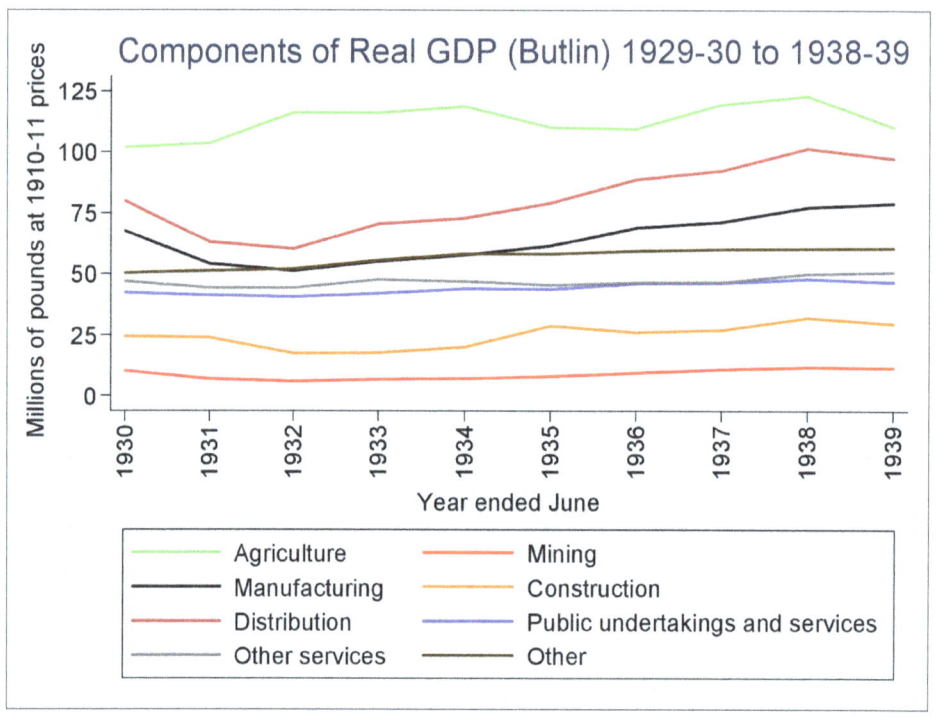

Figure 8.2

Unemployment, as indicated by the trade union returns, is shown in Figure 8.3.[10] Nationally, the unemployment percentage peaked at 30 in the second quarter of 1932. It fell to a minimum of 8 in the first quarter of 1938 and then increased to 10.2 by the second quarter of 1939. The unemployment record is consistent with the GDP estimates, which suggest that the recovery from the Depression stalled in 1937–38. Figure 8.3 indicates that in the main part of the Depression, the severest unemployment was experienced in South Australia (where the percentage reached 35.4). South Australia's relative position improved markedly in the later 1930s. In Queensland, seemingly the

---

[10] Some scholars have constructed unemployment series by treating census and related data as benchmarks and using the trade union statistics to interpolate and extrapolate (Forster 1985). We remain reliant, however, on the trade union data to show the quarter-by-quarter changes of unemployment over time. There is no evidence that they are misleading for this purpose. The 'dip' in the Tasmanian percentage in the last quarter of 1929 (to 7.5) must surely be a mistake. The *Labour Report* offered no comment on this surprising number.

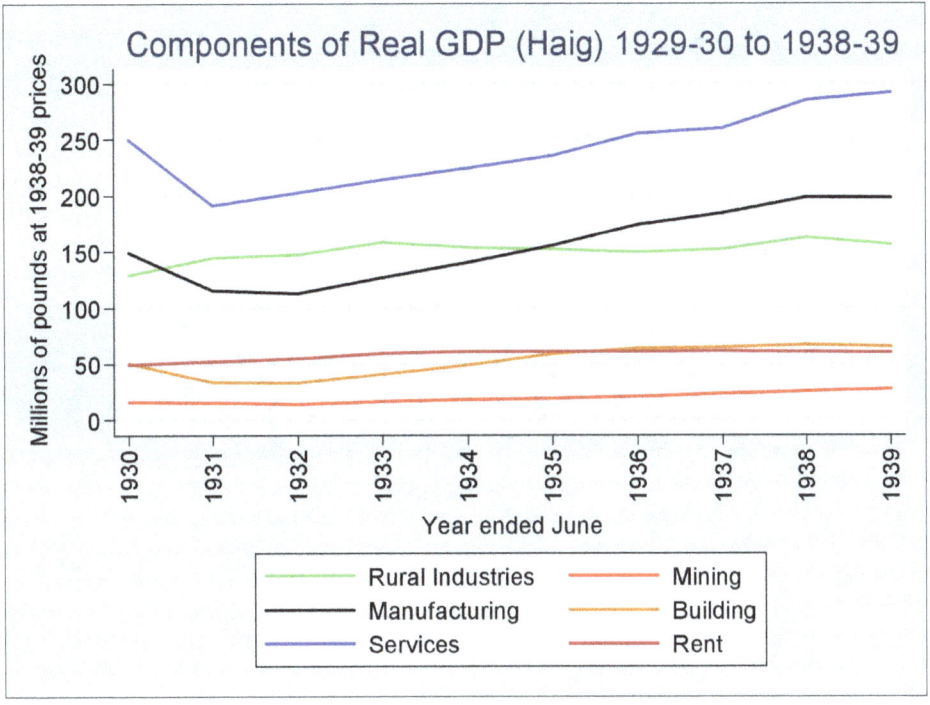

Figure 8.2A

State least affected by the Depression, the unemployment peak was 19.9 per cent.[11] New South Wales generally recorded unemployment percentages above the national average.

---

[11] In the hearing for the 1934 basic wage case, one of the employer representatives (Mann) said that a reason for measured unemployment being low in Queensland was that sustenance workers were required to join unions, which counted them as employed, whereas in other States sustenance workers were counted as unemployed (transcript, pp. 429–430). The credence that should be given to this unverified assertion is unclear. Queensland was a substantial beneficiary of a scheme to assist the sugar industry. The scheme entailed a prohibition of imports of sugar, a subsidy for home production, and export bounties. Coleman, Cornish, and Hagger (2006, p. 137) calculate the budgetary cost of the scheme in 1931 as £8.7 million, which they contrast with £600,000 spent on capital works in schools and £150,000 public expenditure on housing in 1930–31. From time to time, Queensland's favourable economic experience was cited in arguments before the Court. The judges often responded by mentioning the sugar scheme and a kindred scheme for dairying. In August 1937, Beeby said: 'Queensland industrial tribunals in most industries have awarded substantially higher industrial standards than those of other States. Apparently, with the advantage of the sugar subsidy, the State is able to carry higher wage costs in the general run of industry and in operations not subject

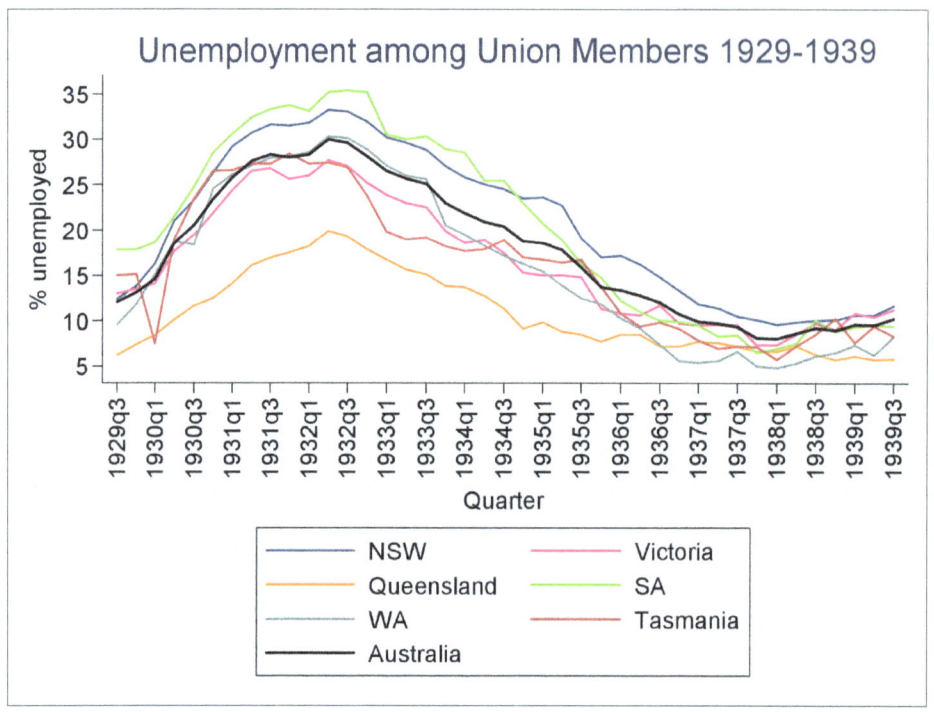

Figure 8.3

8.3 THE DEPRESSION AND THE RECOVERY

It is not my intention, of course, to offer a general history of the Depression.[12] But the Court's decisions and their possible effects cannot be understood without reference to their economic context.

The later 1920s were not a good period for Australia. Business experienced growing pressure on profit margins; unemployment was rising; many farmers could not extract decent livings from their properties; governments (federal and State) encountered difficulties in raising loans and servicing their existing

---

to competition with southern States.' Beeby went on to observe that manufacturing had not developed in Queensland as it had in the Commonwealth as a whole (*Variation—Metal Trades' Awards* 38 CAR 328, 340).

[12] Several histories of the Depression were written in the 1930s, including Copland (1934) and Walker (1933). See also Reddaway (1938). The principal studies from a later perspective are Schedvin (1970), which was the subject of a review article by Hancock (1972); and Gregory and Butlin (1988).

debts; and railway finances—critical to State budgets—were in a dire state. The available data show deterioration in the general economic position. Unemployment among trade union members, which averaged 7.0 per cent in 1927, was 11.1 per cent in 1929, and in the last quarter of that year was 13.1 per cent. We saw in the previous chapter that after 1926 the Court, responding to adverse economic news, became increasingly resistant to union claims; and the restoration of the 48-hour week in the timber industry was in keeping with its perception of a need for severe restraint. Notwithstanding the Court's caution, there was (as we shall see in Chapter 13) an influential body of opinion which held that the arbitration system had raised too high the cost of labour.

Australia slid into full depression during 1930. The Depression was an imported disease, caused by drastic reductions in the prices realised by Australia's principal exports and a virtual cessation of foreign lending to Australian governments.[13] Though part of a world phenomenon, Australia's depression had local characteristics. Prices of wool and wheat, the principal exports, fell more than those of most other commodities and considerably further than those of the bulk of Australian imports. The adverse movement in the terms of trade implied a loss in real income (even without reductions in domestic activity) of the order of 9 per cent between 1929 and 1932 (Gregory 1988, p. 10). The economic impact was much greater than this, however, because of the reduced spending power of the exporters. Elimination of foreign lending led to the curtailment of expenditure on public works, which had been running at high levels in the 1920s. Moreover, governments had serious difficulties in finding the means to service existing debt at a time when their revenues were depleted by the reduced yield of their taxes.

We can conjecture a scenario in which economic activity in Australia carried on as before, with the adverse effects of the external shocks producing

---

[13] Even in the absence of these two effects, the Wall Street collapse would have had real effects in Australia due to the fall in the local equities market and the associated loss of confidence. This aspect of the Depression was little discussed at the time and has been neglected in most of the subsequent literature.

merely a reduction in real incomes. Australian economists attempted to devise and promote policies that, recognising the reality of the 'primary' income-depressing effects, would minimise 'secondary' effects, including unemployment. In the hypothetical world where only the primary effects operated, the real GDP (measuring the total product of domestic industry) would be constant except in response to factors unrelated to the Depression, such as changes in the labour force, productivity, and the seasons. The real national income (measuring the community's command over goods and services) would fall, but only because of the adverse movement in the terms of trade. This is not what happened. A rough indicator of the secondary effects is the growth of unemployment between 1929 and 1932.

In thinking about the policy responses,[14] we should be conscious that at the outset of the Depression there was virtually no economic bureaucracy in Australia (Hancock 2004).[15] Indeed, the tertiary training of economists really began in the 1920s, so that the possibilities of nurturing in-house advice were slender. Governments, therefore, were ill-equipped to deal with a challenge of great severity and complexity. The consequences of administrative inadequacy were exacerbated by political divisions—themselves partly due to the Depression—that rendered some governments (including the Commonwealth Labor Government in 1930 and 1931) ineffectual. There was, in fact, a policy vacuum. Into it stepped several players. One was the

---

[14] For a comprehensive account, see Schedvin (1970).
[15] Coleman, Cornish and Hagger (2006, p. 160) point out that there was a general lack of administrative expertise in the federal public service attributable in part to recruitment policies that entrenched the engagement of youths and militated against the employment of graduates. (W K Hancock had commented on this in 1930: see Chapter 13). They also recount (pp. 73–79) the failed experiment of the *Economic Research Act 1929*. This was passed by the Commonwealth Parliament during the tenure of the Bruce Government. Bruce was influenced by the economists who had participated in the recent inquiry into the Australian tariff. The Act provided for the constitution of a Bureau of Economic Research, with a highly paid Director. It was opposed by the Labor Opposition, largely because of an expectation that the Bureau would advise against the protectionist policies then favoured by Labor, but also because of a broader antagonism to professional economists. The Bureau had not been created by the time of the fall of the Bruce Government, and the Act remained dormant on the statute book until its repeal in 1950.

Court, to which we return in later chapters. Another was the banks, whose influence over the exchange rate and the funding of government deficits was a source of considerable power (Schedvin 1970). Yet another was a small band of economists who proffered influential—even determinative—advice (Coleman, Cornish and Hagger 2006).

The recommendations of the economists were much influenced by the distinction between primary and secondary effects (Cain 1985, 1987a, 1987b; Hancock 2004; Coleman, Cornish and Hagger 2006). Its significance was underscored by L F Giblin's 'discovery' of the foreign trade multiplier, which described a sequence of reductions in domestic spending in response to an initial fall in export proceeds.[16] I discuss this matter in greater depth in Chapter 13. But the lesson drawn from the reasoning about primary and secondary effects was that anti-depression policy should achieve an equal proportional spreading of the initial loss across the entire community. Everyone would be worse off, because exports would finance fewer imports. But otherwise, life could continue as before. 'Equality of sacrifice' became the formula for limiting the effects of the external shocks. One method of pursuing it was to depreciate the Australian currency, so that exporters received more for their produce and the rest of the community had their real incomes lowered by increases in the prices of traded commodities. Exchange rate depreciations occurred in 1930 and 1931, largely through the actions of the banks.[17] Another method was reduction of domestic incomes and prices, which would enhance the purchasing power of the exporters. Here, wage policy was the main weapon, although steps were taken to reduce other incomes such as interest on government debt. During 1930, economists—Giblin, Copland, Brigden, Melville, Shann, Mills and Wood—advocated wage reduction.[18] As

---

[16] Coleman, Cornish, and Hagger (2006, pp. 85–90) offer suggestions as to how the idea of the multiplier entered Giblin's thinking.
[17] But this was in the face of opposition from the Commonwealth Bank, the nascent central bank.
[18] Brigden's *Escape to Prosperity*, published in May 1930, articles by Copland in *The Argus*, published in June, and Giblin's 'Letters to John Smith', published in the Melbourne *Herald* in July, attempted to promote public acceptance of the necessity for wage reductions (Coleman,

we see in the next chapter, it was Copland who presented the argument to the Arbitration Court.

Alongside the quest for equality of sacrifice was a debate about the role of government in ameliorating the effects of the Depression. On the one hand, it might be supposed that an expansion of spending and a reduction of taxes would reduce the secondary effects of the external factors. On the other, conservative thought saw the existing budget deficits as a threat to the stability of the currency—a fear due in part to the German inflation of 1923—and to the prospects of a revival of government borrowing abroad; measures that would increase the deficits could only intensify these risks.[19]

Another anti-depression strategy was promotion of import replacement. Depreciation of the exchange rate contributed to it, but the main measure was a greatly increased protective tariff. This came into effect in 1930, and was the one area of economic policy in which the Labor Government was able to act decisively. There is no doubt that it did encourage import replacement—a process that became more important once economic recovery was under way. By raising exporters' costs, however, it militated somewhat against equality of sacrifice.

The principal attempts at coherent policy were the 'Premiers' Plan' of June 1931 and subsequent adjustments to it, though aspects of the Plan were already in effect because of the actions of the Court and the trading banks. In constructing the Plan, the non-government economists—Copland, Giblin, Dyason, Brigden, and Shann—had a major part. There was a combination of strategies. Wage reduction and exchange rate depreciation were parts of it. But there was a broad acceptance of the conservative view about public finance. State governments did spend modest amounts on the relief of the unemployed (funded in part by taxes on the employed). Generally, however, they tried to rein in their expenditures and increased their taxes so as to minimise their

---

Cornish and Hagger 2006, pp. 111–112; 133–138).

[19] The conservative view was strongly supported by Sir Otto Niemeyer and Sir T E Gregory, the two experts sent by the Bank of England in 1930 to advise the Commonwealth Government.

deficits. In New South Wales, the adoption of conservative policies followed the dismissal of the Premier, J T Lang, in May 1931.

It is self-evident that policy failed to avert secondary effects of the external shocks. To hope that there would be no such effects was plainly unrealistic, for the external forces entailed structural changes that could not have been painless. Were the policies actually adopted ill-conceived? Did they add to or reduce the secondary effects? And by how much? These questions are difficult to answer. The aspects of policy that, from today's perspective, seem hostile to a better outcome were the endeavour to reduce government spending and the related fear of 'inflation' (at a time when prices were tumbling). 'Spreading the sacrifice', however, was an objective that made sense. Its rationale, over and beyond issues of equity, was to avert the collapse of an export sector on which the rest of the economy was heavily reliant. Implicit in the strategy was a hope that export prices would revive. The alternative strategy of autarky (followed to a degree with the tariff increases) might eventually allow recovery in the level of economic activity (though not in the level of real income), but would have entailed severe shorter-term pains of adjustment.

There is a range of interpretations of the recovery. The concept of a business cycle suggests that it was a 'natural' phenomenon, to be expected as the aftermath of any slump. This may well be a correct perspective of the worldwide economic experience. Australia's experience of the business cycle was, of course, much influenced by its working-out in the rest of the world. The Depression in Australia is attributable mainly to the collapse of the markets for its primary exports and the cessation of foreign loans, the effects of these external shocks being exacerbated by errors of policy. Recovery abroad was likely to induce recovery in Australia, with a revival of demand for its exports. Butlin's (1962, p. 456) estimates of prices for the main components of the GDP show pastoral prices falling by 50 per cent between 1928–29 and 1931–32. Over the same period, agricultural prices fell by 31 per cent, dairying prices by 30 per cent and manufacturing prices by 14 per cent. In 1938–39, pastoral prices were 27 per cent below the 1928–29 level, having been only 3 per cent lower in 1936–37; agricultural prices were 2 per cent higher, dairying prices 16 per cent lower and manufacturing prices 1 per cent higher. These percentages are indicative of strong macroeconomic and structural forces. The rise of wool prices between 1931–32 and 1936–37 contributed to the general recovery, and their subsequent fall probably explains much of the deterioration that occurred in 1938 and 1939.

Is the recovery in Australia better understood as a simple reversal of the earlier decline, or as a process of structural change? No one denies that both forces were at work, but there is an issue of emphasis. Schedvin (1970, pp. 10–11) argues for the role of import-replacement, in the form of expanded manufacturing, as a driver of recovery—a process facilitated by higher tariffs. Gregory (1988, p. 26), on the other hand, disputes Schedvin's perspective and accords greater weight to rural revival.[20] Both Butlin's and Haig's estimates of real product in the major sectors of the economy (discussed in the previous section) show that growth was concentrated in domestic sectors—manufacturing, distribution, and services. That fact, however, does not refute the interpretation which depicts domestic expansion as the consequence of recovery in the export industries. The Depression had suppressed forces for growth and structural change inherent in an array of technological developments (Merrett and Ville 2011). External recovery removed the brake on these forces.

Depression and recovery entail, of course, decreases and increases in various components of expenditure. We do not have the data necessary for a comprehensive analysis of the components of expenditure. An important component, however, is investment, which is a volatile category of expenditure. Its fluctuations tend to exceed, in proportional terms, those of the general economy; they may be a prime cause of the general cycle; and they magnify the effects of other causes. Both cause and effect were at work in the 1930s and it is difficult to separate them. Investment outlays were affected by inflow of foreign capital, domestic monetary conditions, and the flow of opportunities

---

[20] The two views come closer together when timing is taken into account. Schedvin accords greater weight to rural revival in the early years of the recovery; and Gregory acknowledges the role of manufacturing growth in later years.

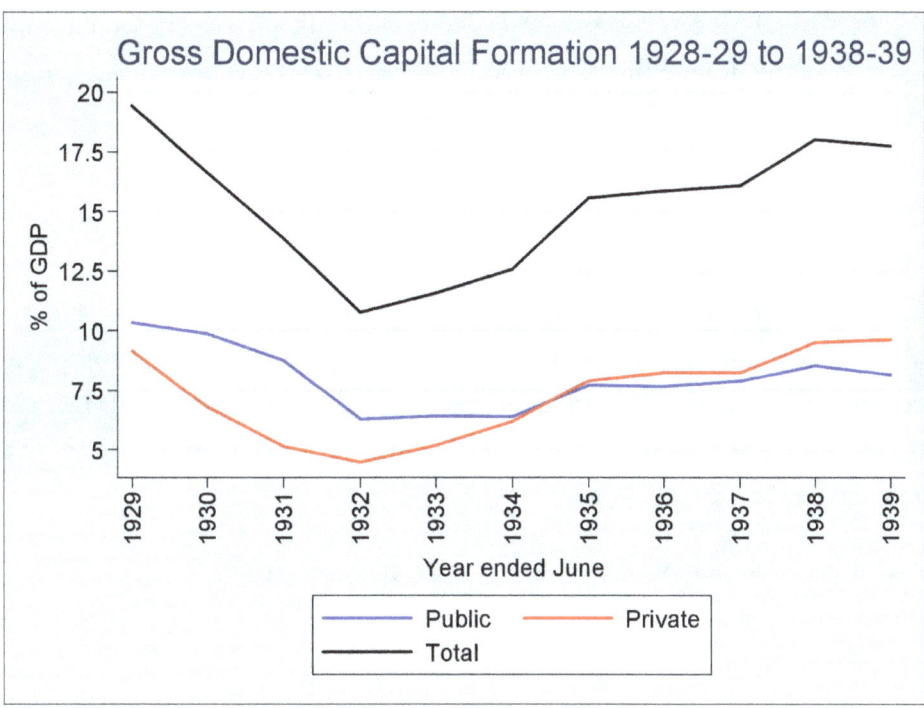

Figure 8.4
Source: Butlin (1962), pp. 11 and 17.

offered by movements in overall economic activity. Butlin (1962) estimated the amounts of gross domestic capital formation. These amounts are not adjusted for price changes; but they can be expressed as proportions of the GDP. Figure 8.4 shows public, private, and total investment as percentages of the GDP between 1928–29 and 1938–39. It appears that both public and private investment fell heavily between 1928–29 and 1931–32. Recovery in private investment began in 1932–33; that of public investment was delayed by a further two years. By the end of the decade, private investment had more than regained its pre-Depression relativity to the GDP, but public investment had not done so. The decline in public—relative to private— investment is likely to have been a consequence of the fall in foreign lending to Australian governments, imposed initially by unavailability of loans and later by a preference to avoid the level of indebtedness that marked the late

1920s. Overall, the expectation that the volatility of investment would both exacerbate the decline into depression and facilitate the recovery seems to be confirmed.

Wages policy in the later 1930s was made in an economic context of significant, but incomplete, recovery. Important contributors to the recovery were a revival of rural incomes and increased investment. The manufacturing sector participated in, but did not lead, the general expansion. Whereas in the years of acute depression the Court saw wage reductions as an appropriate response to the crisis, the partial recovery created expectations of advances in wages and employment conditions with which it had to come to terms. The recovery peaked in 1937–38.

8.4 Wages, prices, and working hours

8.4.1 Nominal wages

The course of nominal wages over the decade is shown in Figure 8.5. For Australia, the lowest average rate was reached in December 1933, when the index stood 21 per cent below its level of September 1929. The greater part of the reduction occurred between September 1930 and September 1932. Clearly, the fall in money wages was a significant feature of the Depression. Between the 1932 trough and the end of 1939, the increase was 18.3 per cent—on average, 3.3 per cent per year. Even with that increase, money wages remained 6.1 per cent below the level reached in the third quarter of 1929. The data for the States show that wages fell most in South Australia and least in Queensland. In New South Wales, where wages were above the national average in the early 1930s, they converged to the average later in the decade. Western Australian wages were close to the average in the early 1930s, but in later years Western Australia became the highest-wage State.

Table 8.1 shows nominal male wages (expressed as percentages of the average) in different industry groups. The percentages are shown for September 1929, December 1934, and December 1939, and the industry groups are ranked according to their wage levels in 1929. Industry rankings

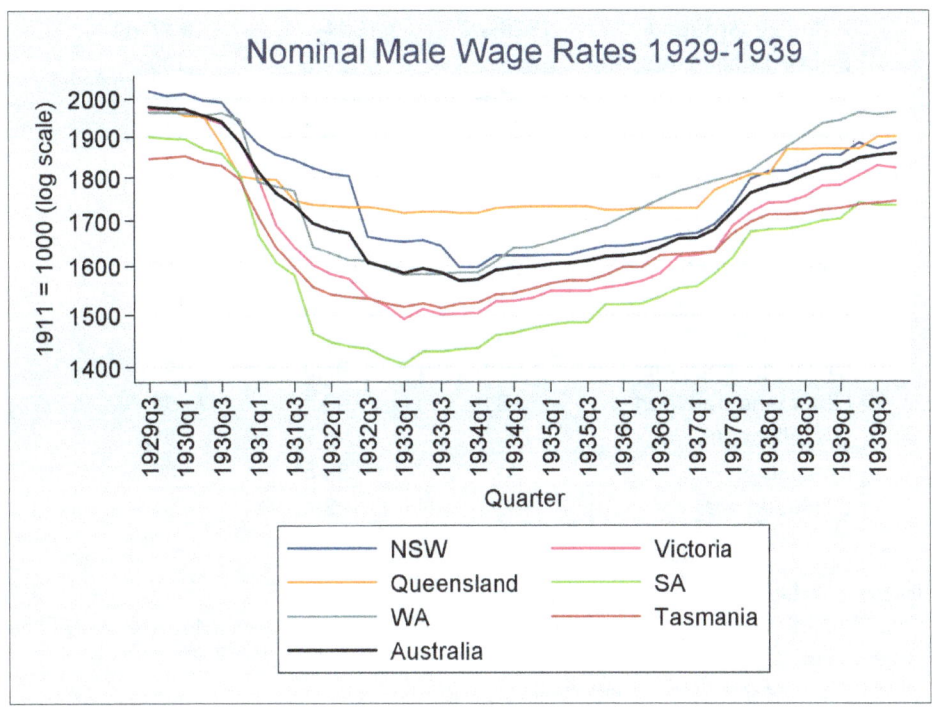

Figure 8.5
Source: *Labour Report*, various numbers.

were generally stable, but there was a notable increase in the relative wage in mining and a decline in agriculture etc. An *a priori* expectation is that the degree of inequality would have widened between 1929 and 1934 because of the fall in the basic wage due to lower prices, with margins being largely unchanged in nominal terms. In the next five years, both the basic wage and margins were increased, and it is more difficult to make an *a priori* prediction. Regression analysis of the data in Table 8.1 suggests that there was a widening of differences between 1929 and 1934 and a narrowing between 1934 and 1939, with a net growth of inequality over the 10¼ years.[21]

---

[21] This statement is based on elasticities calculated by fitting regression equations to the logarithms of the numbers shown in Table 8.1. An elasticity of 1 implies no change (on average) in the degree of inequality; a negative elasticity, a decrease in inequality; and a positive elasticity, an increase. The calculated elasticities are: 1929–34, 1.26; 1934–39, 0.88; 1929–39, 1.08.

Industry Group	1929–q3	1934–q4	1939–q4
Books, printing, etc.	117.6	121.5	120.0
Building	111.9	114.3	111.5
Mining	109.0	119.1	115.0
Shipping, etc.	105.1	103.3	103.6
Railways	103.7	100.9	101.6
Wood, furniture, etc.	103.2	104.1	105.0
Engineering, etc.	102.5	101.5	104.4
Other manufacturing	101.1	99.2	100.5
Food, drink, etc.	99.7	102.1	101.7
Clothing, boots, etc.	98.5	97.5	97.4
Other land transport	96.3	96.1	97.7
Miscellaneous	95.7	95.7	97.5
Agriculture, etc.	94.5	89.5	88.2
Domestic, etc.	92.1	92.4	94.4

Table 8.1 Relative industry wages 1929–39
Note: The industry group names shown in the table are in some cases abbreviations of fuller designations.
Source: *Labour Report*, various numbers.

8.4.2 Prices

The choice of price index was, as we shall see in Chapter 9, an issue in the basic wage cases between 1930–31 and 1933. In this subsection, however, we refer only to the 'All Items' or the 'C series' index. In Figure 8.6, the index is reset with a base of 100 for the Australian average in the third quarter of 1929. The fall in the all-Australia index between then and the first quarter of 1933 was 22 per cent. By the end of 1934, the index was still 20 per cent below its level in quarter 3 of 1929. Over the next five years the rise in prices reduced the fall since 1929 to 10 per cent. Throughout the period, Queensland prices were below those of other States; New South Wales prices were above average; but Figure 8.6 indicates some convergence during the decade.

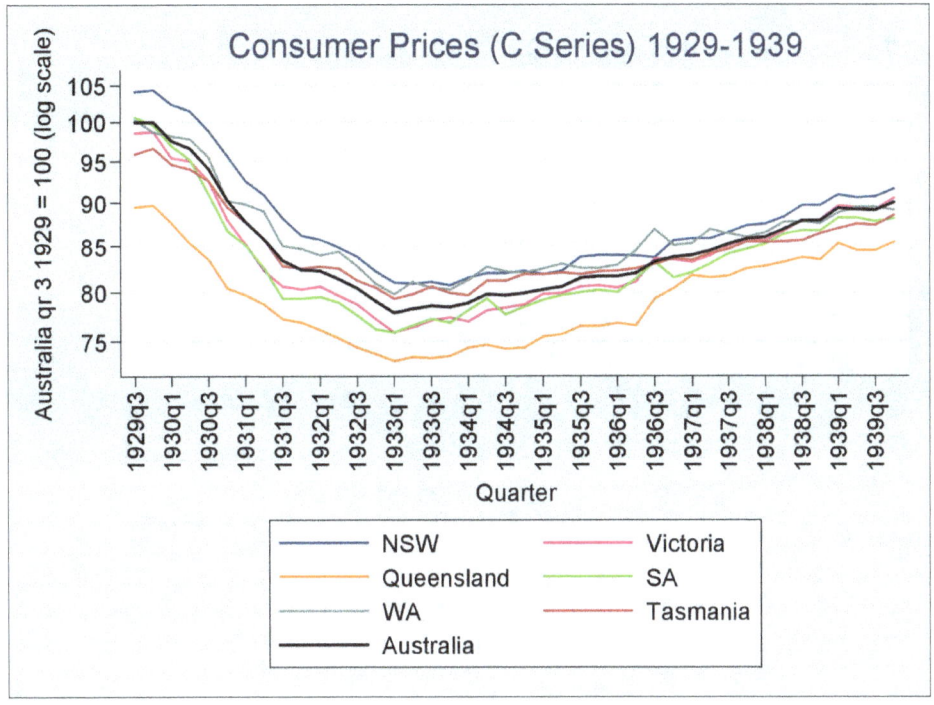

Figure 8.6

8.4.3 Real wages

Figure 8.7 shows the levels of real wages calculated from the nominal wage and price data discussed above.[22] An important feature of this figure is the *rise* in real wages in the early years of the Depression. At no stage during the years 1930–34 was the average real wage in Australia below its level at the end of 1929. In the last quarter of 1930, the average real wage in Australia as a whole was 5.6 per cent above its level of the third quarter of 1929. From 1932 to 1934, there was a gradual reduction, taking it back roughly to the 1929 level. In the last quarter of 1939, the real wage, for Australia as a whole, was 4.3 per cent higher than in the third quarter of 1929. There was an increase of 4 per cent (0.8 per cent per year) between the end of 1934 and the end of 1939,

---

[22] The timing of the wage and price series is not exactly aligned: the former relate to the end of the quarter, whereas the latter represent the quarter as a whole and may be thought of as mid-quarter data. Hence there is a 'gap' of 6–7 weeks.

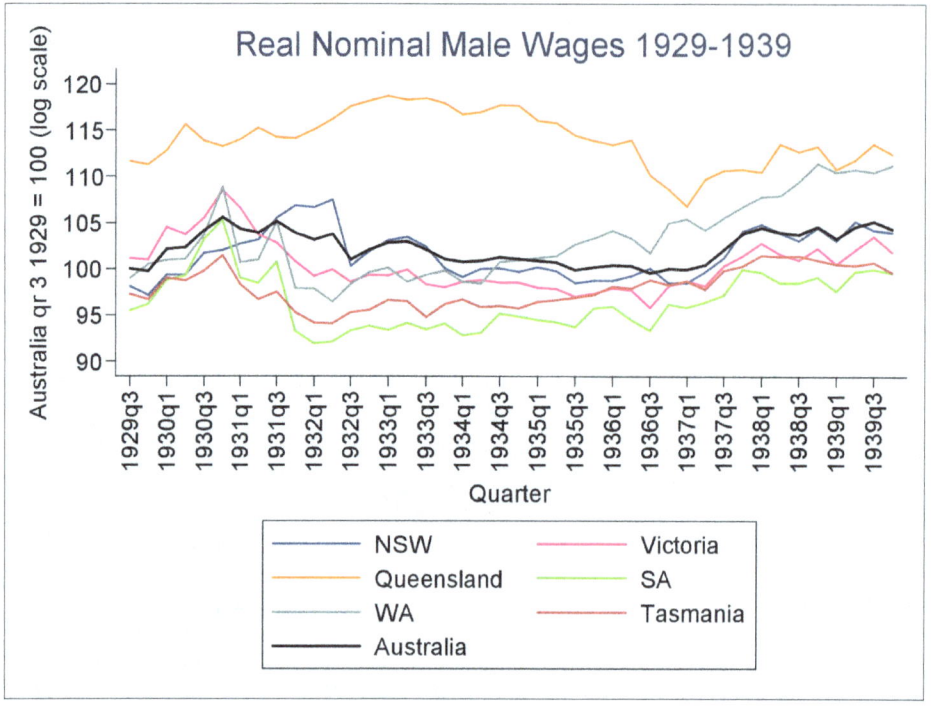

Figure 8.7

concentrated in 1937–38. Of the States, Queensland conspicuously differed from the remainder, with real wages above the average by as much as 16.3 per cent. A reduction of 9.2 per cent between the end of 1934 and the beginning of 1937, however, reduced Queensland's margin above the national average. In the other States, there were diverse experiences. Real wages in New South Wales increased by 9.6 per cent between September 1929 and June 1932, but then fell by 6.7 per cent in a single quarter. South Australian real wages rose by 10.3 per cent over the five quarters to December 1930, but fell by 12.7 per cent in the next five quarters. The real wage in South Australia remained low for the rest of the decade. Western Australian real wages rose strongly in the latter part of the decade. Real wages in Victoria and Tasmania were consistently below the national average.

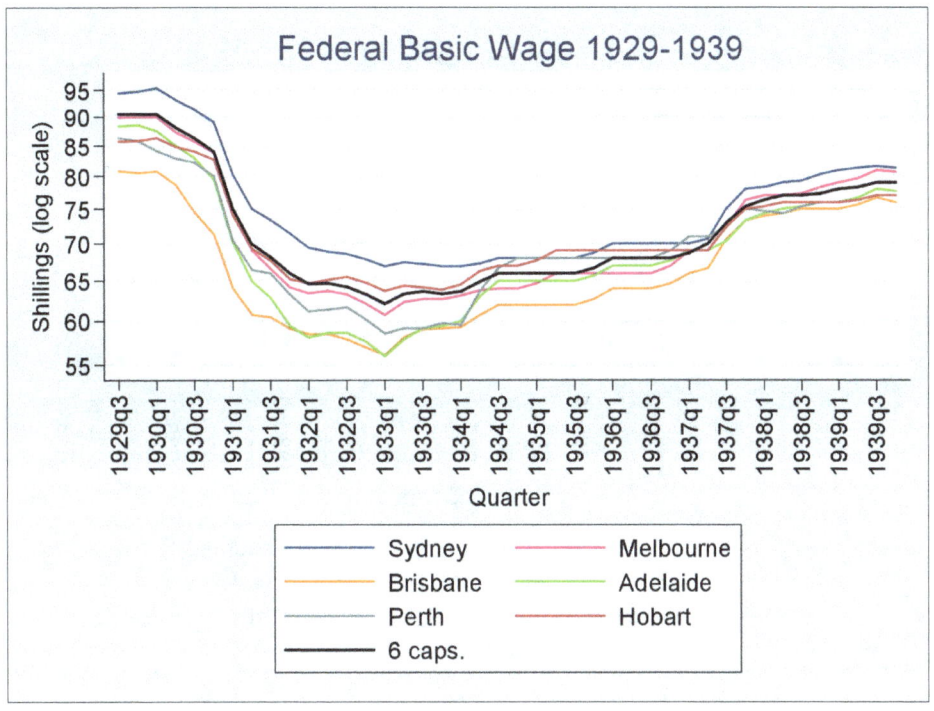

Figure 8.8

8.4.4 The basic wage

Figure 8.8 shows the movement of the Commonwealth basic wage during these years. The six-capitals amount fell from 90s 6d in the third quarter of 1929 to 62s 1d in the first quarter of 1933—a reduction of 31 per cent.[23] This reduction had two causes: the operation of the automatic adjustment system and the 10 per cent reduction imposed by the Court in 1931. Arithmetically, the reduction of 28s 5d can be divided into 6s 11d due to the discretionary reduction and 21s 6d due to automatic adjustments.[24] By the last quarter of 1934, the wage had risen to 63s 7d. Among the capital cities, the peak-

---

[23] As was explained in Chapter 1, the quarterly amounts are calculated after taking into account the dates of wage adjustments within the quarters.
[24] Adding back a 10 per cent reduction to 62s 1d gives 69s, which is 21s 6d less than 90s 6d. Of course, the discretionary reduction may well have intensified the fall in prices, and hence the amount of the automatic adjustments.

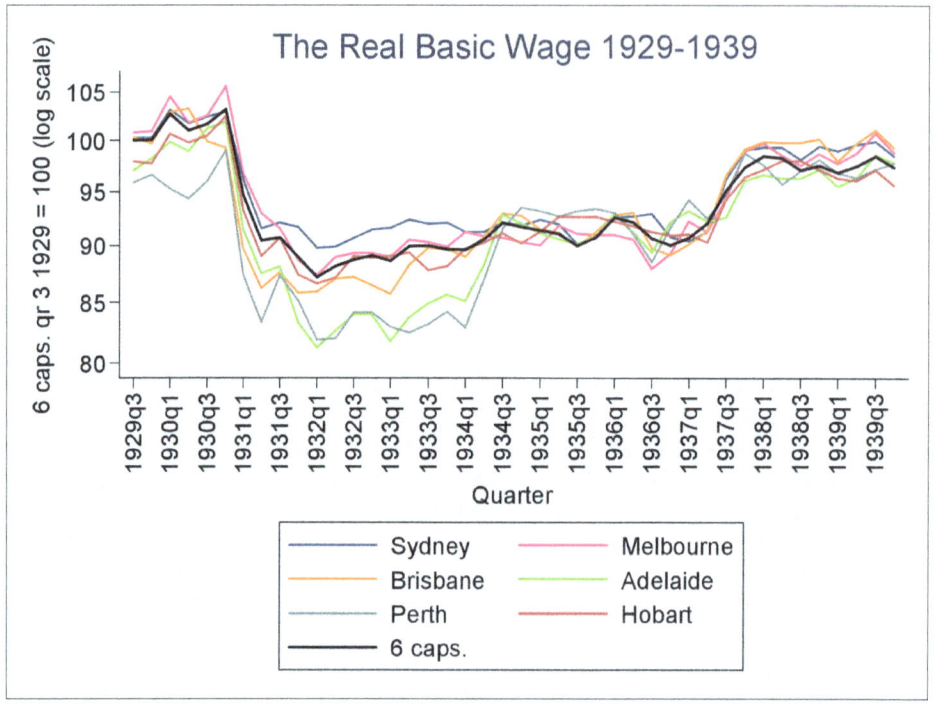

Figure 8.9

to-trough reductions ranged from 29 per cent in Sydney to 37 per cent in Adelaide. In the next five years, the basic wage in the six capitals increased by 13 shillings—19.7 per cent. Approximately 7 shillings of the increase was due to the operation of the automatic adjustment system and about 6 shillings to the 'prosperity loadings' awarded by the Court in 1937. The concentration of the rises in the year 1937 is evident. The figure also shows a degree of convergence of the capital city amounts to the six-capitals amount from 1934 onward, similar to, but more marked than, the convergence of consumer prices.

Figure 8.9 shows the movements of the real basic wage during the period. The peak-to-trough reduction in the six-capitals values (between the last quarter of 1930 and the first quarter of 1932) was 15 per cent. In the last quarter of 1934, the six-capitals real basic wage was 8 per cent below the level of the third quarter of 1929. Between then and the end of 1939, the six-capitals increase was 6.1 per cent, which was wholly accounted for by the increase in 1937. At the end of the period, the six-capitals real basic wage was still 2.6 per cent below the level of September 1929.

It is apparent that before 1934 there were substantial differences between capital cities in the levels of the real basic wage. In 1934, however, these differences virtually disappeared, suggesting that the Court's 'new start' (discussed in Chapter 10, Subsection 10.6.2) succeeded in equalising real basic wage levels. The prosperity loadings granted in 1937 (see Chapter 11, Section 11.2) were larger in New South Wales, Victoria, and Queensland than in the other States, and the unequal movements are apparent in the figure.

Until 1933, the automatic adjustment of the basic wage relied upon a price index confined to food, groceries, and rent (47 items). The Court then moved to the more comprehensive C series index, which included clothing and miscellaneous items as additional categories of spending, having increased the basic wage to offset what appeared to be an excessive reduction due to reliance on the 'All Houses' (A series) index. Figure 8.10 shows that there were indeed significant differences between the two indices. In this figure, the B series index[25] and the C series are compared by expressing the former as a percentage of the latter.[26] For the six capitals, the ratio fell by 7.1 per cent between the third quarter of 1929 and the first quarter of 1933. It is not surprising that the Court chose to take corrective action. Thereafter, the ratio increased. This meant that the switch to the C series index resulted in smaller price-related wage increases than would have occurred if the A series index were retained. Wage earners would have had cause for complaint had not the Court increased the basic wage when it accepted the C series index as the measure of price changes.

---

[25] Differing from the A series because the rent component of the A series index included all houses, whereas the B series was confined to four and five-room houses. There is little difference between the two indices. The B series is used here because full data are published in the *Labour Report*.
[26] Both of the underlying indices are set on a base of six capitals 1923–27 = 1000.

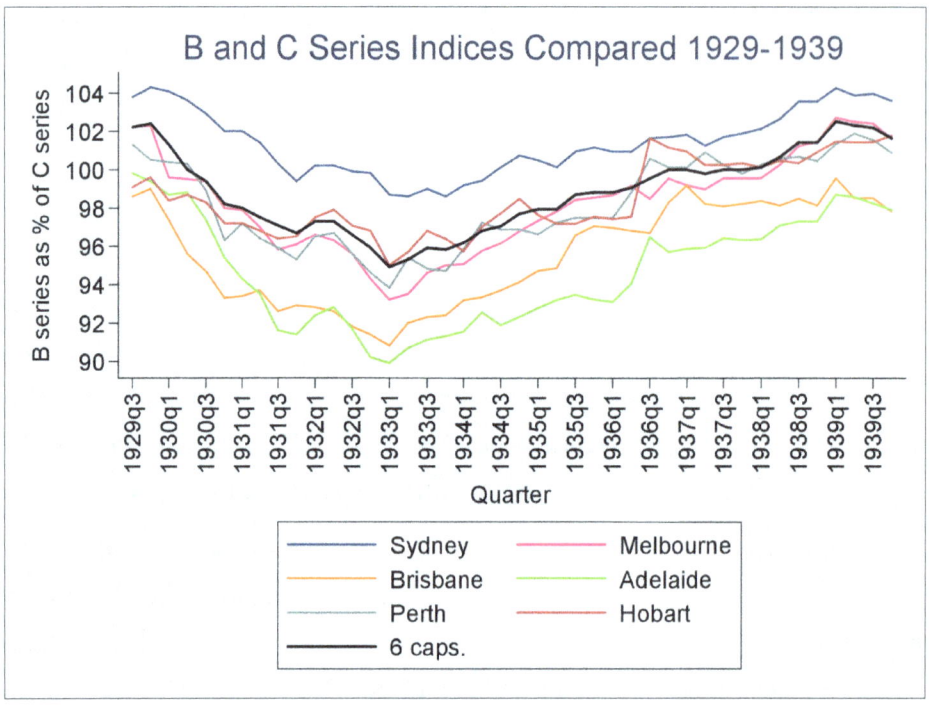

Figure 8.10

The foregoing commentary relates only to the federal basic wage. In New South Wales, Queensland, South Australia and Western Australia, basic or living wages were set by State tribunals. Figure 1.6 in Chapter 1 compares the State basic wages in the capital cities with the respective federal basic wages. It shows that with the onset of the Depression the State basic wages rose sharply, relatively to the federal wage. In Sydney, the State basic wage was 86 per cent of the federal wage in the first quarter of 1930; by the first quarter of 1931 the relativity was 120 per cent. In Brisbane, the percentage rose from 105 in quarter 1 of 1930 to 127 a year later and 133 in quarter 1 of 1933. The State basic wage in Adelaide was 97 per cent of the federal wage in the last quarter of 1929 and 117 per cent in the second quarter of 1931. In Perth, the State wage was 99 per cent of the federal wage in quarter 2 of 1929 and 119 per cent in quarter 3 of 1931. These increases in the State relativity were due partially to the absence of automatic wage adjustments and partially to

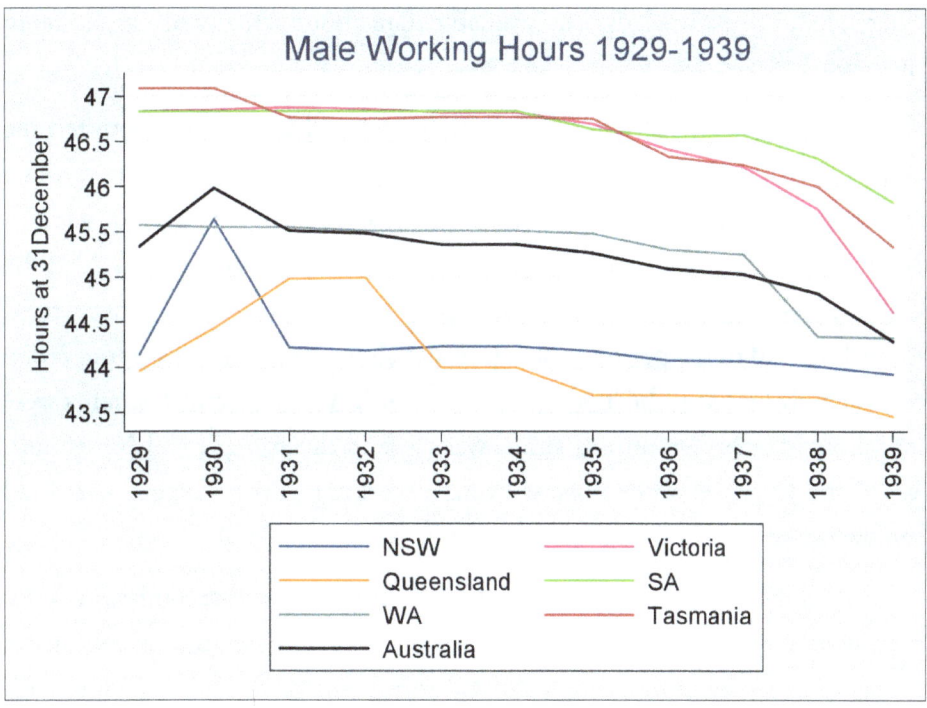

Figure 8.11

the Federal Court's 10 per cent cut of January 1931. They go far to explaining the stability of overall real wages in the Depression years. From around 1933 (earlier in Sydney) the ratios began to fall, as State tribunals made discretionary wage cuts and the federal wage was increased in real terms.

8.4.5 Working hours

Figure 8.11 draws upon the Commonwealth Statistician's data of 'Nominal Hours of Labour (exclusive of overtime) worked by Adult Males during a Full Working Week'. As previously explained, these data show only the working hours prescribed in awards and registered agreements. They do not, for example, reflect variations in time worked as a result of the reduction of overtime and the rationing of work during the Depression. Governments provided relief work, which was invariably less than the normal working week.

There are, to my knowledge, no available data about actual working hours in these years.

There was virtually no change in average full-week hours between the end of 1929 (45.34 hours) and the end of 1934 (45.36 hours).[27] There was a minor increase in 1930, due to the partial restoration of the 48-hour week in New South Wales, reversed in 1931. Nominal weekly hours fell to 44.29 at the end of 1939. Figure 8.11 shows that much of the reduction was concentrated toward the end of the period. The figure also shows that full-week hours varied considerably between the States. Victoria, South Australia, and Tasmania were long-hours States; Western Australia was close to the average; and New South Wales and Queensland had below-average working weeks. The gap narrowed somewhat toward the end of the decade.

Although the statistics of working hours do not distinguish between federal and State awards, a rough indication of the relative provisions is probably given by comparing Victoria, South Australia, and Tasmania with the other States, because the tribunals in the former were more likely to adhere to federal standards (and were less constrained by legislation to do otherwise). The comparison—see Figure 8.11—suggests that workers under federal awards and State awards in Victoria, South Australia, and Tasmania had significantly longer working weeks than employees under State awards in New South Wales, Queensland, and Western Australia.

---

[27] The data can be found in the *Labour Report*; for example, in No. 27 (1936), p. 65.

9

Wage policy and the onset of Depression

9.1 The inception of Depression wage policy

As discussed in Chapter 7, in the late 1920s judges referred from time to time to the need for a fundamental review of the basic wage. Lukin, in particular, was exercised by the continuance of Powers' 3s. Apparently, a general inquiry into the basic wage was delayed by the volume of work claiming the Court's attention. In December 1929, Dethridge, in a case before the Full Court, noted that the basic wage was not an issue in that case, but touched upon a concern to which the Court (and Dethridge in particular) would return in later cases: the need to balance the employment-promoting effects of high wages (due to the spending of the workers) against their employment-destroying effects (due to the costs borne by employers). It was generally recognised, said Dethridge,

> that, in order to minimise industrial depression and unemployment, purchasing power should be widely distributed, which means in effect that as much as possible of the community's production should be paid in wages. With our present means of information, it does not seem possible to measure and state the proportion that can, at any one moment, be so paid, but obviously the amount of that proportion, and therefore of employment, depends nowadays upon the amount of the community's marketable production. The higher that amount the higher is the amount of the proportion that can and should be paid as wages and the lower is the unemployment, but clearly on the other

hand the lower that amount the higher becomes the unemployment. (*Motor Body* case 28 CAR 411, 421)

The *Metal Industry* case (28 CAR 923), which was before Beeby between September 1928 and March 1930, led to the creation of sub-tradesman classifications reflecting the growth of process work within the engineering industry. Dealing with the basic wage in his main decision (December 1929), Beeby referred to a jumble of practices in the selection of the appropriate price index for setting the wage.[1] It was difficult to derive guiding principles from past decisions. 'I have frequently expressed the opinion', he said, 'that the whole basic wage issue, including the continuation or otherwise of the 3s premium, calls for reconsideration by the Full Court.' He would not disturb existing differentials, 'except to remove the glaring anomaly of a higher basic rate for Geelong than for Melbourne' (p. 966). As to margins, the employers did not seriously press their claims for reductions provided that reclassifications were granted (as they were); and the unions had not seriously pressed their claims for increases. Beeby commented: 'If the industry since 1926 had displayed the buoyancy which characterised it during the preceding years, I would not have hesitated to increase margins in some directions in order to restore the ratio of allowance for skill of pre-war days' (p. 967). This was somewhat heretical, because the Court since Higgins' departure had strenuously resisted any appeal to pre-war relativities. As to the unions' claims with respect to holidays, Beeby said:

> However desirable it may be that manual workers of the community should receive the same holiday concessions as the more fortunate clerical and professional workers, the Court must consider the effect of its award. In the present financial position of the industry the cost involved in the granting of such a concession cannot be entertained. (p. 977)[2]

---

[1] In fixing a basic wage for Ballarat, for example, the Court might choose the average price index for 30 towns, the six-capitals average, the Melbourne index, the five-towns index for Victoria, the average index for four towns excluding Melbourne, or the index specific to Ballarat.
[2] In July 1930, Dethridge refused an application for annual leave in the aerated water

Since the reconstitution of the Court in 1926, Beeby had been the Judge most generously disposed to union claims. But by the end of 1929 he was responding to the mounting evidence of economic decline. In March 1930, at the time of finalising his award for the metal trades, he commented on the unions' diagnosis:

> Some union advocates contended that the depression is one of the recurring cycles to which industry and commerce are accustomed. But is it? Can the Court, in the face of existing facts, act on such an assumption? Is it not more correct to surmise that the Commonwealth must face all-round re-organisation, and must rely much more on its own resources and on its capacity for greater and cheaper production? Statements that this re-organisation is impossible without profound economic changes are for the Legislature. The Court operates within the established economic system, and is bound by the Act under which it works to give proper consideration to the present economic situation. In the honest discharge of this direction, I am forced to repeat, and act on my opinion, that in the metal trades group of industries recovery to the level of 1924–1925, and further expansion, are only possible by reduction of costs of production, to which all factors must contribute. It was evident that the unions involved attached very little importance to the analysis of the economic position set out in the stated reasons of the Court for its proposed award. (pp. 1019–1020)

The basic wage in the dried fruit industry was already well below the *Harvester* equivalent (see Chapter 6, Subsection 6.1.2). When Dethridge set a basic wage for dried fruit in January 1930, he substituted 6d for Powers' 3s. He then attempted to compute the *Harvester* equivalent. In doing so, he made a lesser provision for rent than the Statistician's index implied, arguing that the smaller sum more accurately reflected the cost to workers in the industry. On the other hand, he made full allowance for the additional cost of other items. For the Mildura district, he set a basic wage of £4 4s 6d (28 CAR 597, 608). In

---

industry. To grant it would be 'an innovation in the practice of the Court, which ought not to be made in the present state of industrial depression' (29 CAR 288, 293).

real terms, this was probably a little above the amount fixed by Webb in 1925, but below the standard that was likely to apply if no special consideration were given to the industry.

Lukin, in April 1930, inserted a reservation in a new award for manufacturing grocers, enabling him to vary the award once the basic wage had been reviewed by the Full Court. He believed that the review would shortly take place. In previous judgments, he had pointed out 'how unsatisfactory … the judgments and awards of this Court, dealing with the basic wage as laid down by the *Harvester* judgment, have for many years been, both in regard to the method of adjusting its monetary equivalent from time to time, and in regard to the additional Powers' 3s (*Manufacturing Grocers'* case 29 CAR 69, 76).

Dethridge, in July 1930, delivered his decision on an application by employers for variations in the Pastoral Award. The price of wool had fallen from 27.1 pence per pound in 1924–25 and 17.57 pence in 1928–29 to 10.4 pence in the incomplete year 1929–30 (*Pastoral* case 29 CAR 261). At the outset of the case, the Australian Workers' Union had sought Dethridge's advice about the import of section 25D of the Act, inserted in 1928, which required the Court to take into account the 'probable economic effect' of an award or agreement on the community in general and on the industry or industries concerned. Dethridge told the union that 'whether or not section 25D remained in the Act, regard must be had to economic consequences'. This 'always had been the view of the Court subject to special reservation in respect of the *Harvester* basic wage'. In the past, pastoral employers had always conceded that they could pay such rates as the Court thought fair,[3] but Dethridge now was 'faced with the distasteful duty of adjusting wages in accordance with present economic realities'. (In response to what he said, the AWU withdrew from the proceedings.)

---

[3] This concession obviated any requirement to produce financial records. It had been made by various employers, including H V McKay in the *Harvester* case.

The 'probable economic effect', which the Court, according to Dethridge, had to take into account (under section 28D or otherwise), was the effect on the cost of production.

> The Court can only act on the foundation constituted by the existing mode of distribution among the members of the community of the benefit of the production of the community. That mode is a reciprocal process of buying and selling the products. The Court aims at ensuring for wage-earners the *Harvester* basic wage, so far as it lies in its power, but otherwise it is constrained by this process of buying and selling not to make awards which would result in the products of an industry being unsaleable except at a loss. (p. 264)

The price of wool was set in world markets. If capital and management costs were reduced to the least possible, and the cost of production still exceeded the market price, there was 'no escape from the alternatives—either the industry must decrease or wage rates must decrease'. Wool growing was 'the main staple industry of the country, not a parasite that Australia can afford to allow to wither' (p. 265).

Dethridge turned to the argument that wages should not be cut in depression because wage reductions decreased purchasing power and employment. He had some sympathy for it: it was 'sound economic doctrine that at all times, whether depressed or prosperous, the aggregate of employers and capitalists engaged in production and the country generally would profit by distributing in wages as much as possible of the return from industry' (p. 267). But this reasoning could not prevail over the necessity for export industries to produce at costs within the prices set by world markets, over which they had no control; and in the domestic market costs must be constrained by market prices. 'In practice', said Dethridge,

> the economic doctrine of high wages, if applied, works out with these results, manifestly in export industries, and less clearly in other industries—Wages must be kept as high as market prices in the long run permit; they should only be reduced when all other means of keeping

production costs within market prices fail; but, when all these other means fail, wages must be reduced or the industry must collapse. (pp. 267–268)

Much of the rural sector was already outside the coverage of industrial regulation. Federal awards were confined to the pastoral industry and fruit-growing; and State legislation severely restricted the capacity of the respective tribunals to make awards or determinations for rural industries (Copland and Foenander 1932). The applicants now sought to have station hands excluded from the award 'in order that they may be free to engage them at rates substantially less than the true present equivalent of the *Harvester* wage' (p. 272). This, said Dethridge, should be determined by the Full Court. Referring to the terms of section 28D, including the exception made for 'the practice of the Court in fixing the basic wage', he said that 'the following propositions and their respective opposites' called for consideration by the Full Court:

(1) That no 'practice' has been established to meet the position that may possibly arise of the country being unable to continue the equivalent of the *Harvester* wage as the basic wage in industry generally and of the country being thereby compelled to adopt a lower basic wage.

(2) That no 'practice' has been established to meet the position when an essential industry such as the pastoral industry is unable to continue the *Harvester* wage equivalent as the basic wage.

(3) That the Court has established a 'practice' of 'fixing' a 'basic wage' in the pastoral industry, which basic wage is the *Harvester* equivalent, and therefore the Court is prevented by the proviso to section 25D from allowing that practice to be affected by the economic effect of the award.

(4) That the allowance of the 'Powers' 3s' is not part of the 'practice' within the proviso. (I acted on this opinion in the

Fruit-growers case,[4] but it is desirable that the Full Court should consider the point.)

(5) That adjusting the basic wage to fluctuations in the cost of living on the 'food, groceries, and rent' index figures *only* may not be part of the 'practice' within the proviso.

Although the repeal of section 28D rendered irrelevant the issues as to the meaning of the Court's 'practice', this set of propositions was a signal of Dethridge's preparedness to entertain a reconsideration of much of the Court's approach to the setting of the basic wage.

The award prescribed piece rates for shearers. In 1927, when he made the award, Dethridge set the rate by reference to an underlying wage which excluded Powers' 3s but included a margin that was automatically adjusted for price movements from 1911. He now reverted to the 1911 margin of 9s, but restored Powers' 3s, the net effect being a wage reduction. He reduced the piecework allowance from 20 per cent to 10 per cent, raised the average tally from 440 sheep to 480 and reduced allowances for lost time and fares.[5] Although I cannot identify a precise amount, the total of these reductions was clearly considerable. The piece rate for crutching was reduced by 20 per cent.

The Full Court (Dethridge, Beeby, and Drake-Brockman) was convened in August 1930 to deal with applications by Railways Commissioners of New South Wales, Victoria, South Australia, and Tasmania for award variations affecting the computation of the basic wage and the standard hours of some employees. Recent amendments to the Act, however, provided for the appointment of Conciliation Committees and limited the power of the Court (see Chapter 8, Section 8.1). Conciliation Committees had been appointed for the railways. In the Arbitration Court's view, it could not deal with the Railways Commissioners' applications. The Commissioners responded, in September 1930, by applying for the awards to be set aside. On 4 October, the

---

[4] See Chapter 7, Subsection 7.1.2.
[5] Dethridge explained the increase in the tally by reference to the improvements in equipment since it was originally set. Hitherto, the shearers had been allowed the benefit of these improvements, but it was now necessary to be more rigorous.

Full Court held that its power to set aside was not rescinded by the amendment to the Act (29 CAR 464). It agreed to set aside the awards 'except so far as they prescribe the basic wage, except so far as they prescribe standard hours of work and except so far as they abrogate other awards of this Court' (p. 470).

The decision was a response to a perceived emergency. Dethridge said:

> Indisputably the financial position of all the railways in question is extremely bad—in some of the States disastrous. Putting aside that portion of the operations which admittedly must be attended with a deficit even with normal business, the remainder shows a tremendous and increasing deficit. In view of the irrefutable evidence showing the enormous reduction of the income of Australia, due to the fall of all prices of our exports and to the cessation of borrowing—a reduction the effect of which upon industry in general the Court would be fatuous to disregard—that deficit on railway operations will still further increase in the future unless the commissioners are free to make such economies in running costs as are commensurate with the economies and sacrifices which the community in general will have to bear by way of taxation or otherwise. (p. 469)

Beeby was equally forthright:

> The next twelve months clearly will be the most critical year in the history of the Commonwealth. An emergency has arisen which calls for immediate readjustments in all directions; readjustments of costs of government, costs of production, costs of living and of profits and other returns to capital. But foremost is restoration of some measure of stability of public finance and reduction of the alarming losses on railway operations. We are not passing through a customary cycle of depression. The sudden and persisting decline of national income, plus the ever-increasing commitments for interest payments on loans, make our difficulties much greater than those of other countries whose prosperity does not depend, as ours does, on prices received for exported raw materials. For the next twelve months, at least, both Federal and State Governments will be forced to seek emergency devices in adapting affairs to new conditions. Under such circumstances, I think this Court

for twelve months should vacate its industrial control of State railways, leaving each State to adjust railway finances according to the will of its legislature. ... Except as to the basic wage and hours of employment, the application should be granted. The basic wage affects all industry, and should not be altered except after an inquiry at which parties other than railways commissioners if they so desire can be represented. Similarly, hours of employment fixed by this Court ... should not be disturbed without general inquiry. (pp. 472–473)

Dethridge thought that 'each of the four States concerned in these proceedings is faced with a grave financial crisis, and that there is, in fact, a grave danger of the collapse of public credit with all its attendant evil consequences to the community' (p. 475).

The railways matters were again before the Full Court in October 1930. Speaking for the Court, Dethridge said that the Conciliation Committees had stated cases for the opinion of the Court 'as to what, if any, alteration in the basic wage prescribed by the relevant awards or in the principles of computing the basic wage should be made having regard to the applications for variations thereof' (29 CAR 487, 488). Applications as to the basic wage had also been made in other industries. As no Conciliation Committees had been appointed in these industries, the Court retained jurisdiction. 'The Court has intimated', said Dethridge, 'that it invites all organisations or associations of employers or employees who might be interested to take part in the hearing of the question as to whether any alteration in the basic wage such as is applied for should be made, and that it will begin the hearing on 20th October, 1930.'

The times did not lend themselves to advances in non-wage terms of employment. There were few serious applications for them and correspondingly few decisions.

As we saw in Chapter 7, the initial willingness of the Court (in practice, of Dethridge) to extend the decision in the *Main Hours* case of 1927 by awarding the 44-hour week in industries which made similar demands of employees gradually gave way to a sense that deteriorating economic conditions necessitated restraint. In respect of leave, there was no counterpart of the *Main Hours* case. Whereas the Act effectively confined arbitration about standard hours to the Full Court, it left disputes about leave to single members. During the Higgins and Powers periods, the Court had generally granted paid public holidays (8 to 10 per year) or additional pay in lieu. It did not regard annual leave as a normal benefit, but might grant it if special characteristics of the work merited the additional rest. In some instances—typically in white-collar employment—employers consented to shorter hours and periods of leave and the Court either certified agreements or awarded accordingly. For example, agreements in force early in 1930 between the Municipal Officers' Association and the Cities of Brisbane and Melbourne provided for a 38-hour week (worked over 5½ days); 12 days paid annual leave; and leave between Christmas and New Year (29 CAR 9). The difference between the conditions of white-collar and blue-collar workers was recognised by Beeby in his *Metal Trades* decision of December 1929, discussed above.

In May 1930, the Full Court (Dethridge, Lukin, and Beeby) gave a decision about the working week in New South Wales tramways (*Tramway Workers'* case 29 CAR 158). The Commissioners had previously agreed to a 44-hour week, consistent with State government policy; but as there had been a change of government and of policy, they now sought an award provision of 48 hours.[6] Dethridge left undecided the question whether the nature of the work in question met the criteria for a 44-hour week, but said that 'even in the most arduous occupations' the introduction or continuance of the shorter week was 'dependent upon the capacity of the industry in question to maintain itself without decrease caused by the shorter working week'. In this case, he continued,

> the fall of the income of the people as a whole of New South Wales overclouds all aspects other than that of the employees' health. That fall is reflected in the immense loss now occurring in the operation of the transport industry comprising both railways and tramways. … This Court cannot ignore the financial position of the people as a

---

[6] There was some uncertainty as to whether they needed to do so.

whole of New South Wales who are the real employers here—the real persons carrying on the transport industry now in question whatever intermediate managing Commissioners or Boards may be created. (pp. 161–162)

Lukin said that the condition of the industry was not the major consideration. Rather, 48 hours were an appropriate standard, and should apply unless there were 'special or exceptional circumstances' that justified something different (pp. 166–167).[7] Beeby expressed 'no opinion as to what standard hours of the industry should be in any State in normal times', but agreed to the employer's application 'only because I believe that for the time being it is necessary in the public interest and in the interests of the employees involved' (p. 170). The Court's decision to grant the Commissioners' application accorded with its perception of mounting economic problems, affecting in this case the state of public finances.

9.2 THE TEN PER CENT CUT

The Basic Wage and Wage Reduction Inquiry of 1930–31 was among the most important in the history of federal arbitration. I deal with it in some detail. Readers who are interested only in the outcome of the case should proceed to Subsection 9.2.9.

9.2.1 The employers' claim

After a preliminary hearing on 6 October, the Court excluded counsel.[8] The full hearing began on 20 October and continued, with little interruption, until 15 January 1931.[9] The Railways Commissioners apparently saw themselves as the principal applicants and this view seems to have been accepted by other

---

[7] This was Lukin's last significant case in the Court.
[8] R G Menzies KC with Stanley Lewis sought to represent 'the employers generally—Railways Commissioners and others'. The unions successfully objected. When the Attorney-General exercised his right to intervene, he was represented by a barrister. Otherwise, the case was conducted by lay advocates.
[9] The Court repeatedly rejected union applications for adjournment or granted brief adjournments when the unions sought much longer periods to prepare their presentations.

employers, who wished to ensure that any gains made by the railways would extend more generally. At the outset, the Commissioners, through P J Carolan, of the Victorian Railways, defined their objective:

> As already outlined, the railways, generally, are asking for the deletion of the Powers' 3s, and for the basic wage to be ascertained from time to time by taking the *Harvester* 7s and ascertaining the equivalent of that 7s, by taking into consideration the cost of food, groceries, housing—4 and 5 rooms only—clothing and miscellaneous, instead of food, groceries, and housing, all houses. The Court has, up to the present, used the latter table, namely, food, groceries and housing, with the weighted average of the six capitals, equalling 1000, in 1911, as the base. The 'All Items' table, on which the Court is asked to act, conforms in principle with the recommendations of the Royal Commission on the basic wage in 1920, with modifications adopted by the Commonwealth Statistician. … All that the railways are asking for, it is claimed, is what they are entitled to, on a proper calculation of the basic wage, apart from any consideration of finance; but the alarming state of their finances, as already emphasised, has made their position so desperate that they cannot, at the present time, afford to be generous, and they feel that they must now claim that wages should be adjusted on a correct basis, and not on the unnecessarily generous basis which has been in vogue for some years past. (transcript, pp. 62–63)

The Court, during the rest of the hearing, made it very plain that it did not wish the issue before it to be defined in these terms. So defining it invited the unions to dispute the validity of the 'All Items' table and to contest the assumption that the real basic wage of 1907 had been more than maintained. This was an invitation that they willingly accepted. The Court, however, wished to disregard these issues and to focus the attention of the parties on the question whether the current economic circumstances necessitated a reduction of wages.

Carolan told the Court that he wished to have as witnesses C H Wickens, the Commonwealth Statistician, and D B Copland. 'Those two gentlemen', he suggested, 'should be called by the Court because they are in a position where it is thought it would be best for the Court to call them.' The Court, without further discussion, agreed (p. 78).

9.2.2 Wickens' evidence

Wickens was called on the same day. Asked by Carolan about the relative merits of the price index for food, groceries and rent and the 'All Items' index, Wickens said that, 'if you can get each of them equally reliable ... the wider your sample the better your result is going to be'. He 'would say that we have good figures for all the items we are collecting at the present time'. Two of the union advocates—T C Maher (Railway Professional Officers) and H C Gibson (Federated Carters and Drivers)—had been members of the basic wage Royal Commission of 1919–20 and had joined in a recommendation that led the Statistician's Office—somewhat against its will—to produce the All Items (or C series) index. The position now was that adoption of the All Items index would reduce the basic wage by about 5 shillings. Hence while the employers advocated that step, the unions sought to discredit the 'All Items' index, arguing also that even the 'All Houses' series index was too low. The principal complaint against the C series index was that some of the items were not, in fact, repriced each quarter or, indeed, at all; they remained in the index at the prices found by the Piddington Commission. Some of the items were now dearer than they had been a decade earlier, but were in the index at an unchanged price. The following exchanges occurred during Gibson's cross-examination of Wickens:

> Mr Gibson: At the adjournment last night, we were dealing with smoking requisites, under the heading of miscellaneous. Has that 2s per week allowance been adjusted? --- No.
>
> It still remains, in your calculations, at 2s? --- Yes, my recollection is that there has been no variation.
>
> ...

Charles Wickens

The next item is 2s 6d per week allowance for fares? --- Those miscellaneous items have been allowed in all cases.

Does that item still stand at 2s 6d? --- As far as I can recollect, yes, but I will confirm it and let you know later.

…

Do you not think that that item in respect of fares should be increased by at least 75 per cent … I am paying over 100 per cent more, and walking twice as far.

Beeby J: I take it that you are not challenging the original fixation; what you are saying now is that it has been a stationary amount in the regimen, and has not been raised.

Mr Gibson: In regard to these miscellaneous items, I shall endeavour to prove to the Court subsequently that, with the exception of one small group, every item under miscellaneous has had a very strong upward tendency. ... The only ones so far as Mr Wickens has gone that have been adjusted are those which have come down.

Mr Wickens: Not because they have come down, but because they were the items which were available for statistical investigation.

Mr Gibson: With all due respect, here is the point. Take the item 'fares'. It might be called a small item. Let us take Melbourne. The applicants in this case will tell you that since 1920 the price of fares (suburban) paid by the workers has advanced on the average over 35 per cent. Tramway fares have advanced over 50 per cent. Take my own individual case. I am one of those unfortunates who live out in the suburbs [Malvern East]. In 1920, I could come from my home to the Trades Hall for 6d. Today, on a seasonal ticket, it costs me 1s. Therefore, in my individual case it has gone up 100 per cent.

...

Drake-Brockman J: The difficulty, as I understand it from Mr Wickens at present, is that certain of these items do not lend themselves to the collection of statistics by his department as at present organised.

Mr Gibson: Is that to be our funeral: because the department is not properly organised, have the workers to suffer? ... I say with all diffidence, as a member of the body that compiled this, it was a unanimous compilation ... and I respectfully submit that the methods by which it was arrived at are the methods by which it can be adjusted—every item of it; because, there is not one single item which was arrived at by guesswork.

Mr Gibson: I take it that school requisites were treated likewise? --- Exactly.

That is, they still stand in your compilation at the original 3d? --- Yes. (pp. 204–209)

A further criticism advanced by the unions applied to both the A and C series indices. Retailers who submitted returns to the Statistician were asked to provide the prices of the 'predominant' variety of the commodity in question. If incomes were falling (as a result, for example, of unemployment), consumers would substitute inferior and cheaper varieties and the character of the 'predominant' variety would change accordingly. Hence the indices were biased by treating changes in quality as changes in price. The advocate representing the gas employees, Charlie Crofts (also Secretary of the ACTU), raised this criticism with Wickens. 'That is a possibility, undoubtedly', said Wickens. Crofts asked: 'To what extent are you able to say that might affect the result, so that the lower index figure not only represents greater cheapness but also represents a lowering of quality?' Wickens replied: 'I am afraid that our method does not admit of such refinement.' Crofts persisted: 'And can you say whether it would be substantial or insubstantial?' 'I am afraid', said Wickens, 'that nothing of a satisfactory nature could be given in reply to that' (p. 157). In his final address, Crofts claimed that if real wages were reduced directly by the Court's decision, there would be a further indirect reduction by reason of the downward bias of the price index, as workers and their families substituted lower for higher quality items. Dethridge acknowledged the point:

> I have heard no answer to that suggestion as yet, and I do not think that Mr Wickens could give an answer to it. The Court has to recognise that may be the result. I asked Mr Wickens if he could indicate the amount of that effect, but he could not. It seems logical that that will be the case, and assuming a cut in the wages is made, there will be some further reduction in the standard of the workers owing to the manner in which the index figures are compiled. (p. 2164)

In the course of Maher's cross-examination, Wickens said:

> I would say that I do not think that any index number should be used absolutely in fixing a wage. It is something which should inform those that have the fixing, but should not be used simply as an item to determine what the wage should be. I do not want to find fault with what the Court has done in the past; that is my own opinion. (p. 104)

The criticisms made of the price indices, and especially the All Items index, could only reinforce the Court's wish to shift the emphasis of the case from the formula proposed by Carolan (and supported by other employers) to the state of the economy. At the end of Wickens' evidence, Dethridge addressed Carolan:

> Mr Gibson suggests, in effect, that the All Items index number table should not be used. He says first of all that it is unreliable, and secondly that it is unfair in its results, and, therefore, that your suggestion that it should be adopted as a basis for the present proposed reduction of wages is unfair. That is the way he puts it, and I suppose you have to meet that. The position you are in is this: you say that your application is limited to an adjustment, so as to give the present day real equivalent of the *Harvester* wage, and you say that that adjustment which you ask for is to be made by first of all deleting the Powers' 3s, and secondly by using the All Items index figure. Then Mr Gibson says that would not be right, because the All Items table is fundamentally wrong. That is the way he puts it. Mind you, it is just as well to meet that situation, because you have narrowed your application, it may be, in such a way as to limit us to that kind of material, and prevent us from dealing with the really more vital aspect of things, to which I have referred once or twice. I do not say that is so, but it may be. The more vital aspect—let us face it—is that the country cannot afford to pay as a basic wage that which it has been paying for the last few years. That is the fundamental question … the country can no longer afford to pay the *Harvester* wage at the amount at which it has been assessed in recent years. Of course, it may be that your application is so framed as to prevent us going outside a mere matter of adjustment of the *Harvester* wage, and prevent us from dealing with the underlying conditions. (p. 234)

As the case proceeded, the Court seems to have overcome any doubts about its capacity to disregard the employers' formula and to substitute the issue of economic capacity. A factor which made this transition easier was the fact that the employers' formula would cause a reduction of about 10 per cent in the basic wage. The Court—supported by Copland's evidence—was able to shift the focus from the formula to the outcome. The Judges, especially Dethridge, repeatedly hypothesised about a reduction of 10 per cent and challenged the parties to confront the economic case for such a reduction.

They also made it clear that a reduction could not exceed 10 per cent because that would go beyond the limit of the employers' claim.

Wickens was asked about various other matters. Among then was the possibility of adjusting the money supply so as to counteract the fall in prices. That would be done, he suggested,

> by the use of something in the nature of the index numbers, as indicating the trend downward of prices, and not only those index numbers, but all other index numbers, as indicating that you are experiencing a fall in prices which is much too rapid for the general good of the community. It might be possible to devise a scheme by which you would issue notes when you saw your prices were rushing down too rapidly, and not only check the issue of notes but also cancel the notes when you found the reverse position, that is, when prices were coming up. But it would need very careful handling. It is a matter which is not new. It has been put up by leading writers, including J Maynard Keynes. He strongly urged it in 1925. (pp. 161–162)

This was a proposal that would later be argued by union witnesses, supporting their contention that no wage reduction was necessary to deal with the crisis.

Wickens lent his support to the view that Australia in the 1920s had lived beyond its means:

> There was an unduly lavish expenditure. … An eminent Australian economist, Professor Giblin, at the Perth meeting of the Australasian Association gave a public address in which he indicated that at the time there was evidence that we were treading that primrose path that leads to the everlasting bonfire. He was dealing very largely with the expenditure on motor cars and the tendency there was in Australia for unduly lavish expenditure. That was as far back as 1926. (p. 228)

Beeby commented: 'Two years ago I was a super-optimist; but I am trying to find out what has really happened during the last two years and what is going to be the effect of it on the future.' Wickens responded: 'I think your Honour is not alone in that matter' (p. 229).

On 12 November 1930, the Court responded to a union application for the Commonwealth Statistician to be asked to inquire into a variety of matters. The Court thought that the material already provided to the parties by the Statistician was sufficient:

> The suggestion that he should embark upon the extensive further inquiries specified ignores the nature of the applications now before the Court. Those applications are said by the applicants to be made for the purpose of meeting what they allege is the gravest economic emergency in the history of the Commonwealth. They specifically raise the issue that the recent decline in the national income, and the reduction of the spending power of the community, arising from the sudden cessation of loan credits, makes an immediate reduction of the basic wage imperative. That is the main issue raised by the applicants; and it is the only issue which the Court proposes, at present, to hear and determine. (*Basic Wage and Wage Reduction Inquiry* 30 CAR 2, 4)

It is likely that the Court saw the union application as a delaying tactic, and that this perception was accurate.

9.2.3 Copland's evidence

Copland gave evidence on the third day of the hearing.[10] He was concerned to be seen as independent:

> I was approached to give evidence. It was explained to me that I was not to give evidence for either party, but that my evidence would be independent. I was agreeable to give evidence because I had written and said so much about the problem of the basic wage and about the question involved in the economic readjustment. Therefore I felt under an obligation to come here to give evidence, if I was wanted and if I could be of any use to the Court. I am not here for either party. No one has suggested to me what I should say. My statement was prepared independently entirely of anyone else. (pp. 258–259)

---

[10] Copland's statement was based on an article which he had recently sent to *The Economic Journal* and was published in December 1930 (Copland 1930). The statement of evidence is printed in Shann and Copland (1931).

From the outset, the unions made clear their suspicions of Copland and his professed independence:

> Mr Crofts: From the Unions' point of view, I do not know that we would call this witness.
>
> Dethridge C J: I have made it clear that the Professor is a witness of the Court, whose evidence may be used by either side. He is not your witness, but you may use whatever evidence he gives that you wish.
>
> Mr Crofts: I do not know that the Court should call Professor Copland as a witness.
>
> Dethridge C J: If no such witness as he or Mr Wickens had been called, the Court would certainly have to consider calling such witnesses for its own benefit.

Crofts noted that Copland had given a copy of his statement in advance to the employers, but not to the unions. Dethridge told him that if the unions required an adjournment before cross-examining Copland, it would be granted. That is what happened. In the closing stage of the case, Crofts attempted to portray Copland as a biased witness. Among his grounds were Copland's association with E C Dyason and the support given by business to the Faculty of Commerce at Melbourne University, which Copland had founded.

Copland began by identifying problems in the pre-Depression economy. Three of these were of particular importance:

- There was a potential problem in the obligations to the rest of the world caused by the accumulated foreign debt. Copland identified a 'transfer problem'[11] amounting to £4 10s per head—more than in any other country except New Zealand. 'It was the magnitude of this transfer problem', he said, 'that caused concern to competent observers of the economic condition of Australia even in the days of prosperity' (Shann and Copland 1931, p. 91).

---

[11] A term much used in the 1920s in relation to Germany's reparations payments.

Douglas Copland

- Australian prices were misaligned with those of the rest of the world:

    In 1928, British prices as measured by the Board of Trade index number were about 33 per cent above pre-war levels, while Australian were 65 per cent up. While these figures cannot be taken as an accurate measure of the disparity in price movements in Australia and overseas, there is no doubt that the Australian price level was sustained at a high figure, while overseas prices were either falling or stable at a lower level. Two main causes account for this disparity. First, the overseas borrowing increased spending power and the volume of bank credits, and, secondly, the high prices for Australian exports were reflected in high internal prices. The tariff was, of course, a contributing factor in keeping up the prices of manufactured and sheltered goods, but in the absence of the other two main causes the tariff could not have sustained high prices without forcing a contraction of export production and a decline in real wages. (Shann and Copland 1931, pp. 92–93)

The notion that prices in Australia were too high carried the implicit assumption of fixed exchange rates, such as were associated with the gold standard.

- Labour costs were too high:

    The general level of wages was rising. In 1922, there was added to the basic wage what came to be known as the Powers' 3s. This was intended to compensate for the losses incurred by wage earners on account of the rise in the cost of living and the lag in the adjustment of wages, but it was continued after the reason for it had disappeared. Owing to the increase in the number of workers brought within the ambit of arbitration and wage fixing tribunals, including many engaged in state instrumentalities, the basic wage was applied to a larger number of workers. The adjustments in the basic wage have been made on the basis of an index number of retail prices of food and house rents, estimated to cover about 60 per cent of household expenditure. This index number has not fallen to the same extent as a more complex index number, including clothing and other household expenditure. Had the basic wage been adjusted according to movements in the more complex index number, 'the *Harvester* equivalent' … could have been observed with a basic wage 6 per cent less than has been fixed. The steady upward trend of unemployment must be regarded as indication of the development of wage rates somewhat above the capacity of industry. The average unemployment for the years 1922–1929 was 10 per cent with a rising tendency. If unemployment is ignored real wages were 8 per cent higher in 1929 than in 1911, but when allowance is made for the incidence of unemployment the real wage was barely 1 per cent higher. (Shann and Copland 1931, pp. 93–94)

These problems would have required 'very small' economic adjustments: 'A minor alteration in the basic wage, perhaps, a progressive reduction of overseas borrowing over a series of years and an increase in taxation to balance the budgets, in my opinion, would have met the situation' (transcript, p. 270a).

But the position had been transformed by the collapse of export prices which began in mid-1929. Copland's diagnosis and prescription were summarised thus:

> Export industries have sustained a severe reduction in spending power and so have industries that were supplying goods and services to those whose incomes were formerly paid direct from overseas loans. The reduced spending power in these industries has seriously affected all other Australian industries and has caused indirect or secondary losses of national income. These secondary losses are due to the present inequitable distribution of the first loss. It is beyond the scope of this statement to consider in detail all the problems involved in securing the equitable distribution of the first loss. But this distribution is a prerequisite of economic recovery. An essential condition is the spreading of the burden over all wage and salary earners. The first loss of income is at least 10 per cent and it follows that a reduction in wages and salaries of 10 per cent is required to secure its equitable distribution. ... The reduction in wages would promote an equitable distribution of the first loss and would lower costs of production through the whole field of industry. Lowering costs would bring some relief to export industries and to industries competing with imports. Moreover, costs of production in all sheltered industries would also be reduced and the fall in prices would be met by some expansion of demand for the products of sheltered and protected industries. ... As industry expanded, the secondary losses of national income would be made good and the total loss reduced to the amount of the first loss. ... Equilibrium would then be restored at a reduced income per head, but with the loss of income evenly spread throughout the community. (Shann and Copland 1931, pp. 100–102)

Dethridge asked Copland whether he had attempted to assess the secondary loss. He had not—this would be 'quite an impossible thing to get at. You can only take the indications of growing unemployment, reduced profits in industry and things like that, as a rough indication that it is going on' (transcript, pp. 273–274).

Copland told the Court that he favoured a 20 per cent depreciation of the exchange rate. When Dethridge asked whether 'any economist of the comparatively few we have in Australia' had considered the question of exchange rate parity, Copland said that the only one of his colleagues who disagreed with his prescription of a 20 per cent devaluation was Professor Melville of the University of Adelaide. 'If I am pessimistic', said Copland, 'I do not know what he is. What I have suggested [the 20 per cent devaluation] is rather in the line of an encouragement to a quick way out, which he does not agree with' (p. 279).[12]

Drake-Brockman sought to summarise Copland's recommendation to the Court: 'As I understand the Professor, what he has said is this: there is a necessity for a 10 per cent reduction in the basic wage; that a convenient way of arriving at that is to accept the Statistician's index figures, which take into account all items, and to get rid of the Powers' 3s, and that roughly is 10 per cent.' Copland accepted this summary: 'Yes. … What I said, in effect, was that the equivalent of the 7s of the *Harvester* judgment could be obtained today by taking the complete index number, minus the Powers' 3s. That is really the whole basis of my statement' (p. 282).

In his initial cross-examination, Crofts asked Copland whether he was putting it to the Court that all of the unemployed would be absorbed if wages were reduced by 10 per cent. Copland answered: 'That is only the beginning; and you have to consider that aspect in combination with other policies that I have enunciated in other directions' (p. 285).

Copland was recalled on 1 December. The barrister representing the Attorney-General, A M Fraser asked questions going to the 'fairness' of imposing a 10 per cent reduction on wage-earners. Copland answered that wage-earners would be bearing 'their due proportion … if everybody shares

---

[12] An advocate from South Australia, K H Boykett, interjected: 'Professor Melville suggested a drop of 15 per cent at least in wages'.

a loss of 10 per cent in income, it is [fair]'. Fraser put it to Copland that it was necessary to inquire whether a wage reduced by 10 per cent would be 'sufficient for their ordinary and reasonable needs'. 'I am afraid', said Copland, 'that their ordinary and reasonable needs have to be considered in relation to the size of the national income' (pp. 801–802).

Gibson asked whether a 10 per cent reduction would automatically reduce the nation's purchasing power. Copland replied:

> I do not think so. The purchasing power or spending power of the nation is determined by the size of the national income, and the greater the national income the greater the spending power. Of course if you reduce a certain section of the community by 10 per cent you will cause a certain shock to the spending power in that direction, but that will release spending power elsewhere, because it will make production more profitable, which will eventually increase the national dividend and will eventually increase spending. (p. 812)

This answer accorded with Dethridge's understanding of 'spending power'. The following exchange ensued:

> Dethridge C J: ... Is not this the position: The wage is cut by 10 per cent or from 83s to, say, 75s, so that the basic wage earner and everyone who is in employment has 8s less to spend, but the man who would have to pay that 8s if there had been no reduction, that is the employer, has 8s more to spend. The fund from which the wage earner and the wage payer draw the money is, say, 100s. The wage payer instead of drawing only 17s, as he does at present, from the 100s draws 25s, but what does he do with that? He spends it. I grant you that he may not spend it in what may be called the consumption of goods. I suppose that you are quite familiar with the Hobson theory? --- Yes.

> Dethridge C J: The way in which it is spent may have a material effect upon the advantages to and the welfare of the country, but the spending power of the community is the same, and it is unaffected by the reduction of wages.

Mr Gibson: At present I am trying to cross-examine the Professor, but I would like the opportunity to cross-examine your Honour on the subject.

Dethridge C J: I want to be educated as we go along. I want to have this point cleared up as it has been referred to over and over again particularly by Mr Crofts, but not only by Mr Crofts. I may say frankly that I have tried to read everything lately which has been published by both sides, and I saw that it was stated definitely on the question of this reduction of wages that instead of reducing the basic wage it should be put up …

Mr Crofts: That is what they did in America.

Dethridge C J: At present, I am mentioning the arguments which have been put forward, that instead of reducing the basic wage it should be put up, and thereby increasing the spending power of the community. That is the argument, but I cannot see how the spending power of the community would be increased. The spending power of the worker who is lucky enough to retain his employment would be increased, but I cannot see how [that] can be applied to the community. However, I appreciate the force of the Hobson argument, and there may be something in that.

…

Mr Gibson: I will take his Honour's suggestion … that if the worker gets 10 per cent less the 10 per cent is in the hands of the employer and he necessarily spends it? --- [Professor Copland] Yes, I adopt that. Spending may mean the direct purchase of goods, or it may mean putting the money into the bank, increasing his deposits and making credit available to someone else for capital expenditure, and so on.

…

Do I get it from you, then, that money saved immediately goes into circulation? --- Yes, always.

If that is so, why the present depression? --- Because it may be that there is a maladjustment in the amount of spending by one nation and another. Saving is only spending in another form.

> Is not the present depression in the final analysis due to the fact that people are not spending? --- If you like to put it that way, yes, but they have not anything to spend. You have to go behind that. ... The reduction in the wages fund comes because the national income has fallen. The spending power has already declined, and 20 per cent of the workers have no income at all. The maintenance of the wage rate does not increase the spending power of the working classes if that wage is an uneconomic rate. (pp. 812–814)

Gibson asked Copland: 'Does not the circulation of the workers' income supply that prosperity that we so much desire?' Copland replied: 'No. What supplies the prosperity we desire is, fundamentally, the amount of the national income we ... produce' (p. 823).

In addition to pressing Copland on the matter of wages and purchasing power, with little apparent success, the unions put the argument that the Depression was being exacerbated by the deflation of prices. This, indeed, was a recurrent issue throughout the case and there was little or no disagreement that falling prices reduced demand because people deferred expenditure so as to buy at lower future prices. There was less agreement that wages were a price that should not fall. Gibson raised the issue with Copland:

> Is it not rather by reason of the instability of prices that the nation's circulation of money has become temporarily choked up? --- I think so. I explained in my evidence that the faults due to Australia's economic policy accounted for some part of the present trouble, and the faults due to overseas export prices were generally greater.
>
> No one buys on a falling market if they can possibly help it? --- No.
>
> Except for absolute necessities? --- Yes.
>
> If that is so, is not the first necessity to stop falling markets? --- You might do that in any one of a number of ways.
>
> Will the 10 per cent cut in the basic wage have a tendency in that direction? --- The 10 per cent cut in the basic wage will compensate

> people who have been affected by the falling market, and it will help them to meet the costs of the falling market. (pp. 814–815)

Copland's answer seems not to have confronted the question; but evidently he was putting the view that keeping wages high was the wrong way to resist deflation, because it would distort the relative price of labour. It was part of his 'scheme' that deflation should be checked by monetary policy and by depreciating the exchange rate. Relatively higher wages would be tenable if the general price level were buttressed by broader economic policy.

The unions also sought unsuccessfully to get Copland's assent to the argument that a wage reduction should be enforced only if there were a comprehensive set of anti-depression measures, such as Copland advocated. Copland's set of measures included, as well as lowering real wages, balanced budgets, reducing interest rates, depreciation of the exchange rate, and greater availability of bank credit. But he refused to say that the items in the mixture were inseparable.

> Mr Crofts: Would it not be reasonably fair that we should have an inquiry into the whole of your suggestions before anything is done in any one direction? --- Things ought to be done simultaneously.
>
> Dethridge C J: What things? --- The general scheme I have put up from time to time.
>
> But Mr Crofts, I think, is directing his question to another issue.
>
> Mr Crofts: No. The Professor agrees that there should be an inquiry into every aspect of Australian industry? --- No. There is no need for an inquiry. The duty of the country is plain, and it should be done.
>
> …
>
> Mr Crofts: The Professor says there is no necessity for an inquiry, but that they should all happen at the same time.
>
> Dethridge C J: And the authorities who can bring that about should act at the same time as any wage regulation.

Mr Crofts: And nobody should interfere with one part of the scheme without the other bodies doing the same thing? --- Each body has to do its duty.

And you suggest that they should all do it at the same time? --- It would be better if they did. ... In order to clear up the matter I may say that in this *Economic Record*, which is just coming off the press now, you will find the second article, at p. 170, which represents my considered views on the whole position.

...

It might even be dangerous to reduce wages without the other correction you suggested? --- No, I do not think so. (pp. 880–881)

Crofts also challenged Copland to predict the improvement in economic conditions that would occur if his proposals were adopted:

Mr Crofts: I think it is a fair inference to draw that the Professor is advocating a low rate of wages to bring down the cost of production? --- I am advocating the wages which I think the country can afford to pay.

...

Dethridge C J: [Professor Copland] says that there has been that loss, and it has to be borne equally, or as nearly equally as it can be. The employers have suffered, and the unemployed have suffered. Indeed they have suffered more than their share of the loss and the professor says that it is necessary to take from them their undue share of the burden, and spread it among those employees who are at work.

Mr Crofts: And he wants to reduce wages in an attempt to allow the employers to spend more money in the endeavour to employ the unemployed.

Dethridge C J: That is one aspect.

Mr Crofts: I suggest to the Court that if that opinion is expressed there might be something behind it, particularly if it is the opinion of a professor of economics. I say he should be able to inform this Court as to the length of time it will take, if the workers of this country give up

10 per cent of their spending power, to reemploy their comrades. … (To witness): Have you given that matter serious consideration? When can we go to our workers and say 'If you accept a reduction of 10 per cent, all your comrades who are out of employment will be employed within a certain time'? I want to know what time? --- I am not a prophet.

But you have come here, and you have made yourself a prophet. You say in effect 'Do this thing, and something will happen.' Tell us what will happen? --- … My answer is this: If you do this thing—that is reduce wages, and the other things I have suggested—that is balance budgets, and adopt the money and banking policy, I think you will get an immediate alleviation of unemployment.

To what extent? --- It is very difficult to say.

You are advocating that there should be a reduction in wages, but you think something else might happen. I want to go to the workers and tell them what you have said? --- I hope you will tell them truthfully.

I shall read to them what you have said; I shall not rely on my memory? --- I would hazard a guess—and it can only be an intelligent guess—that it will take 18 months to get the unemployed figures down to the average of what they have been since the War.

What has that average been? --- A little under 10 per cent. There is going to be no easy way out. It is going to be a long and arduous job. The sooner these steps are taken the sooner we will get out of our difficulties.

First you advocate a 10 per cent reduction in wages, and then you say perhaps something might happen, but only to the extent that we are going back to a period of 10 per cent unemployment; is that normal? --- No; I say that it will be reduced.

What will bring about a reduction of the other 10 per cent? --- The steady improvement in business conditions, and efficiency in production.

Not a lowering in wages? --- I hope not.

Assume that we get a reduction of something like £30 million in the spending power of the people as a result of this application being granted in full? --- That is a wrong assumption. The spending power of the people is determined by the national income. The mere reduction of 10 per cent in the wages of those employed does not reduce the spending power of the people; it reduces the spending power of those whose wages have been reduced.

...

What would you call a normal percentage of unemployed? --- The lowest percentage of unemployed in Australian history is 4.7; that was in 1911. The average for the period before the War was about 5.9. I should say you would be very fortunate if you get it down to an average of 6½ per cent under existing conditions of the rapid changes in industry. (pp. 896–898)

Crofts subsequently stood aside to allow Gordon Massey to cross-examine Copland. Massey was a salaried officer of the Victorian Railways (and a Councillor of the Australian Railways' Union) who apparently had some acquaintance with economics.[13] He was exceedingly respectful to Copland, but conducted a lengthy and at times tortuous cross-examination.

Massey began by alluding to the view of Dethridge that 'spending power' was synonymous with the national income. The unions, he said, regarded the 10 per cent cut in real wages as unreasonable 'and further that from a national viewpoint it is unsound inasmuch as the reduction of wages reduced the spending power of the people, and consequently further reduce the national dividend'. He continued:

---

[13] In 1930 Massey published a pamphlet entitled *The Last Shilling: Australia's Destiny and Australian Money*. The thrust of it was that the imported economic problems were being needlessly worsened by the behaviour of the monetary system. Copland wrote an Introduction (dated 27 October), but indicated, both in the Introduction and in his evidence, that he disagreed with some of the contents. Massey told the Court that the unions had not decided to ask him to cross-examine Copland until some time after Copland had made his statement and that he had received the statement only five days earlier (p. 964). Early in 1931, he published a series of articles in *The Railways' Union Gazette*, including one of 10 February entitled 'The Arbitration Outrage'. (I thank Trevor Dobbyn, Victorian State Secretary of the Rail, Tram and Bus Union, for sending me copies.) I have not found any biographical information about Massey.

> Let us consider the latter—what His Honour the Chief Judge has defined as a very popular fallacy at the present moment. His Honour has expressed the fallacy in essence by saying that purchasing power depends upon the amount of marketable production, and not upon the amount of wages paid, that is to say that the total production is consequently divided and spent in various proportions among the worker, the entrepreneur, and the rentier. Therefore, though you may increase proportionate shares, you cannot make any one part larger if by doing so you make the parts greater than the whole. Therefore the total spending power remains constant for a given production, though its incidence may vary. That is a correct statement of the principle I take it?
>
> Dethridge C J: Substantially, but, in order to avoid any misunderstanding, I may say that when I put it in that precise form I am not ignoring the possibility of a division of the national income. If we take two divisions of the national income, it may be that by giving a greater share to the working classes in the one mode of the division than in the other mode of division, you do increase the real welfare of the community. I am not ignoring what Karl Marx pointed out many years ago in connection with that matter—that if you allow the entrepreneur or rentier class to take a large share that encourages luxury trades, and attracts capital to those luxury trades necessity trades [sic], [illegible] the working classes may be injured in that way. But that is a refinement which I have not bothered about.
>
> Massey: That is the substance of your statement?
>
> Dethridge: Yes. (pp. 947–948)

Massey prefaced a question to Copland by referring to 'the fallacy alluded to by his Honour—that is to say, that the spending power will remain constant for a given production, though its incidence may vary':

> I am referring to the distribution of the income. It may be all there, but a different class may spend it. It has occurred to me that there is some confusion of ideas in reference to the fallacy. Is not the incidence of trade due to the spending power of the workers; that is to say, if the

workers have to spend less they will spend less upon the things which it is desired they shall spend money upon? --- That is true. I am not proposing to suggest anything which will decrease the percentage share of the national income which goes to the workers. They will have the same proportionate influence in demand as they had before.

I take it that is so, but the effect of that upon the reduced spending power of the worker will be reflected in the trades in which the workers spend their money. For instance the present obvious reduction in real income is materially affecting trade and commerce? --- Yes.

And a reduction in the income of the workers, either in the form of unemployment, or in the form of a reduction in wages would have the same effect? --- No—not the same effect. The same immediate effect on the workers' spending, but it might mean quite a different ultimate effect if the reduction of real wages was one of the remedial measures required to reduce unemployment. (pp. 949–950)

Massey returned to the issue of whether a reduction of wages entailed a reduction of the national income:

Mr Massey: Is it obvious that if a proportionate share of the wage earners were varied, the incomes of those trading with wage earners would correspondingly vary, and that would affect the incidence of production? --- Certainly. If you altered the proportion of income going to wage earners that would alter the nature of the demand for goods and services, and would alter the nature of production.

In effect, that would introduce the unemployment factor? --- It would cause a disturbance in the period of adjustment and transition.

In effect, it would reduce the national dividend? --- No.

Not in terms of money? --- In terms of money—if it were accompanied by a fall in the price level it would reduce the income, but not in terms of real goods. ... I do not agree [that there would be a fall in real goods and services], except in the respect that there would be a short period of disturbance due to the alteration of the nature of the demand for production, in which there would probably be a reduction of national income.

…

Dethridge C J: That is to say that the working classes who were previously getting the money under the proposed decrease would cease to spend upon clothing and things of that kind, such as they are in the habit of buying? --- Yes.

The class which gets the money might delay for some little time spending it upon any other class of goods or services. It would be diverted to what we call luxuries or capital goods? --- That is what it comes down to.

Mr Massey: The point I am desirous of making is that it will have a deflationary effect and change the present stabilisation upon which trade, particularly retail trade, and many allied trades, are organised in Australia.

Dethridge C J: There is no doubt that there will be a disturbance, but it will be a transitory disturbance? --- You might get the same result with a great inflation where wages did not follow the price level. (pp. 952–953)

Copland argued that a 10 per cent reduction of real wages would not reduce the wage-earners' share of the national income, since there was a general fall of at least 10 per cent. There was, he implied, a choice between maintaining existing real wages but employing fewer workers or reducing the real wage and restoring the employment of workers who had been displaced by the fall in the aggregate level of spending. This issue generated the following exchange:

Dethridge C J: … The way I understand the Professor suggests [the fall in income] can be equalised is that we have to recognise that the wage earners as a class are already suffering at least a fall of 10 per cent in their income, the same as every section in the community have already suffered that loss. We have to spread that loss. We have to spread the workers' diminished share as well as we can. At present, it is being taken by employed wage earners, and by them only. The unemployed are getting practically no part of it. We have to spread that diminished share, and the only way in which we can do that is by giving something less to the employed workers, and giving a chance to the unemployed workers to get employment and to get their proportion of the diminished share which goes to the working classes.

Mr Crofts: That is not what the Professor says. He says that we should give the 10 per cent to the employer? --- No; I do not say that.

…

Dethridge C J: … Mr Crofts has suggested that this 10 per cent is to be taken away from the wage earners and given to the employers or the capitalists, if you like to so term them.

…

Mr Crofts: And the Professor agrees to that? --- That is not my proposition; I have never said that.

Dethridge C J: Without any corresponding benefit for the working classes—I understand that is what is attributed to the Professor? --- Yes, and that is quite wrong.

…

Mr Massey: The point I am endeavouring to make is that if the real wage is reduced it tends to become a permanent deflationary measure, perpetuating the deflation which has already taken place. Is that so? --- I do not think it is.

It is a reduction of real wages? --- It is a reduction of real wages, and it is a permanent one until the income recovers.

Then it becomes the perpetuation of the present deflation? --- No. If this Court calls me in three or four years' time and there is a recovery in the national income, I will be the first person to say that wages ought to be increased. (pp. 954–955)

Massey moved on to the threat of deflation, which was potentially the unions' strongest argument:

> Mr Massey: Any form of deflation has the effect of decreasing capital value, and with that decrease in capital values, as long as the deflation continues, the tendency is to prevent advances or credit from going out and there is a condition of arrested business or development? --- I think that is true.
>
> The effect of that would be to tend further to increase unemployment? --- If you had a period of rapidly falling price levels on Australia, that would be the effect.
>
> Has not that condition arisen today? --- I do not think so. Our price level has fallen about 10 per cent to 12 per cent all round in the last 12 months, and compared with England, the fall has been practically double there.
>
> Has not the rise in exchange rates had some retarding effect on the Australian price level? --- Yes.
>
> Had that not operated, that retardation would not have taken place and the price level would have gone still lower? --- Yes, I think so. (pp. 956–957)

Massey apparently thought that to avoid the ill-effects of deflation, it was necessary for wage reductions to be embedded in a comprehensive economic plan. In pursuing this point he was rather more subtle, and more effective, than Crofts had been:

> Mr Massey: You have made certain proposals in a general strategical plan evolved by yourself, Mr Dyason and Dr Gordon Wood? --- Yes.
>
> I think it can be said that it is a considered opinion from expert knowledge? --- We hope so.
>
> The plan is directed to bringing about the welfare of the people of Australia as a whole, not one section? --- That is so.

That is to say if sacrifices are involved they are not to be made for the benefit of one class by another? --- No.

They are entirely for the benefit of the nation? --- Yes.

I take it that the plan cannot be separated piecemeal, that any one portion can be picked out and another portion disregarded? --- I agree with that.

If that were done, the plan would not be effective? --- The plan would not be as effective as if it were done as a whole.

...

That is to say, all your evidence here has been keyed into your plan? --- I think that is true.

It is completely interlocked into it? --- I think so.

You presuppose the entire support and cooperation of all concerned? --- I urge it. I cannot presuppose it, because I am not getting it.

The point I am putting on this question is that as far as the wage reduction proposals are concerned, you have admitted that they are part of your general plan? --- Yes, but I believe that whatever is done real wages in this country will fall 10 per cent, whether it is done by legislative action now, by a decision of the Court or not, it will be done by the sheer force of economic law. (pp. 956–957)

Massey referred to the charge levelled against the banks of withholding credit and suggested that the banks were 'not in a position to extend credit in a falling market'. Copland replied that the banks 'have in fact extended credit very greatly' (p. 958). Though he assented to a significant degree to Massey's argument that the major present threat was deflation, he did not agree that this told against the case for a wage reduction:

There is also the factor of the less [sic] monetary value of assets, which is another point I wish to bring out. They are capital losses but, in effect, they will have to be paid out of income, and they are being paid back out of income? --- That is part of the difficulty of the deflation process, part of the difficulty you have been mentioning.

It is another feature. That money which is being paid back is also sterilised—it is not going into use? --- That is so.

That is further increasing unemployment? --- Yes. I think we can say that the deflation of the price level does cause real difficulties for a country.

The major decline in the national dividend is due to the cumulative effects of falling values? --- It is.

And it is correct to say that the loss in the national dividend due to deflation under the present condition of instability is many times greater than what we describe as being our loss from borrowing and our loss from wool sales? --- I would not say that. It has not reached that point yet. The loss from value and the falling value of exports amount to £70 millions, and I take it that you would not suggest that the loss of national income is many times greater than that. ... If you have a rapid fall in the price level, the immediate relief from a wage reduction would not be as great as if you reduced the wages without a rapid fall in price levels. ... In my opinion, a wage reduction has to be made. If you can make a wage reduction, and put the other part of the plan into operation at the same time, you will achieve a better result than if you make the wage reduction without doing that. (p. 959)

Copland said that the primary producer would benefit from a wage reduction in two ways: the direct effect on his own wage bill and the lower costs of transport and other services for which he paid (p. 960). He agreed that a free exchange rate would help to spread the burden of the loss that had to be borne, but in response to Massey's suggestion that the exchange rate was 'really the true means of distributing the burden', he replied: 'A free exchange rate is one of the parts of my plan; but I do not think that a free exchange rate can bring us an alleviation of our troubles, without the other parts of the plan.' Dethridge interposed that

the Court is only concerned with the wage question. I assume that the other constituents of the professor's scheme are receiving consideration from those bodies whose duty it is to consider them. It is not our job. … We cannot introduce a free exchange. (p. 963)

When Massey later put it to Copland that 'rapid deflation will produce a position of chaos in the country', he replied 'I think it will'. The evidence continued:

> Notwithstanding that the condition of the wage earner today is bad, and they are suffering in common with everybody, you propose to continue that condition? --- No; I want to spread the loss evenly over the whole of the workers, not make the unemployed bear the whole burden.
>
> You consider that the incidence of your wage reduction proposals is deflationary? --- Just in respect of people who are selling goods to the workers affected—not generally. (p. 992)
>
> …
>
> Assuming that wages are brought down in terms of money, that is deflation, that will affect the revenues of all public utilities? --- That is your definition of deflation all the time, and you have to realise that.
>
> I can assure you that I have no mental reservations? --- I have.
>
> My application of deflation is general; I do not like the word, and I am merely using it here because apparently it conveys an idea? --- It is a very ugly word.
>
> Personally, I am hostile to the word? --- Yes. I am very hostile to the process.
>
> My definition of deflation means an arbitrary alteration in the amount in terms of money of all utilities, used in the economic sense? --- A serious and continued drop in the price level is deflation. I think that is the proper definition.
>
> …
>
> The dropping of wage rates in terms of money is deflation? --- I do not think it is. I am speaking of the price of commodities. (p. 998)

Though the definition of 'deflation' was in part a semantic issue, there was more to it than that. Massey was surely right in arguing that cutting money wages would have effects normally associated with 'deflation': increasing the real value of debt and of charges that were sticky in nominal terms; and causing deferral of expenditure in the expectation of obtaining goods and services (including labour services) at lower future prices. In one answer that he gave, Copland implied, but did not elaborate on, a monetarist theory of deflation: 'It is the credit policy which causes the fall of the price level, and the fall of the wages' (p. 999). Copland would have been on firmer ground if he had simply said that reducing wages was necessary, *despite its deflationary effects*, in order to spread the burden of the reduced real national income.

After Massey had completed his cross-examination, Crofts and Maher pursued several minor matters with Copland. Maher sought his agreement that his contentions were simply 'your personal opinions as a professor of economics'. 'No', said Copland; 'they are a logical argument. My opinion does not count.' Challenged as to whether there were in Australia 'two professors who agree as to your particular remedy', Copland replied 'that every professor of economics in the country believes that what I have put forward is correct'.

Apart from the general persuasive power of Copland's evidence, its principal effect was to entrench in the Court's thinking the idea that the central issue in the case was a 10 per cent reduction in the basic wage. During his evidence, there was brief reference to the fact that reducing the basic wage by 10 per cent did not imply a 10 per cent reduction in wages because margins would be unaffected.[14] That matter remained dormant, however, until near the conclusion of the hearing. The Court repeatedly affirmed that the sole issue in the case was whether or not the state of the economy necessitated a 10 per cent basic wage reduction.

---

[14] Drake-Brockman said to Copland: 'Your proposal touches only the basic wage; it does not touch the secondary wage at all, which is very considerable'. Copland replied: 'I had forgotten that. The total would not be 10 per cent of the wage bill; it would be something less than 10 per cent' (p. 894). There was no recognition of the fact that, with prices falling, the real value of margins was actually rising.

9.2.4 What evidence was relevant?

The employers called numerous witnesses to testify about the poor state of particular industries. As this evidence proceeded, the Court manifestly became impatient with it. Its impatience was increased when the unions attempted detailed rebuttals. At no stage did the Court accept that this was a railways' case. The basic wage was a general wage and had to be dealt with as such. Evidence about particular industries had no more value than as confirmation of what might be derived from broader indicators. At the end of Copland's evidence, Maher asked whether railway officers 'should be specially signalled [sic] out for a special wage reduction as against other employees in the community'. 'I should say no', said Copland, 'but I am not in the position of having to answer for the railway industry …' Maher continued: 'But you are giving evidence in regard to the whole of these matters before the Court, and the railways represent the major portion of the case'. Dethridge intervened: 'No, do not make a mistake about that; they are not' (p. 1015).

On the next day (Thursday 4 December), the employers closed their case. Crofts alleged that this was a tactic: he understood that there were to be other employer witnesses, and the unions had prepared to cross-examine them. Dethridge commented: 'It may be that they have taken notice of what I said yesterday and that is that, so far as I am concerned, the evidence of value is the evidence of witnesses who are able to give evidence relevant to the position of the country as a whole. That means the evidence of men who can speak as expert economists and statisticians' (p. 1055). When the employers protested about the unions' unwillingness to commence their case forthwith, Dethridge said:

> The position may have become somewhat confused by the way in which the case has shaped itself, as it went along. I think [the unions] may reasonably have felt somewhat doubtful as to what they were called upon to do in the earlier part of the case. … They want, perhaps, some time to prepare such evidence as the Court will regard as necessary, relevant and valuable, and it may be that the employees cannot get

that evidence ready by tomorrow. What I am saying now is not to be taken as indicating that the Court is going to admit detailed evidence as to a number of particular industries because the Court will disregard detailed evidence of either side of that kind. We have to recognise that, if the general condition of the country is such as to require an alteration of the basic wage, that alteration is not going to be held up by enquiries stretching out over months and, it may be, years into the detailed conditions of a number of particular industries. (pp. 1058–1059)

At this point Fraser referred to a 'foregone conclusion'. Rebuked 'as counsel' by Dethridge, Fraser explained himself:

What I was proposing to say is that probably the only one in Australia who can give valuable and proper evidence as to the national dividend is the person charged with collecting statistical information with regard to that point; and unless Mr Wickens' conclusions can be thrown overboard—they undoubtedly show a decline in the national dividend—and if that decline is such as to render it imperative that 10 per cent of that decline should be spread over the employees … it does seem, in my opinion, that it would be a foregone conclusion. (p. 1059)

The Court adjourned until Monday 8 December in Sydney, where it would hear union witnesses. The Court sat for a week in Sydney.

Healy (for the Australian Workers' Union) said at the beginning of the Sydney hearings that he would be calling an accountant to deal with the balance sheets of various companies. Dethridge said to Healy:

Probably the position will be this, that no evidence of that kind will be necessary for the Court's purposes … The position as it appears to the Court at present is that the outstanding fact or facts which face the Court, face the public, and face everyone concerned in this community are these: a tremendous fall in the national income and a tremendous rise in unemployment in the community. … The fact that some companies—I do not dispute it for a moment—have, until this last year, earned considerable profits, is not of the weight which attaches to the tremendous falls in our export values and the fact that we cannot borrow any more money from abroad. (pp. 1066–1067)

When Fraser said that some of the 'industry' evidence related to pastoral companies, the following exchange ensued:

Dethridge C J: The outstanding fact with regard to the pastoral industry is that wool, last season, averaged something under 11d per lb—very considerably less than it has brought for a number of years past. This year, up to now, it has averaged something under 9d. Now, whatever the wool companies concerned have done in the past, whatever profits they have made, it will not alter the fact that wool at the present moment is bringing an average of under 9d per lb, and it will not alter the fact that it costs ever so much more than 9d to produce that wool ... Past wealth, past profits, do not alter that position. This country has to go on producing—if it is going to produce at all; if it is not going to lie down and pass out of existence—and face a world market showing prices of that kind.

Mr Fraser: It is going to come back to this: Apparently, in that view, so far as I see it, it seems very difficult to see what evidence can be called by the respondents, if they are going to be limited in that way.

Dethridge C J: I shall be very glad instead to hear evidence going to prove that wool ... is going to bring 15d or 16d on an average. Bring that evidence, and the Court will be relieved of a lot of difficulty.

Mr Fraser: So it comes down to this, that the evidence at present is undisputed—it is very doubtful if it will ever be disputed—as to the decline in the national income; so it follows that wages must be reduced.

Dethridge C J: It does not follow. We are waiting to hear evidence that a reduction of wages, even in face of that fact, is inexpedient ...

...

Drake-Brockman J: Does the decrease in the national income justify a decrease in wages: the employers say yes and we are waiting to hear your answer, because that is the issue, and the only issue, before the Court. (pp. 1068–1071)

Healy said that the unions were having difficulties in getting appointments with the economics professors. Dethridge replied that 'any economist who is worth his salt' would recognise the gravity of the issue before the Court and 'would disregard everything else for the few hours that will be necessary in order to enable him to place his evidence before the Court'. He told Crofts: 'If you mention any name or suggest the name of any economist, the Court itself will call that economist. It will treat that economist in the same way as it treated Professor Copland' (p. 1082).

9.2.5 Irvine's evidence

The Court, at the unions' request, spent the week of 8 to 12 December in Sydney. On the last day of the week, R F Irvine gave evidence. Though formally called as the Court's witness, he was the principal witness on the union side, just as Copland had been on the employer side. Irvine was the first occupant of a Chair in Economics in Australia, having been appointed to it by the University of Sydney in 1912.[15] He was an unorthodox economist, something of an outcast from the emerging body of professional economists in Australia, and a political radical. He left the University, under pressure, in 1922.[16] At the time of the Inquiry, he was a director of the government-owned Primary Producers' Bank.

Irvine stressed, first, the international origin of the Depression. Australia could do very little to modify world conditions; but there was no reason, 'other than the prevalence of an obsolete economics', why the industrial situation in Australia should be as bad as it was (p. 1322). People unable to earn livings, except for charity and public relief, were 'a reflection upon our intelligence in

---

[15] Irvine (1861–1941) was born in Scotland and educated in New Zealand. He became a school principal in New South Wales and later joined the State public service.
[16] Ostensibly, Irvine's removal from the University was due to his adultery, but Bruce McFarlane (Irvine's biographer in the *Australian Dictionary of Biography*) suggests that it may have reflected the unpopularity of his political utterings.

a country like Australia, which can produce an abundance of the necessaries of life and many of the luxuries of life and at the same time export enormous surpluses of primary products abroad' (p. 1323).

No one who was aware of the fall in world price levels since 1924, and especially in the past 18 months, could fail to come to the conclusion that the root cause of the Depression 'is to be found in our monetary system'. Australia's experience was but one consequence of the global problem:

> There may no doubt be circumstances in any particular country which aggravate the ill-effects of this world movement. It is of course patent to everyone that low prices for wool and wheat are the immediate cause of the drop in our national income, measured in money, and our exchange difficulties. Local discussion, however, scarcely concerns itself with ultimate causes, but fastens on certain local conditions like arbitration, high wages, high cost of production, extravagance, public and private, any and all of which may or may not have helped to aggravate the situation. It is overlooked, however, that altering these things or leaving them alone cannot affect the world's prices for wheat and wool, nor stop the deflation which is accompanied by, and, in my opinion, is the primary cause of world depression and an appalling unemployment. (p. 1324)

What was the cause of the worldwide deflation?

> To some small extent this decline [in prices] may be attributed to the over-production (or under-consumption) of some important commodities, but basically ... it is to be regarded as the sudden outcrop of a period of accumulating deflation. In other words, the slump in the general price level has for its principal cause an appreciation in the buying power of money units, in the last resort gold. The supply of gold, allowed to function in the monetary system, and the credit money linked to it, have not only not kept pace with the volume of goods to be exchanged, but have seriously fallen behind. (p. 1326)

The problem was exacerbated by the accumulation of hoards of gold in the United States and France. 'These two things, chaotic movement of gold and maldistribution, have led', said Irvine, 'to the sterilisation of a considerable part of the existing gold supply. This is the initiating cause of the slump in prices and the world-wide business depression' (p. 1327).

Reducing wages would have little or no beneficial effect; for 'the vast mass of unemployment is more due to business dislocation brought about by deflation than to the resistance of the workers to wage reduction. Even if all wages were adjusted to the new cost of living, and in accordance with our reduced national income, industries starving for orders would be unable to absorb any great percentage of unemployed' (p. 1328). Insofar as the problem had a local component, it was due to the behaviour of the monetary system:

> [A]ll classes, influenced by fears for the future, have begun to hoard and restrict their normal rate of expenditure—a so-called thrift policy which gives the finishing touches to the ruin already wrought by deflation. The piling up of fixed deposits in banks—though very acceptable to the banks—is the barometer which shows clearly the fears of the non-wage earning classes. They are spending much less than usual, and they have practically lost the spirit of enterprise. In the meantime, the banks, following a time honoured—or should we not rather say, a time dishonoured—practice in periods of depression begin to call up overdrafts, and generally to contract credit.
>
> The pressure they bring to bear upon their clients—the entrepreneur class in all industries—compels the latter to unload securities on the market. The result, as we saw some months ago, a slump in the share market and a drop in property values of between 25 per cent and 50 per cent. ... Naturally deposits have gone down. Bankers did not seem to realise that the deposits would go down with the cancellation of overdrafts, but that is the inevitable effect; so the money available for expenditure has been correspondingly reduced. ... The banks, it may be said, had no choice, and in truth their problem was far from easy. They needed cash to preserve a safe ratio between cash and demand liabilities and most of all they wanted money in London. But however justifiable it may be from a purely institutional point of view, contracting credit at

a time like this is like throwing a monkey-wrench into the productive mechanism ... (p. 1329)

Irvine now moved on to recommend a monetary policy of controlled inflation. Before doing so, he asked for the Chief Judge's guidance, because 'it may not be quite relevant to your inquiry'. Dethridge replied that the Court would be glad to hear Irvine's comments on the general situation. 'The more the Court has proceeded with this inquiry', he said, 'the more it feels the difficulty of separating any mere wage issue from the general situation' (p. 1330). That was not a stance consistently taken by the Court. At times, it emphasised that its role was confined to setting wages and that other authorities were responsible for wider policy.

Conscious of the bad odour then attaching to the idea of 'inflation', Irvine said that 'inflation pushed to extremes, as we know from the oft-quoted historical examples, has little to recommend it'. But the fear of inflation was itself a danger:

> Impressed by these evils of extreme inflation, many people are strong in the conviction that even the slightest tendency to inflation must be ruthlessly checked. This has given them a bias in favour of deflation. Australia and most other countries are having a taste of deflation and the medicine has brought them to death's door. ... On occasion it may be necessary to inflate or deflate. Just now, in Australia, it is practically a question of life and death to stop deflation and initiate a movement in the opposite direction. (p. 1332)

Irvine then advanced specific proposals:

> The first step is to make available to primary producers, manufacturers and commercial businesses sufficient credit to enable them to get going again. There must be nothing indiscriminate in this; nor do we need to put into force any novel principles. The banks should control the use of the new credit and should secure advances in the ordinary way. The process, in fact, should be identical with that used by banks in creating bank credit. ... If a suitable amount of credit be made available, in

this way, it will soon begin to absorb the unemployed … as demand for commodities increases. … Every unemployed worker taken on again and every business enabled to start again or extend its operations will produce more wealth and at the same time provide a market for increased output, because they provide markets for each other. There is a fair amount of truth in the old adage about taking in each other's washing. … Increased demand in the consumption market stimulates the demand for capital as well as consumption goods. With normal credit facilities restored and signs of increasing demand, business men take heart and timid capitalists venture into the arena again. … Confidence is restored. The banks who advanced the credit and the business men who borrowed it are now justified by all-round renewed activity. The downward movement of prices is checked. That in itself is an encouragement. But presently … prices recover sufficiently to make enterprise profitable. (p. 1333)

The expansion of credit would be achieved in the following manner:

> The Government may arrange, through the Commonwealth Bank, for the issue of notes in such quantities as may be considered necessary and prudent—a matter which should not be left to political guesswork, but should be determined by a monetary council, consisting of statisticians, economists, bankers, etc, competent to assemble facts and apply scientific principles to their interpretation. Hitherto Australian Governments have entrusted the investigation of economic matters to prominent business men or lawyers, with the result that even if the relevant facts are assembled, the inferences to be properly drawn from them … are left to minds without specific training in handling the order of facts. … I should not allow any bank, not even the Commonwealth Bank, to determine what amount of credit we should have. The work of the bank is to use the credit. It is not their work to determine the policy. … A large part, if not the whole, of such issue as may be made on their advice of the 'Monetary Council' should naturally be allotted to the commercial banks. … I would issue to the commercial banks, because they are in touch with the whole business community, and their experience lies in this direction. That is the granting of credit on

good security. They can carry out that job better than any government department can. (p. 1334)

Irvine had a breathtaking faith in the powers of economic diagnosis and prescription: 'The collection of price statistics and facts indicating other economic tendencies is now so complete that there is little difficulty in estimating the effects of quantitative changes in the volume of currency and credit. These effects are not a matter of opinion or traditional expectation, but of fact and scientific measurement' (p. 1335).

The picture thus painted by Irvine was one of an economy affected by external deflation which had failed to protect itself against the effects of the deflation but might do so with a well-conceived monetary policy. It is very likely, indeed, that the monetary response to the Depression seriously exacerbated it. That was certainly Copland's opinion. But the problem with Irvine's diagnosis was its failure to allow for the loss of real income inherent in the fall in the terms of trade and directly evident in the decimated incomes of the rural sector and the loss of real resources due to the cessation of foreign loans. How should these real losses be absorbed and distributed? Irvine's principal response to this question was to dispute the significance of the losses. The goods that Australia exported were merely 'surpluses' to be disposed of after satisfying the requirements of the local population:

> We have got into the habit of depreciating the importance of our domestic production and consumption, and of exaggerating the importance of the surplus. We have allowed the surplus ... to dominate the internal situation; in other words, we have let the tail wag the dog. Now, the surpluses over and above what we have reserved for a high standard of living have undoubtedly enabled us to borrow freely for developmental purposes, and, in addition, to import a large volume of goods. From that point of view, the surplus is important, but it has still to be regarded as something over and above what we produce for our own consumption ... (p. 1337)

Dethridge asked whether the loss of £60 million did not work 'to our real detriment'. Irvine replied that an increased volume of exports was necessary to service the debt and to pay for any given quantity of imports. But the Government had acted to curb imports; and 'the imports must be regarded as the only benefit which we got by exporting our surplus'. Dethridge made the seemingly obvious comment:

> Undoubtedly, but the imports did not represent a mere superfluity which we could do without, without much inconvenience or loss; but they did, in effect, I think, mean a substantial gain to the community, in this way that the imports, or the proceeds of those imports, enabled, for instance, a lot of constructional work to be done by the Government and so on; and, without those imports, we have not got the means to keep the AWU men—Mr Grayndler's people—going on construction work …? (p. 1338)

Irvine replied that if Dethridge meant machinery which Australia could not make for itself, then it was essential; 'but I fancy that our imports were largely things which we could very well have done without—things which do not really touch the Australian standard of living'. Dethridge interposed: 'There is a good deal of truth in that', encouraging Irvine to continue:

> And it looks to me as if the situation now is that, in Australia, if we like to employ all our people in the ordinary way, we can produce a very solid banquet for all our people. … I am inclined to think that we may work to a large extent independently of what you may call the international or foreign parity in prices and things of that kind. … We have rather considered that the world's parity should control the whole situation in Australia. I do not think it should. In my opinion, we might establish a price quite different from the world parity, in order to secure to the farmer at least a fair return on the local consumption. Then the rest is surplus that we do not want, and we have to put it away. It might then pay us to burn it; but it is the surplus which we send abroad and get the best price we can for. (p. 1339)

When Beeby observed that 'we must send something abroad', Irvine replied: 'Yes, to pay for our obligations abroad. I mean, the interest on borrowed money, and that kind of thing; but I think that we shall have to ignore other countries, and really organise our own industries independently of them'. The evidence continued:

> Beeby J: We will have to evolve a price level of our own for local consumption? --- Undoubtedly.
>
> And a corresponding wage level? --- Yes. You see, if we do not do that, we may be steadily reducing our whole population down to the standard of China or some other country—a very low standard of living. That is not necessary in Australia. (p. 1339)

Thus the real loss, which was so central to Copland's evidence, was to Irvine a minor inconvenience. The imports which had been made available by exports and foreign borrowing were, to a large extent, dispensable. It was true that the Scullin Government had adopted a policy of curtailing imports by tariffs and direct controls. What was not true, however, was that the supplies forgone were irrelevant to the country's ability to support a standard of living. Irvine had not answered Copland's contention that the reduced capacity to import was a real loss which had, somehow, to be shared among the population.

Dethridge asked whether Irvine had 'formed any view or opinion on the question of employment and unemployment in the reduction of wages'. Irvine's answer was:

> I do not think that the idea that, if you reduce wages you take up a large number if the unemployed, because it would pay industries to take them at a reduced rate, would affect the situation very much. Those industries are not deterred by that just now. They are deterred by two things. First of all, they cannot get credits from the banks to go on with, and, secondly, they have no orders. (p. 1340A)

This, of course, accorded with Irvine's stress on the monetary aspects of the Depression. When Beeby asked whether credit might be more easily obtained by producers whose costs were reduced, Irvine replied: 'Then, if you have tried all other methods of reducing costs, you may have to fall back on labour, if you simply cannot carry on; but, in view of the situation in Australia where we have an abundance, we do not want to reduce the real wage. There is no necessity for it, in my opinion' (p. 1340A). Asked how the pastoral industry could carry on without some reduction in its costs of production, including wages, he answered: 'Going on those lines an industry might require no labour cost at all or only the cost of a little rice sufficient to keep its labour alive; if you want that kind of industry in Australia I do not think it is worth discussing' (p. 1344).

Irvine's trivialising of the diminished capacity to import left the Judges uneasy, as is apparent in the following exchange:

> Beeby J: I am very much concerned about the question of the national income, whether it is merely a change of money values or not. We have 30 millions of interest to pay in London and we want £15 millions worth of goods which we cannot make.[17] So in exchange for these goods we send to London 200,000 bales of wool and 17 million bushels of wheat. But London now says they won't do that any longer, but want 300,000 bales of wool and 100 million bushels of wheat; is that not a definite fall in our national income? --- In this way, we have got to give so much away to the public creditor, that limits the amount of goods we can get as a return for our exported surplus.
>
> Dethridge C J: And those goods may be indispensable to us? --- They may be necessary or they may be luxuries.
>
> ...
>
> Drake-Brockman J: Surely under the circumstances that obtain at the present time ... there must be a very serious loss to the country? --- I have admitted that there may be a decrease in the national income ... but we still have got a lot of unused labour here, people who could be set to work.
>
> ...
>
> Dethridge C J: That involves the other question as to whether something else should not be done, that is to say, whether credit in some way or other should not be released to start that work going. And what has been

---

[17] The '£15 millions' is probably a transcript error. It is likely that Beeby said '£50 millions'.

said is certainly very weighty indeed, but then comes the question that, assuming that to be done, and assuming we get back to the position we were in a few years ago, and that there was no normal unemployment, then superimposed on that condition of things we have this real loss to the community because the world outside is not giving us as much as it was. ... Assume that the world outside says 'No longer do you get that £50 millions worth of goods'. Isn't that a serious loss to the community; does it not hit everyone? --- I should say it is a loss undoubtedly.

And a real loss? --- I would still like your Honour to impress my view that what we export from Australia is really in the nature of a surplus.

But for that surplus we are getting these real goods? --- After we have had a very high standard of living, and then that surplus is thrown on the world market for what it will fetch.

Drake-Brockman J: But we must not forget that that high standard of living was brought about as a result of that surplus? --- Undoubtedly. (pp. 1346–1347)

Several questions by employer representatives suggested that it was only fair for the basic-wage earner to carry his share of the burdens that the community had to bear. Irvine's answer was two-fold. First, there was the issue of effectiveness: although one had to admit 'the suffering of the unemployed and the suffering of the farmer', the question was 'how are we to get rid of that; and I cannot see how the reducing of wages is going to make any improvement' (p. 1355). Second, there was the issue of ability to 'pay'. Carolan argued that higher income recipients had to bear much of the burden of taxation and providing for capital requirements. Irvine replied:

It is the ability to bear which you have to consider. When you reach the lowest rung, the ability to bear more is very little, whereas, the higher you go, the ability to bear more is greater. I think that has to be considered in the question of making everybody share alike or share in a percentage. ... In one case, it might be absolute deprivation of necessary food, clothes and so on. In the other case it might only mean the price of a cigar, or some comfort of that kind. (p. 1357)

Irvine did not, at this stage of his evidence, repeat his earlier argument about the minor importance of the fall in the terms of trade. He did, however, return to his contention that the abundance of production was such as to support a rising standard of living for workers. Asked by Crofts for his opinion about an announcement by J T Lang, Premier of New South Wales, that the 44-hour week would be restored in the State railways and wages probably increased, Irvine declined to give a direct answer, but continued:

> I think there is one point perhaps I did not bring out this morning, and it is this, that with an increasing power of production taking place everywhere in the world today, wages and earnings ought to be going up. In other words, if wages are not going up then leisure ought to be going up, because the movement now really is in the direction of a tremendous improvement in the technique of production, so that in quite a short time the industries of the world ought to be able to do all their work in a very few months of the year. There is no Utopia about that, they can do it now. (p. 1370)

9.2.6 Other 'economic' evidence

At the beginning of the Sydney hearings, Crofts told the Court that 'there are men who are not political economists teaching in Universities, men such as Mr Gordon Massey, men who have given much time and thought to political economy and who can express themselves, and with their practical knowledge, may be of more value as witnesses than these men who are attached to Universities' (pp. 1084–1085). Beeby urged him to call them. The following is a brief account of the evidence given by such witnesses.

J A L Gunn, a chartered accountant, had (jointly) written a booklet, *Is This Depression Necessary?* He agreed with Copland's evidence 'as to the facts presented', but not with his inferences. Copland had not given proper weight to falling prices. The banks' failure to adjust the exchange rate with sufficient speed and to a sufficient extent had the effect that the fall in prices received by exporters caused a drastic fall in their incomes, which flowed through to other sectors. All this generated a falling internal price level. When Beeby described as 'a very obvious truism' the proposition that rising prices cause optimism and falling prices caused pessimism, Gunn replied:

> Yes, I wish to stress that particularly in connection with wages. ... Coming down to the wage earner, this spending power is reduced through unemployment, intermittent employment, a fear of loss of employment, and the necessity to maintain some cash balances to pay for fixed charges out of deplenished income thereby causing a falling off in the spending power. There is the loss of health and strength of the worker through diminished spending power, and a loss in efficiency. A permanent fall in wages would bring about a change in the habits of the people. There would be a lowering of the standard of living and a consequent tendency to destroy the home market. ... A reduction in wages cannot solve or help to solve unemployment where you have falling prices. ... There is a real contraction in the currency through a change in the habits of the people. Men, and women more so, tend to hold larger cash balances in the household itself. That itself tends to destroy the velocity of money, and a real contraction of the exchange of goods and services. ... A reduction in wages will reduce spending power, and that in turn will reduce orders, so that any possible gain to the employer ... is wiped out by a still further slowing down in production—a still further break down in the mechanism of exchange. Next thing, the employer will ask for a further reduction because the last reduction was inadequate; and so I contend that the vicious process can go on until every worker can starve in his backyard ... (p. 1109)

Although Gunn promised several times that he would propose an alternative strategy, he failed to do so, except perhaps for the implied support for devaluation and the insistence on not reducing wages. Dethridge and Beeby pressed on him the need to react to the fall in real spending power. Gunn argued that the fall in income should be regarded as temporary and claimed to have a cable from J M Keynes saying that everything depended on whether the fall was permanent or temporary. When Beeby said 'Then you are assuming that the fall in our income from exports is only temporary', Gunn replied:

'Yes, I hope so, because I believe that the remedy lies in restoring the internal value of our export prices to their 1928 level' (p. 1116).

C A Alison was an 'engineer and manufacturer'. He had an engineering degree, but had not done economics at the university. His evidence was rather similar to Gunn's, which is not surprising, as he and Gunn were joint authors of *Is This Depression Necessary?* He was more concrete about the adverse effects of wage reduction and the virtues of expanding the currency. Copland, he said, had not 'interpreted the psychological factors of monetary policy in the proper manner'. A wage reduction

> would be disastrous for the manufacturer as it would rid him of a considerable quantity of the purchasing power of the people that he now has. He may, for instance, think that he is getting a benefit by a reduction in wages, but it would only be in apparent self-interest, and it would be a sacrifice of the real self-interest and it would not annihilate the unemployment that is with us today unless prices started to rise again. But if you have a reduction of the actual wages as they are at the present time, I think that such a thing has a psychological effect upon the average man of such a nature as to make him draw in his horns as far as spending it goes. And that will cause a very great diminution in the velocity of money, and, if you reduce wages with the idea of spreading the money over a greater number of people, as is commonly thought, I consider that it would not help the situation in the slightest. It would be disastrous. (pp. 1138–1139)

Alison favoured an expansion of the money supply (induced by an increase of currency). This would directly stimulate spending and would also cause increases in the prices of exports and imports. The Depression 'would be over in a few months, because the primary producer would then be getting a price for his products which would be the price at which most of most of the money contracts over the last few years have been made'. Dethridge commented:

> The primary producer, for the purpose of his purchases in Australia, would be getting a price for his own goods similar to that which you

say has ruled for some time past; but he would be furnished with that purchasing power by whom—by the rest of the community here. That is how it would work out, surely. ... It may be that it would not be unjust that the primary producer should be subsidised in that way, but let us recognise the fact that the subsidy would be granted at the expense of the rest of the community here not being primary producers? (pp. 1143–1144)

Alison said that 'if our monetary system had been properly correlated here—that is, exchange rates had been allowed to move—the fall in prices abroad would not have affected us to any great extent, except as regards paying back the debt interest, I will admit'. Dethridge pursued the point of the unavoidable real loss:

> Dethridge C J: It is not a matter of financing only. It is a question of not having exchangeable goods? --- We have the same quantity of goods to send overseas.
>
> You know what I mean. We have not the same quantity of goods in their result, because we can only get half as many British goods or British settlements for that same quantity of goods. That is the difficulty ---
>
> Mr Crofts: And the witness is trying to show the Court how we can get ---
>
> Dethridge C J: If the witness can satisfy the Court that, by some internal arrangement of our monetary and credit system we can get the equivalent of shiploads of goods coming into Sydney harbour, Hobson's Bay, and all the other ports, then his theory may have something to be said for it; but that is the real thing. (pp. 1192–1193)

G V Portus, from the University of Sydney, attended the Court, apparently at the behest of the unions.[18] Crofts told the Court, however, that Portus could not assist it: 'We have found that out, and Mr Portus, if I may say it without any disrespect to him, is an economic historian, and does not know the subject in the same way as Professor Copland or other economists

---

[18] Higgins, in *A New Province for Law and Order*, thanked Portus 'for his encouragement and valuable assistance in preparing this little book for the press' (Higgins 1922, p. vi).

know it.' Dethridge expressed 'regret to Mr Portus for giving him unnecessary trouble' and was on the point of bidding him adieu when Fraser suggested that 'the Professor can give some light on the subject, at any rate as to one or two arguments against a reduction in wages' (p. 1179). Portus was duly called as a Court witness. Overall, his evidence was rather equivocal, which may be the reason why Crofts was reluctant to call him.

Though he agreed with Copland's statement of the facts, Portus thought that there were arguments against a general reduction of wages. One was its limited capacity to offset the decline in export incomes:

> I do not think a reduction of wages is going to help primary industry. … Our primary industries depend on world markets, and all world markets for primary industries are contracting, the prices are falling because there is so much surplus stuff all over the world. … But I do not think any 10 per cent reduction in wages is going to affect the size of the market overseas for Australian primary products. (p. 1200)

Another argument called for a long-run approach to wage-setting. It also invoked the idea of the 'standard of living':

> But I think there is a broad social aspect which to my way of thinking, we cannot altogether disregard, although it is rather hard to get it before people, because if you speak like this people generally regard it as mere socialism … But it does seem to me that even if a substantial wage reduction effected a slight increase in employment (and that is very doubtful) on broad social grounds there are reasons why it would not be justified.
>
> Now this country has adopted an ideal of a high standard of living for its workers. This is quite a commonplace to anyone who has troubled to read the records of wage fixation in the Courts of this country. It is also realised by those people that it is necessary for the community to exert continuous pressure on the employers to insure that they shall pay the highest possible wage. … It seems to me that if you take a long view, there is something to be said for sustaining that pressure on the employers even at the expense of slight unemployment in times

of adversity, for this reason, that if you attempt to reduce wages and conditions, in times of prosperity you will find that when trade gets back to its old levels and the workers again realise it, you are going to have all sorts of difficulties, all sorts of industrial disputes, in the attempt to get back to their old standards. … And it does seem to me this is a thought that should give us pause before as a community we consent to reduce the basic wage. It is a living standard here. I don't think it is a living standard of a very high sort, but it is high in comparison with that of other countries in the world. All these arguments must stand up to the test of unemployment, and if unemployment continues, that indicates that wages are too high. But generally I feel that the prospect of recovery from this depression merely through a reduction in wages is not a very rosy one. (p. 1201–1202)[19]

F A A Russell KC was formerly a Lecturer in Commercial and Industrial Law and also in Economics at the University of Sydney. Before taking up law, he had completed a Master's degree in political philosophy among other subjects, 'and at that time I was also a student of economics, though there was no school in the University at that time'. He had lectured for Irvine. And he had been the Chairman of many Industrial Boards in New South Wales.[20]

The thrust of Russell's evidence was the necessity of a stabilisation of the value of money. Want of stability 'is injurious to industry, more particularly, I think, with falling prices than with rising prices, because in the case of falling prices, the producer is always selling on a falling market' (p. 1223). He quoted with approval an article of J M Keynes reprinted in the *Sydney Morning Herald* in 1928: 'The Treasury and the Bank of England,' said Keynes, 'have made the fundamental blunder of believing that, if they looked after the deflation of prices, the deflation of costs would look after itself. Regarding these two different things as though they were practically the same thing they did not

---

[19] In his autobiography, Portus said that the Court, with the exception of Beeby, showed little interest in his evidence (Portus 1953). The transcript belies this. Dethridge and Drake-Brockman engaged him in quite extensive discussion; it was Beeby who had little to say.
[20] In 1914, while he was Chairman of the Industrial Boards, Russell presented a paper to the British Association, which met in Sydney. His paper was published in the *Economic Journal* (Russell 1915).

hesitate to commit the country to a deflation of costs without having any idea or any plan as to how it was to be brought about, yet it is extraordinarily difficult to deflate costs' (p. 1230).

There were, said Russell, some prospects of international monetary change. But in the meantime,

> it would be correct and sound to use some local palliative which might be called inflation. I have used the word 'inflation' here because I am facing the question that it would mean some increase of paper money, but it would not be a real or harmful inflation if it were applied in the production of marketable goods. At least, I do not think so, and my view is that, psychologically, the situation is such that there should be an attempt to do something of that kind. (p. 1236)

The banks, Russell concluded, should be encouraged to issue their own notes.

Russell made no comment on the issue of a wage reduction. The point of his evidence, from the unions' viewpoint, was to show the Court that other measures were appropriate to the economic problems confronting the country.

H W Parkinson was a member of the Institute of Civil Engineers, a Fellow of the Royal Economic Society and author of a pamphlet, *Unemployment: Its Cause and Cure*. He regarded Copland as 'a very dangerous witness'. He read from a critique of a paper on 'The Restoration of Economic Equilibrium' which Wood, Copland, and Giblin had delivered to the Sydney branch of the Economic Society.[21] The Depression, said Parkinson, was worldwide:

> That fact alone shows that the local effects tabulated in the paper are not the real cause of the trouble; and obviously the remedies suggested are of local, not worldwide application; they may be regarded as special palliatives for the special case of Australia. As such there is much to be said for some of them, much against others. That taxation of incomes derived from property and some reduction in land values is necessary, may be accepted, but that real wages should be reduced is, I believe, an egregious error. The apparently fair proposal that all should suffer

---

[21] I have not been able to locate this paper.

the loss of an equal proportion of income is founded on the erroneous assumption that everyone is equally entitled to his present income; that the idle man (or the industrious man) is as much entitled to his dividends … as the worker is to his salary. The thesis is untenable. (p. 1311)

Parkinson drew on J A Hobson's *Wealth and Life* to support a reallocation of income from savers to consumers.

Unemployment, at home and abroad, has already reduced the purchasing power of consumers and brought on a trade depression and so it is gaily proposed to still further reduce purchasing power—on the homeopathic principle! If real wages, that is, the quantity of commodities and services given to the bulk of the population, are reduced, it is obvious that a smaller proportion of the national output will be taken by workers. The authors make no attempt to show that reduced wages would be more than offset by greater numbers employed—in fact, the idea is absurd. (p. 1312)

The primary producer should receive a bounty—a natural corollary to the protection of secondary industries: 'Of course, it should be hedged around. The primary producer, like the worker, should be put on a living wage. He should be helped until he gets, at any rate, £250 or so a year' (p. 1317).

C E Martin, a Bachelor of Economics and a member of the Royal Economic Society, had recently been elected to the Legislative Assembly in New South Wales. Before that, he was a University District Tutor 'lecturing to the various classes in economics in addition to attending to the general administration of that work' (p. 1373).

No economist, he thought, could present evidence to the Court on the matter before it without referring to the increase in machine production. Economists were coming to the conclusion that there would be 'a very definite and permanent displacement of man power'. Related to this was the problem of 'getting purchasing power to the people'. Martin did not draw any specific deduction from this, but presumably he (like Parkinson) perceived a need for a distribution of income that was more, rather than less, favourable to wage-earners.

The monetary policy then being pursued was, said Martin, deflationary, and undue haste had been evidenced by the authorities in Australia attempting to revert to the gold standard. It was essential to have 'a carefully managed dose of inflation'. Martin wanted 'to introduce the Court to the question of interest':

> The interest rates at present in existence are not only pressing heavily upon Governments, but in particular are pressing heavily upon the farming community. ... I would like to point out that actually the interest rates and the interest charges on the farmer are a far greater and more difficult charge for him to bear than are the wages costs that we hear so much about. ... I just read a very brief extract from the 'Index of the Svenska Handelsbanken' an article on 'The Future of the Rate of Interest' by J M Keynes the eminent Swedish [sic] economist. He says, 'The slump is due to a retardation of new real investment so that it is falling seriously behind the level of current saving. This is the natural and inevitable result of maintaining, year after year, a rate of interest which would have been considered high at almost any time during the nineteenth or early twentieth centuries, and is surely preposterously high in an environment so well equipped as is the contemporary world with fixed investment of every description'. (p. 1375)

Dethridge asked whether Keynes had explained how interest rates could be brought down. Were they not 'the subject of competition just as are other services or commodities'? Keynes, said Martin, had not explained this. Beeby suggested that 'now we have the associated banks there is no competition'. Martin said that since the war there had been a psychology of high interest rates, 'and until there is a general settling down I am afraid the interest rates will remain high' (p. 1375).

He asserted that the Court 'should endeavour to maintain a definite and real standard of living in Australia'. There was much room for increased efficiency (including in the wool industry) and reduction of distribution costs:

> I suggest that, if your Honours adopt the course of refusing to consent to wage reductions, you will force upon employers these very necessary economic changes. It has been observed in American industry repeatedly, that, when they face a difficult situation, they turn around and examine the question of reducing other expenses, and, in many cases, they do it successfully. I do not want to suggest that that is always the solution.

Dethridge commented: 'It means they look around, and one of the first things they tackle is labour costs. They put in machines instead of men, and increase the technological unemployment' (p. 1378).

Gordon Massey, who had cross-examined Copland for the unions, was called as the Court's witness.[22] His statement and his evidence contained much verbiage which has to be penetrated to find the essential contentions. The following passage encapsulates his main points:

> Though there has been a real loss of income from export commodities, it is suggested that the amount of loss has not been ascertained sufficiently to form a reliable opinion upon the position, and though there has been a cessation of loan credits, this cannot be regarded in the nature of a loss, but rather as a situation of pause in the development of national assets which—taking all the circumstances into account—is an immediate benefit.

Discussing the fall in export prices, Massey said that the proper response was adjustment of the exchange rate, which presented 'a far more equitable and essentially practical opportunity of spreading the real loss of revenue, than any other means' (p. 1424). The cessation of foreign loans was beneficial because of the tendency for the exchange rate to respond to 'a deficiency of purchaseable [sic] sterling claims on London' and the 'transfer to Australia of the need of manufacturing or otherwise providing for the replacement of imported commodities'. Hence 'consideration of the reduction of £30 millions

---

[22] Fraser told the Court that Massey was apprehensive about his treatment by his employer, the Victorian Railways. Dethridge thought that the Court's *subpoena* should be ample protection (p. 1408).

in loan moneys as a cause for reducing living conditions within Australia is fallacious' (p. 1424).

The policy of reducing real wages, recommended by Copland, would exacerbate the problem of deflation. Its beneficial effects on the level of activity were presumed, not demonstrated. In fact, it would be disruptive:

> Industry, trade and commerce within Australia, have been built up, particularly since the inception of the Commonwealth, upon a policy of high wages ... Therefore, consideration of any reduction or re-distribution must take into account the disorganisation and dislocation which must arise—and the consequent destruction of capital values—arising from any re-division of the national dividend.
>
> But one of the chief results arising out of a re-division of the national dividend will arise from a serious decrease in the velocity of flow of money. The purchase of the cheaper consumer commodities by wage earners greatly facilitates the flow of money and there is little doubt that this factor had a considerable effect upon the prosperity of the United States until the present fall in the price level affected the economic situation as in this country.
>
> Taking all the considerations into account, it is contended that the resultant dislocation of trade and commerce brought about by a re-division of the national income will outweigh any apparent economic benefits. (pp. 1439–1440)

Later in his evidence, Massey provided what was probably the strongest statement of the case against the Copland prescription:

> The community income or spending money is alleged to have suffered a loss, and it can be said in respect of the alleged loss that
>
> 1. Part is no loss at all—namely, £30,000,000 which alleged loss, in the writer's firm opinion, is a great national benefit at the present moment and is likely to be still more beneficial as events proceed.
>
> 2. Part is immediately correctible—namely, that part due to losses from internal trade and commerce.

3. Part is real, inasmuch as the reduced value of wool and wheat give the community less claim than heretofore on sterling or commodities in London or elsewhere.

...

The loss to be regarded as real for the time being is, therefore, only that loss arising from the decline in values of wool and wheat. ... No one, so far, appears to have successfully attacked the problem of the means whereby farmers and graziers are to be induced to produce the additional volume of export commodities demanded. ... [I]f inducements are to be offered, they must be of the nature of a re-establishment of price levels upon the 1929 basis, and a spreading of the apparent monetary loss over the whole community by means of the incidence of exchange rates. Under these circumstances, the national dividend in respect of the proportion derived from internal sources will increase ... [L]oan money having ceased, the local consumer commodity pool will require replenishment from local sources, and the replenishment will require the absorption within consumer commodity production, of the workers hitherto engaged on capital works. ... If stabilisation does not take place the export industries will not export and no function which this Court can exercise will then effect any good purpose. If stabilisation does take place, the incidence of exchange will spread the loss automatically over the whole of the community. (pp. 1628–1629)

This was a coherent argument and it is unlikely that Copland would have challenged its logic. The idea that workers engaged in the 'production' of public works (funded from foreign loans) would be transferred to the production of import-replacing consumption goods was repeated by W B Reddaway in the 1937 basic wage inquiry (see Chapter 11, Subsection 11.2.2). Massey duly recognised that the fall in export prices entailed a real loss and did not resort to the specious arguments of Irvine and others about the irrelevance or unimportance of the exported 'surplus'. Copland would have agreed—and did elsewhere—that, in principle, the spreading of the loss could have been effected entirely by depreciation of the exchange rate. Indeed, Copland and his fellow economists (with the initial exception of Melville) advocated depreciation, but saw a *sole* reliance on exchange rates as impractical. The one logical flaw in Massey's analysis was his reluctance to confront the fact that spreading of the loss necessitated a reduction of the real wage, unless wage-earners were to be exempted. This required that the money wage rise less than or fall more than prices. Massey offered no advice to the Court as to how that could be effected. In cross-examination, he had little answer to the point that merely restoring the internal price level to the 1929 level would leave the prices received by wool-growers far below their pre-Depression levels (p. 1661).

The unions called various other witnesses. The Court's treatment of these witnesses ranged from frustration at union time-wasting to a readiness to engage with them about the import of their evidence. Much of this evidence was of very low quality. An example is that of W J Riordan, the Queensland Branch Secretary of the Australian Workers' Union. Riordan said that the award covering rural workers in Queensland had been cancelled about 18 months earlier (except in respect of shearers). The evidence proceeded:

> Mr Crofts: Can you say as to whether there has been any increase in unemployment since the setting aside of the awards? --- There have [sic] been a considerable increase in unemployment in Queensland during the last 12 months.
>
> In the rural industries? --- Yes, in every industry.
>
> And wages have been reduced in practically every industry, have they not? --- They have been reduced in every industry.
>
> And that has not only not relieved the unemployment market, but has actually increased it? --- Very nearly doubled it in the last 12 months, and there have been two reductions in the [State] basic wage during that period. (p. 1149)

H C Gibson gave evidence about inaccuracies in the price indices and his own estimates of price changes (pp. 1394 et seq.). A E Williams, Secretary of the Federated Clerks' Union, New South Wales Branch, said that the main reason why clerks were unemployed was the calculating machines that were invading their work (p. 1397). C Pescia, the State Secretary of the Motor

Employees' Federation, said that a wage reduction would reduce spending power and be the end of mass production of motor vehicles (p. 1508). Asked whether machinery had affected the industry, Pescia replied: 'Yes, It has had a wonderful effect. As a matter of fact, I think that 65 per cent of men in our industry are unemployed today. Of course, that came about by over-production by mass production' (p. 1511).[23] C G P Trevelyan, the General Secretary of the Musician's Union of Australia, said that wage reduction would not increase employment in his industry: 'The bulk of my members are out of employment not through stress or distress in the industry, but through other means—the introduction of mechanical music and talkies, lack of courage and mismanagement' (p. 1514). T Jewell, the General Secretary of the Australian Tramways' Union, argued that a general wage cut would have a particularly adverse impact on the financial position of public utilities because of the reduced ability of wage-earners to use their services and because the burden of fixed payments associated with past borrowing would be increased (pp. 1854, 1859).

G Dupree, Secretary of the Victorian Branch of the Tanning and Leather Dressing Section of the Australian Saddlery and Tanners' Federation, said that wages were only 16 to 17 per cent of the value of output; hence a 10 per cent cut would represent less than 2 per cent of the value of output. Drake-Brockman pointed out that wages were more than 50 per cent of the value of production (pp. 1518–1519). Dethridge addressed the advocate for the union:

> You may take it that the Court is already aware of the difficulties confronting your industry, and I think you may take it also that the Court recognises that those difficulties, in your industry, probably cannot be surmounted by any mere reduction of wages. But the argument put forward in support of the application is this; the applicants say that taking industry as a whole, at present, and having regard to the loss of income and so on, industry as a whole cannot afford the present basic wage. They do not speak of any particular industry, because they

---

[23] Dethridge observed that Pescia's evidence implied that there should be no wage reduction for men who were able to run motor cars and doubted that there were many such workers.

recognise, just as well as we do, that some industries are suffering from causes such as the witness has referred to, which are quite apart from questions of wages, and can be very little affected by any alteration of wages. ... Then it is true that evidence was given as to some industries, and it was suggested that a reduction of wages would facilitate the recovery of those industries from the present position. That evidence, in most instances ... was not very convincing. (p. 1523)

Crofts called A C a'B Chomley, an engineer whose chief occupation at the time was Lecturer in Economics to the National Credit Union. This was a body 'that has grown out of the Citizens Education Fellowship, that has been studying economics' (p. 1557a). 'The whole problem of wages', he said, 'is bound up with the question of the creation of new money which functions as purchasing power but which is not part of incomes' (p. 1559). Chomley's views were along the lines of Douglas Credit, although he expressed disagreements on points of detail with Major Douglas. In particular, he saw the primary source of the economic difficulties of the time as the failure of banks to provide the funds necessary for people and businesses to buy the output of industry. Reducing real wages would exacerbate the tendency for buying power to fall behind the growth of productive power (p. 1576). What was required was government action to expand the supply of currency to fund the purchase of the products of industry. When Dethridge inquired how this process could be controlled, Chomley replied that 'Mr Wickens could do it on his Sundays' (p. 1611). The treatment of Chomley by the Bench—notably Dethridge and Beeby—was surprisingly sympathetic, even if in the end it took the view that the adoption of Chomley's arguments was a matter for Government rather than the Court. Beeby said to Chomley: 'If you can get the Governments of Australia to adopt your scheme, and Mr Crofts asks for a week's adjournment, I do not think the Court would oppose it.' Dethridge added: 'I quite agree, Mr Chomley, that what you have been saying is the subject of thought by a lot of men whose opinions are worth respecting, not only here but in other countries where this aspect has been considered seriously' (p. 1612). Chomley was emboldened to tell the Court:

I may mention that I asked Professor Gregory, whose real name I understand is Gugenheimer, two or three questions which he hedged in a most magnificent manner, but it was quite sufficient to show me by his attitude and his reaction that he knew exactly what I was driving at. I had the greatest admiration for the manner in which he hedged as an efficient tactician. (pp. 1613–1614)

Beeby remarked: 'All I can say in conclusion is that it looks wonderful, but, to quote a famous phrase, I am sure there is a catch in it somewhere. However, I am going to consider it very closely.' When Beeby repeated that Chomley had 'given us food for thought', Chomley replied: 'It is more than that. It is complete proof' (p. 1699).

J F Chapple, the Acting General Secretary of the Australian Railways' Union (also an advocate), gave evidence in reply to claims of the Railways Commissioners about the state of the industry's finances. The main effect of his evidence was to cause a discussion of the relevance of the railways' position to the case:

> Beeby J: How much of this is there? I am wondering in what way it relates to the issue as to whether or not we are passing through an economic crisis which calls for some readjustment of wages? --- There is a fair amount of it.
>
> We are all familiar with it. It has been put before the Court in different ways. ...? --- But the Commissioners came here with very strong evidence of a 2½ million deficit in their working, and, even if it were that figure, we feel that we should be allowed to present strong argument to show why it should be disregarded.
>
> ...
>
> Mr Crofts: I want to put this: The employers of this country would not have been before this Court at the present juncture if it had not been for the fact that the Commissioners of Railways had a case before the Court. The Court would not have been hearing the basic wage case at all.

Dethridge C J: That is your inference and your statement, but I am not sure that it is correct. ... You assume that the employers in this particular proceeding would not have moved if the Railways had not started the ball rolling. I doubt if that is so.

...

Beeby J: I had referred the matter into Court. I was asked to reduce the basic wage in the Metal Trades case, but I refused to do it, and referred the matter to the Full Court, so the matter was before the Court in that particular trade.

...

Dethridge C J: I may indicate that personally I do not propose to go over a lot of the Railways evidence again; as a matter of fact, I propose to forget a lot of it. ... But what we are concerned with is the question as to whether the basic wage, which is common to all industries, should be reduced. That, properly speaking, to my mind, should be attacked as a national question, and should not be dealt with incidental to particular industries. Properly speaking, to my mind, consideration of the basic wage should be kept apart from industrial disputes. ... [I]t should be dealt with upon a consideration of the capacity of Australia as a whole to bear any proposed basic wage. But unfortunately this Court cannot deal with it in that way; we have to deal with it in this piece-meal fashion. As a result we get a lot of detail evidence concerning particular industries which is not of much value. Unfortunately we feel that we cannot reject that evidence altogether; we have to admit it, and then forget it. (pp. 1748–1751)

9.2.7 The best method of fixing the basic wage?

Before the addresses began, Crofts protested about a document which had been given to him by a representative of the employers and was, apparently, to be furnished to the Court. It comprised 30 pages of typed foolscap written by Copland, a Bank of New South Wales circular containing an article by Copland, and another article by Copland. 'What I do complain about', said

Crofts, 'is that the employers prepared the professor to give evidence for them. He was put in the box and accepted as the Court's witness. ... The statement ... comments on the evidence by Professor Irvine and other witnesses and, I am informed, it does not do them justice' (pp. 1869–1870).

This led to the following response by Dethridge:

That is the disadvantage about a Court, as I have said before, having the function of determining the basic wage. I have repeated myself over and over again upon that most unsatisfactory provision. The ideal body to decide upon the amount of the basic wage is a body composed of a number of representatives. Such a body would comprise, say, two or three men like Professor Copland, and two or three men like Professor Irvine, or, at any rate, one man like Professor Irvine; one like Professor Copland; a man like Mr Gordon Massey; it may be one or two representatives of employers; and one or two representatives of labour. They should not sit in public at all. They should get together and exchange views after deliberation, lengthy and expert consideration, but with each side represented by experts, so that they could formulate their conclusions without being subject to all sorts, what shall I say, of propaganda, in the Court and outside of the Court. It is useless to disguise the fact that this Court ... is being subjected to all sorts of propaganda, to some extent in the Court, but to a much greater extent outside of the Court ... in the press by various views, meetings of various kinds by parties interested, statements by employers, statements by union secretaries of a pronounced kind, some of them somewhat impolite, and statements by politicians, all with a view to influencing the decision of this Court ... However, the job is ours until the law is altered. ... Therefore, we have to do the best we can. In doing that, we desire to be assisted by expert opinions, either in the Court or outside of the Court. We must do the best we can to weigh the value of these opinions ... If we see what appears to be an exposition by an expert economist or an expert of another kind ... we will take that into consideration; we are entitled to do that; we are bound to do it, and we propose to do it. We want to have these expert opinions as far as possible subjected to critical examination by both sides. Professor Copland, for instance, is unquestionably an expert. You may suggest that he is a partisan expert. Very well, suggest that, and we will remember that suggestion. (pp. 1870–1871)

Crofts maintained his protest, saying that the witnesses whom Copland had criticised believed that he had done them an injustice and wished to reply. Dethridge said that they should send their replies along to the Court.[24]

9.2.8 The parties' addresses

I do not intend to summarise the arguments of the various advocates and the one barrister. I shall, however, refer to some of the issues that were raised and the Court's responses in the course of the hearing.

C E Mundy, for the Amalgamated Engineering Union, said that the Court's remarks during the case had indicated an intention 'to fix any new basic wage on what the financial position of the country justifies', with the standard of living a secondary consideration. That had not been the Court's principle in the past and it should not be adopted now. Dethridge replied that the Court did not propose to go below the equivalent of 7 shillings per day in 1907: 'We are not asked to do that, and we do not propose to do it.' Mundy then referred to the possible use of the All Items table instead of the price index limited to food, groceries, and house rents. We have seen earlier that in the early stages of the case, and especially when Wickens was in the box, criticisms of the C series index were made by union representatives. Gibson was foremost among them, and some of his criticisms seemed to have force. Mundy now submitted 'that if the All Items table is going to be used, seeing that it is a departure from the present system or custom which the Court has adopted for the past 23 years, that system should not be adopted until such time as an inquiry has been made as to its correctness or otherwise'. Dethridge's response was that 'we shall assume that both [the A series and the C series indices] are compiled correctly, until a further investigation has been made. They are official tables which have been published for years, and

---

[24] I have not been able to locate either the document tendered on behalf of Copland or the replies.

we will assume that they have been compiled correctly'; and 'Government publications have to be regarded presumably as correct. If that were not so, the Court could not act on any Government publication' (pp. 1884, 1886). In the event, as we shall see, the Court did not adopt the C series index until 1933.

Gibson challenged the assumption that the wage reduction sought by the employers would not take the basic wage below the *Harvester* standard. In the initial computation of the (A series) price index, the value for 1910 was set at 1000, and the Statistician produced a single number for 1907 of 875. Gibson (who mentioned that he had first appeared in the Court in March 1907) disputed the reliability of this retrospective estimate:

> With the exception of firms like Moran & Cato in Melbourne, and McIlwraith's in Sydney, I know of no firms which keep or issue a monthly price list of commodities which they sell. The same thing applies in regard to the other services taken beside food and groceries, in regard to an authentic price list which can be referred to. When we come to dairy produce, and look at such items as onions and potatoes, and the many things which enter into the meat regimen, we find it almost impossible to get actual data as to the prices at which the respective joints were selling for three years prior to the investigation. I know that Sir George Knibbs, if he were present, would probably refute as ridiculous my assertion that the prices ascertained for the purpose of computing that figure of 1000 which he gave in 1907 were largely based on guess work and assumption. But to my mind it is more than a coincidence that the figure found for 1907 was 875; it is more than a coincidence that the figure of 875 divides actually by 7 … For accountancy purposes 125 can be made equal to 1s. I am a little bit surprised that he did not fix the figure at 840, and thus make the calculation a little bit simpler. But whether it be 875 or 840, I think the contention is almost irrefutable that the figure itself was a matter of conjecture and guess work. (p. 1947)

Gibson also spoke of the manner in which the Court had circumscribed the issues in the case.

> I think it would be idle for anyone to stand up at this table and seek to refute that the national dividend or the national income has diminished, or seek to refute that cessation of public borrowing overseas … is not, temporarily at any rate, the position. Therefore, if those are the issues, to my way of thinking—and I say it with all humility, and without the slightest intention of being offensive—we might just as well refrain from addressing the Court any further … (p. 1944)

Dethridge replied that even if the facts were incontrovertible, it did not necessarily follow that there should be a reduction of the basic wage. Beeby likewise said that 'the issue is, is wage reduction a remedy or a partial remedy for the new economic position which has arisen? That, to me, is the issue. … I was waiting anxiously to get argument on that point' (p. 1944).

Crofts complained about the Court's acceptance of the statement by Copland replying to union witnesses such as Irvine and Gunn. Dethridge rebuffed him: 'I told you the other day that the Court holds itself free and in duty bound to exercise freedom to inform its mind in the way it thinks fair and just' (p. 1971). Dethridge expanded on the point:

> I know there is a difficulty in connection with investigations of this nature, but to let the parties know everything that influences the Court's mind … is quite out of the question. To do that, taking my own case, for instance, it would be necessary for me to inform you of the result of my economic reading, which began quite a considerable number of years ago at the University of Melbourne, when I took Economics as one of my subjects, and I have kept up contact with economics to some extent ever since. Well, how can I inform you of the influence of that upon my mind? It is going to influence me, I can assure you. (p. 1973)

When Chapple attempted to discuss the condition of the railways, the Court's patience was strained. The railways, said Dethridge, were a barometer of the general position of the country, and only in this sense were they relevant; but

> the evidence of greatest weight rests in two categories, namely, (1) national income and (2) unemployment. … I think I may say that at

> present it appears to me that the main thing, and probably the only thing, which this Court should consider is how far will any action that it takes … affect the amount of unemployment in this community at the present time. So far as we are concerned, unemployment is the evil to be remedied. (p. 1986)

Dethridge said later: 'It will probably turn out that we will have to come to the conclusion that the only justification for a reduction of the basic wage is whether that reduction will tend to check the increase of unemployment, and to create more avenues of employment' (p. 2032).

Beeby demanded a sense of perspective that was larger than the details of errors made by the Railways Commissioners—whether they had 'wrongly built a bridge somewhere in the back country'. No one, he said,

> can deny what has happened so far as our national income is concerned and with unemployment, that is what Mr Gibson put to the Court, and that is what I am interested in, namely, is a wage reduction the remedy, and if it must come, must it be part of a general scheme? That is what I am directing my mind to. I do not like constantly to be interfering and appearing to be irritable, but when we are dealing with a great national issue of that kind, to listen to trifling details of this nature is exasperating, and I have just about reached my limit. (p. 1986)

Beeby's reference to a 'general scheme' was an allusion to Copland's advocacy of a set of economic reforms whereof a wage reduction was one element: Gibson (and other union advocates) contended that a wage reduction should only be countenanced as part of an overall package, most aspects of which were outside the Court's control. Copland himself had said that the wage reduction would have the greatest benefit if it were implemented as part of a wider plan, but had maintained that the reduction was necessary even if the other measures were not taken. Beeby said that the union argument which appealed most to him was Gibson's contention that 'this Court should not accept the old-fashioned principle that the first thing to do in the time of depression is to reduce wages; if economic forces do force a reduction of wages, it should come not first, but should be part of a general scheme to bring about a re-establishment of things on a new basis, if it is to come at all' (p. 2025–2026).

During Grayndler's submissions, attention reverted to the question of 'spending power'. Grayndler submitted:

> Naturally, no one denies that there has been a drop in the national income. The reason for it is not only that there are no markets overseas for our products but that our local markets are not being supplied because the people have not the money to purchase the things which we grow and manufacture. Therefore, a drop in wages would only accentuate the trouble. (p. 2064)

Dethridge said that there was 'a great deal of confusion as to spending power':

> Many people think that money constitutes spending power, but there is no getting away from the fact that it does not. Money, after all, is only a tool to be used in the exercise of spending power, which is derived from marketable goods and services. Once we get that point clear in our minds we can see what follows from the fact that what constituted our spending power in the past—our wheat and our wool—is no longer spending power. (p. 2066)

The following discussion ensued:

> Beeby J: I have never yet had this illustration properly met. Leave money out of the consideration altogether, and assume that for a hundred bales of wool we were getting 1000 boxes of tea in exchange. Now, the people from whom we get our tea say 'We want 150 bales of wool in exchange for a thousand boxes of tea.' That is what the whole question comes down to, it is a question of goods. ... To that extent our spending power has been reduced.
>
> Mr Grayndler: Let us admit that, let us say that it is a fact. Then we have the position that when the 150 boxes of tea arrive here, there is nobody to use it, or the people cannot buy it.
>
> Beeby J: That is another matter.

> Mr Grayndler: The great majority of the working class have not the necessary tokens with which to buy the tea.
>
> Dethridge C J: That may be, although it is hard to believe. There is no doubt that money is only a tool, nothing else, which we use in the exercise of our spending power. It may be that the supply of the money tool is insufficient; but that is a matter for considerable argument. The real spending power, as shown by the illustration which my brother Beeby just put, is the wool. (pp. 2066–2067)

Beeby added that a wage reduction entailed 'no cutting down of the aggregate spending power, but simply a transfer of spending power from employed wage earners to other people'.

> True, it may be that that transfer of spending power will stick to the employers. If it does, my personal opinion is that then the transfer will be of no benefit to the community. That is my own personal opinion, because to be of benefit to the community, that spending power must be transferred from the employed wage earners and the employers to the other section of the community. It is questionable whether it will be, but that point has to be argued out.

'That', said Drake-Brockman, 'is the problem in a nutshell' (p. 2068).

The comments from the Bench reported above suggest that the Judges were not fully alive to the *secondary* effects of the fall in export prices and foreign borrowing. Beeby's homely example was to the point so far as it went: the decline in the terms of trade necessarily entailed a fall in the national income. The issue that remained, however, was whether this was to be the extent of the fall. Copland's evidence squarely raised that issue. Copland proposed various measures to minimise the secondary effects, including a wage reduction. Other passages in the hearing, and the decision itself, leave little room for doubt that the Court did understand the distinction between primary and secondary effects, even if the exchange with Grayndler suggests otherwise. What the Judges were apparently unable to accept was the possibility that purchasing power might be 'injected' as one way of minimising the secondary effects. In a pre-Keynesian world, of course, they were not alone in this.

Crofts raised the issue of excessive dependence on the rest of the world. He referred to a statement of W M Hughes (in a pamphlet, *Bond or Free?*) that 'we should maintain existing standards and concentrate upon making ourselves a self-contained nation'. 'The Court', said Crofts, 'will remember that that really bears out what Professor Irvine has put'. Beeby agreed, but emphasised the problems of transition:

> We may have to face the position that we simply cannot look to the future to maintain our prosperity by prices for the surplus products which we send abroad. We may have to concentrate on becoming more self-contained. I think that is inevitable. The difficulty is the period of transition—while we are changing over and finding employment for people who are out of employment now on account of the falling away of primary production. It is the period of transition to the new order. (p. 2116)

Dethridge made the point that a need for and possibility of restructuring did not make the current wage level viable:

> Our national spending power … has materially been diminished as a result of the fall in our export prices and the cessation of borrowing. There has been a consequent loss of employing power. As a result a great many men are out of employment … To employ them will mean either the development of existing industries, or the extension of existing industries, or the creation of new. It may be that the only way to bring about that extension of existing industries, or that creation of new industries, will be by reduction of wage costs. (pp. 2121–2122)

Crofts and Dethridge discussed further the case for autarky:

Mr Crofts: But as to Professor Irvine, he referred to books. He said that we may say to the wool grower or to the wheat farmer, 'You are growing too much wool and too much wheat.' But he said that we import books, for instance, and that we should do this work for ourselves in the future; we may not get as good a cover as the imported, but ours will be as serviceable as the imported, and it will keep our people employed. And he said that there are many industries to which he could refer in that way on which we could employ workers from the land more profitably than in growing wool.

Dethridge C J: It may be that there is a great deal of force in that, but the difficulty about all suggestions of that kind is that it will take a very long time to develop those new industries …

Mr Crofts: I disagree with that. Industries are being built up from day to day …

Dethridge C J: Unfortunately, unemployment is increasing more and more.

Crofts: We say that the reason is fear; the employers will not unbutton; and some of the employers would do so, but the banks will not allow them. (pp. 2126–2127)

A reference by Crofts to an article by R C Mills, based on a paper given to the Commonwealth Government's Industrial Peace Conference in February 1929, led to discussion of the economic merits of 'high wages' and the associated issue of productivity (Mills 1929). Dethridge produced a copy of the *Economic Record* containing Mills' paper and read from it. Mills said that 'there exists the too-common tendency here as elsewhere, especially in time of depression, to attack wages and standards, first as a method of reducing costs when it really should be the last resort to be undertaken only when other methods have been explored as an alternative to something worse' (p. 2153). Crofts described Mills as being 'in extreme opposition to Professor Copland'. Dethridge responded:

> He is not. All he says there might be quite consistent with what Professor Copland said. The position is that Professor Mills simply says that real high wages [sic] are desirable, and I suppose all reasonable men agree with that. Then he goes on to say that high wages are not a cause of prosperity. … He says that high wages are not themselves the cause of prosperity, but are a result of prosperity. That is to say, high wages and high productivity run together. You cannot have high wages without high productivity. It does not matter what your money system is. And that, I am afraid, goes to a good deal of what you have been

CHARLES A. CROFTS, Secretary, A.C.T.U., 1927–1943.

Charles Crofts

saying. It does not matter a scrap what your money system is, what your currency methods are; unless you have high productivity, you cannot have high wages. It may be, I grant you, that your monetary system is very defective, and it may be that your monetary system is so defective as to militate against high productivity, but you cannot have high wages without high productivity. (pp. 2155–2156)

Crofts said that wages, in the past, had not been higher than the productivity of Australia warranted. Dethridge noted 'some suggestion in the evidence here that, during the last 8 or 9 years, anyhow, wages have outstripped productivity per head of population, and that has shown itself, even before this pronounced slump at the present moment, in an increasing rate of unemployment' (p. 2156). There ensued an exchange as to what had happened to productivity—a debate unaided by any specific definition of productivity, and much uncertainty as to what the numbers actually showed.

According to Dethridge, there may have been some increase in productivity during the 1920s, but it did not regain the level of 1911; and 'assuming there has been an increase from 1920 in the production per head [of population], the suggestion is that during that ten years, there has been a still greater increase in effective wages' (p. 2162).

Crofts challenged the legitimacy of the Court's taking into account the problem of unemployment. 'All this Court has to do', he said, 'is to settle a dispute and to say what is a reasonable wage for men who are in employment and who are going to be employed in industry' (p. 2165). He also said that it was not the Court's business to take into consideration the inability of Government to borrow overseas: the response to that was a matter for the Government, not the Court (p. 2168). Dethridge said—with particular reference to unemployment—

> It is a problem I have been considering ... The matter is a little bit troublesome at present. ... The position is that this is another of the absurd results of the absurd system of fixing a basic wage in the Commonwealth sphere. I am waiting to hear what can be said in regard to the proposition that this Court can only arbitrate in actual disputes; that it cannot deal with matters which are of nation-wide importance; and that it cannot attempt to remedy evils which are not directly situated in the industrial dispute with which it is concerned. ... It may be that the ultimate answer to the question is that this Court has no right, and never had any right, to fix a basic wage at all. ... That all it can do is to deal with conditions between the parties to a dispute, and should not attempt to introduce anything in the nature of a general rule as to a minimum wage. As to a minimum wage in an industry, yes, but not as to a basic wage for general application. ... It may be that we have gone beyond the constitutional limits. If so, it has been condoned by the legislature. ... If we have the power to introduce a basic wage as a matter of general application, then I should think that it would follow that we have, or ought to have, the power to consider general unemployment; one hinges upon the other. (pp. 2165, 2168)

This exchange raised squarely the capacity of the Court to base its decisions on macroeconomic criteria and to pursue macroeconomic objectives. Whatever doubt Dethridge may have expressed here does not seem to have altered the Court's course of action. The issue was resolved conclusively by the High Court in 1953 (*R v Kelly; Ex parte Australian Railways' Union* (1953) 89 CLR 461).

Dethridge, during Crofts' submissions, repeatedly affirmed the cogency of unemployment as evidence that wages were too high. 'I shall be very delighted', he said,

> to come to the conclusion that there is this productivity which has been, in a way, secretly annexed by employers or capitalists, or some other class than the wage earners. ... Supposing this share has been annexed by the capitalist classes ... What do they do with it? They do not put it away in oil drums in their backyards. They spend it. They may spend it in luxuries, but they spend it; and, if they spend it in luxuries, they give employment ... It comes back to that. All money spent can only be spent, ultimately, by giving some men employment. Very well, if we find a considerable amount of unemployment and increasing unemployment, it rather suggests that this secret commandeering does not now exist. (pp. 2179–2180)

A subsequent exchange went as follows:

Mr Crofts: Has the Court before it any information regarding any particular industry other than the railways? Twenty-two organisations of employers are represented here, but what evidence has come from them; there is no evidence.

Dethridge C J: No, but we have the evidence of what is alleged to be a considerable fall in the national income. We also have the other evidence, which is of much more significance, in regard to the frightful increase in the number of unemployed, in the rate of unemployment.

Mr Crofts: And every industry is to get the benefit of the reduction?

...

> Dethridge C J: The only reason for an adverse decision will be if we come to the conclusion that it will be beneficial to wage earners chiefly, and to industry, and not to employers directly, except in regard to the restoration of industry. (pp. 2208–2209)

'But the difficulty, and the ominous problem', said Dethridge subsequently, 'is the gradual increase of unemployment. That is the only thing that is of moment.' Crofts replied that increased productivity might mean more unemployment. Dethridge responded:

> No. Speaking broadly, the more productivity there is, the more employment there is. The more productivity, the greater the spending power and the greater the employing power. I am making allowance for people running Home, and spending money in Paris on luxuries and so on; but the greater part of increased productivity—if there is any—is spent at home. ... Increased productivity, due to different or new methods, may mean less employment in a particular industry. But let us assume that the whole of the increased productivity is spent in the country producing; then that must mean employment in that country. ... Reason it out. I am asking you to assume that in a self-contained country from which they cannot get away with the profits which they have filched from the working classes, they have to spend those profits in order to get any use out of them. They may spend part in further unnecessary capital goods; but apart from that, they have to spend it on consumption goods; and it may be they will spend it in all of various ways, but it all means employment. Anything that is spent means employment of some kind. (pp. 2245–2246)

An obvious flaw in this argument is the failure to recognise that with an increase in productivity, a given level of output could be achieved with fewer workers. This error was probably due to the lack of any definition of 'productivity'. I defer for later comment the presumption, repeatedly asserted, that production automatically generated commensurate spending.

Unsurprisingly, Crofts asserted a positive relation between wages and purchasing power—a contention that was at odds with Dethridge's circular-flow analysis of production and spending power. Dethridge said that Crofts was assuming 'that you can increase purchasing power by increasing wages'. 'It cannot be done', he said.

> The only thing which will increase purchasing power, or which constitutes purchasing power, is a marketable product or service. There is nothing else constituting purchasing power. If you double, treble, or quadruple wages without increasing marketable products, either goods or services, you do not increase the purchasing power one scrap. (p. 2254–2256)

Dethridge saw the 'purchasing power' argument for higher wages in the same light as monetary schemes:

> I am meeting your argument that an increase in wages would at once lead to an increase in real purchasing power. It would simply mean an all round increase in prices, and everybody would be where he started from ... That is the flaw, to my mind, in all these arguments which are put forward by Mr Chomley, Professor Irvine and other writers of the Douglas school and others who have a system of financing the working consumer by somehow or other handing out money to the wage earners. It simply means that prices are put up all round. (p. 2259)

On the issue of the automatic expenditure of spending power generated by production, Crofts attacked Copland, accusing him of both ignorance and bias:

> [Professor Copland] was asked, 'Do I get it from you, then, that money saved immediately goes into circulation', and he replied, 'Yes, always.' Well, of the authorities, Hobson says different, and Professor Irvine says different. Professor Irvine says, as Hobson says, that it does not always go into circulation, and, as the balance-sheets show, a lot of it is hidden; a lot of it is put away in reserves and buildings, and then depreciation is taken off, etc, etc. Much of it, particularly in this country, does not go into circulation—certainly not immediately—so again it shows that this Professor of Economics, as I have said, is not a Professor of Economics. He is Chairman of the Chamber of Manufactures and Chamber of

Commerce school of teaching young fellows to run businesses profitably, and he tells them that they can only run their businesses profitably by reducing wages. I am putting it that the Professor apparently does not know his subject, or he was not prepared to put the whole of his cards on the table when he came to this Court. (p. 2353)

But Crofts was here in a difficult position. Not merely was he attacking Copland's evidence: he was criticising a contention that Dethridge had repeatedly articulated as if it were a truism—that production automatically generates equivalent expenditure. Neither of the other Judges indicated any disagreement with Dethridge on this point.[25]

Dethridge summarised the case for a wage reduction:

I agree that, with regard to subsisting industries, the mere transfer of spending power from the present employed wage earners to employers will not have any very beneficial effect, except so far as that spending power is passed on from the employers to other sections of the community who are now short of spending power … But the main possible result of a reduction of the basic wage is that it will enable other industries to be established which will absorb the at present unemployed. That cannot be done at once, of course. It must be a slow process, in any event. Professor Copland himself indicated that any process of that kind is going to be fairly slow in its results, but, apparently, it is the only way of meeting the present situation. … A mere increase of money wages, such as has been suggested from your end of the table, Mr Crofts, will not have that effect unless it is accompanied by a greater real spending power. A mere

---

[25] Crofts extended his criticism of Copland, though shifting from the accusation of bias to one of inhabiting an ivory tower: 'May I put this in favour of Professor Irvine? I feel that he is an independent witness. I think his papers show that he has kept abreast of the position so far as economics are concerned, and I think he has the added experience over Professor Copland that he has practical business experience, and that is increased by the fact that it is in connection with banking. Therefore, I say that … he is more likely to be of value to the Court than a man who has simply made himself a teacher. Teachers get into a groove. They get the old masters, and they very seldom like to break away. It is particularly hard for them to break away, especially if they are in a university, where they have the textbooks year in and year out. They simply follow that line of thought.' Beeby retorted: 'I do not think that can be said of Professor Copland. He does not rely on textbooks. He writes his own' (p. 2371).

increase of wages without a corresponding increase of power to transfer real goods and services simply means an increase in prices; that is all. … But the point we have to deal with is an urgent present situation, and that is, in some way or other, to get our present export industries maintained. … There is no means of immediate adjustment. Professor Irvine and Mr Gordon Massey seem to assume that it is a simple thing to be done, but it is going to be a most laborious and lengthy process to substitute other industries for our wool and other export industries. … It is for that reason only that this proposed reduction of the basic wage calls for the most serious consideration. Without that, I should not think there was any real case made. A mere transfer of spending power from the wage earners to the present employers, unless it tends to prevent the further disastrous decrease of our present industries, and also tends to encourage the growth and creation of new industries, would, I agree, be injurious to the community, rather than beneficial. (pp. 2303–2304)[26]

It was on 8 January 1931—a week from the completion of the hearing and two weeks from the decision—and during Crofts' submissions, that Dethridge alluded to the possibility of a decision affecting all wages, and not just the basic wage:

[I]f the Court does make an alteration in the basic wage, it will automatically in most cases, in the absence of very special circumstances, apply the alteration to all other awards of this Court which are in existence. That is the position. It may be that a better way to meet the situation, if any alteration in wages is to be made in view of the condition of the country, would be by a percentage cut on all wages, to be regarded as a measure to operate until things improve. It may be that would be a better way to go about the job which the Court has before it. Whether the further relief claimed in the summonses before

---

[26] In a later remark to Crofts, Dethridge appears to resile somewhat from his criticism of monetary solutions: 'I may say that it is quite a relevant and legitimate argument for you to say that the unemployed here at the present time are not in that position through wages being too high but because of insufficient credit facilities. That is a legitimate argument which the Court will have to consider' (p. 2331).

> us enables that to be done may be worthy of consideration. You may take it that, so far as the basic wage is concerned, if any alteration is made, it will be made in these proceedings as to all matters listed, but as to other matters not listed they will have to be brought up subsequently in separate applications. (p. 2349)

The 'further relief claimed in the summonses' referred to catch-all terms added to the primary applications, which called for reduction of the basic wage via the adoption of the C series index and the removal of Powers' Three Shillings. Crofts evidently failed to appreciate the significance of Dethridge's 'hint' and did not respond to it.

Mindful, no doubt, of the industrial and political pressures bearing upon him, Crofts came to a truculent, if forlorn, conclusion:

> Not for ever are we going to come pleading to this Court not to reduce the basic wage. We are going to demand it and we shall resist to the very last, and we shall not have taken away from us what it has taken 40 years to obtain. We have been preaching arbitration—many of our comrades with greater ability than we in this Court tell us we are wrong—but we have taken some risks even in our positions in our attempts to show the workers of this country that arbitration is right. But I never thought that I would have to stand up here to defend the meagre basic wage that we have got after 40 years of struggle. (p. 2406)

L C Meagher, for the Victorian Chamber of Manufactures, responded to the union contention that the Court should not move unless and until other authorities took the steps which the situation demanded:

> It is inconceivable to think that a Court such as this is, charged with one specific duty, namely the settling of disputes, should refrain from exercising its function if it is convinced that its function should be exercised. If it is convinced that the applicants in this case have made a good claim for the reduction of the basic wage by 10 per cent, surely it should not influence the Court one jot whatever any other authority charged with other duties sees fit to do or not to do. ... It is also to be borne in mind in this connection that one, already, of the three things

suggested by Professor Copland has to all intent and purposes been done, that is to say the liberating of the exchange rate, and if this Court were to find that we have substantiated our claim for a reduction of the basic wage, then a complete half of Professor Copland's rehabilitation scheme will have been carried out and the remaining duty will devolve upon the Government—the duty of balancing its Budget. (pp. 2426–2427)

Meagher, the first of the employer advocates to address the Court, sought to downplay the employers' initial reliance on the substitution of the All Items table for the All Houses index (confined to food, groceries, and rent):

> I want to say, on behalf of the private employers, that we lay no great store by that particular table. If the Unions want the Court's order … to exclude reference to that table, I do not see that we can have any very serious objection to it. If they think that that particular table is an integral part of our application … that is not so. If the Court thinks that our case has been substantiated, we are prepared to take an order from the Court in another form altogether, and it follows from what I have said about the things which have been grafted on to the *Harvester* standard since 1907 that there is a money amount quite sufficient for the purpose of the application which can be deducted from today's basic wage without in any way infringing upon the *Harvester* standard as laid down by Mr Justice Higgins. … Your Honour the Chief Judge said that, under no circumstances, in these proceedings, would the decision of the Court order a wage which went below the equivalent of 7s a day in 1907. (pp. 2429–2430)

Dethridge replied: 'In substance, yes. We want to keep as near that as we can.' The problem for Meagher was that in the initial arguments, the employers *had* relied upon (1) removing Powers' three shillings and (2) substituting the C series for the A series index to justify their claim that the basic wage could be reduced by about 10 per cent without taking it below *Harvester*. The removal of Powers' three shillings alone was not sufficient. If the substitution of indices were abandoned, how could the remainder of the reduction be effected within the limit of *Harvester*? Meagher introduced a quite new consideration. The *Harvester* wage was 7 shillings *per day*. A worker in 1907 might not get 42 shillings per week, because he might not have employment for 6 days. Since the time of *Harvester*, the Court had provided in its awards for weekly wages. This benefit had been assessed by Powers as having a value of 5 shillings per week—an estimate that had been endorsed by Quick and Beeby. Hence there was an amount of about 5 shillings that could be removed without going below *Harvester*. Crofts interjected (accurately) that the *Harvester* standard had been determined by Higgins as 42 shillings per week, though expressed as 7 shillings per day. That Meagher's argument elicited no response from the Bench is probably a good indication that the Judges had lost interest in the *Harvester* benchmark and were focusing their attention almost exclusively on the economic aspect of the case.

F H Corke, representing various employer groups in New South Wales, sought to emphasise the pre-eminence of primary production:

> There seem to be two Australian obsessions; one is the standard of living and the other, which is the considered policy of Australia which must not be disputed, is high protection. And we can hardly consider the position that has arisen in Australia without some reference to the effects of the tariff—as to the tariff reacting on arbitration and arbitration again reacting on the tariff ... In considering this larger question we have to bear in mind, as so much has been said about world conditions and world finance, that this is the only country where wages are so completely regulated and, as I contend, which is the least able to bear it. ... I submit that this country, being entirely dependent on primary products, should have avoided such a definite regulation of wages in the cities. (p. 2486)

The theories advanced by Irvine and others, said Dethridge, assumed that it was 'a comparatively easy thing to substitute for the export industries we now have running ... other industries which will supply the country with sufficient marketable production ... to enable the wages which they think should be maintained to be maintained and paid' (p. 2493).

Corke regretted that the applications before the Court allowed for only modest wage reductions. The reduction should be at least 25 per cent. Better still would be a suspension of all awards for a definite time:

> Then we would find the proper basis upon which we could carry on under the present conditions, something that the country could pay and yet absorb all the unemployed. It may be, and I think the Court would certainly hold that having found the basis by which all could be employed, we might have to build up again from that basis, and perhaps build up rapidly. But it would have the advantage of providing employment for all, and at the same time finding our real position. (p. 2543)

Dethridge disagreed:

> That is very questionable, in my opinion. A very radical reduction of wages, in my opinion, would probably do more harm than good. We have to remember that any reduction to the wage earners in the aggregate hits the necessity industries, and a wholesale reduction of wages would close up ---
>
> Mr Corke: It would temporarily disorganise everything, but ---
>
> Dethridge C J: Undoubtedly it would, and one has also to recollect that the home industries are the larger part of our industries. They may depend for their very existence upon the continuation of the primary industries. They are secondary industries in that sense, and they cannot continue to exist unless we have some fundamental industries still in existence, but we have to recollect that, although that be so, a wholesale reduction of wages, more than that which is necessary for the sustenance of the fundamental industries, would lead to mischief. ... we have to find the balance. Too great a reduction, to my mind, would not only lead to a mere temporary dislocation, but would lead to a permanent disabling of a great part of the industry of this country. (pp. 2543–2544)

Corke accepted that 'what is in the mind of the Court and everybody else is 10 per cent'. This equated to 8 shillings, 'and that, of course, is made up, we submit, by the 5 shillings and the 3 shillings addition'. The 5 shillings was 'the equivalent of the weekly wage'—the contention previously put by Meagher (p. 2545). At this point—in the second-last day of the hearing—Drake-Brockman asked whether the wage reduction should be confined to the basic wage. 'A great deal of your discussion', he said to Corke, 'and, certainly, the attitude of Professor Copland, was based on a reduction of wages rather than a reduction of the basic wage. What about dealing with it on some such lines as that, rather than on one section of the wage?' Fraser pointed out that the original application was for the railways, where only the basic wage could be affected (because the award regulation of margins had been suspended) (p. 2546). Dethridge indicated some sympathy for Drake-Brockman's implicit suggestion. When Beeby questioned whether the Court could go outside the limit of the claims, Corke invoked the 'further relief' terms of most of the applications. In the ensuing discussion, Corke referred to the effect of the Court's decision on women's rates. Drake-Brockman said that if the case were confined to the basic wage, women would not be affected at all, 'or it looks like that'. But if the order were for a general 10 per cent reduction, women would be covered by it. This comment led the representative of the Clothing and Allied Trades' Union, to say that before there was any decision affecting women, he wanted to be heard; he had acted 'on the assumption that the question of the female workers is not before the Court at present' (p. 2548). This was an obvious point of natural justice which (to judge from the transcript) was ignored by the Court. The same point could have been made about margins, but the unions let it pass.[27]

The Commonwealth Government had publicly expressed its opposition to a wage reduction. This is the background to the following incident reported in the transcript:

> Mr Crofts: I now desire to refer the Court to a statement in this morning's *Argus*.

---

[27] At the conclusion of the case, Crofts inquired whether it was open to the Court 'to meet the desires of the employers in some way other than that asked for in their application'. 'Can the Court make an order reducing wages, say, by 10 per cent, without ---'. Dethridge interposed: 'We have to consider the position. That is all I can say, Mr Crofts' (2620).

> Dethridge C J: Oh, dear me ---
>
> Mr Crofts: You have taken quotations from the other side, and I want to quote what the Prime Minister of this country has said.
>
> Dethridge C J: I object. I prohibit you from going further. I forbid you to make reference to anything of that kind. Sit down! (His Honour here ordered the Court crier to bring a policeman.) If you do not sit down, I shall have you removed from the Court. Do you undertake not to proceed with the reference to the Prime Minister? Do you undertake not to proceed with the reference to the Prime Minister?
>
> Mr Crofts resumes his seat. (p. 2553)

On the next and final day of the case, Dethridge spoke directly to Crofts:

> If you attempt, as, in my opinion, you obviously were doing yesterday, to improperly influence this Court by calling attention to a statement by the Prime Minister concerning a matter which is in issue in this Court, the Court must object to it. ... This Court has nothing to do with what any Minister of the Commonwealth, with what any person on the legislative side, or the Executive side of the community, might say. You must understand that. I do wish you would try to realise that we are here as Judges, and we must resist most strongly any attempt to coerce us on the part of the Executive of the country, either directly or indirectly. (p. 2603)

The Government did, however, appear as of right in the Court, its views being put by Fraser. His instructions were 'to submit here certain arguments, and to make whatever observation the evidence renders necessary, against the present application' (p. 2554). His submissions do not suggest that he was supported by significant expert advice. Rather, he seems to have attended to the evidence given in the Court and placed the best possible construction upon it from his client's viewpoint.

Fraser argued that the Court could not take into consideration general unemployment. It was the Court's function to settle disputes. In doing so, it might take into account unemployment within the industry concerned, but not more generally. Drake-Brockman asked:

> Supposing there were a dispute in the shipping industry which resulted in a cessation of work and that cessation of work brought about, not by strike but by absence of employment, unemployment in other industries, and there were repercussions from those other industries to yet other industries … could not the Court take into consideration the unemployment brought about by that dispute? (p. 2558)

'I submit not', replied Fraser. Dethridge pressed him:

> Do you see where you are driven by your argument …? Supposing it to be established beyond a doubt that no sensible man could come to any conclusion other than that the basic wage is destroying industries wholesale, and leading to unemployment of an appalling nature. … On your argument or suggestion, this Court would have to disregard that effect of the basic wage, and still maintain it, let it go on doing its destructive work.

Fraser preferred 'not to go as far as that' (p. 2562). But he assented when Dethridge put it that, on Fraser's understanding, the basic wage 'cannot be decreased in any circumstances however injurious it may be shown to be' (p. 2563). Beeby asked what provision of the Act led to this interpretation. Fraser answered that the legislature first made explicit reference to the basic wage in 1926. By then, the basic wage had a well-defined meaning in the Court's practice, which the legislature implicitly recognised. 'A recognition', asked Dethridge' 'as meaning a wage irreducible by the Court?' 'Yes', said Fraser (p. 2563). When Beeby put it that, on this view, the basic wage could not be increased, either, Fraser disagreed:

> No, I do not suggest that as the meaning of the term 'basic wage' at all. It is the minimum below which we must not go. … But it does not say that we are prevented from going higher. (p. 2566)

'The Court', said Fraser, 'is not the remedy for all the ills of the body politic. The legislature has cognisance of the position, and of the decline in the national income, and of the Depression, and if the legislature considers that one of the operating causes is a high basic wage then the legislature can interfere' (p. 2567).

In what was, in effect, an alternative submission, Fraser said that the burden of showing that a basic wage reduction was necessary rested on the employer applicants. 'But what', he asked, 'do the applicants do?'

> [T]hey put forward one claim, and one claim only, and that is Professor Copland's scheme. He described his scheme in the article appearing in the *Economic Record* as a scheme that should be put into force as a whole; he said it was almost imperative that the whole scheme should be put into operation. (p. 2577)

The Court should not contemplate a wage reduction unless the applicants satisfied it that all other necessary steps to deal with the economic situation had been taken. Fraser did not acknowledge Copland's statement from the witness box that the basic wage should be reduced *even if* the other recommended steps were not taken. Drake-Brockman noted a further problem with the submission:

> Drake-Brockman J: If we were to follow on the lines of your suggestion that the onus is on the employers to show that everything else has been done that could possibly be done, before they are justified in asking that this Court should deal with the only element it can deal with, there are certain things to be considered. For instance, there are some people who say that the tariff should be altered; some say that there should be prohibition of imports. Others say that there should be complete free trade. Then we come to the question of exchange. Some people say that the exchange rate should be pegged at a high level; some say it should be at a low level, and some say that it should be free. Where do we get to? How are we going to decide that all the things that should and could be done have, in fact, been done, when we come to deal with the one and only factor we can deal with?

Mr Fraser: It has been said in this Court that a reduction of this nature should be the very last resort; therefore, is it not necessary for the applicants to show first that all the other avenues have been explored?

Drake-Brockman J: But my difficulty is to know when we have come to the very last resort. (p. 2578)

During Fraser's address, Dethridge put the view that the unemployment level was the issue which cut through all others:

> Then I suppose you get back to this—and I think it comes down to this—that the main evidence the present wage level is too high—so high as to make industry unprofitable for any available market—is the high amount of unemployment. If you have a market available—and in this case it means partly the home market for home industries and partly, of course, the export market—and if the costs of industry are sufficiently low to give a reasonable chance of running industries at a profit to supply those markets, there will be no abnormal unemployment. That is the argument. And when you get down to a national position of this kind, it is practically the only argument—the only evidence that is of any use. It is true that unemployment may be due to other causes as well; but at any rate one knows that if you do have too high a wage level, make the costs of production too high for the available market, of course unemployment results. (p. 2574)

9.2.9 The decision

At the end of the hearing, Corke asked when the Court would give its decision. Dethridge replied: 'We cannot say. Our minds are still in a state of great complexity. We cannot say now what is the wisest thing to do in the circumstances of this case. I will not say we are in a state of bewilderment, but we are still seeking some definite conclusion …' (p. 2624). The Court, nevertheless, took just a week to finalise and publish its decision—testimony to its sense of urgency about the coming reduction.

The Court recognised that 'a proposal to reduce wage standards, laboriously built up by organised labour during the last quarter of a century, naturally met with strenuous opposition' (*Basic Wage and Wage Reduction Inquiry* 30 CAR 2, 8).

> But however desirous a Court with wage fixing powers may be to maintain standards largely created through its instrumentality it cannot accept the principle enunciated that under no circumstances should there be reductions. In the past the Court has been compelled by economic circumstances to refuse to apply those standards to particular industries, and in some industries to reduce standards which previously it had prescribed. Always it has been necessary and always it will be necessary to entertain applications to vary awards on the ground of substantial change in economic conditions. (p. 8)

The essence of the crisis was the deterioration of the external accounts. A major aspect was the fall in the terms of trade:

> All the theorising in the world cannot alter the fact that in goods we are at present receiving £40,000,000 worth per annum less than we received two years ago in exchange for our exports. To quote a simple illustration: before 1929, for 100 bales of wool or 1000 bags of wheat we received in exchange, say, 1000 boxes of tea; now, for the same quantity of wool we can only exchange 600 boxes of tea, or for the 1000 boxes of tea we are asked to provide 140 bales of wool or 1600 bags of wheat. (pp. 8–9)

This was the essence of the current account problem. But it was compounded by the capital account:

> Before the present disturbance we were able to borrow £30,000,000 per annum for use in developmental and other labour-employing works. Now we cannot borrow money from abroad ... It is true that this £30,000,000 per annum is not in the true sense of the term national income; it is true that ultimately we may be better off if public borrowing comes from internal wealth. But for the moment and for some time to come we have £30,000,000 less to spend, making, with the loss from fall in prices, a total of £70,000,000 as compared with 1928. (p. 9)

The £70 million corresponded to what the economists saw as the primary loss. But, said the Court, the disaster did not end there.

> Such a violent change in spending power reacted in all directions. It immediately reduced income derived from services, particularly those controlled by State railway and tramway authorities whose receipts declined rapidly and whose deficits increased month by month at an alarming rate. This with other declines in public revenue left the State and the Commonwealth Governments unable to balance their budgets. Grave governmental deficiencies created a general air of financial insecurity which increased the general stagnation. Then again the contraction of purchasing power traceable to a direct loss of income led to further decline in productivity. The first loss was added to by further losses the extent of which cannot be calculated. Opinions differ as to the actual money figure for these repercussions. Some economists are of opinion that they equal the original loss, but this probably is an exaggeration. It can be safely said, however, that for the moment they exceed 50 per cent of the primary loss making the reduced spending power of the community over £100,000,000, or in the vicinity of one-sixth of the average national income of the preceding five years. (p. 9)

Some of the decline was 'psychological in origin'. The prevailing uncertainty, the precarious state of public finance and falling prices were responsible for much of the commercial and industrial stagnation. 'But taking the most optimistic view, it is clear that the bulk of the lost spending power is a harsh reality, and the restoration of the customary value of our productivity will be a long and laborious process.' It was difficult, said the Court, to get the unions to accept this harsh reality (p. 11).

The Court referred to Irvine's advocacy of a greater detachment of the Australian economy from the rest of the world. It was unimpressed, for reasons of both a long-term and a short-term character:

> To achieve that ideal we must do without mineral oils, rubber goods, cotton fabrics, and many other commodities which we regard as necessaries, and must also repudiate our foreign interest liabilities …

> Complete isolation may be desirable to some, but it is clear that its achievement means the adoption of all-round standards of living much lower than those now enjoyed. ... However interesting speculation as to the future possibilities of the social order may be, none of this class of evidence faced the real problems of the moment. What is to be done immediately, even if temporarily, to meet the sudden reduction by at least one-sixth of the Commonwealth's spending power? (p. 13)

Thus the Court's perception was that the standard of living of wage-earners had been sustained until recently by the combination of favourable export prices and high levels of external borrowing. This led it to ask whether, without these supports, the level of real wages could have been justified by productivity. It chose to pursue that question by a comparison of 1907 and 1928–29. 'We assume' said the Court, 'that Mr Justice Higgins in fixing the *Harvester* wage—and the generally increased wage following therefrom—took into account the productive activity per unit of the population at that time.'[28] There was other evidence that the 1907 standard was justified:

> It has been claimed (probably correctly) that the 1907 standard was about 25 per cent higher than that which had ruled prior to that date. Had it been economically unsound it must have produced a large measure of unemployment, which does not appear to have been the case. (p. 17)

Thus the question to be considered was whether 'productivity' had moved favourably or adversely between 1907 and 1928–29.[29] The Court commented:

> Inspection of the official figures (*Labour Report* No. 20, p. 84) discloses that the index number for 1911 was taken as 1000. The relative figure for 1907 was 948, while the figure for 1928–29 was 937, which disclosed that the productivity per head of population for the last named year was slightly less than in 1907. According to the evidence before the Court the relative figure for the year 1929–1930 will be somewhere in the

---

[28] An assumption at odds with the realities of *Harvester*. See Chapter 3, Subsection 3.2.2.
[29] The inference about the effect of the 1907 decision was simplistic. An obvious question, for example, is how many workers were affected by it.

> vicinity of 800, and for the year 1930–1931 may be expected to be even less. (p. 17)

The Court drew the inference that productivity had declined since 1907, leaving no buffer against the effects of the external problems. The index numbers were taken from a table in the *Labour Report* entitled 'Estimated relative productive Activity in Australia for the years specified, 1871 to 1929'. In constructing them, the Statistician relied on estimates of the value of material production in primary and secondary industries. The next number of the *Labour Report* announced the discontinuance of these statistics because of their unreliability (see Chapter 1, Subsection 1.2.2).

The Court dealt at some length with arguments about purchasing power and (what would now be called) the propensity to consume.

> One of the main arguments of the respondents against the proposed reduction was, as first put, based on the supposition that it would reduce the spending power of the community. This is plainly fallacious in that the reduction would leave the spending power of the community unaltered in quantity, although it would, as to such wage-earners as are still in employment, effect to the extent of the reduction a transfer of part of their spending power to their employers. But the argument as finally put was that this would result in the transferred spending power being exercised less beneficially to wage-earners in the aggregate and that it would lead to an increase instead of a decrease in unemployment. The argument in this form was advanced with such earnestness and evident sincerity that it calls for serious consideration ... (p. 19)

In its 'serious consideration', the Court articulated (as Dethridge had done in earlier cases) a concept of balance between the beneficial and the adverse effects of higher wages—the former focusing on wage-earner spending and the latter on producer costs. All intelligent people accepted

> the principle that the general wage-rate should be as high as the marketable productivity of the country permits, and that in a time of depression the last remedy to be sought is a lowering of that wage level.

> They realise that in the home market of the most vital industries of the country, that is to say, the necessity industries, wage-earners provide the largest consumption, and that a forcing down of the wage level below the highest point which the country's marketable productivity enables it to attain, tends to weaken those vital industries and to lower the welfare of the whole community. They accept the proposition that such a forcing down of the wage level must cause 'under-consumption' of the products of those industries and diminishes distribution of those products among the people who sorely need them. But they are also compelled to recognise that if a country attempts to force or maintain a wage level at a point higher than the country's marketable productivity allows, there will be an irresistible tendency to ever-increasing unemployment with ever-increasing 'under-consumption' … If it is too high then a reduction, although causing an unfortunate transfer of spending power away from wage-earners now in employment, would act as a stimulus of general industrial activity, thus giving work to men now unemployed, with consequential benefit to *all* industries. (p. 21)

Other arguments about spending, advanced by witnesses, related to the adequacy of the supply of money. Some witnesses, said the Court, 'advocated a system involving the distribution of "new money" to consumers, somewhat similar to that enunciated during the last ten years by Major Douglas and his followers' (p. 22). The role of the financial system, and the relation between it and the government, were at the time the subject of intense political contest. The Court said:

> Many eminent economists and statesmen to-day support the idea that the control of money should be a state function rather than a field of dividend-making. But banking reform is a matter beyond the province of the Court. It is, however, material for the purposes of this inquiry to examine the contention that our local banking policy has been the main cause of the present depression. … It was submitted that the banks, notwithstanding the prosperous run they have had since the war, were unnecessarily contracting credit, and were dictating the financial policy of enterprise all in the direction of forcing reductions of wages. … In

> order to test this argument the Court secured from the Commonwealth Statistician an analysis of banking statistics between the years 1914 and 1930 with a view of determining whether there had been any undue contraction of credits during recent years ... (pp. 23–24)

The judgment contains a table, based on the Statistician's analysis, which shows that the ratio of bank advances to deposits had substantially increased. 'It will thus be seen', the Court said, 'that during recent years, particularly the last two years, there has been no contraction of credits by the banks.' Some witnesses had put forward the theory 'that consumption of goods would be stimulated and industry revived by an increase in the volume of money in circulation, irrespective of the country's productivity'. What these witnesses 'really meant'—though some disputed it—'was that inflation of the currency would have immediate beneficial effects. On this dangerous controversy it is not the function of the Court to express personal opinions' (p. 25). Here, the Court cited the evidence of Copland who 'pointed out that whatever policy may be ultimately adopted on this issue Australia's problem is not a mere monetary adjustment'. Copland had contended that

> there has been a severe and, at present, irreparable loss of income. It is therefore all the more important that in the process of re-adjustment this loss of income should be given first consideration; monetary re-adjustment may be made later. ... The first step is the equitable distribution of the loss of income. Export producers, unemployed wage-earners, and recipients of profits from Australian businesses are bearing the main part of the burden at the moment. But the burden is too great to be borne by a few groups, comprising only a section of total producers. (p. 25)

Irvine, said the Court, differed from Copland 'on one or two material points'. He saw it as 'practically a question of life and death to stop deflation and initiate a movement in the other direction, that is, to re-trace our steps by way of a carefully guarded inflation'. The first step was 'to make available to primary producers, manufacturers, and commercial businesses sufficient credit to enable them to get going again'. Irvine's position in this respect was not far removed from that of other witnesses:

> There was almost unanimity in the opinions of witnesses that in some form banking policy should be changed, and that there should be a limited note issue. Professor Copland, Mr F A A Russell, KC, one time Lecturer in Economics at Sydney University, Mr Portus, of the Sydney University, Mr Dyason, by way of his contributions to economic literature, and many others are in agreement that if the risks of indiscriminate inflation can be avoided the position can be substantially assisted by a change in the banking policy, carrying with it abandonment of the attempt to maintain parity of exchange and a note issue for the sole purpose of facilitating some stabilisation of price levels. (p. 26)

The thrust of this evidence, which seemed to carry the Court's implicit endorsement, was contrary to the orthodox stance recently urged by the Bank of England advisers, Niemeyer and Gregory, and presaged important elements of the forthcoming Premiers' Plan.[30]

Although the judgment canvassed a wide range of issues and developed detailed arguments as to why a wage reduction was necessary, it was surprisingly light on the issues of quantum and method. For the former, the Court seems to have relied very largely on Copland:

> Professor Copland admitted that wage reduction alone would by no means meet the situation, and attached great importance to stabilisation of price levels, reduction of the costs of Government, and a temporary departure from the effort which up to the time of his evidence had been made to establish exchange parity. But he was convinced that whatever else was done, there must be at least 10 per cent reduction in real wages. (p. 27)

---

[30] In one of his Marshall Lectures of 1933, Copland said: 'We have to turn to a semi-official body, viz. the Arbitration Court, to get the first authoritative statement of the case for a reduction in costs. It is well to remember, however, that the Court itself hinted that its acceptance of the policy of reducing money costs was to be regarded as part of a general policy embracing both deflationary and inflationary action' (Copland 1934, p. 118).

As to the form of the wage cut, the Court did briefly consider the role of the basic wage. It discussed the assumption of a family of five as the unit for which the wage was supposed to provide:

> During the proceedings the Court stated, and still adheres to the statement, that the finding of what is known as the Piddington Commission was an accurate estimate of the cost of living of a unit of man, wife, and three children according to reasonable standards of comfort, and the application of later index numbers enables the Court to correct the estimate arrived at in accordance with present price levels. But the function of the Court is not merely to ascertain what is the cost of living of the predominant family unit. It carries the responsibility of fixing a basic wage for adults, single, married without children, or married with children whatever the number may be. Whatever the ascertained cost of living at a certain standard of comfort may be, the Court in fixing a wage must of necessity consider the productive capacity of the Commonwealth. A basic wage to provide for the needs of a man, wife, and three children, extended to all single men and to men who have no children, is admittedly beyond the capacity of industry. (p. 30)

If the basic wage were to persist as a component of the wage-setting system, 'national consideration of a system of child endowment appears to be the only method by which the wage can be equitably fixed' (p. 31). We may note in passing the implicit repudiation of the stance of Higgins and Powers, who had rejected the Piddington finding about the wage required to support a family of five.

Consistent with the thinking which emerged toward the end of the hearing, the Court decided not to confront the issues before it in terms of the basic wage:

> The Court refuses to make any variations in the basic wage or in the present method of calculation thereof without further inquiry, but after much anxious thought it is forced to the conclusion that for a period of twelve months and thereafter until further order a general reduction of wages is necessary. ... The issue actually debated by the parties during

the proceedings, and to which the evidence and the arguments on the applications were mainly directed, was whether in the present condition of industry some such reduction was necessary. This issue was fought out regardless of the form of the applications. ... [O]rders are now made for variation of the awards covered by the applications by the reduction of all wage rates therein prescribed by 10 per cent, for a period of twelve months and thereafter until further order ... (p. 31)

The effect of these orders was that both the basic wage and margins were reduced by 10 per cent. This did not, however, constitute parity of treatment, because the nominal basic wage had been and continued to be subject to additional reductions in line with the decline of retail prices.

9.2.10 The aftermath

In response to the decision, the Labor Government tried to persuade the Court to defer the wage cut for three months, 'on the ground that the Government, in consultation with banking authorities, is engaged in the formulation of a scheme to ensure that the burden of the loss arising from the decline on national income and spending power shall be equitably distributed over all sections of the community, and that the immediate enforcement of the Court's order would embarrass the Government in completing its proposals for economic rehabilitation'. This was heard as an *ex parte* application 12 days after the main decision and decided on the next day (30 CAR 74). It was supported by an affidavit of the Attorney-General. Anderson outlined its terms:

> The Attorney-General in his affidavit stated that the Government realised that wage reductions alone would not materially alter the existing situation; that many other changes must be made before economic stability could be restored; that the Government was then engaged on the details of a scheme which was primarily concerned with the reduction of unemployment and the maintenance of national solvency; that there must be a sacrifice by all persons in Australia, and that such sacrifice must be equitably apportioned and made concurrently in all cases; that the Government was collaborating with banking and

other authorities in a comprehensive scheme of economic monetary and financial rehabilitation; that any alteration of the wage standard in advance of the commencement of the operation of the policy indicated would have the effect of unbalancing such plan, creating an atmosphere of distrust and/or defiance, and rendering it extremely difficult, if not impossible, of execution. The Attorney-General could not, however, give the Court details of the proposed plan—consultations were proceeding, but had not reached the stage at which details of the proposals could be announced. (Anderson 1931, p. 120)

Having said that the application required 'grave consideration', the Court rejected it, stating that 'any scheme dealing with present conditions must, in order to provide a remedy, comprise a reduction of wages such as has been ordered by the Court, and nothing has been adduced in this proceeding which leads the Court to the conclusion that delay in making that reduction will conduce to the success of such a scheme' (p. 75). Less than three weeks later, the Government repeated the application, with the same outcome (30 CAR 169). As it had done during the hearing, the Court asserted its independence of the executive government.

Subsequent decisions implementing the wage cut are discussed in the next chapter.

10

The depths of the Depression

10.1 Applying the cut

The decision to cut wages did not immediately take effect across the totality of the Court's awards. Except for the applicants in the main proceedings, employers had to apply for the reduction clause to be inserted into their awards. Such applications were being made throughout 1931, and a set of applications was granted as late as January 1932. I do not know the numbers of workers subject to the wage cut at specific times, but clearly the process of enforcing it was protracted.

There were a number of instances in which the reductions in the price index took it below the levels allowed for in the existing adjustment tables. By inserting new bands of index numbers, the Court allowed the basic wage to fall below the previous minima. There were also cases where the Court was asked by employers to insert automatic-adjustment clauses into awards which lacked them. These were awards in which the adjustment clauses had been omitted by agreement. In one such case, for storemen and packers, Beeby refused to insert an adjustment clause on the ground that the agreed wage rates may have reflected the absence of an adjustment provision (*Storemen and Packers'* case 30 CAR 467). In another, about maltsters, Dethridge said: 'The employers thought it convenient not to have the adjustment clause, and, throughout the last ten or eleven years, the parties, thinking it suitable for themselves, have done without an adjustment clause in their agreements or awards, and I do not think that I should introduce one now to the detriment of the employees' (*Variation—Maltsters (Victorian Award)* 30 CAR 702).

In a decision about banking, in July 1931, the Full Court said that at the time of the hearing which preceded the 10 per cent cut, the impact of the economic crisis on banks was unclear, and 'the Court therefore deemed it advisable to reserve the applications for further consideration until the results of operations for the year ending 30th June, 1931, were known' (*Variation—Bank Clerks' Award* 30 CAR 482). The position had since changed:

> As the result of a Premiers' Conference ... a scheme for the economic and financial rehabilitation of the Commonwealth has been adopted. This scheme aims at a reduction of costs of Government to the extent of 20 per cent, and includes substantial reductions of Civil Service salaries. It also provides for reduction of interest on Government securities and on future bank overdrafts, and imposes on banks the necessity of carrying increased holdings of Government stocks at lower rates of interest until a balancing of Commonwealth and State Budgets is achieved. Insurance companies and banks now carry over £100,000,000 of Government stock, and the reduction in rates of interest materially reduces their earning power. Such information as is available also discloses a noticeable fall in current accounts at banks and an increase in fixed deposits on which interest is payable. ... Under the new circumstances the Court can see no valid reason why bank officers should not be included in the rule that all must participate in the effort to re-establish affairs on a new level. (pp. 482–483)

Although the 10 per cent cut was thus applied to bank clerks, the terms of the decision implied that it might not be imposed where the employers were still prosperous.[1] This was confirmed in later decisions, some of which

---

[1] In September 1931, the Full Court made a similar decision for insurance (*Variation—Insurance Staffs' Awards* 30 CAR 484), but the High Court in November 1931 held that this decision was beyond its jurisdiction because the reduced salaries were below the amounts proposed by the employers when the underlying dispute came into existence. (Salaries had already been reduced by automatic adjustments of the basic-wage component.) In January 1932, the Full Court set aside the salaries clauses of the award, the companies having

are discussed below. It was at odds with the concept of the wage reduction as a means of spreading the losses of the export sector across the community, confusing macroeconomic strategy with a focus on the financial position of the employer or the industry—a confusion which the Court had strenuously resisted during the main hearing.

The problems of the pastoral industry, which had already been considered in depth by Dethridge in mid-1930 (see Chapter 9, Section 9.1), were the cause of a Full Court decision of May 1931. This was on an employer application to suspend the award provisions for station hands or, alternatively, to reduce their wages by 50 per cent (*Pastoral* case 30 CAR 301). The Court noted that most station hands were not union members and therefore fell outside the coverage of the award, threatening the employment of the union members whose wages and conditions were set by the award.[2] It accepted the 'manifest necessity for reducing *in all directions* the cost of production therein if the [pastoral] industry is to be maintained'. Although rural workers lacked amenities enjoyed by dwellers in towns, they had 'the compensating advantage, especially valuable in bad times like the present, of escaping many of the expenses incurred by wage earners living there'. The Court was unwilling to leave station hands 'without any recognised standard wage to serve as a barrier to some extent against possible sweating conditions'. But the crisis in 'this vital export industry', which had led Dethridge in July 1930 to reduce the shearers' rates by 20 per cent, caused the Court to reduce the station hand's rate also by 20 per cent (inclusive of the general 10 per cent cut) (pp. 302–303).

By the end of 1931, the Court was making decisions about the application of the emergency reduction to particular employers, taking into account their specific circumstances and especially their power in the product markets. In the gas industry, the Court granted the reduction to some employers, but not to others. An employer, to succeed, had to persuade the Court either that it

---

undertaken to apply the rates prescribed in them less 10 per cent (*Variation—Setting Aside Insurance Awards* 31 CAR 104).

[2] Whereas workers in non-rural industries who were not covered by federal awards were likely to be regulated by State awards and determinations, rural workers were commonly not protected by State instruments.

was in financial difficulty *or* that the benefit of cost reductions would flow fully through to consumers. Unless there were convincing evidence that 'privileged and prosperous monopolies' would themselves make no gain from a wage reduction, the Court would not grant it (*Variation—Gas Employees Award* 30 CAR 770, 773). The Court also granted a union application to rescind the reduction for the Colonial Sugar Refining Company (*Rescission of Wage Reduction—Colonial Sugar Refinery* 30 CAR 780). Here, the consideration that weighed most heavily was that the skilled employees of the company who worked under the Court's award had suffered the wage cut, whereas the unskilled workers under State awards had not. Dethridge and Drake-Brockman said:

> Except possibly to a small extent in South Australia and Western Australia no reduction of real wages as distinguished from adjustments to lower cost of living have been made by the State wage authorities or tribunals in the wages of the company's employees not covered by federal awards. In consequence the employees under federal awards who comprise practically all the skilled men in the refineries, and who are in number much less than one-third of the total employees in those refineries, now receive wages, in many cases, little more than those of the unskilled labourers employed there ... We think the necessity for the 10 per cent reduction of wages is by no means at an end, and that this necessity will very soon become apparent to State wage tribunals and others. When it appears that all and not merely a minority of the refinery employees of the company are to be called upon to share the sacrifice imposed by Australia's shrinkage of income, steps may be taken for the renewed application of this Court's orders. (p. 784)

10.2 THE FIRST APPLICATION TO CANCEL THE CUT

Early in 1932, unions applied to the Court for cancellation of the emergency reduction. The case was heard in March and April, but not decided until June—a delay that can be contrasted with the Court's speed in January 1931. Using unemployment as a guide, we can now see that the decision came at the very depth of the Depression, for it was in the second quarter of 1932 that

Australia-wide unemployment (measured by trade union returns) reached its maximum of 30 per cent. 'In the inquiry just concluded', said the Court (in a unanimous decision), 'there was no evidence of economic recovery. On the contrary, evidence disclosed that, during the year 1931, the further decline in national income and spending power was much greater than even the most pessimistic of economists had anticipated' (*Application for Cancellation— Emergency Reduction of Award Rates* 31 CAR 305, 315).

To a very large extent, the unions' case was an attempt to rebut what the Court had said in January 1931. They tried unavailingly to turn the deterioration to their advantage. Their principal advocate, Crofts, said in his opening address:

> What I am submitting to the Court is that there should be hardly any need for the unions to go further than to say to the Court 'Your dictum has failed; you tried to do the right thing, we give you credit for trying to do the right thing, but you must acknowledge that something has gone wrong with the scheme'. ... I think that the witness, Professor Copland, whose word was taken against so many experts, has proved to be wrong. (transcript, p. 35)

In a later reference to Copland's 1930 evidence, Crofts said:

> I asked him whether I could go to the men who are in work and tell them that, if they gave up 10 per cent of their real wages, their comrades, who were out of work, would be taken back into employment. He said: 'No'. I asked 'Why?' He said: 'I am not a prophet.' I said: 'You are a Professor, and you are telling this Court that if they reduce wages the men out of work will be taken back into industry.' He said: 'Not immediately. ... It may come to something like a normal position in about 18 months' time.' I said: 'Can I say that all the unemployed over a period of 18 months will be re-absorbed in employment?' He said 'No.' I said: 'What will happen?' He said: 'Australia will be very fortunate if ever she gets back to the time when she has less than 10 per cent of her working population unemployed.'[3]

---

[3] Crofts described Copland as 'the Court's witness'. Dethridge responded: 'I think you are

Copland was unavailable to give evidence in this case. At the behest of the employers, the Court invited G L Wood, of Melbourne University, to be a witness. Wood had refused to give evidence for the employers, but was prepared to attend as an independent witness.[4] The thrust of his evidence[5] was that:

- The high-wage theory, propounded by economists such as G D H Cole and J A Hobson and commended by the unions, was inapplicable to Australia's circumstances, partly because the share of labour in the national income was already high and partly because of Australia's economic dependence on the rest of the world.
- Measures to restore the real purchasing power of farmers, including reduction of the domestic price and cost levels, were essential to economic recovery.
- The failure of the 10 per cent cut to achieve economic recovery was due largely to the continued high level of wages in New South Wales State awards.

The Court summarised the unions' arguments as follows:

1. That the combined effect of periodic adjustments of the basic wage arrived at on data which do not correctly reflect the cost of living, of the 10 per cent reduction, and of greater intermittency

---

making a mistake. The Court paid great respect to the evidence of Professor Copland and still does. It paid considerable respect to some of the witnesses called on your side, some of the men with more or less economic knowledge, but it exercised an independent mind, and we are not tyros in economic matters. ... He was accepted as being an honest and capable witness and, having regard to the Court's economic knowledge, other witnesses were not accepted as sound witnesses, although they had some economic pretensions' (p. 46). Crofts was right. Copland was called as the Court's witness, as were a number of other witnesses, including Irvine.

[4] In asking the Court to call Wood, F P Derham (for the employers) acknowledged that 'all those Professors' had signed a 1930 economists' memorandum calling for measures that included wage reductions. Dethridge commented: 'At that time, undoubtedly. I do not know whether Mr Melville was in it. I think he took rather stronger views than the others. He thought the cut would have to be greater than it was' (p. 607).

[5] Beginning at p. 845 of the transcript.

of employment has been to bring the earnings of many employees below a bare living standard.

2. That the method of calculating and adjusting the basic wage is erroneous and unjust and should be revised.

3. That … industry can now carry at least the wage standards existing before those orders were made.

4. That monetary reform would be the most effective cure for recurring cycles of depression and would exclude necessity for wage reductions.

5. That the restriction of purchasing power resulting from wage reductions has retarded rather than assisted economic recovery.

6. That the distribution of sacrifice imposed by the depression has not been equitable, but so far has fallen most heavily on wage-earners.

7. That the orders for reduction have tended to increase rather than decrease unemployment, and that events subsequent to the orders support the original contention of employees that wage reduction was not necessary, and would not effectively contribute to economic rehabilitation. (decision, pp. 306–307)

The unions argued that the wage cut had driven households affected by it on to 'near-starvation' living conditions. They produced affidavits (read to the Court) which movingly described the hardships of the workers and their families. After hearing them, Dethridge remarked:

> You make a very effective and feeling appeal … and I may say that each one of us here … cannot help but feeling sore hearted about it, but what is to be done? … It is not for want of sympathy that one does unpleasant and distasteful things; but whatever is done by people who have any human feeling is done to mitigate distress, however harsh the measures they have to adopt may appear to be to other people. Those who take those measures have also to take the misjudgement which follows. (transcript, p. 935)

In the judgment, the Court spoke of the impossibility of providing for families of diverse compositions:

> Any system of wage regulation which ignores the necessity of graduations of minima according to domestic responsibility must result in anomalies. Some will get too much and some too little. It becomes more evident every day that by means of child endowment or some other device the aggregate amount which industry can pay to wage-earners as a whole must be more equitably divided. (decision, p. 308)

The main issue was whether the pre-reduction wage standard was sustainable:

> But whatever system of distribution of the nation's income may be adopted … only that can be distributed which is produced. For this Court to fix a basic wage at an amount which would procure an average standard of living for wage-earners such as the Court would very gladly see prevailing, would be worse than futile if the nation's income is not large enough to maintain the prescribed standard. However grievous the lowering of a customary average standard may be to those with heavy family or other responsibilities, and however painful it may be to this Court to have to declare that such a lowering is for the time being unavoidable, the Court must perform that duty, if, after full deliberation, it is forced to conclude that the occasion for lowering has arisen. (p. 309)[6]

The unions complained that the price index used by the Court to adjust the basic wage, comprising food and groceries and house rent, had exaggerated

---

[6] In the hearing, Dethridge said of the 1931 decision: 'the position was that the income of Australia was not sufficient to enable the preceding wage to be maintained at that time, and it took into consideration the desirability of spreading the actual income not only amongst those who were then in employment, but also among other men who were looking for employment and who were unable to get it at the prevailing rate of wage. That is what the Court did. The Court did not intend to take a penny away from the wage earners. It intended to spread among the whole of the wage earners, as far as possible, that which was available for wage earners' (transcript, p. 100). Responding to reasoning such as this, Crofts said that 'it is not the function of this Court to give some of the wages of the men in work to men out of work. That is the function of the Government' (p. 171).

the fall in prices. On this issue, the Court heard evidence from Giblin, who was then the Acting Commonwealth Statistician. Giblin had already published a pamphlet, *Wages and Prices*, which defended the index against a variety of criticisms.[7] The Court concurred in Giblin's conclusions, as stated in the pamphlet:

> (a) That the index for food and housing makes in general a fairly satisfactory measure of retail prices generally.
>
> (b) That the index for food and housing if not always perfectly satisfactory for retail prices generally is still the best measure of them that can, in practice, be made.
>
> (c) That the error in using food and housing as a general index of prices will be now one way, now the other, so that it will not accumulate to any serious amount in any moderate period of years.

The decision did less than justice to cross-examination of Giblin by H C Gibson. One of his contentions (which he had also argued in 1930) was that the direction from the Statistician to retailers to report the prices of the 'predominant' grade of an item caused the index to fall with reductions in quality, which were occurring as households responded to lower incomes by more austere living. Giblin acknowledged the point, and said that the instruction to retailers had been amended, but argued that the reverse effect had applied in the 1920s, when incomes were rising, so that recent losses would merely have cancelled earlier unintended gains. Neither Gibson nor Giblin attempted to quantify the error.[8]

R F Irvine had written a statement, *The Basic Wage*, from which Crofts quoted at length. The thrust of his argument was that the source of the current economic problems was the monetary system and that the case for adjusting real incomes was contradicted by the unrealised productive potential of technology.[9] Beeby commented during the hearing that some of Irvine's

---

[7] This document was included, as an appendix, in the *Labour Report*, No. 21, 1930.
[8] Transcript, especially p. 317.
[9] The unions also called witnesses who ascribed the Depression to the malfunctioning of the monetary system and contended that higher wages would tend to offset it.

statements were 'as extraordinary as the evidence which Professor Irvine gave in the original case'. He added:

> I argued that position out with Professor Irvine when he was in the witness box [in 1930], and he held to one opinion which I think is untenable, but he sticks to it still. His whole contention is monetary, that we get less in exchange for the goods which we send Home; but it is not monetary where a country relies on the export of its surplus products. ... I am referring to our export of surplus goods, and we get less goods in exchange for them. (p. 84)

'Mr Irvine', said the Court, 'thinks "that engineers and other technicians can double, treble, or even quadruple the output of ordinary necessities in a very short period."' This notion was espoused by a number of writers 'whose ideas as to potential production seem to have been coloured by their familiarity with increase of production effected by modern methods in factories' and who found the reason for the non-attainment of the productive potential in 'an insufficient supply of monetary instruments'. Irvine, said the Court, seemed largely to have accepted the doctrines of Major Douglas. This was not the place for an exhaustive commentary on Douglas' proposals 'or any other cognate proposals for changes in the monetary system':

> But mention should be made of the fact that economic thinkers of eminence of diverse political and economic views, but all sympathetic with the claims of wage-earners for advancement, have rejected those proposals as fallacious. Mr J M Keynes, the famous authority on money, Mr J A Hobson, the high-wage advocate, Mr G D H Cole, a leading British socialist, and Messrs Foster and Catchings, prominent American economists, more or less discard the Douglas theory and its varied offshoots. (decision, pp. 311–312)[10]

---

[10] Dethridge said during the hearing: 'I think it would be very desirable if an economist of real standing like Keynes or Stamp and others did apply his very considerable understanding of economic principles to this Major Douglas suggestion and say what he has to say upon it. But they simply class it as unworthy of notice, call it the "Douglas heresy" and say nothing about it' (transcript, p. 88). In *The General Theory* (Keynes 1936), Keynes did discuss the Douglas proposals.

It might be true, the Court said, that the world Depression had a monetary origin, but Irvine overlooked the fact that the prices of Australia's exports of primary products had fallen more than the prices of imports, depressing the real income of Australia.[11]

The Court was correct in pointing to the decline of the terms of trade, which had an obvious adverse effect on real spending power. We may wonder, however, whether too much was made of the point by economists such as Copland and Giblin and by the Court. Imagine that the prices of *both* exports and imports had fallen in the same proportion as the prices of exports, relative to the local price level. Could the Depression then have been averted or significantly mitigated? Without other adjustments, the competitive positions of both exporters and import-competing businesses would have been drastically eroded. The other adjustments might have been a depreciation of the exchange rate, a reduction of domestic money incomes (including wages), or both. If these fell short of the required levels, severe structural problems would have remained. It is doubtful that the Australian economy had the flexibility to absorb the price shocks coming from abroad without such structural problems emerging. To what extent the structural impact of the shocks was exacerbated by the terms-of-trade effect is unknown and probably unknowable. The cessation of foreign loans was, of course, an additional 'imported' cause of depression.

The Court attached much weight to the state of public finances. Commonwealth and State deficits had been funded by short-dated bank loans, including Treasury Bills held by the Commonwealth Bank, and the banks' ability to lend for industrial and commercial purposes was correspondingly reduced. A persistent and important cause of the deficits was a fall in railway revenues without corresponding reductions of working expenses and interest charges. A rise in wages would increase the railways' deficiencies. It was difficult,

---

[11] Referring to Irvine, Dethridge said: 'The position is this. If anyone comes along and says "The ordinary rules of arithmetic are unsound," and someone else comes along and says "the rules of arithmetic are sound, and two and two still make four," the Court, I suppose, is inclined to accept the evidence of him who said that two and two make four and not four and a half' (transcript, pp. 246–247).

said the Court, to get the union advocates to appreciate the importance of the government's budgetary problems (p. 316).

The general economic situation was far worse, in the Court's view, than it had been when the 10 per cent cut was ordered, despite some improvement in public finances due to the Premiers' Plan. Under any economic order, Australia would depend for a long time on exports of primary produce. While low prices continued, it was imperative for costs to be brought to a level at which increased primary production was possible (p. 318).

The Court then discussed the 'theory of high wages', which 'plays an important part in modern economics, and is supported by many distinguished economists'. 'None', it said,

> can contest the broad theory that the more that is drawn from production by wage-earners, so long as sufficient is reserved for necessary capital and other requirements, the more prosperous a community becomes. Wages maintained at the highest possible level stimulate consumption, and steadily increasing consumption means increased employment with improving standards of living. (p. 318)

J A Hobson, a distinguished exponent of the high-wage theory, argued that depression was caused by excessive spending on investment relative to consumption. The Court said that Hobson's version of the theory was disputed by (among others) J M Keynes in his *Treatise on Money*. Keynes saw the source of the problem in a deficiency of investment relative to saving and thought that this might be remedied by 'a creation and issue of credit for purposes of industry to an amount equal to current uninvested savings'. Notwithstanding such disagreements, 'most experts of any standing in the economic world agree that payment of the highest wages consistent with sufficient reservations to attract competent management, enterprise, and capital should be the aim of industry'. The old school of economists, 'who preached low wages and long hours of employment as the inevitable foundation of industry', were no longer heeded (p. 319). But the union advocates refused to recognise any relation between wages as a cost of production and unemployment. Even if the high-wage theory were accepted in its entirety, it might still be the case that existing standards were unsustainable.[12]

Not surprisingly, the unions argued that the continued reduction of employment demonstrated the futility of the wage cut. The Court's response was to blame the State tribunals which had not followed its lead:

> The 10 per cent reduction was not universally adopted. In Victoria except in some sheltered industries it was applied to Governmental services and was adopted by Wages Boards dealing with employees in key industries not covered by this Court's awards. In the State of New South Wales the policy of the Government has been to prevent any wage reductions as part of a scheme of rehabilitation. In Queensland, where industrial conditions are mainly controlled by a State Tribunal, the basic wage has been reduced to £3 14s 0d per week as against this Court's present minimum of £2 18s 6d. In South Australia the minimum has been fixed by the State Tribunal at £3 3s 0d per week as against this Court's £2 19s 0d per week, and in Western Australia at £3 12s 0d per week as against £3 1s 9d. ... The Court is still of opinion that the uniform adoption simultaneously in all States of a 10 per cent reduction in actual wage costs ... would have had a marked effect on employment. ... Hesitancy in its adoption can only make recovery slower and more painful. (p. 323)

Crofts had observed that the State tribunals which had set and maintained basic wages higher than the federal Court's wage 'know all the facts this Court knows'. Dethridge responded: 'I take it that they know the economic facts,

---

[12] During the hearing, Dethridge put it to Crofts that, if the union argument were correct, 'it would be not only desirable to restore the ten per cent, but it would be desirable to increase all wages, all salaries (including those of judges) and all endowments in the nature of family endowments by one hundred per cent, because the spending power of the community would thereby be increased correspondingly. ... Does not it seem to follow from your argument?' Crofts retorted that, on the Court's logic, wages should be reduced to nothing. 'The answer to that', said Dethridge, 'is quite clear. Wages should not be brought down below the amount which the productivity of the country permits to be paid' (transcript, p. 461).

but they also know certain political facts. It is just as well to be frank. ... This Court is independent of political influence' (transcript, p. 121).[13]

The unions' application was refused. 'After the expiration of the present year', said the Court, 'circumstances may justify further consideration, particularly as to those who have no margins above the basic wage' (p. 324). No reason was given for the hint of a possibly brighter future. We may speculate about a division of opinion within the Bench. One member—Beeby being the most likely—may have been uncomfortable with the generally negative tenor of the decision.

10.3 Administering wage restraint 1932–33

The decision in the 1932 emergency reduction case required no follow-up action. The period between that case and the next general decision on the 10 per cent cut was one of relative quiescence in federal wage setting.

In August 1932, Beeby dealt with applications by the Victorian Government for the removal of award terms that might impede the employment of men on relief works (see *Suspension—Metal Trades' Award—Unemployment Relief Work—Victoria* 31 CAR 515 and subsequently reported decisions). Specifically, the Government wished to be able to employ all such workers at basic wage rates and to ration work. Beeby refused the former request. He accommodated the latter by suspending the operation of the awards so far as they applied to relief workers, but subject to the requirement that the hourly rates paid, including margins, accord with the weekly rates prescribed in the awards.

The Full Court in September 1932 refused to apply the 10 per cent cut to workers on the waterfront and in railway sheds in the Northern Territory

---

[13] Dethridge noted 'the tremendous evil that does arise from those discrepancies; and we have thought that possibly by some joint action between the State tribunals and this Court something might be done to mitigate that evil. But there we are faced with the difficulty that in some of the States the tribunals are bound by State legislation, so that they are bound to take a particular course which may inevitably result in the wages being higher than those determined by this Court and, it may be, higher than are economically sound' (transcript, p. 660). I am unaware of any consultation between the Court and the State tribunals.

(*Port Darwin—Emergency Reduction* 31 CAR 571). The reason given was the hopelessness of the employment situation in Port Darwin:

> By far too many men are sharing what little work is available at Port Darwin, and no effort appears to have been made by those who employ labour to devise some scheme of organisation to meet the peculiar needs of the port. A reduction of the earnings of those who share the work … will make no appreciable difference to the people of the Northern Territory. The local unemployment problem and the unfortunate position of many men who cling to the town in the hope of restored prosperity call for decisive action before wage rates are reduced.

In the same month, the Full Court dealt with an application by the Transport Commissioners for New South Wales which can be attributed to a change of government in the State (*Variation—Railway and Tramway Awards, NSW* 31 CAR 579). The Court, in 1930, had limited its regulation of employment in railways to the basic wage and standard hours (see Chapter 9, Section 9.1). The New South Wales Railways Commissioners, at the direction of the recently elected Labor Government, withdrew their application for wage reductions which the Court, in respect of other employers, had met with the 10 per cent cut. After another change of government, the Transport Commissioners now sought the reduction. In the course of its decision, the Court commented on the argument of the unions that railway deficits were due to the existence of lines that had been constructed for developmental purposes. The Court accepted 'that many of these lines should not be taken into account in estimating the final railway results'. But 'even if the total cost of these non-paying lines in New South Wales were written off, and the interest on the balance of the borrowed money used in railway construction were reduced by 25 per cent, there would still be a deficit in railway revenue which could not be allowed to continue' (p. 582). The majority of the employees were already covered by general awards, not specific to railways, in which the reduction was in force (though not observed while the Labor Government was in power). It was inevitable that the Court would grant the application: 'the balance of railway servants affected by these applications cannot expect to escape the general lowering of standards which for the time being has become inevitable in all occupations'.

On the other hand, the Court (also in September 1932) cancelled the emergency reduction as it applied to the Bendigo Gas Company (*Variation—Gas Employees' Award* 31 CAR 636). No reasons were given, and we can only surmise that the decision reflected the financial condition and monopoly position of the company. On the same day, the Full Court gave its decision in a rubber industry case (*Rubber Industry—Application to Vary Award* 31 CAR 638). The evidence, it said, indicated 'a noticeable improvement in the financial outlook of the companies concerned', but the recovery was insufficient to justify cancellation of the emergency reduction.

In December 1932, Dethridge finalised the new pastoral award (*Judgment—Pastoral Industry* 31 CAR 710). The evidence suggested that the cost of production of wool had fallen from about 11d per pound in 1930 to 9d; but the price of wool had fallen also—from 8.36d in 1930–31 to 7.72d in 1931–32. Although the current price-cost relation was unsustainable in the long run, Dethridge favoured a measure of restraint in responding to the situation:

> No possible reduction of wages in the industry will be sufficient in itself to replace the industry in prosperity, but wage-earners cannot escape some lessening of their share of the industry's returns. At the same time we must remember that employers, because in prosperity they may have the chance of reaping high profits, have in adversity to carry a corresponding burden of loss. ... No very great lowering of a previously attained standard of wages can be made suddenly, although in the long run no standard of wages can be maintained above the durable economic capacity of an industry. If that economic capacity is permanently lowered, the standard of wages must, of course, ultimately fall with it. But until it appears that there is such a permanent lowering and not only a depression, which, though severe, will probably disappear, thus leaving the way open again to profits, employers must be prepared to

> pay wages somewhat above those that would accompany a permanent fixation of the industry upon the prices which prevail in the pit of a depression. (p. 713)

Dethridge made only minor changes to the prescribed wages, which had been heavily reduced in 1930 and 1931. The basic wage would be set on the basis of average prices in the year to September 1932 and remain fixed until March 1934.

A case of some policy interest, also decided by Dethridge in December 1932, was about an industry—food preserving—whose fortunes had evidently undergone some improvement (*Variation—Food Preserving Employees' Award* 31 CAR 833). The case afforded Dethridge the opportunity to state unequivocally principles that were implicit, but perhaps less clearly articulated, in decisions of the Full Court. It was part of the union's case for suspending the emergency reduction that the price index had exaggerated the fall in the cost of living. The argument involved a comparison of the All Items (C series) Index and the All Houses (A series) Index used by the Court. While it was true that the latter had fallen more than the former since 1929, it was possible, said Dethridge, that the All Houses Index was too high in 1929 and that what had since occurred was a correction. As the Full Court had done in June, Dethridge cited Giblin's pamphlet as a reason to conclude that the index was satisfactory.

Dethridge then discussed the adjustment of wages to prices. He drew a distinction between price reductions that were due to increased productivity and those that were not. Clearly, the latter predominated in the Depression period. Dethridge said:

> It is clear that some adjustment of wages to a great fall in the general price level is unavoidable where that fall is not due to increased productivity per head of a nation's population. That price level expresses, roughly, in terms of money the contents of the flow of commodities from which the shares of wage-earners and employers are both drawn, and therefore

those shares must be measured in money proportionately to the measurement of those contents, that is to say, to the general price level. Whatever may be said of the principle of a basic wage fixed in relation to the cost of living, the system of adjustment adopted by this Court probably tends to produce a due relativity of wage level to price level, inevitable in the long run, with as little friction as any method that could be devised. I am not prepared to depart from a practice which has been so serviceable to the community. (p. 835)

This was an important statement, because it depicted the price level as a rough measure of capacity to pay and emphasised that aspect rather than the aspect of family needs. Where a fall in prices was due to greater productivity, different considerations applied:

But if the fall in the general price level is due to increased productivity of the community, it may not be just that the wage-earners who have contributed to that increase should, by having their wages reduced in accordance with the fall in prices, be deprived of a share in that increase. Mr Clarey referred to the report of the British Economic Commission, which expressed the opinion that the Australian basic wage fixed in relation to cost of living was wrong in principle for this reason, and because, as was thought, the wage-earners' incentive to increase productivity was thereby destroyed.[14] How far experience justifies this opinion is a question of difficulty for the consideration of which this is not an appropriate occasion. (p. 835)

Dethridge's commentary on the adjustment of wages to prices has added interest because of remarks made by the Court in 1953 (at the time of abolishing automatic adjustments of the basic wage) to the effect that the adjustment system had become an anachronism in 1931, when the 10 per cent cut recognised the dominance of the capacity-to-pay criterion. There was an implication that the Depression-period Court had absent-mindedly continued automatic adjustments. It is evident that Dethridge saw the adjustment system,

---

[14] Dethridge should have said 'British Economic Mission' (see Chapter 13, Subsection 13.1.2).

which delivered large wage reductions during the Depression, as entirely consistent with the capacity principle.

The union put once more the familiar argument about wages and purchasing power. Dethridge noted that this argument had been fully considered by the Full Court, but again depicted the issue as one of balance:

> For the best economic distribution of the national income, what is to be sought is the nearest possible approach to a state of balance, in which the wage level is as high as is necessary to enable the employed wage-earners to provide their *full* proportionate part of the market for the community's products, but is *not* so high as to put the prices of those products above the purchasing power of the other consumers who have to be relied upon to provide the remainder of that market. No one can say exactly what wages should be at any particular time to procure that ideal balance, but, broadly, inferences as to the necessary trends of wage levels may be drawn with reasonable safety. To determine precisely the utmost amount that can be paid as wages in an industry without destroying its power to continue to produce and sell its products is impossible, but the extent of unemployment does furnish some guidance as to when wages should be increased or decreased. (pp. 836–837)

Dethridge then turned to the condition of the industry before him, and the evidence persuaded him that it had undergone some recovery. 'Where wages have been reduced because of depression in an industry', he said, 'it is fair that with a return of prosperity to that industry the wage-earners engaged therein should share in that prosperity …' (p. 837). He had thought it proper to consult his Full Court colleagues, who agreed with his intended order. In respect of the basic wage, the 10 per cent reduction was cancelled, but Powers' 3s was removed. The effect was to raise the rate by 3s, or just under 5 per cent. For margins, the 10 per cent cut was replaced by one of 5 per cent. On the same day, the Full Court made a similar order for the glass industry (*Variation—Glass Workers' Award* 31 CAR 844). These decisions confirmed the Court's willingness to dilute the broad principle of the 1931 decision, which emphasised the spreading of sacrifice, with an industry-by-industry approach whereby some workers fared better and (in the pastoral industry) some worse than the standard.[15]

Four days later, Beeby made an award for the wool and basil industry with no adjustment clause. He thought that there should be no further automatic wage reductions until the whole method of basic-wage fixation and adjustment had been reviewed. In saying this, he was not to be taken as expressing the opinion of the Full Court.

> When the 10 per cent reduction was ordered I, personally, did not anticipate such serious further reductions as have resulted from changes in the Commonwealth Statistician's index numbers. I therefore have arrived at the wage schedule not so much on a base rate with margins that are to be regarded as final as on consideration of the net earning power of individuals in the industry as now conducted. For this reason I have not included an adjustment clause, but reserve leave to either side to apply if there are further fluctuations in the cost of living or if the position of the industry materially changes. (*Judgment—Wool and Basil Industry* 31 CAR 846, 852)

10.4 THE 1933 INQUIRY

In April 1933 the Court heard a further union application for the rescission of the 10 per cent cut. It gave its decision on 5 May (*Application (No. 2) for Cancellation Emergency Reduction of Wage Rates* 32 CAR 90).

In the preceding quarter, unemployment (calculated from the trade union returns) was 26.5 per cent, compared with 28.3 per cent a year earlier and 30 per cent at the peak, registered in the second quarter of 1932. On the evidence of unemployment, then, there had been a very modest improvement.

The Court, which had been unanimous in 1931 and 1932, now divided. Dethridge and Drake-Brockman gave a majority judgment, with Beeby favouring a slightly different outcome.

---

[15] In February 1933, Beeby made a consent order for the Melbourne and Metropolitan Tramways Board, providing that any further reductions in wages due to price reductions would be offset by equivalent wage increases (*Tramways' Award—Variation* 32 CAR 21).

The unions again argued that the reduced level of wages left families in hardship; and Dethridge and Drake-Brockman once more spoke of the inequity of a system that rewarded the man with large family responsibilities no more than the single man. 'But', they said, 'this Court cannot remedy that evil' (p. 92). The unions also argued the inequity of subjecting workers under the Court's awards to the reduction, when many other workers escaped it. Dethridge and Drake-Brockman, 'while deploring the inequality of treatment, and realising that it results in a tendency on the part of wage earners to put themselves outside the awards of the Court and to seek a place under those of State industrial tribunals', refused to remove the inequality 'except so far as that removal is consistent with what we regard as a necessary adaptation of wages to the present industrial position of Australia' (p. 93). They estimated that about a half of Australian wage-earners had been subject to the reduction. This estimate took into account the membership of federally registered unions—about one-third of all workers—and the predominant acceptance of the Federal Court's lead by wages boards in Victoria and Tasmania (p. 98).

The Court was moving further from the notion of the basic wage as a 'needs' wage and closer to an explicit recognition of the preponderant weight of economic criteria. During the hearing, Dethridge responded to a reminder that the *Harvester* basic wage was supposed to be 'sacrosanct' with the observation that 'nothing is sacrosanct against the impossibility of fulfilment' (transcript, p. 196); and when told of the hardships that wage-earners were experiencing, he replied:

> Mere appeals to sympathy are not of much use. ... Of course, the Court recognises as it has already said that the man on the basic wage, with family responsibilities, is suffering most extreme hardship. ... but because the Court sympathetically recognises the painful position that wage earners are in, it would be absurd for the court to allow its eyes to be blinded by tears to the real facts. (pp. 201–202)

In a more direct repudiation of the Higgins legacy, Dethridge said:

> The judgments [of the South Australian Board of Industry] contain a number of good, sound dicta, in my opinion. ... I do not know that the New South Wales Court has given the same attention as the South Australian Board to economic factors, that is to say, given attention to the unavoidable relationship of the basic wage to the production of the country. The South Australian Board does in fact indicate that you cannot divorce the basic wage from the marketable production of the country. I am afraid in this Court in the early days that inseparability was not emphasised as it might have been. The result is that there has grown up a kind of notion that the basic wage is independent of the actual production of wealth in the country. But it is not, and it never can be independent. However, there seems to be an idea that it is independent. (p. 356)

Though yet again rejecting union arguments about wage reductions and purchasing power, Dethridge and Drake-Brockman were a little more equivocal than the Court had been in 1931 and 1932.[16] Not only did the union advocates argue for wage increases to increase spending power, 'but they were able to find support for those views in the statements of some prominent employers, and in the judgments of some members of State industrial tribunals, and also what they regarded as support in expressions of some economists, written however in relation to world conditions and not to the special present conditions of Australia' (decision, pp. 93–94). The majority Judges proceeded to state 'why in our opinion this "purchasing" or "spending" power proposition lacks the cogency which by many people ... it is supposed to have; [and] at the same time the extent of its real validity will be indicated' (p. 94). The fallacy of the purchasing-power argument lay in its assumption that a reduction of *workers'* spending power equated to a reduction in *aggregate* spending power:

---

[16] During the hearing, Dethridge said to Crofts: 'You can take it that I at any rate agree with you to this extent, that if you attempt to give the wage earners too small a share of what may be conveniently called the purchasing power, then the whole purchasing power of the community is reduced detrimentally to the whole community. If you attempt to give them too much you have the converse problem, so this Court, together with other tribunals, has to feel its way, so to speak, with doubt all the time as to whether what it is doing is the right thing' (p. 31).

> If by awards of this Court we could effectively raise wages so as to transfer the whole profits, rent and interest to the wage earners, we would not increase purchasing power, but would only transfer it. Conversely, when wages are reduced, there is a transfer of spending power from those employees who suffer the reduction, but there is no reduction in the aggregate spending power.

The main cause of the prevailing lack of purchasing power was the depressed incomes of the primary producers, together with the cessation of foreign loans. Unless the spending power of the primary industries were increased, 'the purchasing power of the whole of Australia must continue lowered and no increasing of wages in factories, railways, shops or theatres will raise it' (p. 95).

A hint of equivocation can, however, be found in the following passage:

> But although a reduction of wages does not of itself diminish the aggregate of the purchasing power of the community it may possibly so affect the rapidity with which that power is exercised as to diminish the extent of the willingness to buy which is necessary for absorption of production. If the purchasing power which was transferred to employers by means of the 10 per cent reduction has been hoarded or allowed to be idle, or has not been promptly used directly or indirectly either to maintain or increase employment *in some form* somewhere in Australia or to cheapen such products or services of the factories, transport, shopkeeping, or amusement industries to which the 10 per cent applies as are required by the farming and mining industries, and thus make the lowered spending power of these two industries more effective, then to that extent the reduction of wages has been economically unsound. (p. 95)

Dethridge and Drake-Brockman's acceptance of the possibility of hoarding was a concession relative to the stances that they (with Beeby) had taken in 1931 and 1932. But they did not see it as one of practical importance.[17] Any such

---

[17] During the hearing, Mundy asserted that the national income could be kept much closer to its pre-Depression level if internal production were sustained by the circulation of money. Dethridge commented: 'That blessed term "Circulation of money" is like the blessed word "Mesopotamia"' (transcript, p. 85). A little later, Mundy claimed that his position was

effects that may have followed the wage reduction were 'negligible compared with the increased efficiency thereby given to the lessened purchasing power of the primary exporting industries'. The emergency reduction had not restored 'equilibrium' between the purchasing power of the primary producers and the costs of Australian industries, but 'has certainly brought us nearer to it'.

'What signs', asked Dethridge and Drake-Brockman, 'are there of renewed prosperity?' 'All that can be said', they tautologically answered, 'is that the country has hitherto just succeeded in staving off an even worse industrial disaster than has been suffered'. The continued high level of unemployment was the strongest evidence of incomplete adjustment of outgoings to income and costs to markets. While favourable seasons had boosted production, this gain was far from offsetting the falls in prices: since 1928, wheat prices had fallen by 50 per cent; wool prices by 55 per cent; butter prices by 40 per cent; and mutton prices by 44 per cent. There was, in short, 'no possible foundation for suggesting that alterations since 1931 justify any restoration of the reduction then made' (p. 98).

Dethridge and Drake-Brockman thought, however, that the fall in real wages that had occurred exceeded what was intended in 1931:

> It was not our intention to exceed a reduction of 10 per cent in the actual real wages existing before the fall of income, even though by reason of the use in adjustment of the All Houses Price Index Table and of the Powers' 3s, the 'basic wage' element ... may have come to exceed in its purchasing power that of the '*Harvester*' 7s in 1907 in Melbourne.

They were now 'seriously concerned with the question whether by the use in adjustment of the "All Houses" table that intended 10 per cent reduction of real wages may not since have been exceeded'. Whereas in 1932 the Court had accepted Giblin's assessment that the All Houses Index provided 'in general a fairly satisfactory measure of retail prices generally', they now thought that

---

supported by a number of economists whom the Court regarded as unorthodox. Asked to name them, Mundy mentioned Keynes. Dethridge said that he did not regard Keynes as unorthodox, adding that Keynes, whether orthodox or not, was 'pretty sound'; and Beeby said that orthodoxy was 'not always the test of truth' (p. 96).

it did not measure accurately the fall in prices since the end of 1929. The All Items (C series) Index—more comprehensive because of the inclusion of clothing and miscellaneous items—was to be preferred.[18]

Dethridge and Drake-Brockman accordingly adopted a formula which, in effect, took as its starting point the basic wages in the awards as they stood in the last quarter of 1929. These were then reduced for the movement in the All Items Index between the whole of 1929 and the first quarter of 1933. (This adjustment was applied to Powers' 3s, as well as the *Harvester* equivalent.) The resultant amounts remained subject to the 10 per cent reduction. The immediate effect was to raise the six-capitals basic wage from 61s 8d to 64s 2d—an increase of 4.1 per cent (p. 101). Subsequent quarterly adjustments were to be based on the same principle, that is, updating the wage in the fourth quarter of 1929 according to movements in the C series index by comparison with the yearly average for 1929. This arrangement lasted until the 1934 case (see below).[19]

The majority Judges left open the possibility that specific inquiry into individual industries might lead to further wage increases in those industries (p. 103). During the hearing, Dethridge had contemplated step-by-step restoration of the wage cut, dependent on the conditions of particular industries:

> A basic wage common to all industries can only be paid if industry as a whole can stand the payment of that wage. It does not matter what is laid down by any tribunal or any Court. In the past history of this Court, and also in connection with legislation governing State tribunals, an attempt has been made—and I am not condemning the attempt at

---

[18] Gibson repeated the contention that the Statistician's reliance on 'predominant' prices had biased the index downward. This criticism, he said, had been accepted by the Statistician, who now sought prices of items of constant quality; but there had been no retrospective correction of the index. It may be that Gibson's submission influenced the Court's perception that the price index had exaggerated the fall in prices (transcript, p. 138).

[19] Although the thrust of the majority decision about cost of living adjustments is accurately summarised above, the adjustment clause by which the Court gave effect to it was quite complicated.

all—to prescribe a minimum living wage, and, of course, it is a very desirable thing to have a minimum living wage as high as possible for every wage-earner in the community. But an attempt has been made to introduce that principle, and, to some extent it has been successful; but it has only been successful up to now because the income from industry in the country has been able to pay it. If that income from the industry of the country had been unable to pay it it would not have been paid, and the attempt to pay it would have resulted in continually increasing unemployment. ... As a matter of fact, it seems to me that that is the working principle which will have to be applied to industries as they become more prosperous than they have been recently. As soon as they can afford to pay the hitherto recognised basic wage, let them pay it. If they can afford to pay more, and they get on to some more satisfactory basis of assessment, let them pay it as long as the payment does not militate against the continuance of the necessary expansion of the industry. (transcript, p. 196)

Beeby began by deploring the chaotic situation caused by the divergent policies of the different tribunals:

The conflict between State and Federal Tribunals, the impossibility in the existing state of the law of securing purely national consideration of wage fixation, and the inability of tribunals to grade minimum wages according to the size of family units makes equitable fixation of a national minimum wage impossible. ... The Court [in 1931] anticipated that its analysis of the economic situation ... would, within a reasonable time, lead to similar declarations by State tribunals and result in universal 10 per cent reduction of 'real' as contrasted with nominal wages. But after two years State tribunals (except Tasmanian Wages Boards) have not deemed it necessary to reduce wage standards, but have been content to make reductions only in proportion to the reduced cost of living. (pp. 103–104)

A comparison of the federal basic wage (after an impending cost of living adjustment) and State basic wages for capital cities showed:

	Federal	**State**
Sydney[20]	64s 7d	68s 6d
Adelaide	54s 10d	63s 0d
Brisbane	54s 10d	74s 0d
Perth	56s 7d	72s 0d

In Melbourne, the federal rate was 58s 4d. This rate, said Beeby, was generally adopted by the wages boards. In Hobart, the federal rate of 66s was also generally applied by the boards (p. 104). Beeby, like his colleagues, estimated that the 10 per cent cut applied to only about half of the industrial population. This was a 'startling anomaly', but he did not think it 'sufficient reason for this Court to go back on its conclusion that a general reduction of standards by at least 10 per cent was, on the date of its original orders, and still is, unavoidable' (p. 105).

The union advocates' attack on the All Houses Index had crystallised his doubts as to whether that index accurately measured the fall in the cost of living. The time had come to abandon the adjusted *Harvester* standard. Beeby did not set out, as the majority did, an adjustment formula, but he proposed some basic-wage amounts slightly above those chosen by the majority. These rates would operate for six months or until further order, and the method of wage fixation would be the subject of further inquiry and conferences with the State tribunals.

In May and June 1933, the Full Court gave two unanimous decisions affecting railways and tramways. In the former of the two, it removed an existing limitation (presumably inserted by consent) which prevented the basic wage in New South Wales from falling below the State award level, and imposed the adjustment clause prescribed in the main case (*Variation— Railway and Tramway Awards, NSW* 32 CAR 316). In the latter, the Court made a statement which may well have reflected discussion within the Bench arising from the different approaches in the main case:

> We have given thought to the introduction of a less complicated system of adjustment based upon the 'All Items' Index Numbers only without

---

[20] Workers with children also received child endowment.

reference to the 'All Houses' Index Numbers but fear that such a change would at present cause confusion in other directions. Some system of adjustment to fluctuations in cost of living is indispensable for a basic wage prescribed to provide a standard of living. When industrial affairs emerge from their present precarious condition into apparent stability so that a basic real wage may be re-assessed with some assurance that as so re-assessed it can be maintained, a simple system of adjusting that wage to changes in cost of living will have to be adopted by the Court.[21]
(*Award—Basic Wage—Commonwealth Railways* 32 CAR 371, 380)

10.5 Restraint moderated

By the first quarter of 1934, unemployment fell to 21.9 per cent. Obviously, the economy remained severely depressed, but there were signs of slow recovery. The Court responded with sporadic and specific concessions to labour claims.

As noted in Section 10.9 below, the Full Court in June 1933 granted a 44-hour week for the textile industry. In the same decision, it refused to rescind the wage reduction.

In August, by consent, it cancelled the reduction for several companies bound by the Metal Trades' Award: Australian Glass Manufacturers, Australasian Paper and Pulp, Australian Paper Manufacturers, and Cumberland Paper Board Mills and nine companies in the food-preserving industry (*Variation—Metal Trades' Award* 32 CAR 487). In September, the Court granted a union application to cancel the reduction in respect of the Adelaide Electric Supply Company (*Variation—Metal Trades' Award [Adelaide Electric Supply Co Ltd]* 32 CAR 514). It referred to and apparently accepted the union's argument 'that the saving of labour cost resulting from the wage cut seems to have resulted in a benefit mainly only for those interested as stock-holders in the concern,

---

[21] In September 1933, the Full Court varied the awards for New South Wales railways by adding Powers' 3s to the basic wage. Powers had omitted this, by consent, in 1925 because of other benefits provided. The Court now felt that the value of additional benefits had diminished to such an extent as to justify observance of the standard wage provision (*Variation—Railway and Tramway Awards, NSW* 32 CAR 516).

and that the financial position of the company is such that it can carry on and make reasonable profits notwithstanding the rescission of the wage reduction …' (p. 515).

The Court, on the other hand, refused in September a union application for wage increases in the pastoral industry which would have reversed the various reductions that had been imposed in and since 1930. It acknowledged that there had been some increase in the price of wool, but regarded it as insufficient to justify the higher wages (*Variation—Pastoral Award* 32 CAR 522). On the same day, it refused an application to vary the fruitpickers' award so as to apply the decision in the main case. It accepted the employers' contention that 'the industry … is in such a critical condition that no increase whatever in labour costs can be carried' (*Variation—Fruit-Pickers' Award* 32 CAR 525, 526).

I refer later to a handful of decisions about standard hours.

10.6 THE WAGE CUT RESCINDED

The exceptions made for specific industries generated a number of applications for the removal of the 10 per cent cut. In October 1933, the Court put some of these 'on hold' to await a general review early in 1934. In fact, the Court sat in December 1933. The hearing occupied 19 days, and the decision was given on 17 April 1934 (*Basic Wage Inquiry 1934* 33 CAR 144).[22]

10.6.1 The hearing

The nature and purpose of the basic wage

The whole tenor of the hearing indicated an expectation that the Court would not merely cancel the emergency reduction but would also put the basic wage

---

[22] In a decision of 9 February 1934, Dethridge said that the Court would soon decide what was to be done about the 10 per cent reduction and also about the basic wage. 'It may be', he said, 'that the Court will put the basic wage, whatever the amount, upon a somewhat clearer basis as to the Statistician's figures, and a simpler basis as to adjustment, than has been the case hitherto' (*Interpretation—Agricultural Implement Award* 33 CAR 7, 8).

on a new footing. There was sporadic discussion of the need for a basic wage, the principles underlying it, and the method of its adjustment.

Early in the hearing, the Judges expressed general agreement that they did not want any more family-budget inquiries: they already had the results of inquiries by Piddington and others (transcript, p. 6). There was, initially, some questioning of the automatic adjustment system. Dethridge said:

> I am inclined to think, as I have already stated in judgments of the Court, that the more appropriate method of adjustment of the basic wage is one based upon what is known as the 'All Items Table' rather than upon the 'All Houses Table'. Assuming that to be so—assuming that the all items table is the one which more accurately serves as a measure, one finds that there are discrepancies in the basic wage as between different capitals or different States. If we adopted the all items table, it would mean, apparently, that a re-adjustment of the wages as between the different capitals or States would have to be made. ... and I may say also, it may be that it is an opportune moment for introducing a rather better system of adjustment than we have had. I am not at all sure—here again I speak for myself—that we have not made too many adjustments. I am not at all sure that the quarterly adjustment is not a source of embarrassment; that it harasses business people unnecessarily ... (pp. 4–5)

After the hearing had proceeded for several days, Dethridge reverted to the question of automatic adjustments:

> I have it in mind that possibly the best course is this: to have adjustments made once every six months, but to have those adjustments made upon the last preceding quarter's figures. That has appealed to me, but I have an open mind upon it and I want to hear what can be said. By adopting that method, it appears to me that you do have the advantage of getting the most recent cost of living figures for the period you are adjusting for ... and at the same time you do away with what may be—I have to hear you upon this—a too frequent adjustment by means of quarterly adjustment. (pp. 181–182)

Beeby contemplated a larger departure from existing practice:

> I was hoping to hear argument on another possibility to which I have been giving consideration: whether a better method would not be to abandon the mechanical adjustment and for this Court once a year to, as briefly as possible, survey the situation and declare the wage for that year.

Dethridge had thought of this but saw it as impractical. 'It might be feasible', he said, 'for a Court acting in one State to have a yearly examination of the actual cost of living and so on, but for this Court to undertake the examination of the cost of living all over Australia would take all our time' (p. 182). Beeby was not convinced: 'Surely if this Court changed its principle and settled down to a new method the considerations as to whether or not there should be a variation ought not to be a very extensive matter once a year.' P J Clarey, one of the union advocates, said that the unions wished to retain quarterly automatic adjustment, but proposed that no adjustment be made until the amount was at least two shillings. Dethridge was attracted to this. He said (on the next day): 'I am inclined to think that if that were introduced, we could then adhere, generally speaking, to the quarterly adjustment because that in itself would diminish the necessity for such frequent adjustments ... and, at the same time, as you say, would enable the basic wage to meet any sharp change in the cost of living' (p. 204).

The issue of wage adjustment was further discussed later in the hearing. Beeby asked whether 'until we get some traditional stability would it not be better for the Court, after having arrived at a basic wage, to have a short review every six months, and cut out the adjustments? ... There may be some violent changes in the economic circumstances again calling for a reconsideration of the basic wage' (p. 470). He thought that there were some industries in which the 10 per cent cut could be restored, 'but the automatic universal system is a very difficult one to cope with' (p. 471). Dethridge was reluctant to take so large a step:

> I may say that my present feeling is that we should as far as possible get at the basic wage which should be applied ordinarily, and should come to a decision as to whether the 10 per cent cut generally should be removed either wholly or in part, and, having announced what we regard as being the rule for the general application of that wage we should then call upon those concerned in any industry who wish to do so, to show cause why that generally should not be applied. I am inclined to think that that would meet the situation which my brother Beeby has in mind … My present view is that the Court should be slow to discard the principle of a basic wage to be used in ordinary circumstances. It is true that originally there was no statutory direction to the Court to adopt any such principle, or to arbitrate within the limits of any such principle; but the principle was adopted early in 1907, and it has been recognised, in my opinion, by the Legislature in some later amendments. (p. 471)

Dethridge assured Crofts: 'I think you may take it that I have not in my mind anything which will lead to the discarding or the abandonment, either ostensibly or otherwise, of the basic wage as the normal minimum wage for the adult male' (p. 472). Beeby retreated somewhat from his suggestion:

> I am not putting that forward as a practical proposal at present. All I am saying is that we have not reached the limit of schemes for wage regulation. If the system persists, and we could get some cohesion between those tribunals which fix wages, we could get a much better scheme than that which exists today. (pp. 472–473)

Crofts sought to rehabilitate the idea of the basic wage as a minimum sum for a family of five.[23] He attributed the practice of birth control to the

---

[23] He found some support in a 1926 basic wage decision of Mr Justice Dwyer in Western Australia. 'A wage which does not provide for three children', said Dwyer, 'should not be tolerated in a sparsely populated country such as this. We as a community are prepared to mortgage our resources to the extent of millions of pounds to bring in immigrants, and everyone agrees that an Australian baby is the best immigrant. We cannot be guided absolutely by statistics. Every man has not three children, neither has every man a wife, but every man who marries requires a whole wife of his own. If we award a wage by statistics, then we should fix it at a figure which would support only a decimal fraction of a wife, to be exact, .49. This would not be satisfactory, so we should refuse to have what might be called a bigoted regard

inability of workers 'to bring up families in decency and comfort', causing Dethridge to comment:

> It is not so much the wages awarded by this Court that affects the rate of births. It is the general income of the community, speaking broadly, and the standard which that community chooses to adopt. In Australia hitherto the capacity of wealth-production has been, I might say, reasonably high, so that people have also adopted a comparatively high standard of living, and accordingly, taking it by and large, they have to cut their family according to the wealth of the community. ... It comes back to this: it is the general wealth-production of the community, the income, in the broad sense of the word, and the standard which that community chooses to seek which brings about birth control. That is from the economic point of view. There may be other reasons for birth control, but that is the chief reason. (p. 35)

Two of the Judges—Dethridge and Drake-Brockman—later asserted the irrelevance of the family standard. There could be a high standard for a small family or a lesser one for a larger family. The following discussion ensued:

> Dethridge C J: Cannot we cut this short? Mr Justice Higgins purported to fix a basic wage for a family unit of five which was in my opinion a low standard, but Mr Justice Higgins endeavoured to fix that which was the best possible standard for a family of five or a family of four or a family of three. He endeavoured to fix the best possible standard and that I think is the aim that we should make for. It then becomes somewhat trifling, if I may say so, to say that that is the standard for a family of five, or four, or three, it is the best possible standard. All this discussion as to the family unit is perhaps somewhat beside the question.
>
> Mr Crofts: I desire to cut this question of the family unit short, but I am bound to point out the employees' viewpoint. That family unit has not only been used by myself, but generally by those who have been sitting

---

for statistics and award to each man enough to keep a whole wife' (Dwyer quoted by Crofts, transcript, p. 34).

in positions such as you are sitting in now. It has been declared from time to time that the basic wage provides for a unit of so and so.

Dethridge C J: I know that such declarations have been made, and I think it is just as well to say that I attach very little value to those declarations.

Clarey commented on the stagnation of the basic wage since it was set in 1907. 'I think', said Drake-Brockman, 'you are overlooking the fact that, although the basis for the basic wage was established in 1907 there was in fact between 1907 and 1930 a general increase in wages taken as a whole of about ten per cent.' Clarey—renowned for his open-mindedness—responded:

> I can see exactly what Your Honour means. Probably that may have come about in this way that, the standard once having been established, it took some time before the effect of the standard was actually felt in the community. The Court decided in 1907 that the basic wage should be 42s per week, but that did not apply to all industries for a start. First of all the *Harvester* people secured it and then gradually, as industry after industry came before this Court, they also secured it. Then in Victoria under the Wages Board system a long period of time elapsed before finally that system reached the *Harvester* standard, so that from 1907 to 1918 approximately speaking, slowly but surely the actual standard of living given to the workers was being brought into line with the *Harvester* standard and that, of course, is equivalent to saying that the amount given in wages has been increased.

There was, thought Drake-Brockman, a little more to the matter than this. He was speaking of wages in total, not just the basic wage. The increase 'was brought about partly by a great number of semi-skilled people going off the basic wage and getting a margin, and others getting more margin' (p. 205).

Clarey pressed the Court to agree that there should be periodic inquiries so that the basic wage could be adjusted for rising productivity. The Judges were inclined to say that productivity was a matter for the Statistician to determine, rather than for the Court's inquiry. Clarey explained that he was speaking of the translation of productivity movements into wages, which was a matter for the Court. 'It is better', he said, 'if we fix the basic wage now, to have that determine that standpoint and from now on measure our wage level, not from the 1907 standpoint, but from the 1934 standpoint, and every two years, say, make an investigation at the beginning of that year into whether industry can pay a higher wage' (pp. 206–210). Clarey's willingness to abandon 'the 1907 standpoint' must surely have been a breath of fresh air. A little later, Dethridge declared: 'We are making a fresh start' (p. 265).

The employer representative, L R Mann, criticised the continuance of Powers' 3s. As we have seen, the Court in 1931 did not adopt the original employers' proposal to cancel it and to substitute the C series for the A series index, but instead simply reduced award wages by 10 per cent, leaving the Powers' 3s as a component of the reduced basic wage. Mann was, no doubt, apprehensive of the Court deciding to cancel the emergency reduction without taking any step to offset any part of the resultant wage increases. The Court, he said, had dallied over a long period with the question of removing the Powers' 3s. Its original purpose was no longer relevant (p. 464). Beeby thought that the original purpose had long ago ceased to be the reason for maintaining the 3s. 'The Court continued the Powers 3s because they thought the general prosperity of industry justified them in paying something more than the bare basic wage.' Dethridge agreed (p. 465).

The partial recovery

Unemployment, though it had fallen somewhat, remained a potential barrier to higher wages. Clarey argued that the Court should treat as normal unemployment of about 10 per cent. 'Your suggestion, said Drake-Brockman, 'is that for the purpose of reckoning the effect of the depression on unemployment we should not take the figure 25.1 per cent but 25.1 less 10 or thereabouts.'[24] Clarey agreed:

> I suggest, first of all, that unemployment is always with us, and when we speak of the unemployment being 25.1, at the very best we could not

---

[24] Recorded unemployment was 25.1 per cent in the third quarter of 1933. This, apparently, was the most recent available statistic. In the first quarter of 1934, the percentage was 21.9.

reduce that to, say, 8.7.[25] The chances are that because of our improved methods of production and greater supervision, the lesson we have learned during the last three years, the number of people employed in any given industry will not be the same as in the past in the production of certain commodities. Assuming that 10 per cent will always be unemployed, it is only 15 points above that when we say 25. ...Your Honour has crystallised what I desire to submit ...

'Somewhat the same sort of thought has gone through my mind from time to time', said Drake-Brockman, '—that that is the proper way of looking at it' (p. 154).

The hearing took place at a time of a substantial recovery in the price of wool. J W Allen, the General Secretary of the Graziers' Association of New South Wales, provided the following statistics of the price per pound (pp. 294–295):

1927–28	19.5d
1928–29	16.44d
1929–30	10.29d
1930–31	8.59d
1931–32	8.46d
July 1933	8.04d
January 1934	19.4d

According to Allen, the depreciation of the exchange rate accounted for 3.12d of the recent value. He attributed the remainder of the increase to a poor season. Evidence given by A J King, a Director of the Victorian Wheatgrowers' Corporation, indicated that there had been no improvement in the price of wheat (p. 412).

Mann told the Court that there had been an improvement in building activity. This, he said, was due partly to the investment locally of funds which might otherwise have been transferred abroad, especially in city buildings.

---

[25] The average of 1923–29.

Low interest rates had encouraged investment in suburban properties. But in the case of suburban dwellings, low wages had been a major factor:

> I am dealing here with actual facts, and not with rates prescribed in awards. It is to some extent regrettable, because it has enabled some proportion, at any rate, of sweating to take place. But in suburban dwellings ... the award rates of this Court were avoided by gangs engaging as contractors. ... The unemployment was such in the building trade that no awards could hold it, and people contracted out of the awards ... (p. 426)

Recently things had improved and 'the award rate has been gradually approximated' (p. 427).

When Mann produced statistics showing a fall in the ratio of bank advances to deposits, Dethridge said that this showed that people did not want credit:

> Business people and others do not want to borrow money; they prefer to leave the deposits in the banks; but that may indicate this: that the community is not spending much—that the people who have been in the habit of borrowing money from the banks have ceased to spend money, and therefore have not borrowed money from the banks. That being so the power to spend should be transferred to the wage earners, because they will spend more money and thus balance consumption with production. That is an argument which might have been put, although I am afraid it was not put in that form before on previous occasions, but it might still be put. (p. 441)

This was a surprising comment in the face of repeated union claims in earlier cases that wage reductions would reduce spending. Dethridge then referred to the views of J M Keynes:

> Keynes says that the investing classes are not investing; they are not doing what they should do to balance production with consumption. If they were doing what they ought to do they would take the benefit of all the capital which is being bound up in bank deposits, and spend it .... and once you have more spending the world is cured. If the investing classes

are not doing it then somebody else must do it. Let the Government step in, and as soon as the Government steps in and starts spending, that will inevitably cause a certain amount of movement in business, and encourage other people to take their part in getting hold of the available savings and spending them. That is Keynes' argument. I quite agree, however theoretically sound that argument may be, spending by Government has not had a very encouraging history. ... That, I take it, is the reason why in Great Britain in the present time Mr Keynes suggestion has not been accepted. They think that the spending by Governments which he advocates would be more than counterbalanced by all kinds of evils. (pp. 442–443)

Employer resistance

W C Myhill, for the New South Wales employers, claimed that 'the time is not ripe for a general restoration of the 10 per cent; [and] that it should not be restored even in individual industries, because restoration of the 10 per cent in any particular industry gives the employees in that industry an advantage over their fellow workers' (pp. 575–576). Dethridge commented:

> There we are faced with the position that, in some industries, outside the Court altogether, employers have restored the full 10 per cent. The flour millers restored the 10 per cent, including the Powers' 3s, and there are other instances of a similar kind. ... The position is that, in those industries, the employers have thought that they could afford to restore the full 10 per cent. The flour millers apparently thought so, and the paper millers ... I think are in the same position. The banks—I do not know how far they have gone in making the full restoration—only lately have they thought the position enabled them to make some restoration of their salary rates. There we are faced with restorations of that kind.

Drake-Brockman added that the Commonwealth Government had restored part of the cut to the public service. Dethridge continued: 'The importance of those things is this: They were not brought about as the result of direct action. ... Those wages have been granted by employers, presumably because they felt that the economic position justified that restoration. That is where the importance of them presents itself' (p. 576). Myhill replied that the employers in question were either monopolies or in sheltered industries (p. 576a).

Myhill described the relief from award standards that had been provided to primary producers:

> With the primary producer we find that generally they are exempt from the awards of this Court, possibly with the exception of shearing. If we take wheat, or butter, or the production of eggs or honey, and other primary products such as those, we find they are exempt from the awards of this and other Courts, so that from the point of view of actual production, taking wheat as an illustration, the actual production of that wheat is no more costly in Australia than, say, in the Argentine, but the farmer's trouble starts as soon as he has to transport his wheat. That is where his costs come in. He has to pay for transport and other essential services. (p. 583)

Myhill might have added to 'transport and other essential services' goods manufactured in Australia under award wages and conditions and with the help of the protective tariff.

Carolan said that the Victorian Railways Commissioners had 'explored every avenue of bringing costs closer to the revenue, and every channel for increasing the revenue, and they depend upon the Court to refrain from adding to their difficulties by withdrawing the relief which the Court granted' (p. 525). The Court would appreciate 'that the Railway position has a dominating influence upon the financial position of the State'. Carolan described the jumbled arrangements for wage-fixing in the Victorian Railways. Some of the employees were entirely under the control of the Court; some had their wages controlled by the Railways Classification Board; and some depended on the Court for the basic wage and the Board for margins. A few grades, such as bricklayers, plumbers, and masons in the building trade, were covered by Victorian wages boards, and in respect of the conditions the Railways Classification Board covered practically the whole field. The Board has adhered strictly to Court standards on wages; but the Commissioners gained some benefits in respect of conditions (p. 526).

State and federal standards

There was some, though not extensive, discussion of the disparate treatment of wage-earners under Commonwealth and State awards. If the State tribunals—perhaps subject to legislative direction—would not follow the Court's lead, was it fair that workers under Commonwealth awards be placed at a disadvantage? Drake-Brockman referred to the fact that although the Court had reduced wages by 10 per cent, average wages had risen slightly in real terms. (Presumably he was referring to the Nominal Wage index.) This led him to comment:

> Now, obviously the other tribunals who operate in this industrial sphere, and all of the Legislatures of Australia, disagreed with what we had done; and the thing that worries me is, why should this small and diminishing number ... continue to carry this load, when nobody else will distribute it evenly in every other sphere in Australia in this regard. (p. 678)

Crofts presented the issue starkly:

> Other wage fixing tribunals and parliaments have decided differently. In New South Wales, there have been three Parliaments, two National and one Labor, in office since this Court took away the 10 per cent, and they have had the right to alter their Act to allow their Court to fall in line with this Court's judgment, but they have not done it. They have said, in effect, 'No, we are not prepared, and the electors have told us that that we are not to give our wage fixing tribunal the opportunity of doing what the Federal Arbitration Court has done.' Two Governments have been in power in Western Australia, and they have not altered the Act. In Queensland, a Nationalist Government did not alter the Act. South Australia has had a National Government which has not attempted to influence the Court, so that this Court is not only running up against a section of employees in this country who can see others

getting better treatment by other tribunals, but it is running up against the Governments which have said, 'This thing shall not be done'. (p. 814)

Geographical divergences

A vexed issue in this case was geographical differences in the basic wage. It related to both differences between capital cities and regional differences within States. Adoption of the C series index would entail some alteration of inter-capital differences, generally in the direction of 'flattening' them. (Although the Court in 1933 adopted the C series index, it was applied to the wage levels in force in 1929. Hence 1929 disparities were preserved.) The items in the A series index—food, groceries, and rent—differed more as between cities than did clothing and miscellaneous items included in the C series. Dethridge observed that the Sydney rate would fall and the Adelaide rate rise if the index were changed (p. 605). *Apart from* the effects of changing the index, Dethridge did not contemplate any revision of inter-capital differences:

> I am not sure that it is suggested by anyone, or is going to be suggested by anyone, that the Court should lay down a rigid rule, either that differential rates will be adopted in future, or that there should be a flat rate adopted in future. I do not know what Mr Wright [for South Australian employers] is going to suggest—whether he is going to suggest that there should be a general practice of differentiating the basic wage in the various States according to their local index numbers. All I have to say is that he is not at all likely to succeed. That would involve a departure from the practice of the Court, which it had acted upon until quite recently, in its latest award; and so, if he is going to suggest that, he has not much hope ... We are inclined to think that we should leave the question of differential basic wages and flat basic wages to be dealt with in each case as it comes before the Court. (p. 607)

Wright said that 'we in SA are extremely concerned at the possibility of the loss of the relative advantage between our rates and Melbourne'. The following exchange ensued:

> Dethridge C J: What you are asking for, in substance, is this: That there should be maintained in permanence a different basic wage, that is a lower basic wage, in Adelaide than in any other place. ... The position in Adelaide is that at present, speaking in round figures, the basic wage is somewhere about 3s less than Melbourne. Is that correct?
>
> Mr Wright: Yes.
>
> Dethridge C J: Now, taking the All Items index figures ... that difference of 3s in favour of Adelaide as against Melbourne deprives the Adelaide wage earner of commodities to the value of 3s per week. It may be that the 'poverty' of Adelaide as compared with the 'wealth' of Melbourne necessitates some differentiation of wage payment in Adelaide. It may be that is unfortunately the case: but if that is the case, let that be recognised and let it be said that Adelaide cannot afford to pay the same basic wage, real purchasing power, as Melbourne ... It may be ... that the way to approach that position is this: that the basic wage for Adelaide for some time to come be 3s less in real value ... than that of Melbourne; that after the expiration of some particular time it should become 2s less; that after the expiration of another time it should become 1s less, and after still another time become the same in real purchasing power as that of Melbourne. It may be that something of that kind should be done, but at any rate if that were done it would recognise and state the real reason for the distinction between the basic wage in Melbourne and that of Adelaide, and it would get away from any glossing over of the position by a lot of juggling ... with figures. (pp. 632–633)

Dethridge noted that the State basic wage in Adelaide (set by the Board of Industry) was above the federal rate. Wright acknowledged this, but commented: 'When you take into consideration that this Court almost invariably awards payment for 10 days a year for holidays and a sort of optional six days for sickness, there is not much difference between State and Federal awards there' (p. 636). Dethridge said later: 'Beyond a doubt, if the All Items table is applied, that is going to result in a flattening out of the wage between States, as far as the basic wage is concerned. There is no doubt about that. And if the principle of the basic wage is to be maintained at all, such flattening out is called for by justice' (p. 665A).

Intra-state differentials were the subject of submissions on behalf of Victorian country employers, who were concerned that the change of index would obliterate or reduce differences between regional and metropolitan rates. 'It may be said', their representative (Derham) contended,

> that the C series, or any series the Court adopts, does not show a difference between cities and provincial towns, but there are some considerations which do not appear in cold print differentiating the country cost of living and the city. For instance, generally speaking, the houses are better: that is, they are not so congested and are on large blocks, whereas, for living purposes, they are just as good in the country as in the city. (p. 611)

Moreover, said Derham, the country worker paid no fares to work; and 'there is not the same opportunity of spending money in those places, such as trips to the seaside and trips out of town, as in the city' (p. 612). And the country employer faced higher costs for transportation and city representation. He was asking for 'a fixed differential lower rate for these towns irrespective of what the cost of living figures actually amount to' (p. 615).

Clarey told the Court that the unions did not favour a flat-rate basic wage for the capital cities; but they 'would be prepared to accept a flat rate for a State provided that the flat rate was the rate determined for the capital city, and further provided that in certain areas where, because of peculiar circumstances the cost of living is very much higher than in Melbourne, those expensive country district areas should not be brought down to the Melbourne level' (p. 754). He cited Yallourn as a country town where high living costs called for a basic wage above the metropolitan equivalent. Dethridge referred to and defended the Court's *refusal* to enforce a higher basic wage in a town—Mildura—where the cost of living was above that of the capital:

> As you know, the Court at Mildura almost invariably adopts the Melbourne figure when dealing with ordinary industry. It is recognised

that the cost of living on the Statist's figures would be rather higher than the Melbourne rates, but invariably the Court has said that, on the whole, the Melbourne index number should be acted on for Mildura, the reason undoubtedly being that it is thought undesirable to put too great a wage cost on a place like Mildura. ... In the fruit picking industry, of course, wage costs cannot be made very high. I had to deal with that two or three years ago and considered the position very carefully. If you were to put on a wage cost, prescribed rates of wage for the men engaged in fruit picking such as were suggested by the local index figure, it would have been disastrous. So the Court in the past has not acted with a rigid adherence to the index figures in places like Mildura and, I think, in one or two other places. ... and I must confess, in the case of Mildura certainly, the Court acted with great commonsense. (p. 759)

'spreading the burden'

During his final reply, Clarey spoke of the goal of 'spreading the burden', which had actuated the Court since 1930. He thought that the Court would now realise that the task was too big for it: 'It is a job that requires the full powers and responsibilities of the Governments of Australia in order to see that the burden is spread equally amongst those who are in a position to help' (p. 741). Clarey elicited from Dethridge this reflection on the Court's role:

> Yes, that may be so, but you must not overlook the fact that Governments have to rely upon the citizens of the country for the means of doing what has to be done. It is a question of money. They can do nothing unless they can levy upon the community for the means of doing what has to be done. The power that the Government has to levy depends upon what those upon whom the levy is made have to give, and what they have to give depends upon what they make out of the industry in which they are engaged, and what they make out of the industry in which they are engaged depends upon the costs of production in that industry, and the costs of production in that industry depend upon, amongst other things, the wages that have to be paid in it, and the wages that have to be paid in it depend to a fairly considerable extent upon what

is prescribed by this Court. So you have the power of the Government to assist the primary producer dependent upon the wages prescribed by this Court. ... It is like the house that Jack built. Ultimately you get back very largely to what this Court does. So while this Court feels that it is not desirable to make in wage rates any changes which do not appear to be clearly necessary, nevertheless changes in wage rates may become necessary for the purpose of bringing about the object we have been discussing, that is, the helping of the primary producer. ... (p. 741)

Beeby and Drake-Brockman agreed.

Female wages

The unions, anticipating a decision that would raise the basic wage, asked the Court to consider its implications for females and sought a decision that the minimum female rate in any award be not less than 60 per cent of the male basic wage. Although there was no female basic wage in the Court's awards, the lowest rate set for women could, by arithmetic, be expressed as a percentage of the male basic wage. There was, however, no mechanism whereby the women's wage would rise or fall with the male basic wage. Hence, as the male wage rose or fell, the percentage that the minimum female rate bore to the basic wage moved in the opposite direction. In some of the State jurisdictions, female basic wages were explicitly provided and usually varied by the tribunal when it altered the male rate.

Drake-Brockman had recently made a new textiles award. The minimum female rate was equal to just under 54 per cent of the basic wage. 'But', he said, 'that was only an accident. I went into the matter pretty carefully, examined a whole lot of budgets, got costs of what actually these women, in Melbourne at all events, paid for board and lodging, and so on; in fact I did a lot of work on it.' Wright, representing South Australian employers, was apparently apprehensive that the Court might adopt a percentage similar to that in textiles:

I am not unmindful of the fact that comparatively recently the Court has given consideration to this matter in the textile case ... We consider

> that the system of the percentage wage for a female is very defective, yet we realise that the Court must have some regard to the relationship between the male and female wages, and I am afraid that we are not in a position to suggest any alternative to a percentage fixation until the Court feels disposed to conduct some sort of inquiry into the requirements of women workers, such as has been done in the case of State tribunals ... There has, as far as my knowledge extends, been only one thorough investigation by this Court into the subject, and ... it appears probable that in that case His Honour Judge Drake-Brockman did not purport to fix a female wage as a percentage of a male wage. It of necessity bore a percentage relationship to the male wage, but I think I can demonstrate to the Court that that percentage did not really represent the percentage that my friends, the union advocates, have suggested. (p. 620)

The minimum female rate set by Drake-Brockman was, said Wright, equal to 53.6 per cent of the basic wage. This, however, included a 2 shillings holiday allowance, with which Wright disagreed. If that were excluded, the percentage would be 51.3. Wright recounted decisions of the South Australian Board of Industry presided over by Jethro Brown and Raymond Kelly wherein the female basic wage was set below 50 per cent of the male rate; in December 1931, the percentage was exactly 50 (pp. 625–629).

Crofts, on the other hand, had studied the records of 26 Victorian wages boards:

> The Court will find that in the majority of cases the female percentage is above 55 per cent of the male rate and it goes as high as 80 per cent in the tobacconist trade, and in the jewellery trade there is an equal rate for males and females. In the electrical trade the female percentage is 65 per cent of the male wage, for storemen and packers it is 57 per cent, for charworkers it is 87 per cent, for cigar makers it is 62 per cent, for commercial clerks it is 62 per cent and for brushmakers it is 47 per cent. (p. 846)

10.6.2 The decision

The Court's decision was delivered on 17 April (33 CAR 144). There were majority and minority judgments.

Dethridge and Drake-Brockman took first the question of the status of the basic wage:

> Although the fixation of a general basic wage is not a necessary part of the Court's activity and was not adopted until 1908, it has proved of value as a starting point to work from in the settlement of industrial disputes. It has been recognised by the Legislature ... as a constant element in the practice of the Court, and is now almost invariably incorporated by parties in their claims. A statement was made during the hearing that this Court, unlike State Industrial Courts, is free to abandon the principle of a basic wage if it so thinks fit. This is true, but no sufficient reason for taking that course was suggested. (p. 147)

The two Judges turned then to the question of the criterion by which the basic wage should be fixed: 'the cost of living of a labourer's family' or 'national productivity'. They continued:

> Inasmuch as the source of all wages is the national productivity, and inasmuch it is just that the share of wage-earners as a whole should be proportionate to the national productivity for the time being, the latter proposition is theoretically the sounder. But its practical application is full of difficulty, and the working out of a feasible scheme, even if possible at all, would probably take years in normal times. In the present precarious position of industry no such scheme could be successfully devised and applied. In 1925, a commission, consisting of Mr J T Sutcliffe and Professors Mills and Brigden, investigated the question of adjusting wages according to variations in productivity, and made a report to the Queensland Industrial Court recommending a scheme. No action was taken upon the report. Hitherto Australian Industrial Courts have substantially assessed their basic or living wage on the cost of living of a family unit ... In the long run, if due consideration be given to economic conditions, this process will probably give a resulting

> basic wage in amount fairly close to that which would be indicated by a method founded on national productivity. (p. 147)

A notable aspect of this passage is the implication that it is desirable for the wage-earners' 'share' to be proportionate to national productivity. That was, in principle, the premise of the Queensland Economic Commission (which complicated its prescriptions to take account of problems of measurement and timing). The juxtaposition of 'share' and 'national productivity' makes sense only if the latter is conceived to be a money amount. That is, the wage would rise or fall with the price of the product as well as the quantity produced. The Economic Commission was clear on this point, and it is also implicit in the assumption of Dethridge and Drake-Brockman that adjusting wages for movements in the cost of living will, 'if due consideration be given to economic conditions', give a result that approximates the setting of wages according to national productivity.

Moving to a discussion of economic conditions, Dethridge and Drake-Brockman said:

> There has undoubtedly been some improvement in the industrial position of the Commonwealth during the last year. The price of wool has substantially increased and there is a rise in some minor products. But our other substantial exports, wheat and butter, cannot realise payable prices abroad and the dried and canned fruits export trade is meeting with such keen competition that its condition is perilous. The government finances of the States are still far from being in a satisfactory condition, chiefly because of railway deficits. It is not necessary to discuss in detail these conditions which are now matters of general public knowledge. The position may be summed up by saying that there is now an increase of confidence among the community resulting in freer expenditure and some increase of investment in industry, but that former prosperity is far from being restored. Unemployment though decreasing is still very great. (pp. 147–148)

The question to be faced was whether the signs of recovery warranted a change in wage rates. Having posed the question, Dethridge and Drake-Brockman decided that the 10 per cent reduction would cease to operate. At the same time, however, there would be a change in the method of fixing the basic wage which would lessen the increase in wage levels.

The majority judges reviewed the notion of the basic wage as a family wage. They claimed that Higgins in 1907 had been 'compelled to accept a hazy opinion then prevalent that the number in [an average labourer's] household was about five'. He appeared 'to have concluded that inasmuch as labourers' households of average size had in fact somehow been maintained upon the wage of 7s a day paid by reputable employers in sheltered industries, he could reasonably take that amount as being sufficient to provide for a family unit of five' (pp. 148–149). Subsequent investigations had revealed that on average the dependants supported by the worker were fewer than four. The average family of a married worker contained about 2.8 people. 'But whatever the family unit adopted by a wage-fixing body', said Dethridge and Drake-Brockman,

> the power of that body to endow that unit with any desired standard of living depends on the productive capacity of the community as a whole. With few exceptions the determinations of industrial tribunals shows that this limitation has been realised—though perhaps it has not been sufficiently acknowledged by them. Generally speaking, however, it may be said that the outcome of this realisation is that the basic or living wage prescribed would have been about the same in amount, regardless of the size of the family unit ostensibly adopted. The larger the family assumed as the unit, the lower the possible standard of living prescribed, the smaller the family assumed, the higher the standard prescribed. (p. 149)

Having thus called into question the relevance of the family, Dethridge and Drake-Brockman immediately rehabilitated it:

> This suggests that the adoption of a family unit is not necessary, and that what should be sought is the independent ascertainment and prescription of the highest basic wage that can be sustained by the total of industry in all its primary, secondary and ancillary forms. That no doubt is the object, but the adoption of something like the real

average family as the unit to be provided for is not without its use in the attainment of that object. There is no clear means of measuring the general wage-paying capacity of the total industry of a country. All that can be done is to approximate, and one of the methods of approximation is to find out the actual wage upon which well situated labourers are at the time maintaining the average family unit. We may be pardoned for saying that Mr Justice Higgins very wisely used this criterion in the *Harvester* case. Moreover, if the average size families of such well situated labourers have become accustomed to enjoy, and do actually enjoy, a certain standard of living in our community, it may reasonably be assumed that such a standard for all labourers is probably not beyond the capacity of industry in general to provide. Therefore in determining the amount of a living or basic wage, there is sound economic warranty for the ascertainment of the real average family unit and of the cost of providing something like the standard which such families of well employed labourers have already reached. (pp. 149–150)

Despite the risk that the wage set might be too high, the highest possible level of wages should be sought for economic as well as humanitarian reasons. The Judges here returned to the notion of 'balance' which had been articulated in earlier decisions, especially by Dethridge:

For economic welfare total production must be substantially balanced by total consumption, and balanced as promptly as possible. If so-called savings are quickly spent upon industrial enterprises, this spending helps to balance consumption with production just as effectively as if the wage-earners had taken a larger share and no savings had been made. But if savings … are not used speedily, then the necessary prompt balancing of production and consumption is not achieved. Economically, the community might be better off if the savings had not been made and the wage-earners had received more in wages and had spent it. To this extent the purchasing power argument for the maintenance of wage rates is valid. A wage level fixed too low may be as detrimental as one fixed too high. (p. 150)

It was possible (though there was no satisfactory evidence on the point) that the benefit of the 10 per cent cut had been less than it might have been—'that the transferred spending power was not used by employers or capitalists quickly or abundantly'. The cut had helped many industrial concerns 'to weather the economic blizzard, thus preventing unemployment from becoming greater than it actually was' (p. 150). Moreover, the Court's practice in adjusting the basic wage to prices had 'rendered to the community during the recent calamitous industrial crisis the very valuable service of a large part of the required adaptation automatically' (p. 152). The present challenge was 'to estimate, as nearly as we can, what level of wages will promote the active exercise of spending power, and at the same time avoid chilling the now slightly rewarmed industrial courage' (p. 150).

The earlier adjustment of the basic wage by the All Houses Index had caused differences between the States which were excessive when compared with cost of living differences indicated by the All Items Index. Dethridge and Drake-Brockman readjusted the amounts for the six capitals by use of the latter index, producing a Six-Capitals amount of 65s. The Melbourne wage of 64s was identical to the *Harvester* equivalent. Before the decision, the basic wage was subject to the 10 per cent cut, which now ceased. The increase was partially offset, however, by the abolition of Powers' 3s, which 'is not in our opinion now justifiable'. Because of the condition of the local economies, the basic wages for South Australia and Tasmania were subject to deductions of 3s and 2s respectively. These deductions would expire in June 1935. In net terms, the Six-Capitals basic wage was raised by 1s 3d, or just under 2 per cent. The basic wage for non-metropolitan towns in each State was to be 3s below the respective capital-city amount. Future quarterly adjustments would reflect movements of the C series index, subject to the requirement that the minimum adjustments be 2s.

The majority decision allowed State legislatures to reduce the wages paid to employees of transport authorities where like reductions were imposed on other State employees. The judges said:

> Employees in general of the State can fairly claim that the State legislature should not require them to make sacrifices out of proportion to those required of the rest of the community. And if the legislators demand more from State employees than the community thinks is fair, the legislators responsible may be ejected from office. But should the State legislature think fit to reduce or make a reduction from the remuneration generally of the employees of the State, those engaged in its transport services have no moral claim to escape a reduction or deduction equal in degree to that imposed generally upon other employees of the State in similar grades. All that they are entitled to is that they be treated no worse. (p. 158)

Dethridge and Drake-Brockman also decided that no orders would be made for various sectors. In some cases—bond stores, felt hatters, Victorian marine stores, Launceston tramways, and some municipal employees—there had been no adjustment of wages for the reduced cost of living. The Court's order stated generally that the cancellation of the reduction did not apply where the wage had not been subject to cost of living adjustments. The pastoral industry was excluded, because the matters at issue were wider than the restoration of the 10 per cent and remained to be heard. Fruit-growing was excluded because of the critical state of the industry. No explicit reasons were stated for excluding printing at Broken Hill and mining at Mount Lyall.

Beeby agreed that a 'fresh declaration' was necessary, but disagreed with his colleagues' methods and the results. He concurred in the cancellation of the emergency reduction. He would also have set basic wages for the various locations below the levels that the mere rescission of the cut would have yielded, but the amounts would have been slightly above those set by Dethridge and Drake-Brockman.

In his opinion, the economic position was much better than it had been a year earlier, but the recovery was 'not sufficient or permanent enough to justify belief that the Commonwealth can get back to pre-depression standards':

> We still have more than 20 per cent of our population unemployed or depending for bare existence on relief works. The prices offering for base

metals are barely sufficient to meet costs of production. The prices which we can obtain for two of our main lines of export—wheat and dairy produce—are lower than in 1931, and difficulty in finding markets for our surpluses have increased. Economic nationalism hampers exchange of our surpluses for other goods far more than in 1930. On present indications, unless world co-operation improves, we will have to greatly reduce our exports of foodstuffs, and primary producers will have to rely more and more on local markets. Unless local consumption is greatly increased production will probably of necessity be reduced. Until there is some indication of stabilisation of price levels by international action, Australia's position remains precarious. (p. 165)

Beeby proceeded to question the efficacy of the 1931 order. Data for manufacturing showed that the wage share of value added had fallen from 54.6 per cent in 1927–28 to 50.2 per cent in 1932–33. Had the reduction of the wage-earners' share contributed to recovery? If the transfer of spending power caused an immediate and commensurate increase in investment or in consumption from non-wage incomes, the employee class would benefit from reduced unemployment. On the other hand, the money transferred might be used to reduce debt or simply be hoarded. In that event, there might be no adequate offset to the reduction of wage-earner spending. What were the facts?

> Of course immediate spending of the saved wages was not and could not be expected. It is impossible to estimate whether at the present time the amount transferred to employers is being spent on commodities or is being re-invested but the indications are that it is not. The most reliable test is unemployment. At the height of the depression the proportion of unemployed was about 30 per cent. Today it is approximately 22½ per cent. But the absorption of unemployed up to a few months ago was entirely due to expenditure of public money on relief works. Within recent months revival of activities in the building trades and the motor and some other industries has undoubtedly reduced unemployment. Higher wool prices have appreciably increased national income and re-established a measure of confidence. But it is extremely doubtful

whether reducing the real wages of a section of the workers materially contributed to the partial recovery of the past year. (p. 168)

Beeby still accepted 'the broad theory that reductions of real wages do not reduce total spending power but only transfer it from one group to another', but the experience of the past three years convinced him 'that in times of economic panic and uncertainty such transfer is not conducive to recovery unless it be part of a planned scheme of re-organisation which guarantees that the transferred amount is either immediately spent on commodities or re-invested in labour-employing concerns' (p. 168). In other countries, notably the United Kingdom and the United States, reduction of real wages was out of favour; and 'the universal trend of economic thought from low wage to high-wage theories and to shortening working hours as one of the remedies for unemployment should be closely considered by a national tribunal exercising quasi-legislative functions' (p. 169).

In 1931, said Beeby, the Court had taken 'a leap in the dark—at the time apparently a very necessary leap'. But now there was 'a little more light'.

> Full cancellation of the 10 per cent reduction order would not be an admission of error. It would only be proof that this Court at all times will act as it thinks just in circumstances existing at the time of its decisions and on consideration of results flowing from previous decisions. (p. 169)

In terms of wage outcomes, Beeby's difference from the majority was slender. He agreed with the abolition of Powers' 3s. The Six-Capitals basic wage awarded by Beeby would have been 66s, rather than 65s, the difference being due to larger increases in Brisbane, Adelaide, and Perth. He supported the special provision to enable the States to impose lower wages in the railways.

Dethridge and Drake-Brockman appended to their decision the following paragraph:

> By the courtesy of Beeby J we have been able to read in advance his judgment herein. His comments upon the judgment and order of 1931 ... and the adjustment order of 1933 are of course intended to

> indicate only his own present opinion thereon. Inasmuch, however, as the judgment and order of himself and us making the reduction was unanimous, we think we should make it clear that these comments are not intended to indicate, and in some respects do not indicate, our present views on the subject. (p. 160)

Evidently, they did not 'buy' Beeby's equivocal repudiation of the 1931 decision.

Three years later, the Court (similarly constituted) estimated that the effect of the 1934 decision on the basic wage was to restore its real value to that of the *Harvester* basic wage, exclusive of Powers' 3s (*Basic Wage Inquiry 1937* 37 CAR 583, 585). Inasmuch as it is possible to compare real wages over a period of 27 years, this was probably an accurate assessment.

Cancellation of the emergency reduction had the effect that margins were generally restored to their monetary levels as at the beginning of 1931 and, in most instances, their pre-Depression amounts. With prices having fallen by more than 20 per cent, this represented a substantial real increase. I have referred, in Subsection 8.2.1, to statistical evidence of a change in wage relativities favourable to higher-paid workers. This, of course, was a partial reversal of the compression of relativities in the two preceding decades by reason of the reluctance of the Court and State tribunals to adjust margins for increases in the price level. The Court took no specific decision about female rates. Since the rescission of the 10 per cent cut applied to them, their nominal value was restored to pre-Depression levels, except where they had been reduced by decisions specific to particular awards. Both because the (male) basic wage had fallen heavily in nominal terms and because its real value was not fully restored by the 1934 decision, this implied some narrowing of the gender pay gap.[26]

---

[26] Between December 1929 and December 1934, the average nominal wages of males fell by 19 per cent. For females, the corresponding reduction was 17.7 per cent. Though it is surprising that the difference between the two reductions was not greater, it is to be remembered that most females worked under State awards and determinations. Under some of these, female rates were subject to the same proportional reductions as male rates.

10.7 Continuing caution

In the remainder of 1934, the Court's decisions were a mixture of continued restraint and mild relaxation.

Ten days after its decision on the 10 per cent cut, the Full Court delivered a decision about wages in the pastoral industry (*Variation—Pastoral Award* 33 CAR 503). As we have seen, wage reductions imposed in this industry were more severe than the general 10 per cent cut. The relevant orders were now rescinded, but the Court adopted a new set of arrangements for the basic wage of station hands, reflecting the Court's opinions that (a) living costs for pastoral workers were 10 to 15 per cent below those of town workers, and (b) there should be greater uniformity in wages than in the generality of industries. There would be a single rate for all locations. For adjustment purposes, the index would be the '30 towns' average of the 'C series' index, but there would be no alteration of the wage unless the price index indicated a change of 4s or more. The amount of the basic wage so calculated would be subject to a constant deduction of 8s. Initially, the uniform rate was 60s.

On the same day, the Full Court gave its decision on an application by the Mount Lyall Mining Company for a basic wage below the regular amount and for retention of the 10 per cent cut in margins. The Court granted the former, but not the latter. In explanation of the lower wage, the Court said that it could not disregard harsh economic facts:

> Copper production in Australia is doomed unless world conditions change. The Court feels that it is better to let the working people engaged in copper production know that their means of livelihood are perilously endangered, and not to hold out any hopes of an early restoration of old wage rates. (*Variation of Awards—Mount Lyall Mining Operations* 33 CAR 517, 519)

Dethridge, in May, dealt with a union application affecting margins in the railways (*Interim Award—Railways, South Australia* 33 CAR 531). The Court in October 1930 had set aside the railways awards except in respect of the basic wage and standard hours, leaving the Railways Commissioners (subject to direction or influence by State governments or regulation, in Victoria, by the Railway Classification Board) to determine other terms of employment, including margins. Before the setting-aside, the margins had been as determined by Quick in an award of March 1930. These had partially replaced the margins set by agreement in a 1926 award. After the setting-aside, the practice of the Commissioners had been to observe the margins set by the Court, but with a deduction of 10 per cent. The unions now claimed the restoration of the 1930 margins, but their claim was resisted by the Railways Commissioner for South Australia. They had succeeded in getting employer consent to the consequent increases in other States, and this may have forced Dethridge's hand:

> I am now asked to make an interim or provisional award only—not to make a final determination whether the margins should continue to be as prescribed by Sir John Quick D P, a matter which will have to be left to the Judge who makes a new award upon them. As to the margins agreed to in 1926 I should say that there is a very strong presumption that they should continue. The others may be less defensible, but nevertheless were prescribed after very full investigation by the deputy president, and have just been acceded to by the Commissioners of New South Wales and Tasmania. ... For the Commissioner, however, great stress was laid upon the financial position of the South Australian Railways, and in view of this the recently devised clause enabling general public service reductions to be applied to Federal award rates should certainly be made applicable. (p. 533)

Beeby gave two decisions about the spreading of available work. In June, he extended a provision of the Metal Trades Award allowing the payment of wages on an hourly basis, so as to accommodate relief work. 'The unemployment problem', he said, 'still continues, although it appears to be gradually abating; but money is still being spent in large sums on relief work, and I propose to extend this order for a further twelve months in the hope that the renewal of this application will then be unnecessary' (*Variation—Metal Trades Award* 33 CAR 596, 597). In December, Beeby dealt with the rationing of work in the Adelaide tramways (*Variation—Tramway Employees' Award* 33 CAR 1071). 'One of the things with which I have been most pleased all through the present industrial crisis', he said, 'has been the readiness with which working men, rather than have their mates placed on the unemployed market, have agreed to rationing, and the Adelaide tramway men have not been behind others in that regard.' But now the union sought to have rationing abolished. The choice that Beeby had to make was 'whether I should ask these men, who have done a big service in the past in accepting rationing, to continue a little longer, in the hope that a change may come, or have 64 of them placed on the unemployed market'. In rejecting the latter option, he noted particularly the slight recovery of South Australian industry.

In July, Dethridge revisited the familiar issue—dating back to the early years of Higgins' regime—of a request by a particular employer (in this case a maltster) for wage relief to help overcome its financial problems (*Variation— Liquor Trades Award (Maltsters Section, NSW)* 33 CAR 636):

> Assuming for the moment that if the bulk of the malting industry in New South Wales were in a similar financial difficulty there would be good reasons for reducing wage rates as proposed, it does not follow that this application by a single concern comprising only a small proportion of the industry should be granted. This Court has never except by consent in such a case prescribed for such a concern lower wage rates than those prescribed for the industry generally, nor, conversely, has it prescribed higher wage rates than the general rates for a single prosperous concern.
> (p. 637)

Dethridge did not comment on the relation between this decision and the Full Court's decision in the Mount Lyall case. On the face of the matter, they seem difficult to reconcile. If he had discussed the question, Dethridge might perhaps have referred to the significance of the Mount Lyall company, both as a component of the copper mining industry and in the region, compared with the relative unimportance of a single maltster. The Mount Lyall decision seems to be at odds with the stance of Higgins in the Broken Hill case of 1909, but

Powers had breached the principle of that case in the Moonta and Wallaroo case of 1921 (see Chapter 6, Subsection 6.1.2).

Several notable decisions were given in December 1934, reflecting perhaps the Judges' wish to 'clear the decks' before the summer vacation.

In one of these, Dethridge made a new award for gold mining in Victoria (*Judgment—Gold-Mining Industry (Victoria)* 33 CAR 1106). With the departure from the gold standard and the depreciation of the Australian pound against sterling, the price of gold rose well above its pre-Depression level. But the industry's condition remained problematic. Dethridge said:

> The search for gold has been stimulated in Victoria, as elsewhere, by its present high price, and mining enterprise has become lively, but that enterprise has not yet gained a commensurate reward. Except in one or two cases gold is not yet being obtained in quantities nearly sufficient to give a profit. ... Investment has become somewhat brisk with a very beneficial increase of employment in the industry. The claimant union says that the investors are at heart gamblers, and that they should not be allowed to gamble with underpaid workers as their pawns. Quite true! The probable lack of success in a mine does not justify sweated wages, but it is also true that wages can only be usefully prescribed at such amounts as the average returns of the industry can maintain, while permitting some profit here and there to the lucky investors. The court in determining the amounts of wages must act according to these governing limits; on the one hand maintaining wages at the worst not very much lower than those prevailing in other industries of the community, and on the other refraining from prescribing wages so high that only the rare exceptionally fortunate venture can pay them and carry on. Similar comments apply to conditions of employment other than wage rates. (p. 1107)

Dethridge rejected a union claim for an additional 6s per week to be paid to workers in profitable mines, consistent with a differential previously granted by Powers (see Chapter 6, Subsection 6.1.2). The Court, so far as it considered at all the wage-paying capacity of an industry, should act upon its average capacity (pp. 1108–1109). Some relaxation of restraint was evident in Dethridge's grant of 3s a week to labourers working underground. These workers already enjoyed a 44-hour week, whereas surface employees worked 48 hours. A 1928 agreement had given miners a 9s margin. Dethridge raised the margin to 12s, maintaining the 9s differential between the miner and the labourer. Because of the fall in the basic wage since 1928, the proportional relativity between the miner and the labourer was significantly increased.

In another December decision, Drake-Brockman took a more guarded approach to pleas for special treatment of the railways than had characterised earlier Depression-period decisions. This decision was about the wages of locomotive enginemen in Victoria, Tasmania, and South Australia (*Judgment— Locomotive Enginemen* 33 CAR 1033). Representatives of the Railways Commissioners had urged Drake-Brockman to take into account the state of railway finances in the three States. He was unconvinced:

> Railways are not business concerns but are provided to run, in a very large measure, for the purpose of opening up and developing the country. This part of the reason for their existence has created very large taxable assets in both the State and Federal spheres. For this reason, when considering the question of railway finances, it is necessary to look beyond the railways themselves; first of all to the State finances; ultimately to the general conditions of the finances of Australia as a whole. I am encouraged in this attitude of mind by reason of the fact that the federal Parliament has accepted the principle of partial responsibility for the deficit of necessitous States such as South Australia and Tasmania whose financial difficulties are in a very large measure due to railway deficits. Having these views in mind I have no hesitation in rejecting the plea of the Commissioners that wages for railway employees should be put on a low basis reflecting the finances of the several systems when viewed alone. (p. 1036)

The felt-hatting award contained no automatic adjustment clause and was one of the awards in which the 10 per cent remained in force. In December 1934, the Full Court rejected a union application to remove the cut

(*Variation—Felt Hatting Awards* 33 CAR 1150). In response to an employer application, it reduced the basic wage from 77s 5d (after the 10 per cent cut) to 69s (but added 3s for lost time).

The Full Court acceded to an application of the Sydney Harbour Trust Commissioners for an award provision allowing them to make deductions in wages equivalent to those applied to other State employees (*Award Variation—Sydney Harbour Trust* 33 CAR 1075).

10.8 Wage relativities

There were few attempts in the Depression period to alter margins for skill. In federal awards, margins were subject to the 10 per cent reduction, but otherwise were generally unaltered. These arrangements could be expected to increase the relative rewards of the more skilled workers. It was, of course, the reverse of what had happened in earlier years, when the margins of the more skilled workers rose much less, in proportional terms, than the basic wage. The general implication was that periods of rising wages tended to enhance the relative position of the less skilled and periods of falling wages to improve the relative position of the skilled. This simple generalisation must be qualified by recognising that between 1907 and 1930 margins had been granted to many categories of workers who initially had been treated simply as basic-wage earners.

There were few commentaries on relativities. During the hearing of the 1932 application to rescind the 10 per cent cut, there was some discussion of the matter. Crofts remarked that, apart from Powers' 3s, there had been no advance in the basic wage relative to the *Harvester* standard, and that the worker had gained little benefit from pre-Depression prosperity. Drake-Brockman replied that a valid comparison should take into account the many grants of margins to workers who in 1907 would have received only the basic wage. 'That', he said, 'has come out of prosperity.' Dethridge thought that unskilled workers had, before the Depression, gained at the expense of the more skilled. This trend might now have gone into reverse:

> It is gradually getting back to the old relationship with the cost of living falling, but the skilled worker I think can say that he has not had a prosperity allowance or an increase of wage with any supposed increase in productivity. I have always regarded that as being an undesirable position. Assuming for a moment that the amount which can be paid out of the total production of the country to the wage earners is limited to a particular amount, the more the unskilled workers take out of that share the less is left for the skilled workers. It may be that has been the position in this country. (transcript, pp. 474–475)

In general, however, the issue of wage differences was subordinate to the larger concerns about wage levels. The widening of differentials was a by-product rather than an intended consequence of these concerns.

10.9 Hours and leave

Nor did the times lend themselves to advances in non-wage terms of employment. There were few serious applications for them and correspondingly few decisions. I have discussed in Section 9.1 decisions of the Court in 1930 about working hours and leave—decisions reflecting the Court's pessimistic view of economic conditions.

Dethridge in October 1931 dealt with an employers' application affecting 'front of the house' employees in picture theatres (*Variation—Theatrical Employees Award* 30 CAR 675). The existing award provided that a weekly employee should have one free night (after 6pm) per fortnight, but the employers now asked that the employee be required to work every night. Refusing the application, Dethridge said:

> The employees concerned are women and girls whose working hours are 48 per week with a long daily stretch of hours. I am convinced that the cessation of the night off would tend to reduce the zeal and efficiency of these employees while at their work ... While recognising that the picture theatre industry is suffering severely from the depression, and that every reasonable reduction in labour-cost is essential in order to

maintain it to as great an extent as possible, I am not convinced that if the variation were made there would be any net reduction of labour cost sufficient to give real support to the industry. (p. 676)

Dethridge did, however, reduce overtime rates from time-an-a-half to time-and-a-quarter. He reduced travelling allowances by 10 per cent (p. 677).

In a decision of December 1932 about employment in the Commonwealth Railways, Drake-Brockman said that all parties to the dispute had asked him to make provision for annual leave and that some of the unions had sought long service leave (*Judgment—Commonwealth Railways Dispute* 31 CAR 815). Despite the parties' partial agreement, Drake-Brockman was reluctant to endorse either proposal:

> I have decided to continue the existing practice as to annual leave until the end of the financial year only and have directed that thereafter this subject shall be a matter for managerial determination. My reason for taking this course is that annual leave is a matter of privilege. If provision for it is placed in the award it ceases to be a matter of privilege and becomes a matter of right and so a factor the value of which must be assessed in the fixation of wage rates. For the same reason no provision is made in the award for long service leave. (p. 822)

In June 1933, the Full Court granted a 44-hour week in the textile industry (*Variation—Textile Workers' Awards; Standard Hours and Basic Wage, Textile Industry Disputes* 32 CAR 470).[27] It was influenced by the prevalence of 44 hours in New South Wales; the fact that most of the employees were female; and the impracticality of a longer working week for males. Moreover, the financial condition of the industry had improved—more so in the woollen section than in cotton. It had benefited from a higher tariff imposed in 1929. In the following December, the Full Court refused to extend to males the 44-hour week prescribed for females working in the rope and cordage industry. An application for reduced hours would be dealt with at 'a more appropriate time' (32 CAR 764).

---

[27] The 44-hour standard already applied in the clothing trades.

The Full Court in June 1933 also made orders affecting standard hours in New South Wales railways and tramways (*Standard Hours—Railway Employees—New South Wales* 32 CAR 491).[28] Dethridge and Drake-Brockman outlined the complex history of the matter:

> Of those employees engaged in the kind of work done by the members of the Australian Railways Union, the greater part belong to that union and are covered by the award for that union made by this Court. A considerable number, however, are not in that union and are covered by State awards or enactments which prescribe in effect a 44 hour week. Notwithstanding that a 48 hour week has been prescribed by the award of this Court, the NSW authorities have ever since 1925 except during one rather short period conceded a 44 hour week to all railway employees covered by this Court's award, thus putting them on the same footing as to hours as that of employees covered by State awards or enactments. This was the position until 16th April, 1933, when the authorities required all the employees to work the hours prescribed by awards applicable to them, and thus caused that section of employees covered by the award of this Court to revert to 48 hours while the uncovered section continued to work only 44 hours. (p. 493)

Similar prescriptions had applied to the Electrical Trades' Union and the Australian Timber Workers' Union. Virtually all tramways employees belonged to the Australian Tramway Employees' Union and had been put on to 48 hours. These facts entailed 'a present disparity of working hours among similar employees which is absurd and likely to lead to friction and disturbance in the work to be done' (p. 494). But New South Wales could not be considered in isolation. The Court was concerned with railways and tramways in several States 'and a decision of this Court directly or indirectly affecting the standard hours of working in one State is certain to be regarded as a precedent for each of the other States'. Neither the nature of the work nor the financial condition of the employer justified a 44-hour week and the award provisions for 48 hours were not altered.

---

[28] The reasons were given in August.

The union submissions included a contention that a general shortening of working hours was now appropriate. This proposition, said Dethridge and Drake-Brockman, could not appropriately be debated in the context of the immediate case. Nevertheless they added:

> Material prepared by the International Labour Office and others relating to this thesis was furnished to the Court and is of much interest. It all goes to show, however, the great difficulty and danger of action in that direction by one country alone, and also the enormous obstacles to international co-operation. That consumption of products, and consequently production and trade, would be stimulated by such a shortening is very doubtful. Whether production has become so ill-balanced by reason of modern methods as to make a shortening of working hours necessary in order to spread or ration employment is another question. If nations become more and more self-contained this may become inevitable, but its corollary is that wages also will be rationed. Both employment and wages will then be spread more evenly but also more thinly. (pp. 495–496)

Dethridge and Drake-Brockman thought that it would be possible in the future to reduce hours so as to lessen the hardships of workers' lives. But the scope for reduction was restricted by the requirements of 'economic safety', the limits of which were 'somewhat narrowly fixed ultimately by (1) Australia's large dependence on exports of primary products and (2) the aim to preserve a reasonably high standard of living for its citizens'. Beeby reflected on the Commissioners' vacillation about working hours, corresponding to the varying policies of State governments. The appropriate response, in his view, was for the Court to strike out of its awards all provisions about working hours so far as they related to New South Wales, leaving the matter to the State Industrial Commission. If the Court were to continue to prescribe hours, tramway workers on footboard cars should not be required to work more than 44 per week (p. 498).

The Full Court in February 1934 dealt with applications by the Electrical Trades' Union for extension of the 44-hour week (*Variation—Metal Trades and Electricians' Awards* 33 CAR 56). The claim succeeded in part. 'Employees engaged in process manufacturing', the Court said,

> are in our opinion as much entitled to a shortening of their hours of labour as many others in factory occupations who have already obtained it. Similar comment is justified in the case of electrical fitters and mechanics or wiremen who have as great a claim to the shortening as those in the metal and building trades. ... But we do not think a sufficient case has been made to justify us in reducing the ordinary working hours of any of the other classes of employees covered by the application ... (p. 57)

There was no discussion of economic or industry issues.[29] On the same day, the Court decided by majority (Dethridge and Beeby) that the standard week of male workers in the rubber industry would be reduced from 46½ to 44 (*Variation—Rubber Workers' Award* 33 CAR 60).

In October and November 1934, Dethridge refused two union applications—both for carters and drivers—for annual leave. He said that the claim for employees such as retail milk carters would be strong if industry were more prosperous, but under present conditions he would not be justified in granting it (*Judgment—Carters and Drivers' Award* 33 CAR 857, 871). Carters and drivers in oil stores already enjoyed one week's leave, which had been conceded 'a year or two ago' by the employers because of the irregularity of working hours. The union now claimed a second week. Dethridge expressed reluctance to make a decision which might discourage employers from voluntarily granting leave. He had granted higher penalty rates to discourage irregular hours and did not feel that he could increase the amount of leave beyond that granted by the employers (*Judgment—Carters and Drivers (Oil Stores)* 33 CAR 965, 966–967).

The Full Court in December 1934 made several decisions about working hours. Carpenters and joiners in mixed industries were to have a

---

[29] Railways were initially reserved from this decision, but in May 1934 the Court rejected the Commissioners' attempt to delay its application (*Variation—Electricians' Award—Standard Hours, Railway Employees* 33 CAR 521).

44-hour week, unless they were employed in conjunction with timber mills (in which case the 48-hour week would continue) (*Variation—Carpenters and Joiners' Award* 33 CAR 1085). The Court granted the 44-hour week in tanning (*Variation—Tanning Award* 33 CAR 1143), the glue and gelatine industry (but with provision for 176 hours to be worked over four weeks) (*Variation—Saddlery (Glue and Gelatine) Award* 33 CAR 1145), and in felt hatting (*Variation—Felt Hatting Awards* 33 CAR 1150). In the tanning case, the Court said that it had reached its decision after 'anxious consideration', but it had regard to the unpleasant working conditions and 'the general trend towards the shortening of working hours of wage earners' (p. 1144). In a decision for coachmaking (*Variation—Coachmakers and Metal Trades' Awards* 33 CAR 1089), the Court recalled that in 1929 it had refused a 44-hour week because of economic conditions, but that Dethridge had said that he would support the shorter week if the parties were to intimate their acceptance of piecework. No such intimation had been given. The industry was now brisk, with plentiful employment; and in the American industry, hours had fallen from 48–50 in 1929 to 40. Proceedings for a new award would be before the Court early in 1935 and the 44-hour week would not be implemented until the new award was made. It would be a term of the award that any union sanction against a member on piecework would be nugatory and a breach of the award (pp. 1091–1092).

10.10 STATE POLICIES

There were, in the Depression years, significant differences between the decisions of the Federal Court and those of the State tribunals in four of the States: New South Wales, Queensland, South Australia, and Western Australia. These differences affected principally the basic (or living) wages and, to a lesser degree, working hours.

The statistical relation between federal and State basic wages is summarised in Figure 1.4 and discussed in Chapter 8 (Subsection 8.4.4). In none of the States—New South Wales, Queensland, South Australia, and

Western Australia—wherein local tribunals prescribed basic or living wages was there a straightforward adoption of federal policy.

In the Depression years, New South Wales attracted the severest criticism for maintaining State-fixed wages at too high a level, undermining the effects of the Commonwealth Court's policies. Because of the size of the New South Wales economy and labour force, its divergent policies obviously had a bigger effect on national aggregates than did the policies of smaller States. But Figure 8.7 suggests that similar criticisms could also have been directed at the wages policies of Queensland, South Australia, and Western Australia.

The New South Wales story is closely related to the vagaries of State politics and the composition of the State Tribunal, as Sheldon recounts:

> Due to an unpredictable combination of legislative design, government policy, and judicial strategy, the Living Wage did not change between December 1929 and August 1932 and, in fact, no hearings or adjustment process occurred. Knowing that such inquiries would result in Living Wage reductions, Piddington [as President of the State Commission] struggled against holding them. This brought him into conflict with Bavin [the Premier until October 1930] (and his judicial colleagues) but into harmony with a Labor government that also worked to stymie any possibility of such an inquiry. Under Piddington's influence, the Commission rejected calls for a further Living Wage inquiry on the pretext that the government was proposing legislation to reshape New South Wales industrial relations institutions. Labor's bill failed, but [Premier] Lang successfully either cowered or out-manoeuvred Piddington's judicial colleagues to ensure that the Commission would not investigate the Living Wage. Steady money wages meant rising real wages. (Sheldon 2007, pp. 256–257)

After the defeat of the Lang Government, the Commission was reconstituted (Piddington having already resigned). In August 1932, the tribunal reduced the living wage by 15 per cent—a lesser reduction than the preceding cumulative fall in the Commonwealth wage. Thereafter it made half-yearly declarations which broadly corresponded with movements in the cost of living (Sheldon 2007, p. 257).

In Queensland, a non-Labor Government was in office from early 1929 until June 1932. It replaced the Board of Trade with an Industrial Court and immediately suspended rural industry awards; and in 1930, it removed other groups, including miners, public servants, and railway employees from the arbitration system. After the return of a Labor Government, many of these groups were restored to coverage (Sheldon 2007, p. 267). The State basic wage had been set at 85s in 1925 and remained at that amount until August 1930. The Court in March 1930 refused an application for a reduction, citing a provision of the State Act which forbade the fixing of a wage below the *Harvester* standard. There was a reduction of 5s in August 1930, a further reduction of 3s in December 1930 and another reduction, also of 3s, in July 1931. These were the only changes during the Depression period. The total reduction of 11s between December 1929 and December 1934 compared with a fall of 18s 6d in the Commonwealth wage for Brisbane over the same period.

The South Australian living wage was set by the Board of Industry, which comprised a Judge, two employer representatives, and two employee representatives. This structure effectively made the judge the arbiter of the living wage. The Board was empowered to declare a living wage as it saw necessary, subject to a minimum interval of six months between declarations. The living wage was constant at 85s 6d between July 1925 and October 1930, when it was reduced to 75s A further reduction, to 63s, was made in August 1932. The wage remained at this level until late 1935. In the two years from the end of 1929 to the end of 1931, the living wage, set by the State Tribunal, fell by 22s 6d, while the Commonwealth basic wage for Adelaide was reduced by over 30s. Over the next three years, the State-fixed wage was unchanged, while the federal counterpart increased by about 7s.

In Western Australia, the State basic wage was set by a tripartite Court of Arbitration presided over by a Supreme Court Judge. The Court had been required to make annual declarations, but a 1930 amendment to the legislation (secured by a non-Labor government) provided for quarterly reviews whenever the State Statistician indicated a change of 1s or more in the cost of living. These reviews were discretionary: adjustments were not automatic. A *Financial Emergency Act*, passed in 1931, provided for all-round wage reductions of 18 per cent. This was repealed after the return of a Labor Government in 1933. The basic wage had been constant after 1926 until June 1929, when it was raised by 2s to 87s. Between the end of 1929 and the end of 1931, the fall in the State-fixed basic wage for Perth was 9s; the Commonwealth wage fell by over 20s. In the next three years, the State wage fell by a further 2s 6d, while the federal wage increased by about 6s.

Typically, the State tribunals resisted the kind of economic 'management' on which the Commonwealth Court embarked, and in the 1934 hearing before the Federal Court Crofts dealt at length with State pronouncements which seemed at odds with the Commonwealth decision. The Queensland Court showed considerable scepticism about any beneficial effects of wage reductions on unemployment and, indeed, lent some support to the purchasing-power argument typically invoked by the unions. In October 1932, for example, it published a statement of 'Opinions of the Court', which read in part:

> The Judge and Mr Ferry [employee member] have agreed to adjourn the application of the employers for a reduction of the basic wage until a date in February next to be fixed.
>
> Meanwhile an effort will be made to secure further information as to the probable effect of a general reduction of wages on employment, with a view to enabling the Court to discharge with greater certainty its statutory obligation to consider the economic effect on industry. If more definite information is not forthcoming, the Judge thinks the Court may have to consider the necessity of taking those risks to which Mr Brigden refers but which the Judge thinks are not warranted at present.
>
> It is not contested that a reduction of the purchasing power of the wage-earners as a whole will increase unemployment. But, as Mr Brigden

points out, a reduction of the basic wage by, say, 3s means that 4,116 additional men must be employed at the reduced wage to keep the aggregate fund at the present level. Mr Wallace [employer member] thinks—sharing Mr Brigden's apparent optimism in this regard—that while such a commensurate increase in employment may not be a reasonably probable result of a reduction in the basic wage, a reduction will probably stem the tide of increasing unemployment; but the Judge and Mr Ferry cannot concur in such a conclusion. (transcript, p. 79)

Mr Justice Dwyer, in the Western Australian Court, in June 1932 noted the State Act's definition of the basic wage: 'A sum sufficient to enable the average worker to whom it applies to live in reasonable comfort, having regard to any domestic obligations to which such worker would be ordinarily subject.' He continued:

> It seems to me to follow from the foregoing that it is not our present duty to consider, whether as a general scheme of industrial regulation or otherwise, the rehabilitation of the financial system of the Australian States or over-production in industry or interstate competition or other cognate matters. Questions, therefore, dealing with the balancing of the national ledger, the difference between our exports and imports, the alternation [sic] of the rate of exchange, though very interesting, are outside the scope of this inquiry, or only remotely connected with it. … With regard to the 10 per cent reduction claim, this may be disposed of summarily by stating that there is no power in this Court under the law as it stands to ascertain a standard of living and then deduct or add ten or any other percentage. (transcript, pp. 44–45)

The South Australian Board of Industry, in June 1930, said (presumably in the words of Acting-President Kelly):

> The Board cannot choose any one or more of the remedies or initiate any of the methods of adjustment advocated by economists. Its function is circumscribed by Statute. It has to take the facts as it finds them and is charged with the clear and single duty of providing for the average employee, as already defined, a wage sufficient to meet the

normal and reasonable needs—normal and reasonable in view of all the circumstances existent of time and place.

The provision of such a sum is the sole purpose of its declaration. The remedy of economic ills, the rehabilitation of declining industries, the elimination of unemployment, these are matters with the attainment of which the Board is not charged. The desirability of their attainment may indeed be relevant in the discussion of what are the average employee's reasonable needs when the State is in the throes of industrial and financial depression, when an increasing proportion of the citizens are suffering unemployment. But when that is said, all has been said. (transcript, p. 98)

Thus the Board of Industry, though eschewing the opinions of economists, contemplated some elasticity in setting the living wage by allowing that the 'reasonable needs' of employees might be affected by the state of the economy. Although the *prima facie* estimate of the cost of living was 13s 5d per day, the Board declared a wage of 12s 6d. It referred to evidence that the fall in prices was greater than indicated by the official statistics and that the community was adjusting its standards to changing realities by (for example) retaining clothes for longer use. It spoke also of 'the need for economy on the part of all sections of the community, including employees receiving the living wage' (transcript, p. 99–100). In April 1933, Kelly noted some signs of economic improvement and said that he had 'come to the conclusion that justice and expediency require that no special contraction of the normal and reasonable needs of the living wage earner should now be enforced on the ground of that stringent need for economy which existed during that period' (p. 106).

In Victoria, there was no State-declared basic wage. The common assumption, however, is that the wages boards generally adopted Federal Court decisions. On a broad view, this is true, but the position was somewhat 'messy'. In the 1934 Federal Court hearing, Clarey analysed the deliberations of the boards:

Altogether in Victoria the Wages Boards that have been created total 182, but of those Boards 9 have made no determination. ... Of those Boards in force—173—several have made determinations many years ago which have never been altered ... They are the Brewers, Flour, Ham & Bacon Curers, Meat Preservers, Soap and Soda, Candlemakers, Flour (Country), Malt, Miners (Coal), Starch, Enginedrivers (Mining), Glassworkers, Marine Store, Miners (Gold), and Tie Makers. Some of those determinations were made as far back as 1913–14 ... and must be disregarded. That brings the total number of Boards in operation at the present moment down to 158. Of those 158 determinations 27 have been in force for three months or less ... 15 determinations have been in force for over three months but less than 6 months ... 15 determinations have been in force for more than 6 months but not more than 9 months ... 8 determinations have been in force for 9 months but not more than 12 months ... 27 determinations have been in force for more than 12 months but not more than 18 months ... 11 determinations have been in force for 18 months but not more than 2 years ... 55 have been in force for more than two years ... (transcript, p. 175)

Thus, although Boards may generally have followed the Commonwealth Court's awards, there was often a substantial delay in their doing so. In 1934, the situation described by Clarey was corrected by the passage of a new *Factories and Shops Act*. This required the wages boards to adopt Commonwealth award rates wherever applicable and empowered the Secretary for Labour to adjust wages according to cost of living index numbers without convening the wages boards (Sheldon 2007, p. 262).

As to Tasmania, the *Labour Report* (no. 25, 1934, p. 87) stated: 'There is no State basic wage fixed by any authority in Tasmania, but Wages Boards follow, to a large extent, the rates of the Federal Court and adjust wages in accordance with variations in retail price index numbers.' It made essentially the same statement about Victoria, however, and the kind of 'compliance' with federal determinations described by Clarey may also have obtained in Tasmania.

10.11 Conclusion

The year 1934 saw some signs of relaxation of the Commonwealth Court's policy of reducing and holding down labour costs. There was a modest improvement in economic conditions as indicated by the rate of unemployment. But there was still a distance to travel. The Judges may well have sensed that they had taken the policy of restraint to its practical or equitable limit, given especially the failure of State tribunals to recognise the federal Court's leadership.

Was the policy of reduction of labour costs sound in the Depression context? The question does not lend itself to a ready answer. The issue has to be approached with full regard to the enormity of the economic forces that that bore down on Australia in these years. A presumption that reducing the price of labour takes advantage of downward sloping demand curves is an insubstantial contribution to the debate. For a given industry, it may be true; but when the reduction in pay is widely spread, the contrary effect of reduced purchasing power may well be significant. Moreover, the deflation of prices, to which falling wages contribute, was very likely to depress demand. The case for cutting wages has, rather, to be embedded in an overall understanding of the need for structural adjustment, brought about by the catastrophic fall in export prices and the drying-up of capital inflow.

The economists—Copland, Giblin, Dyason, Shann and others—were essentially correct in their diagnosis of the problems. They were correct in identifying the inevitability of an overall reduction of real incomes. They were right, too, in arguing for a sharing of the burden so that it did not remain wholly with the exporters and the industries that had depended on capital inflow. Primary export industries were fundamental to the structure of the pre-Depression economy. The collapse in their income-generating capacity might in the long run be offset by restructuring the economy, but in the short term the case for policies to aid their survival was strong.[30] Depreciation of the exchange

---

[30] Dethridge said during the 1933 hearing: 'Let us be frank about it: if the primary industries go crash, there is nothing to sustain the secondary industries, and they will go crash, too. That is the difficult situation we are in. It is not a simple situation such as these gentlemen—who, I see, are Bachelors of Science and Bachelors of Medicine—think it is. It is most astonishing

rate was the least painful method of adjustment. The Australian pound was devalued from parity with sterling to 1.25 Australian pounds to the pound sterling, and this entailed a larger devaluation against the US dollar.[31] If the devaluation had been greater, the need for internal price and wage adjustment would have been less. The reasons for resistance to a larger devaluation are a topic that lies outside the scope of this study. Income adjustment was a difficult alternative, for two reasons.

First, what was required (because of the reduction in the real GDP and the cessation of foreign loans) was reduction of real incomes, and not merely money incomes. Policy acts directly on money amounts. To affect real incomes, it depends on the leverage that fixing money incomes exerts over real incomes, that is, the 'stickiness' of prices. In an economy with a large tradeable sector, leverage certainly existed, but the necessary reductions of money incomes exceeded considerably the loss of real income. With money illusions rife, this was a difficult process. Resistance to wage reductions was inescapable. Explicit decisions to reduce wages inevitably generated hostility. When reductions were mandated by automatic adjustment provisions, they gave rise to arguments about the accuracy of the price index.

Second, inasmuch as the reductions were successfully resisted in respect of some incomes, either other sectors had to bear larger reductions or the relief to the export and capital-importing sectors would not occur. As we have seen, the 10 per cent cut imposed by the Federal Court was not followed in several of the State jurisdictions; and some State tribunals showed a reluctance even to match the fall in prices. There was no overall reduction in the real value of prescribed wages. What might be said for the Court's action is that, without it, real wages would probably have risen, making the process of structural adjustment even more difficult than it was.

---

how many men with scientific and engineering training, like Major Douglas and others, think that the world can be cured by their panaceas. It is not to be done in that easy fashion' (transcript, pp. 56–57).

[31] For most of 1931, the sterling exchange rate was at 1.3 Australian pounds to the pound sterling.

There has been some debate about the reasons for the downward rigidity of real wages in Australia (see, for example, Gregory, Ho and McDermott (1985), and Sheldon (2007)). Gregory et al. (1985, pp. 13–19) reject the 'standard' explanations, which 'were first put forward by Giblin (1931) and have been repeated by Hancock (1972) and Schedvin (1970)'.[32] Those explanations relate to the divergent policies of federal and State authorities, lags in the adjustment of the basic wage to falling prices and the stability (in nominal terms) of margins. (Federal award margins were subject to the 10 per cent cut, but not to indexation.) Gregory et al. contend that the stability of real wages shows that *the market* rejected the policies of the wage-setters. A major difficulty with their argument is that the wage data used by all participants in the discussion, including Gregory et al., are about *institutionally prescribed* rates of pay. It is conceivable that 'the market' set *actual* rates that were significantly different.[33] But since the available data describe formally prescribed wages, it is entirely appropriate to relate them to the practices of the institutions which set them. Hence the explanations for real-wage rigidity proposed by Schedvin and Hancock are apposite.[34] Figure 1.4 in Chapter 1 and the analysis of State policies in the previous section of this chapter indicate the importance of the States' failure to act upon the Court's decisions.

The principal arguments against the endeavour to cut real wages by reducing money wages were those that ran in terms of 'purchasing power' and the 'circulation of money'. These arguments, as we have seen, were always presented by union advocates and repeatedly discussed by members of the Court. The unions were supported in the 1930–31 case by R F Irvine and

---

[32] Giblin did not, in fact, discuss the issue—at least, not in the reference cited by Gregory, Ho and McDermott (1985). This is not surprising, because at the time Giblin would not have known the future course of real wages.

[33] In the circumstances of the Depression, the 'market' was surely more likely to have set rates *below* rather than *above* prescribed rates. Little evidence exists about avoidance of the awards. I have referred above to Mann's comments during the 1934 basic wage case hearing about under-payment in the building industry.

[34] Little weight should be given, however, to the lags in basic wage adjustment. Their effect was far outweighed by the use of A series index for adjustment purposes (see Chapter 8, Subsection 8.4.4). In relation to the C series index, the real basic wage fell substantially.

various union witnesses. J M Keynes, in the article which appeared in a number of Australian newspapers in 1932, also lent some support to the purchasing-power argument (see Chapter 13, Subsection 13.1.5). J B Brigden, one of the founders of the profession of economics in the 1920s, became Director of the Queensland Bureau of Industry and Statistics, and in that capacity furnished reports to the State Industrial Court. In the 1933 hearing before the Federal Court for restoration of the 10 per cent cut, Crofts cited a 1931 report by Brigden, who said:

> While the Federal Court asserted that wage reduction ought to be the last resort, it has been adopted as the first resort, and it has accomplished none of those things which it was expected to do. It will be contended that if wage reduction has failed to reduce unemployment, it is because the reductions have not been sufficiently drastic. On this point that noted economist Mr J M Keynes states, 'The advantages to employers of a general reduction of wages are not as good as they look. Each employer sees the advantage to himself of the reduction of wages which he himself pays, and overlooks both the consequences of the reduction of incomes of his customers, and of the reduction of wages which his competitors will enjoy. Anyway, it would certainly lead to some injustice and violent resistance, and it would greatly benefit some classes of incomes at the expense of others. For these reasons, a policy of contraction sufficient to do any real good may be quite impracticable.' (transcript of the 1933 restoration hearing, p. 175)

As we saw in the previous section, the Queensland Court itself held the view that the State basic wage ought not to fall with the decline in prices because of the adverse effect of wage reductions on spending.

To pursue the matter at greater length would take us into issues of macroeconomics that lie beyond the limits of analysis supportable by the available data. For the purpose of this study, the important fact is the realisation by the Court and others, including the emerging band of professional economists, of the Court's role as an institution of economic policy. A recognition that wage levels and employment conditions were constrained by economic circumstances had for many years been implicit—and often explicit—in decisions of the Court. But despite the episode of the Piddington report, there had remained a certain ambivalence about the relation of the economy to the basic wage. The 10 per cent cut was certainly an affirmation of the significance of economics. That might conceivably have been interpreted as a temporary response to an exceptional circumstance; but the 1934 decision went far to enshrining the dominance of economic criteria.

11

The basic wage in the recovery

———•———

11.1 Pre-1937 issues

After the four, virtually annual, basic wage cases of the Depression years, there was no further application for a general review until 1937. The interval may have reflected union priorities for raising margins and for resuming the movement toward a general 44-hour week, as well as a judgment about the likely attitude of the Court toward the degree of economic recovery.

There were, however, cases dealing with subsidiary issues.

11.1.1 Geographical differences

There had emerged over the years of basic-wage prescription a diverse set of basic-wage rates as between localities. In most awards, the rates applying in the capital cities corresponded to the price relativities indicated by the Statistician's index numbers. The substitution of the C series for the A series index altered these relativities, the principal change being a rise in the relative wage in Adelaide. There were, however, awards wherein uniform basic wages applied across States. Textiles were an example. The reason for uniformity in these awards was interstate competition in the product markets. For non-metropolitan areas, the Court had applied various deviations from the strict index-related rates, usually in recognition of economic difficulties of non-urban producers. In 1934, it adopted a rule that basic wage rates in country areas would be equal to the amounts indicated by the price index *minus* 3s. This was in recognition of disadvantages—associated especially with transport costs—of country employers competing with metropolitan firms.

In November 1934, the Full Court observed that where a provincial city was conveniently served by a port there might be no justification for the lower wage; and accordingly, in May 1935, it raised the Newcastle and Port Kembla basic wages to the Sydney level (*Variation—Metal Trades and Carpenters and Joiners' Awards* 34 CAR 642, 643). In July 1935, the Court said:

> In giving its decision in the recent Port Kembla and Wollongong case the Court intimated that, because of what it regarded as sound economic reasons, only in very exceptional cases would a basic wage be prescribed for a provincial place higher than that for the metropolis of the State concerned, even though the index number for the provincial place was higher than that for the metropolis. It now confirms that statement. (*Variation—Metal Trades and Timber Workers' Awards* 34 CAR 817, 819)

The issue of *interstate* differences was bedevilled by the existence of different practices in different awards. In some, the capital cities' basic wages differed in accordance with the respective levels of the price index. In others, there might be a uniform basic wage corresponding to the six-capitals average of the price index. Though there was no firm rule, the latter was most likely to occur where employers in the different States were in significant competition with each other, as in textiles. Dethridge discussed the issue in September 1935 in connection with a possible coverage of Queensland by a commercial printing award. The employers wanted the basic wage in the award to be the six-capitals amount, then 66s. At the time, the basic wage for Brisbane set by the State tribunal was 74s. It was fair to assume, said Dethridge, that the basic wage in a federal award for printing would be 66s. The Brisbane employers, he continued,

> have a substantial reason for desiring to be placed on an equal footing in respect of labour costs with their competitors in other States—a reason

which is likely to become still more cogent in the future. ... Where considerable interstate competition prevails as in these commercial printing and allied industries now in question, there can be no doubt that the federal jurisdiction should operate if an interstate dispute of substance is shown to exist. (*Judgment—Commercial Printing* 36 CAR 738, 740–741)

In November 1935, the Full Court confronted objections from South Australia to the imposition of a uniform basic wage. The Food Preservers' Union and the Commonwealth Jam Preserving and Condiment Manufacturers' Association had reached partial agreement about an award for food preserving. This included a flat-rate basic wage of 75s, which would not to be subject to adjustment before June 1937. (At the time, the six-capitals basic wage was 69s 6d.) The Court set out the issue in dispute:

> Mr Wright, who appeared for respondent employers engaged in the industry in South Australia, objected to the proposed award chiefly because of the proposed flat base rate of 75s per week and stated that his clients desired that the wage rates should be founded upon the Court's basic wage to be assessed and adjusted from time to time for each metropolitan or provincial district upon the relevant index number. ... [T]he dispute so far as concerned with the base rate came before the Full Court. The Government of the State of South Australia then sought and obtained leave to intervene for the purpose of objecting to the prescription of a flat base rate for South Australia in common with other States. It presented criticism of the action of the Court in prescribing a flat basic wage in the textile workers award of 1933 and of the views expressed by this Court when making that award. Unemployment in South Australia is a very serious problem, the capacity of primary industry there to absorb unemployed persons is small, the natural conditions there for secondary industry are generally poor, and therefore this Court should in its awards allow employers in that State who are competing with employers in other States the benefit of any advantage that may be derivable from discrepancies in

the money amounts of this Court's basic wage for the different States. So ran the argument, which in an appropriate case would deserve very serious consideration. (*Judgment—Food Preserving Industry* 35 CAR 481, 483–484)

But the argument, the Court thought, was inappropriate to the current case. Flat rates had operated in the industry's awards since 1924, except that until 1932 there were lower rates for some Victorian provincial districts. In December 1932, the employers consented to the removal of the differentiation within Victoria. South Australian employers did not then object to the uniform rate. 'Until now', said the Court,

> South Australian employers have made no attempt to obtain a differential basic wage, although for a considerable part of the time since 1924, this Court's basic wage for Adelaide was substantially lower than that for other places covered by the award. We see no reason at present for departing from the practice long established in the awards for this industry of a flat rate wage. (p. 484)

Though the point was not much discussed, it seems that the Court equated 'fair competition' between employers with equal money wages rather than equal real wages. Where the competition was intense, it was likely to apply a flat-rate basic wage, typically based on the six-capitals figure.[1]

11.1.2 Employers not subject to the 10 per cent cut

We saw in Chapter 10 that some employers either were excluded from the 10 per cent reduction or had it reversed before the 1934 decision. In 1931, unions had successfully applied for the exclusion from the cut of the Colonial Sugar Refinery (CSR), chiefly on the ground that the great majority of the Company's employees, covered by a State award, were not subject to the cut. This exclusion meant that the CSR workers subject to the federal award received a basic wage comprising the *Harvester* equivalent plus Powers' 3s. In November 1935, the Full Court dealt with a dispute as to whether that form

---

[1] If the award applied to only some States, the flat rate might be the average for those States.

of basic wage should continue or be replaced by one consistent with the 1934 decision. The Court opted for the latter. The unions, it said, claimed

> that the company is very prosperous, that the saving of wage cost which will result from substituting the new basic wage will only be about £8,000 per year, which is a trifling amount compared with its enormous operations, and that the saving of this amount will have only a negligible effect upon either the price of sugar to the consumer or the price paid for cane to the grower. All this is true, but the Court must act on consistent principles in respect of its basic wage. The mere fact that an employer is very prosperous and wealthy does not justify discrimination against him. Such discrimination has always been regarded by this Court as unsound and inexpedient in general, but possibly an exception should be made in the case of a prosperous monopoly where the prescription of a bonus in addition to the basic wage may perhaps be justified. (*Variation—Metal Trades and other Awards,* re *Basic Wage Colonial Sugar Refining Co Ltd and Jam and Food Preserving Companies* 35 CAR 504, 505)

The issue as to whether a company bonus should be awarded as an addition to the basic wage was avoided by a finding that CSR was not a monopolist in the relevant sense. An award prescription of such a bonus would have been a novel step.

11.1.3 Provision for 'keep'

The principle had long been accepted that the basic wage should be reduced when the employer provided 'keep'. But there was always a potential for disputation about the amount of the reduction.

This issue arose in November 1935 in connection with maritime awards. The decision warrants notice because of the Court's use of the finding of the Royal Commission on the Basic Wage in 1920. The unions contended that the Commission's assessment of the food requirements of a family of five as £2 6s should be related to its overall 'basic wage' of £5 15s 8d, which contrasted with the then-prevailing basic wage of only £4 14s. The food allowance, said the unions, should be reduced in proportion to the difference between the actual basic wage at the time of the Royal Commission and the recommended amount. The £2 6s would then be replaced by £1 17s 10d. The male breadwinner's share of the food requirement, according to the Royal Commission, was one-third, and a third of £1 17s 10d was 12s 8d. Applying the price index to that amount led to a weekly food 'bill' for the male worker of 8s 3d. This, said the unions, was the amount by which the seaman's wage should be reduced because of the provision of food. The Court disagreed, maintaining the deduction at the higher amount of one-sixth of the actual basic wage:

> There is no reason to suppose that the actual expenditure of a wage earner in October, 1920, upon food for a family unit of five was not on the average about the amount found by the Commission to be sufficient for the food constituent of its proposed basic wage. The amount which was found by the Commission to be desirable for a basic wage was higher than the prevailing basic wage mainly by reason of the increase or inclusion of other items than food. (*Judgment—Deduction for 'Keep' and Basic Wage—Maritime Awards* 35 CAR 442, 444)

Implicit in the Court's reasoning was an assumption that the generosity of the Piddington 'basic wage' was not due to an all-round liberality in the amounts allowed for different kinds of spending, including spending on food. Rather, it was the result of the Royal Commission's allowance for other items. In other words, the Court assumed that the actual basic wage in 1920 consisted of 46s for food plus 48s for all other items, whereas the Piddington 'basic wage' consisted of 46s for food plus 70s 8d for other items. This, in fact, was substantially correct, though the unions may have seen it as sleight of hand. The sum allowed by Higgins for food and rent, adjusted by the price index, slightly *exceeded* the amount computed by the Royal Commission. The difference between the *Harvester* and the Piddington standard did reside in their unequal allowances for other items.

11.2 The 'Reddawage'

11.2.1 Introduction

The *Harvester* case, the Court's refusal in 1921 to adopt the Piddington standard, the 1922 decision to introduce the system of automatic adjustments, and the decisions of 1931, 1934, and 1937 were the major mileposts in the evolution of basic-wage policy—and *a fortiori* wage policy at large—before World War II. We turn our attention to the last of these.

The unions applied for award variations to raise the basic wage. They asked that the C series index number 1000 be equated to 93s instead of 81s, as it then stood.[2] They also applied for a female basic wage, to be set at 60 per cent of the male rate. The applications were heard in May and June 1937, and the Court delivered its decision on 23 June (*Basic Wage Inquiry 1937* 37 CAR 583). The data presented in Section 8.2 of Chapter 8—especially the unemployment data—suggest that the case came six to 12 months before the peak of the economic revival. The principal issues in the case were whether the economic recovery justified full restoration of losses previously sustained by basic-wage earners; whether some additional increase might be justified to counter an incipient investment-driven boom; and the amount of the increase consistent with the Court's findings on these two subjects.

11.2.2 Expert evidence: W B Reddaway

At the inception of the hearing, Crofts, for the unions, asked whether the Court intended to call any economic expert as a witness. Crofts, no doubt, was mindful of the role played by Copland in 1930–31. This inquiry produced the following exchange:

> Dethridge C J: The difficulty about the Court endeavouring to select an economist is this: there are economists and there are economists. The man I think is an economist my learned colleagues may think is not an

---

[2] The six-capitals index number for the March quarter was 864. For 1000 = 93s, this implied a basic wage of 80s. The actual wage was 70s. Hence, the unions were seeking a 10s increase, not 12s as was commonly said.

economist. Any man selected as an economist may not be regarded as an economist by the gentlemen on the other side. Nowadays it is a matter of fancy, and I think it is unlikely that the Court will take upon itself the function of selecting any economist to assist. ... Do not misunderstand me ... If you desire that some witness should be called as an expert and it appears that that witness would prefer to be called by the Court, so as to appear to be quite impartial, then the Court will certainly consider calling such witness. ... Personally I should welcome any suggestion of that kind from either side.

Mr Crofts: If this side suggested an economist and the Court accepted him as the Court's witness, or an impartial witness, it might be suggested that he was not impartial. To obviate that, I suggest that if the Court wants the assistance of an economist it should itself ask the University to send along a man.

Dethridge C J: I think I know the reply the University would give. They would say 'It is not our job.' ... I think the best thing for you to do if you desire to have an economist or any expert witness who dislikes being called by either side is to submit his name to us. It need not be submitted in public. Then we will consider whether we should make him our witness. That applies to both sides. (transcript, p. 7)

Dethridge invited the parties to see the Court in chambers.[3] The discussion and any negotiations that may have ensued are unreported. Three days later, however, Dethridge announced: 'We have a gentleman coming from the University tomorrow to give evidence at half past ten. He is being called as a witness by the Court' (p. 171).

The gentleman was W B Reddaway. A Cambridge graduate who had been supervised by Keynes and was subsequently employed at the Bank of England, Reddaway held a two-year appointment as a Research Fellow at the University of Melbourne (Millmow 2003; Hancock 2004).[4] He had been in

---

[3] Beeby interposed: 'So long as you do not impose any Douglas Credit people upon us, we shall be glad to have an economist' (p. 14).
[4] Reddaway's appointment was funded by Giblin, drawing on his fee as a member of the Board of the Commonwealth Bank.

Australia for about 15 months.⁵ In all probability, he had been recommended to the Court by Giblin, Copland or Wood. Before he commenced his evidence, Dethridge said to him:

> You understand, Mr Reddaway, you are being called as the Court's witness, identified with neither side? ... You know the subject matter of this proceeding. The Court considered that it would be advisable to have the assistance of some trained mind ... and, that being so, we thought it desirable to have you as a witness. Your expression of views will be framed by yourself absolutely. (p.172)

Reddaway prefaced his evidence with this explanation:

> I have prepared a memorandum in writing on what I thought would be the most useful points for an economist to deal with. I have shown this memorandum to Professors Giblin and Copland and to Dr Wood of the University, and they have authorised me to say that it represents substantially their views also. So that anything that appears in writing here really represents the unanimous opinion of the principal members of the Economic Staff of the University. (p. 172)⁶

At the beginning of his statement, he called for an increase in the basic wage:

> The case for a revision of the basic wage must rest primarily on the increased prosperity of the country, which enables employers to pay a larger amount. The Court is in effect faced with the converse position to that which led it to decide on a reduction in 1931, and all economic arguments then advanced in favour of a reduction should now⁷ be

---

⁵ In cross-examination (by S C G Wright), Reddaway was asked: 'Can you say that you have had any specialty study, or has it been general research work which you have done?' He replied: 'I have been working on this sort of problem, the current position of Australia.' 'With particular reference to wages?' asked Wright. Reddaway answered: 'With particular reference more to the question of checking a boom, and the general measures for dealing with the situation.'

⁶ In its decision, the Court spoke of 'an able economist called as a witness by the Court— Mr Reddaway—who, as well as his own opinion, voiced that of eminent economists of the University of Melbourne, well acquainted with Australian conditions ...' (p. 587).

⁷ The transcript has the word 'not' rather than 'now', but that is inconsistent with the terms

reversed and used in favour of an increase. The national income has risen so much as to require some increase in the basic wage. (p. 173)

Reddaway declined to nominate the amount of the increase: he postulated that the Court might think that increased prosperity justified an increase 'between x shillings and y shillings'. Within such a range, the Court should be influenced by 'the urgency of the worker's need for a higher income'.

It was sometimes argued, said Reddaway, that Australia's prosperity and its capacity to pay wages were now less than before the Depression by reason of the cessation of overseas loans. That argument, he told the Court, was fallacious:

> The effect of overseas borrowing was that men were employed in what was virtually export industry. They were producing public works of various sorts, and although these were not physically exported, yet the same immediate effect was obtained by exporting corresponding Government obligations. ... When the borrowing ceased this particular export industry was, of course, extinguished. The *immediate* effect was disastrous, because the Australian economy could not be re-adjusted in a day. But if time were allowed for adaptation, then there need be no permanent fall in employment, and the effect on consumption should be quite small. Previously men had been producing public works for export, and obtaining manufactures in exchange; they had now to be transferred to other export industries, or to producing manufactures in Australia. Once this was done there would only be a loss of consumption in so far as the new occupations were less productive; and of course any loss on this account might be more than offset by improved efficiency in other industries. (pp. 173–174)

The adjustment process was virtually complete:

> The new method of manufacturing the goods in Australia (instead of importing them in exchange for the equivalent of public works) may not yield quite such good immediate results; we see this in the fact the new industries receive protection, so that £100 will generally not buy as

---

of the statement and is obviously a mistake.

much of their products as it would of imports. But this is a comparatively small matter, representing a loss of real income of perhaps £5 millions; it has been much more than offset by increased efficiency in production as a whole which has been secured since 1929 … [w]hilst there is a very large item to be entered on the credit side, in the fact that there is no longer a risk of sudden dislocation due to a restriction of loans. (p. 174)

Reddaway discussed at some length the issue of railway finances. It was possible that these might 'be used as an argument for a smaller, rather than a larger, increase in wages'. The relevance of railway statistics, said Reddaway, was limited to two aspects: the usage of the railways was roughly correlated with the general level of activity; and it affected the budgetary position (but 'we must be careful to avoid counting both a railway deficit and a budget deficit which includes it'). There were two reasons why the railways might be in deficit at a time when higher wages were justified. One was that much railway construction had been undertaken for non-commercial reasons:

> It may have been justified as a means of developing the country, but it should no more be expected to cover its loan charges than should investment in school buildings. Moreover, the railways have not always been run on commercial lines, unduly low freights have been charged for political reasons, and insufficient provision made for depreciation; there is obviously no reason for fixing wages at a level which will permit 5 per cent to be earned on lines neither constructed nor run on a commercial basis. (p. 175)

The other, and 'more fundamental', reason was:

> Railways have proved a bad investment in Australia, as they have in other countries, largely because of the growth of road competition. … Where they are in private ownership this has meant either a drastic reduction of capital, or simply the passing of dividends on a great part of it. The Australian owners (that is, the general taxpayers) must similarly recognise that their investment has proved a bad one, and will not return them the anticipated 5 per cent. They cannot expect wages to be held down to a level which will cover up their mistakes. (p. 175)

The relationships between the railways and the Treasuries should be revised and the existing maladjustments 'should have no influence on the relationship between the railways and their employees; still less should it affect the general basic wage'.

Turning to the financial condition of the farmers, Reddaway argued

> that with export prices at present levels the farmers' financial difficulties mostly arise out of the excessive prices at which they bought their land. If they had paid for it in cash they would simply have found they had made a bad investment, and would naturally have had to take the consequences in getting little return on their capital. In fact they largely borrowed the money, so that when their equity margin disappeared, they were immediately in difficulties. This created a grave social problem, but it is not one which should or can be rectified by adjusting wages ... Wages only affect the current position and this is for the most part satisfactory; sale prices are about at pre-slump levels, whilst money wages and the cost of living are considerably lower. (p. 176)

Next, Reddaway considered 'foreign competition and the balance of payments'. In the case of exports, the position was clear-cut: the rise in export prices had left the exporter 'in a position to meet a very substantial rise in costs'; and the relation of prices received to costs was decidedly more favourable than it had been before the Depression. Moreover, the efficiency of the export industries had increased under the stimulus of lower prices. Hence there was 'little danger of export production being reduced because of the rise in costs' if wages were raised; and there would be 'a margin of safety to cover a considerable fall in export prices'. In the case of industries competing with imports, the 'margin of safety' might be less. But foreign producers in many cases were 'so busy meeting the swollen demand in their local market that they are unable to compete for more export business'. In recent years, production in competition with imports had expanded greatly, even when demand was depressed; now that demand had increased, it seemed unlikely that producers would be put out of business by a small rise in relative costs. Since costs were rising overseas, 'they should be able to stand an appreciable rise in Australian wages' (p. 177). Thus Reddaway dealt with the positions of both exporters and import-competitors by asking, and answering in the affirmative, the question whether or not the producers in question could survive an increase in costs. We might have expected an eminent economist to pose the question in terms of 'more or less' rather than 'either/or'. A rise in wages, one would think, should make the positions of both exporters and import competitors less favourable than if there were no rise.

The witness statement then has a section headed 'Prevention of an Unhealthy Boom'. The real income of the community was increasing substantially, bringing with it a potential problem:

> A part of this increase is going to labour in the form of wages to those previously unemployed, but if the wage rates are not increased, then the greater part will be concentrated on profits and rents. Business will be very profitable and many people will be anxious either to start new enterprises or expand existing ones. Up to a point this is of course an excellent thing, but it is capable of producing a most unhealthy boom if carried to excess, particularly when unemployment has been reduced to normal. Moreover, it is always accompanied by a rapid rise in the price of existing assets, such as land or ordinary shares, because people compete for those sources of high profits. Not only does this mean some undesirable speculation, but it will cause trouble if there is a subsequent decline. (p. 177)

This process, said Reddaway, was already at work in both the rural and the urban sectors. 'A rise in real wages', he said,

> would be extremely valuable as a restraining influence both on the price of existing assets and the excessive construction of new ones. Of course other controls are needed as well, but a rise in wages is almost indispensable, if we are to maintain a steady level of prosperity and avoid an unhealthy boom. ... A rise in wages would curb the rise in profits in existing businesses, and might reduce men's estimates of future profits from new ones by a greater amount. These are largely influenced by the continuous rise in demand which has been associated

with the period of recovery. Such a great expansion cannot be expected to persist beyond the point where full employment is reached; men must cease thinking in terms of rapid recovery, and adjust their estimates to a condition of steady progress. But this changed outlook will not be secured automatically—rather will optimism feed on itself. Hence the great advantage of a rise in real wages, which will not only raise the costs of construction, but also forcibly direct attention to the improbability of ever-rising profits. (p. 178)

In his conclusion, Reddaway returned to the amount of the increase. At the minimum, it should be large enough to restore the real basic wage to its 1929 level. But 'in view of the desirability of checking the boom and securing a distribution of income which would help to preserve the present level of prosperity I think a somewhat higher figure would be much more satisfactory—say two or three shillings higher'. If the Court were deliberating between a higher and a lower amount, 'then my opinion as an economist is that the higher is preferable, not only on humane grounds, but in the general interest'.

The expedience of a wage increase to avert a boom had been the message of a lecture given by Copland on 23rd April. L R Mann, one of the representatives 'of employers generally', had attended the lecture. He referred to it in his cross-examination of Reddaway (p. 246). The evidence does not disclose whether the idea of raising wages to combat a boom originated with Copland, Reddaway, or someone else. A reasonable conjecture is that Reddaway was its principal author, but Copland had certainly lent his considerable support to it.[8] 'I cannot speak as to what he said in his lecture', said Reddaway in cross-examination, 'but I can say this, that when I submitted my first draft of my evidence to him for comments, and so on, I had not then written any conclusion, and he wrote, as a memo, "I suggest that you end up by saying very much on the lines of what I finally said"' (p. 247).

---

[8] The idea was mentioned several times by the Judges before Reddaway entered the box. No doubt Copland's lecture received publicity. I cannot say whether the proposal was 'in the air' before the lecture.

On the next day, Reddaway made a statement to the Court. In it, he said:

> There was also one matter yesterday with regard to Professor Copland's views on the question whether wages should be raised to meet increases in productivity or merely to check a boom. I referred this matter to Professor Copland and he asked me to read out the comment which he actually wrote when I submitted my first draft to him. ... This is what he wrote:
>
> On page 2 you virtually say that the problem is not whether a rise should be granted but how great the rise should be. The argument that follows suggests that the rise should be little more than the bare amount required to restore wages per head to the 1929 level. That, however, is a general inference the reader or the Court would have to make. You do not come down in any way decisively on one side or the other. I suggest that you might tie up the whole argument by saying something like this: 'On the whole, there is a case for restoring the real wage to the 1929 level on the grounds of restored income. In view, however, of the desirability of checking investment and encouraging consumption so that the present level of prosperity may be long lived, the case for raising wages a little above the 1939 level is very strong'.
>
> Professor Copland gives that as being his views—views with which I am in agreement. (pp. 332–333)

Mann challenged Reddaway's attitude to foreign borrowing. Reddaway agreed that the sudden cessation of loans before the Depression had had a disastrous effect, 'and even if you allow time for adaptation, there may be some increased wage-paying power if you borrow rather than if you produce manufactures in Australia'; but 'in view of the long time that has elapsed I should say that is scarcely worth considering' (p. 230).

Questioned about the continuance of relatively high unemployment, he replied:

> On the matter of the unemployment figures, I do not think I should accept them as conclusive evidence partly because they are not very

good figures to follow [and partly] because the general tendency is for unemployment to rise the world over owing to certain rigidities, and that is what one would expect, in considering that sort of percentage.

'You share the opinion', said Dethridge, 'that what may be called the normal rate of unemployment, assuming something like a steady prosperity continued over a number [of years], shows a tendency to increase on account of those rigidities?' 'Yes', said Reddaway. 'I do not think it is wholly undesirable, because workmen have greater reserves and so are able to wait for a better job rather than scramble for anything that may be going' (p. 243).

Mann asked whether Reddaway agreed with Copland that it was time for a substantial reduction of internal government borrowing. 'Yes', he replied, 'for the same reason that I want an increase in wages to check a boom.' The unemployment which this might cause would be countered partly by increased consumption and partly by the increase in private investment. 'The reason one is so anxious to cut down public works is that private investment may become too big' (pp. 255–256). Mann suggested that a wage increase might cause a boom in the consumption industries. Reddaway agreed that it would cause increased production of consumption goods: 'That is what economic activity is for. The existing equipment will be used to the full, and some extra equipment will be put up.'

Dethridge interposed: 'Assuming the wage is not increased, then you anticipate there will be over-confidence amongst investors, and they will proceed to invest their money in superfluous capital equipment?' This, said Reddaway, was very likely: 'In general, they will put up factories in such large quantities that unless, as the factories are put up, you rapidly engineer more spending power, they will prove to be redundant when they have been put up.'

Mann asked: 'With regard to the damping down of the boom, the suggestion in England is that it should be done by an increase in taxation?' 'That is certainly one way', said Reddaway, 'and I dare say it might be a better way than by raising wages; but in this Court we are considering wages' (p. 257). A very helpful element in checking the boom would be the securing of a budgetary surplus—'You have to attack a boom on all fronts' (p. 258). On the other hand, a rise in interest rates would be a very poor way to check a boom—'If it does anything at all, it is likely to produce a lot of other troubles in the way of loans, and attractive high rates of interest, which are unfortunate' (p. 261).

Another employer representative, C H Grant, asked whether Reddaway would support a wage increase even if it were proved that the 'effective' [real] basic wage was at the same level as in 1928–29. Reddaway replied that he probably would, 'because my conclusion is based mainly on the current position, rather than on a comparison with 1928–29 ... If the current income has increased over the last year or so, I should still advocate an increase in the basic wage for those grounds' (pp. 266–268). The main reason why industry could pay better wages was 'to be found in the improvement in terms of trade, and also in better reorganisation of [the] economy' (p. 273).

Reddaway told Wright, representing 'South Australian employers generally', that the 'right' basic wage could be determined 'within a margin of error of 5 per cent'. This led to the following exchange:

> Dethridge C J: Perhaps you will allow me to follow you more closely in that. Supposing you had no past history at all of the state of industry except that coming within the last three years, and you were asked to make an estimate of what is the basic wage in your opinion, approximately, what factors would you take into account? --- ... The main factor to take into account would be the rise in export prices in the last three years, and the progressive adjustments of the system to what has been a major shock. I do not know whether I should take three years particularly.
>
> It does not matter much what the period is, you can take one year if you like; you go back to the beginning of that year and you say 'I find that the basic wage at that time was so-and-so'? --- Yes
>
> And then I suppose you would say 'Since the beginning of the year there have been certain changes ... And as a result of those changes I think the basic wage should go up, or possibly, down'? --- Yes, I think that

would be so. One uses past history, otherwise it would be so exceedingly difficult to work it out.

It would be practically impossible? --- It would be impossible.

So I thought. Then in the present case you have the advantage of a longer history? --- Yes. I think back to about 1927 is helpful. I do not think there is any great use going back beyond 1927.

I agree with you. I think all the rest is too ancient and you need not bother about it. So that going back to 1927 you start with your basic wage at an ascertainable amount … And you make a certain presumption about that amount at that time; and you assume that as it existed the presumption is that it was something about the correct thing? --- Yes, Your Honour.

And then you look at subsequent stages from their starting point and say, 'Now, do those changes indicate a rise or a fall as being desirable in the basic wage'? --- That is really what it comes down to.

And that is substantially the way in which you have approached the problem here? --- Yes, Your Honour. I found that, as compared with 1928 or 1929, a lot of the factors are very similar, and the level of export prices is very much the same, and although borrowing has ceased I find according to Mr Melville's investigations that has been very nearly compensated for and I also find that profits were high in 1928–29, and possibly too high, and that there is a risk of looking at more recent history giving boom development, and for that reason one chooses a level rather higher than 1928–29 than lower. (pp. 277–278)

Reddaway said that the current equivalent of the pre-Depression standard should be calculated by use of the C series index. Copland, in his lecture, had shown that, on that basis, the current basic wage was 5 per cent below the 1928 level. 'In effect I said "We want 5 per cent higher plus a bit more." … I ought to emphasise once more that my figure of 2s or 3s higher was for purposes of illustration' (pp. 282–283). In response to a further question from Wright, Reddaway proposed that 'the increase, supposing it was in this year, should be done in two steps' (p. 284). (This, in fact, is what happened.)

Wright asked what would be the best way of adjusting the basic wage to changing conditions. Reddaway replied:

> Well, for short run adjustments I see no objection to the present method of following the C series; but I think one must recognise that any real wage that is fixed may have to be altered at comparatively short intervals and there should be a general determination, or perhaps I should say re-determination, of the starting point at intervals of not more than three years; and if there was some special reason for wanting to change owing to something happening beyond the normal, then there would have to be a difference. (pp. 285–286)

Although he agreed with Wright about the importance of export prices, he rejected a suggestion that the wage should be reviewed at six-month intervals because of the fluctuations of export prices,

> because if you left the whole price system of a country fluctuate in accordance with export prices you would meet with greater disparities in all sections. ... The people in an export industry know that they are in an industry where the returns fluctuate, and if they enter that industry of their own accord then it is only natural that they should take the first shock of changes both upwards and downwards. ... If there are indications that export prices were going to be low or high for a number of years then that would be one of the main reasons I would have in mind for having an adjustment of the basic wage. I do not think it is good for a temporary adjustment at all. ... (p. 286)

When Wright suggested that exporters needed more opportunity to recover the losses that they had sustained in earlier years, Reddaway responded:

> My answer to that is that there has been a loss in the Depression, and you cannot get away from that loss. You might as well propose that the basic wage should be raised to make up the leeway, that the wage earners failed to receive in those years of the depression—that amount which they would have received if the 1929 conditions had continued. You cannot do it; that is my answer. ... If the settler cannot pay his current expenses, leaving out all consideration of mortgage or interest

or anything of that nature, if he cannot manage, then he obviously should not be there. (p. 287)

In his memorandum of evidence, Reddaway referred to the growth in national income. Wright asked him whether he relied for his measurement on 'the Sutcliffe method' which involved the use of the Statistician's estimates of value of production in primary and secondary industry, to which were added percentage amounts to allow for the product of the rest of the economy. Reddaway answered:

> I did not take the Sutcliffe method, because I think the Sutcliffe method is very full of dubious hypotheses, and that the figures when produced are worth less than looking at general indications. ... I prefer to look at such things as employment, export prices, sales tax, wool and so on, and then form a general impression, rather than to mislead myself into thinking for a more accurate method than I have. ... [T]he Sutcliffe method is not a good one. The difficulty with it is that it assumes a constant relation between things which one knows are not constant. (pp. 290a–291)[9]

Dethridge put it to Reddaway, who agreed, that 'the basic wage can only be fixed proportionately to the productivity of the country'. Dethridge continued: 'It does not matter what the family's needs may be?' Reddaway replied: 'That is what you must go by, that is what you give them. The other is only a way of persuading yourself that one is better than the other when frankly you do not know which is which.' 'At least' said Dethridge, 'we are getting a clear statement upon that' (p. 292).

W J Home, for the Cities of Hobart and Launceston, asked Reddaway how a wage increase would be paid—'out of surplus profits?'. 'It will be paid', said Reddaway, 'in some cases by higher prices which will be met finally through the higher prices received from outside the system in the form of

---

[9] Dethridge commented that in England and the United States of America attempts had been made to measure the national income. Reddaway responded: 'Yes, and Mr Colin Clark is one of the latest exponents in England; he is coming to Australia very shortly, and I daresay he will produce some better way for Australian conditions' (p. 291).

higher export prices. Part will be paid out of the reduction in costs which arises from working capacity and part out of profits.' Hume put it that many semi-governmental bodies, including municipalities, had no profits or surpluses. 'Yes', said Reddaway,

> it may be that there will be a case for a higher rate, although in a great many cases the result of greater prosperity will be that their collections will be better and the rateable values will be raised. ... If it is necessary to raise the rate, then there will be an extra amount of money collected from the taxpayers to meet it, but they will have higher incomes as a result of greater prosperity, and to some extent it will fall on the wage earners themselves.

When Dethridge asked about the source of the greater prosperity, Reddaway named two sources: higher export prices and 'the re-adjustment of the economy from the shattering blow it received at the beginning of the slump'. Dethridge continued: 'Not a greater prosperity due to wage increase?' 'No, not due to the wage increase', replied Reddaway (p. 331). The point was of some importance to Dethridge, who had consistently resisted union contentions that higher wages would generate increased production and employment.

On the issue of the competitive capacity of local industries, Reddaway said (in answer to Wright) that 'by taking the wage costs relative to 1928 in a common currency, you find that money wages in Australia have fallen relatively to those of Great Britain, expressed in local currencies, and on top of that you have the 25 per cent exchange. ... There is the question of the tariffs as well' (p. 335).

Asked by Wright to elaborate on the concept of an 'unhealthy boom', Reddaway explained:

> If you get beyond a certain rate of expansion, nearly always there is trouble ahead, and it may come from a variety of reasons. It may come because prospects have been over-estimated, and when these factories come into production there will be found an insufficient demand for

their products. I give an illustration of what the excess may be due to … where I say there are two principal dangers in such a situation, firstly, room for development beyond particular lines of activity which are now very considerable, and that a number of independent people may decide to construct their own factories and blocks of flats, imagining that they are the only people to benefit by the activity demanded. … If you reach the state of nearly full employment, and investment is still expanding, that is almost certain proof that it is becoming excessive. (p. 337)

Asked whether conditions were now 'in disequilibrium', Reddaway replied that 'if wages are not raised now we shall get unfortunate results' (p. 338).

11.2.3 The employers' counter

The principal rebuttal of Reddaway's evidence was a statement read to the Court by F P Derham. The statement was entitled 'Considered Views of New South Wales Employers Represented by Mr F P Derham'. It was obvious to all that the 'considered views' of the employers were, in fact, written by an economist as a critique of Reddaway's evidence. This anonymous economist, by not giving evidence, avoided cross-examination. His identity is a matter for conjecture. The most likely contenders, in my view, are Leslie Melville and J B Brigden. The 'Melbourne group' surrounding Copland can be excluded. Melville, from Sydney, was likely—to judge from previous utterances—to be unsympathetic to union aspirations. His role as economist at the Commonwealth Bank—then government-owned and functioning as a nascent central bank—would be a reason for anonymity. Brigden was still Director of the Bureau of Industry in Queensland and, on that account, may have preferred not to be identified as an employers' spokesman. His views had, however, shifted in an anti-union direction and he may have been willing to do what he could to assist the employers. Of the two, Melville appears the more probable 'candidate', but is no 'sure thing'.[10]

---

[10] An 'outsider' in the race is Sutcliffe, then manager of a textile company.

The expert said that Reddaway's evidence was likely to impress the Court,

> as the case for higher wages has never been presented to the Court in arguments of such refinement. Abandoning altogether the view adopted by Trade Union advocates at earlier inquiries, that wage increases would foster recovery by sustaining and augmenting purchasing power, Mr Reddaway assumed that a substantial wage increase would prove a brake upon enterprise, and claimed that this is necessary to prevent the development of an unhealthy boom. His suggestion is that unless wages are raised substantially the recent improvement of economic condition will be followed by speculative tendencies, and 'general over expansion', to be followed by a slump. (p. 855)

But certain questions had to be considered:

1. To what extent do depressions in Australia result from unhealthy developments in the internal economy, and to what extent are they initiated by overseas influences?

2. Is there any evidence that the present progress of recovery is producing conditions which are likely to cause depression here, independently of world developments?

3. In the event of another depression, is a high wage level likely to diminish its effects upon Australia or to render them worse?

4. If a wage increase can slow up the present rate of recovery, is there not a danger that too great an increase in wages will itself produce the depression which Mr Reddaway's advice is designed to avoid?

'A consideration of these questions', said the expert, 'tends to undermine Mr Reddaway's argument which, at first glance, appears so plausible.'

The economic improvement which had occurred was due largely to the combination of higher export prices and good seasons, and reversal of either of these favourable trends 'would be sufficient to initiate another depression, and no present wage policy can prevent such an event'. Reddaway was right to say that the absence of government borrowing abroad contributed to stability, but he neglected the inflow of foreign capital on private account. A check to that inflow 'would tend to produce a slump in Australia in the same way as interruption of oversea borrowing has done in the past'. It was reasonable to suppose 'that the next depression in Australia, like those of 1890 and 1930, will be caused principally by the impact of a world depression rather than by reaction from a local boom'. Reddaway himself, 'in his evidence before the Royal Commission on Monetary and Banking Systems, stressed the fact that Australia is a "dependent economy"' (p. 855).

It could not be denied, said the expert, that the effects of an external slump would be made worse by unhealthy internal developments. But the evidence of an incipient boom was lacking. Profitability had not regained the 1928 level. The recovery of share prices, though due partly to increased profits, had 'been aided by growing confidence in the security of investment in Australian enterprises among people who preferred during the depression to invest in Government bonds, and by the importation of capital'. And scarcity of labour in some trades 'does not indicate a state of over-expansion, but reveals the effects of the depression upon apprenticeship and training generally':

> This is a world-wide problem. But the scarcity will be alleviated as the increased number of boys now in training under the new system become qualified. One difficulty is to obtain a sufficient number of youths to undertake apprenticeship, and it is submitted that a substantial increase in the basic wage for unskilled labour is likely to perpetuate this situation and help maintain the scarcity of skilled labour.

The current level of construction of capital assets was due to the depreciation and non-replacement of capital during the Depression. It was due also to the expansion of import-replacing industries because of the decline in foreign borrowing and the depreciated exchange rate. 'These', said the expert, 'are not unhealthy tendencies—they are essential to recovery, and in any case this construction will diminish as the industries become established.'

When the next depression came, higher wages might afford no protection. Workers might have better reserves 'in the form of clothing, savings deposits and the like' and therefore be better able to survive reduced incomes. But they would also have more liabilities 'in the form of mortgaged homes and goods bought on time payment' (p. 858). Australia's reserves of gold and foreign currencies were now much depleted by comparison with their 1929 level. This would make it more difficult to withstand an imported depression. The foreign reserves needed to be increased, and this required fewer rather than more imports.

> The speed at which imports will rise depends partly upon wages policy. A large increase in the basic wage is likely to stimulate imports in two different ways. In the first place, it raises the costs of local manufacturers relatively to foreign competitors, and renders the tariff and present exchange rate less effective in protecting local industry. In the second place, the increased wages lead wage earners to direct more of their demand towards imported wares, especially in view of the tendency of prices of local goods to rise, owing to the increase in labour costs. At the same time a larger increase in wages would involve a rise in costs to exporters, so that the increase in imports would not be offset by a commensurate increase in exports. … It would appear, therefore, that an unduly large increase in the basic wage would check the establishment of adequate international currency reserves and leave the Australian economy in a less secure position in the event of adverse developments overseas. (pp. 858–859)

Several Melbourne academics, 'including Professor Copland, Professor Giblin and Mr Reddaway', had recently issued a manifesto in favour of freer world trade. A large wage increase 'would be likely to create conditions which would make it difficult for [Australia] to take part in a general reduction of tariff barriers'.

The expert did not explicitly advocate a zero wage increase. It was difficult, however, to estimate the amount of increase 'which would slow up the process of recovery to such an extent as to turn it directly into depression'. There was already a tendency for wages to rise faster than award rates, as employers competed for skilled labour. This natural rise in the ruling rate for skilled labour might itself be sufficient to slow up the process of recovery and to keep it conformable to the available resources. '[T]he greater the rise in the basic wage, the greater the danger that a sharp check to recovery will be imposed.'

The employers' expert concluded:

> Mr Reddaway says 'It may seem strange for an economist to be preaching the need to curb investment'. The latest book on 'The Trade Cycle', by Mr R F Harrod, contends that any sudden curb upon investment during recovery must cause a depression, because recovery itself has led in the capital producing trades to the expansion of equipment to a level at which it can only be fully employed so long as investment continues at a high level; and even continues to expand. Mr Reddaway agrees that we do not even want to have a smaller amount of investment than before, but pleads for "restraint" lest we have too much. According to the economist, we seem to be between the devil and the deep blue sea. A sudden fall in investment, due to large a rise in wages costs, would plunge us back into the sea of depression. On the other hand a certain rise in wages is said to be necessary to prevent the devil from leading us on to the peak of a boom, from whence he would push us into the same sea. The points elaborated above, however, suggest some doubts as to whether the devil really exists. (pp. 860–861)

11.2.4 Reddaway returns

On the next day, Dethridge announced that Reddaway was in the Court and wished to comment on the expert's statement. He would do so from the witness box.

Reddaway did not wish to make debating points: 'I have too much respect for the economist whose influence I rather fancy I see inspiring certain parts of it.' He pointed out that the expert had almost entirely limited himself to one aspect of Reddaway's evidence—the case for a wage increase to avert a boom:

> There is one thing I should say right at the start: this memorandum deals almost entirely with the arguments which I advanced, not for giving an increase in wages at all, but for giving a bigger one than one would do merely on the state of the prosperity of the country. I said at the start of the evidence on the case for a revision, that the basic wage must rise, primarily on the increased prosperity of the country, which enables the employers to pay a larger amount. ... A boom is an argument for going a little further than one would do on the current situation. I think it perhaps may be helpful to put this in more in perspective—what I would do if I were actually fixing the wage. I did not consider it my province to do so before, but since considerable publicity has been given to my figure of 2s or 3s, which was purely illustrative, I should like to do so now, particularly as on a closer examination I feel I should have preferred to have written 1s or 2s, rather than 2s or 3s. (p. 865)

'The objective', said Reddaway,

> is to fix the highest wage which will not cause unemployment by destroying the entrepreneur's incentive to produce. The figure can only be estimated by looking to the past and allowing for changes and expected future developments. At present we can usefully make two approaches, one by comparing the present conditions with those of the immediate past, and a second by taking the last more or less 'normal' year before the slump. (p. 866)

Beginning with the latter criterion, Reddaway said that external conditions were remarkably similar to those of 1928. Export prices were a little higher, import prices virtually unchanged. The cessation of public overseas borrowing was 'offset by increased home production of manufactures'. 'Since productivity has improved and the basic wage paid in 1928–29 had not been increased for some years it appears conservative to say that industry could pay the same real wage now as in that year'. (Reddaway provided no evidence of the increase in productivity.) Turning to the immediate past, Reddaway discerned 'a very great improvement in the terms of trade with other countries and in the readjustment of the national economy to the dislocation of the slump'. There was ground for 'a considerable rise in real wages on grounds of increased prosperity and income, quite apart from the need to check the boom'. To restore the real basic wage to its 1928–29 level required an increase of about 5s, or 7 per cent: 'I would say that the improved position of industry justifies an increase of about this amount, but to avoid sudden dislocation would suggest that it be given in stages' (p. 866). To check a boom and to secure 'a distribution of income which would help to preserve the present level of prosperity', a somewhat higher figure would be justified.

Dethridge asked whether increases in margins should be taken into account in assessing the scope to raise the basic wage. This, replied Reddaway, would be 'a little hard on the basic wage earner, unless it is proved that there is some reason why margins were too low in 1928–29' (p. 867). Dethridge said that the reason why the Judges had been raising margins was indeed that, in their view, 'the time had come when they should be restored to something like the same proportion as had existed in days gone by' (p. 867a). Reddaway commented that this might have to be taken into account as one of the factors that had changed since 1928–29; but so too should the fact that labour had become 'less obstructive', as was evidenced by the statistics of strikes (p. 868).

Reddaway moved to the expert's arguments about the boom:

The writer of this memorandum apparently took my advocacy of higher rates as a means of dealing with a boom, solely in its negative aspect, and solely from the point of view of reducing the amount of capital construction. That is very far from what I had in mind. I am not sure whether I made it clear, but there are two aspects on this question of wages and booms. First of all, you want to restrain the amount of investment but secondly, most important, you want to ensure that what investment there is would be justified so that the factories, which you are putting up this year, and which will come into operation next year ... will be found to meet with an adequate demand. If it is found not to meet with an adequate demand, while possibly investors may manage to struggle along, the incentive to investment would be very materially reduced, even disastrously reduced, so that investment would then fall off. This memorandum also refers to Mr Harrod's book on

> the Trade Cycle. It was actually that book which crystallised my own ideas on the means of making consumption rise hand in hand, so to speak, with investment. If you raise wages, you will also to some extent reduce investment now, but you will also provide a basis with which to justify that investment when the factories and so on come into use. (pp. 871–872)

This was a more complex and subtle version of the anti-boom argument than Reddaway had offered in his opening statement. He contended that Australia, with its wage-fixing machinery, was in the fortunate position of being able to adjust real wages so as to tame the trade cycle—a facility enjoyed by few other countries. 'Mr Harrod', he said, 'took a rather pessimistic view, that in a country without any means of stepping up real wages in this way, there was nothing to do about it, and that is why he thought the trade cycle was so inevitable' (p. 872).

Though depressions came from outside, it did not follow that internal policies had no role in ameliorating their effects. Wage policy, judiciously used, was a significant instrument of control:

> The last depression was met partly by a cut in wages. If you refuse to apply wholeheartedly a reversal of that policy when you get into a boom, with favourable export conditions, then it is going to be a lot harder for the authorities generally to induce labour to give way again … should there be a move for a cut in wages. I would say that a demonstration that this is not a one-way traffic, but a two-way traffic, would increase the probability of Australia meeting any subsequent depression from overseas in an orderly manner. … I feel that it is important in the interests of social rest as opposed to unrest that this Court should be prepared to take the lead in an experiment upwards, in the same way as it took the lead in an experiment downwards. (p. 873)

It was important, as the expert had contended, to attend to the balance of payments. But London funds were expected to rise by £10 million in the year. This afforded 'a certain margin', and 'I would not want to keep down the real wage in order to increase London funds at a rate of more than ten millions a year' (p. 874). Reddaway thought that a wage increase of the order that the Court might grant would have little effect on exports. As to import-competing industries, it was not easy to generalise, but average money wages in Australia had fallen since before the slump by something like 17 per cent. On top of that was an exchange depreciation of 25 per cent, so that, in competition with Great Britain, there had been a sizeable shift in trading conditions favourable to the Australian producer.

The debate between Reddaway and the anonymous expert was a rare explicit discussion of the counter-cyclical role of wage policy. It was true, as Reddaway observed, that the Court's 1931 decision was an endeavour to ameliorate the downward phase of the imported cycle. The expert was correct in pointing out the inconsistency of the unions in opposing the reduction but now embracing the counter-boom advocacy of Reddaway and his Melbourne supporters. His argument against Reddaway turned on the non-existence and the unlikelihood of the apprehended boom. Was there, *in fact*, an actual or an incipient boom? Butlin's estimates of the real GDP indicate increases of 4.7 per cent between 1934–35 and 1935–36; 4.4 per cent between 1935–36 and 1936–37; and 6.2 per cent between 1936–37 and 1937–38 (Butlin 1961, p. 462). In the same years, gross private investment grew (in real terms) by 15.3 per cent, 8.7 per cent and 16.0 per cent (p. 463). Haig's estimates show an increase in the real GDP of 6.1 per cent between 1934–35 and 1935–36; 3.0 per cent in the next year; and then 7.1 per cent. These numbers seem to support Reddaway's position. On the other side may be set the unemployment percentages. Unemployment among trade union members was 9.7 per cent in the second quarter of 1937. It fell to 8 per cent in the first quarter of 1938 and thereafter increased. Of course, these percentages represent an enormous improvement since the depth of the Depression. But is 8 to 10 per cent unemployment consistent with a boom? We must, I think, conclude that the evidence for a boom is mixed.

The issues generated by Reddaway' evidence dominated the hearing, but there were subsidiary topics.

11.2.5 Geographical variations

At the beginning of the hearing, Crofts told the Court that the unions were seeking flat-rate amounts within States (but not between them). The flat rate for a State would be the capital city amount as calculated from the price index, but if the index showed a higher amount for any non-metropolitan town, the latter should be adopted for the town. This claim was not seriously entertained. Toward the end of the hearing, Dethridge made the statement:

> Up to now, nothing has been adduced before the Court to induce it to change its opinion that there should be a differentiation between the basic wage for the metropolitan area, and maybe in certain other specified areas, and the same kind of basic wage for industries carried on in the provinces. That is to say, the principle which the Court indicated in its 1934 judgment, which so far as that is concerned was unanimous, is to continue a differentiation of about the same amount as was then made. ... It may shorten proceedings if that is indicated now. (p. 834)

Some New South Wales employers sought the elimination of interstate differences so as to equalise competitive opportunities. This request was not strenuously pressed and seems to have fallen on deaf ears.

The principal subject of contention was the request of the South Australian Government, railways, and private employers to be excluded from all or some of the wage increase which the Court might grant.[11] One argument was that the cost of living in Adelaide was less than the index suggested. This argument was supported by the evidence of Gilbert Seaman, a statistician in the audit department and a Bachelor of Economics of the University of Adelaide.[12] Seaman did not dispute the accuracy of the index numbers. His contention was that citizens of South Australia did not require the same quantities of goods and services to achieve a standard of living equal to that

---

[11] The case of the South Australian Government and employers was somewhat weakened by the fact that the living wage declared by the State Board of Industry was slightly above the federal basic wage for Adelaide.

[12] Seaman later became the Under-Treasurer of South Australia. He gave evidence in major post-war wage cases.

of other cities.[13] Adelaide citizens, he said, needed less electricity and shorter carriage by public transport than citizens of other capitals; and he estimated the 'saving' as 1s 3d per week. Beeby chided the counsel who was leading Seaman for 'piling up matter on a very small issue, whether or not there is 1s 3d too much for the basic wage in South Australia' (p. 716). Dethridge later said (to different counsel): 'You are now assuming that the Seaman thesis is established, but the Commonwealth Statistician has told me that that is not so. ... He has told me that, at the present time, the C figures do, so far as any index figures can, as between Capital cities, fairly represent the purchasing power of money' (pp. 819–819a). This did not squarely deal with Seaman's point, trivial though it may have been.

A second argument was that a basic wage increase would drive the State budget into deficit. This was the subject of evidence by the Under-Treasurer, R R Stuckey. At the time, the budget was showing a small surplus. Stuckey explained that this had been achieved only by the special grants from the Commonwealth, made on the recommendation of the Commonwealth Grants Commission. Without these grants, 'the annual deficits shown in the State accounts would have been of such dimensions that the State, from its own resources, would have been unable to cope therewith, and would have been placed in a position where default was inevitable' (p. 685). The argument appeared to have little impact. Crofts put it to Stuckey that if a wage increase placed the South Australian Government at a disadvantage relative to other State governments, the Grants Commission would protect the State (p. 707). And Dethridge said: 'Supposing we put up the basic wage, which means that the South Australian government will have to find more money somehow or other in order to keep up its services, then you might expect, as Mr Crofts suggests, that the Commonwealth out of its revenue would increase its subsidy' (p. 709).

---

[13] 'My memorandum does not in any way make an attack upon the index numbers as such. ... It is the recognised practice amongst all statistical authorities that they adopt a common regimen in all cities. It is also recognised that necessary consumption to maintain the same standard of living may differ between cities, and if that necessary consumption to maintain that similar standard does differ between cities, the index numbers computed upon a common regimen cannot give an absolutely correct comparison between towns at any one time' (p. 715).

Stuckey's reply to both was that the Grants Commission's recommendations were just recommendations, which the Commonwealth might or might not accept. Clarey spoke of the implications of Grants Commission assistance:

> Having received that assistance, we cannot have those State Governments coming to this Court and asking the Court in addition to give the further advantage of a relief by the postponement of any ruling this Court may give in relation to the basic wage. In other words, I suggest to the Court that the South Australian Government is asking for it both ways. It gets the assistance because of its alleged financial position, and its difficulty in competition with other States because of federation, but having got that assistance it then uses it as a reason why the wage should not be increased. (p. 936)

The third argument was that South Australian industry needed assistance by way of limitation of any wage increase that the Court might award. In Wright's words:

> In regard to the position in South Australia in particular, I submit that the situation calls for some modification of any decision which the Court may base upon the average of all Australian conditions ... on account of its conditions generally being below the average of all Australia ... We feel that we are deserving of some concession from this Court compared with the more highly developed States. The Court recognised that disability in 1934, and gave us a measure of relief. It was temporary, and it has since gone, but I feel that it did have the effect of helping us to weather the storm better than we could have done, if we had had to take the full effect of the new wage standard in 1934. (pp. 817–818)

Counsel from South Australia spoke of the danger of the motor-body industry being lost to other States. Beeby intimated that he had some sympathy for this argument.[14]

---

[14] 'There is only one feature of South Australia's position which appeals to me, that is, what expense can this Court avoid by its action in encouraging a disturbance of the present organisation of industry, that is, encouraging the transfer of major industries from one State to another, and that is giving me concern. If the motor industry in South Australia is put

11.2.6 The female minimum wage

There was, at this time, no general basic wage for females working under federal awards. Some State awards did provide for female basic or living wages. In those federal awards that recognised the employment of women, there was, of course, a minimum female rate, typically between 50 and 55 per cent of the male basic wage. Unions with female members now sought a decision by the Court to raise the minimum female rate to 60 per cent of the basic wage. Outlining the claim, Crofts said:

> We have stressed time and time again that the amount allotted to females is insufficient, in view of the class of work that the females are called upon to do, in view of which the amount sometimes should be equal to the male rate. Apart from that, we feel that the female wage, which is 52 per cent or 53 per cent of the male rate, generally is insufficient to give females a proper standard of living, particularly when they have to live away from home. (p. 23)

Dethridge, quite early in the proceedings, expressed the opinion that this claim was not 'a basic wage matter'. None the less, he proceeded:

> The Court should not go below a reasonable minimum to pay to women, who have not to carry the responsibilities of a family, such as the basic wage men are presumed to have in the ordinary course of events. It may be that things are altering and that women will have to go out to do the work, while the men stay at home and occupy themselves usefully in housework and minding the children. In that event, of course, women should get the basic wage, while the wage of the men should come down according to our present day custom. I think the tendency is towards an equality of wages as between men and women; but it is a very slow moving tendency. I will not live to see it, but that will be the ultimate outcome in our Western society, if it continues to exist. (pp. 69–70)

---

on exactly the same footing as in other States, there is a possibility of that industry being transferred to the other States, and that does concern me' (p. 936).

The unions called in support of their claim Muriel Heagney, then employed in New South Wales by the Queensland Tourist Bureau but previously (in her words) 'secretary of the unemployed girls'.[15] Heagney cited a number of instances where both federal and State awards and determinations had fixed minimum female rates above the normal proportion of the basic wage. She summarised in two points the arguments for raising the proportion:

- '[W]omen are entering industry in ever increasing numbers and are qualifying for many occupations that were closed to their predecessors, consequentially it is essential that in the interest of the community unfair competition between the sexes must be eliminated through the enforcement of equal occupational rates for persons of either sex'; and
- 'Women's definite social needs and obligations must be recognised and provision made for the normal pleasures of women young and old, so that they may not be debarred through poverty from participating in the amenities of life whether they be social or educational. The prominence given to "lipstick" and "cigarettes" in newspaper publicity during a recent cost of living case in New South Wales had a derogatory effect on uninformed public opinion and is resented by the great mass of women workers whose wages are affected' (pp. 371–371a).

Beeby remarked that Heagney was really arguing for equal pay, whereas the unions were seeking only 60 per cent. Dethridge then made a comment which illustrates the problems confronting those who tried to persuade the tribunals to move toward equal pay:

---

[15] Her entry in the *Australian Dictionary of Biography* reads: 'Alarmed at the plight of jobless women during the Depression, Heagney, in 1930, formed the Unemployed Girls' Relief Movement which established sewing centres where women worked for unemployed families in return for a relief allowance. She also set up a jam factory. To counter propaganda against employment of women in the 1930s, she undertook a survey for the Victorian branch of the Open Door Council and published *Are Women Taking Men's Jobs?* (1935); the book made equal pay a serious national issue, but brought no practical results.'

> You approach this question, it appears to me, chiefly from the point of view of needs—what the woman wage earner needs for maintenance, and, it may be, for the maintenance of dependants that she has—but the chief point of view which I am glad to see has been brought into prominence in this Inquiry, in a way never before accomplished in any basic wage inquiry, is this: What is the wage-paying capacity of industry? Mr Reddaway, who gave evidence which was most admirable in every way, plainly showed that wage paying depends upon economic capacity, and that, unless there is economic capacity, any attempt to meet the needs of wage earners by increasing wages is doomed to absolute failure. That point of view must not be lost sight of in connection with women workers. If women are put upon the same basis as male workers, then the question arises, can industry pay them the same rate? That depends upon the rate which is common to both. … That is to say, the male wage may have to come down, in order that the female rate may be brought up to the level of the male wage. Now you see the ugly position the community is in when dealing with any proposition that women's wages should be the same as men's. I think I may say here that, having regard to the increasing employment of women in industry … the trend is towards equal payment of both sexes, and that equal payment may be a very desirable thing. I am inclined to think it is a very desirable thing, but it can only be brought about … by making the wage level common to both sexes consistent with economic capacity, and, also, it can only be brought about by some extremely difficult social arrangements in respect of the married women and children. … Here, fortunately, as my brother Beeby points out, we are only asked to give what is called a basic wage for women—a minimum wage, I prefer to call it—of 60 per cent of the man's basic wage, so that we are not faced with the frightfully difficult problem which equal wages will present to the community. (pp. 372–373)

Beeby—perhaps to counter the negative tone of Dethridge's remarks—added: 'And, in support of the 60 per cent, I can only say that yours is a most admirable statement.'

While Heagney was in the box, there was some discussion of events in New South Wales in the previous year. On the application of the State Public Service Federation, the Industrial Commission had conducted a special inquiry into the male and female basic wages in State awards. It had separately investigated the two amounts and arrived at a declaration which entailed a female basic wage equal to only 51.4 per cent of the male rate. The previous practice had been to award a female rate equal to 54 per cent of the male wage. The decision had been overturned by legislation, which prescribed a ratio of 54 per cent.

Heagney referred to the practice of some textile firms of putting women on piece-rates and, when output increased, reverting to time rates with an expectation that the higher output would be maintained. Drake-Brockman was sympathetic:

> They have attained their speed by first of all having piecework to encourage them to the speed, and then they expect the same output for the ordinary weekly pay. If they do not get the same output, the girls get put off. It is one of those wretched expedients which has been adopted in the clothing trades—where there is more dishonesty in this sort of way than in any other industry, I think.

When an employer's representative complained that 'Miss Heagney makes a general statement which reflects on the industry', Drake-Brockman replied: 'She could make very much stronger statements on some in the industry. I will not be at all surprised if I am making some of them myself before very long' (pp. 388A–388B).

11.2.7 The amount of the increase

What alteration of the basic wage, if any, was now desirable? Three main considerations were debated in the hearing:

- the need for an increase to restore the real value of the basic wage to its pre-Depression level;

- the ability of the economy and industry to pay more than the present wage; and
- the expedience of adding something to the wage so as to avert an imminent boom.

The union representatives, especially Crofts, sought to argue that a succession of decisions by the Court had cheated the workers of their 'entitlements'. The *Harvester* standard was itself deficient because it provided inadequately for the needs of a worker's family. Powers' 3s had only partially redressed the deficiency. Then the decisions of 1931, 1933, and 1934, taken together, had left the basic wage below the *Harvester* equivalent. One element in the unions' complaints was the substitution of the C for the A series index. They told the Court that they did not seek to reverse this change because that would inevitably delay the proceedings and any wage increase that might emerge from it. Dethridge denied that the substitution of indices had lowered the standard:

> We adopted the C figures not for the purpose of lowering the basic wage at all. We adopted the C figures because, according to experts, and the report of the basic wage commission presided over by Mr Piddington, that was the proper measure to have. ... The way I feel about it is this: supposing we put the basic wage up to the full extent that you suggest, then I still think that we should apply the C figures, and not the A figures. (pp. 11–12)[16]

Dethridge also rejected the comparison with *Harvester*:

> We cannot measure the present basic wage with the *Harvester* basic wage of 1907 because the C index numbers are not there for the earlier period, and therefore it is not easy to make a comparison. However, what I gather is that, in this inquiry, we are asked to arrive at what we think is the highest basic wage which industry can stand. It does not matter what the past history is ... If we can stand a basic wage higher than the *Harvester* wage, good. I do not care how much higher it is if

---

[16] He might have added, but did not, that the basic wage had been increased in 1933 *because* the C series index had fallen less than the A series index.

we can stand it. That is the point, past history is not important. ...The measuring instrument is one feature; the basic wage is another. Let us fix the highest basic wage we can, and then let us consider what is the best measuring instrument to provide for fluctuations in the cost of living. (pp. 13–13a)

Later, Dethridge seemed to resile a little from this stance:

If the present basic wage in real commodities is worth less than the original *Harvester* wage without the Powers' 3s, as you suggest, I say that it is a matter which calls for the most serious consideration. I go further and say, although not with the same emphasis, that if the present basic wage is less in real value than the *Harvester* wage plus the Powers' 3s, that also calls for serious consideration. What more do you want? ... I thought it was obvious that if the A series, plus the Powers' 3s, were applied now, you would get 6s more than you are getting under the C figures. That speaks for itself, but how far you fall short of getting the equivalent in real value of the original *Harvester* wage, or the original *Harvester* wage plus the 3s, is not clear. It depends on the correctness of the A figures on the one side, and the C figures on the other side as the measuring rod. (pp. 39–40)

Later again, Dethridge became terse with Crofts (as he often did). When Crofts spoke repeatedly about the workers' 'entitlements', he told him: 'You are not entitled to any more than Australia can give you. If Australia has not got it to give you, then you are not entitled to it' (p. 67). This was a recurrent theme through the hearing. But the issue whether the basic wage was below the pre-Depression standard, let alone *Harvester*, was not wholly put aside. Dethridge asked rhetorically:

Is it suggested—I want to know this because it is going to be important—that the present day real basic wage ... is 5 per cent lower than the real basic wage before the Depression? If that is suggested, I want it shown. If it is contradicted, I want to have that shown also. ... I may say this; I realise there may be great difficulty in satisfactorily establishing it one way or the other. I cannot help feeling that on the past, on what we heard the other day about our index number, and until quite recently, neither set of index numbers was a very satisfactory guide. I am afraid one has to come to some such conclusion. I think the method of calculating that has been improved very much since the census of 1933, but in respect of prior years, I am very doubtful. (pp. 755–756)

The following exchange took place within the bench:

Drake-Brockman J: I do not think those comparisons matter very much. What we have to determine now is what we can pay now, and not what could have been paid in 1928 or 1929.

Dethridge C J: Except that the amount of unemployment at a past time as compared with the amount of unemployment at the present time, in relation to prevailing wages at each of those times, may be of some assistance to us.

Drake-Brockman J: In that connection, that quotation … from what Professor Copland said at that time calls for consideration, namely that probably we got a little ahead of ourselves in the matter of wages, and that that was reflected in the unemployment.

Dethridge C J: I am not satisfied that that is correct. Unemployment figures are unsatisfactory, as we know, and it seems to me to be doubtful whether until the slump began in 1929, or late in 1928, there was anything more than the unavoidable amount of unemployment. … If that is so, it would indicate that the real wage at that time was about right. Then, if we compare present day conditions with the conditions today [sic], what do we get? In that way, past history is valuable in order to make a comparison. But we have to be certain that our index figures, whichever set we use, give a fair measuring instrument. I am doubtful about the A index figures, and I am a little doubtful about the C index numbers during those years, so it makes a comparison rather difficult. … But, assuming that we could make an accurate comparison, then the real wage at the present day should not be less than it was during that five years period [before the Depression]. It may even be that it should be a little more. (pp. 780–781)

Reddaway's advice, as we have seen, was that the Court should restore the real basic wage to its pre-Depression level and add a little to inoculate the economy against an investment-led boom.

The employers generally gave the impression of recognising the inevitability of an increase but seeking to minimise it. Their principal contention was that producers who had been devastated by the Depression needed more opportunity to repair their fortunes.

11.2.8 The decision

The Court, echoing Reddaway, summarised the principal issue in these terms:

> The application was made mainly on the ground that since 1934 economic recovery as reflected in increased productivity and national income and the restoration of the level of export prices had been great enough to justify more than full restoration of the basic wage operating at the time the 10 per cent reduction was made. In the main, restoration of productivity and of national income to the 1929 level notwithstanding alterations in the economic structure was established. The Court in effect was confronted with the converse position to that which led it to decide on a reduction in 1931 and it was contended that 'all economic arguments then advanced in favour of a reduction should now be reversed and used in favour of an increase'. (*Basic Wage Inquiry 1937* 37 CAR 583, 585)

The Court observed that the employers' expert 'did not dispute that there should be some rise in the wage level but sought to discount the facts and theories applied thereto on which Mr Reddaway based his contentions'. The opinions of experts were not conclusive.[17] 'But those offered in these proceedings by Mr Reddaway unchallenged as they were by any other economist willing to disclose his identity were more impressive than usual' (p. 589).

---

[17] A point made with some vehemence by Dethridge during the hearing. Dethridge also denied that he had followed Copland's advice in 1931 (transcript, p. 803).

The Court found that both rural industries and manufacturing had fully regained their pre-Depression levels of activity. Public finances had vastly improved:

> States still have budgetary difficulties to contend with mainly owing to deficits in railway undertakings. These difficulties have been taken into account in fixing the railway rates as hereafter appear. Increases of revenue which keep pace with general increase in prosperity, provided due economy is shown and there is no undue haste in remitting emergency taxation, should before long enable governments to pay their way. (p. 586)

The financial condition of business had steadily improved since 1934, and recent rises in share prices suggested that the improvement was likely to continue. The employers' representatives, however, had contended that the prosperity was unlikely to endure; and the rise in export prices and the growth of import-replacing manufacturers might be transitory. This, said the Court, 'may or may not be true'. But 'the upward trend since 1935 has, on the whole, brought the Commonwealth to at least pre-depression levels with the advantage that it does not now rely on a large expenditure of overseas public borrowings' (p. 588).

Reddaway's statement, the Court said, was 'an endorsement of the theory that one of the causes of cycles of depression is a recurring lack of balance in the application of the money income received by the members of the community' (p. 590). Whether Reddaway welcomed this characterisation of his evidence is unknown. The Court's elaboration of the 'theory', in terms of achieving a distribution between wage-earners and capitalists that generated an appropriate flow of expenditure, was pure Dethridge: he had articulated the notion frequently on transcript and in published decisions. It accorded with the views of J A Hobson, with whose writings Dethridge and Beeby were both familiar. But the Court also adopted Reddaway's argument for discouraging excessive investment and thereby averting a subsequent slump.

The Court's conclusion—reached 'after grave consideration'—was that 'the present degree of prosperity in the Commonwealth and the existing circumstances of industry make desirable appreciable increases in the basic wage' (p. 593). But it did not follow that the increases granted should be uniform.

> The principle of equality in commodity value was appropriate for a basic wage, the main policy of which was to secure a particular standard of living for wage earners whatever might be the conditions of the industry or the district in which they were engaged. The establishment of such a standard was thought to be socially desirable. Even though some industries might find it difficult to provide the wage, it was nevertheless deemed to be better to impose upon them that wage standard, and if they could not naturally sustain it, either aid them in some other way or let them perish. The standard of living aimed at must always be limited by the productivity of the country generally and therefore inasmuch as the Court cannot differentiate between the wage earners according to their dependants, the basic wage earner with a large family must often suffer and see his family suffer lamentable deprivations. So far as the basic wage is imposed for the purpose of providing for fundamental needs it should be substantially uniform in real value. But where an addition is to be made to the basic wage because of prosperity which may not exist to the same degree nor at all in some States, there is not the same reason for uniformity in the addition. (pp. 593–594)

The 'needs' basic wage (that is, the existing basic wage, subject to cost-of-living adjustments) would be preserved, but there would also be loadings 'because of present prosperity and of stabilising reasons'. These would not be adjusted for price movements. The loadings would be at two levels—a higher level for New South Wales, Victoria and Queensland and a lesser one for South Australia, Western Australia and Tasmania. The Court commented particularly on the position of South Australia:

> South Australia financially is the weakest of the States and has only one highly developed manufacturing enterprise, motor body building,

established in the days when a lower wage level to some extent balanced the disadvantages of distance from the eastern market.

The result of imposing a basic wage which would bring South Australian wage costs to the same level as those of other States would probably accelerate the tendency to concentrate the motor industry in one of the eastern capitals. The Court is anxious not to take any action which of itself may disturb the present distribution of industrial activity amongst the States.

In the South Australian Railways it also seems likely that too high a rise in wage costs would probably result in curtailment of services which must outweigh benefits of increased nominal wages. Similar considerations apply to Tasmania and Western Australia.

The special attention paid to railways was at odds with Reddaway's advice.

The loadings granted were:

Sydney, Melbourne, Brisbane:	6s
Adelaide, Perth, Hobart:	4s
Six capitals:	5s
Railway awards—New South Wales and Victoria:	5s
Railway awards—South Australia and Tasmania:	3s

For country districts, the existing differential of 3s below the relevant metropolitan rate was retained. The wage increases would be phased, with half coming into effect on 1 July and the remainder on 1 October. The existing ratios of minimum female rates to the male basic wages should continue. The average increase in federal award rates caused by the decision was about 5 per cent. Over the three quarters from the second quarter of 1937 to the first quarter of 1938, real award wages (federal and State) rose by about 4 per cent. The 'Reddawage' decision was probably the major source of this increase.

If the nominal basic wage is deflated by the C series index, and the six-capitals numbers are used for the calculation, the increase granted by the Court was not sufficient to restore the real basic wage to its pre-Depression levels (see Figure 8.9). The increase granted therefore fell short of the amount which Reddaway's reasoning seemed to imply.

The Court reported that the Commonwealth Statistician had expressed to it a concern that his role was being misunderstood: because the basic wage was varied with the price index, there was a perception that the Statistician was fixing wages. He suggested that the Court publish its own index, based on the Statistician's index numbers. It accepted this advice. It also acceded to a union request that the basic wage be adjusted to the nearest 1s, instead of 2s.[18]

11.3 Sequel

Dethridge, in September 1937, dealt with an application to raise all rates in the award for journalists with metropolitan daily newspapers. This was not strictly a basic wage matter, because the rates prescribed in the award were total amounts. An increase of 9s was sought, however, on the basis that the basic wage had risen through automatic adjustments by 4s since the making of the award and by a further 5s as the prosperity loading. Dethridge granted an increase of 5s. The parties had agreed in 1934 that rates would not be adjusted in line with movements in the basic wage. Dethridge presumed that they had taken into account their estimate of likely basic wage movements. The prosperity loading, however, had been granted 'by reason of the unexpected prosperity of the community and for other economic reasons, namely to ensure a stable progress or, at any rate, not an excessive speculative advance'. The parties would not have anticipated it. It seemed 'not unreasonable' that

> although it will not make very much difference to many of them, having regard to their rates of pay, they should share in this unexpected increase of the community's prosperity. I think I may assume that, generally speaking, the newspaper industry, and the employers in that industry, will benefit by that prosperity just as other business undertakings have

---

[18] In June 1937, the Full Court considered the basic wage in the pastoral award. It noted 'that all parties concerned in the industry prefer the present method of estimating the future average amount of the basic wage and of avoiding adjustment for an inconsiderable change in the cost of living'. It therefore set a 'needs' basic wage of 72s (2s above the current indexed level) and a loading of 5s (*Variation—Pastoral Awards* 37 CAR 666, 667).

benefited. (*Variation—Journalists' (Metropolitan Daily Newspapers) Award* 38 CAR 238, 241)

In October 1937, the Full Court reconsidered the basic wage in the fruit-picking industry—for long a 'basket case' among the industries regulated by the Court (*Variation—Fruit Pickers' Award* 38 CAR 352). Employers had in 1931 sought a reduction of wages because of depressed conditions generally and specifically in the industry. This led to a cut of 7½ per cent (over and above the 10 per cent) in the basic wage, which was still in force in 1937. The Court was now asked to rescind the reduction and to increase the basic wage. It cancelled the special reduction and set basic wages for various districts which were, in nominal terms, less than the Melbourne basic wage by amounts ranging from 1s to 4s. The differences reflected approximately the relative levels of the C series index. In future, the district rates would be adjusted by the Melbourne C series index and thus be permanently below the Melbourne rate.

The Court in April 1938 again confronted issues about interstate differences in the basic wage. It did so in dealing with the textile award (*Variation—Textile Workers' Award* 39 CAR 114); and the same issue arose, with the same outcome, for the clothing trades (*Variation—Clothing Trades' Awards* 39 CAR 126). In the main basic wage case, some South Australian employers had signalled that they wished to argue later for full account to be taken of the lower level of prices in their State. The applications now before the Court sought to apply this principle to textiles. The existing flat rates, said Dethridge and Drake-Brockman, were due mainly to the existence of keen interstate competition:

> The Court recognised that the adoption of this flat rate would involve the receipt by wage-earners in one State or place of a real basic wage somewhat less than that which the Court considered proper for that State or place, and the receipt in another State or place of a real wage somewhat greater than the Court's real wage for that State or place. But it then thought that the existence of strong interstate competition in an industry would justify a flat money wage … The fact that in some

awards the parties had agreed to adopt a flat basic wage also inclined the Court to adopt it in the Textile awards. ... In substance [the South Australian employers] ask that the then current awards should be varied and that the impending awards be framed so as to prescribe a basic wage for Adelaide based on the Adelaide index number with the South Australian loading of 4s instead of that based upon the five capital cities index number with the five capital cities loading of 5s and a provincial basic wage of 3s less for other places in South Australia. (pp. 115–116)

The Court was divided. Dethridge and Drake-Brockman were in broad agreement with the employers. For the needs basic wage, the appropriate policy normally was to set an equal *real* wage in different places:

> Inasmuch as the basic wage is in theory awardable to all adult males without regard to the presence or absence of any peculiar merit in any of them, presumptively it should so far as is reasonably practicable be awarded by the Court equally for all, that is, should be of equal real value to each of the wage-earner recipients in purchasing power and not merely of equal money amount. ... At best not more than an approximation to equality in any two or more areas is possible. But in view of the disparity in cost of living in different places the assessing of the money amount of the basic wage so as to give this approximately equal real wage is thought to be juster than awarding a flat money basic wage. (pp. 117–118)

Interstate competition was not irrelevant, but its implications required consideration:

> Competitive power depends upon the presence of human ability and other natural resources the amounts of which as between one area and another are subject to constant change. To deprive one area of part of its higher competitive power and to add to the lower competitive power of another area is a process which could not be well performed by any legislative body and certainly not by this Court. For instance, to attempt by means of differential rates of wages and conditions to equalise competitive conditions for steel making in New South Wales and South Australia would be plainly absurd. No one would suggest

that the real needs wage should be raised in New South Wales because coal is produced there, or should be lowered in South Australia because coal has to be imported. But the cheaper supply of food and shelter in South Australia for men in industry is economically the same kind of competitive advantage for that State as the cheaper supply of coal in New South Wales for machines in industry is for the latter State. (p. 119)

The 1937 loadings had been awarded, said Dethridge and Drake-Brockman, 'because the Court thought that industry generally could sustain the additions and considered that the wage earners are fairly entitled to any such sustainable additions; and partly to help in checking what then appeared to be a likely imminent boom and consequent slump' (p. 121). The lesser amounts set for some States, including South Australia, had not been devised to assist those States to compete with other States, but were awarded in recognition of their lesser prosperity. It was not the Court's function to assist one State to compete with another. As the prosperity loadings were not a reflection of living costs, it was appropriate that in competitive industries they be equal. Hence the six-capitals loading should apply.[19]

Beeby strongly disagreed:

From my experience I know that State fixations of wage rates and conditions in industries subject to interstate competition had always been influenced by this lack of facilities to create uniformity. When the Federal Court was created this weakness in the system of industrial regulation was the subject of public agitation. It was one of the 'grievances

---

[19] Dethridge and Drake-Brockman did not proceed to make orders in favour of the South Australian employers, because there were no applications from other States. 'The Court', they said, 'has indicated the principle, and parties can apply as they see fit' (p. 122). In two other decisions given on the same day, Dethridge and Drake-Brockman preserved identical money rates: in food preserving, because of the prevalence of piece-rates, and for theatrical employees, because of the existence of numerous rates for different kinds of work. They said, in the latter case: 'With so many rates ranging through small and large amounts the resulting inconvenience would far outweigh any benefit to the parties from an attempt to equalise in all the States and districts concerned the purchasing power of such rates' (*Variation—Food Preservers' Award* 39 CAR 131; *Variation—Theatrical Employees' Award* 39 CAR 134).

to be remedied' when the federal legislature decided to exercise its power in the field of industrial regulation. That exercise of power was mainly to create an authority which could control industrial conditions from a national as opposed to State points of view. This interpretation of federal legislation is borne out by a long series of decisions of this Court. ... In effect the Court is now asked to over-ride these decisions and declare that interstate competition should not be considered in the making of awards. (p. 122)

Beeby was unfair to his colleagues. If the goal of equalising wages and conditions were accepted, the question remained whether the wages to be equalised were *money* or *real* amounts. The majority did consider that question; Beeby avoided it.

In August 1938, the Full Court dealt with claims for a new award in the pastoral industry in circumstances where the industry's prosperity had diminished since the main basic wage case (*Judgment (Standard Hours and Basic Wage)—Pastoral Industry* 39 CAR 607). Employers sought the removal of the prosperity loadings; the union asked that the station hand's rate be increased to the level of the basic wage for shearers.

The employers' case was based on the combination of a low average price of wool, competition from artificial substitutes, and drought in parts of New South Wales, South Australia and Western Australia. The cumulative effect of these evils was so great in the Western Australian pastoral industry that the Court felt 'compelled to suspend in the new award until further order the prosperity loading for that section of the industry' (p. 609). In New South Wales and Western Australia, however, there were areas that were not drought-stricken and where removal of the loadings was not warranted. Areas which were drought-affected were contiguous to drought-free areas and the removal of the loadings was 'not practicable'. In relation to the union claim, the Court recalled that in 1931 it had reduced the station hands' rate by 20 per cent, 'expressing the view that no index numbers could be relied upon as a guide to the cost of living of such employees and that in such employment they gained some advantages which urban workers did not receive'. In 1934, the Court set the station hand's rate 8s below the shearers' basic wage; and in 1937 it granted prosperity loadings of 5s to shearers and 3s to station hands. Refusing the claim, the Court said:

> If the pastoral industry were at present in a flourishing condition, the relation of the station hands rate to that of other pastoral employees might deserve reconsideration, at any rate in respect of the prosperity loading, but in view of the difficult conditions in which the industry is now being worked, the Court does not think it would be for the benefit of station hands themselves to increase their existing rates in any of the States. (p. 610)

This was the last significant basic wage matter before the outbreak of war.

11.4 STATE POLICIES

Four of the States—New South Wales, Queensland, South Australia and Western Australia—continued to rely predominantly on quasi-judicial industrial tribunals. In Victoria and Tasmania, wages boards remained the authorities with the primary capacity to set the terms of employment. Save for possibilities of appeal to industrial courts, the wages board system did not lend itself to centralised policy-making. In Victoria, however, the *Factories and Shops Act 1934* required all wages boards to adopt federal award rates where applicable in all determinations. It also provided for the Secretary for Labour to make adjustments of wages according to cost-of-living index numbers, without convening the Boards, if the determinations included adjustment clauses (*Labour Report*, No. 29, 1938, p. 80). Tasmanian wages boards, like those of Victoria, were commonly thought to have conformed closely to the lead provided by federal awards.[20] Whichever system operated, State governments could by legislation impose procedures and outcomes on

---

[20] Heyward (1936, p. 110) wrote: 'Where there are Federal Awards covering part of the field it has for some years been the policy of Wages Boards to avoid the evils of overlapping by adopting the Federal Award as their determination. The same result would follow if the Federal Award was a common rule.'

the tribunals. They commonly did so. For example, as previously noted, the Industrial Commission of New South Wales in May 1936 increased slightly the male basic wage and reduced the female basic wage. The *Labour Report* records that 'strong protests made to the Government against the reduction in the female rate resulted in an amendment of the *Industrial Arbitration Acts*, providing for the female rate to be 54 per cent of the male rate or £1 17s 6d retrospectively as from the date of the original declaration' (*Labour Report*, No. 27, 1936, p. 88).

The failure of the New South Wales Industrial Commission to adopt the 10 per cent wage cut of 1931 had been a source of concern to the Federal Court and to economists. For several years, wages were higher and hours shorter for workers under New South Wales awards than for those who were covered by the Federal Court's awards. In respect of pay, this problem had ceased to exist by the end of 1934, with the cancellation of the 10 per cent cut and wage reductions in New South Wales awards leaving federal award workers slightly better paid than their State counterparts. The most important development, however, was the decision of the New South Wales Government, in response to the 1937 federal basic wage decision, to discontinue the system of periodic review of the State basic wage and to adopt the federal basic wage (including automatic adjustments).

Queensland, since the early 1920s, had maintained employment standards well ahead of those embodied in federal and other State awards and determinations. Its ability to pursue this policy, while maintaining low unemployment, was generally attributed to the prosperity of its primary industries, which differed in composition from those of the southern States, and especially to the federal government's protectionist measures for the sugar industry, which prohibited imports and imposed a levy on Australian consumers that was used to subsidise exports. Figure 1.6 in Chapter 1 shows that in the later 1930s the State basic wage in Brisbane remained ahead of the federal wage, but the gap narrowed significantly as the Commonwealth basic wage was increased. Figure 8.7, in Subsection 8.3.2 of Chapter 8, shows that real wages in Queensland, previously well above those of other States, moved closer to the levels elsewhere in the later 1930s.

South Australia maintained the procedure whereby a living wage was declared at intervals of at least six months by a Board of Industry comprising a judge and four Commissioners. The living wage was not automatically adjusted. Late in 1937, the Board increased the basic wage from £3 9s 6d to £3 14s, equal to the federal basic wage for Adelaide.

In Western Australia, the Court of Arbitration was required to declare before 14 June of each year a basic wage to operate from 1 July. A 1930 amendment to the Act provided for quarterly adjustments by the Court, when an official statement supplied by the State Government Statistician showed that a variation in the cost of living of one shilling or more had occurred. The Court's obligation to make an annual declaration remained. In 1938 it granted an increase of almost 7 per cent in the real wage.

12

Other aspects of wage policy 1935–1939

12.1 Wages above the basic wage

During the Depression, the Court had left margins for skill virtually constant as money amounts, save for the operation of the 10 per cent cut. Cancellation of the cut in 1934 meant that most margins were restored to their pre-Depression levels. Since the basic wage had fallen along with prices, the net effect was to increase the relative level of margins. As the Depression receded, the Court moved gradually to an even more generous treatment of margins, and there is no evidence that it was restrained by the widening of relativities that had occurred almost fortuitously in the years 1929–34. The change in approach had two main aspects: (1) a willingness to increase margins due to a view that economic necessity had hitherto compelled the Court to keep them too low and that industries were now able to bear higher wages; and (2) a resumption of the practice of assessing margins on the basis of the work performed. These two sources of change were not entirely separate: in some cases both were at work. It will, nevertheless, be convenient to discuss them as distinct processes.

12.1.1 The move to higher margins

The Court's willingness to approve higher margins was due partly to a general relaxation of wage restraint and partly to a conviction that more highly skilled workers were underpaid. All of the judges, to varying degrees, invoked both reasons for granting increases.

Metal trades (1)

Beeby in April 1935 gave the first of several decisions about a new metal trades award (34 CAR 449). (He had been hearing the case since July 1934.) Looking back on the period since 1930, when he had made the consolidated award, he said that 'economic changes of profound significance' had occurred:

> When making the award the Court realised that critical times were ahead, and sought to reorganise industrial considerations in such a way as to encourage the development of new industries without reducing opportunities for employment of skilled mechanics. At that time Australia's main competitor, Great Britain, had by amalgamation of plants and by the extension of mass production methods reduced costs of production to an extent which enabled her to undersell Australian manufacturers in their own market. The position had become so critical that some change in Australian methods was imperative if we were to find work even for the reduced number of artisans then employed. The Court therefore introduced provisions for mass production methods, but continued existing conditions for ordinary engineering operations. After five years the wisdom of this change has been established. Manufacture of machinery and electrical appliances and metallic articles by mass production methods has greatly increased, and, as anticipated, while these methods have added to the ranks of unskilled, semi-skilled and junior labour, they have largely increased opportunities of employment for skilled mechanics as die and tool makers, machine setters and makers of machinery used in repetitive processes. (p. 452)

A major contributor to the improved state of the industry was the increased tariff. The industry was likely to expand further. In 1930, Beeby said, he had been convinced that the margin for the skilled artisan was too low, but was deterred by economic conditions from increasing it. The tariff revisions had begun to affect the demand for skilled workers in 1933–34, and the market outlook for these workers was now strong: 'Turners, fitters, electrical fitters, first grade machinists and some others just now can pick and choose employment' (p. 453). There were fewer skilled men in the metal trades than in 1930, but the opportunities for employment were greater.

What should the tradesman's margin be? In *Harvester*, Higgins had fixed a tradesman's wage of 10s per day, compared with 7s for the unskilled labourer. The *Harvester* ratio would be restored by fixing a margin of 28s per week. But the Court had 'abandoned the idea that the *Harvester* standard was an irrevocable starting point':

> It is now accepted that wage fixation and standards of living are largely controlled by changing economic circumstances and that in these days of economic fluctuation and uncertainty principles adopted during periods of comparative stability cannot apply. The Court can only feel its way to the best conclusion under circumstances of the moment relating to particular industries. Common action of all judges as to the base rate is of course provided for by Statute. But in dealing with margins and conditions of labour awards cannot be standardised. The nature of the work done, the financial position of the industry, the extent to which the industry is protected from overseas competition and many other matters must be considered. (p. 454)

The judges of the Court, said Beeby, were agreed that wages should be the highest that industry could afford to pay, 'but unfortunately the Court is not in possession of complete statistical data to enable it to give reasoned effect to this truism' (p. 455). Beeby increased the skilled tradesmen's margins by 3s to 27s. This increase was 'within the margin of safety'. Beeby declined, however, to disturb the margins of 'the bulk of labour employed.' He commented:

> Various unions of employees in urging that the margins of other groups should be proportionately increased evidently did not give proper consideration to the reasons stated by the Court for proposing to grant any wage increases. The Court did not come to the conclusion that the general improvement of the industry was sufficient to justify an all round increase in wage rates. It did, however, think that there had

been sufficient recovery to justify the long postponed re-adjustment of margins for skill. (pp. 455–456)

A selection of the margins prescribed in the new award was:

Aero mechanic holding A & B certificates	40s
Patternmaker	36s
Toolmaker	33s
Tradesman	27s
First-class machinist	27s
Motor mechanic	24s
Second-class machinist	18s
Third-class machinist	12s
Process worker	6s

Beeby refused an application by the South Australian Government for a general exemption of the State from the increases in margins; but he excluded the South Australian Railways (in future to be dealt with by Drake-Brockman) and continued a partial exemption for sheet metal in South Australia 'after perusal of the balance sheets of Simpson and Co' (p. 456).

Bank officials

Dethridge in July 1935 varied the bank officials' award (*Variation—Bank Officials' Award* 34 CAR 843). 'During 1935', he said, 'the position of the banking business in Australia shows signs of progressive improvement'. It was 'closely approaching a degree of prosperity, lower than that enjoyed in the period before the recent depression, but sufficiently high and stable to ensure a profit adequate for the enterprise and capital by or for whom it is carried on'. The award did not contain an automatic adjustment provision, but the basic wage in force at the time when it was made had been used in setting the sixth-year rate for a bank clerk (assumed to be 21 years of age). An emergency decision in 1932 had suspended salary increases for all clerks who were already above the sixth-year rate. Dethridge now reduced the sixth-year rate from £180 to £175—a modest recognition of the fall in the nominal basic wage since the award was made—but removed the suspension of increases after the sixth year. He thus restored the full benefits of the incremental salary scale to clerks receiving more than the basic wage.

Motor bodies (1)

A new award for motor-body building was made in December 1935 (*Judgment—Motor Body and Coach Building Industry* 35 CAR 599). The previous award had been made in 1927. Reviewing the industry's financial position, Beeby said:

> The confidential information supplied discloses that up to the beginning of the depression the industry was profitable. Then for nearly three years heavy losses were sustained by most of the employers who, however, were able to survive by using their reserves. In 1934 the industry began to revive and has become re-established with astonishing rapidity. Some of the balance-sheets disclose meagre profits since recovery began. These results however are not traceable to wage costs, but to limited turnover and unprofitable contracts in a market which has become more competitive. I doubt if any employer would have shown much better results on lower wage costs. So far as it is possible to judge, results for the current year will be much better and without some economic disturbance of universal effect, the industry will soon pass the peak year of 1926–1927. (pp. 609–610)

Beeby had 'no hesitation' in granting to tradesmen the 3s increase awarded in the metal trades, but 'found it impossible to continue tradesman's rates for some processes for which they are now paid'. Union representatives had realised the inevitability of some declassifications; but as they could not make admissions, 'the unenviable task of devising a new wage code for the industry became my responsibility' (p. 610).

Agricultural implements

In making a new award for the manufacture of agricultural implements, Beeby in April 1936 noted that employers had opposed any alteration of margins set by Deputy President Quick in 1925. A perusal of Quick's reasons suggested that he had been influenced by the requirement for the industry to pay a basic wage which included Powers' 3s: in the absence of that requirement, he would have granted higher margins. The position had changed since 1925 and further information was now available:

> Foreign competition is not so serious. The Australian amalgamation of H V McKay Pty Ltd with its chief competitor Massey Harris Pty Ltd (except as to dairying appliances) has given local manufacturers better command of the market. The preferment, even at higher prices, given by some farmers to foreign imports is dying out with realisation that the quality of Australian manufactures is equal to that of imported machinery. ... The disparity in direct wage cost compared with American and Canadian competitors has been greatly modified, if not eliminated. By further improvements in methods and by reason of the reduced basic wage, direct wage cost, as related to selling prices, in mass production plants has been reduced to approximately 15 per cent of total costs. In 1934 the Tariff Board, after a lengthy inquiry into the working of the industry, published information which was not available in 1925 and disclosed that wage cost was not the main determinant of selling price. (*Judgment—Agricultural Implement, etc Industry* 36 CAR 39, 41–42)

Beeby decided that, in general, the margins prescribed in the metal trades should apply in this award. He adopted the 27s tradesman's rate. He also raised from 3s 6d to 5s an allowance for lost time due to seasonal fluctuations.

Commercial printing

In April 1936, Dethridge determined several matters referred to him by the parties who were negotiating a new award for commercial printing (*Judgment—Commercial Printing* 36 CAR 738). These included the margin for hand compositors. This had been fixed at 24s by Webb in 1925 and maintained at that level (subject to the 10 per cent cut) by Coneybeer in a new award made in 1932. The employers now sought a reduction to 16s, but in the hearing made it clear that a continuation of 24s was acceptable. The union pressed for a margin of 30s. Dethridge judged that, although the special qualifications required of the compositor had not changed since 1925, he now had 'to use those qualifications under rather greater stress and with quicker decision than formerly' (p. 743). In searching for the suitable margin, he discussed the issue of comparisons between industries and skills:

> There is no doubt that this Court and other industrial tribunals have, in assessing margins for one kind of skilled craftsmen, been unable to avoid being influenced by the margins prevailing at the same time for other classes of skilled craftsmen and have tended to fix one amount for those margins unless there is an obvious disparity in the special capacity requisite. In assessing margins I think I should take into consideration margins being paid to skilled craftsmen in other industries, while at the same time giving due weight to differences in economic and other conditions. (p. 744)

The unions had stressed Beeby's recent decision to raise the metal tradesman's margin to 27s. Dethridge concluded 'that an increase of the hand compositor's margin from 24s to 27s would be justifiable if the industry be in what may be regarded as a normal state'. In his opinion it had 'about recovered ordinary prosperity', and he awarded 27s (p. 745). He referred to a recent decision by an Industrial Board in Western Australia (upheld by the State Court) which fixed the hand compositor's margin at 30s:

> The decision seems to have been influenced somewhat by the then existing prosperity of the industry. It is not sound in principle in my opinion that an addition to a marginal wage intended to remain as a permanent standard should be made because of what may be a passing wave of prosperity. Such a permanent addition should not be made unless there is ground for feeling assured that it can be maintained for a considerable time in the future throughout the economic fluctuations of the industry. If an addition to wages is to be made because of unusual prosperity it seems desirable that it should be expressly made for a limited time or until further order so that its temporary nature is understood. Such temporary additions are probably better left to negotiations

with individual employers rather than imposed by ordinance upon all employers alike whether prosperous or struggling. (p. 745)

There may well be a hint here that, in Dethridge's view, the 27s tradesman's margin was a standard that the Court should not exceed.

Carpenters and joiners

Similarly, in July 1936 Dethridge raised the margin for carpenters and joiners from 24s to 27s (*Variation—Carpenters and Joiners' Award* 36 CAR 324). The employers had opposed this on the ground that the skill required of a metal trades craftsman exceeded that of the carpenter or joiner. Dethridge rejected fine distinctions, discerning a 'tendency in the long run towards equality of wage rates of craftsmen of various kinds'. He referred to this decision in September 1936 in relation to ships' carpenters and joiners (*Variation—Ship Carpenters' Award and Agreement* 36 CAR 460). The real point, he said,

> was that the work of carpenters, broadly speaking, is on the same grade as that of other skilled tradesmen generally, and that carpenters had not yet got back to the relative position occupied by skilled tradesmen compared with unskilled workers. That was the main reason why the increase was given, not only in connexion with carpenters, but in connexion with other apprenticed craftsmen as well. I thought, and I am inclined to think that my brother Beeby also thought in regard to work of a similar order in the Metal Trades, that the day had now come when the skilled worker in the apprentice class should be restored to something like the superiority in rates which he formerly enjoyed. ... I see no reason why the increase in margin which I recently prescribed in connexion with carpenters generally should not be extended to ship carpenters. (pp. 460–461)

Motor bodies (2)

Dethridge also raised some margins at the sub-tradesman level. In October 1936, he reviewed the rate for the second-class panel beater:

The margin of 12s, having regard to the dexterity required for the removal of such warping or denting as there is, is somewhat on the low side. I think it is more than mere repetitive filing, and work requiring some dexterity and judgment, which is hardly covered by the margin of 12s at present being paid. I think the present classification is not appropriate for this particular class of work, and what is necessary is a new classification to cover it ... One cannot compute with mathematical exactness a margin, but an estimate by comparison with other work has to be made. I propose to fix a margin of 17s per week for the work in question. (*Variation—Motor Body and Coach Building Award* 36 CAR 525)

Storemen and packers (wool stores)

In the same month, Dethridge adjusted margins for storemen and packers in wool stores (*Judgment—Storemen and Packers (Wool, etc, Stores)* 36 CAR 565). Since 1920, there had been a minimum industry rate of 3s above the basic wage. This was originally set by consent and was continued in a new award made by Dethridge in 1928. He was now persuaded by 'much evidence and a number of inspections of the operations in concern' that the industry minimum should be raised to 4s above the basic wage (p. 568). He also granted modest increases in specific margins.

Actors

In a decision of November 1936, Dethridge altered the award rates for actors (*Judgment—Actors* 36 CAR 673). Rates of pay and conditions set in a 1929 award had been abandoned by agreement in 1932. Lower rates and longer hours were then adopted. Actors Equity now sought a reversion to the 1929 terms. Opposing this, the employers contended that the 'live show' business was still depressed. There was no doubt, said Dethridge, 'that the people in Australia who seek theatrical entertainment have largely abandoned their former demand for "live shows" and seek other kinds of distraction' (p. 674). Any increase in rates was attended with some risk, but those set in 1932 were very low. Dethridge had decided to increase them; but the new amounts would be 'below the present day equivalent of the rates prescribed in my award of 1929'.

Builders' labourers

Drake-Brockman in January 1937 noted that hitherto awards for builders' labourers had provided a uniform margin for all who worked under the awards. The union had now abandoned the principle of uniformity. Drake-Brockman adopted a two-tier structure. A higher classification, with a margin of 12s, would be created 'on the same basis as to margins as assistants to tradesmen under other awards of this Court'. The other classification 'comprises men who at different times perform work varying in value from that of base wage workers up to tradesmen's assistants and a flat rate of 6s per week appears to me to fairly meet the general average value of the work performed by them' (*Judgment—Builders Labourers* 37 CAR 5, 7).

Tally clerks

In February 1937, Beeby made a new award for tally clerks on the waterfront (*Judgment—Tally Clerks* 37 CAR 164). Tally clerks previously had a casual rate of 2s 6½d per hour—the same rate as for waterside workers. Beeby thought that the correct approach was to disregard the waterside workers' award and to fix 'a marginal addition to the basic wage on consideration of the experience, training and knowledge required and the circumstances under which the work is done'. He awarded, without explaining the choice of amount, a margin of £1, added to the six-capitals basic wage to give a total of 88s. (The casual rate for waterside workers was set on the basis that they could expect 30 hours work in a week, implying a notional wage of 75s.)

Metal trades (2)

Also in February 1937, Beeby delivered his decision on a union application to vary the Metal Trades award by further increasing margins (*Variation—Metal*

Trades' Award 37 CAR 176). This decision preceded the 1937 basic wage inquiry. Much evidence had been tendered to demonstrate the improvement in general economic conditions over the previous two years. That evidence, said Beeby, was more appropriate to a basic wage inquiry and he confined his attention to the metal trades group of industries:

> In this area the evidence submitted disclosed marked recovery. Nearly all important firms are now working to full capacity; unemployment has steadily fallen until today employers have difficulty in obtaining skilled men. Competition for the services of high grade mechanics is keen and a substantial number of employees are paid more than the award rates. Some employers, particularly in the moulding section of the industry, owing to pressure which is inevitable when labour is scarce, have agreed with the union to pay increased margins. Nearly all manufacturers are now making profits, the recovery of some of them in this regard being beyond the expectations of 1935. Notwithstanding tariff revisions resulting from the Ottawa agreement employers at present seem able to meet foreign competition and imports are relatively less than in 1929. I therefore feel free to adjudicate on the merits of the applications without, as in the past, being oppressed with the fear of imposing an extra wage cost that may materially reduce manufacture and opportunities for employment. (pp. 182–183)

Beeby recounted that in 1921 Higgins had made the first attempt to bring the major sectors of the engineering industry within a single national award. In doing so, Higgins had fixed a margin of 36s for tradesmen on a basic wage of 84s. 'I have never acceded', said Beeby, 'to the contention that the 1921 award made by Mr Justice Higgins was an extravagant over-valuation of the relative value of the work of skilled and unskilled workmen.' Whether it had been justified in the economic circumstances of the time was a question on which he expressed no opinion. Looking back at his own 1930 award, he said:

> The award made on that occasion was mainly directed to a reclassification of callings to permit freer use of mass production methods in

manufacture. It was not an award made for a normal industry able to meet foreign competition. It was largely of an experimental nature and introduced, particularly into the engineering trade, provisions for the subdivision of labour which had always been strongly resisted by unions of employees. For that reason I never regarded the 1930 award as a reasoned determination of value of skilled and unskilled labour in a normal industry or as a final settlement of other important conditions of employment which affected earnings. (p. 181)

He raised the tradesman's margin by 3s to 30s.[1] In 1935, when Beeby increased the margin from 24s to 27s, he deferred action on margins below the tradesman level. He now increased these lower margins by a uniform 3s. Only the labourer, who remained on the basic wage, received no benefit from this decision.

There were two cautionary terms to the decision. One was to provide for a review after six months (after the outcome of the anticipated basic wage case was known). The other was to indicate that the increases in tradesmen's rates should not be generalised to other awards:

> I have never agreed that margins for skill should be uniform in all occupations. Some callings call for more intensive training and more knowledge than others. Independent investigation of different industries is necessary in assessing margins for degrees of skill, knowledge and experience. My decision in this group of industries is not therefore to be taken as an opinion that margins in all industries should be similarly assessed. I have always regarded skilled mechanics engaged in metal manufacture and in the generation and supply of electric light, heat and power as entitled to somewhat higher margins than those working in wood and other fabrics. While routine work in all skilled occupations may for purposes of wage assessment be similar, the metal turner and fitter and the electrician must acquire knowledge and exercise precision appreciably greater than usually required. (p. 183)

---

[1] The six-capitals basic wage at the time was 78s. Thus the tradesman's rate was fixed at 1.38 times the labourer's rate. In *Harvester*, Higgins set a tradesman's wage of 10s per day—1.43 times the labourer's rate of 7s.

This clearly conflicted with Dethridge's reluctance to differentiate between apprentice-based trades. It may have been because of Beeby's caution that his 1937 decision for the metal trades did not generally flow to other industries, but it is also likely that Dethridge and Drake-Brockman thought that Beeby had gone too far. I return below to this matter.[2]

Drake-Brockman, in March 1937, applied Beeby's decision to metal trades grades within the Victorian railways (*Variation—Metal Trades' Award, Victorian Railways* 37 CAR 209). He noted the improved financial performance of Victoria's railways and was even more impressed by the better budgetary position of the State government. Evidently feeling liberated from financial constraint, Drake-Brockman moved to a commentary on wage differences:

> I have been impressed from time to time with the fact that since industrial tribunals were established in Australia, there has been quite a considerable tendency to level up the wages of the unskilled and the semi-skilled without a corresponding improvement in the wages of skilled employees. The general tendency has been to bring them nearer together in amount. I think that this is regrettable, and it is desirable if possible to restore, as far as can be done, the relative payments that were paid for the skill of the types of employees concerned. (p. 210)

In May 1937, he had to decide whether to apply the Beeby increases to the South Australian Railways (*Variation—South Australian Railways Metal Trades Grades Award* 37 CAR 431). The union application for higher margins was opposed by the Commissioner for Railways on the grounds of adverse railway and State finances. But Drake-Brockman recalled that in 1935 and 1936 he had refused to allow the union to present evidence in support of claims that went beyond the terms of the general metal trades award. He may well have caused the union to understand that matching any movement in metals would be a formality. 'Accordingly', he said, 'I think that I cannot refuse the

---

[2] Beeby did not refer in his judgment to the existence of over-award payments in the metal trades. But it is known that over-award payments of 3s were common (see Chapter 8, Section 8.1).

application of the unions for corresponding increases to those recently granted by Judge Beeby in the Metal Trades industry generally' (p. 433).

Metal trades (3)

In August 1937, Beeby returned to metal trades issues, consistent with his limitation of the February decision to six months (*Variation—Metal Trades Awards* 38 CAR 328). The Full Court had increased the basic wage (in New South Wales, Victoria and Queensland) by 3s in July, with a further increase of 3s to take effect in October. 'The main point for consideration in these proceedings', said Beeby, 'is whether the wage level which will be reached in October next will be beyond the capacity of the industries involved.' The employers did not contend that it would, but were apprehensive of the future, foreseeing an increase in import competition from British producers. Beeby was unmoved: 'I do not think that the Court should reduce wage levels merely in anticipation of some future possible change in economic circumstances' (p. 331). It is unclear what *might* have happened in the basic wage case that would have caused him to reverse or modify his February decision about margins.

Textiles

Beeby made a new award for the textile industry in December 1937 (*Judgment—Textile Workers* 38 CAR 791). In doing so, he took a more conservative position than for the metal trades. Textiles had made reasonable progress since the Depression, but there was evidence of a reduction of employment over the previous few months. This evidence 'was sufficient to justify the [employers'] contention that the granting of claims resulting in serious increase of production costs might retard future progress'. Beeby found it impossible

> to entertain seriously the union's claim for all-round increases in wage rates on top of the recent basic wage fixation. As the commodities produced are used by all classes of the community retail prices largely control consumption. The industry is one of those in which an

appreciable rise in retail prices inevitably results in reduced consumption. Articles of every-day clothing, usually, can be made to last a little longer if prices are increased. The two main determinants of prices are cost of raw material used and wage cost. The former has been on the up grade for the past two years while the wage level has been raised by the Full Court's recent basic wage fixation. (p. 793)

In this case, then, the basic wage increase emerged as an obstacle to increases in margins. 'The marginal allowances for skill and experience' appeared to Beeby 'to be on the low side.' Average earnings, however, were augmented by piecework. Beeby's main concern was for 'the small groups of employees in all mills who must of necessity work on time rates, and therefore on the margins prescribed can earn very little above the basic wage'. Machine processes which required no long period of training could not carry margins much above the basic wage. But the employees performing these tasks became more valuable with experience. Some, but not all, employers recognised this. 'I therefore sought', said Beeby,

> some way of securing an allowance above marginal rates for experience, and in the draft minutes submitted a proposal that certain groups should be paid an experience allowance. From the comments made, after further reflection I fear that the proposal might not achieve the purpose in view. The industry is so competitive that many employers, particularly in slack times, would probably give preference to employees of shorter experience. ... I with reluctance have decided that the extra cost of the proposed allowance for experience at present cannot be imposed. I, however, commend to employers the wisdom of a wide extension of merit increases to married men on low margins. If this advice is unheeded, I will entertain application for allowances for experience after these awards have been in operation for twelve months. (pp. 793–794)

We may note the irony of Beeby's concern about 'married men on low margins' in a predominantly female industry.

Glue and gelatine workers

In April 1938, Beeby made a new award for the glue and gelatine industry (*Judgment—Glue and Gelatine Workers* 39 CAR 104). There was only one respondent: Davis Gelatine (Aust) Ltd. The work—often wet—had serious disabilities which had not been fully recognised in pay rates:

> When margins were fixed in 1934 the Commonwealth was emerging from the depression and as Davis Gelatine (Aust) Ltd was finding difficulty in securing markets for its products I deliberately refrained from imposing any increased wage cost which might materially affect its operations. On this occasion I am freed of this restraint. The company with an expanding business now carries only normal stocks and is prosperous. I think that considering the disabilities of the work and the responsibility which at times rests on most of the employees there should be a minimum margin of 6s … with maintenance of the grades above that margin as in the existing award. This means an all-round increase of 3s per week. (p. 105)

The highest margin under the new award was 8s. With the basic wage increase and the higher margins, the workers employed by Davis enjoyed total wage increases during a ten-month period of 9s, or more than 12 per cent.

Boot trade

Beeby made an award for the boot trade in September 1938 (*Consolidated Award—Boot Trades* 39 CAR 940). Wages in this industry, originally set by Higgins, had long been depressed by foreign competition, which was now alleviated (and could be countered further) by tariffs:

> The fear that increased wage costs would directly lead to increased importations undoubtedly influenced the learned judge in not bringing wage rates more into line with those of other skilled trades. Assuming that importations can now be kept within reasonable limits and that any increase in local prices is not sufficient to reduce consumption, there is no reason why workers in this industry should not begin to emerge

from the backwash into which they were forced twenty years ago. ... I do not think that the danger of influx of foreign products is sufficient to deter the Court from prescribing what it deems to be proper wage rates and conditions of employment for the industry, and feel confident that the Tariff Board will recommend such tariff re-adjustments as may be necessary. (pp. 946 and 948)

The principal impediment to profitability in the industry was, not foreign competition, but 'excessive competition between factories'; and 'the Court can and does say that living standards of employees should not be depressed because of business methods for which they are not responsible' (pp. 949 and 950). I refer in the next subsection to Beeby's evaluation of the work in this industry.

Furnishing

In October 1938, Drake-Brockman dealt with a union application for an all-round increase of 3s in margins in the furnishing trades (*Variation—Furniture Trade Awards* 39 CAR 1051). In 1928, when he had classified the employees in the industry, he awarded to some of the classifications margins equal to those of tradesmen in the metal trades. These classifications continued to have a margin of 24s, which Drake-Brockman now increased to 27s. That, as we have seen, was the tradesman's margin in the metal trades set by Beeby in 1935. Drake-Brockman did not adopt, or even comment upon, the margin of 30s set by Beeby in 1927. He refused any increase to workers on margins below 24s.

Stonemasons

Dethridge in November 1937 confronted explicitly the question whether the 30s margin in metals should be applied to another trade—in this case stonemasons (*Judgment—Stonemasons (Victoria and South Australia)* 39 CAR 1129). He acknowledged that the craft required apprenticeship of five or six years. The Stonemasons' Society sought a margin of 30s, but the employers contended that it should be 27s—'the amount now assessed for carpenters in this Court's award'. Dethridge continued:

> In my opinion the margin for skill should not be assessed only upon a judge's comparison of the degree of skill in question with that of another vocation—he must also consider the question whether the proposed amount of any marginal wage will tend seriously to prevent the community from purchasing the products of that skill. If it is likely to have that effect that objection outweighs any opinion he may have that the skill in question is so high as to make the proposed amount desirable. Inasmuch as the mason's craft is one of about a five-year apprenticeship prima facie the margin should not be less than 27s per week. But I am not satisfied that it should be assessed at a higher rate than that of the carpenter. ... More important than my opinion as to skill is the likely decline in the demand for mason's work. The present economic position in Australia indicates that we are about to suffer a decline in building activity particularly of that class in which masons are required. Already stone work is subject to the keenest competition from substitutes. In the monumental section of the industry also demand seems to be falling and cheaper moulded substitutes are displacing the mason's work. For these reasons I think that I should not assess the mason's margin for skill at more than 27s per week. (p. 1130)

Dethridge here advances two reasons for rejecting the 30s standard: (1) the doubtful market prospects for the products of the stonemasons' work; and (2) the carpenters' rate of 27s. He makes no direct comparison, in either respect, with metal tradesmen. There is a strong suspicion that Dethridge (and probably Drake-Brockman) disagreed with Beeby's second round of metal trades increases. There was no possibility of appeal from the decision of a single Judge about margins, and the only available way of indicating disapproval was to decline to follow his decision.

Rope and cordage

In June 1939, Beeby made a new award for rope and cordage workers (*Award—Rope and Cordage Workers* 40 CAR 347). The industry had last been reviewed in 1935, when 'employers produced balance sheets which convinced me that at that time appreciable additions to wage costs were inadvisable'. The position had improved, the employers now tendered no balance sheets, and 'I was free to regard the industry as one which had regained normal prosperity'. Beeby could therefore 'increase marginal allowances and female and junior wage rates to the level which I would have established four years ago but for financial reasons'. The margins set ranged up to 22s, but there was no explicit discussion of the amounts chosen.

12.1.2 Work value

In the less-constrained circumstances of the later 1930s, there was a return to the practice of identifying the 'worth' of particular jobs, especially on a comparative basis. I have already referred to some decisions wherein commentary on the nature of the work performed was combined with an assessment of the economic condition of the industry concerned in justification of increased rates. Beeby, for example, took both factors into account in his metal trades decisions.

Tanning

In February 1935, Beeby made a new award for the tanning section of the saddlery industry (*Judgment—Saddlery Industry (Tanning Section)* 34 CAR 111). In the existing consent award, made in 1928, there was an industry margin of 1s 6d, justified by the wet and offensive conditions of work and the irregularity of employment. The unions sought to increase this to 6s. Beeby granted an industry margin of 3s 6d. This reflected the requirements of the work:

> The specialised processes which have superseded the work of curriers are by no means purely mechanical. In many of them the machine is in

reality a tool of trade, the product of which depends on the manipulation of the operative. While no high measure of skill may often be necessary, experience increases the value of the operation. I have always acted on the principle that the operative, even when on a purely mechanical machine, should get some margin above the basic wage. When the machine is not purely mechanical, but is a tool of trade, margins should be fixed according to the judgment and experience which the operative requires to give a satisfactory output.

Rope and cordage

Beeby, in his judgment of May 1935 about the rope and cordage industry, commented on the idea of relating margins to experience. He noted that there was little turnover of labour in the industry:

> I have always considered that long service, if it is widely prevalent in an industry, should be considered in fixing margins, but find it difficult to arrive at any principle of assessment. If margins are graded according to years of service the jobs of old hands might become insecure. Then again employers who might be inclined to recognise long service are afraid that concessions voluntarily made may be used against them in application for all-round wage increases. I think it unwise to state any fixed amount as an extra wage for increased value of labour arising from long service, but in fixing margins have taken this feature of the industry into consideration. (*Award—Rope and Cordage Workers* 34 CAR 355, 356)

Bus and tram drivers

In May 1935, Drake-Brockman considered the relative pay of bus drivers and tram drivers:

> With regard to the drivers of the buses, I am impressed with the fact that they are called upon to exercise slightly more skill and undergo slightly more strain, and are under the necessity of taking appropriate cautions for the protection of the public who ride in the buses, in a way

slightly different from that which is imposed upon the driver of a tram. (*Variation—Tramway Employees' Award* 34 CAR 447, 448)

Tram drivers had a ten-year incremental scale. Drake-Brockman decided that the bus driver's wage should correspond to the maximum wage of tram drivers.

Engine drivers and firemen

In June 1935 Beeby dealt with margins for engine drivers and firemen (*Judgment—Engine Drivers and Firemen* 35 CAR 1). He was unwilling to treat the existing margins simply as a platform to be raised in response to improvement in trading conditions. Those margins had come about, in part, because of the union's exercise of the bargaining strength conferred on it by the strategic role of its members:

> The union being dissatisfied with Sir John Quick's [1924] award, under the able leadership of their late secretary, Mr Gibson, adopted a clever campaign of isolating employers. Apart from the slight improvement of conditions secured, particularly in Victoria, as the result of strikes, various firms were induced to make agreements rather than have trouble with a small group of their employees who held key positions. The actual wage cost involved was small when compared with total wages paid. Employers were evidently willing to pay extra rates to secure contentment in their engine-rooms. The union undoubtedly made the best of this strategic advantage ... These agreements, while they must be considered in arriving at a common award, cannot be accepted as a deliberate assessment by the parties of the status of engine-drivers in the industrial world or of the value of their labour. (p. 4)

The engine-driver's work had, in fact, been simplified by improvements of equipment: automatic lubrication, automatic feeding of fires and improvements in the construction of engines and their auxiliaries had lessened the work done. In terms of the skill and training required, existing margins 'would appear to be liberal'. But the work also carried significant responsibility for the protection of both life and property. There was agreement that the margins of some of the lower grades ought to be increased.

High-tension linesmen

In July 1935, Drake-Brockman granted increased margins to high-tension linesmen, taking into account their skill, the risks of their work, and experience:

> It is true that they have not been apprenticed to any particular trade, and that they have acquired their knowledge, which is admitted to be very considerable and useful, in the ordinary course of their occupation. It is admitted on all sides that there is a considerable hazard attached to their occupation, and in my view the degree of skill required in the work itself and the hazard inseparable from a great deal of that work, entitles them to a higher rate of pay than is provided for other linemen. I think, moreover, that the value to the department of these men substantially increases with increasing experience, and, to some extent, I propose to recognise that and to make provision for it. I intend, therefore, to include in my award provision that these men on first appointment as linemen shall receive 3s 4d per day by way of margin, and that after twelve months they shall receive 4s 4d per day. (*Variation—Metal Trades Victorian Railways' Award* 35 CAR 118, 119)

Thus the high-tension linesman's margin was equal (after a year's experience) to 26s per week—fractionally below the normal rate for apprenticed tradesmen.

Motor bodies (1)

In the motor bodies' case of 1935, discussed in Subsection 12.1.1, Beeby was asked to grant an allowance of 5s in recognition of intermittency of employment in the motor body and coach making industry. In his decision, given in December 1935, he refused this claim, distinguishing between types of intermittency:

> Where, owing to fluctuations in trade, some employees in an industry are dismissed until trade revives, it is impossible to provide them with a full year's earnings by an increased rate applying to all. If the employees are expected to stand by and immediately answer a call to resume work,

as in the knitting section of the textile trade, a lost time allowance should be made. But that does not occur to an appreciable extent in this industry. As in the metal, building and most other trades, hands are from time to time shortened and men must seek other employment. This loss of time and earnings for which workmen are not directly responsible is a social injustice which can only be remedied by some form of unemployment insurance, and not by granting increased wage rates to those whose employment is continuous as well as to those who lose time. (*Judgment—Motor Body and Coach Building Industry* 35 CAR 599, 602)

Beeby also rejected an attempt to reclassify tasks so as to reduce margins in recognition of the 'assembly-line' nature of the work:

> Observations on inspections convinced me that specialised processes 'on the chain' were entirely different from assembling as defined in the Metal Trades award. The difference arises when tools of trade are used. The employers' proposed classifications which would in the end de-grade great numbers of tradesmen to the ranks of superior process workers have therefore been rejected. (p. 609)

Agricultural implements

Similarly, in April 1936, Beeby decided that the provisions of the award for agricultural implements should be aligned with those of the metal trades award:

> I see no reason why the Metal Trades award, with certain variations to meet peculiar circumstances, should not be applied to this industry in the two States [Victoria and South Australia] in which disputes exist. The industry is a manufacturing one in which skill has been modified or eliminated in many processes by modern mass production methods. But as in motor body building, skill of varying degrees is necessary in many processes. (*Judgment—Agricultural Implement, etc Industry* 36 CAR 39, 44)

In so deciding, Beeby overturned earlier findings that tradesmen's work in argricultural implements demanded less in skill than ordinary metal trades work (see Chapter 6, Subsection 6.2.2).

Motor bodies (2)

Dethridge in October 1936 reviewed the margin of 'dent-knockers' under the motor body and coach building award. The margin for the second-class panel beater, or dent-knocker, was too high for work performed in connection with garnish moulds. That was one side of the picture. On the other side,

> I do not think the work can fairly be called vyceman's work … The mere fact that the article, during some of these operations, or part of these operations, has to be fixed in a vyce, does not bring it appropriately into the class of vyceman's work as generally understood. … But at the same time the work is not only filing or hammering. … A certain amount of experience and dexterity are required to get rid of the warping, if I may call it so, in the metal, and to get the material to the proper shape after removing that warping, or bending, or whatever it may be called. The margin of 12s having regard to the dexterity required for the removal of such warping or denting as there is, is somewhat on the low side. I think it is more than mere repetitive filing, and work requiring some dexterity and judgment, which is hardly covered by the margin of 12s at present being paid. (*Variation—Motor Body and Coach Building Award* 36 CAR 525, 526)

What was required was a new classification: 'One cannot compute with mathematical exactness a margin, but an estimate by comparison with other work has to be made. I propose to fix a margin of 17s per week for the work in question.'

Radio employees

Drake-Brockman in March 1937 made the first award for professional radio employees. 'The work and operations of the several radio stations concerned varies considerably', he said. 'I have therefore classified the stations into four groups and provided rates of pay for technical staffs varying in accordance with the station classification which I think meets the requirements of the circumstances indicated and the differing degrees of skill and responsibility involved' (*Judgment—Professional Radio Employees* 37 CAR 215, 216). For each category of radio station there would be three grades—technician in charge, technician, and control-room operator.[3] The margins ranged from 75s for the technician in charge in grade A stations to 30s for control-room operators in grade D (p. 219). The decision contains no discussion of the actual amounts chosen.

Aircraft manufacture

In July 1938, Beeby made an award for another 'new' industry—aircraft manufacture. The award prescribed higher rates than those prevailing in the metal trades. Fitters, for example, were awarded a margin of 33s (*Judgment—Aircraft Manufacturing* 39 CAR 512). In June 1939, Beeby varied the award (*Variation—Aircraft Industry Award* 40 CAR 471). The Civil Aviation Board provided for examination of employees after two years on aircraft construction. Employees could then be licensed to certify the airworthiness of fuselages, engines, instruments, and electrical equipment. Tradesmen so licensed were awarded a margin of 45s.

Timber workers

When Dethridge made the timber workers' award in April 1937, most of the award had been settled by agreement—a far cry from the experiences of the 1920s, when timber workers were at the heart of industrial disputation. The union had sought a general industry addition of 3s, but Dethridge did not think this justified. The union then argued for a 3s margin for block stackers, orderman's assistants, yard labourers, pullers out on machines, and employees in vats and steaming chambers. 'I think', said Dethridge, 'that block stackers are required to use a slight degree of skill and care which entitles them to a

---

[3] 'Technician-in-charge' was not included for the lowest category of stations.

small margin of 2s, but that none of the others are so entitled' (*Judgment—Timber Workers* 37 CAR 273, 277). An increase from 21s to 24s in the margin of some machinists was made largely so as to conform to margins prescribed in the furniture trades and motor body and coach building awards of the Court. Those machinists who set up their machines received an increase of 6s to 8s, 'because I think any setting up of such machines deserves the higher amount'. Other changes were made 'because they appear to me to be fair in the circumstances and a similar comment applies where no change is made' (pp. 278–279).[4]

Woolclassers on stations

Woolclassers working on stations were outside the Court's awards until July 1937, when Dethridge set rates for them (*Judgment—Woolclassers* 38 CAR 68). In the awards for textile workers and wool stores, margins of 21s and 18s, respectively, applied to woolclassers. But the woolclasser on a station was different in that he was 'vested with much greater responsibility and is also required to exercise a considerable degree of supervision over other employees':

> He is entrusted with the duty of so classing and separating the component parts of the clip as to make its get-up attractive at the wool sales. And he has to so arrange the work of the employees under him—the pickers-up, fleece-rollers and pressers—as to facilitate the procuring of the most satisfactory get-up. The satisfactory performance of these functions depends entirely upon his own judgment cultivated by such an amount of training and experience as will enable him to make his decisions speedily and accurately. It is conceded that his work is important. One evidence of this is that the important wool broking firms for the purpose of assisting them in arranging their wool sales obtain reports

---

[4] In December 1937, Dethridge fixed margins in the timber workers' award in relation to the production of sporting goods. 'Some of the margins', he said, 'have been assessed by the parties in negotiation. The others are assessed by myself endeavouring to maintain a fair relative proportion having regard to my estimate of the skill, etc, involved' (*Variation—Timber Workers Award (Re Sporting Goods)* 38 CAR 686, 687).

from woolclassers concerning the clips classed by them and also make suggestions to them about the future classing of particular clips. (p. 69)

The rates were fixed per thousand sheep shorn, precluding an exact identification of a margin; but the guaranteed minimum earnings of woolclassers on stations ranged from £7 5s to £8 5s (p. 78). For the times, these were high wages, implying that Dethridge gave much weight to the aspects of responsibility outlined in his decision.

Road construction

Dethridge drew the line against margin 'creep' in a decision of July 1938 about road construction (*Judgment—Road Construction, etc Workers* 39 CAR 859). In doing so, he rejected any presumption that all basic wage work was or should be equal. A strong appeal had been made for a margin for 'the pick and shovel man'. Dethridge commented:

> It is true that he has to work exposed to the wind and sun and his toil is more arduous than that of other adult males who receive the same basic wage as he gets. But a man of average strength can do pick and shovel work without any training, and he has not to exercise any judgment or responsibility or incur unusual risk or work in noxious surroundings. Some definite attribute of this kind must exist to justify a margin in the practice of the Court otherwise awards would abound with inconsistencies. It is true that some unskilled work less arduous than that of the pick and shovel man is awarded the same basic wage by the Court, but this is because the basic wage is adopted as a minimum not as a measure of the relative value of different sorts of unskilled work, but for reasons of general social welfare. (p. 864)

Such a policy was, of course, implicit in the decisions of Higgins and Powers, but it had been eroded during the 1920s by the spread of small margins paid to workers of low skill. The 'pick and shovel man' must have been close to the limiting case. Had a margin been conceded, the basic wage would have retained little credibility as an actual wage in payment.

Bank officials

The relation between the basic wage and 'skill' was also considered by Piper in a decision about banking published in June 1938 (*Judgment—Bank Officials* 29 CAR 1012). As we have noted, Quick had structured the incremental scale for male bank clerks so that the 21-year-old clerk received the basic wage (at the time of the award). Did this imply that the 21-year-old clerk had no skill?

> In Sir John Quick's judgment there is neither a discussion of nor a finding on the question whether the bank clerk of 21 years of age has acquired any skill or not. But his wage seems to have been fixed on the assumption that at that age he has not sufficiently mastered the duties which he may be called upon to perform during his career as a bank clerk to be called 'skilled'. It seems a necessary conclusion from the close relation of their wages that this Court has found that the clerk at 21 years of age has attained only the same degree of ability in his vocation as that possessed by any unskilled navvy in an industry in which brawn and muscle earn the wage rather than brain and hands. In other words this Court has acted on the principle that a bank clerk of 21 years of age is unskilled. If this conclusion is not correct one would expect to find that the adult bank clerk would have been given a higher minimum wage than the unskilled navvy. ... I realise of course that an unskilled navvy if suddenly called upon to perform the duties of a bank clerk of 21 years of age would be unable to perform them with any degree of efficiency, but on the other hand, the same result would follow if the bank clerk were suddenly called upon to do the work of the navvy. Both require a certain amount of knowledge and ability in their respective spheres. ... The basic wage is designed to protect all classes of unskilled adult employees irrespective of the type of unskilled work they have to perform or of the industry in which they perform it. (pp. 1024–1025)

Piper did not consider—in this case it was unnecessary for him to do so—the position outlined by Dethridge in the *Road Construction* case: that 'unskilled' workers receiving the basic wage need not be equally unskilled.

Batteries

In his August 1937 review of the metal trades award, Beeby referred to the specific case of wet-battery making, which he had excluded from the increased margins awarded in the previous February. In the interim, he had thought about the reasons, related to health, which had originally caused him to award these workers more than process workers under the award:

> I was satisfied then that the element of actual danger had been removed, but in spite of that the occupation was unhealthy. It was not a mere fancied unhealthiness, but a definite atmosphere which kept the men a little below par and compelled them to take special precautions to maintain ordinary health. For that reason, I decided they were entitled to margins substantially above those of ordinary process workers. (*Variation—Metal Trades Awards* 38 CAR 328, 334)

Beeby could now see no reason why the wet-battery margins should not be increased to preserve the previous relation with the margins of process workers.

Boot trades

Beeby, in his decision of September 1938 for the boot trades (discussed in the previous subsection), compared the skill requirements of this and other industries:

> It was not disputed that bootmaking is a skilled trade—skilled in the sense that knowledge of the qualities of materials used and high manipulative ability acquired by years of experience is necessary in most of the processes. ... On inspection I was impressed by the candour of some large employers of labour. One stated voluntarily that the trouble in the trade was that its margins had always been too low. With wage rates nearer those of other skilled trades a better type of workman would have been attracted to the industry. ... From the employees' point of view boot manufacturing has always been the Cinderella of skilled trades. ... Trades in which skill is only manipulative cannot, of course, be on the same footing as those which also call for mental effort, such

as engineering, electrical and carpentering. But boot operatives, with justice, claim that at least they should be on a higher level than the ordinary run of semi-skilled workers. (*Consolidated Award—Boot Trades* 39 CAR 940, 945–946)

For 27 years there had been a flat marginal rate in the award (then 12s), and the union wished to preserve the flat-rate principle. The employers, on the other hand, asked the Court to impose 'an elaborate classification of margins', which Beeby rejected:

> The employers' claim … sought to impose on the Court the impossible task of assessing the comparative value of almost every process. Where a product in course of manufacture passes from one trained operative to another, where all processes call for the same speed and vigilance and where most of the processes are entrusted to tradesmen or apprentices, such refinement of classification would be both unjust and impracticable. … Relative value of work could not be determined by mere observance of processes. (p. 950)

Beeby concluded that due recognition of levels of skills implied that, for some tasks, margins would have to fall. The minimum margin would be 9s; the maximum (and predominant) margin, 18s (p. 950).

Rubber

We have noted in passing various instances of Judges fixing margins without providing more than superficial explanations of the amounts chosen. Another example is Drake-Brockman's decision of November 1938 about the rubber industry (*Judgment—Rubber Workers* 39 CAR 1098). He pointed out that the parties had not reached agreement about margins. The following is, in its entirety, his commentary on the amounts prescribed:

> These margins have been fixed by me. They do not embody very substantial departure from the margins heretofore obtaining. The few alterations in the amounts now made should bring the respective

Harold Piper

margins into a better relationship *inter se* having regard to the skill necessary for the performance of the respective operations concerned. (p. 1099)

The margins set were thus a product of previous practice and unexplained judgments about the need for modification.

Health inspectors

In December 1938, Piper increased the salaries of health inspectors because of the increased demands of their positions (*Judgment—Health Inspectors* 39 CAR 1301). The control of public health had become more rigorous; the work of prevention of disease and limiting its spread had become more onerous;

and the public, whose conscience on health matters had been aroused, was becoming more reliant on the inspectors. 'It is not claimed', said Piper, 'that health inspectors in fact work longer hours than formerly but I think that the present position may be summarised as follows—that compared with 1927–1928 the health inspectors have been given a more prominent place in the public life of the community and this entails greater responsibility, greater preparation for the position, a wider knowledge and further study in matters pertaining to health' (p. 1309).

Train drivers

The relative job requirements of drivers of electric and steam trains were considered by Drake-Brockman in February 1939 (*Variation—Locomotive Enginemen's Award* 40 CAR 65). The existing margins of steam train drivers were higher than those of electric train drivers, but the union wished to raise the electric drivers' margin to the level of the steam drivers'. On several previous occasions, Drake-Brockman had refused such requests 'because I have not been convinced that the same measure of skill has been required by the electric train driver as has been required by the steam locomotive driver' (p. 65). Moreover, he had been influenced by the stated attitude of the Victorian Railways Commissioners about the recruitment of the two kinds of drivers, which implied that less skill was required to drive electric trains. The Commissioners, however, had not acted on this basis. Rather, their recruitment practice implied that the electric train driver 'did in fact require the skill and particularly the road sense that is required by the steam locomotive engine driver'. For this reason, he proposed to raise the electric train driver's margin to equality with the steam driver's (the margin would be 4s per day in the first year, rising to 8s in the sixth (p. 66)).

Meat

In May 1939, Beeby made a new award for the meat industry (*Judgment—Meat Industry* 40 CAR 192). Among the issues to be determined was the margin for general butchers working in shops. The existing margin was 18s 6d, including allowance for clothing. The union sought a margin of 27s plus a clothing allowance of 7s 6d. In Beeby's view, the work was not such as to merit the margin paid to skilled mechanics. But it was definitely skilled work:

> Employers who gave evidence were almost unanimous in their opinion that it took from four to five years to turn out a reasonably competent general butcher. In cutting without waste—getting the maximum quantity of saleable meat from a carcass and making the final product attractive—more skill and longer experience are necessary than is popularly supposed. In addition to this a majority of employees are called on to act as salesmen and for that period to purchase, launder and maintain white coats and aprons. (p. 193)

Beeby awarded 24s for shopmen and 21s for butchers not required to serve (inclusive of allowance for clothing and knives).

Summary

The members of the Court, freed to some extent from economic restraints, resumed in this period the traditional practice of evaluating jobs by processes of comparison—both vertical and horizontal. With few exceptions, however, there was little attention to the nature of the wage structure that the Court had produced. The exceptions included Beeby's concerns about the relative position of the tradesman and Drake-Brockman's more broadly expressed regret about the degree of compression of relativities. In neither case was there a consideration of underlying economic forces which may have tended to render earlier relativities obsolete. The Act, the method of procedure and, perhaps, the lawyer's mind did not lend themselves to the raising of issues relevant to the demand and supply for different levels of skill. Attention to 'work value' in terms of the characteristics of jobs militated against a broader policy of wage relativities.

12.1.3 The aggregate impact

It is impossible to quantify precisely the contribution of higher margins to the increase in wages in the pre-war years. The following calculations, however, may throw some light on the matter. The *Labour Report* provides data of the rates applying for particular occupations. I have selected eight low-wage occupations, and compared the rates applying on 31 December 1934 and 31 December 1939.[5] The comparison is limited to Melbourne to minimise (but not eliminate) complications arising from the operation of State awards and determinations. Over the five-year period, the (unweighted) average increase in wages for these jobs was 11s 11d. The average increase in Victoria, for all occupations covered by the nominal wage index, was 14s 9d (*Labour Reports*, No. 25 (1934), pp. 149–158; No. 30 (1939), pp. 57 and 167–176). A tentative inference is that increases in the basic wage accounted for about four-fifths of the overall rise in wages, with higher margins representing the balance.

12.2 STANDARD HOURS

As we saw in Section 10.5 of Chapter 10, the question of working hours returned—to a limited degree—to the Court's agenda in 1933 and 1934. In the next five years, the piecemeal transition to the 44-hour week gathered pace. A significant impetus to this process, at least in the earlier years, was the operation of the shorter week in New South Wales State awards.

An early case involved railways. Drake-Brockman, in March 1935, gave a decision for the daily paid general grades in the New South Wales railways (*Judgment—Daily Paid General Trades, New South Wales Railways* 34 CAR 209). The unions and the railways had been negotiating the terms of awards, but had reached a deadlock on the matter of hours. Ordinarily, a decision about hours would be reserved to the Full Court, but the parties had agreed to Drake-Brockman acting as a private arbitrator and undertook to accept his

---

[5] The occupations are: sawmilling labourers; agricultural implements—labourers; aerated waters—packers; confectionery—storemen; pastrycooking—carters; textiles—general labourers; tanning and currying—linemen and yardmen; railway porters (minimum).

decision. He decided that in the awards concerned the working week should be reduced from 48 to 44 hours. He was much influenced by the fact that two-thirds of the railway employees already worked a 44-hour week under State awards. The difference between awards was a cause of serious discontent (pp. 210–211). But he also took note of an improvement in the financial outlook. The railways' deficit had decreased from £4.5 million in 1931–32 to £1.5 million in 1933–34. The continuing, but smaller, loss led Drake-Brockman to say:

> When considering railways finances it is impossible to altogether divorce them from the finances of the State because railway services are in a very great measure created for the purpose of development, and have not to any extent been provided or run as business enterprises. In the circumstances, it is almost inevitable that they should be run at a loss, and that that loss should be borne by the State Treasury. (p. 212)

The State deficit had fallen from £14 million to £3 million, despite a £6 million reduction of taxes. Financial stress was no longer an insurmountable obstacle to the reduction of hours. In the following July, Drake-Brockman (acting again as a private arbitrator) granted the 44-hour week to daily paid workers in the New South Wales tramways. There were, he said, about 2000 people whose hours were regulated, 'half of whom have been working 44 and the other half 48 hours a week which, of course, is absurd' (*Award—New South Wales Tramways Daily Paid Grades (Australian Railways Union) (Other than Traffic Section)* 34 CAR 744).

The Full Court in June 1935 granted the 44-hour week to coachmakers employed by the Commonwealth Railways. The case of plumbers and carpenters working for this employer was more complex, leading to a mixed outcome:

> In the other railway systems of the various States the practice as to the working hours of these tradesmen is fixed, as to carpenters, by Federal or State awards, and as to plumbers by State awards or determinations. No consistent principle can be found governing the hours for these tradesmen working in connexion with the railways. On the

Commonwealth railways covered by this award, when working outside they frequently collaborate with men working a 48-hour week, and we think this fact is important so far as outside work is concerned. On the other hand, when working in the Commonwealth Railways Workshop, their conditions seem to be substantially similar to those of other workshop employees who have a 44-hour week. For the purpose of this particular award we think the working week of these tradesmen should be 44 when working in the workshop and 48 when working outside. (*Variation—Commonwealth Railways Award* 34 CAR 688, 689–690)

On the next day, the Full Court awarded 44 hours to woodworkers in New South Wales 'because in the furniture-making industry in New South Wales 44 hours is the prevalent working week and has been very largely assented to by the employers in that trade' (*Variation—Timber Workers' Award* 34 CAR 692).

In December 1935, the Full Court delivered a number of 'hours' decisions on a single day. It granted the 44-hour week to gas industry workers (*Variation—Gas Employees' Awards and Agreements* 35 CAR 684), adult males in the rope and cordage industry (*Rope and Cordage Award—Variation (Hours)* 35 CAR 693) and furniture trades workers (*Variation—Furniture Trades' Award* 35 CAR 699). In the case of timber workers, the Court was of the opinion that

> no substantial distinction can be made between [their] work and other work for which the Court has prescribed a 44-hour week. The question to be determined therefore is whether any reduction of the working hours prescribed by this award should be made having regard to existing financial considerations. … [Financial documents provided to the Court] show that the industry has suffered greatly during the depression. That it is now improving but has as yet on the whole only a very moderate degree of prosperity. We think that there will probably be some increase in its welfare but the prospect is not such as to warrant a present reduction of the ordinary working hours from 48 to 44 per week. Some reduction can, however, in our opinion, be made without imperilling the stability of those engaged in the industry. We have

concluded that the proper order here is that the award be varied so as to substitute a 46-hour week for the present 48. (*Variation—Timber Workers' Award* 35 CAR 696, 697)

Further consideration would be given to hours in this industry after two years. The Court also decided that the nature and condition of the work of employees in agricultural implement manufacture 'entitle them to a shorter week at least as much as any other section of the metal trades industry to which the reduction has been allowed', but its consideration of the financial position of the industry led it to conclude that it could not, 'without serious risk of injury to the parties concerned', reduce hours below 46 per week (*Standard Hours— Agricultural Implement, etc Industry* 35 CAR 707, 708).[6] In South Australia, the 46-hour week for workers in the agricultural implements industry would come into effect in March 1938. The Court returned in October 1937 to the question of standard hours in agricultural implement manufacture. It now decided to reduce the working week to 44 hours with effect from March 1938, except in South Australia, where the 46-hour week was to take effect in March 1938 and 44 hours would apply from March 1939.

Having 'given careful thought to the evidence as to the nature of the work of railway employees and also as to the financial position of the South Australian Railways', the Court refused to reduce hours below 96 per fortnight.[7] (*Variation—Railway Daily Paid Grades Award (South Australia)* 35 CAR 686)

The Full Court in January 1936 dealt with an application by the Electrical Trades' Union seeking the 44-hour week for those of its members covered by the metal trades award who did not so far enjoy it. It undertook a case-by-case examination of the various classifications of workers, with the implication that there needed to be something about the work to justify the shorter hours. In the case of linesmen, for example, it said:

---

[6] The reduction was deferred until 1 July 1936, except for South Australia, where it was deferred until 1 July 1938. Early in 1936, the parties to the railways' award in Tasmania agreed to reduce hours from 96 per fortnight to 44 per week (*Award—Daily Paid and Salaried Grades, Tasmanian Railways* 35 CAR 766, 767).

[7] For some employees, even the 96-hour fortnight constituted a reduction of hours. This reduction was deferred until 1 July 1936.

> If linesmen were required to work upon the standards or poles substantially the whole of their time, there would be no question that the 44-hour week should be allowed. The evidence shows that probably they do not average more than 6 hours a day upon the standards. Some portion of their time is spent upon preparatory work, and a portion in travelling to or from the job. All of them have to do some work close to high tension wires but the proportion of such work varies greatly; such work is nerve racking and adds weight to the claim for the 44-hour week. The relative amounts of live-wire work will probably increase with increasing congestion of service. Efforts to reduce time spent in travelling and in preparatory work will tend to become more successful. On the whole we think the case for a 44-hour week for the linesman has been established and the award will be varied accordingly. The same working hours will be prescribed for the linesman's labourer. (*Variation—Metal Trades Award* 35 CAR 718, 720)

The impression suggested by this and other decisions is that while the nature of the work remained a relevant consideration, it would be a less exacting criterion than hitherto.

In December 1936, the 'nature-of-the-work' criterion was discussed in a case about wool stores (*Standard Hours—Storemen and Packers (Wool, etc Stores)* 36 CAR 736). The parties had debated the effects of the 1927 metal trades decision, wherein Dethridge, as the deciding Judge, had limited the 44-hour week to classifications for which the conditions of the work warranted a reduction of hours below the norm of 48 per week. The Full Court did not think it necessary 'to expatiate upon this point' and took note of the gradual spread of 44 hours. Since 1927,

> the Court has admitted other elements in some cases as a justification for reducing ordinary working hours to an average of 44 per week, among them being unusually disagreeable circumstances of the work. A considerable part of the work done by the employees here in hide and skin stores is offensive and monotonous. In the wool stores however it is questionable whether the intrinsic nature and surroundings of the work is such as to establish any special claim to a shortening of working hours.

> But the 44-hour week is already worked by a considerable number of these classes of employees in Australia as well as by an increasingly great number of other wage earners whose work is certainly not more arduous nor deserving of greater leisure that that now in question. This consideration cannot be ignored. ... On the whole we think a case is made for the provision of an average 44 hour week ... (p. 737)

In March 1937 the Full Court reduced to 44 hours the standard week in the saddlery, leather, and canvas industry. A difficulty had been created by a High Court decision excluding South Australian employers from the underlying dispute. Employers in other States objected to the competitive advantage that the South Australians would enjoy if the 44-hour week were granted. The Court acknowledged the problem but nevertheless acceded to the union's application (*Variation—Saddlery, Leather and Canvas Workers' Award* 37 CAR 234).

Dealing in June 1937 with an application to vary awards for railway workers in Victoria and South Australia, the Full Court (delivering judgment on the same day as it published its basic wage decision) referred again to the history of the 44-hour week:

> In 1927 the Court delivered judgment in what has come to be known as the main hours case and therein laid down certain principles which have been accepted as a guide in the granting or withholding of reduced working hours. Between 1927 and 1933 no applications for reduction were granted on account of the depressed condition of industry in Australia. Since 1933 many successful applications for reduction have been made to the Court. The principles laid down in the main case have been elaborated and extended in subsequent decisions and to some extent the Court has been influenced by the general trend in Australia towards a uniform working week of 44 hours. In all cases dealt with by the Court the financial condition of the industry concerned has been taken into account and in certain cases where the financial condition was doubtful, the decrease asked for has been withheld—or postponed—even though the working conditions comply generally with

the principles that have guided the Court in this regard. (*Variation—Victorian and South Australian Railways Awards and Agreement* 37 CAR 937, 938)

In response to the railway employers' plea of financial incapacity, the Court reiterated the argument (by now blessed by Reddaway in the basic wage case) that the developmental purposes of railways made normal financial criteria less relevant, but it took into account the budgetary conditions of the States. These had improved, but (especially in South Australia) were still not fully satisfactory. The Court was

> convinced of the desirability of establishing, as soon as practicable, uniformity as to hours in each railway system considered separately. The Court therefore determines, in principle, that the hours of railway employees in the States of Victoria and South Australia shall be 44 per week or 88 per fortnight. Having regard, however, to the financial conditions already touched on, and having regard also to the altered basic wage provided for in a judgment delivered to-day, and to the necessity for allowing sufficient time for the States concerned to make necessary financial adjustments, the Court makes the following orders ... As to the South Australian railway employees concerned in these proceedings, other than steam engine drivers and firemen, the introduction of the 44-hour week or 88-hour fortnight is indefinitely postponed. As to Victorian railway employees concerned in these proceedings, other than steam engine drivers and firemen, the 44-hour week or 88-hour fortnight shall come into operation as and from the commencement of the first pay period after the 1st day of January, 1938. (p. 939)

Also on the same day, the Court published its decision about standard hours of wool and basil workers (*Variation—Wool and Basil Workers' Award* 37 CAR 959). The Court had refused applications for shorter hours in December 1934 and November 1935. The noxious nature of the work justified a reduction of hours, but the Court had refused to take any action that might increase the tendency to send abroad skins for treatment and wool for scouring. Since the earlier decisions, the danger of contraction of local production had, if anything, increased. The Court therefore refused a reduction of hours. It returned to the matter in October 1938 (see below).

In September 1937, the Full Court refused a reduction of hours for engine drivers and firemen not employed on shift work (*Variation—Engine Drivers' and Firemen's Award* 38 CAR 303) and granted a reduction to municipal employees (but with effect from the following January) (*Variation of Award—Municipal Employees* 38 CAR 306). In neither case did the Court give explicit reasons for its decision.

In a decision of November 1937 about shift workers employed by the State Electricity Commission in Victoria, the Court made a somewhat complicated alteration in working hours. In essence, it reduced the standard hours from 48 to 44, but provided for a week of 43 hours and 5 minutes if the shifts included Sundays *unless* the employer provided at least one week of annual leave (*Judgment—Engine Drivers and Firemen (State Electricity Commission of Victoria)* 38 CAR 641, 643). Since the employer had already provided two weeks leave voluntarily, the practical effect of the decision seems to have been limited to the introduction of a 44-hour week.

In November 1937, the Full Court revisited working hours in the timber industry (*Variation—Timber Workers Award* 38 CAR 644). As we have seen, it had in December 1935 reduced hours in this industry from 48 to 46. This was to operate for a period of two years, which was now near to expiry. Financial information supplied by the employers caused the Court to have some doubt about a further reduction of hours in the bush-milling section of the industry, 'but after weighing the considerations for and against the introduction of the 44-hour week we have concluded that the better course in existing circumstances is to make the reduction from 46 to 44 hours throughout all the sections covered by these awards, the reduction to come into effect on 1st January, 1938' (p. 645). It will be recalled that Higgins had granted the 44-hour week to timber workers in 1921. The 48-hour week was partially restored in 1929. The process of moving from a 48-hour standard to one of 44 hours in this industry had indeed been tortuous.

The Full Court gave several decisions in April 1938 reducing hours to 44 per week in the South Australian Railways with effect from 1st October (for example, *Variation—Engine Drivers and Firemens' Award (South Australian Railways)* 39 CAR 198). It also introduced the 44-hour week in the glass, aerated waters, and yeast and vinegar industries (*Variation of Award—Glass Workers* 39 CAR 211; *Variation of Award—Liquor Trades (Aerated Waters Section)* 39 CAR 212; *Variation of Award—Liquor Trades (Yeast and Vinegar Section)* 39 CAR 213). Few reasons were given. In the aerated waters decision, the Court said that there was some risk of damage to the industry, but 'we cannot overlook the fact that in New South Wales, Queensland and Tasmania they are working 44 hours per week'.

Drake-Brockman, presumably acting with the employer's consent, in May 1938 adopted a recommendation of the Victorian Railways Classification Board that the hours of shunters, leading shunters, signalmen (1st class), and signalmen (special) be reduced to 84 per fortnight (*Variation—Railway Employees Award, Victoria* 39 CAR 258).

In a brief decision of May 1938, the Court applied the 44-hour week to the meat industry (*Variation—Meat Industry Award* 39 CAR 274).

Dethridge in July 1938 commented on the position of road construction workers in South Australia (*Judgment—Road Construction, etc Workers* 39 CAR 859). Thier work had hitherto been regulated by State awards. Although Dethridge thought that State regulation should continue, working hours presented a special problem. In every part of the Commonwealth except South Australia, the 44-hour week now operated for road construction. If longer hours were to continue in South Australia, the 'discriminating contrast' was likely to cause friction. 'I think', said Dethridge, 'that until the 44-hour week is adopted for these employees in the service of the State of South Australia, this Court's award should apply and that State is accordingly bound in respect of ordinary working hours' (p. 860).

A further union application for a 44-hour week for wool and basil workers led to a Full Court decision of October 1938, wherein the Court concluded, somewhat grudgingly, that the time had come to make the change:

> In 1934, 1935 and 1937, the Court dealt with similar applications by this Federation and while stating that the nature of the work was such as to make the proposed reduction desirable felt compelled to refuse it because of the difficulty experienced by the industry in coping with foreign competitors. That difficulty still exists; it is not improbable that in this industry the adoption of the 44-hour week will lead to a loss of business for employers and a loss of employment for employees. But the Federation, though warned by the Court of this danger, is so averse to working a 48-hour week while the 44-hour week prevails in other industries that it disregards this risk. Since the Court's decision of 23rd June, 1937, the members of the Federation in New South Wales were able to bring such pressure upon employers in that State that in August, 1937, the 44-hour week was adopted and has ever since continued in operation. There seems to be no doubt that since August, 1937, in this industry the drift of business away from New South Wales employers and employees to foreign employers and employees has increased. ... So long as the 44-hour week continues in New South Wales this Court cannot expect that in other States this industry can be treated as an exception to the prevailing standard of 44 hours for work of the kind in question even though the industry may be unable to maintain itself with the 44-hour week. Whether we grant or refuse the 44-hour week the industry will meet trouble. We think that in the long run the lesser evil for the industry will be the reduction of the ordinary working week to 44 hours, the reduction to come into operation on 1st January, 1939. (*Variation—Wool and Basil Workers Award* 39 CAR 1056, 1057)

This was but one of a number of cases in which the momentum toward shorter hours, gathering strength case by case, became a telling factor in the Court's decisions.

Beeby (now Chief Justice) in March 1939 made an award whereby porcelain enamelling in Victoria and South Australia came under an award of the Court for the first time. In New South Wales, he said, men engaged as dusters and dusters' assistants worked between 36 and 40 hours per week; but in Victoria they worked 48 hours. 'Their hours', he said, 'will now be 44 per week and I will ask the Full Court to decide whether there should be a further reduction' (*Judgment—Oven, Stove, Bedstead and Fender Making* 40 CAR 104, 109). In May, on the other hand, he refused a 44-hour week in the ham and bacon section of the meat industry in a decision that savours of punishment for past industrial misbehaviour:

> Employers complained that margins were considerably in excess of those originally prescribed and had been forced up to their present level by direct action in defiance of awards of this Court, first by 6s per week and later by another 2s 6d per week. When employees resorted to direct action employers agreed to pay this extra wage under circumstances which suggest that the industry could carry higher wages than those awarded and the additional rate has persisted both by agreement and award up to the present. At a later stage, a further addition of 2s 6d per week was secured by employees in Victoria. Employers disputed the justice of this addition but to avert industrial trouble during the busy season it was awarded by Mr Commissioner Coneybeer. Without comment on the action of the Commissioner I think it would be unjust to load employers with the extra cost of a 44-hour week as well as the last increase in wage rates. (*Judgment—Meat Industry* 40 CAR 192, 195)

The Full Court (Beeby, Piper, and O'Mara) in May 1939 revisited the hours worked by engine drivers and firemen. These workers typically had the role of supplying steam or power to the industries of their employers; and it had been the practice of the Court to fix hours of work that matched those of the industry concerned. In cool stores, most workers were employed for 44 hours, but men engaged in the delivery of ice worked 48 hours and the employers argued that a 44-hour week for the engine drivers whose work was necessary for the supply of the ice would disturb their operations and cause considerable expense. 'The expense involved in such a change', said the Court, 'is not sufficient to justify denial to engine drivers of the now generally accepted standard 44 hours. ... In order, however, to facilitate the rostering of shiftmen the hours are fixed at 88 per fortnight with a direction that not more than 48 hours shall be worked in any one week' (*Variation—Engine Drivers and Firemen's (Cool Stores) Award* 40 CAR 276, 277).

In June 1939, the Full Court, similarly constituted, dealt with the working hours of Victorian tramways' employees (the matter having been referred by Drake-Brockman) (*Variation—Tramway Employees' Award (Melbourne and Metropolitan Tramways Board)* 40 CAR 306). Beeby and O'Mara said that the main arguments advanced in support of a reduction were 'that this Court has extended 44 hours to most industries including railway traffic services and that most similar services in Australasia had adopted the 44-hour week' (p. 307). In opposing a reduction of hours, the Melbourne and Metropolitan Tramways Board had invoked its financial position. Beeby and O'Mara noted, however, that the Board's deficits arose from 'extraneous obligations imposed on the Board by the Act', namely, making payments to the Queen's Memorial Infectious Diseases Hospital Board, the Metropolitan Fire Brigades' Board, and certain municipalities (pp. 309 and 312). The Board's finances compared 'not unfavourably with those of public utilities to which a 44-hour week has been applied' and did not justify the withholding of the shorter working week. They granted an 88-hour fortnight, to take effect in October (p. 315). Piper agreed with this outcome.

In June 1939, Drake-Brockman made a new award for the coal industry (*Judgment—Coal Mining Industry* 40 CAR 367). The background was a strike lasting for more than six weeks in September and October 1938. During the strike, the unions were informed that once work was resumed, the Court would promptly deal with all matters in contention which were of an industrial character. Hours were among them. Drake-Brockman said that, while the Act reserved to the Full Court the function of *varying* hours, there was 'no limitation imposed which prevents the Court from fixing the hours of work of employees in an industry'. He declared that there were no standard hours in the industry, no hours having ever been fixed by the Court. After discussing, with some sympathy, a union argument that shorter hours would lead to more employment, he stated that this was not a reason for his decision:

> The small reduction in hours made by the awards issued herewith is not made with any intention of correcting unemployment; but because of the nature of the industry and of the conditions under which the majority of employees in it are compelled to work. All work underground is hard and hazardous. Superimposed on the hard and dangerous character of the work is the constant fear of these men of contracting lung diseases … In similar cases in other occupations the Court has considered that a complete absence from dust-laden atmosphere for as long as possible in each week was the best means available to it to reduce the risks of contracting silicosis and other lung infections. I propose to follow the same reasoning in this case. I have as a consequence provided that there shall be no work underground on Saturdays and Sundays except for essential services and safety of mines. (p. 378)

The decision was to award, for underground work, a 40-hour week to be worked over five days. The case for shorter hours above ground was 'not so strong', but as some employer witnesses supported uniformity of hours in the industry, Drake-Brockman provided for a general 40-hour week. This was later reviewed by the Full Court which, by majority (Beeby and Piper, with Drake-Brockman dissenting) limited the 40-hour week to underground work (*Variation—Coal Mining Industry Awards* 41 CAR 37, 47, 49).

The Full Court (Beeby, Piper and O'Mara) in August 1939 published two decisions which effectively announced that the 44-hour week was now the norm. In one, relating to carters and drivers, Beeby and O'Mara said that the employers had resisted the reduction of hours because of their financial position. 'It was urged', they said,

> that a decrease in hours would result in increased costs which could not be passed on, particularly in the case of master carriers in competition with owner drivers, who escape any regulation of hours. The evidence on this point was fragmentary and unconvincing. Such competition

Thomas O'Mara

undoubtedly exists, but it was not proven to be great enough to justify refusal ... of the now usual standard. (*Variation—Carters and Drivers Awards* 40 CAR 524, 525)

Piper, in a longer judgment, discussed the submission of S C G Wright, counsel for the South Australian respondents, who claimed that since 1927 the Court had observed a concept of 'equation of leisure'. This concept was implicit in the judgment of Dethridge in the *Main Hours* case. Piper acknowledged that Dethridge did say:

> A just standard of hours of labour in industry is that which places the workers in all industries on what is really, and not merely superficially, the same footing in point of leisure. Inasmuch as in some industries the day's work deprives the workers of opportunity and capacity for enjoyment more than in others, the number of hours to be worked must vary accordingly to secure general fair treatment. (p. 527)

Dethridge's position had prevailed, not because it was a shared view of the Court but because of the divergent positions of Beeby and Lukin. Because of this division, Dethridge's approach was adopted for some time. Piper continued:

> But after 1933 and with the change in the constitution of the Court other factors gradually came to be taken into consideration. Beeby J had never at any time approved of the test of the equation of leisure as the only ground for granting reductions though at times he applied it. Drake-Brockman J has never stated expressly his approval of it as stated by Dethridge C J in 1927. After a very careful and full consideration of the decisions of the Court since 1933 I do not think it can be said that the Court has recently acted on the doctrine of equation of leisure as laid down in 1927. ... With regard to the nature of the work the Court, including Dethridge C J, particularly in the last two or three years, has granted many applications in which the work has not been like that of a factory worker on concentrated repetitive work. Gradually the reduction has been extended ... (p. 538)

In Piper's view, 'the doctrine of the equation of leisure had been discarded by this Court by the end of 1938'. The Court had 'adopted the 44 hour week as the standard for industry under its control' and would grant it unless satisfied that special circumstances existed. Two such special circumstances were implicit in 'the reasonable applicability test and the economic principle, and I do think that the Court has or should cease to take them into account or under proper circumstances refuse to apply them' (p. 539). He was not persuaded by the attempt of the principal employers' counsel to plead that a general deterioration of economic conditions warranted refusal of the union application. The Court might 'be faced with the necessity of giving consideration to the present wage cost in industry'; but this was not a ground 'for refusing to bring this industry into line with general existing standards with regard to hours' (p. 540).

In the other decision published on the same day, for storemen and packers, it was Beeby and O'Mara who wrote at length (*Standard Hours—*

Storemen and Packers (General Stores) 40 CAR 544). The award before them applied to South Australia and Tasmania; in all other States, the operative awards prescribed a 44-hour week. Reviewing the history traversed by Piper in the carters and drivers case, Beeby and O'Mara said:

> The doctrine of the equation of leisure was never adopted by a majority of the bench as the only or as the main test to be applied, and we do not consider the Court obliged to regard the decision in which the test was first promulgated as being more than persuasive. The question now before the Court is the same as that under consideration in 1927 only to the extent that a shortening of the 48-hour week is sought. In other respects the situation is vastly different. Circumstances have changed, and what Dethridge C J felt was 'fraught with danger to the workers themselves' and Lukin J regarded as 'spelling retrogression' has taken place, namely, a general shortening of the 48-hour week, and with such change has gone the need for relying on any original doctrines stated by individual judges.
>
> We are forced to the conclusion that the ultimate conclusion reached by the Court was that the 44-hour week should be accepted as the standard for Australian industry with such exceptions as special circumstances demanded. A declaration to that effect is now explicitly made by the Court. (pp. 548–549)

Thus after 12 years of case-by case change—sometimes halting, sometimes accelerated—the 44-hour week was declared to be the standard for federal awards. Deviations were possible, but required special justification. Significantly, Beeby and O'Mara added: 'The mere fact that a reduction of hours will involve employers in extra costs is not sufficient to justify refusal of this now accepted general standard' (p. 550).[8] It was with this standard that Australia, 19 days later, entered World War II.

---

[8] On the same day, the Full Court deferred a decision about the introduction of the 44-hour week for tugs, lighters, dredges, etc because it had been told that a reduction of standard hours would have no effect except to increase overtime payments. It thought that a decision about hours should await a full review of the award by a single judge (*Variation—Merchant Service Guild Award* 40 CAR 553).

It would be easy, however, to exaggerate the reduction of working hours during this period. Under some State awards, notably in New South Wales and Queensland, the 44-hour week was largely achieved during the 1920s; and it was partially achieved under federal awards after the metal trades decision of 1927. The Commonwealth Statistician's statistics of nominal hours of labour were, like the data of nominal wages, based on the provisions of awards and formal agreements.[9] Chapter 8 noted that average hours of adult males at the end 1929 and the end of 1934 were virtually identical: 45.34 and 45.36 respectively. At the end of 1939, they were 44.29. By States, the reductions in male hours over the five years and the averages at the end of the period were:

	Reduction in Hours	**End 1939 Hours**
New South Wales	0.31	43.92
Victoria	1.21	44.61
Queensland	0.54	43.46
South Australia	1.00	45.83
Western Australia	1.18	44.33
Tasmania	1.44	45.33

Thus New South Wales and Queensland, the States with the smallest reductions, remained the States with the shortest working weeks, confirming that in those States the reduction of hours had largely been accomplished by 1934 (and in fact by 1929).

In the 1930s, unions were developing a campaign for a 40-hour week. The 1937 Congress of the ACTU gave its support to this campaign (Hagan 1981, p. 102; Beever 1985). In 1936 the International Labour Organisation adopted a Convention in favour of a 40-hour week. To the embarrassment of the government, its representative, Sir Frederick Stewart, voted in favour of the resolution (Beever 1985, p. 4). The 40-hour week was not, however, an objective that was seriously pressed in the Arbitration Court, possibly because

---

[9] The hours data exclude two industry groups—shipping and agriculture—which are included in the wage data. The Statistician stated that in the two excluded groups 'working hours have not been generally regulated by industrial tribunals'. See, for example, *Labour Report*, No. 30, 1939, p. 66.

unions were aware that the prospects of success were negligible, except in industries with special characteristics.

12.3 Recreation leave

Since Higgins' time, the Court had generally adopted the practice of providing in its awards for paid public holidays.[10] It did not award annual leave (except when the parties agreed to it) unless the work had some adverse feature for which leave might be an offset. There was, however, a significant range of employment, largely in the public sector, where the employers had voluntarily conceded annual leave. In April 1936, Dethridge described the 'state of play':

> This Court has frequently been asked to award annual leave on full pay but has hitherto not done so except in cases where employees have to work on Sunday, or suffer some other deprivation by reason of isolation or other cause, or in cases where such leave has become the custom generally by the practice of most of the parties concerned. The State awards and registered agreements in New South Wales appear to follow substantially the same practice, but with some extensions to other cases of limited extent. In Queensland and Western Australia the State awards in general frequently provide for paid annual leave. In Victoria, South Australia, and Tasmania paid annual leave in private employment seems to be rare in factories. In all the States, employees of the State or of State instrumentalities or municipalities obtain annual leave on full pay, whether or not they have to work on Sundays. In all the States employees of banks receive some such leave, and so also do most shop employees. (*Judgment—Commercial Printing* 36 CAR 738, 746)

Dethridge then proposed a cautious change of policy:

> Unless an industry is finding difficulty in maintaining itself, in my opinion the institution of paid annual leave is a very desirable boon for employees. ... The introduction of annual leave with pay should not however be made in an industry unless at the time there is a

---

[10] A typical provision was for holidays on New Year's Day, Easter (three days, including Saturday), the Sovereign's Birthday, union picnic day, Christmas Day, and Boxing Day.

> reasonable certainty of stable prosperity in the industry. As a remedy for unemployment it would, like the reduction of weekly working hours, almost certainly be valueless, and it might indeed be harmful. … [The commercial printing] industry has I think recovered from the depression, but its restoration is recent and may not be lasting. … I have decided to prescribe annual leave for a week with full pay for the employees in this industry, but to defer its operation until the expiration of a year from the commencement of the award. The prescription will then begin to operate unless the employers concerned satisfy a judge of the Court that the financial position of the industry then will be such that such operation will imperil the maintenance of the industry. … I think there should be at least six months service before any right accrues. In the Soviets the right does not accrue until the worker has worked five and a half months in the same undertaking. (p. 747)

Initially, Dethridge's attitude was at odds with that of Drake-Brockman, who saw annual leave as a 'privilege' which employers might grant but which should not be awarded except by consent. As we saw in Section 10.9 of Chapter 10, Drake-Brockman had articulated this view, in a Commonwealth Railways case, in December 1932. He reasoned that since the wages awarded to different groups of workers did not take into account benefits such as leave, those benefits ought not to be part of the Court's normal agenda. His distinction between entitlements and privileges was set out in a decision of March 1936 about Tasmanian railways:

> I propose to do what the parties ask in this regard. I point out, however, that there are many provisions in the agreement which I have indicated, from time to time, I will not include in railway awards. Many matters I regard as matters of privilege, to be granted or withheld by the Commissioner or the Parliaments of the States concerned, and not to be ordered by the Court. Long-service leave is one such matter. I am glad to see the employees get such leave and the Commissioner consent to it, but it is not a matter which this Court awards. Where the Commissioners agree to it, and the Parliaments are willing to provide the money involved, I do not propose to omit the agreed provisions from

> a consent award. ... Such matters as long-service leave and free passes over the railways are not taken into account when assessing wages, and therefore should not be included in adjudicated awards. Railway wages are assessed on the same basis as the wages of all other wage-earners in the community who do not enjoy free passes over the railways or long-service leave. (*Award—Daily Paid and Salaried Grades, Tasmanian Railways* 35 CAR 766, 767)

In another decision of March 1936, Drake-Brockman stated his opinion that 'the question of annual leave is not a matter that should be determined by this Court, particularly since this Court does not take it into account when fixing margins for employees' (*Interim Award—Railway Employees—South Australian Refreshment Rooms, etc* 35 CAR 793, 794).

Despite Dethridge's innovation in the commercial printing case, movement was initially slow. Beeby, in making his award for the textile industry in December 1937, made a modest provision for leave. He explained:

> Chief Judge Dethridge in his Printing trades award made provision for a week's holiday on full pay to come into operation at a future date. State tribunals in Queensland and New South Wales are also moving cautiously in the same direction. The justice of the claim of industrialists to a concession largely enjoyed by all other sections of the community cannot be disputed. The granting of such claims however depends on the financial condition of the industry concerned. In this industry I think the time is opportune for a holiday concession. (*Judgment—Textile Workers* 38 CAR 791, 796)

Beeby's 'concession' was to prescribe a 'break' from Christmas Day to New Year's Day, but to delete two of the listed public holidays. The net effect, he said, was to provide two days of extra leave.

In June 1938, Dethridge convened a Full Court to consider the award of annual leave in commercial printing (*Variation—Commercial Printing Award* 39 CAR 553). He explained: 'Inasmuch as constant service leave in such a case as the present is an innovation in the practice of the Court, I thought it desirable to ask my colleagues to sit with me upon this application.' Speaking for himself, he said that the material and arguments before the Court had 'not changed my opinion expressed when making this award that such leave should be prescribed where it is feasible nor have they satisfied me that the economic position of the industry is such as to justify a postponement of the operation of the leave provision'. But he was prepared to consider an application to vary the award by inserting a clause similar to that in the textiles award. Beeby agreed: 'I think that leave on full pay ... is desirable and its extension should be continued, subject to the economic circumstances of the industry in which application is made.' Drake-Brockman also concurred, making no reference to 'privileges'. Dethridge subsequently varied the award so as to allow employers to meet the leave requirement by granting the days between Boxing Day and New Year's Day (p. 555).

Dethridge, in his decision of July 1938 about road construction workers, said that annual leave was 'a great boon which tends in the long run to the better and smoother carrying on of operations' (*Judgment—Road Construction, etc Workers* 39 CAR 859, 865). The award provided a week's leave in addition to public holidays. Drake-Brockman, in September 1938, prescribed 14 days leave for professional radio employees. This appeared from the evidence to accord with the existing practice of country radio stations (*Award—Professional Radio Employees (Broadcasting)* 39 CAR 597). In November 1938, Drake-Brockman prescribed a period of leave for rubber workers 'over the normal Christmas period'. Employees required to work during that period were to have a week's leave at some other time (*Judgment—Rubber Workers* 39 CAR 1098, 1100, 1109). Beeby, on the other hand, in May 1939, refused an application for annual leave for retail butchers:

> I regret being forced to the conclusion that the industry is not one in which a full week's holiday should be universally awarded. The disturbance of the business of small shops in which contact between the customer and the shopman is essential would be too great. Then again the margin of profit at present is too low to justify imposing the extra cost on all employers. A studied proposal, made when the industry is

more prosperous, to secure annual leave in shops in which more than a certain number of employees is employed will be considered in the future. (*Judgment—Meat Industry* 40 CAR 192, 195)

Thus there were relatively few arbitral decisions about annual leave. It was frequently provided by agreement. There are, however, no available statistics that indicate its prevalence.

12.4 FEMALE RATES

Between 1935 and 1939, decisions about the relative wages of females and males were rare. The few exceptions included the following:

- In August 1935, Dethridge set new rates for female clerks under the Municipal Officers Award for Victoria (*Award—Municipal Officers (Victoria)* 35 CAR 133). Under the previous award, the rates ranged from £75 per annum for girls aged less than 17 to £160 for women who were 22 years or older. These rates had not been subject to reductions for falling prices. Dethridge rejected the employers' proposal that they be reduced in proportion to the fall in the basic wage, because part of the wage (unspecified) could be seen as a margin. But the rates 'must come down to less than they were when the current basic wage for males was £4 12s'. The basic wage had fallen by 24 per cent. The new award prescribed a range for female clerks from £60 to £150 — reductions of 15 per cent at the minimum and 7 per cent at the maximum.
- The Full Court in November 1935 approved a 'flat' basic wage (not varying by location) of 75s in the food preserving industry. The female minimum would be 41s (54.7 per cent of the basic wage) (*Judgment—Food Preserving Industry* 35 CAR 481). In December 1937 the Full Court varied this award along lines agreed by the parties. The award now provided, for males, 'a flat basic wage of £3 11s (assessed on the combined

index number for Sydney, Melbourne, Adelaide, and Hobart) plus a constant loading of 5s and an industry allowance of 2s'. The corresponding amounts for females were 39s, 2s 9d, and 1s 3d—a total of 43s (55.1 per cent of the male minimum) (*Judgment—Food Preserving Industry* 37 CAR 833).

- In the basic wage case of 1937, the unions sought minimum rates for females equal to 60 per cent of the basic wage. The Court, however, was content to indicate that female minima should rise so as to maintain existing proportional relativities with the basic wage (see Chapter 11, Subsection 11.2.6).

- In June 1938, Drake-Brockman varied the award for Tasmanian railways by prescribing a rate of 39s 6d per week for 'buffet attendants (female)'. He said that there should be no margin for this classification. In setting the rate, he had 'taken into account the value of the food and other privileges provided for them by the Commissioner' (*Variation—Tasmanian Railways Award* 39 CAR 415).

- Making an award for rope and cordage workers, Beeby, in June 1939, said that improvements in the fortunes of the industry enabled him 'to increase marginal allowances and female and junior wage rates to the level which I would have established four years ago but for financial reasons. ... The minimum wage payable to females has been fixed at 54 per cent of that of males and a morning rest period has been awarded' (*Award—Rope and Cordage Workers* 40 CAR 347).

There was, so far as I am aware, little or no commentary in the Court's decisions on the rationale for unequal wages for males and females, although the issue was discussed, as we have seen, during the hearing of the basic wage case.

THE ECONOMIC CRITIQUE

13

The economics of wage regulation

13.1 Contemporary commentary

13.1.1 Introduction

Wage regulation, at its inception, was neither blessed nor opposed by professional economic opinion, because there was none. At the beginning of the 20th century, Australian economics was close to non-existent. Those few people in other disciplines—such as philosophy, history and law—who had interests in the subject scarcely merited description as 'economists' (La Nauze 1949; Goodwin 1966).[1] Two decades would elapse before a significant group began to form. The first appointees as academic economists seem to have been R F Irvine and E O G Shann. Irvine, after lecturing part-time for several years, moved from the State Public Service to become Professor of Economics at Sydney University in 1912. His economics were unorthodox. In 1922, at age 61, he resigned his Chair (under pressure).[2] Although he remained active until the 1930s, Irvine was completely disregarded by the newly emerging mainstream.[3] As we have seen, he was the principal 'expert' witness relied upon

---

[1] In the 19th century, the economist Stanley Jevons spent time in Sydney as assayer of the mint. La Nauze (1949) discusses the economic thought of Jevons and of W E Hearn, a Professor of Law at Melbourne University, and David Syme, editor of *The Age*.

[2] A brief biography of Irvine is provided by McFarlane (1964). Irvine's successor in the Sydney Chair of Economics was R C Mills.

[3] McFarlane (1964, p. 18) says that he advised E G Theodore, the Treasurer in the Labor Government, and assisted with speeches delivered by Theodore in 1931. In 1933 Irvine

by the unions in the 1930–31 basic wage case. Though treated courteously by the Court, he failed to counter the evidence of Copland. Shann was appointed Professor of History and Economics at the University of Western Australia in 1912. He was apparently an effective teacher of economic principles, but not until the late 1920s did he emerge as a participant in wider economic debate.[4] Herbert Heaton, an economic historian of note, had an appointment in adult education at Adelaide in the late 1910s and early 1920s, but had no apparent impact on economic thought in Australia.[5]

The British Association met in Sydney in 1914. Papers about wage determination were presented to the economics section (and subsequently published in the *Economic Journal*) by George Beeby (1915), F W Eggleston (1915), and F A A Russell (1915). Beeby spoke of 'the tendency ... for the regulation of details steadily to increase, and each year industrial regulation has become more complex and inelastic' (p. 323). He believed that the existing system obstructed efficiency, 'mainly owing to fixing standard rates instead of minima, and to the failure of our Courts to popularise payment by results with reasonable safeguards against sweating or undue "speeding up"'. Apprenticeship was discouraged by union-imposed restrictions and by the high wages prescribed for apprentices, which caused employers to rely on immigration as a source of skilled labour (p. 326). Beeby looked forward to a time of fewer regulations, 'which will amount to the prescribing of a universal bare living standard, below which there will be no competition for employment'. He believed that, when this occurred, 'the old economic forces will again come into play, and that education, with the maintenance of easily accessible tribunals for arbitration, will lead to industrial peace far more rapidly

---

published privately *The Midas Touch* (Hassal Press, Adelaide), criticising orthodox remedies for economic depression. I have not seen this book; but it was sympathetically reviewed by Foenander (1934).

[4] For a summary of Shann's career, see Snooks (1991).

[5] He did, however, publish an account of basic wage prescription, observing that 'for nearly thirty years the Australian experiments in wages regulation have attracted the attention of students of economic problems the world over' (Heaton 1921, p. 309). Heaton later published an Australian version of his well-known textbook (Heaton 1925). This contains a (largely descriptive) account of the wage-fixing system.

than the compulsory laws with which we have been experimenting' (p. 328). Eggleston was a major figure in Australian social science in the first half of the century.[6] His paper had some economic content, discussing the possibilities and the realities of adjusting income shares by wage regulation. Russell's had none. He was Chairman of the New South Wales wages boards and described the development of wage-fixing machinery in New South Wales.[7]

The Australian tribunals (especially the Victorian wages boards) attracted a good deal of notice from abroad. Among the visitors who came to learn about them were the Americans Clark (1906; 1909), Hammond (1913), and Sells (1924); and the Britons Aves (1908) and Rankin (1916).[8] Of these, Rankin provided the most 'economic' appraisal of conciliation and arbitration. Though prepared to concede a moral case for legal intervention to counter 'sweating', she was otherwise hostile to the system. The state, in her view, had no legitimate role beyond facilitating the 'higgling' of the market.[9] Commentators from afar included Alfred Marshall, who did not necessarily condemn the Australian innovations but resisted their translation to Britain:

> And the proposal that a minimum wage should be fixed by authority of Government below which no man may work, and another below which no woman may work, has claimed the attention of students for a long while. If it could be made effective, its benefits would be so great that it might gladly be accepted, in spite of the fear that it would lead to malingering and some other abuses; and that it would be used as a leverage for pressing for a rigid artificial standard of wages, in cases in which there was no exceptional justification for it. But, though great improvements in the details of the scheme have been made recently,

---

[6] He was later knighted. Among the offices that he held was the (inaugural) chairmanship of the Commonwealth Grants Commission (1933–41).
[7] Russell, like Irvine, gave (pro-union) evidence in the 1930–31 basic wage case (see Chapter 9, Subsection 9.2.7). By then he was a King's Counsel. Beeby commented favourably on his earlier encounters with Russell.
[8] Sidney and Beatrice Webb, during their visit to Australia in 1898, learnt something of the Victorian wages boards, commenting that 'by far the most interesting institution in Victoria is the fixing of a minimum wage by law in certain sweated trades' (Austin 1965, pp. 78–86). I thank Professor William Brown, who brought this to my notice.
[9] See also Chapter 3, Section 3.1.

and especially in the last two or three years, its central difficulties do not appear to have been fairly faced. There is scarcely any experience to guide us except that of Australasia, where every inhabitant is part owner of a vast landed property; and which has been recently populated by men and women in full strength and health. And such experience is of but little use in regard to a people whose vitality has been impaired by the old Poor Law, and the old Corn Laws; and by the misuses of the Factory system, when its dangers were not yet understood. A scheme, that has any claim to be ready for practical adoption, must be based on statistical estimates of the numbers of those who under it would be forced to seek the aid of the State, because their work was not worth the minimum wage. (Marshall 1961, p. 715)

Paul Douglas, the renowned American labour economist (later a United States Senator), published in 1923 an article about 'Wages Regulation and Children's Maintenance in Australia', but this had little economic content. It was an account of the development of minimum wage prescription with special reference to social issues such as the assumed size of families (Douglas 1923).

There are few examples of economic 'advice' or opinion about wage policy before about 1923. George Knibbs, the first Commonwealth Statistician, was a physicist and educational administrator. We saw in Chapter 3 that in 1920 he was asked to advise Prime Minister Hughes whether the country could afford to act on the finding of the Piddington Commission about the basic wage needed to provide fair and reasonable living standards. He said that it could not. This, perhaps, was economic advice. The head of the Labour and Industry Bureau in the Statistician's Office was J T Sutcliffe, who did contribute to economic thought—with emphasis on measurement—in the 1920s.[10]

---

[10] Sutcliffe left the Commonwealth Public Service for the Queensland Public Service in 1924 and entered private industry as General Manager of a textile company in 1927. This information was supplied to me by the late Ian Castles, former Australian Statistician.

The most important single step toward the emergence of an Australian economist was the appointment of D B Copland to the University of Tasmania in 1917. Copland, a New Zealander, became Professor of Economics in Tasmania in 1920, moving to Melbourne in 1924. From the early 1920s until World War II, he was a key figure in virtually all economic debate in Australia. From being unnoticeable at the beginning of the 1920s, the body of mainstream economists grew rapidly in influence, importance and sophistication. In a talk that he gave in 1950, Copland said of the influence wielded by pre-war economists: 'That this influence was considerable will be generally admitted, though many people may doubt whether the chief participants had much claim to be considered economists of distinction in the classical sense or were more than highly skilled opportunists in respect of their public activities.' The changes that came over the economic scene in the late 1920s and early 1930s

> afforded the economists unusual opportunities for going over the trenches in the grand manner to occupy positions that had hitherto been beyond their reach. This they did with an air of confidence that is sadly lacking in these more buoyant days of full employment when one would have thought that the world was the economist's oyster; they did it with something of a missionary zeal, always a dangerous attitude of mind, and they did it with a more or less united front. (Copland 1950, p. 1)

When Copland left Tasmania in 1924, he was succeeded in the Chair of Economics by J B Brigden, who was to be a major 'player' in Australian economic debate.[11] L F Giblin, whose role in formulating Depression policy was central, moved to Melbourne University in 1929, as the first Ritchie Professor, from the post of Government Statistician in Tasmania. Thus Tasmania contributed to the economic debate several of its principal participants (Coleman, Cornish and Hagger 2006).

Because the various tribunals were so conspicuous a feature of the labour market, it is not surprising that the economists, in their analyses of the Australian

---

[11] Some seven years older than Copland, Brigden had been a Lecturer for the University of Tasmania at Queenstown since 1922.

economy, assigned them—and especially the Commonwealth Court—an important role. We might expect that there would have been antagonism, in principle, to interference in the market; but little of that was expressed. E O G Shann's pro-market preconceptions would undoubtedly have led him in this direction. I have not found an explicit call by Shann for abolition of the Arbitration Court, and he joined with other economists in advocating a Depression strategy that assigned an important role it.[12] Overtones of hostility to the system are obvious in *An Economic History of Australia* (Shann 1930), which has a chapter on 'The Origins and Extension of Wage-Fixing'. Shann wrote with a fervour that is typical of converts from the Left to the Right. 'In 1907', he said,

> a Judge of the High Court of Australia presiding over a Federal Arbitration Court, took high moral ground in claiming for the workers a wage independent of supply and demand. A glow of idealism warmed what had seemed a class egoism. (p. 375)

Referring to the post-1913 adjustment of the basic wage for prices, Shann wrote:

> Thus through all the vicissitudes of war and post-war prices, those who drew the basic wage were secure of their real wages, of the normal needs of the average employee regarded as a human being, so far as the *Harvester* judgment covered those needs. It may be hard to regard that average as divine, but it has certainly been placed, so far as laws can do it, upon a pedestal of privilege. (p. 381)

'*Fiat justitia*', he said,

> is a high doctrine. The danger involved is that wage-fixing tribunals may raise their conception of justice more rapidly than the price which can be allotted from the joint product of the industry to the contributors

---

[12] Snooks (1991) has no doubt of Shann's hostility to wage-fixing, and I do not disagree. Stone (1991) also recounts Shann's antagonism to labour market regulation but, like Snooks, cites no actual recommendation of the Court's abolition. This reticence is the more remarkable when viewed against the background of the Bruce Government's having put the issue squarely, if unavailingly, on the political agenda.

E O G Shann

of routine service. Prices, even of routine and skilled manual service, are ultimately encouragements or discouragements to persistence in that service. If sacrosanctity and increase of wages go hand in hand, more may be attracted into the callings so blessed than can be found regular employment in them. Fluctuating wages have a social function to perform in minimising unemployment and sending labour to Sydney or the bush. (p. 385)

In the same year that Shann's *Economic History* appeared, the historian W K Hancock published *Australia* (Hancock 1930). Over the subsequent decades, this attracted much favourable attention. His commentary on arbitration in many ways mirrored Shann's, though it was rather more nuanced.[13] Hancock wrote of the interdependence of minimum wages and tariff protection:

> The Australian conception of 'fair and reasonable' is ethical, like the mediaeval idea of the just price. To those who object that such a standard

---

[13] Hancock had worked under Shann's leadership at the University of Western Australia and held Shann in high regard. He records that 'Edward Shann's pioneer book was "twenty years a-growing"' (Hancock 1954, p. 76).

may conflict with economic possibilities, the courts reply that Australia is 'not quite so bankrupt in resources of material or of mind or of will' as to be unable to provide for workers 'the bare necessaries of life in a supposedly civilised community'. ... Manufacturers must learn to seek economy through efficiency, rather than efficiency through parsimony; they must make economic facts conform to the idea of justice. If an industry is unable to achieve this, it must die—unless the State chooses to intervene in order to prolong its existence. With this saving clause the argument completes its circle; it has led back to Protection. Does this mean that the distinctive ethics of Australian democracy are dependent, after all, upon its distinctive economics?

The Australians have always disliked scientific economics and (still more) scientific economists. They are fond of ideals and impatient of technique. ... The mechanism of international prices, which signals the world's need from one country to another and invites the nations to produce more of this commodity and less of that, belongs to an entirely different order. It knows no rights, but only necessities. The Australians have never felt disposed to submit to these necessities. They have insisted that their Governments must struggle to soften them or elude them or master them. (pp. 85–86)

Hancock spelt out his misgivings about the basic wage:

Since 1913, the Commonwealth Court of Conciliation and Arbitration has followed the practice of restating the wage of 1907 in terms of the changed purchasing power of money, as indicated by the Statistician's price-index numbers. This restated wage is called the *Harvester Equivalent*. ... In so far as we really use the basic wage as a measuring rod, we have created, to all intents and purposes, our own original iron law of wages. It is a monstrous achievement.

'Fair and reasonable', 'fair and average', 'normal needs'—all these phrases are intelligible only as they are relevant to conditions of time and place. They depend, and must depend, on custom. But is the reward of labour for ever to be governed by the custom of 1907? In 1919–20 Australia sought to free herself from the dead hand of

W K Hancock

the past by modernising her definition of needs. One result of this attempt was to place new emphasis on something which the Courts had always realised and sometimes stated—the futility of considering needs without considering also the capacity of industry to satisfy them. Some economists have suggested that the wage-fixing authorities should frankly accept 'capacity to pay' as the chief criterion. But this criterion, too, has its economic critics. Nor will Labour accept it. Capacity to pay fluctuates both upwards and downwards, and Labour plays for safety. The rigid standard of wages may increase unemployment in bad times and rob the workers of their fair share in the enjoyment of good times; but it is something definite and tangible, a rallying-point in the class struggle, a trench to man against the attacking forces of capitalism. If Australia were an exhausted country of dwindling resources this would be good tactics. But the tactics seem hardly suitable in a vigorous new country which has not yet reached its 'optimum' population. What America began to enjoy a few years after the war—a steady rise in wages unaccompanied by a corresponding rise in prices—would seem to the Australians a fantastic miracle. Australia's policy might seem to have been specially designed to persuade the Australian workman of what is nevertheless untrue—that he has no interest in low costs. For, to outward seeming, he has no real interest in low prices. If his efficiency helps to reduce prices, he is rewarded by a scaling-down of his wages. This is the anti-climax of Labour's struggles; the burlesque conclusion of that practical Australian logic which has so persistently elaborated its generous postulate of justice. (pp. 184–186)

It is a reasonable conjecture that the conservative Leslie Melville (trained as an actuary) would have endorsed Shann's and Hancock's criticisms of wage regulation. But as a group, the economists were concerned more with understanding the effects of wage policy and influencing the tribunals' decisions than with challenging their existence.

A comprehensive analysis of the economics of arbitration was provided in Frederic Benham's *The Prosperity of Australia*, written while he worked at Sydney University and published in 1928 (Benham 1928). Benham does not seem to have exerted much practical influence during his Australian sojourn.[14] His long chapter on 'Wage-regulation' is, however, of much interest. It can be understood as an attempt to understand the interaction of the forces of 'the market' and regulation. Benham seems to have believed that in the long run the 'economic' forces tended to assert themselves, whereas in the shorter period the regulators had more scope to impose their priorities. In neither case, however, was the predominance wholly one way. Benham expounded the standard neoclassical presumption against market intervention:

A wage is essentially a *price*. Wages form part of the price-mechanism, which plays such an important and useful part in our economic life. Interference with the price-mechanism, unless very skilfully carried out, is likely to have harmful consequences. If the price of anything is raised too high, less will be bought; and if the price of labour is raised too high, less labour may be bought. In other words, wage-regulation may tend to increase unemployment. Again, differences in wages (in the

---

[14] Benham did give evidence in the *Main Hours* case of 1926–27 (see Chapter 7, Subsection 7.3.2). I have not been able to access the relevant pages of the transcript.

absence of regulation) provide incentives to effort and divert the flow of labour towards those occupations and industries where it is relatively most needed. Here also wage-regulation clearly has its dangers. (p. 170)

In practice, the conflict between market and regulators was softened by the weight that the regulators, 'consciously or unconsciously', had given to economic considerations. There were, nevertheless, two adverse consequences of regulated wages:

- a greater level of unemployment than would otherwise have obtained; and
- a compression of wage differences which discouraged the acquisition of skill and encouraged young people to enter 'dead-end' but seemingly well-paid jobs.

Benham cites the *Royal Commission on National Insurance* of 1926 for the finding that unemployment was heavier among unskilled and casual workers than among the more skilled and claims that the position of the less skilled would be still worse but for the employment provided by governments and local authorities. He attempts an analysis of the relation between unemployment and the wage share in the value of manufacturing production over the period and claims (rather unpersuasively) that there is an inverse correlation. He accepts that unemployment under arbitration may have been little more than it would have been under collective bargaining, 'although the percentage of unemployment has been somewhat higher in Australia than in most countries during recent years' (p. 213).

Benham did not advocate the abolition of wage regulation, but 'whilst wage-tribunals serve a useful purpose in their capacity as arbitrators, preventing or settling industrial disputes, yet the fixing of wages, which is an inevitable accompaniment of that function, is a very delicate matter' (p. 234). He made several recommendations.

First, there should be no rigid adherence to the 'cost of living' principle:

Unless the standard of comfort is altered from time to time this principle tends to establish for all time a standard arrived at perhaps

> many years ago, and then, possibly, upon somewhat meagre evidence. … If prosperity increases, then wage-earners have a right to share in that increase. In point of fact they do share in it in the long run, whatever wage-tribunals do. (Thus, with growing prosperity, *hours* have been reduced during recent years.) But basic wages awarded in accordance with a fixed standard make the 'long run' longer that it would otherwise be. On the other hand, if real wages are maintained at a given level whilst prosperity is declining, the result will be to injure wage-earners (as a whole) by increasing unemployment … Nor will constant alterations of the standard solve the difficulty, unless they are made very frequently (sometimes upwards and sometimes downwards), which logically amounts to discarding the 'cost of living' principle altogether. (pp. 234–235)

There was no one single principle to replace the cost of living: 'The real solution is for wage-tribunals to recognise clearly all the factors involved, to form their opinions concerning present and probable future conditions, and to award those various wages which they consider will produce the best consequences, without being bound by any fixed 'principle' at all—except that of maximising prosperity.'

Second, Benham was critical of 'capacity to pay' (such as was recommended by the Queensland Economic Commission)[15] as a guide to wage-setting:

> *In the long run* money wages will tend to vary with average value produced per worker. But wage-regulation is concerned mainly with the short run. In Australia, especially, considerable fluctuations occur from time to time in the value of production per worker. The main risk of these variations from the general trend—the bulk of the gain in 'good' years and of the loss in 'bad' years—is borne by owners. It is part of their function, and they are better prepared for such variations than are wage-earners. (pp. 235–236)

---

[15] See Subsection 13.1.3 below.

Moreover, the idea of a uniform 'capacity to pay' was misconceived. Capacity varied geographically, between industries and between firms:

> The conception of a *rigid* minimum or basic wage, applying to all industries, districts, and workers should be definitely abandoned. ... The Queensland model of distinguishing between industries of 'more than average', 'average' and 'less than average', prosperity, might be generally adopted. Fine distinctions between industries and districts would not be practicable, but greater plasticity than at present is possible. Thus some workers would be attracted away from the less prosperous and towards the more prosperous industries (and districts). (p. 237)

Third, the compression of relativities should be resisted:

> As between occupations, a 'margin for skill' sufficient to attract adequate members [sic] to enter each particular 'skilled' occupation should be awarded. If at any time there was a marked shortage of workers in a particular occupation, wages in that occupation might be somewhat raised. (The fact that workers in one occupation, but in industries of differing prosperity, would be receiving different rates would tend to promote desirable movements from less productive towards more productive industries.) (p. 238)

No attempt should be made to reduce wage inequality by wage regulation. If inequality was a problem, it should be tackled by public finance.

Fourth, firmer attempts should be made to induce payment by results where practicable. Resistance to it might be diminished by a scheme of unemployment insurance.

The foregoing is a selective summary of Benham's chapter. Overall, it can be seen as a blend of a theoretical preference for free markets and a pragmatic recognition of the practical role of wage regulation. Benham's reasoning was unsympathetic to the concept of the basic wage in the sense of a more or less uniform foundation wage spread across industries and occupations. He explicitly rejected the principle that industries that could not pay the basic wage should be allowed to fail. He did not explore the process by which skill differentials had been squeezed over the past two decades, but he was opposed to the result (without actually adducing evidence of ill-effects). Benham's analysis was the most thorough attempt to that time to set wage fixation in an economic context. It is intriguing that it attracted so little notice. Benham (who left Australia in 1930) seems never to have gained entry to the select club of influential economists led by Copland, Giblin, Brigden, Mills, Melville, and Shann.

13.1.2 The British Economic Mission and employer opinion

Early in 1929, a critical commentary on the wage-fixing system was offered by a group of British businessmen, selected by the British Government to visit Australia at the request of the Commonwealth Government (British Economic Mission 1929). The Australian Government's request was due in part to the limited success of policies adopted in the 1920s to raise the population through immigration and development. It also reflected the government's hostility to existing industrial arrangements, which culminated later in 1929 in its attempt to abolish federal arbitration (save for the maritime industries).

I refer in Subsection 13.1.5 to the Mission's criticism of the relation between wage-setting and the tariff. That criticism, of course, entered into its broader assessment of the wage-fixing system. But the Mission also saw the system as seriously flawed in other respects. It reported a widespread and shared discontent:

> In every capital city of Australia we have had the advantage of meeting the leaders of the Trade Union movement. We have been much struck by the strength of that movement, reinforced as it doubtless is by the homogeneity of the people and by the active and intelligent interest which they take in all matters affecting their welfare. We have had frank and interesting discussions with the leaders of the movement; and we have found that practically on every occasion the subject of the Arbitration Acts and of the Courts established thereunder has come up during the course of these discussions. By workmen's representatives, not less emphatically than by representatives of the employers, it has

been consistently represented to us that the Arbitration Acts are not achieving their purpose and that a system designed to arrive by judicial decisions at fair and prompt settlement of industrial disputes such as could be freely accepted by both sides must be held to have failed. (p. 17)

The reasons for these discontents were: a view that the arbitral system imported the antagonisms between the parties that were a characteristic of litigation; the delays inherent in the process of assembling and presenting evidence; the expense and the absorption of time in arbitration; and the complexities of simultaneous operation of federal and State tribunals. The parties consulted believed, moreover, 'that the subject matter of the questions which are brought before the Courts is not of a nature with which judicial tribunals, necessarily unversed in the practical problems of industry or in the economic questions to which they give rise, are best fitted to deal'. The Mission endorsed these complaints:

> The indictment of the system of the Arbitration Courts which we have heard is a heavy one; and we feel that it is well founded on many grounds, and particularly on the ground that the system has tended to consolidate employers and employees into two opposing camps, and has lessened the inducement to either side to resort to round table conferences for that frank and confidential discussion of difficulties in the light of mutual understanding and sympathy which is the best means of arriving at fair and workable industrial agreements.

This was an early instance of the oft-repeated fallacy of contrasting a real-world 'dirty' arbitration system with an idealised and unlikely world of mutual understanding and co-operation.[16]

The Mission also condemned the adjustment of the basic wage to the cost of living:

> Further, a system of wage fixation resting upon a basic money wage which rises or falls with a varying index figure of the cost of living is

---

[16] Of course, Higgins and others committed a similar fallacy when they contrasted the grubby realities of union-employer conflict with the new province for law and order.

> open to the gravest criticism, as tending to deprive employees of any interest in the prosperity of the industry with which they are connected. Let us assume that by better, more energetic, and more willing work on the part of all concerned from the highest to the lowest, the output of Australian industries were increased with no increase in overhead cost. The natural economic effect would be that prices all round would fall and that consumption and profits would rise; but as the cost of living would fall the basic wage would also fall, and with it all wages fixed by the Arbitration Courts in relation to the basic wage with margins for special skill and the like. Thus the system is such as to give the worker in industry no interest in a cheaper cost of living, and no inducement to that increased efficiency which would tend to bring it about. In such a case as we have imagined it would be only right that wages should rise and that the workmen should share in the increased prosperity so largely attributable to them. It is only if all concerned in industry genuinely feel that their own fortunes are bound up with its success or failure that that solidarity in industry which is essential to its prosperity can be achieved. (p. 18)

The unargued presumptions that prices varied inversely with productivity[17] and that the worker within a workplace would be motivated by this correlation to greater on-the-job effort require little comment.

The Mission's report mirrored employer opinion in Australia. Plowman (1989) recounts that as economic conditions deteriorated in the later 1920s, employer demands for the abolition of arbitration intensified. In 1928, a Conference of the Central Council of Employers' Associations resolved:

> That this conference is of the opinion that compulsory arbitration has largely failed, and that it has not achieved the purpose for which it was introduced. Having this view, we consider that it should be abolished. (Plowman 1989, p. 76)

These sentiments, Plowman reports, were shared by other employer bodies. According to the *Employers' Review*, arbitration was the 'major cause of

---

[17] A presumption also made by W K Hancock (see above).

depression in general; it reduces output since wages are paid to employees irrespective of their worth; it causes high unemployment, high tariffs, high production costs, industrial chaos and industrial conflict in particular' (Plowman 1989, p. 77).

Plowman also describes a transformation of employer views over the 1930s. Employers became strong advocates of the system. In December 1938, the *Employers' Review* declared:

> We Australians, employers and employees alike, are a type—we should know how to work together, and if differences do arrive, we have an Arbitration Court to settle them. In our arbitration system we have machinery for settling disputes. This machinery has been built up over the past 30 years. It has stood the test of the Great War and the Great Depression. (Plowman 1989, p. 80) (See also Hagan 1981, p. 67)

13.1.3 Capacity to pay

By the time that economists began to talk about wage policy—about 1923—they were broadly aware of the significant fall in real wages between about 1917 and 1920 and the enormous increase of 1921–22. These changes were due mainly to a lack of synchronisation of wage and price movements. Prices rose rapidly after 1916, and although the tribunals took account of this, they were for various reasons slow in doing so; and so money wages lagged behind prices. Then in the early 1920s, wages went on rising quite fast, as they were adjusted to earlier price movements, although prices were actually falling. Copland, in 1923, gave a paper to ANZAAS, which was substantially reproduced in the *Economic Journal* (Copland 1924). It was concerned mainly with the business decline in 1920–22. Copland attributed this to two factors: widely divergent movements of retail and wholesale prices and the poor timing of wage movements. Because retail prices fell much less than wholesale prices, the adjustment of wages to retail prices meant that for many producers there was a wage-price squeeze. And the slow adjustment of wages to price movements meant that real wages had fallen during the period of rising prices and risen when prices were falling. Copland concluded that the cost of living was a bad criterion for wage adjustment. 'Arbitration', he said, 'has been a costly experiment for Australia, but failure to apply a principle soundly should not, as many suppose, warrant the condemnation of that principle. The productivity of industry is the final source of wages, and arbitration cannot be successful if it ignores this factor' (p. 45).

We now use the term 'productivity' to describe something like real output per worker or per hour worked (with or without allowance for other factor inputs). That is not what Copland meant. He was talking about value added per worker, measured in money (not real) terms. This was the main determinant of businesses' capacity to pay their workers. Unless wages were raised or reduced at a similar rate, the tribunals were either imposing increased burdens on business or depriving workers of wages that business could afford to pay. To put the point differently, their objective should be to stabilise the wage share of value added. (Copland did not use that language.)

Copland's reasoning assumed, tacitly, that the prices paid by employers for their non-labour inputs and the prices that they received for their output were given extraneously. There was no consideration of the possibility that business might offset increases by raising their prices, because prices were taken as given. This assumption is explicable by two of the characteristics of the economy at the time. One was its high dependence on foreign trade, the other Australia's adherence to a fixed exchange rate with its main trading partner—the United Kingdom.

Copland's views caught the attention of the President of the Queensland Court of Industrial Arbitration.[18] The Queensland basic wage (more correctly, basic wages) and the principles upon which Queensland award wages were set were already rather different from those of the Commonwealth Court. Wages under State awards were significantly above the Commonwealth standards. The President instigated an Economic Commission on the Queensland Basic Wage. Copland was asked to serve on it, but was unavailable. The members

---

[18] T W McCawley was a judge of the Supreme Court and part-time President of the Industrial Court. He had published an article in the *International Labour Review* (McCawley 1922).

were Sutcliffe (as chairman), Mills, and Brigden.[19] The topics referred to the Commission included 'the productivity of Queensland year by year from 1913 to 1924 and the estimated productivity for 1925'; 'real wages compared with productivity for the same periods'; 'to what extent it is practicable in adjusting wages to have regard to productivity'; 'whether an increase in wages would be likely to affect adversely the growth of any, and what, Queensland industries'; and 'such other matters of an economic nature as in the opinion of the Commission may be of assistance to the Court in determining the basic wage' (Economic Commission on the Queensland Basic Wage 1925). The Commission reported that

> the capacity of all industries to pay wages depends primarily upon their net aggregate production. The only possible measure of this is value. The aggregate value is found from the value of production and the price of a unit. ... The aggregate value of production then may vary from two separate sets of causes—those which affect volume of output, and those which affect price. (pp. 15–16)

The Commission produced a complex formula of 'capacity to pay'.[20] Its basic purpose was to measure changes in the value of production per head in Queensland.[21] The cause of complexity was the lack of current data. Hence the index took into account both the data of the previous year's production (primary and secondary, but not tertiary) and an estimate of the current year's production, based mainly on factors affecting the value of rural production. The Commission recommended to the Court that it apply the formula with

---

[19] The Commission was appointed on 30 December 1924, assembled in Brisbane on 19 January 1925, and reported on 21 February. Brigden observed a few months later that this was 'the first occasion when professional economists had been made use of in Australia', and although he had welcomed the opportunity to participate, it was 'not the business of University teachers to spend their vacation in this manner' (University of Tasmania 1925, p. 22).

[20] The formula was trenchantly criticised by H B Higgins, partly on the ground of its complexity but also because 'it is, in essence, an attempt to make the worker share in the losses as in the gains of the industries generally; of industries in which they are not consulted or concerned as owners' (Higgins 2001, pp. 184–185).

[21] The equation of capacity to pay with value of production per head was criticised by Gifford (1928, pp. 51 and 53), who said that other factors also affected the willingness of employers to employ labour at given wages.

discretion, having regard to (1) the desirability of curbing fluctuations in wages and (2) changes in the level of unemployment.

The Commission was critical of the Commonwealth Court's adherence to the *Harvester* standard 16 years after its adoption:

> In effect the rough measure of capacity to pay determined by Mr Justice Higgins in 1907 has been stereotyped, and the level of wages in that year has determined the level of wages ever since. It is true that the conditions of employment have improved; hours have been reduced, and the wages of juniors have been increased, but the basic wage has tended to remain rigid. (p. 27)

Brigden subsequently was more forthright:

> It was no wonder that the Federal Arbitration Court was the most criticised institution in Australia; the wonder was that it had succeeded at all. When to its defective powers under the Constitution, its inability to prevent conflicts before they became inter-State, its inability to enforce its awards, was added a weak personnel and a vicious principle of wage regulation, it was not surprising to find chaos. In the circumstances, the principle of compulsory arbitration seemed to have survived every possible obstacle. (University of Tasmania 1925, p. 28)

Very little came of this early venture into the economic analysis of capacity to pay. In Queensland, factors militating against the adoption of the Commission's proposals were the complexity of the formula and the death of the President before they could be put into effect. More generally, retention of 'old' ways, especially *Harvester*, was probably due largely to the much greater stability of retail prices after the turmoil of 1917–22.[22]

Sutcliffe (1925) expressed a further objection to the gearing of wages to the cost of living: that it deprived workers of all incentive to contribute to

---

[22] A point of interest is the similarity of the underlying reasoning to that used 35 years later by Eric Russell and Wilfred Salter, who gave evidence for the ACTU in the 1959 basic wage case. Russell and Salter advocated wage adjustment for prices and physical productivity, corrected for movements in the terms of trade. There was the same implicit objective of holding constant the wage share of the national income.

greater production, because they neither gained nor suffered from changes in the fortunes of the industries that employed them. In Queensland, there were broad differentiations between industries, with wage levels under State awards related to their prosperity (though not to any assessment of the workers' efforts), and this may have informed Sutcliffe's contention. The view that he put became a familiar one. As we have seen, it was an opinion expressed by the British Economic Mission, probably mirroring comments heard during its consultations; and W K Hancock (see above) offered a similar view.

13.1.4 The tariff

The issue whether Australia would be free trade or protectionist, left open at federation, was resolved by 1906 in favour of protection. The Tariff Board was established in 1921 to recommend the granting or withholding of protection.[23] There was an interrelation between the tariff and wage policy, because protection affected the attainable real wage. It did this partly by its (uncertain) effects on the productivity of the economy and partly by creating possibilities of income transference between unprotected exporters and the protected industries.

In the early numbers of *The Economic Record*, which began in 1925, there was an important debate, involving Brigden, Benham and Giblin. Brigden (1925) confronted full-on the question whether the tariff was, in the round, beneficial. (He did not discuss specific tariffs.) An affirmative answer, of course, flew in the face of economic orthodoxy. Brigden had no sympathy with the arguments that had been used by protectionists in Australia. They had all of the flaws that had been identified by standard economics. Moreover, Brigden was alive to the exploitation of consumers by manufacturers and labour raising prices and wages behind the tariff wall. Nevertheless, he asked whether, in relation to the benefits and costs of protection, 'the intuition of the protectionists is sounder than their logic, and that they may be right to a degree in spite of it'? (p. 32)

---

[23] For political aspects of tariff-setting in the 1920s, see Hagan (1981, pp. 27–28).

His answer was 'yes'. He took into account the objective of a larger population and the presumed facts of diminishing returns in agriculture and increasing returns in manufacturing. Because the last two mainly take the form of externalities, they are inadequately factored into decisions taken at the microeconomic level. (Brigden did not use the language of externalities, but the idea is implicit in his argument.) Without intervention, the expansion of agriculture, where diminishing returns prevailed, would go too far and the growth of manufacturing, where there were increasing returns, would be unduly retarded. Just as free trade was appropriate to the circumstances of Britain in the 19th century, protection was right for Australia in the 20th. Free trade, in Britain's case, and protection, in Australia's, countered the effects of diminishing returns in agriculture.

It would be unfair to say that Benham (1926) merely asserted the conventional arguments for free trade. Probably his main ammunition was a denial of diminishing returns in agriculture. He talked about the past and likely future reductions in labour requirements for producing increasing volumes of agricultural output. He made the point that the growth of cities in the 19th century was made possible by the increased productivity of agriculture. Benham also made a good deal of the statistical evidence that in New South Wales, under free trade in the latter decades of the 19th century, manufacturing had grown faster than in protectionist Victoria.

Brigden (1927), in his rejoinder to Benham, talked particularly about the distributive effects of combining population growth with free trade. The principal distributional contest was between labour and land. Capital and management, being the most mobile of factors, would be affected least of all.

> Labour has been protected at the expense of land ownership. It is true that Protection has caused a rise in city and urban site values, and that the net result is difficult to measure. The argument is as usual one of tendency, and I merely allege that Protection has relieved the demand for land in general and increased the demand for labour. Thereby it has reduced the strength of land ownership and increased the bargaining power of labour. (pp 108–109)

Giblin (1927), then Government Statistician in Hobart, joined the fray. One of his main points was that the statistics used by Benham, though published in such worthy places as the *Commonwealth Yearbook*, were worse than useless. For example, the 'evidence' that manufacturing had grown faster in New South Wales than in Victoria was spurious. 'Mr Benham', said Giblin, 'reaches conclusions so opposed to common sense that one is rather surprised at his accepting them without a close scrutiny of the meaning of the figures on which they are based' (p. 148). But, really, recourse to statistics was unnecessary:

> Professor Brigden's assumption seems to me axiomatic, though it may not have been wise to tie the red rag of 'diminishing returns' to it. If 100,000 farmers are making a living in a given State, and 20,000 more with the same average capital and ability are added to them, it seems clear that in general they will not make so good a living; otherwise the first 100,000 are proved to be fools, which is contrary to hypothesis. That is all that is required for Mr Brigden's argument, and it hardly seems open to question. (p. 151)

Moreover, Benham had failed to account for the public assistance to agriculture by way of railways and roads: 'This point is vital, and makes further discussion unnecessary so far as Mr Brigden's argument is concerned' (p 151).

Late in 1927, the Prime Minister, S M Bruce, asked a group of people to undertake an inquiry into the tariff. He initially approached E C Dyason, a stockbroker, Giblin, and C H Wickens, the Commonwealth Statistician. Subsequently, Brigden and Copland were added. In his foreword to the Report, published in 1929, Bruce wrote:

> They not only agreed to undertake the work, but they insisted that they should do so on a purely voluntary basis. The report is a free gift to the Australian people. Some indication of the measure and the quality of this rare act of public service is to be found in the fact that their investigations and the preparation of their report have kept the Committee continuously and heavily engaged for over eighteen months. (Brigden et al. 1929, p. viii)

The Brigden Report, as it is generally known, was a significant contribution, not only to Australian but to wider economic thinking. It was, of course, more detailed and contained many more elaborations and qualifications than the original Brigden article. But the basic conclusion was the same: Australia could not have supported the population of the day at the then-existing standard of living without the tariff. The committee said:

> We have to recognise in the tariff as a whole, in spite of its undoubted extravagances, a potent instrument in maintaining at a given standard of living a larger population than would have been otherwise possible. It seems certain that without the tariff we could not have offered the same field for immigration, and would not have been able to maintain our growth of population. (p. 84)

The tariff did more than divert resources from the export industries into the sheltered industries. It also caused a redistribution of income between the two sectors. And it provided scope for the raising of real wages in the sheltered industries. Australia's standard of living was high, primarily because of the productivity of its primary industries. The tariff helped to sustain their productivity by restraining their growth. But it also caused some of the benefits of rural productivity to be transferred. In that context, wage regulation played a part:

> The standard of wages is high, therefore, primarily because the income per head is high. But it can be, and is, made a little higher than naturally it would be, by pressure of various kinds upon other incomes. There is room for such pressure ... There are maximum and minimum payments which can be made for labour, neither of which can be established with certainty, and between which there is room for variation. Free competition is liable to reduce wages to the minimum, and regulation can compel the maximum payments, provided the by-products of regulation have not absorbed too much of the income available. (p. 96)

The view that emerges, then, is that the tariff, as well as protecting real income against the threat of diminishing returns in the major export industries, also facilitated transference of income from which wage-earners in the sheltered industries benefited. It would be wrong to suppose that Brigden and colleagues saw the arbitration tribunals as playing a large part in the overall scheme of maintaining real income and redistributing it. But they played some part, and the thinking that the tariff debate generated almost certainly contributed to the economists' prescriptions for wages in the Depression. These were intended to put the transference process into reverse.

These were 'big picture' analyses of the tariff. At a more pragmatic level, there was an issue as to the interaction of tariffs and wage increases. The Tariff Board itself, in the later 1920s, was the principal source of alarm about this issue. In its 1926 report, the Board said:

> As a result of the investigation into the iron and steel industry ... the Tariff Board was so impressed with the critical nature of the industrial position into which Australia was drifting, and indeed has drifted, that a suggestion was advanced that the recommendations for increases in the Tariff which were absolutely essential to the maintenance of the industry should be granted only on condition that assurances were obtained from the various industrial unions connected with the industry that no further demands would be made for wage increases or any other action taken which would have the result of defeating the effect of any increase in duties recommended. It was pointed out that that the principal applicant employers had given guarantees that the prices would not be raised, and that the merchants had also agreed not to make any alteration in their selling prices in the event of the requests being granted. It was suggested by the Board that the same assurances should be obtained from the industrial unions. Immediately following upon the increases in the Tariff in regard to woollen piece goods ... with a view to relieving certain sections of the industry which were suffering detriment from external competition, the industrial union embracing the operations in the industry lodged an application before the Federal Arbitration Court for heavy increases in their wages and modified working conditions. The recommendations of the Tariff Board were made on evidence tendered to it in order to assist certain of the different woollen mills in a time of depression, and no provision

was made for an alteration in the existing conditions governing wages. The representatives of the union who appeared before the Board in the woollen piece goods investigation, gave no indication that it was contemplated, in the event of a favourable recommendation being made and Parliament granting such, that the costs of production would be raised by higher wages and different conditions.

This action of the Textile Workers Union seems to have been influenced by the judgment of Mr Justice Powers, wherein it was laid down that his Court could take no cognisance of the capacity of an industry to pay certain wages, but would fix what wages it thought necessary, and the industry would then have recourse to the Tariff Board, which had been created by the Federal Parliament to make recommendations for the granting of whatever protection was necessary. In this case the various unions appeared before the Tariff Board to assist the employers in obtaining necessary increases in order to make it possible to work the mills at a profit instead of at a loss, and then immediately approached the Arbitration Court for their share in these increases.

In this way a precedent is created for passing back and forth between the Federal Arbitration Court and the Tariff Board for increments in wages and duties, which can only result in an ever increasing wage rate, and an ever ascending Tariff. This course must ultimately defeat itself, and by constantly raising the cost of living bring about an industrial paralysis.

From considerations such as the foregoing the Tariff Board is strongly of opinion that the industrial unions of the Commonwealth should be induced to realise the critical position into which the Commonwealth is drifting and the absolute necessity for preventing the wages gap from becoming still wider between the United Kingdom, the continent of Europe, and the Commonwealth, otherwise, the Tariff Board, placed as it is in the position to take a comprehensive and intimate view of all Australian industry, can see nothing but economic disaster ahead, and that at no very distant date. (Tariff Board 1926, pp. 13–14)

In its 1927 report, the Board again discussed this problem. Commenting on 'the abuse of protection', it wrote:

> The Board is profoundly convinced that if Australian industry is to be maintained and safeguarded, it is absolutely essential that the leaders of industrial unions should recognise the serious menace of rising costs of production which the Board has indicated. The Board wishes it to be understood that it is not desirous of taking any side in the industrial disputes … but it cannot be blind to the fact that simultaneously with the Board being asked to consider large increases in duties on such important industries as—
>
> Timber
> Engineering
> Iron and Steel
> Brushware
> Copper (Bonus)
> Butter and Cheese
> Glassware
> Clothing
> Textiles
>
> with the object of enabling such industries to *exist*, applications had been lodged and Arbitration Courts—Federal and State—had been and were being asked to grant not only increased wages but further improved conditions and shorter hours, and State Governments were introducing legislation at the time which further added to the already high cost of production. (Tariff Board 1927, p. 21)

The Board, in its next annual report, said that it was 'again evident that requests for increased wages and improved conditions of employment are not always based upon sound economic principles, and there is an apparent need for co-operation between the authorities fixing the rates of wages and conditions of employment and the framers of the tariff' (Tariff Board 1928, p. 16). The Board deprecated the 'acknowledged hostility between organised employers and organised employees'. It would be 'a good thing for both organisations and for Australian industry if each organisation would exclude from its membership all members whose militancy makes for strife and bad feeling' (p. 18).

In 1929, the British Economic Mission joined in the criticism of the misuse of the tariff:

> But all measures designed for the increase of Australia's wealth production and power of absorbing new population tend to be defeated if there are strong forces within her which operate so to raise her costs of production that she cannot sell her products in the markets of the world, and is restricted within the limitations of her home market. Here we approach the most vexed, and the most important of all Australian questions, that of the combined effect of the protective Customs tariff and of the legislative enactments, both of the Commonwealth and of the States, which we will call, for brevity, the Arbitration Acts. ... [W]e have been strongly disposed to the view that the combined operation of the tariff and of the Arbitration Acts has raised costs to a level which has laid an excessive and possibly even a dangerous load upon the unsheltered primary industries, which, having to sell in the world's markets, cannot pass on the burden to other sections of the Australian community, and, consequently, as between the various States, upon those, notably Western Australia, South Australia and Tasmania, which are poor in manufactures and are principally concerned with primary production. ... We have felt much force in the oft-repeated complaint that successive increases in the tariff which affect prices and the cost of living, following upon, or being followed by, successive advances in the cost of labour as the result of decisions under the Arbitration Acts have involved Australia in a vicious circle of ever ascending costs and prices, and that this condition of affairs is crippling Australia's progress and her power of supporting increased population. There lies no task before the Australian people more urgent than that of in some way breaking the vicious circle and of bringing down costs of production, as is being done in other industrial countries of the world, without lowering the standard of living of the workers as measured not by money but by real wages, which are the reward of labour in the form of goods and services. (British Economic Mission 1929, pp. 13–14)

In 1929, the Tariff Board played a somewhat different tune. It was impressed by 'reports from different sources that there is a growing spirit of co-operation between employers and employees and a more ready acknowledgement that the interests of the two sections are so closely allied that only by mutual consideration can the objective of both, or either, be attained' (Tariff Board 1929, p. 12). There was a return to the former line of comment in 1930, when the Board stated that 'labour costs are seriously higher in Australia than in many other countries'. It was 'impossible to escape the conviction that the costs of production in some industries could be materially reduced if there were greater co-operation between employers and employees to secure increased output' (Tariff Board 1930, p. 17). This may well have been an allusion to the vexed question of piecework.

Thereafter, the Board gave less emphasis to the problems of labour relations and labour costs. In 1935, it cited League of Nations statistics indicating a considerable fall in labour costs in Australia relative to those of the United Kingdom (Tariff Board 1935, p. 19). In its report for 1937, it said:

> The outlook is much more hopeful at present than it has been for years. … During the late twenties, wages, interest and costs generally were rising and prices of products of protected industry were getting more and more out of step with world prices. The Tariff Board year by year sounded this warning, pointing out that this spiral rise in costs and prices must have a reaction ultimately. The position in this regard is markedly better today. (Tariff Board 1938, p. 25)

The Board again compared labour costs in Australia and the United Kingdom, using nominal wage data for Australia and Bowley's wage index for Britain. Between 1929 and 1937, wages had fallen by 15.2 per cent in Australia and had risen by 0.5 per cent in the United Kingdom. The Australian data pre-dated the 1937 basic wage increase. 'It is not easy', said the Board, 'to forecast the full effect of the increase, but from the point of view of its possible effect on the competitive position of local industries, it is not likely to be serious' (Tariff Board 1938, p. 26). In its 1938–39 report, the Board extended to 1938 the comparison of Australian and British wages: Australian wages had since

1929 fallen by 9.8 per cent, while British wages had risen by 3.8 per cent (Tariff Board 1939, p. 16).

It appears that the debate about the tariff-wages issue, which had been so prominent in the later 1920s, was submerged by the Depression and did not revive thereafter.

13.1.5 The Depression

At onset of the Great Depression, Australia lacked any bureaucratic infrastructure for economic advice that could assist governments in understanding the problem and in devising measures to deal with it.[24] Policy focused initially on two concerns: government finance and the funding of a rising foreign-account deficit. The Labor Government, which had been elected in mid-1929 on the specific issue of preserving the arbitration system, sought help from Britain, and this resulted in the visit of Sir Otto Niemeyer (Deputy Governor of the Bank of England) and Sir Theodore Gregory (a monetary economist at the London School of Economics and a member of the MacMillan Committee). Their advice was rigidly orthodox. They were preoccupied with the maintenance of confidence on the part of foreign lenders and saw this as requiring strict adherence to the existing exchange rate and rigorously balanced government budgets. Niemeyer and Gregory had little impact on policy. The Labor Government, however, was torn by conflict over the adoption of the kinds of measures proposed by the mainstream Australian economists, the less orthodox

---

[24] There were at least two reasons. One was the scarcity of trained economists. The other was the recruitment practices of the Public Services. On the latter, W K Hancock commented: 'Democratic sentiment applauds the sound argument that every office boy should have a chance to become a manager, and perverts it into a practical rule that no one shall become a manager who has not been an office boy. Australian Governments insist generally upon the rule that everybody must enter the public service at the age of sixteen or thereabouts. At the same time, by means of an excellent system of scholarships, they cunningly entice the cleverest boys to the Universities. When they have been enticed thither, these boys discover (unless they have entered upon a strictly technical training) that there is nothing for them to do except teach. So they return to school and encourage other clever boys to win scholarships. In this way the State has most ingeniously contrived that its system of democratic education shall not embarrass the public services by introducing into them resplendent talents. There has, it is true, been considerable reform in recent years. Merit is gaining rapidly on mere seniority. Yet it would be very easy to prove that the lack of trained economic forethought is responsible for some of the most costly failures of state enterprise in Australia' (Hancock 1930, p. 142).

measures espoused by the Treasurer, E G Theodore, and the extreme policies pursued by the New South Wales Government of J T Lang.

There was a policy vacuum. The Australian economists—mainly academics or ex-academics—proceeded to fill it. In doing so, they devised policies reflective of local circumstances that stepped around the advice of Niemeyer and Gregory. The scope for their doing so was increased by the sharing of decision-making between the Commonwealth and the States, partly by reason of the paralysis of the Labor Government, but also because of the role played by the Loan Council[25] and because important areas of policy were then State-based.

Among the economists there was a remarkable level of agreement. At the centre of their thinking were the realities of an enormous fall in the incomes of exporters (especially wool and wheat growers) and the inevitability of an overall reduction in real expenditure due both to the adverse movement of the terms of trade and a drying up of foreign credit. The objective of their advice was to limit the fall in real spending to the amount that was inescapable with the fall in the terms of trade and the collapse of foreign borrowing, roundly estimated at 10 per cent. If this were achieved, there would be a fall in the standard of living, but employment would be protected. The economists judged that this best-available outcome required an even distribution of the loss across all sectors of the economy, rather than its concentration upon the export sectors. As we have seen, Copland delivered this message to the Court in 1930.

The intellectual foundation of the economists' view about distributing the burden seems to have been described, rather tentatively, by Giblin (1930a) in his inaugural lecture at The University of Melbourne as Ritchie Professor, given in April 1930. This may well have been the first statement, anywhere, of the multiplier. But whereas the Keynesian multiplier, expounded first by R F Kahn and adopted by Keynes in *The General Theory*, turned on an imbalance of saving and investment, Giblin's concern was with the adjustment of income

---

[25] A Commonwealth-State instrumentality established in the 1920s to coordinate and control government borrowing.

to a level at which imports would equal the lower level of exports. At that stage, the apparent loss of export income was about £50 million. With about one-third of every pound of expenditure going on imports, Giblin's reasoning led him to predict a fall of income of £150 million. He went on:

> The matter is obscure. I confess I do not see my way clearly through the tangle of price reactions that must follow the loss of income. I will only say that my somewhat muddled belief is that the tendency will be broadly to this result, to the extent that the Australian standard of living fails to adjust itself to the diminished income; but that if the loss is evenly spread through the community, it may be very nearly confined to the first direct loss of £50 million, and there need be no serious addition to unemployment. (pp 11–12)

Spreading the sacrifice became a fundamental plank in the economists' program. And this included a cut in real wages.

Giblin's *Letters to John Smith* (Giblin 1930b), published by the Melbourne *Herald* in July 1930, were an attempt to 'sell' this line of thought to the general public. At least one man in every six, he estimated, must be working in export industries. Then there were all the industries which had to compete with imports, which were also unsheltered.

> So that it is clear that a big part of our industry must be unsheltered for many years to come. We must keep this unsheltered industry going. But if we raise wages in sheltered industry, we make it impossible to grow as much wheat and wool or mine as much zinc and lead, and we shall not have exports enough to pay our interest and pay for necessary imports. That is the mess we are in now, with unemployment widespread and growing on every side. And we have not seen the worst of it yet. (p. 7)

'We have', said Giblin, 'been living as a people on more than we earned by a big margin. In future we are going to earn less (unless we work harder) because other people do not want our wool and wheat so much as they did in the last few years and they don't lend us so much money to help out what we can earn ourselves' (p. 10). He attempted some arithmetic, based on the Statistician's wage data, which seemed to show that the total wage bill exceeded

L F Gliblin

the sum available for payment of wages, even before the crisis. The only possible explanation was 'that a great many people not working under a regular award must be getting considerably less than the average of organised labour. These will include wage-earners on farms, and all kinds of people working on their own accounts and particularly the farmer on one-man and two-man farms' (pp. 15–16). The sensible thing was 'to recognise that wage rates in organised labour have been rather above their fair share of the wealth produced in the country. With the fall in the wealth produced, they must come down' (p.17). The wages of organised labour could no longer be sustained by the earnings of unsheltered industry, and the inevitable result was unemployment of workers in the sheltered industries. This was now a reality (p. 21).

I have discussed at length, in Chapter 9, Copland's evidence to the Court, which substantially reflected the contentions agreed upon by the mainstream of Australian economists. It would be wrong to say that the Court simply adopted Copland's arguments: the decision is quite wide-ranging and, for the time, sophisticated.[26] Copland's evidence, nevertheless, served to confirm the Court's determination to reduce wages and lent some precision to its perception of the amount of the required reduction.

About a year later, the Wallace Bruce Committee reviewed the effect of wage reductions. Its report (Wallace Bruce Committee 1932) was prepared by a committee comprising two Under-Treasurers and the economists Giblin, Melville, Mills, and Shann. The falling-off in rural purchasing power had, the Committee said, spread unemployment throughout the community:

> The restoration of employment, as opposed to temporary stimulants, is to be found in bringing into harmony the costs and prices of export industry. This adjustment must involve, for the time, a general lowering of standards in agreement with our loss of real income. … With the present trend of overseas prices, the cut in costs required to restore the balance if this way alone were followed, would involve reductions in nominal wages and interest rates of the order of 50 per cent. The attempt to do this would threaten social and financial stability. To attempt to restore export prices simply by raising the exchange would end in loss of control of the currency and general collapse. There is, however, a probability that a solution can be found by using each method as far as is safe and practicable. The gap between export costs and prices is about 20 per cent. Some of this might be covered by direct cutting of costs, some by raising the exchange and some gained by increased efficiency throughout industry. The re-absorption of all the unemployed is unsustainable until prosperity is regained over a large part of the world. In the meantime the problem of relieving unemployment is pressing. But it is essential that the method of restoring equilibrium between costs and prices should be steadily pursued along with measures of alleviation, and that the latter should be framed so as not to impede but to form the basis of future prosperity.' (pp. 39–41)

---

[26] A view that I share with Schedvin (1970, p. 215).

The policy of cutting real wages by 10 per cent had not been given a fair trial. Workers under federal awards had been subject to the full reduction, but many other workers had not. Nominal wages had been reduced on the average by about 12 per cent since 1928. The average, however, covered a dispersion from about 3 per cent under State awards in New South Wales to over 30 per cent under federal awards in South Australia. Some salaries had not been reduced; others had been reduced by over 30 per cent (p. 56). The Committee called for a general application of the cut. It recognised that wage reductions would lead to price reductions and hence to further wage reductions, so that the total reduction in nominal wages would be much more than 10 per cent. This process would be mitigated by appreciation of the exchange rate (p. 67).

J M Keynes never visited Australia. But he made two interventions into the Australian debate. One was in May 1932, when he wrote an article for the Melbourne *Herald*, which was reproduced in other newspapers (Keynes 1982). This was a commentary on the Wallace Bruce Report. (Keynes had not actually seen it and his comments were based on second-hand reports.) The general thrust of his article was that Australia had already done as much as it was sensible to do, that more 'strong action' might worsen the situation and that it was best simply to await a world recovery, especially a recovery of prices. In relation to wages, he lent his support to the somewhat unorthodox view that wage cuts were a dubious policy, for while they reduced costs they also reduced purchasing power. 'I understand', he said

> that the reductions of money wages so far effected have been unequal. It is of the essence of what has been happening in Australia that there should be equality of sacrifice, and it would seem obvious that New South Wales should be brought into line with the rest of the country. … But a policy of a further general reduction in money wages would be a double-edged weapon. It would tend to curtail purchasing power and, consequently, to aggravate rather than assist the problem of the Budget. I do not clearly see in what way it would help the general situation unless

it were to expand the physical volume of exports, and I should have supposed that in present circumstances it would have no considerable effect in that direction. So far as internal production and consumption are concerned, sales receipts would fall off by just about as much as costs had been cut. The Experts recognise that it is impracticable to reduce costs and debts by a further 40 per cent. But I go much further than this. I do not believe that unemployment would be remedied by measures of this kind even if they could be put into force. (pp. 96–97)

The years 1931–35 were the period when Keynes was moving from the ideas articulated in his *Treatise on Money* to those of *The General Theory*. It is well known that he discussed his emerging theories widely within Cambridge. E R Walker, a Sydney graduate, took his PhD at Cambridge and in 1933 published a book, *Australia in the World Depression*, based on his PhD thesis. It contains a useful factual account of what happened before and during the early years of the Depression. But it also struggles with the question whether the policies adopted in Australia could be reconciled with the ideas being advanced by Keynes. The unions, in the 1930–31 wage case, had put the argument that a wage cut would be of no help, because there would be a more or less equivalent reduction of purchasing power. This argument was encouraged by Irvine. The Court itself rejected it, arguing that purchasing power would not be reduced, but would be shifted from workers to capitalists, who would spend their added purchasing power on their own consumption or on investment. 'Mr Keynes' theories', said Walker,

> encourage scepticism as regards the view that someone's loss is necessarily somebody else's gain. If attempts to share the loss by cutting wages lead only to the reduction of consumers' incomes by the same amount as the cost of production is reduced, the factors determining the general level of unemployment will not have been affected at all. Of course, the view that general wage reductions may be neutral in their effect upon the business cycle is in many quarters regarded as fallacious. Indeed, it is only with its adoption by Mr Keynes that it has gained respectability among English economists. (Walker 1933, p.167)

If Keynes were right, the only measures that could reduce unemployment were those that would alter the balance between investment and saving. There was no reason to suppose that wage cuts would do that.[27]

But the Keynesian analysis, in its simplest form, relates to a closed economy. The Australian economy was open and the Depression was imposed on it from abroad. Given time, it might adjust by shifting resources out of the export industries into import replacement. In the shorter term, a collapse of the export industries, with the consequent drying up of exporters' spending, would be equivalent in its effects to a reduction of investment. The economists' advocacy of wage reductions had to do, not so much with shifting income between workers and employers, but with keeping exporters in business. They would do this by restoring the previous relativity between domestic and external prices. The same effect could be achieved by exchange rate adjustment. The economists did advocate a depreciation of the Australian pound. They were unwilling to rely wholly on it because of the possible effect on foreign confidence. Hence they favoured a mixture of wage reductions and external depreciation. Keynes' article in the *Herald* recognised that wage reductions were meant to maintain export production. He opposed further reductions because of a practical judgment that they would have no effect on exports.

Keynes' second intervention was less direct. It was in *The General Theory* itself. There is a passage in which Keynes rejects the idea of managing the money wage level with a view to altering real wages and thereby employment. The equilibrium level of employment was a product of the level of investment, and the equilibrium real wage was a product of the level of employment,

---

[27] In 1935, Arthur Smithies—just returned from research in Harvard and a teaching post at Michigan University to join the Bureau of Census and Statistics—published an article (Smithies 1935) exploring 'from the "orthodox" point of view' the question whether a wage reduction would increase employment. (The answer was equivocal.) This was a highly theoretical article. Smithies simply assumed that the wage reduction was in real terms. He also assumed that the economy was closed. In a note published in 1936, Walker said that Smithies, by the artificiality of his assumptions, 'clearly forfeits all claim to deal with wages policy in the real world' (Walker 1936, p. 100). Smithies (1936) published a rejoinder.

and not *vice versa*. A successful attempt to fix real wages would cause violent fluctuations of employment and prices:

> If, as in Australia, an attempt were made to fix real wages by legislation, then there would be a certain level of employment corresponding to that level of real wages; and the actual level of employment would, in a closed system, oscillate violently between that level and no employment at all, according as the rate of investment was or was not below the rate compatible with that level; whilst prices would be in unstable equilibrium when investment was at the critical level, racing to zero whenever investment was below it, and to infinity whenever it was above it. ... In the actual case of Australia, the escape was found, partly of course in the inevitable inefficacy of the legislation to achieve its object, and partly in Australia not being a closed system, so that the level of money-wages was itself a determinant of the level of foreign investment and hence of total investment, whilst the terms of trade were an important influence on real wages. (Keynes 1936, pp. 269–270)

Keynes may have heard the 1933 Marshall Lectures, wherein Copland reported that the wage-reduction strategy had failed to reduce real wages at all, despite a massive reduction in money wages. Keynes went on to say that he was 'now of the opinion that the maintenance of a stable general level of money-wages is, on a balance of considerations, the most advisable policy for a closed system; whilst the same conclusion will hold good for an open system, provided that equilibrium with the rest of the world can be secured by means of fluctuating exchanges' (p. 270). Australia's experiment with a managed wage reduction may well have had an important effect on Keynes' thinking.

13.1.6 Recovery

In the last five years or so before World War II, the apparent interest of the economists in wage fixation diminished. This, no doubt, was a result of a general decline in the necessity for economic management as external influences became more benign. The principal exception was the concern of the 'Melbourne group' in 1937 to raise wages so as to avert an investment boom. This concern was articulated for them by Reddaway, whose evidence to the basic wage case is described in Chapter 12. I do not repeat that account, but note the following implications of Reddaway's analysis:

- It entailed a clear perception of the Arbitration Court as an instrument and arbiter of macroeconomic policy. The same perception, of course, was apparent in Copland's evidence in 1930. Like Copland, Reddaway saw the policy as operating via the modification of distributive shares. By reallocating income between rent and profits, on the one hand, and wages, on the other, the Court would moderate the expansionary forces then evident in the economy.
- There was a presumption that good policy required wage restraint in depressed times and generosity when conditions were better. This presumption was generally accepted by the Court and created difficulties after World War II, when it was translated into an environment of full employment and inflation.
- Reddaway spoke of the need to increase the real wage, failing to comment on the Court's ability to control real wages and seemingly taking no heed of Keynes' remarks about the consequences of attempting to fix real wages and the advisability of stabilising money wages.

I return to Reddaway's prescription of a wage increase to stem an incipient boom in Subsection 13.2.4 below.

13.1.7 Retrospectives

This subsection recounts four appraisals of the Court's role and performance in managing wage policy in the 1930s.

The first was by Copland who, in one of his 1933 Marshall Lectures (Copland 1934), gave the following summary of the Court's contribution to anti-Depression policy:

> The Government of the day had been elected on a pledge to preserve the Court. This was interpreted by the electorate as a pledge to preserve the standard of living. Despite important amendments to the Arbitration Act, the Government was powerless to prevent the Court from ordering a reduction in wages, if economic conditions appeared to necessitate such a reduction. The Government did in fact intervene in the case, and was represented by counsel. This was the limit to its authority, and the Court, after hearing evidence that covered the whole economic position of the country, decided to reduce the basic wage by 10 per cent in addition to the normal adjustments of the wage to quarterly decreases in the cost of living. The award of the Court was a survey of the general economic situation at the end of 1930, and it is of more than passing interest to note that the first pronouncement on the crisis from a responsible authority was this award of the Arbitration Court. (p. 89)

In another lecture, Copland noted that the benefit of the Court's decision was diminished by the failure of State arbitration authorities to follow its lead. Nevertheless, the system as a whole facilitated a reduction of money wages that, in the economists' view, was an essential element in the overall economic program. Copland contrasted the Australian experience favourably with that of Great Britain, where wage reductions had been much more difficult to achieve.

The second assessment, by A G B Fisher in 1934, was somewhat similar to Copland's:

> The system of wage regulation which has played such an important part in Australian economic life for many years has frequently been criticised both inside and outside Australia on the ground that it introduced elements of rigidity which did make difficult, if not impossible, rapid adjustment to any change in the foundations of the

Australian economy. The Australian wage structure is still certainly far from displaying that delicacy and elasticity which did delight the hearts of those who admire the free working of a flexible economic system, but the history of recent years has shown clearly that the fears of critics were exaggerated, for prompt adjustments have been made at least as easily in Australia as in most other parts of the world ... Throughout the period, however, the downward movement of retail prices was roughly parallel to the movement of wages, so that apart from the increased risks of unemployment real wages have apparently moved very little. (Fisher 1934, p. 760)

Third, we have the opinion of Reddaway. By early 1938, he was back at Clare College, Cambridge. He published an article reviewing in some detail the Court's policies over the period 1927–37. His broad conclusion was that the Court's ability to conduct a wage policy (including wage reductions) had been a valuable ingredient of the overall policy mix:

[I]s there any advantage in having machinery for fixing the general level of wages, instead of leaving it to emerge from a large number of sectional decisions? The experience of this period surely shows that such a system is very valuable. The employment market in a country such as Australia does not, and never will, bear much resemblance to the text-book version with its perfect competition, equality of opportunity, automatic adjustments, and so on. Without some general system of regulation it is doubtful whether money wages could ever have been reduced sufficiently to preserve the exporter and encourage new manufactures; it is quite certain that the cuts would have fallen most unequally on different sections of the community. The trade unions in sheltered industries would have been able to resist the full cut, relying on the ability of the employers to charge relatively high prices at least for a time; if the unsheltered industries were to be maintained despite these relatively high prices for the things they bought, then the standards of the people engaged in them would have had to be cut still further. To secure the general fall in costs that was vitally necessary, a general system of regulation was almost indispensable. (Reddaway 1938, pp. 334–335)

Reddaway asked the question: 'What principle or principles should the Court apply in determining its policy?' The Court itself had reached the conclusion 'that its main criterion must be, in some sense, the state of industry, and not the attractive but elusive idea of the "needs" of the worker, with or without his traditional wife and three children'. 'This', said Reddaway, 'is obviously sound' (pp. 335–336). But it was difficult to give precise content to the criterion of capacity to pay. The Court, to a large extent, had equated it with unemployment:

> The Court's procedure is to use the extent of unemployment as the main guide in judging whether the wage prescribed in the past was appropriate to the circumstances of the time, and then to investigate whether there have been any material changes in those circumstances such as would justify a revision of the wage. This is clearly the only possible method, but it is still full of difficulties. Unemployment is a complex phenomenon which is influenced by other things beside wage policy; the Court recognised this when it granted a rise in 1934 although the level of unemployment was then above 'normal'. It was obvious that no practicable wage policy could remove the abnormal unemployment overnight, and the Court assessed 'the unemployment situation' dynamically in terms of a rate of progress rather than statically by the absolute level. On a comprehensive view of the situation it decided that a higher wage would be compatible with further reduction of unemployment at a reasonable rate. (p. 336)

Inasmuch as this comment gives the impression that the unemployment percentages were the principal focus of the Court's attention, it is an exaggeration. The judges were, of course, mindful of a firm link between the prosperity of employers and their capacity to employ. They were, however, concerned very much with evidence about the profitability of industry and its vulnerability to increased costs. Employers who adduced such evidence could be confident of careful (and often sympathetic) attention, provided that the evidence had the appropriate degree of generality. The Court, in the 1930s, was impatient with those employers who debated general wage changes by detailing the circumstances of specific industries.

Reddaway accepted that wage reductions had been necessary in the Depression. They provided relief to exporters, and facilitated expansion of secondary industries by improving their capacity to compete with imports. In economic logic, exchange depreciation was an alternative, but the scope for this was limited:

> At that time the virtues of exchange depreciation were not recognised; it was associated in men's minds with the German inflation and regarded as a mere nostrum. Australia did use it, the rate on London rising to 130 in January 1931, and then being reduced to 125 in December. To have raised it further—say to 150—might have created a first-class panic. The political aspect also cannot be ignored. A Labour Government was in power, which would make the adoption of an unorthodox policy appear all the more dangerous to the leaders of industry and owners of capital, whose 'confidence' is unfortunately so essential. It would have been regarded as an expedient to shirk the real issue ... (p. 331)

To Reddaway, the Depression experience proved the value of an institution able to influence the general behaviour of wages. It was important to have a mechanism capable of delivering lower money wages at a time of rapidly falling prices:

> Without some general system of regulation it is doubtful whether money wages could ever have been reduced sufficiently to preserve the exporter and encourage new manufactures; it is quite certain that the cuts would have fallen most unequally on different sections of the community. The trade unions in sheltered industries would have been able to resist the full cut, relying on the ability of the employers to charge relatively high prices at least for a time; if the unsheltered industries were to be maintained despite these relatively high prices for the things they bought, then the standards of the people engaged in them would have had to be cut still further. To secure the general fall in costs that was vitally necessary, a general system of regulation was almost indispensable. (p. 334)

Reddaway discussed the system of automatic adjustments. 'At first sight', he said,

> this might appear anomalous if the wage is to be based on capacity to pay (depending largely on external circumstances) and not on the worker's needs. But it is at least arguable that the adjustment will produce good results, so long as the wage itself is reviewed fairly frequently. If circumstances remain stable, the two systems are identical; if they are changing rapidly, as during the war or at the onset of the depression, then the automatic adjustments will generally be in the right direction, and will be better than nothing until the situation can be reviewed. Moreover the system has the very important support of tradition. (p. 337)

The 'anomaly' of maintaining automatic adjustments alongside a 'capacity-to-pay' criterion formed an important part of the Court's reasoning when it jettisoned the adjustment system in 1953. There is no evidence that, in the 1930s, it saw the price index as a temporary, if inexact, indicator of capacity to pay. The most accurate interpretation, I believe, is that in making a decision about the basic wage it relied primarily on the contemporaneous state of the economy and industries, with perhaps some attempt to anticipate conditions in the medium-term future. Having set the wage, it sought, for reasons of equity, to preserve its real value until the next review. Maintenance of the real wage was seen to be most important for the low-paid. At no time did the Court exhibit a like concern about the real value of margins.

Finally, I note briefly the opinion of W R Maclaurin, an American scholar who had visited Australia in 1934–35:

> Although the labor movement has not accepted the Court's arguments in favour of wage reductions in the depression as valid, the discussion by the Court in 1931 of the necessity for wage reductions in view of the fall in the national income appears to have been of very considerable value in promoting an understanding of the economic situation of the country among a large section of the electorate. From the beginning of the depression the Court has taken more notice of fluctuations in economic

conditions than almost any other official or semi-official body in the country. ... In the regulation of minimum wages we could profit perhaps by Australian experience. Here again, however, it would seem desirable to experiment first with a 'basic' wage designed to provide a 'fair and reasonable' standard of living and leave the provision of margins for skill to the play of market forces. So far as the method of adjusting the basic wage is concerned, I am inclined to think that the Australian system of automatic regional cost-of-living adjustments checked periodically by reference to general economic conditions is the most practical method of administering a national minimum wage. The understanding of general economic conditions shown by the Commonwealth Court in recent years indicates that a properly administered minimum wage may add a valuable element of flexibility and control in the business cycle. (Maclaurin 1938, pp. 74 and 81)[28]

Between these four economists, then, there was a consensus as to the value of a regulatory institution able to influence wages in the direction indicated by the state of the economy. By the late 1930s, so far as I am aware, there was no Australian economist arguing a contrary view.

13.1.8 Conclusion

Wage policy was one topic to which the economists who exerted significant influence over policy before World War II gave their attention. To the best of my knowledge, Australia was unique in the part that wage policy played in economic discourse. This, of course, is attributable to the unique role of arbitration in this country. The economists had a stylised conception of the Federal Court—one that exaggerated its control of affairs. The Court's willingness to listen to the economists was no doubt due partly to its own lack of economic expertise: it was entirely composed of lawyers. The explicit and

---

[28] In a footnote (p. 81), Maclaurin wrote: 'Professor Copland has written to me that the new principle of a prosperity "loading" adopted by the Court in 1937 was worked out largely at the suggestion of the Australian economists. "Apart from the basic economic conditions having justified a rise in wages," Copland writes, "the Court thought an extra amount should be given to workers in order that expansion and investment might be dampened down"'.

implicit affirmations of the economists about the significance of wage policy could only have added to the Court's sense of its own importance.

The economists, of course, did not have the field entirely to themselves. In this section we have noted criticisms of the system by 'practical' men—those associated with the Tariff Board and the British Economic Mission. But it was the economists who struggled to unravel the more intricate cause-and-effect relations between wage-setting and economic performance.

13.2 Economic appraisal

13.2.1 Introduction

The background information provided in Chapter 1 affords evidence, admittedly imperfect, of two notable features of this period: a slow growth of productivity and a modest growth in real wages. Economists would generally expect the latter to flow from the former, though noting various reasons why they might to some extent diverge, including the terms of trade and foreign borrowing and a range of influences which might cause changes in the share of national income accruing to wage-earners. Because of Australia's exposure to foreign trade and, until 1931, the rigidity of the exchange rate between sterling and the Australian pound, there were significant possibilities of variation in income shares. Such variations might or might not affect employment. To the extent that the Court controlled money wages, it might be able to effect changes in the overall claim of labour on the national income. The available statistics, summarised in Chapter 1, suggest that real wages fell substantially in the years of World War I and immediately afterwards but increased dramatically in 1920–21. Subsequent changes were subdued. In this study we have explored the interaction between the Court's policies and economic conditions. Nevertheless, the question as to how, in the long term, those policies affected income shares, productivity growth, prices, and employment is largely conjectural.

The various issues involved in an assessment of the system's performance cannot be divorced from the environment in which it operated. If there had been no intervention by the government or one of its agencies in the functioning of the labour market, would the worst aspects of the market inherited from the 19th century, and characterised by the term 'sweating', have solved themselves? And would trade unions have recovered from the setbacks of the 1890s and expanded their membership sufficiently to exercise a significant effect over the terms of employment? The two questions are obviously interrelated. The original *Commonwealth Conciliation and Arbitration Act 1904* was an attempt to move on two fronts: to encourage the formation of unions and employers' associations so that employment terms would be negotiated rather than set by take-it-or-leave-it offers of employers; and to provide a mechanism whereby disputes between the negotiators could be determined and whereby employees lacking bargaining power could be protected. State laws had similar objectives, and all provided for authorities able to exercise legal power over terms of employment. The mechanisms varied. But federal and State laws all recognised and encouraged trade unions as representatives of labour.

Some of the founders of arbitration may well have envisaged the tribunals as industrial firemen, intervening to douse specific conflagrations and then retiring from the scene to allow the forces of the market and of bargaining to resume their normal determinative course. Others undoubtedly foresaw a wider role than this. That wider role may or may not have been inevitable, but it certainly came to pass. At least two reasons can be identified.

First, as we have noted, the creation and operation of tribunals went hand in hand with an expanded role for unions. The law assisted the growth of unions by providing mechanisms for their registration and for resolving issues as to their coverage. Even more important than this was the removal of the employers' option to refuse to deal with unions. If a union had a legal right to represent the employer's workers, the employer could not act as if it did not exist. An employer who refused to deal with the union could be forced to appear (directly or through an association) before a tribunal and be subject to an award which set standards that must be observed. In practice, most employers came to terms with this reality, and a high proportion of the content of awards was settled by agreement. The growth of unionism and the expansion of the tribunals' role were closely linked. Employers' attitudes to tribunal regulation went through phases, as we have seen. In the 1920s, there was strong resentment of regulation; by the late 1930s, employers were strongly supportive of the tribunals (especially the Commonwealth Court).

Second, the members of tribunals—especially those of the Court type—had a natural inclination toward consistency. They saw inconsistent decisions both as unfair and as likely causes of disputation. Acceptance of prior decisions led into pattern-setting. Arbitrators, in some though not all cases, made their decisions on the basis that the standards being set were likely to be observed more widely. The federal basic wage emerged from this process. In respect of other issues, including working hours and margins, there were recognised key decisions. The federal legislature, beginning in 1921, encouraged this process by reserving some issues to full benches.[29] These attributes of the system caused the emergence, not of absolute uniformity, but of widely prevailing standards.

It is difficult, then, to engage with critics who assert that Australia's economic development would have been better if no arbitration system had existed. Before assessing such a contention one would need to know:

- how the institutions of the labour market, especially trade unions, would have developed in the absence of the tribunal system. Would collective bargaining arrangements have evolved; what form would they have taken; and how wide would their coverage have been?
- the form, the scope, and the effectiveness of legal protections that would have been instituted for workers judged to be disadvantaged in the labour market.

It is pointless to respond to these implicit questions by describing some ideal set of arrangements or postulating a benign labour market. The pertinent question is what *would* have happened, not what *should* have happened.

---

[29] It might have gone further by providing for appeals, but this did not occur until the 1950s.

We must, therefore, retreat to a different and less ambitious kind of question. Take as given the position that arbitration occupied in the labour market. How well did the tribunals, and especially the Federal Court, exercise their powers? In the previous chapters, we have described their actions as a form of economic and distributive regulation. There are, of course, other aspects to be considered—notably the preservation of industrial peace—in an overall evaluation of the tribunals' performance. These, however, are not the subject of this study.

13.2.2 The Higgins era

Higgins, broadly supported by Powers, adopted the concept of a minimum wage as the foundation of the regulated wage structure. A similar principle was accepted by the State tribunal in New South Wales and, a little later, in South Australia; later still, in Queensland and Western Australia. Wages boards in Victoria and Tasmania applied it in a less explicit manner. By 1920, *the* basic wage had become sufficiently recognised as a component of Australian wages for Prime Minister Hughes refer to it in an election policy speech and to appoint an inquiry into its adequacy and mode of adjustment. In the preceding years, the application of the basic wage concept had been strained by wartime inflation and deficient methods of wage adjustment. And in the federal jurisdiction, there was no general basic wage but rather one that varied from award to award according to when the award was made and who made it. The *Harvester* standard was recognised. Aided by Higgins' doctrine that it was 'sacrosanct', and not subject to any test of economy-wide or industry-level capacity to pay, it acquired a somewhat mystical character; but it was not extensively enforced because of the absence of a general basic wage, the infrequency of award making, and the unsystematic responses to price levels. There was little appreciation of the concept of a wage *structure*. Rewards for skill varied inversely, in real terms, to the rate of inflation, although Higgins during the war did advert to the need to restore proportional relativities in more normal times and in 1921 began to do that.

The embryonic wage policy consisted of decided cases wherein some principles or rules gradually crystallised. Apart from those pertaining to the basic wage, the most important were:

- the non-adjustment for inflation of margins for skill and other attributes of the work;
- in the federal jurisdiction, adherence to the norm of a 48-hour working week; and
- the principle that females should receive less than males. Though explicitly defended in terms of unequal need, the differentiation was not confined to the basic wage.

It is difficult to identify the benefits to wage-earners, the cost to employers or the economic effects more generally of the advent of arbitration. Figure 2.7 in Chapter 2 suggests that the period of World War I saw rather violent fluctuations in overall real wages. The Court failed to enforce a basic wage that matched the *Harvester* standard. As we have seen, the wage-fixing practices of the time were ill-adapted to the circumstances of imported inflation.

The end of the Higgins era was marked by a complex set of events. Foremost among these were a depression and a consequent transition from inflation to deflation. Sticky money wages, at a time of falling prices, caused a dramatic increase in real wages to a level well above that of 1914. There is little evidence that the arbitration tribunals were alive to this process while it was occurring. (Indeed, there is little reference to it in later pronouncements.) Higgins showed some disposition to move to more generous labour standards, including reduction of working hours and increased margins. Other members of the Court, however, resisted these concessions. The Court, including Higgins, would not countenance the kind of increase needed to give effect to the Piddington basic wage. It justified its stance primarily by reference to alleged defects in Piddington's letters patent, but was also conscious of the contemporary depression. The general pattern, then, was that the Court acquiesced in the rise in real wages caused by the conjuncture of falling prices and sticky money wages, but would not impose yet additional increases in workers' benefits. To call this 'wage policy' is going too far: confusion was too rife. But it may be that the experience was the genesis of more coherent practices.

13.2.3 The 1920s

An early sign of a more orderly approach—facilitated by the tailing-off of the postwar depression and the inflation—was Powers' efforts to introduce a more systematic method of fixing the basic wage. Automatic adjustments would reduce the scope for large 'chance' variations in the real basic wage such as had occurred over the previous decade. Powers' 3s was an attempt to appease the trade unions at a time when they hoped to continue benefiting from a long lag between (falling) prices and wages. Powers' action in getting approval of his policy from a Full Bench of the Court and subsequently having the Court enunciate a set of principles consolidated the change of direction. It was at this time that it became meaningful to speak of *the* basic wage, notwithstanding variations in practice with respect to locations and the application of the price index.

Powers' rejection of the Piddington basic wage, together with his reversal of Higgins' initial attempts to restore pre-war skill relativities and to introduce a general 44-hour week, indicated a sense that the Court was constrained by economic conditions, even if the contention that the Royal Commission was the victim of faulty letters patent was casuistry.

For the rest of Powers' tenure (until 1926), the Court's tendency to focus on the particular industries to which its awards related, few of which manifested high prosperity, led to continuing caution.

The reconstituted Court faced, as its first significant task, a review of the working week. Division within the Bench produced a hybrid outcome, with the practical effect that the transition from the 48-hour to the 44-hour standard week was a protracted process, spread across 12 years. The decision left the Court free to raise the bar against extension of the 44-hour week as economic conditions deteriorated. By 1928, it was doing just that; and in the celebrated *Timber Workers'* case, it actually reverted from 44 hours (granted in 1921) to 48. The Court's hesitancy about reducing the working week stood in contrast to the situation in two of the States, where 44 hours were enforced by legislation.

There was no generalised attempt to restore skill relativities, reflecting the Court's view that most industries had little capacity to absorb extra imposts. But the Court did award—often by consent—margins to sub-tradesmen grades to which previously the basic wage alone applied. It is not possible to quantify the aggregate effect of these less conspicuous wage increases, but the members of the Court sometimes referred to them in rebutting suggestions of undue parsimony.

The principal criticism that has been levelled at the Court's policies in the 1920s is that they (along with those of State tribunals) entailed a real wage level that was too high for the contemporary economy. Evidence for this is found in an unemployment level that was high by pre-war standards. It appears from the data that nominal wages rose strongly between 1920 and 1922 and that, with retail prices falling, there was a large increase in real wages—an increase that was, to a large extent, unintended. In contemporary discussion, the reality of this increase was not fully appreciated. The basic wage *standard* remained—save for Powers' 3s—at the 1907 level. Surely, it might be (and often was) said, the Australian economy could at least maintain this historic standard. This was to overlook several salient facts:

- The *Harvester* standard, when introduced, did constitute a substantial increase in the wage for unskilled workers, at any rate in the private sector. Higgins spoke of a 27 per cent increase. This implied a prior wage of 5s 6d per day, which was probably below the prevailing standard. Six shillings, implying a *Harvester* increase of 17 per cent, was more realistic.
- The application of *Harvester* was initially narrow. The extension of the basic wage and like wages under State awards and determinations was spread over a decade or more.

- During that period, the impact of the basic wage was mitigated by the failure of the tribunals to preserve its real value. That failure was reflected in Hughes' decision of 1919 to appoint a Royal Commission.
- With the fall in prices of 1921–22, the basic wage—by then applicable to much of the workforce—came into line with *Harvester*, augmented by Powers' 3s.

It is a mistake, then, to think of the advent of the *Harvester* basic wage as a 1907 event. It was a process spread across 15 years; and the requirement to meet the standard was a burden not fully imposed on industry until the 1920s.

The impact of the basic wage on the general wage level was offset, to a degree, by squeezing the real value of margins. But overall, the Nominal Wage Index, though beginning only in 1914, indicates a substantial and not reversed rise in real wages in the early 1920s. The contention that wages in the 1920s were too high for full employment, therefore, is not at odds with the wage and price data. Before attributing to wage policy any particular share of blame for semi-depressed conditions, however, it would be necessary to analyse many other contributors, including the failure of agriculture to support adequately the additional settlers committed to it, the poor performance of some of the infrastructure projects of the period, adherence to a near-fixed exchange rate with sterling (which returned to the gold standard in 1925), and the lack of qualified advice in the formulation of government economic policy.

In the later 1920s, the Court was increasingly concerned about the condition of industries and became reluctant to impose further burdens on them.

13.2.4 Depression and recovery

During 1930, the Federal Court made clear its growing belief that the intensifying depression would necessitate wage reductions over and above those associated with falling retail prices. It was therefore willing to be coopted into the professional economists' plans, which included real wage reduction among a suite of measures to deal with the crisis. As Copland noted in 1933, the Court moved independently of government in formulating its response to the crisis. Its decision of January 1931 came at a time of policy disorder, and may well have been crucial to the economists' capacity to get acceptance of their program. The Court's policy of holding down working standards was sustained for several years. Its main elements were the 10 per cent reduction in the real basic wage, a 10 per cent cut in nominal margins and a freeze on reductions in working hours. In other words, it sought to make labour cheaper; and it pursued this policy to offset the adverse effects on industries—especially primary industries—of reduced export prices and the cessation of foreign lending to Australian governments. The Court's policies were significantly counteracted by those of State tribunals (constrained in some cases by legislation).

It is an intriguing question whether any alternative wage policy would have made much or any difference to the severity of the Depression, as measured (for example) by unemployment. By 1934, Beeby, at least, was entertaining serious doubt about the effectiveness of the 10 per cent cut. Money wages and prices fell by 25 to 30 per cent. The fall in money wages was associated with the automatic adjustment system and explicit decisions of tribunals. Reductions in wages and prices reinforced each other, and we cannot say how far prices would have fallen if money wages had somehow been held constant. There is now a general acceptance that the *process* of price deflation has depressing effects, in terms of real output. From the viewpoint of 1930–31, this would have been a reason to rely on exchange depreciation, rather than wage cuts. That apart, there were two problems in wage reductions:

- the difficulty of converting *general* wage reductions into lower real wages—one of the major points made by Keynes. Of course, it was possible to reduce a real wage if it covered a limited field. The federal basic wage did fall in real terms. But, overall, hourly real wages were not reduced.

- a low macroeconomic elasticity of demand for labour due to (1) the adverse effect on the demand for output associated with reduced purchasing power in the workers' hands and (2) a psychological reluctance of capitalists to contemplate the added investment that might have offset diminished consumption.

Notwithstanding these points, it must surely have been true that the general lowering of the price level (including wages) restored somewhat the relativity of domestic to external prices and that this helped sustain primary producers who would otherwise have gone to the wall. Keynes implied that this policy had been taken to its practical limit, and possibly too far. He may well have been right.

With the exception of the 1937 basic wage case, the wage policy of the later 1930s was less one of economic strategy than one of gradual improvement of working standards, featuring higher margins and increased leisure. It was hardly conceivable that the degree of restraint that characterised the early 1930s would be sustained. There is no reason to doubt that the judges of the Court, and their State counterparts, genuinely wished to preside over a rising standard of living for labour; but if they had not done so, the authority of the tribunals might well have been undermined. There were labour leaders, such as Crofts and Clarey, who believed in arbitration but had to contend with more militant officials who favoured the extraction of benefits by direct action. The judges were well aware of this tension and would have been conscious of the necessity of providing to the moderates evidence that their support for the system was not misplaced.

The 1937 case stood apart from other cases of the later 1930s by reason of the attention given to economic strategy. This was at the behest of the Melbourne group of economists, represented by Reddaway. As the employers' anonymous expert pointed out, Reddaway's evidence contained an endorsement of the thesis that higher real wages operated as a brake on economic activity. The unions were prepared to praise this advice because in 1937 it seemed to favour higher wages, whereas in the cases of 1930–34 they had strenuously resisted it. The Court respected Reddaway and was happy to cite his advice as a factor influencing its decision. Reddaway may, indeed, have exercised some influence over the size and timing of the wage increase. But as the employers plainly realised, it was quite unlikely that the unions would have left the Court empty-handed even if no economic advice were proffered to it. The 1934 decision had not fully reversed the 10 per cent cut in the basic wage; and it was clearly expedient for the Court to demonstrate that, just as bad times had called for a wage reduction, increases would be available when better times arrived.

Reddaway's prescription—blessed and possibly instigated by Copland—of an enhanced wage increase to restrain an impending investment boom presumed that making a major input of production more costly would deter entrepreneurs and investors from undertaking projects which might otherwise have gone ahead. The hypothesis seems to be common sense. But there are problems. One is that the proponents of the idea offered no empirical analysis of its practical importance. Given that Reddaway was talking of adding a shilling or two to the wage increase that would otherwise be granted on equity grounds, we may wonder whether the effect would have been noticeable. A second problem is that the deterrent effect might have been outweighed by decisions to adopt more capital-intensive processes in response to the higher cost of labour. A third problem is that raising real wages was likely to stimulate consumption, which may in turn have engendered more investment. A fourth is that—as the employers' anonymous expert pointed out—any impact of the kind that Reddaway suggested was likely to be submerged by the effects of fluctuations in the prices received for major rural exports, especially wool. Overall, it is difficult to accord much weight to the speculation. This, of course, is a criticism of only part of Reddaway's evidence. His comments on foreign borrowing, railway finances, and rural debt were pertinent.

13.3 Conclusion

The legislation required the members of the Court to be lawyers.[30] None was a trained economist.[31] Did they deliver outcomes that were economically sound?

The Court's primary concerns, in the early years of arbitration, of averting industrial disputation and imposing just wages and conditions naturally gave rise to situations in which the judges had to consider the capacity of employers to bear the standards that unions wished them to impose. To a large extent, that issue was posed in microeconomic terms: what were the resources at the disposal of the particular employers to provide benefits to their employees? The transition from this kind of question to a more comprehensive analysis was gradual, subtle, and never complete. But there were landmarks. One was the rejection of the Piddington basic wage, based on a realisation that such a wage was beyond the capacity of industry as a whole to bear. A second was the reform of basic wage setting instigated by Powers in 1922–23, which reinforced the perception of the basic wage as an economy-wide standard. The *Main Hours* case of 1926–27 raised explicitly the question whether industry at large should be required to sustain the shorter working week: the Court, by majority, answered that question in the negative. Probably the most important landmark was the 1931 basic wage decision, which entailed the Court's assessment—with Copland's assistance—that a general wage reduction would assist primary producers (who were not major employers of labour) and curb the growth in unemployment. The basic wage cases of 1932, 1933, and 1934 were about the degree (if any) to which the overall economy had recovered. Finally, the arguments in the 1937 basic wage hearing were, to a significant

---

[30] An exception was the Conciliation Commissioners. Stewart and Coneybeer were the only persons appointed to this office.

[31] Dethridge pointed out that he had studied economics while pursuing his law degree. (He did not identify his teachers.) He said that he and his colleagues were not 'economic tyros'. Beeby had presented a paper (published in the *Economic Journal*)—see Subsection 13.1.1 above—to the economics section of the British Association when it met in Sydney in 1914. His comments from the Bench and in some of his decisions suggest that he had confidence in his own ability to cope with economic reasoning.

degree, macroeconomic, raising for consideration the Court's ability to regulate the economy by wage-setting.

Many of the Court's decisions can be criticised and some of its reasoning questioned. Overall, however, the history of wage-setting is one of learning by doing. Much progress was made. It may or may not be the case that better economic outcomes would have been produced by an atomistic labour market wherein wages and conditions were matters of individual contract, steered by the forces of competition. That was not an available option. Arbitration operated in a world of institutions and economic power wielded by large employers, employers' associations and unions. In such a world, without arbitration, outcomes would have reflected relative industrial strength. It would be foolish to deny that industrial might played a role in the determination of wages and conditions, despite the presence of arbitrators. Yet the arbitrators also exercised an autonomous role, tempering bargaining strength and intruding notions of fairness and policy. They were important contributors to the texture of Australian society.

References

Anderson, George (1928), 'The Commonwealth Conciliation and Arbitration Act 1928', *Economic Record*, vol. 4, pp. 279–301.

Anderson, George (1929), *Fixation of Wages in Australia*, Macmillan in association with MUP, Melbourne.

Anderson, George (1931), 'Wage Reductions in Australia. National Emergency', *Economic Record*, vol. 7, pp. 117–121.

Anderson, George (1939), 'Industrial Tribunals and Standards of Living', in Eggleston, F W, Walker, E Ronald, Anderson, George and Nimmow J F, *Australian Standards of Living: Studies*, issued by the Australian Institute of International Affairs, MUP in association with OUP, London, pp. 65–112.

Austin, A G (1965), *The Webbs' Australian Diary 1898*, Pitman, Melbourne.

Australian Government Commission of Inquiry into Poverty (1975), Ronald F Henderson Chairman, *First Main Report*, Commonwealth of Australia.

Aves, Ernest (1908), *Report to the Secretary of State for the Home Department on the Wages Boards and Industrial Conciliation Acts of Australia and New Zealand*, Cd 4167.

Beeby, George S (1915), 'The Artificial Regulation of Wages in Australia', *Economic Journal*, vol. 25, pp. 321–328.

Beever, Alan (1985), *The Forty-Hour Week Movement in Australia 1930–48*, Working Papers in Economic History ANU, No. 35.

Benham, F C (1926), 'The Australian Tariff and the Standard of Living: A Reply', *Economic Record*, vol. 2, pp. 21–42.

Benham, Frederic C (1928), *The Prosperity of Australia: An Economic Analysis*, King & Son, London.

Board of Trade (NSW) (1918), *Bulletin of the New South Wales Board of Trade: Living Wage (Adult Males)*.

Brigden, J B (1925), 'The Australian Tariff and the Standard of Living', *Economic Record*, vol. 1, pp. 29–46.

Brigden, J B (1927), 'The Australian Tariff and the Standard of Living: A Rejoinder', *Economic Record*, vol. 3, pp. 102–116.

Brigden, J B, Copland, D B, Dyason, E C, Giblin, L F and Wickens, C H (1929), *The Australian Tariff: An Economic Enquiry*, MUP in association with Macmillan, Melbourne.

British Economic Mission (1929), *Report of the British Economic Mission to Australia : Nominated by His Majesty's Government in Great Britain at the Request of His Majesty's Government in the Commonwealth of Australia*, Government Printer, Canberra.

Burns, E M (1926), *Wages and the State: A Comparative Study of the Problems of State Wage Regulation*, P S King & Son, London.

Butlin, N G (1962), *Australian Domestic Product, Investment and Foreign Borrowing 1861–1938/39*, CUP, Cambridge.

Butlin, N G (1970), 'Some Perspectives of Australian Economic Development, 1890–1965', in Forster, C (ed.), *Australian Economic Development in the Twentieth Century*, Allen & Unwin, London, pp. 266–327.

Cain, Neville (1985), *Keynes and Australian Policy in 1932*, ANU Working Papers in Economic History No. 58.

Cain, Neville (1987a), *Australian Economic Advice in 1930: Liberal and Radical Alternatives*, ANU Working Papers in Economic History No. 78.

Cain, Neville (1987b), *The Australian Economists and Controversy over Depression Policy, 1930-early 1931*, ANU Working Papers in Economic History No. 79.

Cameron, R J, (1953), 'The Role of the Arbitration Court', *Historical Studies of Australia and New Zealand*, vol. 6, 1953–55, pp. 204–214.

Clark, Victor S (1906), *The Labour Movement in Australasia*, Burt Franklin, New York, reprinted 1970.

Clark, Victor S (1909), 'Present State of Labor Legislation in Australia and New Zealand', *Annals of the American Academy of Political and Social Science*, vol. 33, pp. 440–447.

Coghlan, T A (1969), *Labour and Industry in Australia*, 4 volumes, Macmillan, Melbourne.

Cole, G D H (1928), *The Payment of Wages: A Study in Payment by Results under the Wage-system*, Allen & Unwin, London.

Coleman, John and Baum, Gregory (1991), *Rerum Novarum: One Hundred Years of Catholic Social Teaching*, Concilium: SCM Press, Philadelphia.

Coleman, William, Cornish, Selwyn and Hagger, Alf (2006), *Giblin's Platoon: The Trials and Triumphs of the Economist in Australian Public Life*, ANU E Press, Canberra.

Compendium of Living Wage Declarations and Reports Made by the NSW Board of Trade (1921), Government Printer, Sydney.

Copland, D B (1924), 'The Economic Situation in Australia, 1918–23', *Economic Journal*, vol. 34, pp. 33–51.

Copland, D B (1930), 'The Australian Problem', *Economic Journal*, vol. 40, pp. 638–649.

Copland, Douglas (1934), *Australia in the World Crisis 1929–1933*, The Marshall Lectures October and November 1933, CUP, Cambridge.

Copland, Sir Douglas (1950), *Developments in Economic Thought 1924–1950*, address given in May 1950 to celebrate the 25th anniversary of the foundation of the Victorian Branch of the Economic Society and the School of Commerce at the University of Melbourne.

Copland, D B and Foenander, O deR (1932), 'Agricultural Wages in Australia', *International Labour Review*, vol. 25, pp. 765–786.

Dabscheck, Braham (1983), *Arbitrator at Work: Sir William Raymond Kelly and the Regulation of Australian Industrial Relations*, Allen & Unwin, Sydney.

Davey, Patricia Ruth (1975), *Wages Boards in Victoria 1896–1920*, PhD thesis, University of Melbourne.

Douglas, Paul H (1923), 'Wages Regulation and Children's Maintenance in Australia', *Quarterly Journal of Economics*, vol. 37, pp. 643–686.

Economic Commission on the Queensland Basic Wage (1925), *Report*, Government Printer, Brisbane.

Eggleston, F W (1915), 'The Australian Democracy and its Economic Problems', *Economic Journal*, vol. 25, pp. 347–359.

Fahey, Charles and Lack, John (2007), '*Harvester* Men and Women: The Making of the *Harvester* Decision', in Kimber, Julie and Love, Peter (eds), *The Time of Their Lives: The Eight Hour Day and Working Life*, Australian Society for the Study of Labour History, Melbourne.

Finnimore, Christine (1995), *A Woman of Difference: Augusta Zadow and the 1894 Factories Act*, WorkCover Corporation, Adelaide.

Fisher, Allan G B (1934), 'Crisis and Readjustment in Australia', *Journal of Political Economy*, vol. 42, pp. 753–782.

Foenander, O de R (1934), Review of Irvine, R F (1934), *The Midas Touch*, Hassal Press, Adelaide, in *Economic Record*, vol. 10, pp. 131–132.

Foenander, O de R (1937), *Towards Industrial Peace in Australia*, MUP, Melbourne.

Fogarty, Michael (1961), *The Just Wage*, Chapman, London.

Forster, Colin (1964), *Industrial Development in Australia 1920–1930*, Australian National University.

Forster, Colin (1985), *Unemployment and the Australian Economic Recovery of the 1930s*, ANU Working Papers in Economic History No. 45.

Forster, Colin (1987), *The Economy, Wages and the Foundation of Arbitration*, ANU Working Papers in Economic History, No. 83.

Giblin, L F (1927), 'The Australian Tariff and the Standard of Living: A Note on Mr Benham's Statistics', *Economic Record*, vol. 3, pp. 148–156.

Giblin, L F (1930a), *Australia, 1930: An Inaugural Lecture*, MUP, Melbourne.

Giblin, L F (1930b), *Letters to John Smith* (a series of articles in the Melbourne Herald, July 1930, reprinted by the Herald).

Giblin, L F (1931), Wages and Prices, *Labour Report*, No. 21, 1930, pp. 163–180.

Gifford, J L K (1928), *Economic Statistics for Australian Arbitration Courts*, Macmillan in association with MUP, Melbourne.

Goodwin, Crauford D W (1966), *Economic Enquiry in Australia*, Duke University Press, Durham.

Graham, Morris (1995), *A B Piddington: The Last Radical Liberal*, University of New South Wales Press, Kensington.

Gregory, R, Ho, V and McDermott, L (1985), *Sharing the Burden: The Australian Labour Market During the 1930s*, ANU Working Papers in Economic History, No. 47.

Gregory, R G and Butlin, N G (eds) (1988), *Recovery from the Depression: Australia and the World Economy in the 1930s*, CUP, Cambridge and Melbourne.

Gregory, R G (1988), 'Overview', in Gregory, R G and Butlin, N G (eds) (1988), *Recovery from the Depression: Australia and the World Economy in the 1930s, op. cit.*, Chapter 1.

Hagan, Jim (1981), *The History of the ACTU*, Longman Cheshire, Melbourne.

Haig, Bryan (2001), 'New Estimates of Australian GDP: 1861–1948/49', *Australian Economic History Review*, vol. 41, pp. 1–34.

Hammond, M B (1913), 'Judicial Interpretation of the Minimum Wage in Australia', *American Economic Review*, vol. 3, pp. 259–286.

Hammond, M B (1914–15), 'Wages Boards in Australia: I. Victoria', *Quarterly Journal of Economics*, vol. 29, pp. 98–148.

Hancock, Keith (1972), 'Forty Years On', *Australian Economic History Review*, vol. 12, pp. 71–79.

Hancock, Keith and Moore, Kathryn (1972), 'The Occupational Wage Structure in Australia Since 1914', *British Journal of Industrial Relations*, vol. 10, pp. 107–122.

Hancock, K J (1979a), 'The First Half-Century of Australian Wage Policy—Part I', *Journal of Industrial Relations*, vol. 21, pp. 1–19.

Hancock, K J (1979b), 'The First Half-Century of Australian Wage Policy—Part II', *Journal of Industrial Relations*, vol. 21, pp. 129–160.

Hancock, Keith (2004), 'Economists and Australian Wage Policy before World War II', *Australian Journal of Labour Economics*, vol. 7, pp. 411–438.

Hancock, W K (1930), *Australia*, Ernest Benn, London.

Hancock, W K (1954), *Country and Calling*, Faber and Faber, London.

Harley, Bill (2004), 'Managing Industrial Conflict', in Isaac, Joe and Macintyre, Stuart (eds), *The New Province for Law and Order*, CUP, Cambridge and Port Melbourne, pp. 316–352.

Heagney, Muriel A (1935), *Are Women Taking Men's Jobs; A Survey of Women's Work in Victoria, with Special Regard to Equal Status, Equal Pay, and Equality of Opportunity*, Hilton & Veitch, Melbourne.

Heaton, H (1921) 'The Basic Wage Principle in Australian Wages Regulation', *Economic Journal*, vol. 31, pp. 309–319.

Heaton, H (1925), *Modern Economic History: With Special Reference to Australia*, WEA in cooperation with Macmillan, Melbourne.

Henderson, R F, Harcourt, A and Harper, R J A (1970), *People in Poverty: A Melbourne Survey*, Cheshire, Melbourne.

Heyward, E J R (1936), 'The Tasmanian Wages Board System', *Economic Record*, vol. 12, pp. 108–114.

Higgins, Henry Bournes (1922), *A New Province for Law and Order*, WEA, Sydney.

Higgins, H B (2001), 'Industrial Arbitration', *Australian Bulletin of Labour*, vol. 27, pp. 177–191.

The Industrial Unrest and the Living Wage (1913), with an Introduction by the Rev William Temple, MA, The Collegium with P S King & Son, London.

Keynes, J M (1936), *The General Theory of Employment, Interest and Money*, MacMillan, London.

Keynes, J M (1982), 'The Report of the Australian Experts', in Moggridge, Donald (ed.), *The Collected Writings of J M Keynes*, vol. XXI, Macmillan & CUP for the Royal Economic Society, pp. 94–100.

Kirby, Michael and Creighton, Breen (2004), 'The Law of Conciliation and Arbitration', in Isaac, Joe and Macintyre, Stuart (eds), *The New Province for Law and Order*, Cambridge and Port Melbourne, pp. 98–138.

La Nauze, J A (1949), *Political Economy in Australia: Historical Studies*, MUP, Melbourne.

Lee, Jenny (1987), 'A Redivision of Labour: Victoria's Wages Boards in Action, 1896–1908', *Historical Studies*, vol. 22, pp. 352–372.

Macarthy, P G (1968), 'Victorian Wages Boards: Their Origins and the Doctrine of the Living Wage', *Journal of Industrial Relations*, vol. 10, pp. 116–134.

Macarthy, P G (1969), 'Justice Higgins and the *Harvester* Judgment', *Australian Economic History Review*, vol. 9, pp. 17–38.

Macintyre, Stuart (2004), 'Arbitration in Action', in Isaac, Joe and Macintyre, Stuart (eds), *The New Province for Law and Order,* CUP, Cambridge and Port Melbourne, pp. 55–97.

Macintyre, S and Mitchell, R (eds) (1989), *Foundations of Arbitration*, OUP, Melbourne.

McCawley, T W (1922), 'Industrial Arbitration in Queensland', *International Labour Review*, vol. 5, pp. 385–409).

McFarlane, Bruce (1964), *Professor Irvine's Economics in Australian Labour History*, Australian Society for the Study of Labour History.

Maclaurin, W R (1938), 'Recent Experience with Compulsory Arbitration in Australia', *American Economic Review*, vol. 28, pp. 65–81.

McLean, Ian W and Pincus, Jonathan J (1983), 'Did Australian Living Standards Stagnate Between 1890 and 1940?', *The Journal of Economic History*, vol. 43, pp. 193–202.

Maddock, R and McLean, I W (1987), 'The Australian Economy in the Very Long Run', in Maddock, R and McLean, I W (eds), *The Australian Economy in The Long Run*, CUP, Melbourne, pp. 5–29.

Marshall, Alfred (1961), *Principles of Economics*, vol. 1, Ninth (Variorum) Edition with Annotations by C W Guillebaud, Macmillan for the Royal Economic Society, London and New York.

Meredith, D and Dyster, B (1999), *Australia in the Global Economy*, CUP, New York.

Merrett, David and Ville, Simon (2011), 'Tariffs, Subsidies, and Profits: A Reassessment of Structural Change in Australia 1901–39', *Australian Economic History Review*, vol. 51, pp. 46–70.

Millmow, Alex (2003), 'W Brian Reddaway—Keynes' Emissary to Australia', *Economic Record*, vol. 79, pp. 136–138.

Mills, R C (1929), 'Some Economic Factors in Industrial Relations', *Economic Record*, vol. 5, pp. 34–53.

New Protection—Explanatory Memorandum in Regard to (1907), Commonwealth Parliamentary Papers 1907–8, vol. II.

Nyland, Chris (1987), 'Work Time in the 1920s', *Australian Economic History Review*, vol. 27, pp. 37–55.

Palgrave's Dictionary of Political Economy (1906), Macmillan, London.

Phelps Brown, E H (1959), *The Growth of British Industrial Relations: A Study from the Standpoint of 1906–14*, Macmillan, London.

Piddington, A B (1921), *The Next Step: A Family Basic Income*, Macmillan, Melbourne.

Plowman, David H (1989), *Holding the Line: Compulsory Arbitration and National Employer Co-ordination in Australia*, CUP, Cambridge and Melbourne.

Portus, G V (1953), *Happy Highways*, MUP, Carlton.

Pribram, K (1928), 'The Regulation of Minimum Wages as an International Problem', *International Labour Review*, vol. 17, pp. 317–331.

Rankin, Mary Theresa (1916), *Arbitration and Conciliation in Australasia: The Legal Wage in Victoria & New Zealand*, Allen & Unwin, London.

Reddaway, W B (1938), 'Australian Wage Policy, 1927–1937', *International Labour Review*, vol. 37, pp. 314–337.

Ricardo, David (1962), *On the Principles of Political Economy and Taxation*, vol. I, in Sraffa, Piero (ed) with the collaboration of Dobb, M H, CUP, London.

Rickard, John (1984), *The Rebel as Judge*, Allen & Unwin, Sydney.

Rimmer, Malcolm (2004), 'Unions and Arbitration', in Isaac, Joe and Macintyre, Stuart (eds), *The New Province for Law and Order*, CUP, Cambridge and Port Melbourne, pp. 275–315.

Rowe, J W F (1928), *Wages in Practice and Theory*, Routledge, London.

Royal Commission on the Basic Wage (1920), *Report*, Parliament of the Commonwealth of Australia.

Royal Commission on the Basic Wage (1921), *Report*, Parliament of the Commonwealth of Australia.

Russell, F A A (1915), 'Industrial Arbitration in New South Wales', *Economic Journal*, vol. 25, pp. 329–346.

Ryan, John A (1906), *A Living Wage*, Macmillan, London.

Sawkins, D T (1933), *The Living Wage in Australia*, MUP, Melbourne.

Schedvin, C B (1970), *Australia and the Great Depression*, Sydney University Press, Sydney.

Sells, Dorothy McD (1924), 'The Development of State Wage Regulation in Australia and New Zealand', *International Labour Review*, vol. 10, pp. 607–629, 779–799, 962–1004.

Shanahan, M (1999), 'Australian Labour Market Institutions through Time: A Perspective from the New Institutional Economics', *Australian Economic History Review*, vol. 39, pp. 213–238.

Shann, E O G (1930), *An Economic History of Australia*, CUP, Cambridge.

Shann, E O G and Copland, D B (eds) (1931), *The Crisis in Australian Finance 1929 to 1931: Documents on Budgetary and Economic Policy*, Angus & Robertson, Sydney.

Sheldon, Peter (2007), 'State-level Basic Wages in Australia during the Depression, 1929–35: Institutions and Politics over Marhets, *Australian Economic History Review*, vol. 47, pp. 249–277.

Smithies, A (1935), 'Wages Policy in the Depression', *Economic Record*, vol. 11, pp. 249–268.

Smithies, A (1936), 'Rejoinder', *Economic Record*, vol. 12, pp. 101–102.

Snooks, G D (1991), 'Bond or Free? The Life, Work, and Times of Edward Shann, 1884–1935', in Siddique, M A B (ed.), *A Decade of Shann Memorial Lectures 1981–90 & the Australian Economy*, University of Western Australia, pp. 15–33.

Snowden, Philip (1913), *The Living Wage*, Hodder and Stoughton. (Dating based on internal evidence).

Stone, J O N (1991), '1929 and All That …', in Siddique, M A B (ed.), *A Decade of Shann Memorial Lectures 1981–90 & the Australian Economy*, University of Western Australia, pp. 129–163.

Sutcliffe, J T (1925), 'Wages and Production', *Economic Record*, vol. 1, pp. 63–72.

Sutcliffe, J T (1926), *National Dividend: An Enquiry into the Amount of the National Dividend of Australia and the manner of its Distribution*, MUP in association with Macmillan.

Tariff Board (1926), *Annual Report for the Year Ended 30th June, 1926*, Parliamentary Papers 1926–27–28, vol. IV, p. 1605.

Tariff Board (1927), *Annual Report for the Year Ended 30th June, 1927*, Parliamentary Papers 1926–27–28, vol. IV, p. 1621.

Tariff Board (1928), *Annual Report for the Year Ended 30th June, 1928*, Parliamentary Papers 1926–27–28, vol. IV, p. 1647.

Tariff Board (1929), *Annual Report for the Year Ended 30th June, 1929*, Parliamentary Papers 1929, vol. II, p. 2509.

Tariff Board (1930), *Annual Report for the Year Ended 30th June, 1930*, Parliamentary Papers 1929–30–31, vol. III, p. 1215.

Tariff Board (1935), *Annual Report for the Year Ended 30th June, 1935*, Parliamentary Papers 1934–35–36–37, vol. II, p. 1355.

Tariff Board (1938), *Annual Report for the Year Ended 30th June, 1937*, Parliamentary Papers 1937–38–39–40, vol. II, p. 998.

Tariff Board (1939), *Annual Report for Year 1938–39*, Parliamentary Papers 1934–35–36–37, vol. II, p. 1027.

University of Tasmania (1925), *Employment Relations and the Basic Wage: Lectures and Papers Published in Connection with the Pitt Cobbett Foundation*, Hobart.

Walker, E R (1933), *Australia in the World Depression*, King & Son, London.

Walker, E R (1936), *Unemployment Policy with Special Reference to Australia*, Angus & Robertson, Sydney.

Wallace Bruce Committee (1932), 'Report by the Wallace Bruce Committee, a Preliminary Survey of the Economic Problem for the Premiers' Conference, April 1932', in *The Australian Price Structure, 1932*, with an Introduction by E O G Shann and D B Copland, Angus & Robertson, Sydney, 1933, pp. 38–78.

Whillier, R J (1977), *The Piddington Commission 1920 Enquiry into the Basic Wage*, University of Adelaide BA Honours thesis held in the Barr Smith Library.

Wilson, Roland (1937), *Prices, Quantities and Values*, Economic Society of Australia and New Zealand, Melbourne.

Wilson, Roland (1947), *Facts and Fancies of Productivity*, Economic Society of Australia and New Zealand, Melbourne.

Withers, Glenn (1987), 'Labour', in Maddock, Rodney and McLean, Ian W (eds), *The Australian Economy in the Long Run*, CUP, Melbourne, pp. 248–288.

Index

This book is available as a free fully-searchable pdf from
www.adelaide.edu.au/press

A

Age, The 5–6, 653
Alison, C A 414–415
Anderson, George 61, 68, 81, 87, 90, 95, 100, 113–114, 169–170, 190, 209, 242, 462–463
anonymous expert (1937) 564–568, 707–708
Arthur, J A 69
Attorney-General 66, 177, 188, 306, 369, 382, 462, 463
Aumont, Smith 74–75
Australian Council of Trade Unions (ACTU) 323, 374, 644, 672
Australian Railways' Union v Victorian Railways Commissioners 332
Aves, Ernest 8, 655

B

Beeby, Justice and Chief Justice G S 187, 282, 283, 296–297, 299, 300, 305, 306–323 (passim), 326, 331, 332, 333, 335, 336, 339, 340, 359–650 (passim), 654, 655, 706, 709
below-award payments 28, 501
Benham, Frederic 284, 313–314, 662, 663–666, 673–675
Board of Industry (SA) 242, 486, 506, 510, 533, 535–536, 573, 594
Board of Trade (NSW) 10, 105, 110, 116, 119, 166, 187, 242, 289
Booth, Charles 58
Brigden, J B 240, 343–344, 511, 534–535, 541, 564, 657, 666, 671–672, 673–677
British Economic Mission 190, 482, 666–669, 673, 680, 698
Brown, President Jethro 87, 95, 113–115, 166, 170, 510
Bruce, S M 342, 675
Bult, George 79
Burns, Evelyn M 3, 5, 8, 57, 62, 104, 112, 113
Butlin, N G 15–20, 22, 44–48, 190–193, 336–338, 340, 345–347, 572

C

capacity to pay 82, 278, 482, 552, 661, 664–665, 669–673, 696, 701, 709–710
Carlyle, A J 60
Carolan, P J 370, 371, 374–375, 411, 503
censuses 10–12, 25–26, 48, 105, 111, 127, 139, 161, 338, 582
Central Council of Employers' Associations 668
Chapple, J F 427, 432
child endowment 35, 140, 142, 148, 280, 281, 289–290, 461, 472, 491
Chomley, A C a'B 426, 427, 442
Clarey, P J 482, 495, 498–499, 507–508, 536–537, 575, 707
Clark, Victor S 655
Clyde Engineering Company v Cowburn 189
Cole, G D H 327–328, 470, 474
Coleman, W, Cornish, S and Hagger, A 342–343, 657
Commonwealth Conciliation and Arbitration Act 1904 43, 67, 104, 113, 178, 190, 699
Commonwealth Conciliation and Arbitration Act 1928, section 28D 190, 363, 364, 365
Commonwealth Grants Commission 574, 655
Commonwealth Statistician 10, 20, 24, 26, 28, 49, 88–91, 94, 99, 101, 103, 105, 108, 111, 113, 117, 123–124, 127, 133–134, 138, 145, 171, 201, 205, 207, 216, 221, 223, 237, 241, 288, 307, 357, 370, 377, 459, 473, 484, 574, 587, 644, 656, 675
Conciliation Committees 332, 365, 367
Coneybeer, Conciliation Commissioner E H 332, 600, 638, 709
Copland, D B 340, 343, 344, 364, 370, 375, 377–398, 399, 402, 407, 409, 412, 414, 415, 416, 418, 421, 422, 423, 428, 429, 430, 432, 433, 435, 437, 442–443, 446, 449, 452, 459, 460, 469, 470, 475, 538, 549, 551, 556–558, 560, 564, 567, 582, 583, 654, 657, 666, 669–670, 675, 683, 685–686, 690, 691, 692, 697, 706, 708, 709
Corke, F H 447–449, 453
Court of Arbitration (WA) 242, 306, 533, 594
Court of Industrial Appeals (SA) 112
Court of Industrial Arbitration (Qld) 170, 242, 670
Crofts, Charles 214, 215, 230, 306, 307, 374, 378, 382, 384, 386, 387, 389, 393, 394, 398, 399, 402, 412, 415, 416, 424, 426, 427, 428, 429, 430, 432, 436, 437, 438, 439, 440, 441–447, 449–450, 469–470, 472–473, 477, 486, 496–497, 504, 510, 525, 534, 541, 549–550, 573–574, 576, 580–581, 707
Cussen, Mr Justice L F B 169
Custom Tariff Act 1906 64, 66

D

Dabscheck, Braham 8
Davey, P R 7–9, 82
Deakin, Alfred 5, 7, 65–67, 80
deflation 29, 233, 385–386, 393–398, 403–407, 417–418, 422, 459, 538, 702, 706
Derham, F P 286, 470, 507, 564
Dethridge, Chief Justice G J 187, 215–216, 280–281, 283, 284–285, 290–296, 298–300, 303–304, 305 306–321 (passim), 325–327, 331, 332, 359–650 (passim), 709
Dilke, Charles 5
Divini Redemptoris 58
Douglas, C H 426, 442, 458, 474, 539, 550
Douglas, Paul 656
Drake-Brockman, Justice E A 187, 188, 282, 283, 285, 323, 326, 331–333, 359–650 (passim)
Dupree, G 425
Dyason, E C 344, 378, 394, 460, 538, 675
Dyster, B 14–15

E

Economic Commission on the Queensland Basic Wage 307, 512, 664, 670–671
Economic Research Act 1929 342
Economic Research, Bureau of 342
Edmonds, Mr Justice 108
Eggleston, F W 654–655
equation of leisure 309, 641–643
Excise Tariff Act 1906 63, 67–68, 84, 171

F

Factories Act 1894 (SA) 8
Factories and Shops Act 1934 (Vic) 537, 592
Fahey, Charles and Lack, John 64
Fair Wages Resolution 58
family size 23, 79, 85, 100, 112, 116–117, 140, 147, 280–281
female wages and conditions 36–37, 38, 114, 161–171, 176, 177, 270–277, 317, 323–327, 449, 509–510, 519, 527, 549, 576–579, 613, 649–650, 702
Finnimore, Christine 8
Fisher, A G B 692–693
Foenander, O de R 188–189, 190, 323, 332, 364, 654
Forster, Colin 19, 193, 211, 338
Forty-four Hours Week Act 1925 (NSW) 210
Foster, A W 124, 307, 474
Fraser, A M 382, 383, 400–401, 416, 421, 449–453

G

Garde, J B 80
Gavan Duffy, Frank (later Mr Justice) 69–74, 82, 84, 152, 187, 262, 264–265
Giblin, L F 20, 137, 240, 343, 344, 376, 418, 473, 475, 481, 488, 538, 540, 550, 551, 567, 657, 666, 673, 675, 683–685, 686

Gibson, H C 28, 122, 207, 208, 212, 229, 371–373, 375, 383–385, 424, 430–431, 433, 473, 489, 615
Gifford, J L K 24, 206, 671
Goodall, H W 152
Gordon, Mr Justice 112
Graham, Morris 109, 118, 123, 140, 142, 290
Grant, C H 559
Grayndler, E 408, 434–435
Gregory, R G 339, 341, 346
Gregory, R, Ho, V and McDermott, L 540
Gregory, T E 344, 427, 460, 682, 683
Griffith, Samuel 62
Gunn, J A L 412–414, 432

H

Hagan, Jim 188, 265, 323, 644, 669, 673
Haig, Bryan 15–22, 44–47, 190–193, 336–337, 346, 572
Hammond, M B 5, 6–7, 655
Hancock, Keith 44, 340, 342, 343, 540, 550
Hancock, K and Moore, K 262
Hancock, W K 342, 659–662, 668, 673, 682
Harvester case 33, 44, 63, 64–85, 99–100, 111, 124, 133, 181, 223, 362, 514, 549
Harvester standard 28, 64, 84–85, 90, 99, 102, 105, 112, 118, 123, 132, 134, 143, 147, 153, 211–212, 223, 224, 227, 229, 230–232, 234, 236–237, 278, 281, 287–288, 431, 446–447, 491, 498, 525, 533, 580, 597, 672, 701, 702, 704
Heagney, Muriel 577–579
Healy, J 400, 402
Heaton, Herbert 654
Henderson, R F 148
Heydon, Mr Justice C G 64, 89, 95, 99, 104–111, 113, 114, 116, 144
Higgins, Mr Justice Henry Bournes 7, 10, 41, 43, 44, 48, 54, 55–183 (passim), 213, 217–218, 220, 223–226, 229, 236, 243–247, 252, 254, 256, 262–263, 265, 266, 270, 272, 276, 278, 280, 290–291, 301, 304, 318, 324, 326, 360, 368, 415, 446–447, 456, 461, 485, 497, 513–514, 522, 548, 597, 60–606, 610, 621, 635, 645, 667, 671–672, 701–704
High Court of Australia 10, 43, 68, 123, 144, 180–189, 235, 248, 269, 305, 332–333, 440, 466, 633, 658
highest function rule 154
high wages doctrine 300, 327–328, 359, 363, 403, 422, 437–438, 476, 621, 654
Hobson, J A 383–384, 415, 419, 442, 470, 474, 476, 584
holidays (see leave)
Holloway, E J 318–319
Home, W J 562
hours of work 17, 22–23, 37–38, 171–181, 189–190, 209–210,

212–214, 244, 262–270, 274, 276–277, 304–318, 320–322, 325–326, 327, 332, 336, 341, 357–358, 365–369, 412, 479, 524, 526–531, 593, 603, 604, 628–645, 702, 703–704, 706
household budget (see also Royal Commission on the Basic Wage) 73–79, 96–97, 105–107
House of Lords, Select Committee 3–4
Hughes, W M 44, 119, 120–121, 134, 138, 141, 142, 144, 146, 436, 656, 701, 705

I

Industrial Arbitration Act 1912 (SA) 113
Industrial Commission (NSW) 242, 289, 290, 529, 579, 593
Industrial Unrest and the Living Wage, The 5, 60–61
industry allowance 243, 249, 256–257, 258–259, 335, 650
inflation 29, 52, 108–109, 118, 154, 211, 233, 288, 344–345, 392, 405, 418, 420, 459–460, 691, 695, 701, 702, 703
International Labour Organisation (ILO) 61, 644
interstate competition 535, 543, 545, 588–591
Irvine, R F 402–412, 417, 423, 429, 432, 436, 442–444, 447, 455, 459, 460, 470, 473–475, 540, 653, 655, 688

Isaacs, Mr Justice Isaac 43, 163

J

Jewell, T 425

K

Kelly, Acting President and President Raymond 510, 535–536
Keynes, J M 376, 413, 417–418, 420, 474, 476, 488, 501–502, 541, 550, 683, 687–690, 691, 706, 707
Kirby, Michael and Creighton, Breen 1, 188
Knibbs, George 94, 105, 108, 138–139, 141–142, 148, 221, 307, 431, 656

L

labour standards 195, 211–216, 279, 328, 702
Lang, J T 345, 412, 532, 683
Latham, J T 188
Lawrence, Captain 215–216
leave 17, 39, 79, 172–173, 175, 180, 181, 182, 212, 307, 368, 506, 527, 530, 625, 645–649
Lee, Jenny 2, 162
Leo XIII, Pope 57
living wage 3, 9, 10, 35–36, 55–64, 83, 84–85, 86, 96, 98, 99, 101, 102–104, 104–119, 151, 154, 212, 214, 218, 223, 225, 227, 229, 242, 245, 246, 264, 265, 282, 289, 290, 356, 419,

490, 511, 513, 532, 533, 536, 573, 576, 594
Lloyd Thomas, Reverend J M 5
Lukin, Justice L O 187, 235, 281–284, 285, 287, 301–302, 305, 306–322 (passim), 326, 331, 359, 362, 368–369, 642–643
Lyne, William 65

M

Macarthy, P G 64, 76
Macintyre, Stuart 10, 43
Macintyre, Stuart and Mitchell, R 2
Maddock, R and McLean, I W 13, 14
Maher, T C 123, 371, 374, 398–399
Main Hours case 1926–27 214, 266, 304, 306–314, 318, 322, 367, 368, 641, 662, 709
Mann, L R 339, 499–501, 540, 556–558
Marshall, Alfred 58–59, 460, 655–656
Martin, C E 419–420
Martin, Russell 124
Massey, Gordon 389–398, 412, 421–424, 429, 444
McCawley, Mr Justice T W 670
McFarlane, Bruce 402, 653
McKay, George 80, 82
McKay, H V 68–78, 152–153, 171, 181, 362, 600
McLaurin, W R 334–335
McLean, Ian W and Pincus, Jonathan J 22–23
Meagher, L C 445–447, 449

Meeker, Royal 126, 137
Melville, Leslie 343, 382, 423, 470, 560, 564, 662, 666, 686
Menzies, R G 230, 369
Meredith, D 14–15
Merrett, D and Ville, S 191, 346
Mills, R C 343, 437, 511, 653, 666, 671, 686
Mundy, C E 335, 430, 487–488
Myhill, W C 252, 502–503

N

New Protection 65–66
Niemeyer, Otto 344, 460, 682–683
nominal wages 26–28, 30, 34, 49–50, 52, 148, 196–197, 199–200, 335, 348–350, 519, 628, 681, 686–687, 704
Nyland, Chris 209, 304, 317

O

O'Connor, Mr Justice R E 43, 68
O'Mara, Judge Thomas 240, 332, 335, 638–643
Ord, Harrison 6
Osborne, Ethel 130, 177, 325
over-award payments 28, 335, 607

P

Parkinson, H W 418, 419
Payment by Results (see piecework)
Peace Treaty 1919 61, 266, 309
Peacock, Alexander 6, 7
Pescia, C 424, 425
Piddington, A B (see also Royal

Commission on the Basic Wage) 112, 123, 125, 132–142, 146, 147, 148, 217, 220, 222, 281, 289, 290, 532
piecework 216, 302, 314, 318, 319–323, 365, 531, 579, 609, 681
Piper, Justice H B 332, 622, 625, 626, 638–639, 640–641, 642–643
Pius XI, Pope 58
Plowman, David 10, 188, 668–669
population 10–13, 14, 16–17, 161, 193–194, 661, 666, 673–676, 680
Portus, G V 415–417, 460
poverty line 136, 148–149,
Powers' 3s 207, 233, 235, 281–285, 286, 288, 301, 359, 361, 362, 364, 365, 370, 375, 380, 382, 483, 488, 489, 492, 499, 502, 515, 518, 519, 525, 546, 580, 581, 600, 703, 704, 705
Powers, Mr Justice Charles 43, 44, 85–278 (passim), 279, 280, 281, 284, 285, 288, 291, 295, 296, 305, 310, 368, 447, 461, 523, 621, 678, 701, 703, 709
price indices 10–13, 14, 16–17, 28, 29, 33, 34, 51–52, 88–95, 97, 113, 117, 133–134, 143, 196–198, 201–209, 232–234, 237–238, 242, 286–287, 288, 350–351, 355, 360, 371–375, 379, 380, 382, 424, 430–431, 446, 465, 472–473, 481, 484, 488–489, 491–492, 499, 505–508, 515, 520, 537, 539, 540, 543, 544, 548, 549, 560, 573–574, 580, 581–582, 587, 588–589, 591, 592, 660, 667–668, 696, 703
productivity 15–24, 31–33, 44–45, 211, 215–216, 221, 236, 279, 308–310, 312–314, 327–328, 437–439, 441, 455–459, 481–482, 498–499, 511–512, 562, 569, 583, 585, 668, 670–673, 676, 698

Q

Quick, Deputy President John 187–188, 231–232, 233–235, 236, 249–250, 252–253, 255–257, 259–260, 265, 266, 268, 270, 273, 275, 278, 286, 297–298, 303, 447, 521, 599, 615, 622

R

Rankin, Theresa 61, 655
real wages 22–23, 29–31, 31–33, 34–35, 52–53, 88, 109, 148, 197–199, 211, 214–215, 221, 223, 237, 278, 351–352, 374, 380, 386, 391–393, 395, 418–419, 422, 426, 456, 460, 468, 469, 488, 518, 519, 532, 539–541, 546, 555–556, 569, 571, 594, 658, 664, 669, 676, 680, 684, 687, 689–690, 691, 693, 698, 702, 704–708
Rerum Novarum 57, 62
Ricardo, David 56
Rich, Mr Justice George Edward

187, 262, 264, 265
Riordan, W J 424
Rowe, J W F 327
Rowntree, Seebohm 58, 64, 116, 165, 167, 309
Royal Commission on the Basic Wage (Piddington Commission) 29, 85, 100, 103–104, 118–149, 178, 196, 201–202, 205, 207–208, 212, 217–222, 224, 277–278, 280–281, 286, 288, 289, 307, 370, 371, 461, 494, 542, 547–548, 549, 580, 656, 702, 703, 705, 709
Rules of Practice (1923) 267–268, 285
Russell, Eric 672
Russell, F A A 104–105, 417–418, 460, 654–655
Ryan, John A 57–58

S

Salter, Wilfred 672
Sawkins, D T 55, 63–64, 105, 135, 290
Schedvin, C B 340, 342–343, 346, 540, 686
Schutt, William 69–72, 76–77, 80, 83
Sells, Dorothy 655
Shann, E O G 343–345, 538, 653–654, 658–659, 666, 686
Sheldon, Peter 532, 533, 537, 540
Smart, William 59
Smith, Adam 55
Smith, Constance 61
Smithies, Arthur 689
Snowden, Philip 58, 59, 60
Starke, Mr Justice Hayden 43, 59, 60, 143, 159, 160, 168, 169, 178, 239, 243, 245
Stewart, A M 188, 709
Stuckey, R R 574, 575
Sutcliffe, J T 24, 89, 92, 110, 123, 132, 133, 134, 139, 141, 142, 201, 216, 228, 229, 235, 240, 286, 307, 311, 313, 511, 562, 564, 656, 670–673
sweating 3–9, 58, 61, 63, 64, 293, 467, 501, 654, 655, 699
Syme, David 5, 653

T

tariff 64–67, 68, 70, 84, 171, 194, 273, 302, 310, 342, 344, 345, 346, 379, 409, 447, 452, 503, 527, 563, 567, 596, 600, 605, 610, 611, 659, 666, 669, 673, 675–682, 698
Tariff Board 310, 600, 611, 673, 677–679, 681–682, 698
terms of trade 14, 336, 341, 342, 407, 412, 435, 454, 475, 559, 569, 672, 683, 690, 698
Trevelyan, C G P 425

U

unemployment 24–26, 47–48, 147, 181, 195–196, 222, 226, 241, 264, 279, 294, 318, 319–320, 336, 338–340, 342, 359–360, 380, 381, 388, 391, 394, 396,

400, 403, 404, 409, 413, 414, 421, 424, 432–433, 437, 438, 439, 440, 441, 450–451, 453, 456, 457–458, 462, 468–469, 471, 479, 483, 484, 488, 490, 492, 499–500, 501, 515, 517–518, 521, 534–535, 536, 538, 541, 549, 555, 557–558, 569, 572, 582, 593, 605, 640, 645–646, 658–659, 661, 662–664, 668–669, 671–672, 683–685, 686, 687–688, 694, 704, 706–707, 709

W

wage relativities 52–54, 199, 200, 290–292, 290–296, 298, 348–350 519, 525–526, 595–596, 602, 605, 607, 627

wages boards 1, 2, 5–10, 61, 64, 65–66, 81–84, 112–113, 114, 151–154, 169, 174, 219, 240–241, 242, 247–248, 252–253, 269–270, 477, 485, 491, 498, 503–504, 510, 536–537, 592, 655, 701

Walker, E R 340, 688–689

Wallace Bruce Committee 686

Wall Street collapse 341

Webb, Beatrice 166–167, 655

Webb, Deputy President N A 183, 187–188, 213–214, 231–232, 233–234, 235, 236–237, 239, 240, 241–242, 250–252, 253, 254–255, 258–259–262, 265, 266, 271, 272, 273, 274, 275, 276–277, 301–302, 323–325, 362, 600

Webb, Sidney 64, 655

Whillier, R J 118–122, 123, 124–125, 138, 141, 147

Wickens, C H 207–208, 216, 307, 370–376, 378, 400, 426, 430, 675

Wicksteed, Philip H 61

Williams, A E 424

Wilson, Roland 20–23, 31–33

Withers, Glenn 13

Wood, G L 343, 394, 418, 470, 551

working hours (see hours of work)

Wright, S C G 505–506, 509–510, 545, 551, 559–564, 575, 641

Z

Zigliaria, Cardinal 57

www.ingramcontent.com/pod-product-compliance
Lightning Source LLC
Chambersburg PA
CBHW080023110526
44587CB00021BA/3827